Working at a Small-to-Medium Business

CCNA Discovery Learning Guide

Allan Reid

Jim Lorenz

Cisco Press

800 East 96th Street

Indianapolis, Indiana 46240 USA

Working at a Small-to-Medium Business or ISP
CCNA Discovery Learning Guide

Allan Reid and Jim Lorenz

Copyright® 2008 Cisco Systems, Inc.

Published by:
Cisco Press
800 East 96th Street
Indianapolis, IN 46240 USA

Printed in the United States of America

Second Printing July 2008

Library of Congress Cataloging-in-Publication Data

Reid, Allan.

  Working at a small-to-medium business or ISP : CCNA discovery learning

guide / Allan Reid, Jim Lorenz.

    p. cm.

  Includes index.

  ISBN 978-1-58713-210-0 (pbk. w/cd)

  1. Computer networks—Textbooks. 2. Computer networks—Management—
Textbooks. 3. Local area networks (Computer networks)—
Textbooks. 4. Business enterprises—Computer networks—
Textbooks. 5. Internet service providers—Textbooks. I.

Lorenz, Jim. II. Title.

  TK5105.5.R4464 2008

  004.6—dc22

2008015723

ISBN-13: 978-1-58713-210-0

ISBN-10: 1-58713-210-9

Publisher
Paul Boger

Associate Publisher
Dave Dusthimer

Cisco Representative
Anthony Wolfenden

Cisco Press Program Manager
Jeff Brady

Executive Editor
Mary Beth Ray

Managing Editor
Patrick Kanouse

Development Editor
Dayna Isley

Senior Project Editor
Tonya Simpson

Copy Editor
Gayle Johnson

Technical Editors
Bernadette O'Brien, Elaine Horn,
William Shurbert, Glenn Wright

Editorial Assistant
Vanessa Evans

Book Designer
Louisa Adair

Composition
Louisa Adair

Indexer
Tim Wright

Proofreader
Molly Proue

Warning and Disclaimer

This book is designed to provide information about the *Working at a Small-to-Medium Business or ISP CCNA Discovery* course. Every effort has been made to make this book as complete and accurate as possible, but no warranty or fitness is implied.

The information is provided on an "as is" basis. The authors, Cisco Press, and Cisco Systems, Inc., shall have neither liability nor responsibility to any person or entity with respect to any loss or damages arising from the information contained in this book or from the use of the discs or programs that may accompany it.

The opinions expressed in this book belong to the authors and are not necessarily those of Cisco Systems, Inc.

Trademark Acknowledgments

All terms mentioned in this book that are known to be trademarks or service marks have been appropriately capitalized. Cisco Press or Cisco Systems, Inc., cannot attest to the accuracy of this information. Use of a term in this book should not be regarded as affecting the validity of any trademark or service mark.

Corporate and Government Sales

The publisher offers excellent discounts on this book when ordered in quantity for bulk purchases or special sales, which may include electronic versions and/or custom covers and content particular to your business, training goals, marketing focus, and branding interests. For more information, please contact **U.S. Corporate and Government Sales** 1-800-382-3419 corpsales@pearsontechgroup.com.

For sales outside the United States, please contact **International Sales** international@pearsoned.com.

Feedback Information

At Cisco Press, our goal is to create in-depth technical books of the highest quality and value. Each book is crafted with care and precision, undergoing rigorous development that involves the unique expertise of members of the professional technical community.

Reader feedback is a natural continuation of this process. If you have any comments about how we could improve the quality of this book, or otherwise alter it to better suit your needs, you can contact us through e-mail at feedback@ciscopress.com. Please be sure to include the book title and ISBN in your message.

We greatly appreciate your assistance.

Americas Headquarters
Cisco Systems, Inc.
170 West Tasman Drive
San Jose, CA 95134-1706
USA
www.cisco.com
Tel: 408 526-4000
800 553-NETS (6387)
Fax: 408 527-0883

Asia Pacific Headquarters
Cisco Systems, Inc.
168 Robinson Road
#28-01 Capital Tower
Singapore 068912
www.cisco.com
Tel: +65 6317 7777
Fax: +65 6317 7799

Europe Headquarters
Cisco Systems International BV
Haarlerbergpark
Haarlerbergweg 13-19
1101 CH Amsterdam
The Netherlands
www-europe.cisco.com
Tel: +31 0 800 020 0791
Fax: +31 0 20 357 1100

Cisco has more than 200 offices worldwide. Addresses, phone numbers, and fax numbers are listed on the Cisco Website at **www.cisco.com/go/offices**.

About the Authors

Allan Reid is the curriculum lead and a CCNA/CCNP instructor at the Centennial College CATC in Toronto, Canada. He is a professor in the Information and Communications Engineering Technology department and is an instructor and program supervisor for the School of Continuing Education at Centennial College. He has developed and taught networking courses for both private and public organizations and has been instrumental in developing and implementing numerous certificate, diploma, and degree programs in networking. Allan also is a curriculum developer for the Cisco Networking Academy. Outside his academic responsibilities, he has been active in the computer and networking fields for more than 25 years. Currently he is a principal in a company specializing in the design, management, and security of network solutions for small and medium-sized companies. Allan authored the first edition of *WAN Technologies CCNA 4 Companion Guide* (Cisco Press, ISBN 1-58713-172-2) and *Using a Networker's Journal*, which is a supplement to *A Networker's Journal* (Cisco Press, ISBN 1-58713-158-7). Most recently, he coauthored the *CCNA Discovery* online academy courses *Networking for Home and Small Businesses* and *Introducing Routing and Switching in the Enterprise* with Jim Lorenz.

Jim Lorenz is an instructor and curriculum developer for the Cisco Networking Academy. He has coauthored several Cisco Press titles, including *Fundamentals of UNIX Companion Guide*, Second Edition (ISBN 1-58713-140-4), *Fundamentals of UNIX Lab Companion*, Second Edition (ISBN 1-58713-139-0), and the third editions of the *CCNA Lab Companions*. He has more than 20 years of experience in information systems, ranging from programming and database administration to network design and project management. Jim has developed and taught computer and networking courses for numerous public and private institutions. As the Cisco academy manager at Chandler-Gilbert Community College in Arizona, he was instrumental in starting the Information Technology Institute (ITI) and developed a number of certificates and degree programs. Most recently, Jim coauthored the *CCNA Discovery* online academy courses *Networking for Home and Small Businesses* and *Introducing Routing and Switching in the Enterprise* with Allan Reid.

About the Technical Reviewers

Bernadette O'Brien has been teaching in the Cisco Networking Academy in Schenectady, New York since 1998. Schenectady High School is a Regional Academy for CCNA and is a CATC for Sponsored Curriculum, which Bernadette coordinates. Bernadette received her BS degree from SUNY Buffalo and her MS degree in curriculum and instruction from SUNY Albany. She is also CCNA and CCAI certified. Bernadette and her husband and two children live in a Victorian village very near the Adirondack Mountains in upstate New York. They enjoy rehabbing their 120-year-old Victorian house, skiing, and hiking.

Elaine Horn, CCAI, has been teaching in the Cisco Networking Academy since 1998 at TRECA (http://www.treca.org) in Marion, Ohio. TRECA is a CATC for CCNA, a regional academy for Sponsored and Emerging Technologies Curriculum, and a local academy for CCNA. She is currently teaching and supporting academies in Ohio, Kentucky, and Michigan. Elaine received her BS degree in education and an MA in mathematics education from The Ohio State University. She has also coordinated the Skills Ohio Internetworking Competition and worked with Cisco Press as a technical editor for Academy-related materials.

Bill Shurbert is a professor of information technology at New Hampshire Technical Institute in Concord, New Hampshire. He holds a bachelor's degree in technical management from Southern New Hampshire University. He enjoys teaching the Cisco CCNA, Wireless, and IT Essentials classes. In his off time, you can find Bill and Joanne, his wife of more than 25 years, sailing the waters of Lake Winnipesaukee.

Glenn Wright, CCNA, CCAI, is the codirector of the Cisco Academy Training Center (CATC) in Fort Worth, Texas. He has a bachelor's degree in business education from the University of North Texas and 22 years of experience in computer education. He has been involved in many aspects of the Cisco Networking Academy since 1999. He serves the Academy as an instructor and supports the Regional Academies in Texas, Louisiana, Oklahoma, Arkansas, North Carolina, South Carolina, Virginia, and Tennessee. Glenn has also worked with the Academy Quality Assurance Team, reviewing and editing Academy curriculum and assessment. He has developed and edited Packet Tracer activities for the *Discovery* curriculum. He has also worked with Cisco Press as a technical editor for Academy-related materials.

Dedications

This book is dedicated to my children: Andrew, Philip, Amanda, Christopher, and Shaun. You are my inspiration, and you make it all worthwhile. Thank you for your patience and support. —*Allan Reid*

To the three most important people in my life: my wife, Mary, and my daughters, Jessica and Natasha. Thanks for your patience and support. —*Jim Lorenz*

Acknowledgments

We want to thank Mary Beth Ray, Dayna Isley, and Drew Cupp with Cisco Press for their help and guidance in putting this book together. We also want to thank the technical editors, Bernadette O'Brien, Elaine Horn, Bill Shurbert, and Glenn Wright. Their attention to detail and suggestions made a significant contribution to the accuracy and clarity of the content.

We would also like to acknowledge the entire *CCNA Discovery* development team from Cisco Systems for their hard work and dedication to making *CCNA Discovery* a reality.

Contents at a Glance

Introduction   xxxii

Part I: Concepts

Chapter 1   The Internet and Its Uses   1

Chapter 2   Help Desk   19

Chapter 3   Planning a Network Upgrade   49

Chapter 4   Planning the Addressing Structure   73

Chapter 5   Configuring Network Devices   109

Chapter 6   Routing   173

Chapter 7   ISP Services   205

Chapter 8   ISP Responsibility   241

Chapter 9   Troubleshooting   285

Chapter 10   Putting It All Together   353

Part II: Labs

Chapter 1   Lab: The Internet and Its Uses   357

Chapter 2   Lab: Help Desk   367

Chapter 3   Lab: Planning a Network Upgrade   369

Chapter 4   Lab: Planning the Addressing Structure   373

Chapter 5   Lab: Configuring Network Devices   383

Chapter 6   Lab: Routing   487

Chapter 7   Lab: ISP Services   505

Chapter 8   Lab: ISP Responsibility   521

Chapter 9   Lab: Troubleshooting   589

Chapter 10   Capstone Project: Putting It All Together   679

Appendix A   Check Your Understanding and Challenge Questions Answer Key   693

Appendix B   Router Boot and Password Recovery Labs   709

Appendix C   Lab Equipment Interfaces and Initial Configuration Restoration   721

Glossary   725

Index   739

Contents

Introduction   xxxii

Part I: Concepts

Chapter 1   The Internet and Its Uses   1

Objectives   1

Key Terms   1

What Is the Internet?   2

The Internet and Standards   2

 E-Commerce   2

 Communications   2

 Collaboration and Training   3

ISPs and ISP Services   4

Internet Service Providers   4

Delivering Internet Services to End Users   5

 Dialup Access   5

 DSL   5

 Cable Modem   6

 Satellite   6

 Dedicated Bandwidth Options   6

 Point of Presence   7

Internet Hierarchy   7

 Tier 1 ISPs   9

 Tier 2 ISPs   9

 Tier 3 ISPs   9

Identifying the Structure of the Internet   9

ISP Connectivity   12

ISP Requirements   12

Roles and Responsibilities Within an ISP   14

Summary   15

Activities and Labs   16

Check Your Understanding   16

Challenge Questions and Activities   18

Chapter 2   Help Desk   19

Objectives   19

Key Terms   19

Help Desk Technicians   20

ISP Help Desk Organization   20

Roles of ISP Technicians   21

Interacting with Customers   22

OSI Model   24

Using the OSI Model   24

OSI Model Protocols and Technologies   27

Step 1: Upper Layers Create the Data 27

Step 2: Layer 4 Packages the Data for End-to-End Transport 27

Step 3: Layer 3 Adds the Network IP Address Information 28

Step 4: Layer 2 Adds the Data Link Layer Header and Trailer 28

Step 5: Layer 1 Converts the Data into Bits for Transmission 28

Troubleshooting Using the OSI Model 29

Bottom-Up Approach 30

Top-Down Approach 30

Divide-and-Conquer Approach 31

Help Desk Troubleshooting Example 31

ISP Troubleshooting 34

Help Desk Troubleshooting Scenarios 34

E-mail Issues 35

Host Configuration Issues 35

Customer Connectivity Issues 36

Creating and Using Help Desk Records 37

Customer Site Procedures 40

Summary 42

Activities and Labs 42

Check Your Understanding 43

Challenge Questions and Activities 47

Chapter 3   Planning a Network Upgrade 49

Objectives 49

Key Terms 49

Common Issues 50

Site Survey 50

Physical and Logical Topologies 52

Star Topologies 54

Mesh Topologies 54

Network Requirements Documentation 55

Planning the Network Upgrade 55

Network Upgrades 56

Phase 1: Requirements Gathering 56

Phase 2: Selection and Design 56

Phase 3: Implementation 56

Phase 4: Operation 56

Phase 5: Review and Evaluation 57

Physical Environment 57

Cabling Considerations 58

Structured Cable 60

Purchasing and Maintaining Equipment 61

Purchasing Equipment 61

Selecting Network Devices 63

Selecting LAN Devices   63

   Speed and Types of Ports/Interfaces   63

   Expandability   64

   Manageability   64

   Cost   64

Selecting Internetworking Devices   64

   Connectivity   65

   Features   65

   Cost   65

Network Equipment Upgrades   66

Reliability and Availability   67

IP Addressing Plan   68

Summary   69

Activities and Labs   69

Check Your Understanding   70

Challenge Questions and Activities   72

Chapter 4   **Planning the Addressing Structure   73**

Objectives   73

Key Terms   73

IP Addressing in the LAN   74

Review of IP Addresses   74

   Hierarchical Addressing   75

   Classful Addressing   75

   Subnetting Concepts   77

   Classless Interdomain Routing (CIDR)   79

Subnetting a Network   82

   Network Expansion Requirements   82

   Proposed Solution   83

Classful Subnetting   85

Custom Subnet Masks   86

Communicating Between Subnets   90

IPv6   92

NAT and PAT   93

Basic Network Address Translation (NAT)   93

IP NAT Terms   95

Static and Dynamic NAT   97

Port-Based Network Address Translation   99

IP NAT Issues   102

Summary   103

Activities and Labs   103

Check Your Understanding   104

Challenge Questions and Activities   107

Chapter 5   **Configuring Network Devices   109**

Objectives   109

Key Terms   109

Initial ISR Configuration   110

Physical Setup of the ISR   112

Bootup Process   114

Startup Configuration File   114

Running Configuration File   115

In-Band and Out-of-Band Router Configuration   117

Out-of-Band Management   117

In-Band Management   117

Cisco IOS Programs   118

Configuring an ISR with SDM   120

SDM Express   121

Basic Configuration   121

LAN IP Address   122

DHCP   123

Configuring a Serial WAN Connection   124

Cisco SDM and SDM Express   126

Configuring Dynamic NAT Using Cisco SDM   127

Configuring a Router Using IOS CLI   128

Command-Line Interface and Modes   128

Using the Cisco IOS CLI   129

Using show Commands   132

Basic Configuration   137

Configuring an Interface   139

Configuring a Default Route   141

Configuring DHCP Services   141

Step 1: Create the DHCP Address Pool   142

Step 2: Specify the Network or Subnet   142

Step 3: Exclude IP Addresses   142

Step 4: Specify the Domain Name   142

Step 5: Specify the DNS Server IP Address   142

Step 6: Set the Default Gateway   143

Step 7: Set the Lease Duration   143

Step 8: Verify the Configuration   143

Configuring Static NAT Using Cisco IOS CLI   144

Backing Up a Cisco Router Configuration to a TFTP Server   146

Connecting the CPE to the ISP   148

Installing the CPE   148

Customer Connections over a WAN   151

Point-to-Point   151

Circuit-Switched   152

Packet-Switched   152

Choosing a WAN Connection   153

Configuring WAN Connections   154

Initial Cisco 2960 Switch Configuration   155

Standalone Switches   156

Power Up the Cisco 2960 Switch   159

Connecting the LAN Switch to the Router   161

CDP   164

Summary   167

Activities and Labs   168

Check Your Understanding   169

Challenge Questions and Activities   172

Chapter 6   Routing   173

Objectives   173

Key Terms   173

Enabling Routing Protocols   174

Routing Basics   174

Directly Connected Routes   178

Dynamically Updated Routes (Dynamic Routes)   178

Default Route   178

Static Routes   178

Routing Protocols   179

Common Interior Routing Protocols   182

RIP   183

EIGRP   184

Link-State Protocols: OSPF   185

Routing Within an Organization   187

Configure and Verify RIP   190

Exterior Routing Protocols   193

Autonomous Systems   193

Routing Between Autonomous Systems   195

Routing Across the Internet   196

Exterior Routing Protocols and the ISP   197

Configure and Verify BGP   199

Summary   201

Activities and Labs   201

Check Your Understanding   202

Chapter 7   ISP Services   205

Objectives   205

Key Terms   205

Introducing ISP Services   206

ISP Services   206

Reliability and Availability   207

    Reliability   207

    Availability   208

Protocols That Support ISP Services   208

Review of TCP/IP Protocols   208

    Application Layer Protocols   210

    Transport Layer Protocols   211

TCP and UDP   212

    TCP   212

    UDP   212

Differences Between TCP and UDP   214

Supporting Multiple Services   215

Domain Name Service   218

TCP/IP Hosts File   218

DNS   219

    Resource Records and Domain Namespace   220

    Domain Name Servers   220

    Resolvers   220

DNS Name Resolution   221

    Forward Lookup Zones   224

    Reverse Lookup Zones   224

    Primary Zones   225

    Secondary Zones   225

Provisioning DNS Servers   225

    Using ISP DNS Servers   225

    Using Local DNS Servers   226

Services and Protocols   226

Supporting HTTP and HTTPS   227

Supporting FTP   229

    Protocol Interpreter (PI)   229

    Data Transfer Process (DTP)   229

Supporting SMTP, POP3, and IMAP   230

    Simple Mail Transfer Protocol (SMTP)   231

    Post Office Protocol Version 3 (POP3)   233

    Internet Message Access Protocol (IMAP4)   234

Summary   236

Activities and Labs   236

Check Your Understanding   237

Challenge Questions and Activities   239

Chapter 8   ISP Responsibility   241

Objectives   241

Key Terms   241

ISP Security Considerations   242

ISP Security 242
Password Security 243
Extraneous Services 243
Patch Management 244
Application Security 244
User Rights 244
Security Scanning 244

Best Practices for Security 245

Data Encryption 247
Web Servers 248
E-mail Servers 248
Telnet Servers 248
FTP Servers 249
File Servers 249

Security Tools 249

Denial-of-Service Attacks 249
DoS 249
DDoS 249
DRDoS 250

Access Lists and Port Filtering 250
Port Filtering 250
Access Lists 251

Firewalls 251

IDS and IPS 253
IDS 254
IPS 255

Wireless Security 256
Changing Default Settings 257
Enabling Authentication 257
MAC Address Filtering 257
WEP 257
WPA 258
WPA2 258

Host Security 258
Known Attacks 259
Exploitable Services 260
Worms and Viruses 260
Back Doors and Trojans 260

Monitoring and Managing the ISP 261

Service-Level Agreements 261

Monitoring Network Link Performance 262

Device Management Using In-Band Tools 264
Telnet 264
Secure Shell (SSH) 264

Using SNMP and Syslog 265
SNMP 265
Syslog 267

Backups and Disaster Recovery 268

Causes of Data Loss 268
Hardware Failure 268

User Error   269
Theft   269
Malicious Activity   269
Operating System Failure   269

Backup Media   269
Tape Media   270
Optical Media   270
Hard Disk Media   270
Solid-State Media   271

Methods of File Backup   271
Normal (Full)   271
Differential   272
Incremental   273

Backup System Maintenance   273
Swap Media   273
Review Backup Logs   274
Perform Trial Restores   274
Perform Drive Maintenance   274

Backing Up and Restoring Cisco IOS Image Files   275
Using TFTP to Update the IOS Image   275
Using ROMmon to Recover the IOS Image   276

Best Practices for Disaster Recovery   277

Summary   280

Activities and Labs   281

Check Your Understanding   282

Chapter 9   **Troubleshooting   285**

Objectives   285

Troubleshooting Methodologies and Tools   286

The OSI Model and Troubleshooting   286

Troubleshooting Methodologies   289
Top-Down   289
Bottom-Up   289
Divide-and-Conquer   289

Troubleshooting Tools   290
Network Topologies   290
Software Troubleshooting Tools   291
Hardware Troubleshooting Tools   293

Troubleshooting Layer 1 and Layer 2 Issues   295

Layer 1 and 2 Problems   295

Troubleshooting Device Hardware and Boot Errors   298

Troubleshooting Cable and Device Port Errors   301
Excessive Noise   302
Excessive Collisions   303
Excessive Runt Frames   303
Late Collisions   303

Troubleshooting LAN Connectivity Issues   304

Troubleshooting WAN Connectivity Issues   305

   Serial x Is Down, Line Protocol Is Down (DTE)   307

   Serial x Is Up, Line Protocol Is Down (DTE)   307

   Serial x Is Up, Line Protocol Is Down (DCE)   308

   Serial x Is Up, Line Protocol Is Up (Looped)   308

   Serial x Is Up, Line Protocol Is Down (Disabled)   308

   Serial x Is Administratively Down, Line Protocol Is Down   309

Troubleshooting Layer 3 IP Addressing Issues   309

   Review of Layer 3 Functionality and IP Addressing   310

IP Design and Configuration Issues   314

IP Address Planning and Allocation Issues   317

DHCP and NAT Issues   318

Troubleshooting Layer 3 Routing Issues   323

Layer 3 Routing Issues   323

   Connected Route Problems   324

   Static and Default Route Problems   324

   Dynamic Route Problems   324

   Dynamic Routing Errors   325

Troubleshooting Layer 4 and Upper Layer Issues   331

   Layer 4 Traffic Filtering Errors   331

   Troubleshooting Upper-Layer Problems   332

      Step 1: Ping the Default Gateway   333

      Step 2: Verify End-to-End Connectivity   333

      Step 3: Verify Routing Configuration   334

      Step 4: Verify NAT Operation   334

      Step 5: Verify Firewall Filtering Rules   334

   Using Telnet to Check Upper-Layer Connectivity   335

Preparing for Cisco Certification   336

   Knowledge, Skills, and Abilities   336

   Networking Knowledge, Skills, and Abilities   338

   Making the Commitment   341

   Creating a Plan   341

   Practicing Test Taking   342

      Visit the Testing Center   343

      Format of the Examination   343

Summary   345

Activities and Labs   347

Check Your Understanding   348

Chapter 10   Putting It All Together   353

Summary Activity   353

Activities and Labs   353

Part II: Labs

Chapter 1   Lab: The Internet and Its Uses   357

    Lab 1-1: Mapping ISP Connectivity Using traceroute (1.2.3)   357

        Objectives   357

        Background/Preparation   357

        Task 1: Run the tracert Utility from a Host Computer   358

        Task 2: Interpret tracert Outputs to Determine ISP Connectivity   359

        Task 3: Map the Connectivity of Your ISP   361

        Routes Traced Worksheet   363

Chapter 2   Lab: Help Desk   367

Chapter 3   Lab: Planning a Network Upgrade   369

    Lab 3-1: Evaluating a Cabling Upgrade Plan (3.2.4)   369

        Objectives   369

        Background/Preparation   369

        Task 1: Examine the Existing Floor Plan   369

        Task 2: Evaluate the Plan for the New Floor Space   370

        Task 3: Examine the Floor Space and Wiring Plan   370

        Task 4: Reflection   371

Chapter 4   Lab: Planning the Addressing Structure   373

    Lab 4-1: Subnetting a Network (4.1.5)   373

        Objective   373

        Background/Preparation   373

        Task 1: Analyze the Network   375

        Task 2: Calculate the Custom Subnet Mask   375

        Task 3: Specify the Host IP Addresses   375

        Task 4: Consider Other Subnetting Options   376

        Task 5: Reflection   377

    Lab 4-2: Determining PAT Translations (4.2.4)   378

        Objectives   378

        Background/Preparation   378

        Task 1: Determine the IP Address of the Computer   379

        Task 2: Determine the IP Addresses of the Gateway Router or ISR   379

        Task 3: Display Baseline netstat Results   379

        Task 4: Display Active Network Connections   380

        Task 5: Determine Translated Addresses   380

        Task 6: Reflection   381

Chapter 5   Lab: Configuring Network Devices   383

    Lab 5-1: Powering Up an Integrated Services Router (5.1.3)   383

        Objectives   383

        Background/Preparation   383

Part 1: Initial Router Setup and Startup   384

    Task 1: Position the Router and Connect the Ground Wire (Optional)   384

    Task 2: Install the Compact Flash Memory Card (Optional)   385

    Task 3: Connect the PC and Configure the Terminal Emulation Program   385

    Task 4: Power Up the ISR   386

    Task 5: Troubleshoot a Nonworking Router   387

Part 2: Displaying Router Information Using show Commands   387

    Task 1: Display the Router Running Configuration   387

    Task 2: Display the Router Startup Configuration   389

    Task 3: Save the Running-Config to the Startup-Config   389

    Task 4: Display the Router System Information Using the show version Command   390

    Task 5: Reflection   392

Lab 5-2: Configuring an ISR with SDM Express (5.2.3)   393

Objectives   393

Background/Preparation   393

Task 1: Configure the PC to Connect to the Router, and Then Launch Cisco SDM   394

Task 2: Perform Initial Basic Configuration   396

Task 3: Configure the LAN IP Address   397

Task 4: Deselect the DHCP Server   398

Task 5: Configure the WAN Interface   398

Task 6: Enable the Firewall and Security Settings   401

Task 7: Review and Complete the Configuration   402

Task 8: Reflection   403

Lab 5-3: Configuring Dynamic NAT with SDM (5.2.4)   405

Objective   405

Background/Preparation   405

Task 1: Establish a Connection from the PC to the Router   406

Task 2: Configure SDM to Show Cisco IOS CLI Commands   407

Task 3: Launch the Basic NAT Wizard   407

Task 4: Select the WAN Interface for NAT   408

Task 5: Reflection   411

Lab 5-4: Configuring Basic Router Settings with the Cisco IOS CLI (5.3.5)   412

Objectives   412

Background/Preparation   412

Task 1: Configure Host IP Settings   413

Task 2: Log In to Each Router, and Configure a Hostname and Password   414

Task 3: Show the Router Running Configuration   415

Task 4: Configure the Serial Interface on R1   416

Task 5: Display Information About the Serial Interface on R1   417

Task 6: Configure the Serial Interface on R2   418

Task 7: Display Information About the Serial Interface on R2   418

Task 8: Verify That the Serial Connection Is Functioning   419

Task 9: Configure the FastEthernet Interface on R1   420

Task 10: Display Information About the FastEthernet Interface on R1   420

Task 11: Configure the FastEthernet Interface on R2   421

Task 12: Display Information About the FastEthernet Interface on R2   422

Task 13: Save the Configuration on Both Routers   423

Task 14: Check Both Router Configurations   423

Task 15: Verify That the FastEthernet Connection to Each Router Is
  Functioning   423

Task 16: Test Connectivity (Optional Challenge)   424

Lab 5-5: Configuring DHCP with SDM and the Cisco IOS CLI (5.3.7)   425

Objectives   425

Background/Preparation   425

Task 1: Configure Basic Router Settings Using IOS, and Configure PAT Using
  SDM   426

Task 2: Configure and Verify DHCP Using IOS   432

Task 3: Reflection   435

Lab 5-6: Configuring PAT with SDM and Static NAT Using Cisco IOS (5.3.8)   436

Objectives   436

Background/Preparation   436

Task 1: Configure Basic Router Settings Using IOS, and Configure PAT Using
  SDM   437

Task 2: Configure and Verify Static NAT Using IOS   444

Task 3: Reflection   446

Lab 5-7: Managing Router Configuration Files Using HyperTerminal (5.3.9a)   447

Objectives   447

Background/Preparation   447

Task 1: Configure Host IP Settings   448

Task 2: Log In to Router R1, and Configure the Basic Settings   449

Task 3: Display the R1 Router Configuration   449

Task 4: Save the Configuration on R1   450

Task 5: Start Capturing the Running Configuration File   450

Task 6: Stop Capturing the Configuration File   450

Task 7: Clean Up the Captured Configuration File   450

Task 8: Erase the Current Startup Configuration, and Restart the Router   454

Task 9: Reconfigure the R1 Router from the Saved Text File   455

Task 10: Modify the R1 Text File, and Use It to Configure the R2 Router   455

Task 11: Verify That the Network Is Functioning   456

Lab 5-8: Managing Router Configuration Files Using TFTP (5.3.9b)   457

Objectives   457

Background/Preparation   457

Task 1: Build the Network and Verify Connectivity   458

Task 2: Use TFTP to Save a Cisco IOS Configuration   459

Task 3: Use TFTP to Restore a Cisco IOS Configuration   464

Task 4: Reflection   465

Lab 5-9: Planning a WAN Upgrade (5.4.3)   466

Objective   466

Background/Preparation   466

Task 1: Identify the Business Requirements for the WAN Upgrade   466

Task 2: List Available WAN Options for the Business   467

Task 3: Identify the Best WAN Connection Option for the Business   467

Task 4: Group Discussion   467

WAN Upgrade Proposal   468

Lab 5-10: Powering Up a Switch (5.5.2)   470

Objectives   470

Background/Preparation   470

Task 1: Position and Ground the Switch (Optional)   470

Task 2: Connect the Computer to the Switch   470

Task 3: Configure the PC Terminal Emulation Program   471

Task 4: Power Up the Switch   471

Task 5: Troubleshoot a Nonworking Switch   473

Task 6: Reflection   473

Lab 5-11: Configuring the Cisco 2960 Switch (5.5.4)   474

Objectives   474

Background/Preparation   474

Task 1: Connect the Hosts to the Switch, and Configure Them   475

Task 2: Connect the Router to the Switch, and Configure the Router   475

Task 3: Perform an Initial Configuration on the Switch   476

Task 4: Configure the Management Interface on VLAN 1   476

Task 5: Verify Configuration of the Switch   477

Task 6: Verify Connectivity Using ping and Telnet   478

Task 7: Determine Which MAC Addresses the Switch Has Learned   480

Task 8: Configure Basic Port Security   481

Task 9: Connect a Different PC to the Secure Switch Port   483

Alternative Task 9: Change the MAC Address of H2 (Optional)   484

Task 10: Reactivate the Port   485

Task 11: Set Speed and Duplex Options for a Port   485

Task 12: Exit the Switch   486

Task 13: Reflection   486

Chapter 6   Lab: Routing   487

Lab 6-1: Creating a Network Diagram from Routing Tables (6.1.2)   487

Objectives   487

Background/Preparation   487

Task 1: Examine the Routing Table Entries for Router R1   487

Task 2: Examine the Routing Table Entries for Router R2   488

Task 3: Document Router Interfaces and IP Addresses   489

Task 4: Create a Network Topology Diagram   489

Task 5: Reflection   490

Lab 6-2: Configuring and Verifying RIP (6.1.5)   491

Objective   491

Background/Preparation   491

Task 1: Build the Network and Configure the Routers   492

Task 2: Configure the Hosts with the Proper IP Address, Subnet Mask, and Default Gateway   492

Task 3: Check the Routing Table Entries   492

Task 4: Test End-to-end Connectivity   493

Task 5: Configure the Routing Protocol of the Routers   493

Task 6: Show the Routing Tables for Each Router   494

Task 7: Test End-to-end Connectivity   495

Task 8: Use debug to Observe RIP Communications   496

Task 9: Reflection   497

Lab 6-3: Configuring BGP with Default Routing (6.2.4)   498

Objectives   498

Background/Preparation   498

Task 1: Configure Basic Information on Each Router   499

Task 2: Configure the Default and Static Routes   500

Task 3: Configure BGP on Both ISP Routers   500

Task 4: View the Routing Tables   501

Task 5: Verify Connectivity   503

Task 6: View BGP Information on the ISP Routers   503

Task 7: Reflection   503

Chapter 7   Lab: ISP Services   505

Lab 7-1: Editing the HOSTS File in Windows (7.3.1)   505

Objective   505

Background/Preparation   505

Task 1: Locate the HOSTS File in Windows   505

Task 2: Edit the HOSTS File   506

Task 3: Test the New Name Mapping   507

Task 4: Reflection   507

Lab 7-2: Examining Cached DNS Information on a Windows DNS Server (7.3.3)   508

Objective   508

Background/Preparation   508

Task 1: Use the Windows Server DNS Administrative Tool   508

Task 2: Perform a DNS Lookup   510

Task 3: Examine the Cached DNS Entries   510

Task 4: Reflection   511

Lab 7-3: Creating Primary and Secondary Forward Lookup Zones (7.3.3)   512

Objective   512

Background/Preparation   512

Task 1: Create a Primary Forward Lookup Zone on Windows   512

Task 2: Add a Host Record to the Primary Forward Lookup Zone   515

Task 3: Create a Secondary Forward Lookup Zone   517

Task 4: Reflection   519

Chapter 8   Labs: ISP Responsibility   521

Lab 8-1: Securing Local Data and Transmitted Data (8.1.3)   521

Objectives   521

Background/Preparation   521

Part 1: Securing Local Data   521

Task 1: Secure Bob's Files Folder   521

Task 2: Test Joe's Access to Bob's Files   525

Part 2: Identifying a Secure Communication Channel When Transmitting Data over the Internet   525

Task 1: Identify a Secure Web Page   526

Task 2: Examine Secure Access to an Untrusted Source Warning   528

Lab 8-2: Planning for Access Control Lists and Port Filters (8.2.1)   529

Objective   529

Background/Preparation   529

Task 1: Restrict Client A to One Subnet   529

Task 2: Restrict Client B Access to Server A, But Allow Access to Server B and the Internet   530

Task 3: Allow Only Client A to Access the Routers Using Only SSH   530

Lab 8-3: Researching Anti-X Software Products (8.2.5)   532

Objective   532

Background/Preparation   532

Task 1: Identify Three Products   532

Task 2: Compare Pricing   532

Lab 8-4: Interpreting a Service-Level Agreement (8.3.1)   533

Objectives   533

Background/Preparation   533

Task 1: Review Typical Customer Needs   533

Task 2: Analyze a Sample SLA and Identify Its Key Components   534

I. General Terms of the Service-Level Agreement   536

II. Warranty and Liability   536

III. Services Provided to [Client]   536

IV. System Availability   537

V. System Monitoring   537

VI. System Notifications   537

VII. Change Management Process   537

VIII. Penalties for Service Outages   540

IX. ISP Facilities Policies   540

X. Billing   540

XI. Signatures   540

Appendix 1: Services and Pricing   540

Appendix 2: System Requests Contact Lists   541

Lab 8-5: Conducting a Network Capture with Wireshark (8.3.2)   542

Objectives   542

Background/Preparation   542

Task 1: Install and Launch Wireshark   542

Task 2: Select an Interface to Use for Capturing Packets (Optional)   543

Task 3: Start a Network Capture   543

Task 4: Analyze Web Traffic Information (Optional)   543

Task 5: Filter a Network Capture   544

Task 6: Reflection   545

Lab 8-6: Managing Remote Network Devices with Telnet (8.3.3a)   546

Objectives   546

Background/Preparation   546

Task 1: Build the Network and Verify Connectivity   547

Task 2: Establish a Telnet Session from a Host Computer   548

Task 3: Perform Basic Telnet Operations Between Two Routers   549

Task 4: Perform Telnet Operations Between Multiple Routers   552

Task 5: Experiment with Multiple Linked Telnet Sessions   553

Task 6: Reflection   554

Lab 8-7: Configuring a Remote Router Using SSH (8.3.3b)   555

Objectives   555

Background/Preparation   555

Task 1: Configure the ISR to Accept SSH Connections Using SDM   557

Task 2: Configure SSH on a Non-SDM Router (Optional)   559

Task 3: Configure the SSH Client, and Connect the PC to the ISR   560

Task 4: Check the Configuration of the Cisco 1841 ISR   562

Task 5: Log Out of the Cisco 1841 ISR   562

Task 6: Reflection   562

Lab 8-8: Planning a Backup Solution (8.4.2)   563

Objective   563

Background/Preparation   563

Task 1: Choose the Media and Backup Hardware   563

Task 2: Design a Backup Plan and Procedure   564

Lab 8-9: Managing Cisco IOS Images with TFTP (8.4.3a)   565

Objectives   565

Background/Preparation   565

Task 1: Build the Network and Verify Connectivity   566

Task 2: Collect Information About the Router Memory and IOS Image   567

Task 3: Use TFTP to Save the Cisco IOS Image   569

Task 4: Use TFTP to Update a Cisco IOS Image   573

Task 5: Reflection   574

Lab 8-10: Managing Cisco IOS Images with ROMmon and TFTP (8.4.3b) 575

Objectives   575

Background/Preparation   575

Task 1: Build the Network and Verify Connectivity   576

Task 2: Collect Information About the Router Memory and IOS Image   577

Task 3: Use TFTP to Save the Current Cisco IOS Image   578

Task 4: Consider IOS Restoration Options   582

Task 5: Working in ROMmon Mode   582

Task 6: Use ROMmon and tftpdnld to Restore an IOS Image (Optional)   585

Task 7: Reflection   588

Chapter 9   Lab: Troubleshooting   589

Lab 9-1: Organizing CCENT Objectives by OSI Layer (9.1.1)   589

Objectives   589

Background/Preparation   589

Task 1: Access the CCENT Exam Web Page   589

Task 2: Review the OSI Model Layers   592

Task 3: Reflection   596

Lab 9-2: Using Wireshark to Observe the TCP Three-Way Handshake (9.1.3) 597

Objectives   597

Background/Preparation   597

Task 1: Prepare Wireshark to Capture Packets   597

Task 2: Generate and Analyze Captured Packets   598

Task 3: Reflection   603

Lab 9-3: Identifying Cabling and Media Errors (9.2.3)   604

Objectives   604

Background/Preparation   604

Task 1: Review Ethernet Device Cabling   605

Task 2: Build the Network and Configure Devices   606

Task 3: Verify Cabling and Interface Link LEDs   606

Task 4: Verify Interface Status and Connectivity   607

Task 5: Observe the Effects of Using Different Cable   610

Task 7: Reflection   614

Lab 9-4: Troubleshooting LAN Connectivity (9.2.4)   615

Objectives   615

Background/Preparation   615

Task 1: Build the Network and Configure Devices   616

Task 2: Verify Cabling, Interface LEDs, and Link Speed   617

Task 3: Verify Switch Interface Information   618

Task 4: Change Duplex Settings   619

Task 5: Change Speed Settings   620

Task 6: Set Both Duplex and Speed Settings   621

Task 7: Check Settings and Characteristics of Neighboring Devices and Interfaces   622

Task 8: Change Router Duplex Settings   623

Task 9: Reflection   623

Lab 9-5: Troubleshooting WAN Connectivity (9.2.5)   624

Objectives   624

Background/Preparation   624

Task 1: Build the Network and Configure Devices   625

Task 2: Verify Cabling and Interface LEDs   625

Task 3: Verify Router Interface Status and Connectivity   626

Task 4: Change the Clock Rate   628

Task 5: Remove the Serial Cable and Observe the Effects   630

Task 6: Change the Encapsulation Type   632

Task 7: Reflection   636

Lab 9-6: Designing an IP Subnetting Scheme for Growth (9.3.3)   637

Objectives   637

Background/Preparation   637

Task 1: Analyze the Network Topology for Subnetting Requirements   637

Task 2: Develop the Subnet Scheme   638

Task 3: Document Network Device and Host Interfaces   639

Task 4: Reflection   640

Lab 9-7: Correcting RIPv2 Routing Problems (9.4.2)   641

Objectives   641

Background/Preparation   641

Task 1: Build the Network and Configure Devices   643

Task 2: Load Routers with the Supplied Scripts   643

Task 3: Troubleshoot the BRANCH1 Router   646

Task 4: Troubleshoot HQ   650

Task 5: Troubleshoot BRANCH2   651

Task 6: Remove Auto-Summary   654

Task 7: Reflection   655

Task 8: Documentation   655

Lab 9-8: Using Telnet and SSH to Access Networking Devices (9.5.3)   656

Objectives   656

Background/Preparation 656

Part 1. Working with Telnet to Verify Device Configurations and
Connectivity 658

Task 1: Build the Network and Verify Network Layer Connectivity 658

Task 2: Establish a Telnet Session from a Host Computer 659

Task 3: Perform Basic Telnet Operations Between the Routers 660

Task 4: Perform Telnet Operations Between Multiple Routers 661

Task 5: Remove the vty Password from R3 662

Part 2. Working with SSH to Verify Device Configurations and
Connectivity 663

Task 1: Configure SSH on Router R2 664

Task 2: Log In to R2 Using the R1 CLI SSH Client 666

Task 3: Reflection 667

Lab 9-9: Identifying Necessary Knowledge, Skills, and Abilities (9.6.2) 668

Objectives 668

Background/Preparation 668

Task 1: Review the Definitions for KSAs 668

Task 2: Review an Existing Lab 669

Task 3: Identify the Knowledge, Skills, and Abilities Required for the Lab 670

Lab 9-10: Exploring the CCNA Prep Center (9.6.5) 671

Objectives 671

Background/Preparation 671

Task 1: Identify the Tools and Resources Available 671

Task 2: Explore the Cisco CCNA Prep Center Website 672

Task 3: Explore the Exam Study Area and Take Practice Exams 675

Task 4: Reflection 676

Chapter 10   Capstone Project: Putting It All Together   679

Objectives   679

Background/Preparation   679

Part A: Review the Existing Network and Customer Work Order   681

Part B: Develop the Subnet Scheme   682

Task 1: Determine the Number of Hosts and Subnets 682

Task 2: Calculate the Custom Subnet Mask 682

Task 3: Identify Subnet and Host IP Addresses 682

Part C: Document Network Device Interfaces and Physical Topology   683

Task 1: Document the Cisco 1841 Router Interfaces and Host IP
Addresses 683

Task 2: Document the Linksys Interfaces and Host IP Addresses 684

Task 3: Diagram the Upgraded Network 684

Part D: Configure Devices, and Verify Default Settings   685

Task 1: Verify the Default Settings for the Cisco 1841 Customer Router   685

Task 2: Configure the Cisco 1841 Customer Router   685

Task 3: Verify Default Settings for the Linksys, and Set the SSID   687

Task 4: Verify Default Settings for the Cisco 2960 Switch   687

Task 5: Verify That Host PCs Are DHCP Clients   687

Part E: Connect Network Devices, and Verify Connectivity   688

Task 1: Connect the Network Devices   688

Task 2: Verify Device Configurations and Network Connectivity   689

Part F: Configure Port Security for the Switch   690

Task 1: Display the MAC Address Table Entry for the Port to Which the Wired
Host Is Connected   690

Task 2: Clear the Dynamically Learned MAC Address Entry   691

Task 3: Shut Down the Port, Configure It as an Access Port, and Then Issue the
Port Security Commands   691

Task 4: Ping from the Wired Host to the AnyCompanyX Router Default
Gateway   691

Task 5: Display the Port Security Using the show port-security interface
Command   692

Task 6: Remove the Wired Host Cable from the Switch Port and Connect the
Cable from Another PC   692

Task 7: Reconnect the Original Host to Its Port and Restore the Port   692

**Appendix A   Check Your Understanding and Challenge Questions Answer
Key   693**

Chapter 1   693

Check Your Understanding   693

Challenge Questions and Activities   694

Chapter 2   694

Check Your Understanding   694

Challenge Questions and Activities   696

Chapter 3   696

Check Your Understanding   696

Challenge Questions and Activities   697

Chapter 4   698

Check Your Understanding   698

Challenge Questions and Activities   700

Chapter 5   701

Check Your Understanding   701

Challenge Questions and Activities   702

Chapter 6   702

Check Your Understanding   702

Chapter 7   704

Check Your Understanding   704

Challenge Questions and Activities   705

Chapter 8   705

Check Your Understanding   705

Chapter 9   707

Check Your Understanding   707

Appendix B   Router Boot and Password Recovery Labs   709

Lab B-1: Using the boot system Command   710

Task 1: Log in to the Router   710

Task 2: Enter Privileged EXEC Mode   710

Task 3: Save the Existing running-config to the startup-config   711

Task 4: Configure the Router and View the Running Configuration File   711

Task 5: Show Information About the Backup Configuration File   711

Task 6: Display the IOS Version and Other Important Information   711

Task 7: Create the Statements to Perform the Following Functions   712

Task 8: Show Information About the Flash Memory Device   712

Task 9: Specify a Fallback Boot Sequence   713

Lab B-2: Troubleshooting Configuration Register Boot Problems   714

Task 1: Log in to the Router   714

Task 2: Configure the Router Name and Configuration Register Setting   715

Task 3: Save the Existing running-config to the startup-config   715

Task 4: Restart the Router   715

Task 5: View the Running Configuration File   715

Task 6: Reload the Saved Configuration   715

Task 7: Display the IOS Version and Other Important Information   716

Task 8: Change the Configuration Register to Load the Startup Configuration
File from NVRAM, Save, and Reload the Router   716

Task 9: Verify the Configuration Register Setting and Log Out of the
Router   716

Lab B-3: Password Recovery Procedures   717

Task 1: Attempt to Log in to the Router   718

Task 2: Document the Current Configuration Register Setting   718

Task 3: Enter ROM Monitor Mode   718

Task 4: Examine the ROM Monitor Mode Help   718

Task 5: Change the Configuration Register Setting to Boot Without Loading the
Configuration File   719

Task 6: Restart the Router   719

Task 7: Enter Privileged EXEC Mode and Change the Password   719

Task 8: Verify the New Password and Configuration   719

Appendix C   Lab Equipment Interfaces and Initial Configuration Restoration   721

Router Interface Summary   721

Erasing and Reloading the Router   722

Erasing and Reloading the Switch   722

SDM Router Basic IOS Configuration   724

Glossary   725

Index   739

Icons Used in This Book

Command Syntax Conventions

The conventions used to present command syntax in this book are the same conventions used in the IOS Command Reference. The Command Reference describes these conventions as follows:

- **Boldface** indicates commands and keywords that are entered literally as shown. In actual configuration examples and output (not general command syntax), boldface indicates commands that the user enters (such as a **show** command).

- *Italic* indicates arguments for which you supply actual values.

- Vertical bars (|) separate alternative, mutually exclusive elements.

- Square brackets ([ ]) indicate an optional element.

- Braces ({ }) indicate a required choice.

- Braces within brackets ([{ }]) indicate a required choice within an optional element.

Introduction

The Cisco Networking Academy is a comprehensive e-learning program that delivers information technology skills to students around the world. The Cisco *CCNA Discovery* curriculum consists of four courses that provide a comprehensive overview of networking, from fundamentals to advanced applications and services. The curriculum emphasizes real-world practical application while providing opportunities for you to gain the skills and hands-on experience needed to design, install, operate, and maintain networks in small to medium-sized businesses, as well as enterprise and Internet service provider environments. The *Working at a Small-to-Medium Business or ISP* course is the second course in the curriculum.

This book is the official supplemental textbook for the second course in v4.1 of the CCNA Discovery online curriculum of the Networking Academy. As a textbook, this book provides a ready reference to explain the same networking concepts, technologies, protocols, and devices as the online curriculum. In addition, it contains all the interactive activities, Packet Tracer activities, and hands-on labs from the online curriculum as well as bonus activities.

This book emphasizes key topics, terms, and activities and provides many alternative explanations and examples as compared with the course. You can use the online curriculum as directed by your instructor and then also use this book's study tools to help solidify your understanding of all the topics. In addition, this book includes the following:

- Expanded coverage of CCENT/CCNA exam material

- Additional key glossary terms

- Bonus labs

- Additional Check Your Understanding and Challenge questions

- Interactive activities and Packet Tracer activities on the CD-ROM

Goals of This Book

First and foremost, by providing a fresh, complementary perspective on the online content, this book helps you learn all the required materials of the second course in the Networking Academy CCNA Discovery curriculum. As a secondary goal, individuals who do not always have Internet access can use this text as a mobile replacement for the online curriculum. In those cases, you can read the appropriate sections of this book, as directed by your instructor, and learn the topics that appear in the online curriculum. Another secondary goal of this book is to serve as your offline study material to help prepare you for the CCENT and CCNA exams.

Audience for This Book

This book's main audience is anyone taking the second *CCNA Discovery* course of the Networking Academy curriculum. Many Networking Academies use this textbook as a required tool in the course. Other Networking Academies recommend the *Learning Guides* as an additional source of study and practice materials.

Book Features

This book's educational features focus on supporting topic coverage, readability, and practice of the course material to facilitate your full understanding of the course material.

Topic Coverage

The following features give you a thorough overview of the topics covered in each chapter so that you can make constructive use of your study time:

- **Objectives:** Listed at the beginning of each chapter, the objectives reference the core concepts covered in the chapter. The objectives match the objectives stated in the corresponding chapters of the online curriculum. The question format in the *Learning Guide* encourages you to think about finding the answers as you read the chapter.

- **"How-to" feature:** When this book covers a set of steps that you need to perform for certain tasks, the text lists the steps as a how-to list. When you are studying, this icon helps you easily find this feature as you skim through the book.

- **Notes, tips, cautions, and warnings:** These are short sidebars that point out interesting facts, time-saving methods, and important safety issues.

- **Chapter summaries:** At the end of each chapter is a summary of the chapter's key concepts. It provides a synopsis of the chapter and serves as a study aid.

Readability

The authors have compiled, edited, and in some cases rewritten the material so that it has a more conversational tone that follows a consistent and accessible reading level. In addition, the following features have been updated to assist your understanding of the networking vocabulary:

- **Key terms:** Each chapter begins with a list of key terms, along with a page-number reference from the chapter. The terms are listed in the order in which they are explained in the chapter. This handy reference allows you to find a term, flip to the page where it appears, and see the term used in context. The glossary defines all the key terms.

- **Glossary:** This book contains an all-new glossary with more than 260 computer and networking terms.

Practice

Practice makes perfect. This new *Learning Guide* offers you ample opportunities to put what you learn into practice. You will find the following features valuable and effective in reinforcing the instruction you receive:

- **Check Your Understanding questions and answer key:** Updated review questions are presented at the end of each chapter as a self-assessment tool. These questions match the style of questions that you see in the online course. Appendix A, "Check Your Understanding and Challenge Questions Answer Key," provides answers for all the questions and explains each answer.

- **(New) Challenge questions and activities:** Additional—and more challenging—review questions and activities are presented at the end of the chapters. These questions are purposefully designed to be similar to the more complex styles of questions you might see on the CCNA exam. This section might also include activities to help prepare you for the exams. Appendix A provides the answers.

- **Packet Tracer activities:** Interspersed throughout the chapters you'll find many activities to perform with the Cisco Packet Tracer tool. Packet Tracer allows you to create a network, visualize how packets flow in the network, and use basic testing tools to determine whether the network would work. When you see this icon, you can use Packet Tracer with the listed file to perform a task suggested in this book. The activity files are available on this book's CD-ROM; the Packet Tracer software, however, is available through the Academy Connection website. Ask your instructor for access to Packet Tracer.

- **Interactive activities:** These activities provide an interactive learning experience to reinforce the material presented in the chapter.

- **Labs:** This book contains all the hands-on labs from the curriculum plus additional labs for further practice. Part I includes references to the hands-on labs, as denoted by the lab icon, and Part II of the book contains each lab in full. You may perform each lab when you see its reference in the chapter, or you can wait until you have completed the chapter.

A Word About the Packet Tracer Software and Activities

Packet Tracer is a self-paced, visual, interactive teaching and learning tool developed by Cisco. Lab activities are an important part of networking education. However, lab equipment can be a scarce resource. Packet Tracer provides a visual simulation of equipment and network processes to offset the challenge of limited equipment. You can spend as much time as you like completing standard lab exercises using Packet Tracer, and you have the option to work from home. Although Packet Tracer is not a substitute for real equipment, it allows you to practice using a command-line interface. This "e-doing" capability is a fundamental component of learning how to configure routers and switches from the command line.

Packet Tracer v4.x is available only to Cisco Networking Academies through the Academy Connection website. Ask your instructor for access to Packet Tracer.

A Word About the Discovery Server CD

The *CCNA Discovery* series of courses is designed to provide a hands-on learning approach to networking. Many of the *CCNA Discovery* labs are based on Internet services. Because it is not always possible to allow students to access these services on a live network, the Discovery Server has been developed to provide them.

The Discovery Server CD is a bootable CD that transforms a regular PC into a Linux server running several preconfigured services for use with *CCNA Discovery* labs. Your instructor can download the CD files, burn a CD, and show you how to use the server. Hands-on labs that make use of the Discovery server are identified within the labs themselves.

After it is booted, the server provides many services to clients:

- Domain Name System

- Web services

- FTP

- TFTP

- Telnet

- SSH

- DHCP

- Streaming video

How This Book Is Organized

This book covers the major topics in the same sequence as the online curriculum for the *CCNA Discovery Working at a Small-to-Medium Business or ISP* course. The online curriculum has nine chapters for this course, so this book has 10 chapters with the same names and numbers as the online course chapters.

To make it easier to use this book as a companion to the course, the major topic headings in each chapter match (with just a few exceptions) the major sections of the online course chapters. However, the *Learning Guide* presents many topics in a slightly different order under each major heading. Additionally, the book occasionally uses different examples than the course. As a result, you get more detailed explanations, a second set of examples, and different sequences of individual topics, all to aid the learning process. This new design, based on research into the needs of the Networking Academies, helps typical students lock in their understanding of all the course topics.

Chapters and Topics

Part I of this book has 10 chapters:

- **Chapter 1, "The Internet and Its Uses,"** discusses the Internet—how it is evolving and how businesses and individuals make use of it. The importance of the ISP and standards in the continuing growth of the Internet is emphasized. This chapter focuses on the Internet infrastructure, including POPs, IXPs, and the types of devices ISPs use to provide services.

- **Chapter 2, "Help Desk,"** introduces the help desk and the various roles of help desk and installation technicians. It also describes the levels of support provided by these personnel. This chapter reviews the seven layers of the OSI model as they relate to help desk support and their use in troubleshooting network issues. Common tools and diagnostic procedures used by help desk technicians are examined, as well as on-site procedures used to resolve issues.

- **Chapter 3, "Planning a Network Upgrade,"** emphasizes the importance of proper planning when performing a network upgrade, including the use of a site survey, and it describes the steps involved in performing one. An overview of structured cabling is provided, along with the factors you must consider when upgrading LAN and internetworking devices.

- **Chapter 4, "Planning the Addressing Structure,"** describes how IP addressing is implemented in the LAN and compares classful and classless networks and subnets. This chapter explains the process for subnetting a network to allow for efficient use of available IP addresses. In addition, it describes how Network Address Translation (NAT) and Port Address Translation (PAT) are used in modern-day networks.

- **Chapter 5, "Configuring Network Devices,"** introduces the ISR and the methods available for configuring an ISR using both in-band and out-of-band techniques. This chapter introduces SDM and IOS commands and discusses how each is used to configure a Cisco device. The purpose and relationship of the device startup configuration and the running configuration are explained. In addition, Cisco Discovery Protocol (CDP) is introduced. Finally, the types of WAN connections available are discussed and compared in terms of cost and speed.

- **Chapter 6, "Routing,"** describes the purpose and function of dynamic routing and compares the characteristics of different types of routes. The main interior gateway protocols and their key features are introduced, as is the configuration process for RIPv2 dynamic routing, using Cisco IOS. In addition, exterior gateway routing protocols, such as BGP, are introduced, as are the steps required to configure BGP.

- **Chapter 7, "ISP Services,"** builds on network services introduced in the first *CCNA Discovery* course. It describes them in greater detail as they relate to those provided by an ISP. It describes the most common application layer protocols, such as HTTP, FTP, SMTP, IMAP, and POP3, as well as secure versions where they exist. This chapter also compares the UDP and TCP protocols and the types of traffic for which they are best suited. It also provides additional information on the Domain Name System (DNS) and how it functions.

- **Chapter 8, "ISP Responsibility,"** describes ISP security policies and procedures and the tools used in implementing security at the ISP. This chapter describes the monitoring and managing of the ISP, as well as the responsibilities of the ISP with regard to maintenance and recovery.

- **Chapter 9, "Troubleshooting,"** provides a review of Chapters 1 through 8, with a focus on identifying and correcting network problems using the OSI model as a basis. This chapter also provides guidance in preparing for the CCENT certification exam.

- In **Chapter 10, "Putting It All Together,"** you use what you have learned about computer hardware and software, wired and wireless networking components, protocols and applications, and techniques for securing a network to plan and implement a technical solution for a small business.

Part II of this book includes the labs that correspond to each chapter.

This book also includes the following:

- **Appendix A, "Check Your Understanding and Challenge Questions Answer Key,"** provides the answers to the Check Your Understanding questions that you find at the end of each chapter. It also includes answers for the Challenge questions and activities that conclude most chapters.

- **Appendix B, "Router Boot and Password Recovery Labs,"** provides several additional labs to help you learn how to control the router bootup process and troubleshoot configuration register boot problems. Password recovery procedures are also included.

- **Appendix C, "Lab Equipment Interfaces and Initial Configuration Restoration,"** provides a table listing the proper interface designations for various routers. Procedures are included for erasing and restoring routers and switches to clear previous configurations. In addition, the steps necessary to restore an SDM router are provided.

- The **glossary** provides a compiled list of all the key terms that appear throughout this book, plus additional computer and networking terms.

About the CD-ROM

The CD-ROM included with this book provides many useful tools and information to support your education:

- **Packet Tracer activity files:** These files allow you to work through the Packet Tracer activities referenced throughout the book, as indicated by the Packet Tracer activity icon.

- **Interactive activities:** The CD-ROM contains the interactive activities referenced throughout the book.

- **CCENT Study Guides:** Referenced throughout Chapter 9, "Troubleshooting," the six Study Guides and one Preparation Guide provide you with a method to prepare to obtain your CCENT certification by organizing your review of the topics covered on the ICND1 exam.

- **Taking Notes:** This section includes a .txt file of the chapter objectives to serve as a general outline of the key topics of which you need to take note. The practice of taking clear, consistent notes is an important skill not only for learning and studying the material but also for on-the-job success. Also included in this section is "A Guide to Using a Networker's Journal." It's a PDF booklet providing important insights into the value of using a professional journal, how to organize a journal, and some best practices for what, and what not, to take note of in your journal.

- **IT Career Information:** This section includes a Student Guide to applying the toolkit approach to your career development. Learn more about entering the world of information technology as a career by reading two informational chapters excerpted from *The IT Career Builder's Toolkit*: "Defining Yourself: Aptitudes and Desires" and "Making Yourself Indispensable."

- **Lifelong Learning in Networking:** As you embark on a technology career, you will notice that it is ever-changing and evolving. This career path provides new and exciting opportunities to learn new technologies and their applications. Cisco Press is one of the key resources to plug into on your quest for knowledge. This section of the CD-ROM provides an orientation to the information available to you and gives you tips on how to tap into these resources for lifelong learning.

PART I

Concepts

Chapter 1   **The Internet and Its Uses**   page 1

Chapter 2   **Help Desk**   page 19

Chapter 3   **Planning a Network Upgrade**   page 49

Chapter 4   **Planning the Addressing Structure**   page 73

Chapter 5   **Configuring Network Devices**   page 109

Chapter 6   **Routing**   page 173

Chapter 7   **ISP Services**   page 205

Chapter 8   **ISP Responsibility**   page 241

Chapter 9   **Troubleshooting**   page 285

Chapter 10   **Putting It All Together**   page 353

## CHAPTER 1

The Internet and Its Uses

Objectives

After completing this chapter, you should be able to answer the following questions:

- How is the Internet evolving?

- How do businesses and individuals use the Internet?

- What is the importance of standards in the continuing growth of the Internet?

- What is the role of an Internet service provider (ISP)?

- How does the hierarchical structure of the Internet allow the efficient movement of information?

- What are a point of presence (POP) and an Internet Exchange Point (IXP)?

- What types of devices do ISPs use to provide services?

- What is scalability, and why is it important in the ISP network?

- What support teams work at an ISP, and what is their purpose?

Key Terms

This chapter uses the following key terms. You can find the definitions in the glossary.

Internet   *page 2*

electronic commerce (e-commerce)   *page 2*

Request for Comments (RFC)   *page 3*

Internet service provider (ISP)   *page 4*

bandwidth   *page 4*

digital subscriber line (DSL)   *page 5*

Metro Ethernet   *page 7*

point of presence (POP)   *page 7*

Internet Exchange Point (IXP)   *page 7*

Network Access Point (NAP)   *page 7*

Tier 1 ISP   *page 9*

Tier 2 ISP   *page 9*

Tier 3 ISP   *page 9*

Internet Control Message Protocol (ICMP)   *page 9*

transport network   *page 12*

DSL access multiplexer (DSLAM)   *page 13*

cable modem termination system (CMTS)   *page 13*

scalable network   *page 14*

The globalization of the Internet has occurred faster than anyone could have imagined. The manner in which social, commercial, political, and personal interactions occur is rapidly changing to keep pace with the evolution of the Internet. This expansion has created a wider audience and a larger consumer base for whatever message, product, or service can be delivered. Today millions of individuals are connected to this global network, and the number is growing. This chapter discusses the importance of standards in maintaining this rapid growth and provides an overview of the hierarchical structure of the Internet and the role of the ISP.

Part II of this book includes the corresponding labs for this chapter.

What Is the Internet?

The *Internet* is a worldwide, publicly accessible network of networks. Through interconnected computer networks, the Internet enables individuals and businesses to share information, resources, and services. Because no single individual or group of individuals controls the Internet, it is imperative that certain rules and guidelines are adhered to so that it can function efficiently.

The Internet and Standards

In the beginning, the Internet was used strictly for scientific, educational, and military research. In 1991, regulations changed to allow businesses and consumers to connect as well. Since that time, the Internet has grown rapidly and now covers the globe. New technologies are continuously being developed that make the Internet easier and more attractive to use. Online applications are available to the Internet user, including e-mail, web browsing, streaming music and video, online gaming, and instant messaging.

The way people interact, share information, and even do business is changing to keep up with the continuous evolution of this global network. The Internet is creating a wider audience and consumer base for whatever message, product, or service can be delivered. For many businesses, having Internet access has become critical, not only for communication, but also for day-to-day operation. This includes e-commerce, communications, and collaboration and training, as shown in Figure 1-1 and described in the next sections.

E-Commerce

Electronic commerce (e-commerce) is any business activity that can be conducted over the web. This includes using web space for advertisements, brochures, and catalogs, as well as ordering and distribution services. Companies can sell products and services over the Internet from their own websites, through auction sites, or through affiliated websites.

Communications

Communications refers to any electronic method of communication, such as the use of e-mail, instant messaging, and online chat. In addition, many businesses use internal phone systems that operate over the Internet using IP phones and voice over IP (VoIP) technology to reduce phone costs.

Figure 1-1   Common Uses for the Internet

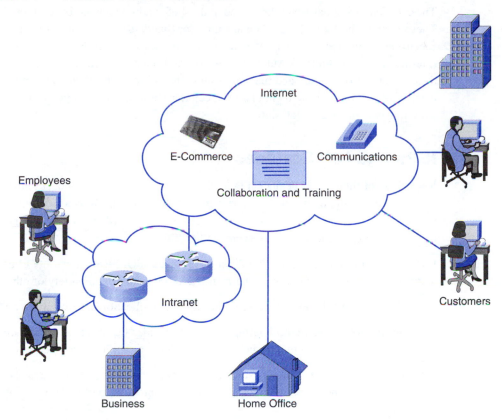

Collaboration and Training

The Internet enables the sharing of documents, presentations, and spreadsheets among users around the world. It allows teams of people to work together virtually from remote locations for business and training purposes. Examples include videoconferencing, virtual meeting places, virtual classrooms, online learning, online bulletin boards, FTP sites, and password-protected databases and applications.

With the increasing number of new devices and technologies coming online, it is important that all users and technologies adhere to a set of rules or guidelines. This allows services such as e-mail to be reliably delivered to all users. These rules and guidelines are known as *Internet standards*.

A standard is a set of rules for how something must be done. Networking and Internet standards ensure that all devices connecting to the network use the same set of rules. By having standards, different types of devices can send information to each other over the Internet. For example, an e-mail message is formatted, forwarded, and received by all devices in a standardized manner. If someone sends an e-mail via a PC, someone else can use a mobile phone to receive and read the e-mail as long as the mobile phone uses the same standards.

An Internet standard is the end result of a comprehensive cycle of discussion, problem solving, and testing. When a new standard is proposed, each stage of the development and approval process is recorded in a numbered *Request for Comments (RFC)* document so that the evolution of the standard is tracked.

Thousands of Internet standards help define the rules for how devices communicate on networks. These different standards are developed, published, and maintained by a variety of organizations. These include the International Organization for Standardization (ISO), Institute of Electrical and Electronics Engineers (IEEE), Internet Corporation for Assigned Names and Numbers (ICANN), Internet Assigned Numbers Authority (IANA), and Internet Engineering Task Force (IETF). Because these organizations create and maintain standards, millions of individuals can connect to the Internet using a variety of devices, including PCs, cellular phones, handheld personal digital assistants (PDA), MP3 players, and even televisions.

ISPs and ISP Services

Regardless of the type of device an individual or business uses to connect to the Internet, the device must connect through an *Internet service provider (ISP)*. An ISP is a company or organization through which a subscriber obtains Internet access. A subscriber can be a business, a private consumer, a government body, or even another ISP.

Users connect to the ISP through a Point of Presence (POP) using a variety of access technologies. In addition to offering connection to the Internet, an ISP can offer a variety of other services:

- **FTP hosting:** The ISP provides the server and application software for a business FTP site.

- **Applications and media hosting:** The ISP provides the server and software to allow a business to provide streaming media such as music, video, or applications such as online databases.

- **Technical support:** Many businesses do not have the in-house technical expertise to manage large internal networks. Some ISPs provide technical support and consulting services for an additional fee.

- **Voice over IP:** A business can save on long-distance telephone charges, especially for internal calls between geographically distant offices, by using VoIP.

- **Equipment co-location:** A business may opt to have some or all internal network equipment physically located on the ISP premises.

- **Web hosting:** The ISP provides the server and application software for storing web pages and web content for the business website.

Interactive Activity 1-1: Which ISP Is Best? (1.1.2)

In this activity, you determine the best ISP for a given scenario. Use file d2ia-112 on the CD-ROM that accompanies this book to perform this interactive activity.

Internet Service Providers

Although ISPs offer their clients many different services, their main role is to provide a connection to the Internet. The actual type of connection varies according to the region. Not all connection types are available in all areas. Some connection options provide continuous connection, and others provide connection only when required. *Bandwidth*, both upstream and downstream, varies between the different options and must match the requirements of the individual or business. Bandwidth is measured in bits per second (bps), kilobits per second (kbps), megabits per second (Mbps), or gigabits per second (Gbps).

Delivering Internet Services to End Users

ISPs offer various connection options for home and business users. The main connection methods used by home and small business users include dialup, DSL, cable, and satellite connections. These are shown in Figure 1-2.

Figure 1-2   Internet Connection Technology for Home and Small Business

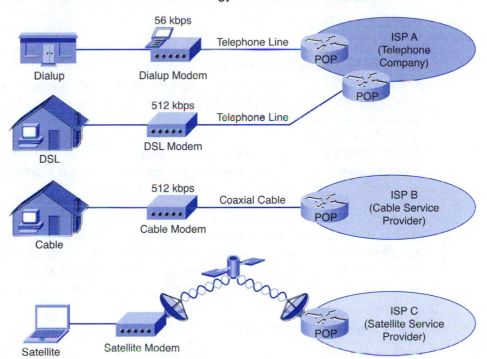

This section describes these connection methods as well as dedicated bandwidth options and the role of a point of presence (POP).

Dialup Access

Dialup access is an inexpensive option that uses a phone line and a modem. To connect to the ISP, a user calls the ISP access phone number. With connection speeds of about 56 kbps, dialup is the slowest connection option. At this speed it would take approximately 12 minutes to download a 5-MB file. Dialup is typically used by mobile workers and in areas where higher-speed connection options are not available.

DSL

Digital subscriber line (DSL) is more expensive than dialup but provides a faster connection. DSL also uses telephone lines, but unlike dialup access, DSL provides a continuous connection to the Internet. This connection option uses a special high-speed modem that separates the DSL signal from the telephone signal and provides an Ethernet connection to a host computer or local-area network (LAN).

Speeds of 512 kbps and higher are common with DSL services. At this speed, a 5-MB file would take approximately one minute to download. Upload and download speeds vary based on geography, distance from the ISP, and the type of service offered by the ISP.

DSL comes in several flavors. Typically, a home user uses an asymmetric digital subscriber line (ADSL), in which the download speed is faster than the upload speed. Because most home users download significantly more than they upload, this type of connection is sufficient. In a business environment, the amount of data uploaded may be equal to or even greater than the amount of data downloaded. For these users, an ADSL line is insufficient; a symmetric digital subscriber line (SDSL) service is more appropriate. SDSL offers the same upload and download speeds.

Cable Modem

A cable modem is a connection option offered by cable television service providers. It offers faster connection speeds than that generally provided by DSL. Cable Internet connections offer speeds of 5 Mbps to 10 Mbps. At these speeds a 5-MB file would take only seconds to download. The Internet signal is carried on the same coaxial cable that delivers cable television to homes and businesses. A special cable modem separates the Internet signal from the other signals carried on the cable and provides an Ethernet connection to a host computer or LAN. Unlike DSL, the distance from the ISP does not affect the performance of the cable connection. Cable is a shared-bandwidth service, so as more customers in an area connect and use the Internet, the speed is negatively affected.

Satellite

Satellite connection is an option offered by satellite service providers. The user's computer connects through Ethernet to a satellite modem that transmits radio signals to the nearest POP within the satellite network. Satellite Internet access speeds range from 128 Kbps to 512 Kbps, depending on the subscriber plan. Satellite connection may be the only available technology in many regions of the world.

Dedicated Bandwidth Options

Business customers often require dedicated, high-bandwidth connections to the Internet. Figure 1-3 shows the three main types of dedicated, high-bandwidth connection options that are used by businesses: T1/E1, T3/E3, and Metro Ethernet.

Figure 1-3   High-Speed, Dedicated-Bandwidth Internet Connections

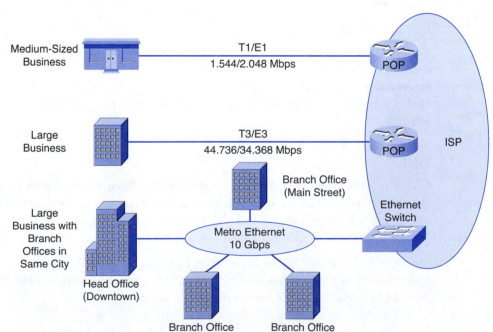

T1/E1 Connections

T1 connections transmit data at rates of up to 1.544 Mbps. They are symmetrical, meaning that the upload bandwidth is the same as the download bandwidth. A medium-sized business may need only one T1 connection for all its connectivity requirements. T1 connections are common in North America and some other parts of the world. E1 is a European standard that transmits data at 2.048 Mbps.

T3/E3 Connections

T3 connections allow data to be transmitted at rates of up to 45 Mbps. Although T3 is considerably more expensive than a T1 connection, a larger business may need a T3 connection to accommodate all its employees or business volume. Large businesses with multiple locations might use a combination of T1 and T3 lines. Quite often the main office or data center has a T3 line, and each branch office has a T1 connection. E3 is a European standard that transmits data at 34.368 Mbps.

Metro Ethernet

Metro Ethernet offers a wide range of high-bandwidth options, including Gbps links. Large companies with many branches in the same city, such as banks, often use Metro Ethernet. Metro Ethernet connects the main office location and all the branches using switched technology. It allows the transfer of large amounts of data faster and less expensively than other high-bandwidth connection options.

Point of Presence

After the type of connection is established, it is necessary to connect to the ISP to get access to the Internet. Individual computers and business networks connect to the ISP at a *point of presence (POP)*. POPs are located at the edge of the ISP's network and serve a particular geographic region. They provide a local point of connection and authentication (password control) for multiple end users. An ISP may have many POPs, depending on the size of the area it services.

Within the ISP network, high-speed routers and switches move data between the various POPs. Multiple links interconnect the POPs to provide alternative routes in case one of the links becomes overloaded with traffic or fails.

Internet Hierarchy

The Internet has a hierarchical structure. At the top of this hierarchy are the ISP organizations. The ISP POPs connect to an *Internet Exchange Point (IXP)*. In some countries, this is called a *Network Access Point (NAP)*. An IXP or NAP is where multiple ISPs are joined to gain access to each others' networks and exchange information, as shown in Figure 1-4. Currently more than 100 major exchange points exist worldwide.

Figure 1-4   Internet Hierarchy

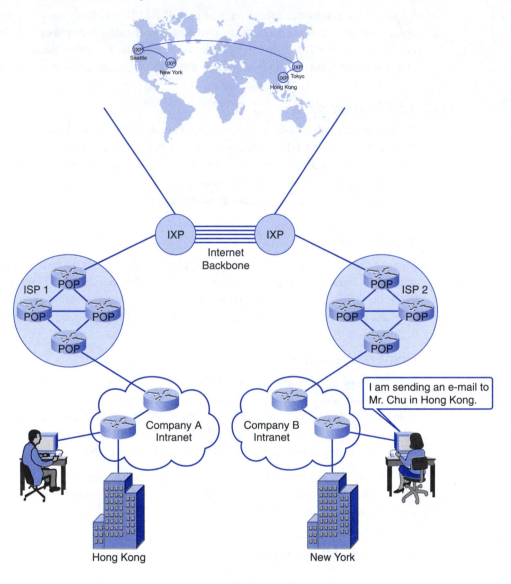

The Internet backbone consists of this group of networks owned by various organizations and interconnected through IXPs and private peering connections. The Internet backbone is like an information superhighway that provides high-speed data links to interconnect the POPs and IXPs in major metropolitan areas around the world. The primary medium that connects the Internet backbone is fiber-optic cable. This cable typically is installed underground to connect cities within continents. Fiber-optic cables also run under the sea to connect cities between continents.

ISPs are classified into different tiers according to how they access the Internet backbone. Three tiers of ISPs are identified.

Tier 1 ISPs

Tier 1 ISPs are at the top of the hierarchy. Tier 1 ISPs are huge organizations that connect directly with each other through private peering, physically joining their individual network backbones to create the global Internet backbone. Within their own networks, the Tier 1 ISPs own the routers, high-speed data links, and other pieces of equipment that join them to other Tier 1 ISP networks. This includes the undersea cables that connect the continents.

Tier 2 ISPs

Tier 2 ISPs are the next tier in terms of backbone access. Tier 2 ISPs can also be very large, even extending across several countries, but very few have networks that span entire continents or between continents. To provide their customers with global Internet access, some Tier 2 ISPs pay Tier 1 ISPs to carry their traffic to other parts of the world. Some Tier 2 ISPs exchange global traffic with other ISPs less expensively through public peering at IXPs. A large IXP may bring together hundreds of ISPs in a central physical location for access to multiple networks over a shared connection.

Tier 3 ISPs

Tier 3 ISPs are the farthest from the backbone. Tier 3 ISPs generally are found in major cities and give customers local access to the Internet. Tier 3 ISPs pay Tier 1 and 2 ISPs for access to the global Internet and Internet services.

Identifying the Structure of the Internet

Network utilities can be used to create a map of the Internet to visualize how ISP networks interconnect. These utilities also illustrate the speed at which each connecting point can be reached.

The **ping** command tests the accessibility of a specific IP address. This command sends an *Internet Control Message Protocol (ICMP)* echo request packet to the destination address and then waits for an echo reply packet to return from that host, as shown in Figure 1-5. It measures the time that elapses between when the request packet is sent and the response packet is received.

Figure 1-5   ping Utility

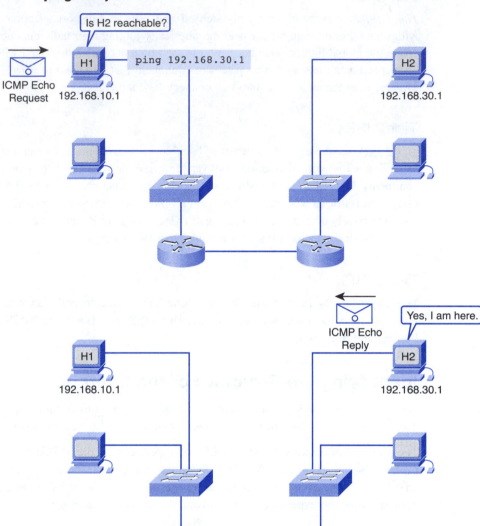

The **ping** command output indicates whether the reply was received successfully and displays the round-trip time for the transmissions. Example 1-1 shows the syntax and result of a successful **ping** command from a Windows-based host. Note that either the IP address or the domain name may be used. If the Domain Name System (DNS) is not functioning properly, the IP address should be used.

Example 1-1 Sample Output from the ping Command

```
C:\> ping cisco.netacad.net

Pinging cisco.netacad.net [128.107.229.50] with 32 bytes of data:

Reply from 128.107.229.50: bytes=32 time=560ms TTL=115
Reply from 128.107.229.50: bytes=32 time=636ms TTL=115
Reply from 128.107.229.50: bytes=32 time=460ms TTL=115
Reply from 128.107.229.50: bytes=32 time=645ms TTL=115

Ping statistics for 128.107.229.50:
```

```
    Packets: Sent = 4, Received = 4, Lost = 0 (0% loss),
Approximate round trip times in milli-seconds:
    Minimum = 460ms, Maximum = 645ms, Average = 575ms


C:\> ping 128.107.229.50


Pinging 128.107.229.50 with 32 bytes of data:


Reply from 128.107.229.50: bytes=32 time=118ms TTL=115
Reply from 128.107.229.50: bytes=32 time=376ms TTL=115
Reply from 128.107.229.50: bytes=32 time=577ms TTL=115
Reply from 128.107.229.50: bytes=32 time=120ms TTL=115


Ping statistics for 128.107.229.50:
    Packets: Sent = 4, Received = 4, Lost = 0 (0% loss),
Approximate round trip times in milli-seconds:
    Minimum = 118ms, Maximum = 577ms, Average = 297ms
```

If a packet does not reach the destination, or if delays are encountered along the way, you can use the traceroute utility to display information about where the packet encountered problems. The traceroute utility displays the path that a packet takes from the source to the destination host. Each router that the packet passes through is called a hop. The **traceroute** utility displays each hop along the way. It also calculates the time between when the packet is sent and when a reply is received from the router at each hop.

If a problem occurs, use the output of the **traceroute** command to help determine where a packet was lost or delayed. The output shows the various ISPs that the packet must pass through during its journey from source to destination. The Windows **tracert** utility works the same way. Also, a number of visual **traceroute** programs provide a graphical display of the route a packet takes. Example 1-2 shows an example of **tracert** command output.

Example 1-2 Sample Output from the tracert Command

```
C:\> tracert cisco.netacad.net

Tracing route to cisco.netacad.net [128.107.229.50]
over a maximum of 30 hops:


  1     1 ms    <1 ms    <1 ms   192.168.1.1
  2     8 ms     8 ms    12 ms   bas1-toronto46_lo0_SYMP.net.bell.ca [64.230.197.216]
  3     7 ms     7 ms     7 ms   dis7-toronto01_Vlan147.net.bell.ca [64.230.202.105]
  4     6 ms     7 ms     6 ms   core1-toronto01_GE3-1-2.net.bell.ca [64.230.161.69]
  5     7 ms     7 ms     7 ms   core3-toronto12_POS13-1.net.bell.ca [64.230.242.157]
  6    16 ms    17 ms    17 ms   core1-chicago23_pos13-0-0.net.bell.ca [64.230.147.18]
  7    17 ms    17 ms    17 ms   bx2-chicagodt_so-2-0-0-0.net.bell.ca [64.230.203.146]
  8    18 ms    17 ms    17 ms   ex2-p6-1.eqchil.sbcglobal.net [151.164.250.241]
  9    68 ms    68 ms    68 ms   ded4-g8-3-0.sntc01.pbi.net [151.164.41.165]
 10    69 ms    68 ms    68 ms   Cisco-Systems-1152786.cust-rtr.pacbell.net [64.161.0.62]
 11    68 ms    68 ms    68 ms   sjc5-dmzbb-gw1.cisco.com [128.107.224.105]
 12    68 ms    68 ms    68 ms   sjc12-dmzdc-gw1-gig1-1.cisco.com [128.107.224.14]
 13    70 ms    69 ms    70 ms   cna-prod-nv.cisco.com [128.107.229.50]
```

```
Trace complete.


C:\> tracert 128.107.229.50


Tracing route to cna-prod-nv.cisco.com [128.107.229.50]
over a maximum of 30 hops:

   1    <1 ms    <1 ms     1 ms  192.168.1.1
   2     9 ms     8 ms     7 ms  bas1-toronto46_lo0_SYMP.net.bell.ca [64.230.197.216]
   3     7 ms     7 ms     7 ms  dis7-toronto01_Vlan147.net.bell.ca [64.230.202.105]
   4     7 ms     6 ms     6 ms  core1-toronto01_GE3-1-2.net.bell.ca [64.230.161.69]
   5     7 ms     7 ms     7 ms  core3-toronto12_POS13-1.net.bell.ca [64.230.242.157]
   6    17 ms    17 ms    17 ms  core1-chicago23_pos13-0-0.net.bell.ca [64.230.147.18]
   7    18 ms    17 ms    17 ms  bx2-chicagodt_so-2-0-0-0.net.bell.ca [64.230.203.146]
   8    20 ms    17 ms    26 ms  ex2-p6-1.eqchil.sbcglobal.net [151.164.250.241]
   9    68 ms    68 ms    68 ms  ded4-g8-3-0.sntc01.pbi.net [151.164.41.165]
  10    68 ms    67 ms    68 ms  Cisco-Systems-1152786.cust-rtr.pacbell.net [64.161.0.62]
  11    68 ms    68 ms    68 ms  sjc5-dmzbb-gw1.cisco.com [128.107.224.105]
  12    67 ms    68 ms    68 ms  sjc12-dmzdc-gw1-gig1-1.cisco.com [128.107.224.14]
  13    69 ms    69 ms    70 ms  cna-prod-nv.cisco.com [128.107.229.50]

Trace complete.
```

Lab 1-1: Mapping ISP Connectivity Using **traceroute** (1.2.3)

In this lab, you use the **traceroute** utility to check ISP connectivity through the Internet. Refer to the lab in Part II of this book. You may perform this lab now or wait until the end of the chapter.

Interpreting **ping** and **traceroute** Output (1.2.3)

In this activity, you interpret successful and unsuccessful **ping** and **traceroute** command output. Use file d2-123.pka on the CD-ROM that accompanies this book to perform this activity using Packet Tracer.

ISP Connectivity

ISPs must be able to provide clients with a reliable connection to the Internet. To accomplish this, they require a variety of equipment and controlled power and environmental conditions. In addition, the ISP must be able to provision and install new services for customers as well as support existing services.

ISP Requirements

An ISP requires a variety of devices to accept input from end users and provide services. To participate in a *transport network*, the ISP must be able to connect to other ISPs. An ISP must also be able to handle large volumes of traffic.

Some of the devices required to provide services are shown in Figure 1-6:

- Access devices that enable end users to connect to the ISP, such as a *DSL access multiplexer (DSLAM)* for DSL connections, a *cable modem termination system (CMTS)* for cable connections, modems for dialup connections, or wireless bridging equipment for wireless access

- Border gateway routers to enable the ISP to connect and transfer data to other ISPs, IXPs, or large business enterprise customers

- Servers for such applications as e-mail, network address assignment, web space, FTP hosting, and multimedia hosting

Figure 1-6   ISP Connection Devices

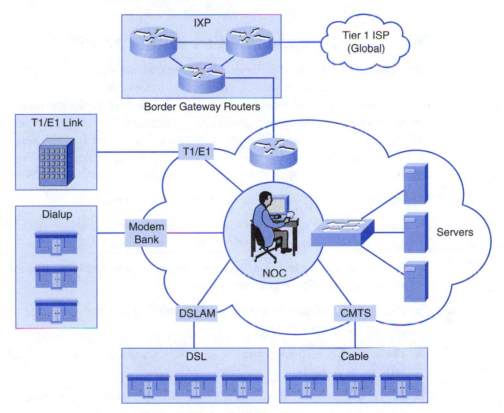

In addition, the ISPs must be able to provide uninterrupted power to the devices and also remove the large amount of heat generated by the equipment. To accomplish this, ISPs also require the following:

- Power conditioning equipment with substantial battery backup to maintain continuity if the main power grid fails

- High-capacity air conditioning units to maintain controlled temperatures

Like other businesses, ISPs want to expand so that they can increase their income. The ability to expand their business depends on gaining new subscribers and selling more services. However, as the number of subscribers grows, the traffic on the ISP's network also grows.

Eventually, the increased traffic may overload the network, causing router errors, lost packets, and excessive delays. In an overloaded network, subscribers can wait for minutes for a web page to load, or may even lose network connection. These customers may choose to switch to a competing ISP to get better performance. Loss of customers directly translates to loss of income for an ISP. For this reason, it is important that the ISP provide a reliable and scalable network.

Scalability is the ability to allow for future change and growth. A *scalable network* can expand quickly to support new users and applications without impacting the performance of the service being delivered to existing users. The most scalable devices are those that are modular and provide expansion slots for adding modules. Different modules can have different numbers of ports. In the case of a chassis router, some modules also offer different interface options, allowing for different connection options on the same chassis.

Identifying Equipment to Meet Customer Requirements (1.3.1))

In this activity you identify the appropriate equipment to meet the business needs of ISP customers. Use file d2-131.pka on the CD-ROM that accompanies this book to perform this activity using Packet Tracer.

Roles and Responsibilities Within an ISP

ISP organizations consist of many teams and departments. These teams are responsible for ensuring that the network operates smoothly and that the services that the ISP offers are available on a reliable basis. Network support services are involved in all aspects of network management, including planning and provisioning new equipment and circuits, adding new subscribers, network repair and maintenance, and customer service for network connectivity issues. When a new business subscriber orders ISP services, the various network support service teams work together to ensure that the order is processed correctly and that the network is ready to deliver those services as quickly as possible.

Each network support service team has its own roles and responsibilities:

- Customer service receives the order from the customer and ensures that the customer's specified requirements are accurately entered into the order-tracking database.

- Planning and provisioning determines whether the new customer has existing network hardware and circuits or whether new circuits need to be installed.

- The onsite installation team is advised of which circuits and equipment to use and then installs them at the customer site.

- The network operations center (NOC) monitors and tests the new connection and ensures that it is performing properly.

- The NOC notifies the help desk when the circuit is ready for operation. The help desk contacts the customer to guide the customer through the process of setting up passwords and other necessary account information.

Interactive Activity 1-2: ISP Teams and Responsibilities (1.3.2)

In this activity, you determine which ISP team is responsible for a particular task. Use file d2ia-132 on the CD-ROM that accompanies this book to perform this interactive activity.

Summary

Businesses continue to adapt to an evolving Internet. They use the Internet for such activities as e-commerce, communications, collaboration, and training. Many businesses rely on the Internet for their very existence.

Standards provide a mechanism to ensure that all devices that connect to the Internet, or that use the services offered on the Internet, follow the same set of rules. This allows different devices to communicate over the Internet.

Businesses connect to the Internet through the services of an ISP. ISPs not only provide connection services but also offer a range of support services:

- Equipment co-location
- Web hosting
- FTP hosting
- Application and media hosting
- VoIP
- Technical support

A number of connection options are available for home and business users. Home and small businesses typically connect using dialup, DSL, cable, or satellite technology. Larger businesses often require more bandwidth than home users and small businesses and therefore use connections such as T1/E1, T3/E3, and Metro Ethernet.

An ISP can be classified as Tier 1, Tier 2, or Tier 3, depending on how it accesses the Internet backbone. Tier 1 ISPs are at the top of the hierarchy and provide connectivity services to other ISPs. The Internet backbone is made up of a group of networks owned by various organizations and interconnected through Internet Exchange Points (IXP) and private peering connections.

To provide reliable services to its customers, an ISP requires a number of devices to accept input from end users and to provide the subscribed-to services. These devices include

- Access devices
- Border gateway routers
- Server
- Air conditioning units
- Power conditioning devices

The ISP's network must be reliable and scalable. A scalable network can quickly expand to support new users and services without impacting current performance. To be able to handle client requests for new services and to efficiently support existing services, ISPs are made up of many teams or departments, each with specific roles and responsibilities. ISP teams can include

- Customer service
- Network operations center
- Planning and provisioning
- Onsite installation
- Help desk

Activities and Labs

This summary outlines the activities and labs you can perform to help reinforce important concepts described in this chapter. You can find the activity and Packet Tracer files on the CD-ROM accompanying this book. The complete hands-on labs appear in Part II.

Interactive Activities on the CD:

Interactive Activity 1-1: Which ISP Is Best? (1.1.2)

Interactive Activity 1-2: ISP Teams and Responsibilities (1.3.2)

Packet Tracer Activity on the CD:

Interpreting **ping** and **traceroute** Output (1.2.3)

Identifying Equipment to Meet Customer Requirements (1.3.1)

Hands-on Lab in Part II of this book:

Lab 1-1: Mapping ISP Connectivity Using **traceroute** (1.2.3)

Check Your Understanding

Complete the review questions to check your understanding of the topics and concepts in this chapter. Answers are listed in Appendix A, "Check Your Understanding and Challenge Questions Answer Key."

1. For what purposes do businesses use the Internet? (Select all that apply.)

   A. E-commerce

   B. Communication

   C. Collaboration

   D. Training

2. Which of the following are services that an ISP might offer? (Select all that apply.)

   A. Equipment co-location

   B. Web hosting

   C. FTP hosting

   D. Application hosting

   E. VoIP

   F. Technical support

3. Which type of Internet connection might be the only choice for an individual in a remote community?

A. Dialup

B. DSL

C. Cable

D. T1/E1

E. Satellite

4. Which type of high-bandwidth connection is often used by organizations with multiple branches in a single city?

A. DSL

B. Cable

C. T1/E1

D. T3/E3

E. Metro Ethernet

5. Which tier of ISP normally has links between continents?

A. Tier 1

B. Tier 2

C. Tier 3

6. Where do multiple service providers join to gain access to each others' networks and exchange information?

A. DSL

B. ISP

C. IXP

D. IPX

7. Which ISP team is responsible for determining whether a customer has sufficient existing equipment or whether new equipment must be installed to support the new service?

A. Customer service

B. Planning and provisioning

C. Onsite installation

D. Network operations center

E. Help desk

8. Which ISP team is responsible for working with the customer to guide the customer through the final setup of a new service?

A. Customer service

B. Planning and provisioning

C. Onsite installation

D. Network operations center

E. Help desk

9. Which ISP team is responsible for testing a new service or circuit and ensuring that it is functioning properly?

   A. Customer service

   B. Planning and provisioning

   C. Onsite installation

   D. Network operations center

   E. Help desk

10. Why might a medium-sized business decide to install a T1 connection in its offices rather than a cable Internet connection?

11. Why is it important that an ISP network be scalable?

Challenge Questions and Activities

These questions require a deeper application of the concepts covered in this chapter. You can find the answers in Appendix A.

1. For what tasks do you use the Internet? What services do you use on a regular basis?

2. Outline the process that a typical ISP follows when a client calls and asks to have a new T1 connection installed in one of its branch offices.

Help Desk

Objectives

After completing this chapter, you should be able to answer the following questions:

- What are the various roles of help desk and installation technicians?

- What levels of support do help desk technicians provide?

- What are the seven layers of the OSI model, and how is the OSI model used to troubleshoot network issues?

- What common tools and diagnostic procedures do help desk technicians use?

- What onsite procedures are used to help resolve issues?

Key Terms

This chapter uses the following key terms. You can find the definitions in the glossary.

help desk 20

escalation 21

outsourcing 21

frequently asked questions (FAQ) 21

remote desktop sharing 22

managed services 22

customer premises equipment (CPE) 22

service-level agreement (SLA) 22

incident management 23

trouble ticket 23

Open Systems Interconnection (OSI) model 24

application layer 25

presentation layer 25

session layer 25

transport layer 25

network layer 25

data link layer 25

physical layer 25

upper layers 25

lower layers 25

protocol stack 26

bottom-up approach 30

top-down approach 30

divide-and-conquer approach 31

Domain Name System (DNS) 33

link-local address 35

Automatic Private IP Addressing (APIPA) 35

loopback address 36

Providing Internet service is a highly competitive business, and poor service can cause the ISP to lose customers to competing ISPs. Having a good help desk ensures that problems are resolved quickly and to the customer's satisfaction. Whether a technician is employed inside the organization as a help desk technician or as an onsite support technician, that person represents the ISP to the customer.

Help Desk Technicians

The help desk function is critical to maintaining the network and supporting end users and business functions. ISP technicians staff the help desk to resolve user problems and keep the network up and running.

This section describes the job of the help desk network technician and how this person interacts with customers.

ISP Help Desk Organization

Connecting to the local network, as well as the Internet, is critical to most business operations. When people cannot access the Internet or local network resources, their productivity can suffer. Solving network problems is a top priority for businesses and ISPs.

Because ISPs provide the Internet connection for businesses, they also provide support for problems that occur with that connectivity. This support usually includes assistance with customer equipment problems. ISP support typically is provided through the ISP *help desk*.

It is important to distinguish between a help desk technician who works within a business to support that organization's own users and a technician who works for an ISP supporting many users from different companies. The internal technician usually deals with a wider variety of issues, including local PC applications support. The internal help desk usually has more direct face-to-face contact with the end user. The ISP technician may provide some of the same support as the internal help desk. However, this person usually focuses only on the services the customer has purchased from the ISP and the access to the resources the ISP provides.

ISP help desk technicians have the knowledge and experience to fix problems and get users connected. ISP help desk technicians provide solutions to customer problems with the goal of network optimization and customer retention. Whether the problem is connecting to the Internet or receiving e-mail, the ISP help desk is usually the first place a user or business turns to for help.

A good help desk team ensures that problems are resolved quickly and to the customer's satisfaction. A typical conversation between a help desk employee and a customer is shown in Figure 2-1.

Figure 2-1   Help Desk Technician and Customer Conversation

An ISP usually has three levels of customer support:

- Level 1 is for immediate support handled by junior-level help desk technicians.

- Level 2 handles calls that are escalated to more experienced telephone support.

- Level 3 is for calls that cannot be resolved by phone support and require a visit by an onsite technician.

In addition to ISPs, many other types of medium-to-large businesses employ help desk or customer support teams within the company. The titles assigned to the technicians may vary from those described here, but the three-level hierarchy is the most common structure.

The process of raising a problem from one level to the next if the previous level cannot solve it is called *escalation*. Figure 2-2 shows the process of escalating a help desk call. Depending on the size of the organization, the help desk can consist of one person who performs all three levels of support, or it can be a comprehensive call center with elaborate call routing facilities and escalation rules. Some ISPs and businesses contract out their help desk functions to a third-party call center company, which provides the services of Level 1 and Level 2 technicians. This is called *outsourcing*.

Figure 2-2   Levels of Customer Support Escalation

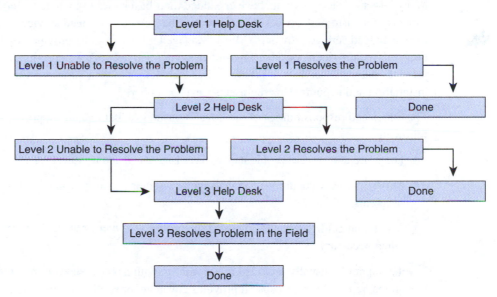

Roles of ISP Technicians

When a user initially contacts the help desk to resolve an issue, the call or message is usually directed to a Level 1 support technician. Level 1 support is usually an entry-level position that provides junior technicians with valuable experience. The duties and responsibilities of the Level 1 technician include the following:

- Diagnose basic network connectivity issues.

- Diagnose and document the symptoms of hardware, software, and system problems.

- Resolve and document any basic user issues.

- Answer *frequently asked questions (FAQ)*.

- Help customers complete online order forms to attain various systems, services, hardware, software, reports, and entitlements.

- Escalate any issues that cannot be resolved to the next level.

The majority of customer issues can be resolved by the Level 1 support technician. Level 2 support typically has fewer agents available, but they have a higher skill level. The duties and responsibilities of the Level 2 technician are similar to that of the Level 1 technician. These agents are expected to solve problems that are more challenging and that require more problem-solving abilities than normal end-user issues.

The duties and responsibilities of the Level 2 technician include the following:

- Diagnose and solve more difficult network problems.

- Use diagnostic tools and *remote desktop sharing* tools to identify and fix problems.

- Identify when an onsite technician must be dispatched to perform repairs.

Some smaller ISPs and businesses may combine Level 1 and Level 2 support, requiring that all technicians have the higher technical capabilities.

Many larger service providers have expanded their businesses to include *managed services* or onsite support of a customer network. Organizations that provide managed services sometimes are referred to as managed service providers (MSP). Managed services can be provided by ISPs, telecommunications service providers, or other types of computer and network support organizations. When an ISP provides managed services, it often requires technicians to visit customer sites for the purpose of installation and support. This represents Level 3 support.

The duties and responsibilities of the Level 3 onsite installation and support technician include the following:

- Diagnose and resolve problems that have been escalated by Level 1 and Level 2 technicians.

- Survey network conditions for analysis by a senior network technician for more complex problems.

- Install and configure new equipment, including *customer premises equipment (CPE)* upgrades, when necessary.

Level 3 support is usually provided in accordance with a *service-level agreement (SLA)*. An SLA is like an insurance policy, because it provides coverage, or service, in the case of a computer or network problem.

Interactive Activity 2-1: Identify Technician Support Level Responsibilities (2.1.2)

In this interactive activity, you identify the responsibilities of each level of network technician. Use file d2ia-212 on the CD-ROM that accompanies this book to perform this interactive activity.

Interacting with Customers

Help desk technicians may be required to provide phone support, e-mail support, web-based support, online chat support, and possibly onsite support. They are often the first point of contact for frustrated and anxious customers. Until the problem is solved, help desk technicians may continue to get calls and correspondence asking for status updates and time estimates to resolve the issue.

The help desk technician must be able to stay focused in an environment with frequent interruptions and perform multiple tasks efficiently and accurately. It can be difficult to consistently maintain a positive attitude and provide a high level of service. The help desk technician must have excellent interpersonal and communication skills, both oral and written. The technician must also be able to work independently as well as part of a team.

It is also important for the help desk technician to be able to handle customer issues with speed, efficiency, and professionalism.

Basic *incident management* procedures should be followed every time a help desk technician receives a call and begins troubleshooting issues. Incident management includes techniques such as opening a *trouble ticket* and following a problem-solving strategy. Problem-solving techniques include using troubleshooting flowcharts, addressing questions in a template format, and maintaining proper ticket escalation procedures.

The help desk technician uses a help desk script to gather information and cover the important facts about a customer incident.

In addition to technical ability, help desk technicians need other skills to be successful. Customer service and interpersonal skills are important when handling difficult clients and incidents. Help desk technicians must greet customers pleasantly and maintain a professional and courteous demeanor, as shown in Figure 2-3, throughout the call until the customer request is resolved or escalated. Technicians must also know how to relieve customer stress and respond to abusive customers. Here are some of the skills that are consistently used in successful help desk communication:

- Preparing with adequate training

- Offering a courteous greeting

- Opening a trouble ticket

- Listening to the customer

- Adapting to the customer's temperament

- Correctly diagnosing a simple problem

- Logging the call

Figure 2-3   Technician Following the Customer Service Policy

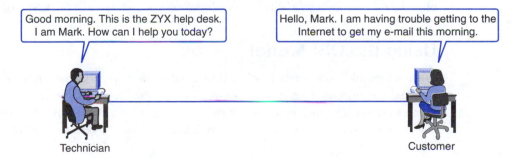

Opening trouble tickets and logging information on the tickets are critical to help desk operation. When many calls relate to a single problem or symptom, it is helpful to have information on how the problem was resolved in the past. It is also important to relay to the customer what is being done to solve the problem. Good information on open trouble tickets helps communicate accurate status, to both the customer and other ISP personnel.

Although many issues can be handled remotely, some problems require an onsite visit to the customer premises to install and troubleshoot equipment. When a technician goes on site, it is important to represent the organization in a professional manner. A professional knows how to make the customer feel at ease and confident in the technician's skills.

On the first visit to a customer location, it is important for the technician to make a good first impression. Personal grooming and how the technician is dressed are the first things the customer notices. If the technician makes a bad first impression, it can be difficult to change that impression and gain the confidence of the customer. Many employers provide a uniform or have a dress code for their onsite technicians.

The language and attitude of the technician also reflect on the organization that the technician represents. A customer might be anxious or concerned about how the new equipment will operate. When speaking with a customer, the technician should be polite and respectful and answer all customer questions. If the technician does not know an answer to a customer question, or if additional information is required, the technician should write down the customer inquiry and follow up on it as soon as possible.

Interactive Activity 2-2: Determine the Customer Support Process (2.1.3)

In this interactive activity, you examine statements and decide to which part of the customer support process they belong. Use file d2ia-213 on the CD-ROM that accompanies this book to perform this interactive activity.

OSI Model

The OSI model can be very helpful in troubleshooting network problems. An understanding of the OSI model layers and their functions provides a good foundation for categorizing and analyzing network issues.

This section describes the layers of the OSI model and some troubleshooting techniques that make use of it, including top-down, bottom-up, and divide-and-conquer. It also describes the protocols, the types of problems, and tools available for troubleshooting at each layer of the OSI model.

Using the OSI Model

When a network connectivity problem is reported to the help desk, many methods are available to diagnose the problem. One common method is to troubleshoot the problem using a layered approach. Using a layered approach requires that the network technician be familiar with the various functions that occur as messages are created, delivered, and interpreted by the network devices and hosts on the network.

The process of moving data across a network is highly structured. It is best visualized using the seven layers of the *Open Systems Interconnection (OSI) model*, commonly called the OSI model. The OSI model breaks network communications into multiple processes. Each process is a small part of the larger task.

For example, in a vehicle manufacturing plant, one person does not assemble the entire vehicle. The vehicle moves from station to station, or levels, where specialized teams add various components. Each station adds its assigned components and then passes the vehicle to the next station. The complex task of assembling a vehicle is made easier by breaking it into more manageable and logical tasks. When a problem occurs in the manufacturing process, it is possible to isolate the problem to the specific task where the defect was introduced and then fix it.

In a similar manner, the OSI model can be used as a reference when troubleshooting to identify and resolve network problems. All aspects of network communication between two hosts can be described and classified using the OSI model. The basic functions of each OSI layer are as follows:

- Layer 7: *Application layer*

  - Defines interfaces between application software and network communication functions.

  - Provides standardized services such as file transfer between systems.

- Layer 6: *Presentation layer*

  - Standardizes user data formats for use between different types of systems.

  - Encodes and decodes user data. Encrypts and decrypts data. Compresses and decompresses data.

- Layer 5: *Session layer*

  - Manages user sessions and dialogues.

  - Maintains logical links between systems.

- Layer 4: *Transport layer*

  - Manages end-to-end message delivery over the network.

  - Can provide reliable and sequential packet delivery through error recovery and flow control mechanisms.

- Layer 3: *Network layer*

  - Defines logical host addressing.

  - Routes packets between networks based on network Layer 3 device addresses.

- Layer 2: *Data link layer*

  - Defines procedures and frame formats for operating the communication links.

  - Detects and compensates for frame transmit errors.

- Layer 1: *Physical layer*

  - Defines physical means of sending data over network devices.

  - Interfaces between the network medium (physical cables and wireless) and devices.

  - Defines optical, electrical, and mechanical characteristics of both wired and wireless media.

  - Includes all forms of electromagnetic transmission such as light, electricity, infrared, and radio waves.

The seven layers of the OSI model can be divided into two groups: *upper layers* and *lower layers*.

The upper layer is any layer above the transport layer. The upper layers of the OSI model deal with application functionality and generally are implemented only in software. The highest layer, the application layer, is closest to the end user.

The lower layers of the OSI model handle data transport functions. The physical and data link layers are implemented in both hardware and software. The physical layer is closest to the physical network medium, or network cabling. The physical layer actually places information on the medium.

End stations, such as clients and servers, usually work with all seven layers. Each host runs a network *protocol stack* that it uses to send and receive messages, as shown in Figure 2-4. Networking devices are concerned with only the lower layers. Hubs operate at Layer 1; LAN switches at Layers 1 and 2; routers at Layers 1, 2, and 3; and firewalls at Layers 1, 2, 3, and 4. Figure 2-5 shows the seven layers of the OSI model and identifies some of the more important protocols, technologies and terminology associated with each layer.

Figure 2-4   Layers of the OSI Model Enable Communication Between Networked Hosts

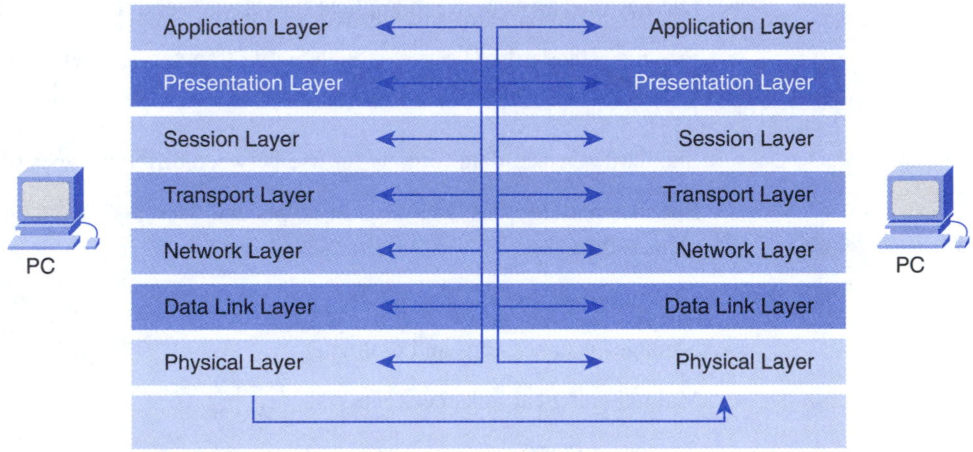

Figure 2-5   OSI Model Layer Chart

Group	No.	Layer Name	Common Protocols and Technologies	Common Network Components Associated with This Layer
Upper Layers	7	Application	DNS, NFS, DHCP, SNMP, FTP, TFTP, SMTP, POP3, IMAP, HTTP, Telnet	Network-Aware Applications, E-mail, Web Browsers and Servers, File Transfer, Name Resolution
Upper Layers	6	Presentation	SSL, Shells and Redirectors, MIME	Network-Aware Applications, E-mail, Web Browsers and Servers, File Transfer, Name Resolution
Upper Layers	5	Session	NetBIOS, Application Program Interfaces, Remote Procedure Calls	Network-Aware Applications, E-mail, Web Browsers and Servers, File Transfer, Name Resolution
Lower Layers	4	Transport	TCP and UDP	Video and Voice Streaming Mechanisms, Firewall Filtering Lists
Lower Layers	3	Network	IP, IPv6, IP NAT	IP Addressing, Routing
Lower Layers	2	Data Link	Ethernet Family, WLAN, Wi-Fi, ATM, PPP	Network Interface Cards and Drivers, Network Switching, WAN Connectivity
Lower Layers	1	Physical	Electrical Signaling, Light Wave Patterns, Radio Wave Patterns	Physical Medium (Copper Twisted Pair, Fiber-Optic Cable, Wireless Transmitters), Hubs and Repeaters

OSI Model Protocols and Technologies

When using the OSI model as a framework for troubleshooting, it is important to understand which functions are performed at each layer. You also need to understand what network information is available to the devices or software programs performing these functions. For example, many processes must occur for e-mail to successfully travel from the client to the server. The OSI model breaks the common task of sending and receiving e-mail into separate and distinct steps:

Step 1.   Upper layers create the data.

Step 2.   Layer 4 packages the data for end-to-end transport.

Step 3.   Layer 3 adds the network IP address information.

Step 4.   Layer 2 adds the data link layer header and trailer.

Step 5.   Layer 1 converts the data into bits for transmission.

Step 1: Upper Layers Create the Data

When a user creates an e-mail message, the alphanumeric characters entered are converted into digital bits within the computer's RAM. When the message is sent, the information in the message is converted into data that can travel across the network. Upper Layers 7, 6, and 5 are responsible for ensuring that the message is formatted in a way that can be understood by the application running on the destination host. This process is called encoding. The upper layers then send the encoded messages to the lower layers for transport across the network. Figure 2-6 shows some of the functions that the upper layers can perform. Transporting the e-mail to the correct server relies on the configuration information provided by the user. Problems that occur at the application layer are often related to errors in the configuration of the user software programs.

Figure 2-6   OSI Upper-Layer Functions

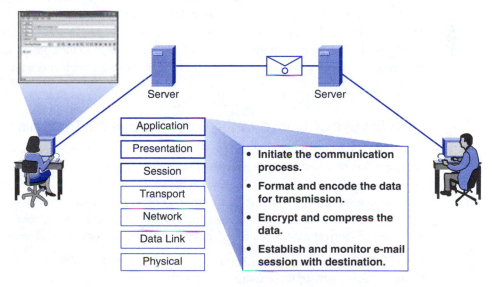

Step 2: Layer 4 Packages the Data for End-to-End Transport

The data that comprises the e-mail message is packaged for network transport at Layer 4. Layer 4 breaks the message into smaller segments. A header is placed on each segment, indicating the TCP or UDP port number that corresponds to the correct destination application. Examples of application layer destination port numbers include port 80 for HTTP and port 21 for FTP session control. When e-mail is sent, the destination application port is 25, which corresponds to Simple Mail Transport Protocol (SMTP). Functions in the transport layer indicate the type of delivery service. E-mail uses TCP segments, so the destination e-mail server acknowledges packet delivery. Layer 4 functions are implemented in software that runs on the source and destination hosts. Firewalls often use the TCP and UDP port numbers to filter traffic. Therefore, problems that occur at Layer 4 can be caused by improperly configured firewall filter lists. The process of adding a transport header to each user data segment is called *encapsulation*. As the user data moves down through the protocol stack, each layer encapsulates the next, until the bits are transmitted onto the medium.

Step 3: Layer 3 Adds the Network IP Address Information

The segments of e-mail data received from the transport layer are put into packets. Each packet contains a header with the source and destination logical IP addresses. Routers use the destination address to direct the packets across the network along the appropriate path. Incorrectly configured IP address information on the source or destination hosts can cause Layer 3 problems. Because routers also use IP address information, router configuration errors can also cause problems at this layer.

Step 4: Layer 2 Adds the Data Link Layer Header and Trailer

Each network device in the path from the source to the destination, including the sending host, encapsulates the packet into a frame. The frame header contains the physical or hardware address of the next directly connected network device on the link. Each device in the chosen network path requires framing for it to connect to the next device. In addition to the header, a trailer is added to the end of the packet to complete the frame. The trailer contains a checksum to help ensure that the frame content received by a device is the same as that which was sent by the previous device in the series.

As data travels through a network, it may pass through many different types of devices. The frame type and physical addressing can change at each device, but the internal contents of the frame do not change. For example, a package that is sent to someone may go from a car to a truck to an airplane to another truck before it reaches the end user. The type of carrier and vehicle identification changes at each step, but the contents of the package being carried do not. Switches and network interface cards (NIC) use the information in the frame to deliver the message to the correct destination device. Incorrect NIC drivers, interface cards themselves, or hardware problems with switches can cause Layer 2 issues.

Step 5: Layer 1 Converts the Data into Bits for Transmission

The frame is converted into a pattern of 1s and 0s (bits) for transmission on the medium. A clocking or timing function enables the devices to distinguish these bits as they travel across the medium. The medium can change along the path between the source and destination. For example, the e-mail message can originate on an Ethernet LAN, cross a fiber-optic campus backbone, and cross a serial WAN link until it reaches its destination on another remote Ethernet LAN. Layer 1 problems can be caused by loose or incorrect cables, malfunctioning interface cards, or electrical interference.

Figure 2-7 shows a completed Ethernet frame ready for transmission over the network to the e-mail server. It takes many of these frames to carry the entire message. A portion of the user e-mail data is encapsulated in a TCP segment. The TCP segment is encapsulated in an IP packet, and the IP packet is encapsulated in the Ethernet frame. On its way to the e-mail server, this Ethernet frame may pass through multiple switches and one or more routers. As the frame passes through each router, the exiting frame header is stripped and replaced with another header. This could be an Ethernet header or a WAN link encapsulation header, depending on the link type to which it is being forwarded.

Figure 2-7   Encapsulated Components Within an Ethernet Frame

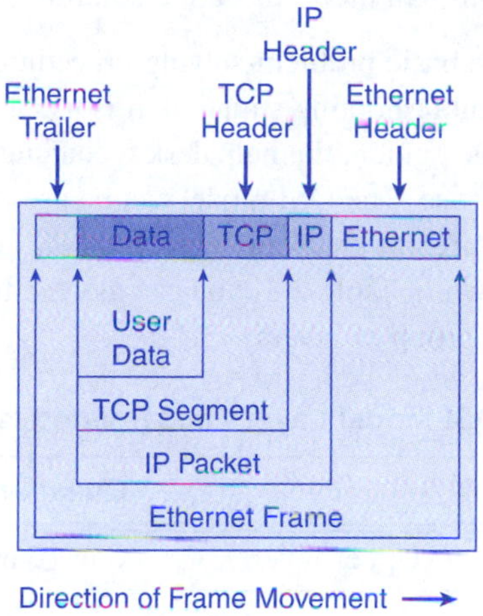

IP
Header

Ethernet   TCP   Ethernet
Trailer   Header   Header

| | Data | TCP | IP | Ethernet |

User
Data

TCP Segment

IP Packet

Ethernet Frame

Direction of Frame Movement ⟶

At the receiving e-mail server, the process described in Steps 1 through 5 is reversed, with the message traveling back up the layers to the appropriate application. The Ethernet frame header is stripped, followed by the IP header and then the TCP header. After all TCP segments have been received and reassembled on the e-mail server, the e-mail message is stored on the server's hard disks. When the e-mail recipient retrieves the message from the server, it starts the process of encapsulation again to transmit the message over the network to the final recipient host. There the frames are de-encapsulated so that the user can read them.

Interactive Activity 2-3: Identify OSI Layer Protocols and Technologies (2.2.2)

In this interactive activity, you identify the layer to which the protocol or technology belongs. Use file d2ia-222 on the CD-ROM that accompanies this book to perform this interactive activity.

Troubleshooting Using the OSI Model

As a theoretical model, the OSI model defines the functions that take place at the seven layers. These then can be associated with the protocols, hardware, and other specifications that operate at these layers.

The OSI model also provides a systematic basis for troubleshooting a network. In any troubleshooting scenario, the basic problem-solving procedure includes the following steps:

Step 1. Define the problem.

Step 2. Isolate the cause of the problem.

Step 3. Solve the problem:

- Identify and prioritize alternative solutions.

- Select one alternative as the solution.

- Implement the solution.

- Evaluate the solution.

- Document the solution.

If an identified solution does not fix the problem, undo any changes, and proceed to the next possible solution. Loop through the steps until a solution works.

In addition to the basic problem-solving procedures, the OSI model can be used as a troubleshooting guide. In any troubleshooting situation, it is usually best to start with the easiest items to check. Using the OSI model as a guide, the help desk technician can query the customer to help define the problem and isolate the cause. The OSI model can be used to analyze and troubleshoot a problem when accessing a website. Different problems at each layer can contribute to the symptoms being experienced. For example, as shown in Table 2-1, you can ask the following questions to help isolate the problem to a specific layer or group of layers.

Table 2-1   OSI Model Layers and Related Issues

Layer	Question
Layers 5 through 7: Upper layers	Can your browser open this website?
Layer 4: Transport	Do you have a firewall configured on your PC?
Layer 3: Network	Can you ping your default gateway?
Layer 2: Data link	Is the link light on your NIC on?
Layer 1: Physical	Is your network cable plugged in and secure?

When troubleshooting a problem using the OSI model, you have three basic troubleshooting approaches:

- Bottom-up
- Top-down
- Divide-and-conquer

Bottom-Up Approach

The *bottom-up approach* to troubleshooting a networking problem starts with the network's physical components and works up the layers of the OSI model. Bottom-up troubleshooting is an effective and efficient approach for situations when the problem is suspected to be physical. Physical problems are usually fairly easy to rule out and can save you time troubleshooting other higher-level issues. For example, if the cable is unplugged, it does not make sense to spend time trying to analyze upper-layer problems.

Top-Down Approach

When you apply a *top-down approach* to troubleshooting a networking problem, you start with the user application and work your way down the layers of the OSI model. The top-down approach is usually the simple route and typically affects only one or a few users. Lower layers, or network infrastructure, usually affect more than a few users.

For example, if a user cannot get to a website, the technician can start at the top of the OSI model and try accessing a different website. If the other website can be accessed, the problem is probably with the first website. If the second site is also inaccessible, the technician can move down the OSI model and check for a firewall blocking ports at the transport layer. The technician could then check IP settings on the host and try pinging the default gateway or the DNS servers to determine if the problem is at the network layer.

Divide-and-Conquer Approach

The *divide-and-conquer approach* is generally used by more experienced network technicians. The technician makes an educated guess targeting the problem layer and then moves up or down the OSI layers based on the observed results.

Help Desk Troubleshooting Example

The help desk technician usually has a standard checklist or script to follow when troubleshooting a problem. Often the script takes a bottom-up approach to troubleshooting because physical problems usually are the simplest to diagnose and repair, and the bottom-up approach starts with the physical layer.

Layer 1 Troubleshooting

The technician should start with Layer 1 issues. Remember, Layer 1 deals with the physical connectivity of the network devices. Layer 1 problems often involve cabling and electricity and are the cause of many help desk calls. Some of the more common Layer 1 problems include the following:

- Device power is off
- Device power is unplugged
- Loose network cable connection
- Incorrect cable type
- Faulty network cable

To troubleshoot at Layer 1, check that all devices have the proper electrical supply and that they are turned on. This seems obvious, but many times a device within the network path from source to destination may be overlooked by the person reporting the problem. If any LEDs display the status of the connectivity, verify with the customer that they are indicating correctly. If the technician is onsite at the customer location, the next step is to visually inspect the network cabling and reconnect cables to ensure a proper connection. Figure 2-8 shows the back of a router with various connections, including an Ethernet cable, console cable, serial cable, and power cord. Any of these can cause Layer 1 problems that might prevent network communication.

Figure 2-8   Cables and Connections

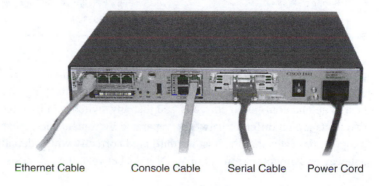

Ethernet Cable   Console Cable   Serial Cable   Power Cord

When remotely troubleshooting a problem, talk the caller through each step. Tell the person what to look for and what to do if an error is found. If it is determined that all Layer 1 issues have been addressed, it is time to travel up the OSI model to Layer 2.

Layer 2 Troubleshooting

Network switches and host NICs perform Layer 2 functions. Layer 2 problems can be caused by faulty equipment, incorrect device drivers, or an improperly configured switch. When remotely troubleshooting a problem, it may be difficult to isolate a Layer 2 problem.

An onsite technician can check whether the NIC is installed and working properly. Reseating the NIC, or replacing a suspected faulty NIC with a known good NIC, helps isolate the problem. The same process can be done with any network switch.

Layer 3 Troubleshooting

At Layer 3, the technician needs to investigate the logical addressing used in the network, such as the IP addressing scheme. If the network is using IP addressing, the technician verifies that the device has the proper settings, such as

- IP address within the assigned network
- Correct subnet mask
- Correct default gateway
- Other settings as required, such as DHCP or DNS

Most network problems usually can be resolved using Layer 1, 2, and 3 troubleshooting techniques. At Layer 3, several utilities can assist with the troubleshooting process. Three of the most common Windows command-line tools are **ipconfig**, **ping**, and **tracert**. Linux and UNIX hosts use **ifconfig**, **ping**, and **traceroute**. Cisco network devices such as switches and routers can also use **ping** and **traceroute**. Examples of the output from the Windows versions of these tools follow.

ipconfig shows IP settings on the computer, as shown in Example 2-1.

Example 2-1 Sample ipconfig Output

```
C:\> ipconfig

Windows IP Configuration
Ethernet adapter Local Area Connection:
    Connection-specific DNS Suffix  . : cisco.com
    IP Address. . . . . . . . . .  : 192.168.1.100
    Subnet Mask . . . . . . . . . . : 255.255.255.0
    Default Gateway . . . . . . . . : 192.168.1.1
```

ping tests basic network connectivity, as shown in Example 2-2. If the IP address 192.168.1.1 is on the same local Ethernet network as the host that issued the ping, the ping demonstrates that the target host is up and configured correctly and that any switches in between are functioning properly. If the two hosts are on different networks, separated by routers and perhaps one or more WAN links, the ping demonstrates that the host is configured correctly with a default gateway. It also shows that the gateway and any other routers or WAN links between the two hosts are functioning properly.

Example 2-2 Sample ping Output

```
C:\> ping 192.168.1.1

Pinging 192.168.1.1 with 32 bytes of data:
Reply from 192.168.1.1: bytes=32 time<1ms TTL=64
```

```
Reply from 192.168.1.1: bytes=32 time<1ms TTL=64
Reply from 192.168.1.1: bytes=32 time<1ms TTL=64
Reply from 192.168.1.1: bytes=32 time<1ms TTL=64
Ping statistics for 192.168.1.1:
    Packets: Sent = 4, Received = 4, Lost = 0 (0% loss),
Approximate round trip times in milli-seconds:
    Minimum = 0ms, Maximum = 0ms, Average = 0ms
```

traceroute or **tracert** determines whether the routing path between the source and destination is available, as shown in Example 2-3. This example illustrates a Windows PC issuing the command. If this were a Linux or UNIX host or a Cisco networking device, such as a router, the command used would be **traceroute**.

Example 2-3 Sample tracert Output

```
C:\> tracert www.cisco.com

Tracing route to www.cisco.com [198.133.219.25]
over a maximum of 30 hops:
<some output omitted>
  1    <1 ms    <1 ms    <1 ms   192.168.1.1
  2     8 ms     9 ms     7 ms   10.44.192.1
  3     7 ms     7 ms    10 ms   gig5-2.rtr3.cisco.com [172.18.234.57]
  4     9 ms     9 ms    10 ms   www.cisco.com [198.133.219.25]
Trace complete
```

Layer 4 Troubleshooting

If Layers 1 through 3 all appear to be operating normally and the technician can successfully ping the IP address of the remote server, it is time to check the higher layers. For example, if a network firewall is used along the path, it is important to check that the application TCP or UDP port is opened and that no filter lists are blocking traffic to that port.

Layer 5 Through 7 Troubleshooting

The technician should also check the application configuration. For example, if troubleshooting an e-mail issue, ensure that the application is configured with the correct sending and receiving e-mail server information, as shown in Figure 2-9. In the figure, the e-mail server name is specified. If the wrong server name is specified, the e-mail client cannot send or receive e-mail. Because the server name must be resolved to an IP address before e-mail can be sent or received, it is also necessary to ensure that *Domain Name System (DNS)* resolution is occurring as expected. This can be done by pinging the e-mail server by name and IP address. If the technician can ping the server by IP address but not by name, there could be a problem with DNS. Further testing can also be performed by pinging the primary and secondary DNS servers to see if they are up. Remote technicians can check higher-layer issues by using other network utility tools, such as a packet sniffer, to view traffic as it crosses the network. A network application, such as Telnet, can also be used to view configurations remotely.

Figure 2-9   E-mail Account Settings

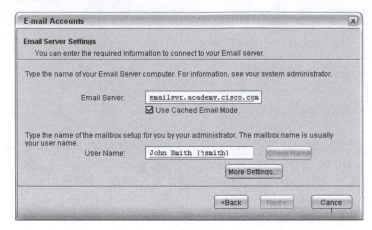

The bottom-up approach works for many situations, but the top-down approach can also be used. The top-down approach simply reverses the order in which things are checked, starting with the application layer.

The divide-and-conquer approach can also be used. With this technique the technician may choose to start the troubleshooting process at a middle layer, such as the network layer. The technician then works up or down the OSI model, depending on the troubleshooting results from that layer.

Interactive Activity 2-4: Identify Network Issues at OSI Layers (2.2.3)

In this interactive activity, you identify whether a network issue occurs at Layer 1, Layer 2, Layer 3, Layer 4, or Layers 5 through 7. Use file d2ia-223 on the CD-ROM that accompanies this book to perform this interactive activity.

ISP Troubleshooting

Network help desk personnel must be prepared for various types of potential end-user problems, but most can be categorized as either e-mail-related or an inability to access a network resource due to connectivity issues. Problems can usually be resolved remotely but may require an onsite visit by the technician. This section covers the use of help desk records, remote diagnostics, and onsite customer procedures.

Help Desk Troubleshooting Scenarios

The number and types of calls received by the help desk can vary considerably. Some of the most common calls include e-mail and connectivity issues.

E-mail Issues

Common e-mail issues include the following:

- You can receive but not send

- You can send but not receive

- You cannot send or receive

- Nobody can reply to your messages

A very common cause of many e-mail problems is using the wrong POP, IMAP, or SMTP server name. It is best to check with the e-mail administrator to confirm the proper name of the e-mail server and SMTP server. In some cases, the same server name for both POP/IMAP and SMTP are used. Also, confirm that the username and password are correct.

When troubleshooting these issues over the phone, it is important to step the customer through the configuration parameters carefully. Many customers are unfamiliar with both the terminology and the values of the various configuration parameters. If possible, connecting to the customer device via remote management software, using in-band management, is preferred. Examples of remote desktop management software include PC Anywhere, LogMeIn, and GoToMyPC. Use an Internet search engine with the keywords "remote desktop management software" to see many others. When the technician uses remote desktop tools, the end user must allow the remote application to access his or her PC. This allows the technician to take control of the customer's PC and perform the necessary steps for the customer.

Another problem that can affect application functionality is a failure of DNS to correctly resolve server names. This can be checked with the command-line **ping** or **nslookup**. A simple web browser check for DNS operation can prevent needless troubleshooting steps.

Host Configuration Issues

A common issue that can prevent connectivity to the Internet or other network resources is improperly configured host addressing information. This can include an incorrect IP address, subnet mask, or default gateway, or a combination of these.

In environments where the IP addressing information is manually configured, it is possible that the IP configuration was simply entered incorrectly. In environments where hosts are configured to dynamically receive an IP address from an assignment server, such as a DHCP server, the DHCP server may fail or become unreachable due to network issues.

If a Windows host is configured to receive an address dynamically, and an assignment server, such as a DHCP server, is unavailable or unreachable, the operating system will automatically assign a *link-local address* to the local host. IPv4 addresses in the address range 169.254.0.1 to 169.254.255.254 (169.254.0.0/16) are designated as link-local addresses. A link-local process will randomly select an IP address within the 169.254.0.0/16 range. But what prevents two hosts from randomly selecting the same IP address?

When the link-local process selects an IP address, it sends an ARP query with that IP onto the network to see if any other devices are using that address. If there is no response, the IP address is assigned to the device; otherwise, another IP address is selected and the ARP query is repeated. Microsoft refers to link-local addresses as *Automatic Private IP Addressing (APIPA)*.

If multiple hosts on the same network obtain a link-local address, client/server and peer-to-peer applications between those hosts will work properly. However, because link-local addresses are in the private Class B address space, communication outside the local network is not possible.

When troubleshooting both manually and dynamically configured hosts, use the host command **ipconfig /all** to verify that the host is using the appropriate IP configuration.

In Figure 2-10, the DHCP server on Network A is down. All Microsoft OS hosts on this network receive an APIPA link-local address. They are able to communicate locally but are unable to access other hosts on other networks. The DHCP server on Network B is up and all hosts on that network receive normal IP addressing. These hosts can communicate with each other and with hosts on the Internet.

Figure 2-10   APIPA Addressing Issues

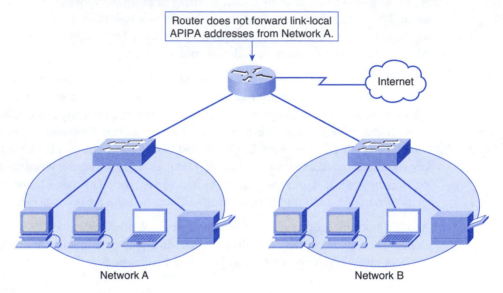

Customer Connectivity Issues

Connectivity problems are more common with new customers trying to connect for the first time; however, sometimes existing customers encounter connectivity issues. First-time customers usually have a problem with the hardware as well as software settings. Existing customers notice connectivity problems when they cannot open a web page or connect to instant messaging or e-mail.

There can be many reasons why a customer has no connectivity:

- Billing account issues

- Hardware failure

- Physical layer problems

- Application settings

- Application plug-in is missing

- Missing applications

In many cases, the problem is a faulty cable, or even a cable plugged in to an incorrect port. These types of issues can be resolved by checking the cable connection or replacing the cable.

Other problems, such as software issues, may be more difficult to detect and might require researching similar issues on FAQs or a knowledge base. One example is an incorrectly loaded TCP/IP stack, preventing IP from operating correctly. The TCP/IP stack can be tested and verified using a *loopback address*. The loopback is a special address, the reserved IPv4 address 127.0.0.1, which hosts use to direct traffic to themselves.

The loopback address creates a shortcut method for TCP/IP applications and services that run on the same device to communicate.

You can ping the loopback address to test the configuration of TCP/IP on the local host. If you are unable to get a response when pinging the loopback address, suspect an improperly configured or installed TCP/IP stack.

Addresses 127.0.0.1 through 127.255.255.254 are reserved for testing purposes. Any address within this block will loop back within the local host. No address within this block should ever appear on any network. Despite the fact that the entire 127.0.0.0/8 network range is reserved, the only address typically used for loopback testing is the 127.0.0.1 address.

Troubleshoot and Resolve Network Connectivity Issues (2.3.1)

In this activity, you troubleshoot and resolve a network connectivity issue. Use file d2-231.pka on the CD-ROM that accompanies this book to perform this interactive activity.

Creating and Using Help Desk Records

When a Level 1 help desk technician receives a call, he or she follows a certain process in gathering information and using a system to store and retrieve relevant information. This is extremely important in case a call has to be escalated to Layer 2, or even needs an onsite visit.

The information gathering and recording process starts as soon as the technician answers the phone. When the customer identifies himself or herself, the technician accesses the relevant customer information. Typically, a database application is used to manage the customer information. Examples of help desk software include Autotask, Help Desk, and HelpSTAR. Use an Internet search engine with the keywords "help desk management software" to see many others.

The information is transferred to a trouble ticket, or incident report. This document can be a piece of paper in a filing system or an electronic tracking system designed to follow the troubleshooting process from beginning to end. Each person who works on the customer's problem is expected to record in the trouble ticket what was done. When an onsite call is required, the trouble ticket information can be converted to a work order, as shown in Figure 2-11, that the onsite technician can take to the customer site.

Figure 2-11   Work Order Form

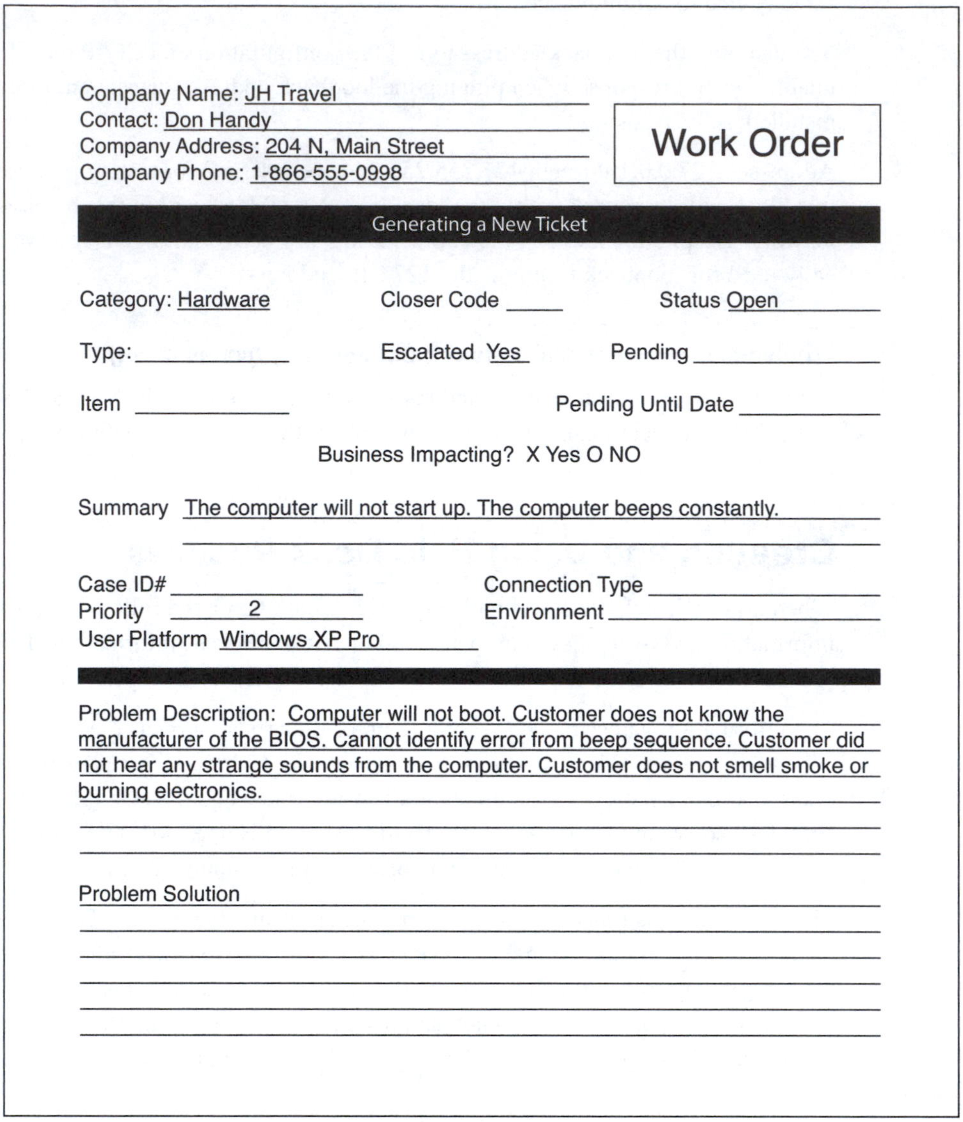

Company Name: JH Travel
Contact: Don Handy
Company Address: 204 N, Main Street   **Work Order**
Company Phone: 1-866-555-0998

Generating a New Ticket

Category: Hardware   Closer Code _____   Status Open _____

Type: _____   Escalated Yes   Pending _____

Item _____   Pending Until Date _____

Business Impacting? X Yes O NO

Summary   The computer will not start up. The computer beeps constantly.
_____

Case ID# _____   Connection Type _____
Priority _____2_____   Environment _____
User Platform Windows XP Pro _____

Problem Description: Computer will not boot. Customer does not know the
manufacturer of the BIOS. Cannot identify error from beep sequence. Customer did
not hear any strange sounds from the computer. Customer does not smell smoke or
burning electronics.
_____

Problem Solution _____
_____
_____
_____
_____
_____

When a problem is resolved, the solution is documented on the customer work order or trouble ticket and in a knowledge-base document for future reference.

Occasionally, the help desk technician may receive a call that cannot be resolved quickly. In this case, the technician is responsible for passing the call to someone who is more qualified to resolve the issue. This is the process of call escalation, in which the call is passed to a Level 2 technician.

Level 1 and Level 2 help desk technicians attempt to solve customer problems using the telephone, web tools, and possibly even remote desktop-sharing applications.

If the help desk technicians cannot remotely fix the problem, it is often necessary to dispatch a mobile onsite technician to the customer premises. It is the job of the onsite technician to visit the customer premises to physically work on the problem equipment. The help desk technician can make an appointment with the customer for the onsite technician to perform the repairs, or it may be the responsibility of the onsite technician to arrange the appointment.

To properly troubleshoot the problem, the onsite technician reviews the trouble ticket to see what was previously done. This review gives the technician some background information, as well as a logical starting point. It also helps the technician decide which tools and supplies to bring, rather than having to leave the customer site to obtain supplies.

Onsite technicians typically work on the network at the customer location. But sometimes the technician is unable to make the needed repairs and must bring the damaged equipment back to the ISP site for repair. In many cases, the technician can install a replacement unit to get the customer up and running. The onsite technician can bring a number of tools to help with the job, such as those shown in Figure 2-12. These can include, but are not limited to, the following:

- **Crimpers:** Used to crimp the connector to the cable.

- **Cable:** Used to run new cable or replace old cable.

- **Cable tester:** Used to determine cable length and whether a cable is good or bad.

- **Connectors:** Used to make new cables or replace broken connectors.

- **Multimeter:** Used to check an electric circuit.

- **Laptop:** Used to test the network through various utility programs.

- **Hub or small switch:** Used to connect multiple computers to a single network.

- **Floppy disk:** Used for boot disks.

- **CD-ROM:** Used to boot and store troubleshooting utilities.

- **USB flash drive:** Used to store files and troubleshooting utilities.

- **Cell phone:** Used to call the office and set up and confirm appointments with customers.

Figure 2-12   Troubleshooting Tools

Customer Site Procedures

An onsite technician should follow four steps before beginning any troubleshooting or repair at the customer site:

Step 1.   Provide proper identification to the customer.

Step 2.   Review the trouble ticket or work order with the customer to verify that the information is correct.

Step 3.   Communicate the current status of any identified problems or issues, as well as the actions the technician expects to take at the customer site that day.

Step 4.   Obtain permission from the customer to begin the work.

The technician must verify all items on the trouble ticket. As soon as the technician is familiar with all the issues, the work can begin. The technician checks all device and network settings and runs any necessary utilities. When necessary, the technician may have to swap out suspected faulty hardware with known good hardware to determine if a hardware problem exists. After the technician determines the cause of the problem, he or she can attempt the repair and observe the results.

When performing any troubleshooting tasks on site, especially when installing new or replacing existing equipment, it is important to minimize the risk of injury by following good safety practices. Many employers offer safety training as part of their employee services.

Different equipment and workspaces require you to take special care while troubleshooting, as follows:

- **Ladders:** Use ladders to reach high locations to install networking cable and to install or troubleshoot wireless access points in places that are difficult to reach. To reduce the risk of falling off the ladder or dropping equipment while climbing on the ladder, work with a partner whenever possible.

- **High or dangerous locations:** Sometimes network equipment and cables are located in high and dangerous places that are not accessible by a ladder, such as on the side of a building, on rooftops, or in an internal structure such as an elevator shaft. Work performed at this type of location must be done very carefully. Using a safety harness reduces the risk of falling.

- **Electrical equipment:** If there is a risk of damaging or coming in contact with any electrical lines when handling hardware, consult with the customer's electrician about measures that can be taken to reduce the risk of electrical shock. Coming in contact with electrical equipment can result in serious personal injury.

- **Awkward spaces:** Network equipment is often located in narrow and awkward spaces. Ensure that the work area is properly lighted. Determine the best way to lift, install, and remove equipment to minimize the risks.

- **Heavy equipment:** Networking devices can be large and heavy. Plan to have the correct equipment and trained personnel when heavy equipment needs to be installed or moved at a customer site.

When finished, the technician communicates to the customer the nature of the identified problem, what solution was applied, and any follow-up procedures. Before the problem can be considered fully resolved, the technician must obtain the customer's acceptance. The technician can then close the trouble ticket and document the solution.

The customer receives a copy of the documentation. The document includes the original help desk call problem and the actions taken to solve it. The technician records the final solution, and the customer acceptance is indicated on the trouble ticket. For future reference, the technician should also record the problem and the solution in the help desk documentation and FAQs.

In some cases, an onsite technician can uncover network problems that require upgrades or reconfiguration of the network devices. When this occurs, it may be outside the scope of the original trouble ticket. These issues usually are communicated to both the customer and the ISP network personnel for further action.

Summary

Help desk technicians provide solutions to customers' network problems. Help desk user support usually exists at three levels. Incident management is the basic procedure followed when a help desk technician initiates the standard problem-solving processes. Help desk operation relies on opening trouble tickets and logging information.

Customer service and interpersonal skills are important when handling difficult clients and incidents. Some of the skills that are consistently used in successful help desk communication include

- Preparation
- Courteous greeting
- Listening to the customer
- Adapting to the customer's temperament
- Correctly diagnosing a simple problem
- Logging the call

A layered approach is used for troubleshooting. The layered OSI model breaks the task of network communication into multiple processes. Each process is a small part of the larger task. The seven layers of the OSI reference model can be divided into two categories: upper and lower layers. Upper layers consist of any layer above the transport layer and are implemented in software. Lower layers consist of the transport, network, data link, and physical layers and handle data transport functions. Using the OSI model, the help desk technician can troubleshoot using a bottom-up, top-down, or divide-and-conquer approach.

Information gathered from the customer is transferred to the trouble ticket, or incident report. Some of the most common customer service calls are about e-mail and connectivity issues.

Level 1 and Level 2 help desk technicians attempt to solve customer problems over the telephone or web or by using remote desktop-sharing applications. Sometimes it is necessary to dispatch a mobile onsite technician, or Level 3 technician.

It is important to document the solution on the customer work order, on the trouble ticket, and in a knowledge-base document for future reference.

Activities and Labs

This summary outlines the activities you can perform to help reinforce important concepts described in this chapter. You can find the activity and Packet Tracer files on the CD-ROM accompanying this book.

Interactive Activities on the CD:

Interactive Activity 2-1: Identify Technician Support Level Responsibilities (2.1.2)

Interactive Activity 2-2: Determine the Customer Support Process (2.1.3)

Interactive Activity 2-3: Identify OSI Layer Protocols and Technologies (2.2.2)

Interactive Activity 2-4: Identify Network Issues at OSI Layers (2.2.3)

Packet Tracer Activity on the CD:

Troubleshoot and Resolve Network Connectivity Issues (2.3.1)

Chapter 2 does not have a Hands-on Lab in Part II of this book.

Check Your Understanding

Complete the review questions to test your understanding of the topics and concepts in this chapter. Appendix A, "Check Your Understanding and Challenge Questions Answer Key," lists the answers.

1. Indicate whether the network function is associated with the transport or network layer by placing a T or N next to it:

   A. Packages data in segments for transmission: ____

   B. Routes packets between networks: ____

   C. Encapsulates data in packets for transmission: ____

   D. Uses UDP for real-time data streaming: ____

   E. Adds port numbers: ____

   F. Adds IP addresses to data packets: ____

2. Using a systematic troubleshooting approach, a help desk technician suspects a problem at Layer 3 of the OSI model. Which two questions could the technician ask to isolate the problem to Layer 3?

   A. Is your PC configured for DHCP?

   B. Can you browse to http://www.cisco.com?

   C. Is your network cable plugged in?

   D. Can you ping your default gateway?

   E. Do you see a link light on your network card?

3. Indicate the OSI layer that each question is associated with if a help desk technician is using a bottom-up approach to troubleshooting. Place the OSI model layer number next to each question to indicate the order in which the technician would troubleshoot. For the application layer, use Layers 5 through 7.

   Is your network cable securely connected? ____

   What mail server is listed in the outgoing server setting? ____

   Is your Windows firewall blocking port 25? ____

   Do you see a link light on your network card? ____

   What is the subnet mask on Local Area Connection 2? ____

4. A customer call has been escalated to an onsite technician because the Level 1 and 2 technicians could not determine the problem. Which three tasks would the onsite technician perform?

A. Open the trouble ticket and enter the customer's information.

B. Replace faulty cables or connections.

C. Check to see if the ISP's e-mail server is working.

D. Correct PC network settings, and run any necessary utilities.

E. Swap out suspected faulty hardware with known good hardware.

F. Check the customer's account payment status.

5. Which two actions should be taken after a customer problem is resolved by the ISP help desk?

A. Delete the trouble ticket from the database.

B. Document the solution in the trouble ticket or work order.

C. Escalate the trouble ticket to Level 2 for future reference.

D. File a work order for customer notification.

E. Copy the solution into a knowledge-base document for future reference.

6. Which two scenarios are common causes of physical network connectivity problems?

A. The monitor is unplugged

B. The Ethernet cable is plugged into the wrong port

C. Incorrect default gateway

D. Unassigned IP address

E. Faulty Ethernet cable

7. Indicate whether each network component or function is associated with the physical, data link, or network layer by placing a P, D, or N next to it:

A. Twisted-pair cable: ___

B. IP address: ___

C. Routing: ___

D. Switching: ___

E. MAC address: ___

F. Hub: ___

8. What two tasks should an onsite technician perform before beginning any troubleshooting or repair at the customer site?

A. Review the trouble ticket with the customer to verify that the information is correct.

B. Take damaged equipment to the ISP site for repair.

C. Document the troubleshooting task performed and the solution.

D. Provide identification, including name and place of employment.

E. Examine cabling to determine if it is faulty or connected to the wrong port.

9. Match the technical skill on the left to the appropriate help desk activity on the right:

Skill	Help Desk Activity
Make notes about the resolution of a help desk case	Providing a courteous greeting
Answer calls in a friendly, professional manner	Adapting to the customer's temperament
Speak in a calm, reassuring manner	Logging the call
Get all relevant information from the customer	Diagnosing a problem correctly
Use analytical tools to provide a problem resolution	Listening to the customer

10. An ISP customer calls to report that the web server web-s1.cisco.com cannot be reached through a web browser. The technician uses command-line utilities to verify the problem and to begin the troubleshooting process. Based on the results shown in the following sample output, what can you determine about the problem? (Choose two.)

```
C:\> ping web-s1.cisco.com

Ping request could not find host web-s1.cisco.com. Please check the name and try again.
C:\> ping 192.168.0.10

Pinging 192.168.0.10 with 32 bytes of data:
Reply from 192.168.0.10: bytes=32 time<10ms TTL=64
Reply from 192.168.0.10: bytes=32 time<10ms TTL=64
Reply from 192.168.0.10: bytes=32 time<10ms TTL=64
Reply from 192.168.0.10: bytes=32 time<10ms TTL=64
Ping statistics for 192.168.0.10:
    Packets: Sent = 4, Received = 4, Lost = 0 (0% loss),
Approximate round trip times in milli-seconds:
    Minimum = 10ms, Maximum = 10ms, Average = 10ms
```

A. The web server at 192.168.0.10 can be reached from the source host.

B. A problem is occurring with the web server software on web-s1.cisco.com.

C. A router is down between the source host and the server web-s1.cisco.com.

D. DNS cannot resolve the IP address for the server web-s1.cisco.com.

E. The default gateway between the source host and the server at 192.168.0.10 is down.

11. A network technician is unable to telnet to a remote server from her workstation. She tries pinging the server and is successful. Next she checks to see if a firewall is blocking Telnet port 23. Finally, she checks to see if the Telnet service is running on the remote server. What troubleshooting approach is she using?

A. Top-down approach

B. Divide-and-conquer approach

C. Bottom-up approach

D. Substitution

12. A technician uses the **nslookup** command to troubleshoot a problem when none of the users at a customer's location can access remote websites. What type of problem can this command help diagnose?

A. The firewall is blocking port 23.

B. An Ethernet cable to one of the customer's hosts is disconnected.

C. DNS is not resolving names to IP addresses.

D. Wireless connectivity issues are occurring.

13. When a computer with a Microsoft OS is configured as a DHCP client and a DHCP server is unavailable, what type of address does the client receive?

_____

14. The TCP/IP software stack on the local machine can be tested using what type of address?

_____

Challenge Questions and Activities

These questions require a deeper application of the concepts covered in this chapter. You can find the answers in Appendix A.

1. In your role as an internal organization help desk technician, you receive a call from a user stating that she cannot access a file server that she normally works with.

   A. Would you employ the top-down, bottom-up, or divide-and-conquer troubleshooting approach?

   B. What questions would you ask the user to help identify the problem?

   C. What other steps could you take to help resolve the problem?

2. In your role as an ISP help desk technician, you receive a call from a DSL/cable customer stating that he cannot access any websites.

   A. Would you employ the top-down, bottom-up, or divide-and-conquer troubleshooting approach?

   B. What questions would you ask the customer to help identify the problem?

   C. What other steps could you take to help resolve the problem?

3. Help desk person interview activity (optional).

   In this activity you will contact a help desk person and, using the following form, ask him a few questions about his job. This will help you better understand the background that a help desk employee has and the nature of his work. This person can be an internal help desk person or one who works for an ISP.

   Use your help desk skills to interview the person. Tell him that you are a networking student and would like a few minutes of his time. Be sure to thank him when the interview is complete.

   Organization: _____

   Person's name: _____

   Position/title: _____

   Length of time with the company: _____

   Number of years as a help desk support person: _____

   Support level provided: _____

   Training/background/preparation:

   _____

   _____

   Primary desktop management software used:

   _____

   _____

Help desk problem resolution software used:

_____

_____

Most common types of problems encountered:

_____

_____

_____

Most challenging problem solved:

_____

_____

_____

Compare your notes with those of other students to try to develop a profile of a help desk technician.

## CHAPTER 3

Planning a Network Upgrade

Objectives

After completing this chapter, you should be able to answer the following questions:

- Why is proper planning necessary when you perform a network upgrade?

- What is a site survey, and why is it necessary?

- What steps are involved in performing a site survey?

- What is structured cabling?

- What factors must you consider when upgrading LAN and internetworking devices?

Key Terms

This chapter uses the following key terms. You can find the definitions in the glossary.

site survey 50

SWOT 55

failure domain 64

Cisco IOS 65

Integrated Services Router (ISR) 65

Fault tolerance 68

As businesses grow and evolve, they may outgrow their existing network and require a network upgrade. To help ensure a smooth transition, a careful look at both the current network and the new network requirements is necessary. This will help determine what new equipment and configurations are necessary to ensure that the new network fully supports both the current and future needs of the company or organization.

Part II of this book includes the corresponding labs for this chapter.

Common Issues

When a small company grows rapidly, the original network that supported the company often cannot keep pace with the expansion. Employees at the company may not realize how important it is to properly plan for network upgrades. In many cases, the business may just add various network hardware devices, of varying quality, from different manufacturers, and different network connection technologies, to connect new users. Often this causes a degradation in the quality of the network as each new user or device is added. If this continues, at some point the network is unable to properly support the types and level of network traffic that the users generate. Only when the network starts to fail do most small businesses look for help to redesign the network. An ISP or managed service provider may be called in to provide advice and to install and maintain the network upgrade.

Before a network upgrade can be properly designed, an onsite technician is dispatched to perform a site survey to document the existing network structure. It is also necessary to investigate and document the physical layout of the premises to determine where new equipment can be installed.

Site Survey

A *site survey* can give the network designer a substantial amount of information and create a proper starting point for the project. It shows what is already on site and indicates what is needed. A sales representative may accompany the technician to the site to interview the customer as well. A proper site survey gathers as much information as possible about the current business and its projected growth. This information is gathered from different people in an attempt to accurately forecast the current and future network requirements. Table 3-1 lists the information sought in a site survey.

Table 3-1   Site Survey Information

Category	Information Sought
Number of users and types of equipment	How many network users, printers, and servers will the network support? To determine the number of network users the network must support, be sure to consider how many users will be added over the next 12 months, and how many network printers and network servers the network has to accommodate.
Projected growth	What is the expected growth in the company or organization? Will the company be hiring new employees who must be provided with access to network resources? Will a new branch office be opened that will require connectivity? A network is a long-term investment. Planning for future growth now can save a great deal of time, money, and frustration in the future.

Category	Information Sought
Current Internet connectivity	How does your business connect to the Internet? Does the ISP provide the equipment, or do you own it? Often with a high-speed Internet connection such as DSL or cable, the service provider owns the equipment needed to connect to the Internet (for example, a DSL router or cable modem). If the connectivity is upgraded, the equipment that provides the connectivity may also need to be upgraded or replaced.
Application requirements	What applications does the network need to support? Do you require services for applications such as IP telephony or videoconferencing? It is important to identify the needs of particular applications, especially voice and video. These applications may require additional network device configuration and new ISP services to support the necessary quality.
Existing network infrastructure and physical layout	How many networking devices are installed in your network? What functions do they perform? Understanding the existing number and types of networking equipment that are currently installed is critical to being able to plan for the upgrade. It is also necessary to document any configurations that are loaded on the existing devices.
New services required	Will any new services be required either now or in the future? Will the company be implementing VoIP or videoconferencing technology? Many services require special equipment or configurations to optimize their performance. Equipment and configurations must take into account the possibility of new services to protect the investment and optimize performance.
Security and privacy considerations	Do you currently have a firewall in place to protect your network? When a private network connects to the Internet, it opens physical links to more than 50,000 unknown networks and all their unknown users. Although this connectivity offers exciting opportunities for information sharing, it also creates threats to information not meant for sharing. Integrated Services Routers (ISR) incorporate firewall features along with other functionality.
Wireless requirements	Would you like a wired, wireless, or wired plus wireless local-area network (LAN)? How big is the area that the wireless LAN (WLAN) must cover? It is possible to connect computers, printers, and other devices to the network using a traditional wired network (10/100 switched Ethernet), a wireless-only network (802.11x), or a combination of wired and wireless networking. Each wireless access point that connects the wireless desktop and wireless laptop computers to the network has a given range. To estimate the number of access points that are required, you must know the required coverage area and the physical characteristics of the location that the wireless network must cover.

continues

Table 3-1   **Site Survey Information**   *continued*

Category	Information Sought
Reliability and uptime expectations	What is the real cost of downtime in the company or organization? How long an outage can the company tolerate before suffering serious financial or customer losses? Maintaining nearly 100% uptime requires complete redundancy in all equipment and services and is extremely expensive to implement. Networks must be designed to reflect the real need for uptime and system reliability. This level can be determined only through intensive investigation and discussions with all the business stakeholders.
Budget constraints	What is the budget for the network installation or upgrade? System performance, reliability, and scalability are all expensive to achieve. The project budget normally is the deciding factor as to what can and cannot be done. A complete cost-benefit analysis must be completed to determine which features and services are the most critical and which could be put off to a later date.

It is a good idea to obtain a floor plan if possible. If a floor plan is not available, you can draw a diagram indicating the size and locations of all rooms. An inventory of existing network hardware and software is also useful to provide a baseline of requirements.

You should be prepared for anything when doing the site survey. Networks do not always meet local electrical, building, or safety codes or adhere to standards. Sometimes networks grow haphazardly over time and end up being a mixture of technologies and protocols. When doing a site survey, be careful not to offend the customer by expressing an opinion about the quality of the existing installed network.

When the technician visits the customer premises, he or she should do a thorough overview of the network and computer setup. There may be some obvious issues, such as unlabeled cables, poor physical security for network devices, lack of emergency power, or lack of an uninterruptible power supply (UPS) for critical devices. These conditions should be noted on the technician's report, as well as the other requirements gathered from the survey and the customer interview. These deficiencies in the current network should be addressed in the proposal for a network upgrade.

When the site survey is complete, it is important that the technician review the results with the customer to ensure that nothing is missed and that the report has no errors. A summary of the questions asked and the information gathered can greatly simplify the review process. If the information is accurate, the report provides an excellent basis for the new network design.

Physical and Logical Topologies

Both the physical and logical topologies of the existing network need to be documented. A technician gathers the information during the site survey to create both a physical and logical topology map of the network. A physical topology, as shown in Figure 3-1, is the actual physical location of cables, computers, and other peripherals. A logical topology, as shown in Figure 3-2, documents the path that data takes through a network and the location where network functions, such as routing, occur.

Figure 3-1   Physical Topology

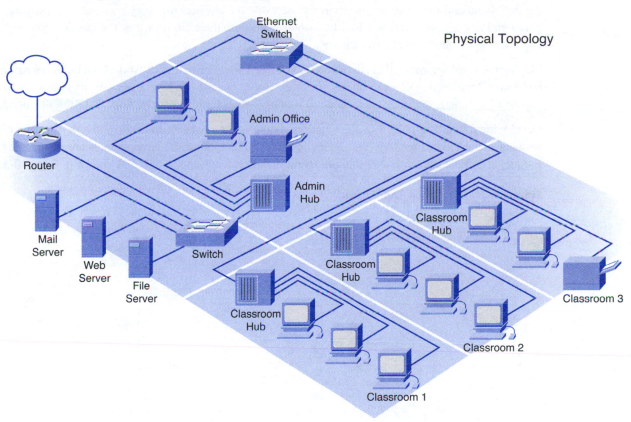

Physical Topology

Figure 3-2   Logical Topology

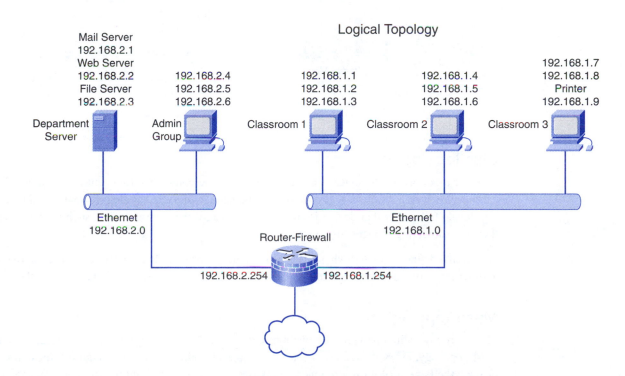

Logical Topology

In a wired network, the physical topology map consists of the wiring closet, as well as the wiring to the individual end-user stations. In a wireless network, the physical topology consists of the wiring closet and any access points that may be installed. Because there are no wires, the physical topology contains the wireless signal coverage area.

The logical topology generally is the same for both a wired and wireless network. It includes the naming and Layer 3 addressing of end stations, router gateways, and other network devices, regardless of the physical location. It indicates the location of routing, network address translation, and firewall filtering.

Developing a logical topology requires understanding of the relationship between the devices and the network, regardless of the physical cabling layout. Several topological arrangements are possible. Examples include star, extended star, partial mesh, and full mesh topologies, as shown in Figure 3-3.

Figure 3-3   Common Topologies

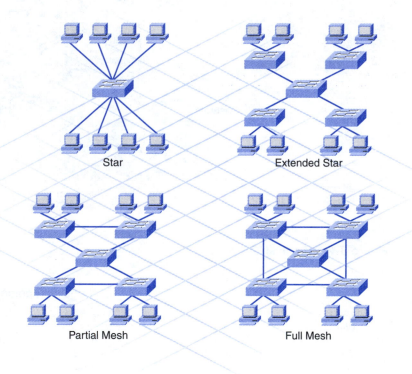

Star Topologies

In a star topology, each device is connected via a single connection to a central point, which is typically a switch or a wireless access point. The advantage of a star topology is that if a single connecting device fails, only that device is affected. However, if the central device, such as the switch, fails, then all connecting devices lose connectivity.

An extended star is created when the central device in one star is connected to a central device of another star, such as when multiple switches are interconnected, or daisy-chained together.

Mesh Topologies

Most core layers in a network are wired in either a full mesh or a partial mesh topology. In a full mesh topology, every device has a connection to every other device. Although full mesh topologies provide the benefit of a fully redundant network, they can be difficult to wire and manage and are more costly.

A partial mesh topology is used for larger installations. In a partial mesh topology, each device is connected to at least two other devices. This arrangement creates sufficient redundancy, without the complexity of a full mesh.

Implementing redundant links through partial or full mesh topologies ensures that network devices can find alternative paths to send data in the event of a failure.

Network Requirements Documentation

Along with creating the topology maps for the existing network, it is necessary to obtain additional information about the hosts and networking devices that are currently installed in the network. Record this information on a brief inventory sheet. In addition to currently installed equipment, document any planned growth that the company anticipates in the near future. This information helps the network designer determine what new equipment is required and the best way to structure the network to support the anticipated growth.

The inventory sheet of all the devices installed on the network includes the following:

- Device name
- Date of purchase
- Warranty information
- Location
- Brand and model
- Operating system
- Logical addressing information
- Connection information
- Security information

Creating Network Diagrams (3.1.3)

In this activity, you create a logical diagram and inventory list for a network. Use file d2-313 on the CD-ROM that accompanies this book to perform this activity using Packet Tracer.

Planning the Network Upgrade

Extensive planning should go into a network upgrade. As with any project, a need is first identified, and then a plan outlines the upgrade process from beginning to end. A good project plan helps identify any strengths, weaknesses, opportunities, and threats. This is called a *SWOT* analysis. The plan should clearly define the tasks and the order in which tasks are completed.

Some common examples of good planning include

- Sports teams following game plans
- Builders following blueprints
- Ceremonies or meetings following agendas

Network Upgrades

A network that is a patchwork of devices strung together using a mixture of technologies and protocols usually indicates poor or no initial planning. These types of networks are susceptible to downtime and are extremely difficult to maintain and troubleshoot. Unfortunately, this type of network is often encountered as small businesses experience rapid, unexpected growth. Even larger organizations often experience unplanned growth in their networks when they acquire or merge with other organizations. Organizations that experience a controlled rate of growth can properly plan their network to avoid problems and give their users an acceptable level of service.

The planning of a network upgrade begins after the initial site survey and report are complete. It consists of five distinct phases:

- Phase 1: Requirements gathering
- Phase 2: Selection and design
- Phase 3: Implementation
- Phase 4: Operation
- Phase 5: Review and evaluation

The next sections describe each phase in greater detail.

Phase 1: Requirements Gathering

After all the information has been gathered from the customer and the site visit, the design team at the ISP analyzes the information to determine network requirements and then generates an analysis report. If insufficient information is available to properly determine the best network upgrade path to follow, this team may request additional information.

Phase 2: Selection and Design

When the analysis report is complete, devices and cabling are selected. The design team creates multiple designs and shares them with other members on the project. This allows team members to view the LAN from a documentation perspective and evaluate trade-offs in performance and cost. It is during this step that any weaknesses of the design can be identified and addressed. Also during this phase, prototypes are created and tested. A successful prototype is a good indicator of how the new network will operate.

Phase 3: Implementation

If the first two steps are done correctly, the implementation phase may be performed without incident. If tasks were overlooked in the earlier phases, they must be corrected during implementation. A good implementation schedule must allow time for unexpected events and also schedules events to keep disruption of the customer's business to a minimum. Staying in constant communication with the customer during the installation is critical to the project's success.

Phase 4: Operation

When the network implementation phase is complete, the network moves into a production environment. In this environment, the network is considered live and performs all the tasks it has been designed to accomplish. If all steps up to this point have been properly completed, very few unexpected incidents should occur when the network moves into the operation phase.

Phase 5: Review and Evaluation

After the network is operational, the design and implementation must be reviewed and evaluated against the original design objectives. This is usually done by members of the design team with assistance from the network staff. This evaluation includes costs, performance, and appropriateness for the environment. For this process, the following items are recommended:

- Compare the user experience with the goals in the documentation, and evaluate whether the design is right for the job.

- Compare the projected designs and costs with the actual deployment. This ensures that future projects will benefit from the lessons learned on this project.

- Monitor the operation, and record changes. This ensures that the system is always fully documented and accountable.

It is important that, at each phase, careful planning and review occur to ensure that the project goes smoothly and the installation is successful. Onsite technicians are often included in all phases of the upgrade, including planning. This allows them to gain a better understanding of the expectations and limitations of the network upgrade and to give the end users a much-improved level of service.

Activity 3-1: Network Planning Phases (3.2.1)

In this activity, you determine at which phase of the network planning process certain events occur. Use file d2ia-321 on the CD-ROM that accompanies this book to perform this interactive activity.

Physical Environment

Before selecting equipment and determining the design of the new network, the network designer must examine the existing network facilities and cabling. This is part of the initial site survey. The facilities include the physical environment, the telecommunication room, and the existing network wiring. A telecommunications room or wiring closet in a small, single-floor network is usually called the main distribution facility (MDF). Figure 3-4 shows a small office environment with a single MDF.

Figure 3-4   Main Distribution Facility

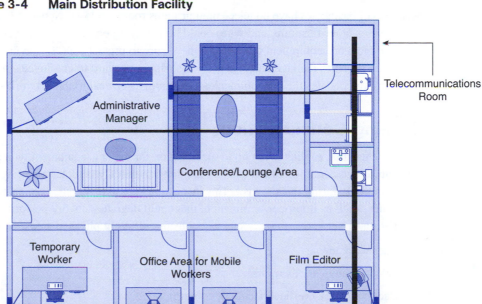

The MDF typically contains many of the network devices, such as switches or hubs, routers, access points, and so on. It is where all the network cable is concentrated in a single point. Many times, the MDF also contains the ISP's point of presence (POP), where the network connects to the Internet through a telecommunications service provider. Figure 3-5 shows the layout of a typical MDF. If additional wiring closets are required, these are called intermediate distribution facilities (IDF). IDFs typically are smaller than the MDF and connect to the MDF with backbone cabling.

Figure 3-5   Typical MDF Layout

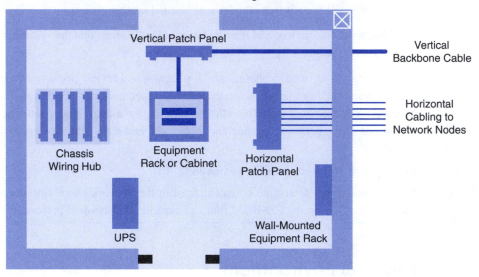

Tip

ISO standards refer to MDFs and IDFs using different terminology. MDFs and IDFs are sometimes called wiring closets. Because normally one MDF distributes telecommunication services to all areas of the building, MDFs are also called *building distributors*. Most environments have one or more IDFs on each floor of a building, so the ISO calls IDFs *floor distributors*.

Many small businesses have no telecommunications room or closet. Network equipment may be located on a desk or other furniture, and wires could be just lying on the floor. This arrangement should be avoided. Network equipment must always be secure to protect data. Loose or improperly installed cables are prone to damage and also present a tripping hazard to employees. As a network grows, it is important to consider the telecommunications room as critical to the network's security and reliability.

Cabling Considerations

When the existing cabling is not up to specification for the new equipment, you must plan for and install new cable. The condition of the existing cabling can quickly be determined by a physical inspection of the network during the site visit. This inspection should reveal the type of cable installed as well as any issues, such as improper termination, that could degrade network performance. When planning the installation of network cabling, you must consider different physical areas, as shown in Figure 3-6:

- User work areas
- Telecommunications rooms
- Backbone area (vertical backbone cabling)
- Distribution area (horizontal cabling)

Figure 3-6   Cabling Areas

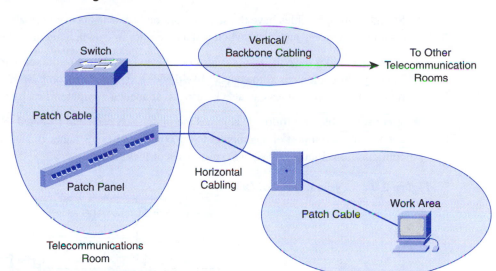

You have many different types of network cables to choose from; some are more common than others. Each type of cable is best suited to specific applications and environments. The most common type of LAN cable is unshielded twisted-pair (UTP). This cable is easy to install, is fairly inexpensive, and has a high bandwidth capability. For long backbone runs or runs between buildings, fiber-optic cable normally is installed. Coaxial cable is not typically used in LANs, but it is widely used in cable modem provider networks. Table 3-2 describes some of the more common types of network cables.

Table 3-2   Common Network Cables

Cable Type	Characteristics
Shielded twisted-pair (STP)	Usually Category 5, 5e, or 6 cable that has a foil shielding to protect from outside electromagnetic interference (EMI). The distance limitation is approximately 328 feet (100 meters).
Unshielded twisted-pair (UTP)	Usually Category 5, 5e, or 6 cable. It does not provide extra shielding from EMI, but it is inexpensive. Cable runs should avoid electrically noisy areas. The distance limitation is approximately 328 feet (100 meters).
Coaxial	Has a solid copper core with several protective layers, including polyvinyl chloride (PVC), braided wire shielding, and a plastic covering. The distance limitation of several miles (kilometers) depends on the purpose of the connection.
Fiber-optic cable	A medium that is not susceptible to EMI and that can transmit data faster and farther than copper. Depending on the type of fiber optics, distance limitations can be several miles (kilometers).

Several organizations provide LAN cabling specifications. The Telecommunications Industry Association (TIA) and the Electronic Industries Association (EIA) worked together to provide the TIA/EIA cable specifications for LANs. Two of the most common TIA/EIA cable specifications are the 568-A and 568-B standards. Both of these standards typically use the same Category 5 or 6 cable, but with a different termination color code.

Three different types of UTP cables are commonly encountered in the network environment:

- Straight-through cables have the same pinout on both ends. They normally are used to connect dissimilar devices, such as a switch and a computer or a switch and a router.

- Crossover cables have the transmit pins on one end connected to the receive pins on the other end. This type of cable is used to connect like devices, such as two computers, two switches, or two routers. Crossover cables can also be used to connect a computer directly to a router interface.

- A console cable or a rollover cable has the pinouts on each end reversed. Normally it is used to connect the serial port of a computer to the console port of a router or switch to perform the initial configuration. Figure 3-7 shows typical uses of these cables.

Figure 3-7   Typical Uses of Cables

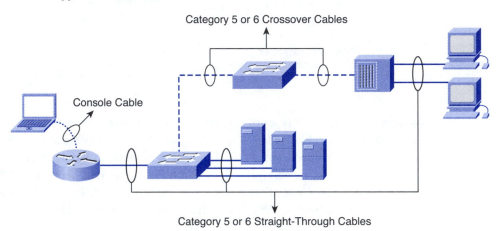

Another type of cable that is common in networks is a serial cable. A serial cable typically is used to connect the router to an Internet connection. This Internet connection may be to the phone company, the cable company, or a private ISP.

Structured Cable

When designing a structured cabling project, the first step is to obtain an accurate floor plan. The floor plan allows the technician to identify possible wiring closet locations, cable runs, and which electrical areas to avoid.

After the technician has identified and confirmed the locations of network devices, it is time to draw the network on the floor plan. Some of the more important items to document include the following:

- **Patch cable:** A short cable from the computer to the wall plate in the user work area.

- **Horizontal cable:** A cable from the wall plate to the IDF in the distribution area.

- **Vertical cable:** A cable from the IDF to the MDF in the organization's backbone area.

- **Backbone cable:** The part of a network that handles the major traffic.

- **Location of wiring closet:** An area to concentrate the end-user cable to the hub or switch.

- **Cable management system:** A series of trays and straps used to guide and protect cable runs.

- **Cable labeling system:** A proper labeling system or scheme that identifies cables.

- **Electrical considerations:** The premises should have adequate outlets to support the electrical requirements of the network equipment.

Figure 3-8 shows a telecommunications room and work area with both horizontal and vertical cabling.

Figure 3-8   Horizontal and Vertical Cabling

Horizontal
Cabling

Vertical/
Backbone
Cabling

Work Area

Telecommunications
Room

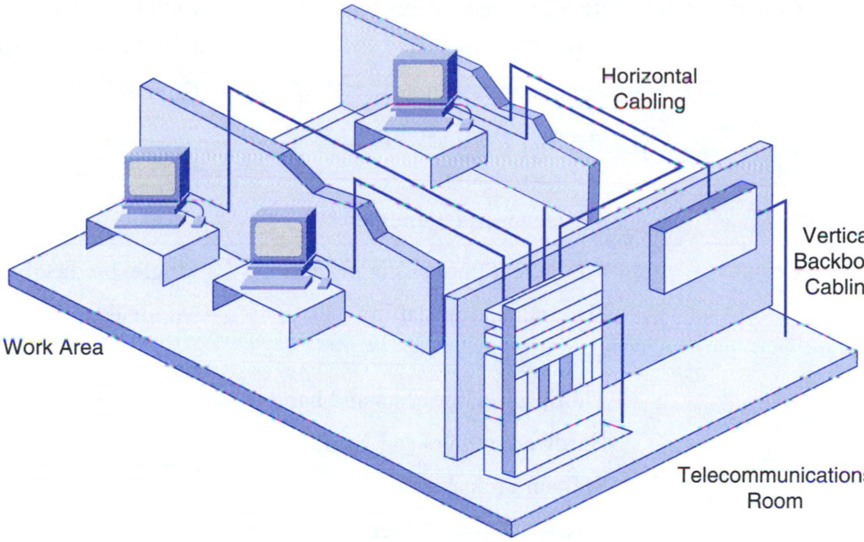

Lab 3-1: Evaluating a Cabling Upgrade Plan (3.2.4)

In this lab, you propose a cable upgrade plan to accommodate extra floor space acquired by a company. Refer to the hands-on lab in Part II of this book. You may perform this lab now or wait until the end of the chapter.

Purchasing and Maintaining Equipment

As the ISP team plans the network upgrade, issues arise related to purchasing new equipment, as well as maintaining new and existing equipment. Generally you have two options for the new equipment: managed service or in-house solutions. With a managed service solution, the equipment is obtained from the ISP through a lease or some other agreement. The ISP is responsible for updating and maintaining the equipment. With an in-house solution, the customer purchases the equipment and is responsible for updates, warranties, and maintaining the equipment.

Purchasing Equipment

When you purchase equipment, cost is always a major factor. A cost analysis of the purchase options must be conducted to provide a sound basis for the final purchase decision. Normally the customer conducts the cost analysis, but this may be done in conjunction with the ISP. Many other factors should be considered in addition to cost. Table 3-3 describes some of the factors you must consider when you're trying to decide if a managed or in-house solution is more appropriate.

Table 3-3   Managed Service or In-house Solution

	In-House	Managed Service
Considerations	Requires many decisions: Type of equipment Equipment location IT organization staffing Network design Maintenance requirements	Initial evaluation and choice of service provider Requirements definition Ongoing evaluation of service provider
Costs	Equipment purchasing or leasing IT organization staffing Training costs Multiple vendor costs and building Hardware repairs and upgrades Software release upgrades Telephone line changes Redundancy and reliability requirements	Single, predictable, monthly recurring bill Minimal up-front costs
Control and responsibility	You have most of the control and responsibility for managing and maintaining your network system	Delegate the level of network management to a qualified service provider based on your needs Keep your core business processes in-house Maintain control of the work flow in your organization Set service-level agreements (SLA) with a service provider
Reliability	You are responsible for keeping your network system available to employees, customers, and partners at all times	Service provider can guarantee availability up to 99.999% A 24-hour help desk is available for remote-access users Service provider management is transparent to the end users
End-user experience	Users are unaware of whether the network is managed by the companyor an external partner	Users are unaware of whether the network is managed by the company or an external partner

If the customer chooses the managed service, the SLA outlines the lease costs as well as other service costs. If the equipment is purchased outright, the customer should be aware of cost, warranty coverage, compatibility with existing equipment, and update and maintenance issues, all of which have an associated cost. This cost must be analyzed to determine the cost-effectiveness of any planned solution.

Selecting Network Devices

After the customer requirements have been analyzed, the design staff recommends the appropriate network devices to connect and support the new network functionality. Modern networks use a variety of devices for connectivity. Each device has certain capabilities to control the flow of data across a network. A general rule is that the higher the device is in the OSI model, the more intelligent it is. This means that a higher-level device can better analyze the data traffic and forward it based on information not available at lower layers. For example, a Layer 1 hub can only forward data out all ports, a Layer 2 switch can filter the data and only send it out the port connected to the destination based on MAC address, and a Layer 3 router can decide which traffic to forward or block based on the logical address.

As switches and routers evolve, the distinction between them becomes blurred. One simple distinction remains: LAN switches provide connectivity within an organization's LAN, whereas routers are needed to interconnect local networks or to form a wide-area network (WAN) environment.

In addition to switches and routers, other connectivity options are available for LANs. Wireless access points allow computers and other devices, such as handheld Internet Protocol (IP) phones, to wirelessly connect to the network or share broadband connectivity. Firewalls guard against network threats and provide application security, network control and containment, and secure connectivity technologies. ISRs combine the functionality of switches, routers, access points, and firewalls in the same networking device.

Selecting LAN Devices

Although both a hub and a switch can provide connectivity at the access layer of a network, switches should be chosen for connecting devices to a LAN. Switches generally are more expensive than hubs, but the enhanced performance makes them cost-effective. A hub generally is chosen as a networking device within a very small LAN, within a LAN that requires low throughput requirements, or when finances are limited. A hub may also be installed in a network when all network traffic is to be monitored. Hubs forward all traffic out all ports, whereas switches microsegment the network. Connecting a network-monitoring device to a hub allows the monitoring device to see all network traffic on that segment. Some switches do provide the ability to monitor all network traffic through a special port, but this is not a universal feature.

When selecting a switch for a particular LAN, network designers need to consider a number of factors, including the following:

- Speed and types of ports/interfaces
- Expandability
- Manageability
- Cost

Speed and Types of Ports/Interfaces

Choosing Layer 2 devices that can accommodate increased speeds allows the network to evolve without your having to replace the central devices. It is a good idea to purchase the fastest ports available within the budgeted funds. A bit of extra money spent now can save a great deal of time and expense later, when it is time to upgrade the network again.

The same can be stated about the number and types of network ports. Network designers must carefully consider how many UTP and fiber ports are needed. It is important to estimate how many additional ports will be required to support network expansion in the future.

Expandability

Networking devices come in both fixed and modular physical configurations. Fixed configurations have a specific number and type of ports or interfaces and cannot be expanded. Modular devices have expansion slots that provide the flexibility to add new modules as requirements evolve. Most modular devices come with a basic number of fixed ports as well as expansion slots.

A typical use of an expansion slot is to add fiber-optic modules to a device that was originally configured with a number of fixed UTP ports. Modular switches can be a cost-effective approach to scaling LANs.

Manageability

A managed switch provides control over individual ports or over the switch as a whole. Typical controls include the ability to monitor operation and change the settings for a device. A managed device can be monitored for performance and security and typically provides enhancements to the monitoring and security features. For example, with a managed switch, ports can be turned on or off as required to control access. In addition, administrators can control which computers or devices are allowed to connect to a port.

Cost

The cost of a switch is determined by its capacity and features. The switch capacity includes the number and types of ports available and the overall throughput. Other factors that impact the cost are the switch's network management capabilities, embedded security technologies, and optional advanced switching technologies.

Using a simple cost-per-port calculation, it may appear initially that the best option is to deploy one large switch at a central location. However, this apparent cost savings may be offset by the expense from the longer cable lengths required to connect every device on the LAN to one central switch. Compare this option with the cost of deploying a number of smaller switches connected by a few long cables to a central switch.

Deploying a number of smaller devices instead of a single large device also has the benefit of reducing the size of the *failure domain.* A failure domain is the area of the network affected when a piece of networking equipment malfunctions or fails.

Exploring Different LAN Switch Options (3.3.3)

In this activity, you determine which types of interfaces are required to connect a new company switch to a router, Linksys wireless router, and hosts. Use file d2-333 on the CD-ROM that accompanies this book to perform this activity using Packet Tracer.

Selecting Internetworking Devices

After the LAN switches have been selected, it is time to determine which router is appropriate for the customer. A router is a Layer 3 device. It performs all tasks of devices in lower layers and selects the best route to the destination network based on Layer 3 information. Routers are the primary devices used to interconnect networks. Each port on a router connects to a different network and routes packets between the networks. Routers can break up broadcast domains and collision domains.

You must consider a number of factors when selecting a router. It is necessary to match the router's characteristics to the network's requirements. Factors for choosing a router include

- The type of connectivity required
- Features available
- Cost

Connectivity

Routers are used to interconnect networks that use different technologies. They can have both LAN and WAN interfaces. The router's LAN interfaces connect to the LAN medium. This medium typically is UTP cabling, but modules can be added to the router to allow the use of fiber-optic cable and other types of media. Depending on the series or model of router, there can be multiple interface types for connecting LAN and WAN cabling. It is important to anticipate an organization's future connectivity requirements and purchase a router that will serve the organization well into the future.

Features

It is necessary to match the router's characteristics to the network's requirements. After analysis, the business may need a router with specific features in addition to basic routing. Many routers provide features such as the following:

- Security
- Quality of service (QoS)
- Voice over IP (VoIP)
- Network Address Translation (NAT)
- Dynamic Host Configuration Protocol (DHCP)
- Wireless access
- Virtual private network (VPN)
- Intrusion detection

Most of these services are contained in the *Cisco IOS* that manages the router hardware and resources. Although normally these are software features, the hardware must be able to support the IOS required.

Cost

When you select internetwork devices, budget is an important consideration. Routers can be expensive. Additional modules, such as fiber optics, can increase the costs. To keep costs as low as possible, the medium used to connect to the router should be supported without the purchase of additional modules.

An *Integrated Services Router (ISR)* is a relatively new technology that combines multiple services into one device. Before the ISR, multiple devices were required to meet the needs of data, wired and wireless, voice and video, firewall, and VPN technologies. The ISR was designed with multiple services to accommodate the demands of small to medium-sized businesses and branch offices of large organizations. An ISR is designed for ease of use. It can quickly and easily enable end-to-end protection for users, applications, network endpoints, and wireless LANs. The cost of an ISR normally is less than if the individual devices are purchased separately.

Packet Tracer
☐ **Activity**

Exploring Internetworking Devices (3.3.4)

In this activity, you determine and install the correct modules in the 1841 ISR to provide network connectivity. In addition, you select the correct cables to connect various network devices to the 1841 ISR. Use file d2-334 on the CD-ROM that accompanies this book to perform this activity using Packet Tracer.

Network Equipment Upgrades

Many small networks were initially built using a low-end integrated router to connect wireless and wired users. This type of device is designed to support small networks, usually consisting of a few wired hosts and possibly four or five wireless devices. When a small business outgrows the capabilities of its existing network devices, it must upgrade to more-capable devices. The devices used in this course and book are the Cisco 1841 ISR and the Cisco 2960 switch, as shown in Figure 3-9.

Figure 3-9   Cisco 1841 ISR and 2960 Switch

Cisco 1841 ISR

Cisco 2960 Switch

The Cisco 1841 ISR is designed to be a branch office or medium-sized business router. As an entry-level multiservice router, it offers a number of different connectivity options. It is modular in design and can deliver multiple security services.

The Cisco Catalyst 2960 series Intelligent Ethernet switches are a family of fixed-configuration, standalone devices that provide Fast Ethernet and Gigabit Ethernet connectivity to the desktop. These switches can provide the high speeds and high-density switching capabilities that the smaller ISRs with integrated switching cannot. They are therefore a good option when upgrading networks built with either hubs or small ISR devices.

The Catalyst 2960 family of switches, shown in Figure 3-10, provides entry-level, enterprise-class, fixed-configuration switching that is optimized for access layer deployments. They provide both Fast Ethernet and Gigabit Ethernet to the desktop and are ideal for entry-level enterprise, mid-market, and branch-office environments. These compact switches often are deployed outside the wiring closet.

Figure 3-10   Cisco Catalyst 2960 Family of Switches

Reliability and Availability

Purchasing network devices and the installation of cabling for a network upgrade is only the beginning. Networks must be both reliable and available. Reliability is usually achieved by adding redundant components to the network, such as two routers instead of one. In this case, alternative data paths
are created, so if one router experiences problems, the data can take an alternative route to arrive at
the destination. For better reliability, all devices and connections should have complete redundancy.
Unfortunately, this is extremely expensive in most environments. Therefore, the network design team
must determine the level of redundancy to incorporate to achieve the necessary reliability. Figure 3-11
shows redundancy in a switched network.

Figure 3-11   Redundancy in a Switched Network

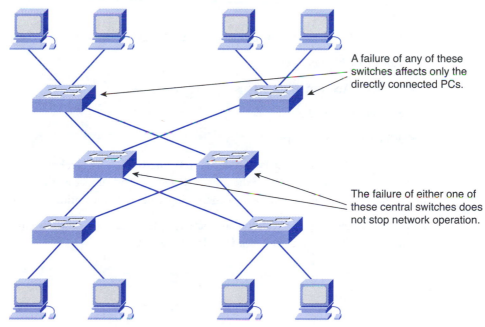

A failure of any of these
switches affects only the
directly connected PCs.

The failure of either one of
these central switches does
not stop network operation.

Availability is the amount of time the network is ready and able to deliver the necessary services. Any increase in reliability improves availability. Ensuring a higher level of availability requires not only redundancy but also equipment and software that have been engineered to provide this level of service. As an example of availability, telephone systems require "five 9s" of uptime. This means that the telephone system must be available 99.999% of the time. Telephone systems cannot be down, or unavailable, more than .001% of the time.

Fault tolerance systems typically are used to improve network reliability. Fault tolerance systems include devices such as UPSs, multiple AC power supplies, hot-swappable devices, and multiple interface cards. When one device fails, the redundant or backup system takes over to ensure minimal loss of reliability.

IP Addressing Plan

Planning for the network installation must include planning the logical addressing. Changing the Layer 3 IP addressing is a major issue when upgrading a network. If the network's structure is changed in the upgrade, the IP address scheme and network information may need to be altered to reflect the new structure.

When developing the addressing scheme, you must consider every device that requires an IP address, now and in the future. Some devices require addresses to carry out their functionality, and others only require an IP address to allow them to be accessed and configured across the network. Hosts and network devices that require an IP address include

- User computers
- Administrator computers
- Servers
- Other end devices such as printers, IP phones, and IP cameras
- Router LAN interfaces
- Router WAN (serial) interfaces
- Standalone switches
- Wireless access points

For example, if a new router is introduced to the network, new local networks, or subnets, are created. These new subnets need to have the proper IP address and subnet mask calculated. Sometimes, this means having to assign a totally new addressing scheme to the entire network.

After all the planning and design phases are complete, the upgrade proceeds to the implementation phase, in which the actual network installation begins.

Summary

Networks often experience unexpected growth and develop in a disorganized manner. When this happens, network performance degrades slowly with each new device added. At some point, the network no longer can support the traffic being generated by the users, so a network upgrade is required.

Whether the network upgrade is forced or planned, the upgrade process must be conducted in an organized manner. The upgrade plan must consider the strengths and weaknesses of and opportunities and threats posed by the network installation.

A network upgrade has five phases:

- Requirements gathering
- Equipment selection and network design
- Implementation
- Operation
- Review and evaluation

Documentation must include the physical and logical topology of the existing network, along with a complete inventory sheet of all equipment. This includes the location and layout of any telecommunications rooms as well as existing network wiring. Customer network requirements are gathered through surveys and interviews.

Cabling has four physical areas to consider: work areas, distribution area, telecommunications room, and backbone. Structured cabling projects deal with the placement of cables, the location of wiring closets, cable management, and electrical considerations.

When new equipment is used in a network upgrade, you have two purchase options: managed service and in-house. Both of these present many advantages and have serious limitations. The choice depends on the current business strengths and weaknesses.

Cost and expandability are two of the most important considerations when upgrading network devices. Generally, a device that functions at a higher OSI layer is considered a more intelligent device.

Activities and Labs

This summary outlines the activities and labs you can perform to help reinforce important concepts described in this chapter. You can find the activity and Packet Tracer files on the CD-ROM accompanying this book. The complete hands-on labs appear in Part II.

Interactive Activity on the CD:

Interactive Activity 3-1: Network Planning Phases (3.2.1)

Packet Tracer Activities on the CD:

Creating Network Diagrams (3.1.3)

Exploring Different LAN Switch Options (3.3.3)

Exploring Internetworking Devices (3.3.4)

Hands-on Lab in Part II of this book:

Lab 3-1: Evaluating a Cabling Upgrade Plan (3.2.4)

Check Your Understanding

Complete the review questions to check your understanding of the topics and concepts in this chapter. Answers are listed in Appendix A, "Check Your Understanding and Challenge Questions Answer Key."

1. What is the purpose of a site survey? (Select all that apply.)

   A. To determine what network resources are currently in place.

   B. To accurately forecast the current and future network requirements.

   C. To repair any malfunctioning network equipment.

   D. To ensure that all purchased networking equipment is still properly installed and functioning.

2. What should a site survey technician do if he or she finds nonstandard network installations during the survey process?

   A. Report the condition to management to make sure that the previous contractor does not get rehired.

   B. Inform management that they are in violation of standards and must pay you to correct the situation, or you will have to report them.

   C. Ignore the situation, and proceed with the survey.

   D. Report the condition to management, pointing out that this often happens when networks grow unexpectedly.

3. What should be done as a first step after the technician completes the site survey?

   A. Use the information contained in the site survey documents to determine the customer's network requirements.

   B. Review the site survey with the customer to make sure that nothing has been missed and everything is accurate.

   C. Use the information contained in the site survey documents to determine how long the planned network upgrade will take.

   D. Ask the technician to summarize the site survey documentation, summarizing only the important facts.

4. What should be contained on a logical topology diagram? (Select all that apply.)

   A. Location of all networking devices

   B. Physical location of cabling runs

   C. IP address information of all devices

   D. Device names

   E. Location of wiring closets

5. What information should you record about devices when performing a network inventory? (Select all that apply.)

A. Device name, brand, and model

B. Physical location

C. Operating system

D. Logical addressing information

E. Connection information

F. Security information

6. What is the correct sequence of steps when performing a network upgrade?

1. Review and evaluation

2. Implementation

3. Operation

4. Requirements gathering

5. Selection and design

A. 1, 2, 3, 4, 5

B. 4, 5, 1, 2, 3

C. 4, 5, 2, 3, 1

D. 4, 1, 5, 3, 2

E. 1, 4, 5, 2, 3

7. What is the name of the location where all network cable is concentrated in a single point?

A. IDF

B. ISP

C. IXP

D. MDF

E. MFD

8. What type of cable typically is used to connect a workstation network interface card (NIC) to the wall outlet?

A. STP

B. UTP

C. Coaxial

D. Fiber-optic

9. Which of the following direct connections normally would require a crossover cable? (Select all that apply.)

A. A PC connected to another PC

B. A PC connected to a switch

C. A PC connected to a router

D. A switch connected to a router

E. A router connected to another router

10. What factors should you consider when selecting an internetworking device?

Challenge Questions and Activities

These questions require a deeper application of the concepts covered in this chapter. You can find the answers in Appendix A.

1. A small company is trying to decide if it should install and manage its own network solution or if it should invest in a managed solution from its local ISP. The company currently is having financial difficulties and does not have an internal IT department. What suggestion would you make, and why?

2. You have asked two new network technicians to recommend a switch for a new department within the company. The department will have 27 users and four networked printers. All devices currently connect at 100 Mbps. The first technician recommends a switch that has 48 10/100-Mbps ports. The second technician recommends a slightly more expensive switch that has 48 10/100/1000-Mbps ports and two fiber-optic uplink ports. Which technician has made the better recommendation, and why?

## CHAPTER 4

Planning the Addressing Structure

Objectives

After completing this chapter, you should be able to answer the following questions:

- How is IP addressing implemented in the LAN?

- What are classful and classless networks and subnets?

- How can a given network be subnetted to allow for efficient use of IP addresses?

- How are Network Address Translation (NAT) and Port Address Translation (PAT) used in a network?

Key Terms

This chapter uses the following key terms. You can find the definitions in the glossary.

high-order bits (HOB)   *page 75*

Classless Interdomain Routing (CIDR)   *page 79*

RFC 1918, Address Allocation for Private Internets   *page 84*

IPv6   *page 92*

Network Address Translation (NAT)   *page 93*

inside local address   *page 95*

inside global address   *page 95*

outside local address   *page 95*

outside global address   *page 95*

Dynamic NAT   *page 97*

Static NAT   *page 98*

Port Address Translation (PAT)   *page 99*

As small-to-medium-sized business networks expand to meet the challenges of new applications and services, they often outgrow their initial design. A key factor when planning the network upgrade is network addressing. Creating a flexible, scalable IP addressing structure that can support new growth is critical to the success of the upgraded network.

Part II of this book includes the corresponding labs for this chapter.

IP Addressing in the LAN

IP addressing is key to moving packets across the Internet and between hosts on local IP networks. This section reviews basic IP concepts, including classful and classless IPv4 addressing, subnetting, and IPv6.

Review of IP Addresses

One of the most important aspects of communications on an internetwork is the logical addressing scheme.

IP addressing is the method used to identify hosts and network devices. The number of hosts connected to the Internet continues to grow, and the IP addressing scheme has been adapted over time to cope with this growth.

To send and receive messages on an IP network, every network host must be assigned a unique 32-bit binary IP address. Because large binary numbers are difficult for humans to read and understand, IP addresses usually are displayed in dotted-decimal notation. In dotted-decimal notation, the 32-bit address is divided into four sets of 8 bits, each of which is called an octet (the prefix "oct" means eight). Each of the four octets is converted into a decimal number separated by a period. For example, consider this IP address:

11000000.10101000.00000001.01101010

This is represented as 192.168.1.106 in dotted-decimal notation, as shown in Figure 4-1.

Figure 4-1   Binary IP Address Expressed Using Dotted-Decimal Notation

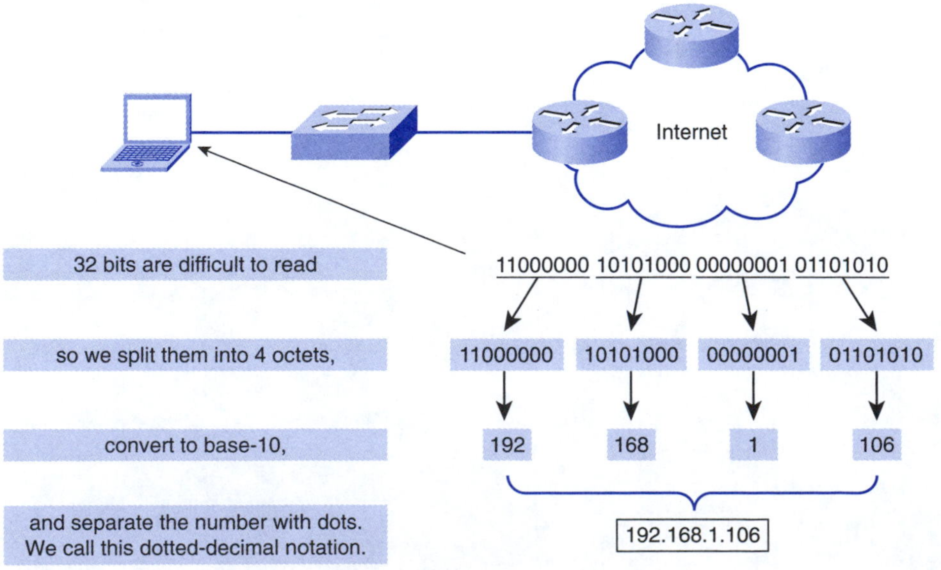

Hierarchical Addressing

IP addresses are hierarchical. A hierarchy is like a family tree with parents at the top and children connected to them below. For a network, this means that part of the 32-bit number identifies the network (parent), and the rest of the bits identify the host (child). In the early days of the Internet, so few organizations needed to connect to the Internet that networks were assigned by only the first 8 bits (the first octet) of the IP address. This left the remaining 24 bits to be used for local host addresses.

The 8-bit network designation made sense at first, because originally people thought that the Internet would be made up of a few very large universities, governments, and military organizations. Using only 8 bits for the network number enabled the creation of 256 separate networks, each containing more than 16 million hosts. It soon became apparent that more organizations, and eventually individuals, would be connecting to the Internet to do research and communicate with others. More networks were required, and a way to assign more network numbers had to be created. Figure 4-2 shows the hierarchical parent/child nature of IP addresses. The network portion of the IP address is the parent, and the individual IP addresses of hosts are the children. Notice that the router interface also has an IP address of 10.1.1.1 and is considered a host on the 10.1.1.0 network, just like the individual PCs.

Figure 4-2   Network and Host Parent/Child IP Address Hierarchy

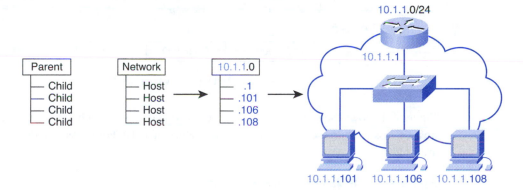

Classful Addressing

To cope with the demand, more unique network numbers were required. To create more possible network designations, the 32-bit address space was organized into five classes. Three of these classes—A, B, and C—provide addresses that can be assigned to individual hosts or networks. The other two classes, D and E, are reserved for multicast and experimental use. Dividing the original 8-bit networks into smaller classes increased the number of available network designations from 256 to more than 2 million.

Until this change, routers examined only the first 8 bits of an IP address for the network ID. If more than 8 bits were assigned to the network, how would routers know to look beyond the first 8 bits to identify Class B or C networks?

In 1981 RFC 791 changed the definition of IP addresses so that they were grouped into three class sizes for commercial host addressing. Dividing the networks in this manner would make it easy for routers to determine the correct number of network ID bits. A network's class is indicated by the values of the first few bits of the IP addresses, called the *high-order bits (HOB)*. If the first bit is 0, the network is a Class A, and the first octet represents the network ID. When the first bit is 1, the router examines the second bit. If that bit is 0, the network is a Class B, and the router uses the first 16 bits (two octets) for the network ID. If the first 3 bits are 110, this indicates a Class C address. Class C addresses use the first 24 bits, or three octets, to designate the network. Figure 4-3 shows the three main commercial address classes—A, B, and C—and the division between the network and host portions of the address.

Figure 4-3   Commercial IP Address Classes A, B, and C

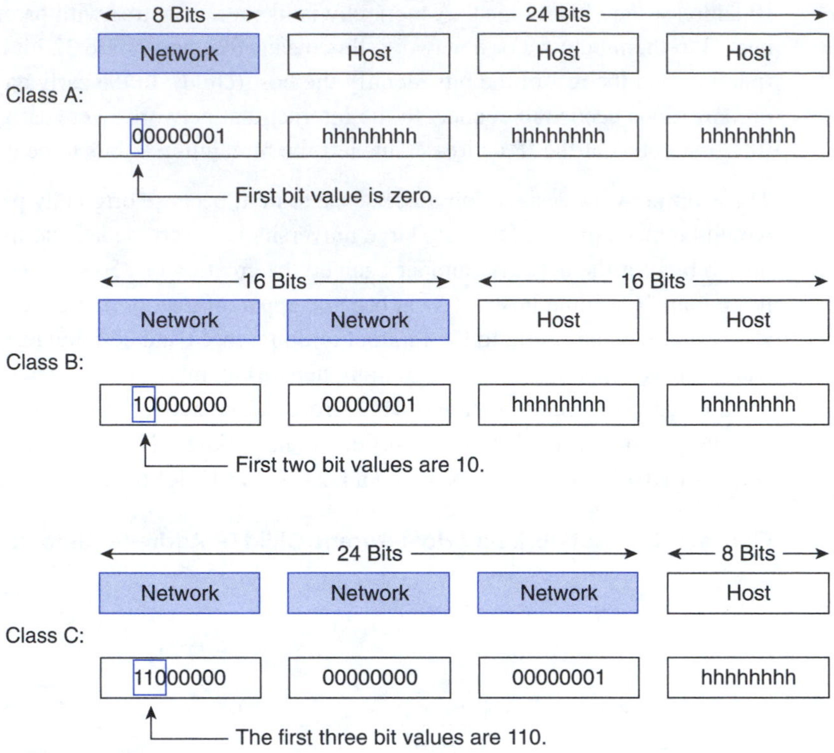

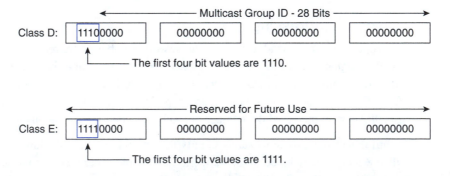

Figure 4-4 shows the special Class D and Class E addresses, which are not used to address regular IP hosts. Class D addresses have the first 4 bit values of 1110. For Class E addresses the first 4 bit values are 1111.

Figure 4-4   IP Address Classes D and E

The following list provides additional information on each of the five address classes:

- **Class A**: The first octet is the network address, and the last three octets are the host portion. Any IP address where the first bit of the first octet is 0 is a Class A address. A Class A address can have a decimal value for the first octet between 1 and 126. Class A addresses are used for networks with more than 65,535 hosts. The Class A address 127 is reserved for loopback testing. An example of a Class A network address is 10.0.0.0.

- **Class B**: The first two octets are the network address, and the last two are the host portion. Any IP address where the first two bits of the first octet are 10 is a Class B address. A Class B address can have a decimal value for the first octet between 128 and 191. Class B addresses are used for networks needing 255 to 65,535 hosts. An example of a Class B network address is 172.16.0.0.

- **Class C**: The first three octets are the network address, and the last octet is the host portion. Any IP address where the first three bits of the first octet are 110 is a Class C address. A Class C address can have a decimal value for the first octet between 192 and 223. Class C addresses are used for networks with 254 hosts or fewer. An example of a Class C network address is 192.168.1.0.

- **Class D**: Used for multicast addressing. Multicast IP addresses have a first octet in the range between 224 and 239. An example of a Class D address is 224.0.0.6, which is a special group address. Multicast clients that join a group are configured to listen for a specific multicast group address and receive all packets sent to that address.

- **Class E**: Reserved for future experimental usage. The first octet range is from 240 to 255.

Subnetting Concepts

Networks began growing rapidly throughout the 1980s and into the 1990s, with many organizations adding hundreds, even thousands, of hosts.

An organization with thousands of hosts should have been well served by a Class B network. Unfortunately, some problems occurred. Organizations with thousands of hosts rarely had them all in one place. Some organizations wanted to separate individual departments from each other for security purposes.

To solve these problems, the organizations leading the development of the Internet chose to divide their larger networks into smaller mini-networks, or subnets, using a process called subnetting. This allows a single Class B network to be split into multiple networks such that each subnet is treated as a separate network.

RFC 917, *Internet Subnets*, defines the subnet mask as the method routers use to isolate a subnet from an IP address. When a router receives a packet, it uses the destination IP address in the packet and the subnet masks associated with the routes in its routing table to determine the appropriate path on which to forward the packet.

The router reads the subnet mask from left to right, bit for bit. If a bit in the subnet mask is set to 1, this indicates that the value in that position is part of the network ID. A 0 in the subnet mask indicates that the value in that position is part of the host ID. Subnet masks always start with some number of 1s on the left side and some number of 0s on the right. 0s are never interspersed between the 1s. Where the 1s stop, the 0s begin. The 1s identify the network portion of the IP address, and the 0s identify the host portion.

Table 4-1 summarizes the five address classes with first octet values, network/host breakdown, and default subnet mask bits in decimal and binary. Also shown is the number of possible networks and hosts per network, as well as the host address range for each class.

Table 4-1   IP Address Classes

Address Class	First Octet Range (Decimal)	First Octet Bits (Blue Bits Don't Change)	Network (N) and Host (H) Parts of the Address	Default Subnet Mask (Decimal and Binary) (Blue Indicates the Network Portion of the Address)	Number of Possible Networks and Hosts Per Network	Notes and Host Address Range*
A	1 to 127*	00000000 to 01111111	N.H.H.H	255.0.0.0 11111111.00000000. 00000000.00000000	126 networks (2^7–2) 16,777,214 hosts per network (2^{24}–2)	Commercial 1.0.0.0 to 126.255.255.255
B	128 to 191	10000000 to 10111111	N.N.H.H	255.255.0.0 11111111.11111111. 00000000.00000000	16,382 networks (2^{14}–2) 65,534 hosts per network (2^{16}–2)	Commercial 128.0.0.0 to 191.255.255.255
C	192 to 223	11000000 to 11011111	N.N.N.H	255.255.255.0 11111111.11111111. 11111111.00000000	2,097,150 networks (2^{21}–2) 254 hosts per network (2^8–2)	Commercial 192.0.0.0 to 223.255.255.255
D	224 to 239	11100000 to 11101111	Not for commercial use as a host	—	—	Multicast (reserved) 224.0.0.0 to 239.255.255.255
E	240 to 255	11110000 to 11111111	Not for commercial use as a host	—	—	Experimental (reserved) 240.0.0.0 to 255.255.255.255

*
  Class A address 127.0.0.0 is reserved for loopback testing.
**
  All-0s and all-1s are invalid host addresses.

The two-level hierarchy of classed addressing includes a network ID and a host ID. In classful subnetting, the network ID is left alone, and the host ID is divided into a subnet ID and a new host ID. For example, a Class B network has a 16-bit default subnet mask of 11111111.11111111.00000000.00000000, or 255.255.0.0. That leaves 16 bits for the host ID. This IP address is divided into only two parts, network (N) and host (H):

NNNNNNNN.NNNNNNNN.HHHHHHHH.HHHHHHHH

One way to divide a Class B address into multiple networks is to use 4 of the host bits as a subnet ID. Subnetting is done by "borrowing" bits from the left side of the host bits. An extended 20-bit subnet mask is used (16 bits for the basic Class B network ID and 4 bits for the subnets). This leaves 12 bits for the host ID. A 20-bit subnet mask is written as 255.255.240.0. The Class B IP address shown previously is now divided into three parts—network (N), subnet (S), and host (H):

NNNNNNNN.NNNNNNNN.SSSSHHHH.HHHHHHHH

Partitioning the host ID this way always results in a fixed number of subnets and a fixed number of hosts per subnet. We started with 16 host bits, which could be used to address up to 65,534 hosts (2^{16}–2). In this case, because we borrowed 4 bits, we can create 16 subnets ($2^4 = 16$). The 12 host bits left can be used to address up to 4094 hosts (2^{12}–2) for each of the 16 subnets.

Classless Interdomain Routing (CIDR)

In a situation where an organization has a Class B network with four subnets, thousands of IP addresses can be wasted if some of the subnets have only a few hosts. To use IP addresses more efficiently, *Classless Interdomain Routing (CIDR)* was created.

With CIDR, there are no more network classes. CIDR uses variable-length subnet masks (VLSM) for subnetting. The network ID no longer has to be on an octet boundary. In a classed addressing system, the network represented by the IP address 192.168.5.0 is a Class C network address. The minimum number of bits that can make up the network ID is 24, and the maximum number of hosts is 254. Using CIDR addressing, sometimes called classless addressing, the number of bits that can make up the network ID is not restricted by class. Networks can be created that use the 192.168.0.0 address space with fewer than 24 bits indicating the network number. For example, the address 192.168.82.174 is part of a network in which the first 18 bits make up the network ID. The network that this host is in would be specified as 192.168.64.0/18, where the /18 indicates an 18-bit subnet mask (255.255.192.0). The slash after the address, followed by the number of bits in the mask, is called the network prefix. This method of specifying the subnet mask is called CIDR notation. To determine which network number the host is on, we first convert the decimal IP address to binary:

Decimal IP address:	192	168	82	174

Binary IP address: 11000000.10101000.01010010.10101110

Next, compare the binary subnet mask of 18 1s, bit for bit, to the IP address from left to right to determine the network number the host is on. Using the ANDing process, combining a 1 bit and a 1 bit results in a 1, and combining a 0 and a 1 or two 0s results in a 0. The result of the ANDing process is the network number:

Binary IP address: 11000000.10101000.01010010.10101110

Binary subnet mask: 11111111.11111111.11000000.00000000

Binary network number: 11000000.10101000.01000000.00000000

Decimal network number:	192	168	64	0

By converting the binary network number that results from the ANDing process, we can see that the network this host is on is 182.168.64.0.

To assist in converting a CIDR mask to dotted-decimal, Table 4-2 lists the most common variable-length subnets from 8 to 30. The CIDR representation form (*/xx*) and the decimal equivalents are shown as are the number of classless host addresses and the number of classful addresses available with each mask. This table is a subset of the one defined in RFC 1878, *Variable Length Subnet Table for IPv4*. Using the /20 CIDR mask from the table as an example, you can see that the CIDR notation mask /20 translates into a dotted-decimal mask of 255.255.240.0 and yields 4096 total CIDR host addresses (4K, or 4 * 1024 = 4096) and 16 Class C network addresses of 256 host addresses each. Also note that the /8 represents a single Class A network, the /16 is a single Class B network, and the /24 is a single Class C network. In Table 4-2, 1 K represents a Kilobyte, or 1024 bytes, and 1 M is a Megabyte, or 1,048,576 bytes.

Table 4-2   CIDR Subnet Mask Values and Decimal Equivalents

CIDR	Decimal	Number of CIDR Addresses	Number of Classful Addresses
/8	255.0.0.0	16 M	1 A
/9	255.128.0.0	8 M	128 B
/10	255.192.0.0	4 M	64 B
/11	255.224.0.0	2 M	32 B
/12	255.240.0.0	1024 K	16 B
/13	255.248.0.0	512 K	8 B
/14	255.252.0.0	256 K	4 B
/15	255.254.0.0	128 K	2 B
/16	255.255.0.0	64 K	1 B
/17	255.255.128.0	32 K	128 C
/18	255.255.192.0	16 K	64 C
/19	255.255.224.0	8 K	32 C
/20	255.255.240.0	4 K	16 C
/21	255.255.248.0	2 K	8 C
/22	255.255.252.0	1 K	4 C
/23	255.255.254.0	512	2 C
/24	255.255.255.0	256	1 C
/25	255.255.255.128	128	1/2 C
/26	255.255.255.192	64	1/4 C
/27	255.255.255.224	32	1/8 C
/28	255.255.255.240	16	1/16 C
/29	255.255.255.248	8	1/32 C
/30	255.255.255.252	4	1/64 C

Figure 4-5 shows a network with four subnets. The base IP network address is 172.16.0.0 with a /19 mask (255.255.224.0). A basic Class B address has a /16 mask, so a /19 mask means that 3 bits were borrowed from the host side. With a standard Class B, the 16 bits can be used to create 65,534 host addresses ($2^{16}-2$). If we borrow 3 bits, we can create eight equal subnets ($2^3 = 8$) of 8190 hosts each ($2^{13}-2 = 8192-2 = 8190$). Classful subnetting requires all subnets to have the same subnet mask (255.255.224.0) and the same number of hosts in each subnet.

Figure 4-5   Network Host Requirements with Multiple Subnets of Different Sizes

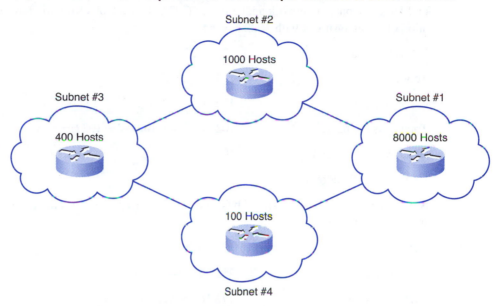

The four subnetworks shown in Figure 4-5 have 100, 400, 1000, and 8000 hosts. Each of the eight subnets we created by borrowing 3 bits has 8190 hosts. Applying one of the eight subnets to the network with 8000 hosts results in very little waste. Applying a subnet with 8190 host addresses to the network that requires only 100 hosts would waste more than 8000 host addresses. Fixed-length subnet masks can waste a significant number of IP addresses.

Variable length subnet masking (VLSM) helps solve this issue. VLSM addressing allows an address space to be divided into networks of various sizes. This is done by subnetting subnets. To accomplish this, routers today must receive routing information that includes the IP address of the network and the subnet mask information which indicates the number of bits that make up the network portion of the IP address. VLSM saves thousands of IP addresses that would be wasted with traditional classful subnetting.

CIDR addressing and VLSM allow for the creation of unequal-sized subnets. With CIDR, subnets can be created based on the number of host addresses required. Care must be taken not to overlap the subnet address ranges.

With the four networks shown in Figure 4-5, we can create four subnets, each with a different mask, all based on the basic network address of 172.16.0.0/16. This greatly reduces wasted addresses, because the mask is selected based on the number of hosts needed.

Subnet #1 has 8000 hosts. Using 3 bits from the host portion enables the creation of a single subnet with 8190 host addresses, as we saw a moment ago. This consumes the first 8190 addresses (172.16.0.0 to 172.16.31.255) for use with Subnet #1.

Network address	172.16.0.0
Subnet mask	55.255.224.0
CIDR notation	172.16.0.0/19 (32–19 = 13 host bits)
Total possible hosts	8190 (2^{13}–2 = 8192–2 = 8190)
IP addresses required	8000
Unassigned IP addresses	190

Subnet #2 has 1000 hosts. We used the first 8190 addresses for Subnet #1, so we will start the second-largest subnet at network address 172.16.32.0. Using 6 bits from the host portion enables the creation of a single subnet with 1022 host addresses.

Network address	172.16.32.0
Subnet mask	255.255.252.0
CIDR notation	172.16.32.0/22 (32–22 = 10 host bits)
Total possible hosts	1022 (2^{10}–2 = 1024–2 = 1022)
IP addresses required	1000
Unassigned IP addresses	22

Subnet #3 has 400 hosts. Using 7 bits from the host portion enables the creation of a single subnet with 510 host addresses.

Network address	172.16.36.0
Subnet mask	255.255.254.0
CIDR notation	172.16.36.0/23 (32–23 = 9 host bits)
Total possible hosts	510 (2^{9}–2 = 512–2 = 510)
IP addresses required	400
Unassigned IP addresses	110

Subnet #4 has 100 hosts. Using 9 bits from the host portion enables the creation of a single subnet with 126 host addresses.

Network address	172.16.38.0
Subnet mask	255.255.255.128
CIDR notation	172.16.38.0/25 (32–25 = 7 host bits)
Total possible hosts	126 (2^{7}–2 = 128–2 = 126)
IP addresses required	100
Unassigned IP addresses	26

Subnetting a Network

As a network grows and traffic increases, it often becomes necessary to subdivide the network into smaller broadcast domains to improve performance, add security, and reduce bottlenecks. Despite these benefits, subdividing the network increases the complexity of the network design and may also require changing from classful network design to a classless one.

Network Expansion Requirements

Figure 4-6 shows a small customer network as it currently exists. All users, including wired and wireless, share a single ISR with an integrated switch. As the number of users has increased, the network has been expanded using hubs to connect to the ISR.

Figure 4-6   Existing Single-ISR Network

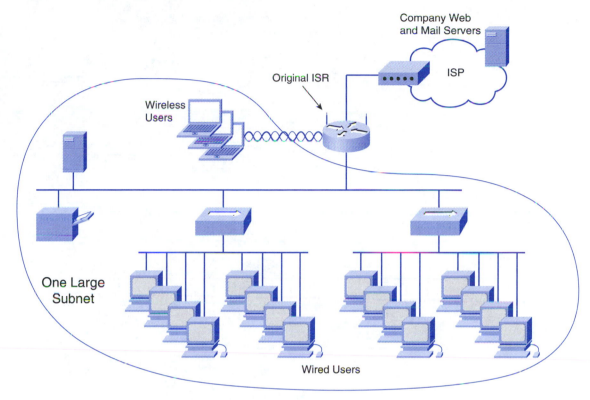

The customer network using the single ISR is badly overloaded. All hosts, wired and wireless, also share one common network address space internally. The single ISR connects to the ISP using a DSL link.

Proposed Solution

To help alleviate the problems of the existing network, a second networking device, a larger ISR, will be added, and the single network will be divided into two separate networks.

For security purposes and to improve performance, the wireless and wired users need to be on separate local networks. The original wireless integrated router can provide the wireless users with connectivity and security.

The new ISR does not have integrated switch ports. It is decided to add a new separate switch to replace the existing hubs for wired user support. The switch will replace the hubs connecting the wired users.

Figure 4-7 shows the proposed network with the new ISR connected to the ISP using a dedicated T1 link to handle increased traffic. The new ISR and switch support the wired users. The existing ISR provides access for the wireless users and a link to the new ISR.

Figure 4-7   New Network Design with Multiple ISRs and Multiple Subnets

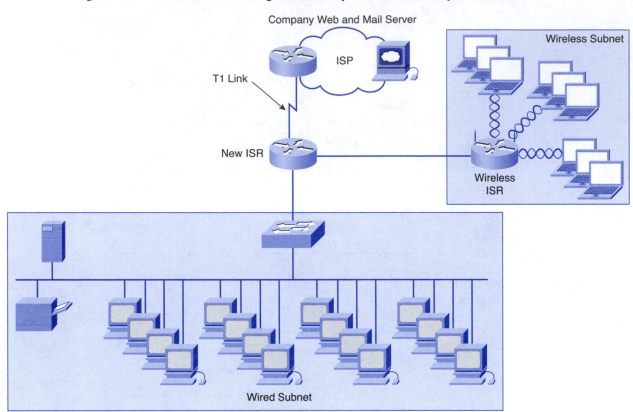

In addition, the new network design subdivides the network into three subnets—one for wired hosts, one for wireless, and one for the link between the existing and new ISR.

During the 1990s, many networks had no connection to other networks or to the Internet. To reduce the number of unique registered IP addresses that were assigned to organizations, the Internet Engineering Task Force (IETF) decided to reserve some of the Internet address space for use by these private networks.

These blocks of addresses did not need to be able to be routed over the public Internet. This meant that all private networks could use the same addresses, and so long as they did not connect to each other, communication could occur normally.

A single Class A address, 10.0.0.0, was reserved for private use. Some Class B and Class C address space was also set aside for private networks. These private address ranges are defined in *RFC 1918, Address Allocation for Private Internets*. They are summarized in Table 4-3.

Table 4-3   Classful Private IP Addresses (RFC 1918)

Class	Address Range	Default Subnet Mask	Number of Networks	Number of Hosts Per Network	Total Hosts
A	10.0.0.0 to 10.255.255.255	255.0.0.0	1	16,777,214	16,777,214
B	172.16.0.0 to 172.31.255.255	255.255.0.0	16	65,534	1,048,544
C	192.168.0.0 to 192.168.255.255	255.255.255.0	256	254	65,024

Most networks today use a private address structure. Only the devices that connect directly to the Internet are assigned registered Internet routable (public) addresses. By default, most consumer networking devices, such as an ISR, give out private addresses through DHCP. Referring to Figure 4-7, the private addresses are used inside the network, and the ISP assigns a public address to the external interface on the new ISR.

Classful Subnetting

A classful IP address hierarchy has two levels: a network and a host. In classful routing, the first 3 leading bit values determine whether an IP address is either Class A, B, or C. After an address is identified by class, the number of bits that make up the network ID and the number of bits that make up the host ID are known. Default subnet masks are used to tell the network and host bits apart.

Subdividing a network adds a level to the network hierarchy. Now there are three levels: a network, a subnetwork, and a host. Figure 4-8 shows the entire internal network with a three-part structure. The wireless network is highlighted to show a single subnet, and a single host is highlighted to show the lowest level of the hierarchy.

Figure 4-8   Network, Subnet, Host Hierarchy

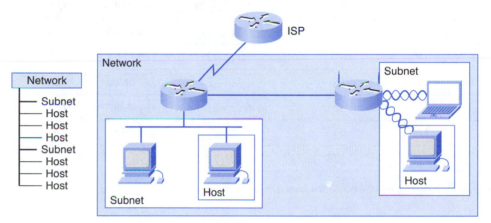

In classful addressing, the number of network bits is fixed. Eight bits designate a Class A network, 16 bits a Class B, and 24 a Class C. That leaves the host bits as the only part of the IP address with any flexibility to be modified. The available host bits can be divided into a subnet identifier ID and a host ID.

In a base Class C network, there are 24 bits in the network portion of the address and 8 bits in the host portion of the address. Each bit in a binary IP address has only one of two possible values, a 0 or a 1. The number of host addresses is calculated using a power of 2. Therefore, the number of host addresses available using an 8-bit address is 2^8, or 2*2*2*2*2*2*2*2. An 8-bit host ID has one network with 254 possible host addresses.

Deciding how many host bits to use for the subnet ID is a big planning decision. You must consider two things when planning subnets: the number of hosts on each network, and the number of individual local networks needed. Figure 4-9 shows the proposed network design and a basic Class C network of 192.168.1.0. With a mask of 255.255.255.0, one subnet and 8 bits are left for hosts, which results in 254 possible combinations. Figure 4-9 shows the binary bit value for the 192.168.1.0 network. Table 4-4 shows the subnet possibilities for the 192.168.1.0 network.

Figure 4-9   New Network Design Requires That the 192.168.1.0 Network Be Subnetted

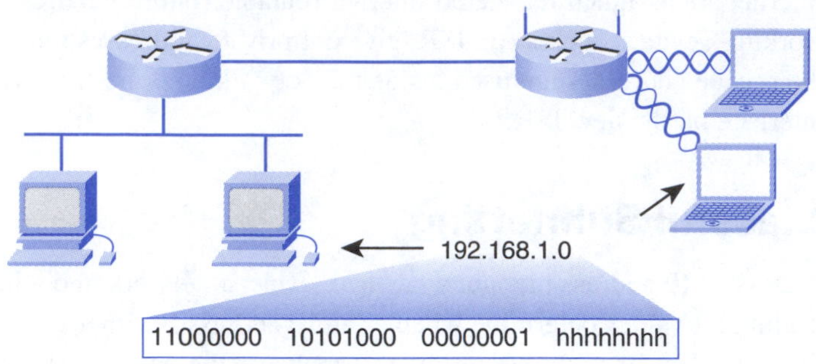

192.168.1.0

| 11000000 | 10101000 | 00000001 | hhhhhhhh |

Table 4-4   Subnetting a Class C 192.168.1.0 Network

Number of Subnet ID Bits	Number of Host ID Bits	Number of Subnets	Number of Hosts Per Subnet	Bit Pattern	CIDR Notation	Decimal Subnet Mask
0	8	1	254 (2^8–2)	hhhhhhhh	/24	255.255.255.0
1	7	2	126 (2^7–2)	shhhhhhh	/25	255.255.255.128
2	6	4	62 (2^6–2)	sshhhhhh	/26	255.255.255.192
3	5	8	30 (2^5–2)	ssshhhhh	/27	255.255.255.224
4	4	16	14 (2^4–2)	sssshhhh	/28	255.255.255.240
5	3	32	6 (2^3–2)	ssssshhh	/29	255.255.255.248
6	2	64	2 (2^2–2)	sssssshh	/30	255.255.255.252
7*	1	128	0 (2^1–2)	sssssssh	/31	255.255.255.254

*
  7 bits cannot be borrowed, because this would leave no host addresses.

Selecting a number of bits for the subnet ID affects both the number of possible subnets and the number of hosts that can be in each subnet. As you borrow more bits to create subnets, the number of hosts per subnet decreases. To calculate the number of subnets, take the number 2 to the power of the number of bits borrowed. To calculate the number of hosts per subnet, take the number 2 to the power of the number of bits left, minus 2. We subtract 2 because the first value (host ID of all-0s) is the actual subnet number, and the last value (host ID of all-1s) is the broadcast address for the subnet. Neither of these can be used as a host address.

As shown in Table 4-4, if we borrow 2 bits from the host field, we can create four subnets ($2^2 = 4$). Six host ID bits are left, which allows for 62 hosts per subnet (2^6–2 = 64–2 = 62). Note that, if we borrow 7 bits for subnets, only 1 bit is left for hosts. This results in only two possible host values, neither of which can be used.

Custom Subnet Masks

Routers distinguish between networks by using the subnet mask to determine which bits make up the network ID and which bits make up the host portion of the address. When a network is partitioned using subnetting, the router needs a modified or custom subnet mask to distinguish the subnets from each other. A default subnet mask and a custom subnet mask differ from each other as follows: Default subnet masks change only on octet boundaries. For instance, the default subnet mask for a Class A network is 255.0.0.0. The default mask for a Class B mask is 255.255.0.0, and a Class C is 255.255.255.0. Custom subnet masks take bits from the host ID portion of the IP address and add them to the default subnet mask.

To create a custom subnet mask, the first question to answer is how many bits to take from the host ID to add to the subnet mask. The simplest example is to look at what happens when we borrow 1 bit. Figure 4-10 starts with the basic Class C network 192.168.1.0/24 (one subnet of 254 hosts) and then borrows 1 bit to split it into two subnets, each with 126 hosts. The two subnets created, 192.168.1.0/25 and 192.168.1.128/25, are shown, along with the host range and the broadcast address for each one.

Figure 4-10   Subnetting a Class C Address to Create Two Subnets

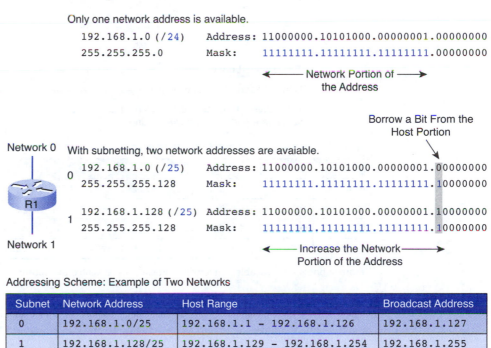

Addressing Scheme: Example of Two Networks

Subnet	Network Address	Host Range	Broadcast Address
0	192.168.1.0/25	192.168.1.1 – 192.168.1.126	192.168.1.127
1	192.168.1.128/25	192.168.1.129 – 192.168.1.254	192.168.1.255

How many bits for a subnet ID will be added to the subnet mask depends on several factors. In this example, those factors have been limited for the sake of simplicity. Not all situations will be so simple. For instance, what if an organization assigned a Class C address has multiple networks—one network with seven hosts, another with 60 hosts, and a third with 34 hosts?

In classful subnetting, all subnets must be the same size, which means that the minimum number of hosts that each subnet must support is 60. To support the minimum number of 60 hosts, at least 6 bits are required in the host ID, which leaves 2 bits for the subnet identifier. Figure 4-11 splits the basic Class C 192.168.1.0/24 network into four subnets of 62 hosts each. The resulting subnet mask, subnet numbers, the number of hosts for each subnet, and broadcast address are listed.

Figure 4-11   Subnetting a Class C Address to Create Four Subnets

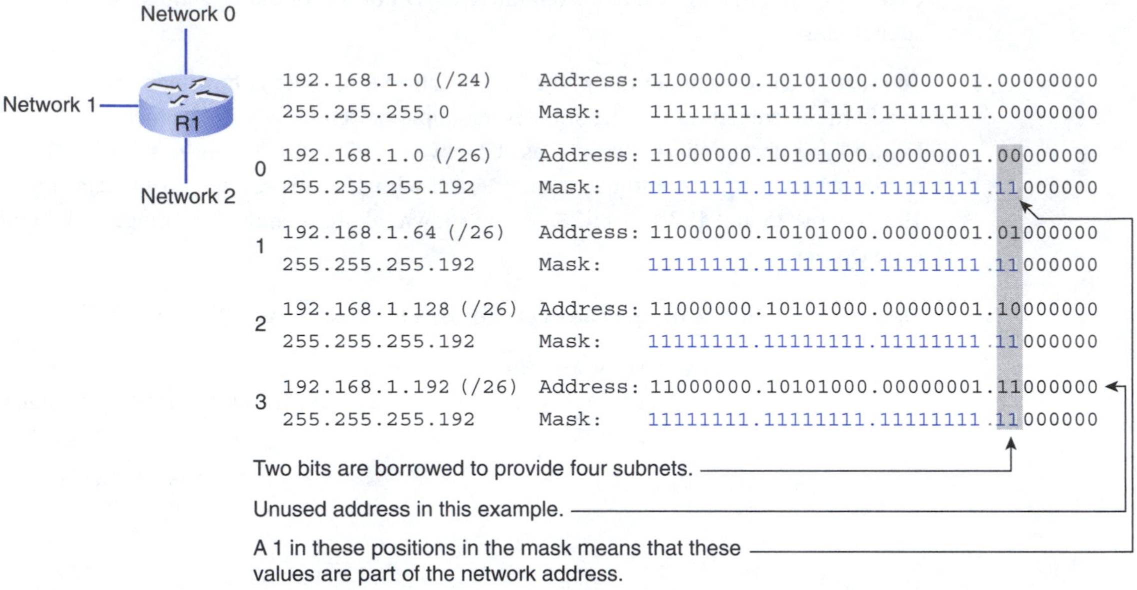

Network 0

Network 1 — R1

Network 2

	192.168.1.0 (/24)	Address:	11000000.10101000.00000001.00000000
	255.255.255.0	Mask:	11111111.11111111.11111111.00000000
0	192.168.1.0 (/26)	Address:	11000000.10101000.00000001.00000000
	255.255.255.192	Mask:	11111111.11111111.11111111.11000000
1	192.168.1.64 (/26)	Address:	11000000.10101000.00000001.01000000
	255.255.255.192	Mask:	11111111.11111111.11111111.11000000
2	192.168.1.128 (/26)	Address:	11000000.10101000.00000001.10000000
	255.255.255.192	Mask:	11111111.11111111.11111111.11000000
3	192.168.1.192 (/26)	Address:	11000000.10101000.00000001.11000000
	255.255.255.192	Mask:	11111111.11111111.11111111.11000000

Two bits are borrowed to provide four subnets.

Unused address in this example.

A 1 in these positions in the mask means that these values are part of the network address.

Addressing Scheme: Example of Four Networks

Subnet	Network Address	Host Range	Broadcast Address
0	192.168.1.0/26	192.168.1.1 - 192.168.1.62	192.168.1.63
1	192.168.1.64/26	192.168.1.65 - 192.168.1.126	192.168.1.127
2	192.168.1.128/26	192.168.1.129 - 192.168.1.190	192.168.1.191
3	192.168.1.192/26	192.168.1.193 - 192.168.1.254	192.168.1.255

More subnets are available, but fewer addresses are available per subnet.

Devices on the network are informed of the subdivision by the use of the subnet mask. Now it is possible to tell what subnet an IP address is in and to design simple classful subnetted IP address schemes.

If a Class C network is subnetted and 3 bits are taken from the host ID to use for the subnet ID, 5 bits are left for host addresses. Five host bits means that there can be 30 hosts per subnet, or 2^5–2. Remember that the all-0s and all-1s host addresses are reserved for the network designation and the broadcast address.

The number of subnets is calculated in a similar manner. If 3 bits are used for the subnet address, the number of subnets is 2*2*2, or 2^3. Subnetting in this manner results in eight subnets (0 to 7) with 30 hosts each, as shown in Figure 4-12. Note that the subnet numbers increase by increments of 32 because that is the number of hosts per subnet (minus 2).

Figure 4-12   Subnetting a Class C Address to Create Eight Subnets

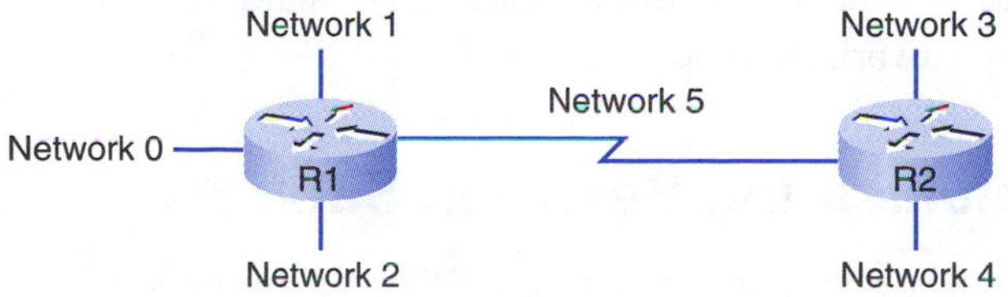

Network 1   Network 3

                  Network 5

Network 0 ──── R1 ──────────────── R2

Network 2   Network 4

	192.168.1.0 (/24)	Address:	11000000.10101000.00000001.00000000
	255.255.255.0	Mask:	11111111.11111111.11111111.00000000
0	192.168.1.0 (/27)	Address:	11000000.10101000.00000001.00000000
	255.255.255.224	Mask:	11111111.11111111.11111111.11100000
1	192.168.1.32 (/27)	Address:	11000000.10101000.00000001.00100000
	255.255.255.224	Mask:	11111111.11111111.11111111.11100000
2	192.168.1.64 (/27)	Address:	11000000.10101000.00000001.01000000
	255.255.255.224	Mask:	11111111.11111111.11111111.11100000
3	192.168.1.96 (/27)	Address:	11000000.10101000.00000001.01100000
	255.255.255.224	Mask:	11111111.11111111.11111111.11100000
4	192.168.1.128 (/27)	Address:	11000000.10101000.00000001.10000000
	255.255.255.224	Mask:	11111111.11111111.11111111.11100000
5	192.168.1.160 (/27)	Address:	11000000.10101000.00000001.10100000
	255.255.255.224	Mask:	11111111.11111111.11111111.11100000
6	192.168.1.192 (/27)	Address:	11000000.10101000.00000001.11000000
	255.255.255.224	Mask:	11111111.11111111.11111111.11100000
7	192.168.1.224 (/27)	Address:	11000000.10101000.00000001.11100000
	255.255.255.224	Mask:	11111111.11111111.11111111.11100000

Three bits are borrowed to
provide eight subnets.

Addressing Scheme: Example of Eight Networks

Subnet	Network Address	Host Range	Broadcast Address
0	192.168.1.0/27	192.168.1.1 - 192.168.1.30	192.168.1.31
1	192.168.1.32/27	192.168.1.33 - 192.168.1.62	192.168.1.63
2	192.168.1.64/27	192.168.1.65 - 192.168.1.94	192.168.1.95
3	192.168.1.96/27	192.168.1.97 - 192.168.1.126	192.168.1.127
4	192.168.1.128/27	192.168.1.129 - 192.168.1.158	192.168.1.159
5	192.168.1.160/27	192.168.1.161 - 192.168.1.190	192.168.1.191
6	192.168.1.192/27	192.168.1.193 - 192.168.1.222	192.168.1.223
7	192.168.1.224/27	192.168.1.225 - 192.168.1.254	192.168.1.255

When determining how many hosts are needed in each subnet, you must include the router interface as well as the individual host devices. Each router interface must have an IP address in the same subnet as the host network attached to it.

Communicating Between Subnets

Think of a subnet as a smaller network. When a network is split into two subnets, there are actually two separate networks. Remember that routers connect networks. For a device in one subnet to communicate with a device in the other, a router is required. The proposed network upgrade discussed earlier has two routers: an existing wireless ISR, which is now connected to the new ISR, and the new ISR that connects to the ISP.

The configuration must ensure that interfaces on routers that connect to each other are assigned IP addresses in the same network or subnet and that clients are assigned default gateways that they can reach.

In our redesigned network, we need three subnets—one for the wired hosts, one for the wireless hosts, and one for the link between the existing ISR and the new one being added. The link between the routers is a point-to-point link and requires only two IP addresses—one for each router interface. Assuming that we have four wired hosts and five wireless hosts, we could borrow 5 subnet bits and create 32 subnets of six hosts each. This scenario is shown in Figure 4-13, with all hosts having a /29 mask, or 255.255.255.248 in decimal.

Figure 4-13   Router Interfaces Are Included in the Subnets

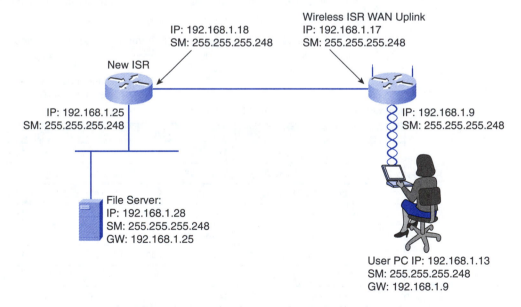

The interfaces that connect the wireless ISR to the 1841 ISR must be on a common network. In Figure 4-13, the common link shows the two routers connected on the 192.168.1.16/29 subnet, with IP addresses 192.168.1.17/29 and 192.168.1.18/29. The user PC (192.168.1.13/29) is on the 192.168.1.8/29 subnet with a default gateway of 192.168.1.9. The file server (192.168.1.28/29) is on the 192.168.1.24/29 subnet with a default gateway of 192.168.1.25. The subnets in Figure 4-13 can be summarized as follows.

192.168.1.0 /24 network subnets (the first four of 32):

- 192.168.1.0/29: Not used

- 192.168.1.8/29: Wireless network

- 192.168.1.16/29: Point-to-point link

- 192.168.1.24/29: Wired network

If the wired and wireless networks need to support 40 to 50 users each, the wired users could use the 192.168.1.64/26 (62 hosts) subnet, and the wireless network could use the 192.168.1.128/26 (62 hosts) subnet. The link between the routers is using a /29 subnet (six hosts), and the wired/wireless LANs are using /26 subnets (62 users each). Because the link between the routers requires only two IP addresses, we could even use a /30 subnet (two users), such as 192.168.1.4/30. In this case we could assign IP addresses of 192.168.1.5 and 192.168.1.6 to the router interfaces with a subnet mask of 255.255.255.252.

This alternative variable subnet scheme can be summarized as follows:

192.168.1.0/24 network:

- 192.16.1.0/26: Not used

- 192.16.1.4/29 or /30: Point-to-point link

- 192.16.1.64/26: Wired users

- 192.16.1.128/26: Wireless users

- 192.16.1.192/26: Not used

Interactive Activity 4-1: Determining Decimal and Binary Network Addresses (4.1.3)

In this activity, you are given a host address and subnet mask and must determine the decimal and binary values for the network the host is on. Use file d2ia-413 on the CD-ROM that accompanies this book to perform this interactive activity

Implementing an IP Addressing Scheme (4.1.3)

In this activity, you subnet an address space based on host requirements and assign host addresses to devices. Use file d2-413.pka on the CD-ROM that accompanies this book to perform this activity using Packet Tracer.

Communicating Between Subnets (4.1.5)

In this activity, you modify the addresses, subnet masks, and device default gateways to enable routing between subnets. Use file d2-415.pka on the CD-ROM that accompanies this book to perform this activity using Packet Tracer.

Lab 4-1: Subnetting a Network (4.1.5)

In this lab you modify the addresses, subnet masks, and device default gateways to enable routing between subnets. Refer to the lab in Part II of this book. You may perform this lab now or wait until the end of the chapter.

IPv6

Subnetting, VLSM, and private IP addressing were developed to provide a temporary solution to the problem of IP address depletion. These methods, though useful, did not create more IP addresses. *IPv6* does that. IPv6 was first proposed in 1998 with RFC 2460.

Although its primary purpose was to solve IPv4 IP address depletion, there were other good reasons for the development of IPv6. Since IPv4 was first standardized, the Internet has grown significantly. This growth has uncovered the advantages and disadvantages of IPv4 and the possibility for upgrades to include new capabilities.

Here's a general list of improvements that IPv6 proposes:

- More address space

- Better address space management

- Easier TCP/IP administration

- Modernized routing capabilities

- Improved support for multicasting, security, and mobility

The development of IPv6 intends to address as many of these requests and problems as possible. Figure 4-14 shows an IP address development timeline from IPv4 to IPv6.

Figure 4-14 Timeline of IP Development from IPv4 to IPv6

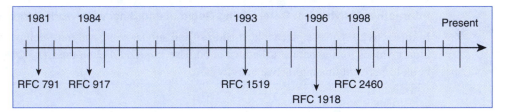

The following summarizes the RFCs mentioned in Figure 4-14:

- RFC 791, *Internet Protocol*, defined IPv4.

- RFC 917, *Internet Subnets*, defined IP subnets.

- RFC 1519, *Classless Inter-Domain Routing (CIDR): an Address Assignment and Aggregation Strategy*, defined CIDR.

- RFC 1918, *Address Allocation for Private Internets*, defined private IP addressing.

- RFC 2460, *Internet Protocol, Version 6 (IPv6) Specification*, defined IPv6.

With IPv6, IP addresses are 128 bits in size, with a potential address space of 2^{128}. In decimal notation, that is approximately a 3 followed by 38 zeros. If IPv4 address space were represented by the volume of a teaspoon, IPv6 address space would be represented by a volume almost equivalent to the planet Saturn.

Working with 128-bit numbers is difficult, so the IPv6 address notation represents the 128 bits as 32 hexadecimal digits, which are further subdivided into eight groups of four hexadecimal digits, using colons as delimiters. The IPv6 address has a three-part hierarchy. The global prefix is the first three blocks of the address and is assigned to an organization by an Internet names registry. The subnet and the interface identifier (ID) are controlled by the network administrator. Figure 4-15 shows the 128-bit address and the groupings of digits.

Figure 4-15   IPv6 Address Notation

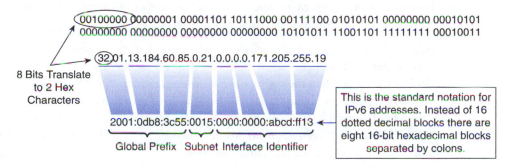

Network administrators will have some time to adjust to this new IPv6 structure. Before the widespread adoption of IPv6 occurs, network administrators still need a way to more efficiently use private address spaces. Some organizations will continue to use IPv4 indefinitely due to its simplicity, especially with the advent of private address space.

Nearly all new computer and network devices operating systems now support IPv6. This makes the transition easier for network administrators who either want to or are required to convert from IPv4 to IPv6.

Example 4-1 is the **ipconfig** command output from a Windows Vista PC showing the IPv4 and IPv6 address. In the output, note that the link-local IPv6 address fe80::4e2:3a49:631a:5d18 has two consecutive colons after the fe80. This notation may be used when there are only 0s in one or more sets of 16 bits (four hex characters). In this case the two colons represent three sets of four hex 0s.

Example 4-1 Windows Vista ipconfig Command Output

```
C:\> ipconfig

Windows IP Configuration
Ethernet adapter Local Area Connection:
   Connection-specific DNS Suffix  . : cisco.com
   Link-local IPv6 Address . . . . . : fe80::4e2:3a49:631a:5d18
   IPv4 Address. . . . . . . . . . . : 192.168.1.100
   Subnet Mask . . . . . . . . . . . : 255.255.255.0
   Default Gateway . . . . . . . . . : 192.168.1.1
```

NAT and PAT

A key development that has helped conserve IPv4 address space is *Network Address Translation (NAT)*. The use of NAT and a variation called Port Address Translation (PAT), in combination with private IP addressing, has contributed significantly to extending the life of IPv4. At the same time, this has delayed the adoption of IPv6. Today, the use of NAT and PAT is common practice with networks of all sizes.

Basic Network Address Translation (NAT)

NAT allows a large group of private users to access the Internet by sharing a small pool of public IP addresses. Address translation is similar to how a company's telephone system works. As a company adds employees, at some point it no longer runs a public phone line to each employee's desk. Instead, the company uses a system that allows it to assign each employee an extension number. The company can do this because not all employees use the phone at the same time. Using private extension numbers enables the company to purchase a smaller number of external phone lines from the phone company. Internal employees share these external lines.

NAT works similarly to a company's phone system. Saving registered IP addresses is one of the main reasons that NAT was developed. NAT can also provide security to PCs, servers, and networking devices by withholding their actual IP host addresses from direct Internet access. Figure 4-16 shows the use of NAT between an internal network with 40 private users and the public Internet. The organization has five public addresses that are used for translation. If private addresses are used internally, NAT is required between the local private network and the public Internet. NAT allows many users in a private network to use a few public addresses.

Figure 4-16   NAT Is Required Between the Private Network and the Public Internet

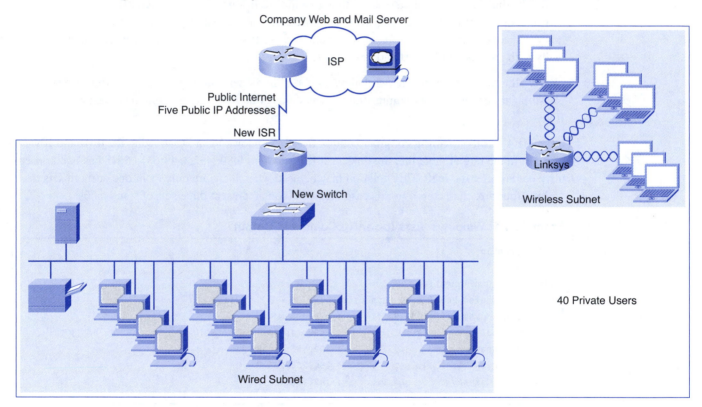

The main advantages of NAT are IP address reuse and the sharing of globally unique IP addresses between many hosts from a single LAN. NAT also serves users transparently. In other words, they do not need to know about NAT to get on the Internet from a private network. Finally, NAT helps shield users of a private network from outside access.

NAT does have some disadvantages. NAT impacts certain applications that have IP addresses in their message payload. These IP addresses must be translated as well, which increases the load on the router CPU. This extra workload on routers hinders network performance. NAT hides private IP addresses from public networks. It performs like access control, which can be desirable, but this can also be bad if legitimate remote access from the Internet to a device on the private network is desired.

The advantages of NAT are

- Public IP address sharing

- Transparent to end users

- Improved security

- LAN expandability or scalability

- Local control, including ISP connectivity

The disadvantages of NAT are

- Incompatibility with certain applications

- Hinders legitimate remote access

- Performance reduction due to increased router processing

IP NAT Terms

When you're configuring NAT on a router, the following terms help you understand how the router accomplishes NAT.

The inside local network refers to any network connected to a router interface that is part of the privately addressed LAN. Hosts on inside networks have their IP addresses translated before their packets are transmitted to outside destinations.

The outside global network is any network attached to the router that is external to the LAN and that does not recognize the private addresses assigned to hosts on the LAN.

An *inside local address* is the private IP address configured on a host on an inside network. It is an address that must be translated before it can travel outside the local network addressing structure.

An *inside global address* is the IP address of an inside host as it appears to the outside network. This is the translated IP address.

The *outside local address* is the destination address of the packet while it is on the local network. Usually this address is the same as the outside global address.

An *outside global address* is the actual public IP address of an external host. This address is allocated from a globally routable address or network space.

Figure 4-17 shows a private internal network with a host that needs to transmit a packet to an external remote server. The source host has an inside local address of 192.168.1.106. The destination remote server has an outside local address of 209.165.200.226. As the packet passes through the router on its way to the remote server, the router converts the 192.168.1.106 internal address in the packet from the source host to an inside global address in a pool from 209.165.202.129 to 209.165.202.130. In this case the 209.165.202.129 address is used. The packets can now be sent to the remote server.

Figure 4-17   NAT: Outgoing Packet

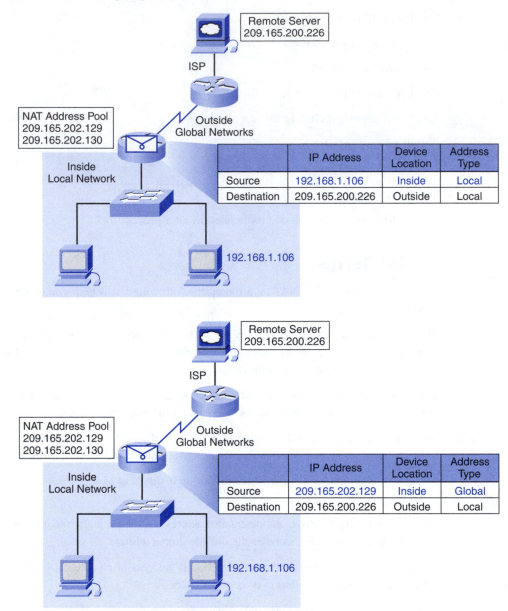

Figure 4-18 shows the reverse process, when the server sends back the packet. In this case the destination address is the inside global address of the local network router's external interface. When the router receives the packet from the remote server, it looks up the inside local address, replaces the 209.165.202.129 address with 192.168.1.106, and forwards the packet to the local host.

Interactive Activity 4-2: Match NAT Terminology to a Datagram (4.2.2)

In this activity, you match the NAT address terminology to the source and destination of the datagram. Use file d2ia-422 on the CD-ROM that accompanies this book to perform this interactive activity.

Figure 4-18   NAT: Return Packet

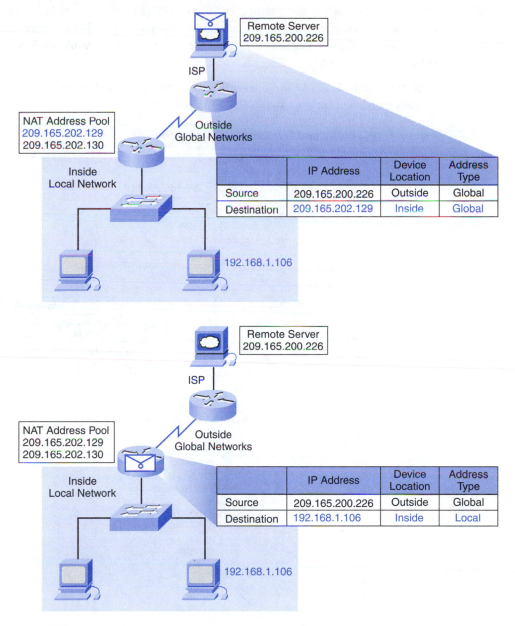

Static and Dynamic NAT

One of the advantages of using NAT is that individual hosts are not directly accessible from the public Internet. But what if one or more of the hosts within a network are running services that need to be accessed from Internet-connected devices, as well as devices on the local private LAN?

One way to provide access to a local host from the Internet is to assign that device a static address translation. Static translations ensure that an individual host private IP address is always translated into the same registered global IP address. It also ensures that no other local host will be translated into the same registered address. This is referred to as static NAT.

Dynamic NAT occurs when a router is configured to assign an IP address from an available pool of global addresses to an inside private network device. As long as the session is open, the router watches for that inside global address and sends acknowledgments to the initiating inside device. When the session ends, the router simply returns the inside global address to the pool.

Dynamic NAT allows hosts assigned with private IP addresses on a network, or intranet, to access a public network, such as the Internet. *Static NAT* allows hosts on the public network to access selected hosts on a private network. This means that when you configure NAT for user access to the outside, you should configure dynamic NAT. If a device on the inside network needs to be accessible from the outside, use static NAT.

Both NAT methods can be installed at the same time if required. Figure 4-19 shows the difference in address translation between static NAT and dynamic NAT.

Figure 4-19   Static and Dynamic NAT Operation

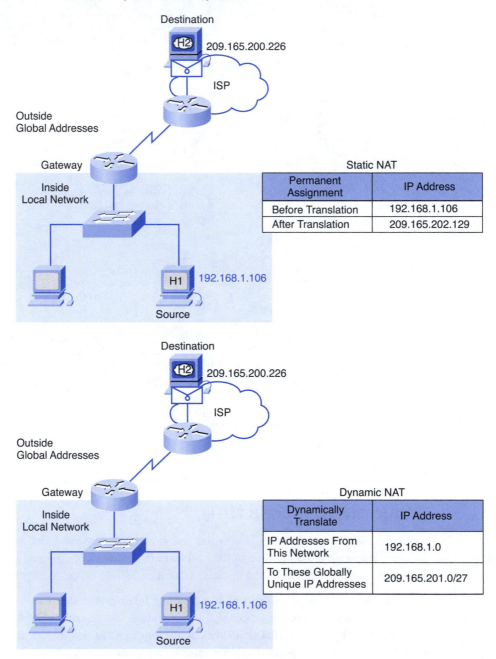

Static NAT

Permanent Assignment	IP Address
Before Translation	192.168.1.106
After Translation	209.165.202.129

Dynamic NAT

Dynamically Translate	IP Address
IP Addresses From This Network	192.168.1.0
To These Globally Unique IP Addresses	209.165.201.0/27

Port-Based Network Address Translation

When an organization has a very small registered IP address pool, or perhaps even just a single IP address, it can still enable multiple users to simultaneously access the public network with a mechanism called NAT overload, or *Port Address Translation (PAT)*.

PAT translates multiple local addresses to a single global IP address. When a source host sends a message to a destination host, it uses an IP address and port number combination to keep track of each conversation with the destination host. In PAT, the gateway translates the local source address and port combination in the packet to a single global IP address and a unique port number above 1024. Although each host is translated into the same global IP address, the port number associated with the conversation is unique.

Responding traffic is addressed to the translated IP address and port number used by the host. A table in the router contains a list of the internal IP address and port number combinations that are translated into the external address. Responding traffic comes back to the external address and is directed to the appropriate internal address and port number. Because more than 64,000 ports are available, a router is unlikely to run out of addresses. Figure 4-20 shows a private network with 40 internal hosts that uses PAT. Each of these hosts can communicate with the Internet using the single public IP address assigned to the external interface of the new ISR router.

Figure 4-20   PAT Operation

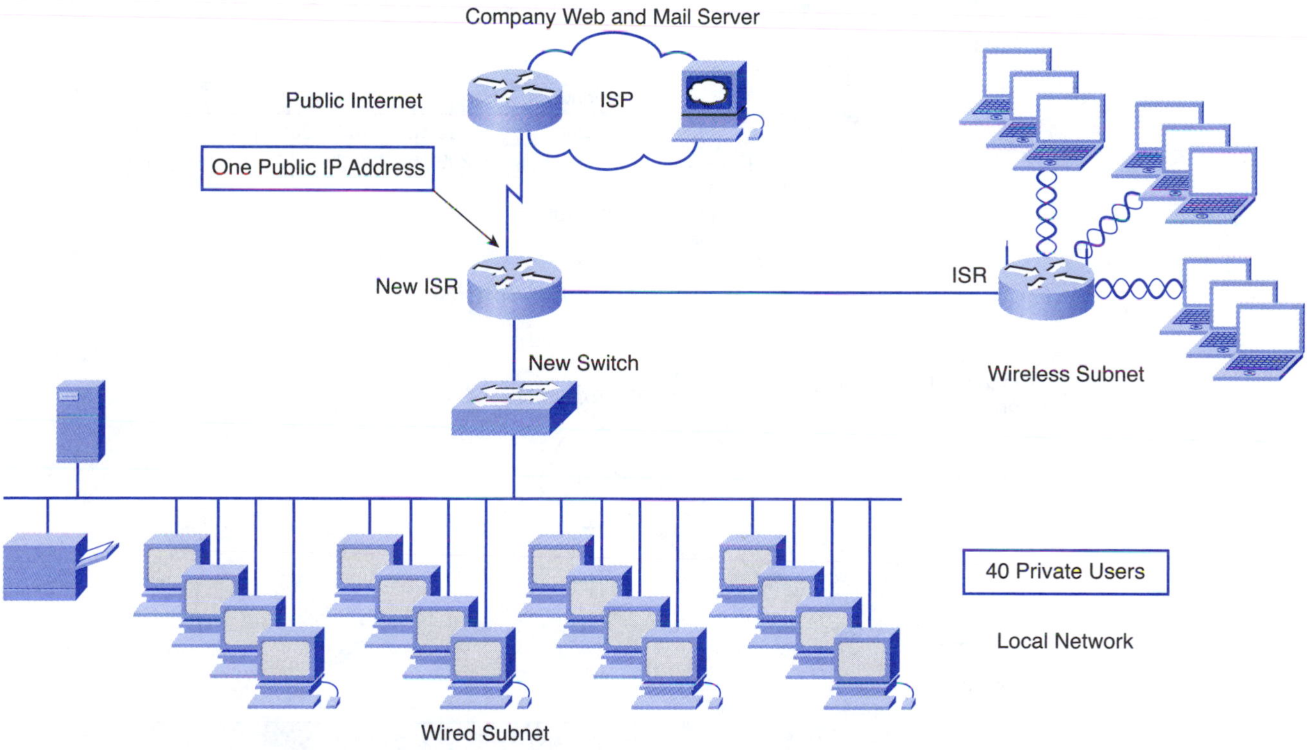

Because the translation is specific to the local address and local port, each connection, which generates a new source port, requires a separate translation. For example, 10.1.1.1:1025 requires a separate translation from 10.1.1.1:1026.

The translation is in place only for the duration of the connection, so a given user does not keep the same global IP address and port number combination after the conversation ends.

Users on the outside network cannot reliably initiate a connection to a host on a network that uses PAT. Not only is it impossible to predict the local or global port number of the host, but a gateway does not even create a translation unless a host on the inside network initiates the communication.

Figure 4-21 shows a private internal network with a host H1 that needs to transmit a packet to an external host H2 using PAT. The source host has an inside local address of 192.168.1.106 and a source port of 7000. The destination host H2 is a web server, and the destination address has well-known port 80 attached. As the packet passes through the router on its way to the H2 server, the router translates the source IP address 192.168.1.106 into the one available public IP address. It then picks a port number from the available ports (any port greater than 1024) and binds it to the public IP address 209.165.202.129 before forwarding the packet to the web server.

Figure 4-21   PAT: Outgoing Packet

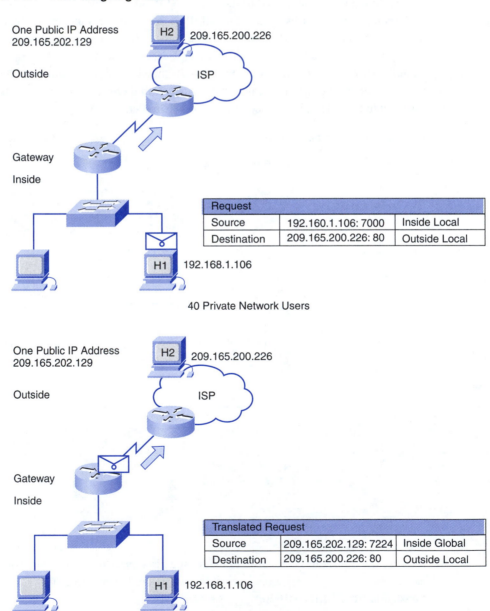

Request		
Source	192.160.1.106: 7000	Inside Local
Destination	209.165.200.226: 80	Outside Local

40 Private Network Users

Translated Request		
Source	209.165.202.129: 7224	Inside Global
Destination	209.165.200.226: 80	Outside Local

40 Private Network Users

Figure 4-22 shows the web server response and the reverse translation process. The server sends back a response to the same host IP address and port combination it received the packet from. The gateway router receives the response and recognizes the IP address and port combination. It translates the combination into the correct IP address, 192.168.1.106, and binds the original port number to it so that the communications loop can be closed.

Figure 4-22   PAT: Return Packet

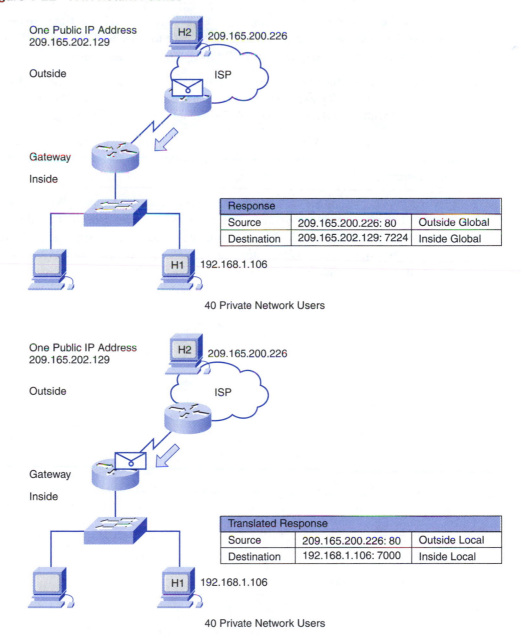

Response		
Source	209.165.200.226: 80	Outside Global
Destination	209.165.202.129: 7224	Inside Global

Translated Response		
Source	209.165.200.226: 80	Outside Local
Destination	192.168.1.106: 7000	Inside Local

Examining Network Address Translation (NAT) (4.2.3)

In this Packet Tracer activity, you examine the contents of the IP header as traffic crosses the NAT border. Use file d2-423.pka on the CD-ROM that accompanies this book to perform this activity using Packet Tracer.

Lab 4-2: Determining PAT Translations (4.2.4)

In this lab you determine the number of PAT translations being performed at any one time. Refer to the lab in Part II of this book. You may perform this lab now or wait until the end of the chapter.

IP NAT Issues

Most of the time, NAT operates invisibly. People access the Internet from private networks without ever realizing the work that the router does to make that happen. The big issue with NAT is the additional work load necessary to support IP address and port translations.

Some applications increase the router's workload because they embed an IP address as part of the encapsulated data. The router must replace the source IP addresses and port combinations that are contained within the data, as well as the source addresses in the IP header.

With all this activity taking place in a router because of NAT, its implementation in a network requires good network design, careful selection of equipment, accurate configuration, and regularly scheduled maintenance.

As a protocol that supports IPv4, NAT has helped delay the complete depletion of the IPv4 address space. It has become so commonplace in integrated networking devices, used in homes and small businesses, that for some people, configuring it is a matter of selecting a checkbox. As businesses grow, they require more sophisticated gateway and routing solutions. Device configurations for NAT and other features and functions can become more complex.

Summary

Interfaces on network devices connected to the Internet need a unique IP address to send and receive messages over public networks. IP addresses are organized into network Classes A, B, C, D, and E and are conserved by the creation of private IP address space.

A network can be divided into subnets. Classful subnetting uses the extension of the subnet mask. Classless IP addressing, part of a method called Classless Interdomain Routing (CIDR), uses a flexible method of subnetting with variable-length subnet masks (VLSM). Subnet masks allow further subdivision of a network by extending the number of bits used.

A subnet ID is created by splitting the host ID into two parts, a subnet ID and a new host. The number of bits in the subnet ID determines how many subnets a network can have. Communication between subnets requires routing.

IPv6 incorporates a 128-bit addressing scheme, whereas IPv4 uses 32 bits.

NAT enables a large group of private users to access the Internet by sharing a small pool of public IP addresses, thereby reducing the consumption of globally unique IP addresses. NAT inside addresses are IP addresses for private network devices. Outside addresses are IP addresses for public network devices. Local addresses are IP addresses in packets that are still in the private network. Global addresses are IP addresses that cross to the outside network. A packet that has been translated and that is in the outside network lists an inside global IP address as source and an outside global IP address as destination.

Static NAT is for permanent one-to-one translations from a specific inside local IP address to a specific inside global IP address. Dynamic NAT assigns inside global IP addresses on a first-come, first-served basis from an available pool of IP addresses to a designated network or subnetwork.

PAT, or NAT overload, translates private internal addresses to a single external global address and adds a port number to the IP address for specific connections. PAT is the most common form of NAT used with home and small business networks.

Network devices that use NAT translate addresses on every packet. This can significantly increase the processing workload.

Activities and Labs

This summary outlines the activities and labs you can perform to help reinforce important concepts described in this chapter. You can find the activity and Packet Tracer files on the CD-ROM accompanying this book. The complete hands-on labs appear in Part II.

Interactive Activity on the CD:

Interactive Activity 4-1: Working with Subnet Masks and Host Ranges. (4.1.3)

Interactive Activity 4-2: Match NAT Terminology to a Datagram (4.2.2)

Packet Tracer Activity on the CD:

Implementing an IP Addressing Scheme (4.1.3)

Communicating Between Subnets (4.1.5)

Examining Network Address Translation (NAT) (4.2.3)

Hands-on Labs in Part II of this book:

Lab 4-1: Subnetting a Network (4.1.5)

Lab 4-2: Determining PAT Translations (4.2.4)

Check Your Understanding

Complete the review questions to check your understanding of the topics and concepts in this chapter. Answers are listed in Appendix A, "Check Your Understanding and Challenge Questions Answer Key."

1. What are three advantages of NAT?

    A. It conserves registered public IP addresses.

    B. It reduces CPU usage on customer routers.

    C. It creates multiple public IP addresses.

    D. It hides private LAN addressing from the Internet.

    E. It permits LAN expansion without additional public IP addresses.

    F. It improves the performance of border routers.

2. What is the default subnet mask for the classful address 172.31.18.222?

    A. 255.0.0.0

    B. 255.255.0.0

    C. 255.255.255.0

    D. 255.255.255.254

    E. 255.255.255.255

3. Which three addresses are valid subnet addresses when 172.25.15.0/24 is further subnetted by borrowing an additional 4 bits?

    A. 172.25.15.0

    B. 172.25.15.8

    C. 172.25.15.16

    D. 172.25.15.40

    E. 172.25.15.96

    F. 172.25.15.248

4. What high-order binary numbers begin a Class C address?

    A. 000

    B. 001

    C. 010

    D. 110

5. Host A is configured with IP address 192.168.75.34, and Host B is configured with IP address 192.168.75.50. Each uses the same subnet mask of 255.255.255.240, but they are unable to ping each other. What networking device is needed for these two hosts to communicate?

    A. Switch

    B. Hub

    C. Server

    D. Router

6. What two pieces of information can be derived from the IP address 192.168.42.135/24?

    A. This is a Class C address, because the high-order bits are 110.

    B. The default subnet mask is 255.255.255.0.

    C. The host portion is represented by the third and fourth octets.

    D. The second high-order bit is a 0, so this is a Class B address.

    E. This host address belongs to the parent 192.168.0.0 network.

    F. This is one host address out of a possible 65,534 addresses.

7. What subnet mask is indicated by the network address 172.16.4.8/18?

    A. 255.255.0.0

    B. 255.255.192.0

    C. 255.255.240.0

    D. 255.255.248.0

    E. 255.255.255.0

8. Draw a line from the IP address on the left to its description on the right.

127.0.0.0	Class A host address
223.14.6.95	Multicast address
191.82.0.0	Class B default subnet mask
255.255.0.0	Class B network address
124.255.255.255	Class C host address
224.100.35.76	Class A broadcast address
61.0.0.255	Loopback testing address

9. An internal web server needs to be accessible from the Internet. Which NAT option provides a method for outside hosts to access the internal web server?

    A. Dynamic NAT using a NAT pool

    B. Static NAT

    C. Port address translation

    D. Dynamic NAT with overload

10. When a network administrator applies the subnet mask 255.255.255.248 to a Class C address, for any given subnet, how many IP addresses are available to be assigned to devices?

A. 6

B. 30

C. 126

D. 254

E. 510

F. 1022

11. An ISP customer has obtained a Class C network address. The network technician needs to create five usable subnets, with each subnet capable of containing at least 20 host addresses. What is the appropriate subnet mask to use?

A. 255.255.255.0

B. 255.255.255.192

C. 255.255.255.224

D. 255.255.255.240

12. For each characteristic listed, check either IPv4 or IPv6:

Characteristics	IPv4	IPv6
Uses a 32-bit address		
Is usually expressed in dotted-decimal notation		
Contains a 24-bit global prefix		
Is usually expressed in hexadecimal notation		
Is in widespread use on the Internet		
Uses a 128-bit address		

13. What is the network broadcast address for a Class B address of 172.17.0.0 with the default subnet mask?

A. 172.17.0.0

B. 172.17.255.255

C. 172.17.0.255

D. 172.17.255.0

14. How many usable hosts are available given a Class C IP address with the default subnet mask?

A. 65,535

B. 255

C. 254

D. 256

E. 128

15. With which IP technology are many internal addresses translated into a single global IP address using different source port numbers?

16. An organization is subnetting the 172.24.4.0/24 network using a subnet mask of 255.255.255.192 to create subnets. What is the maximum number of usable hosts in each subnet?

A. 14

B. 30

C. 62

D. 126

E. 254

17. Which IPv4 address class provides approximately 65,000 hosts per network?

Challenge Questions and Activities

These questions require a deeper application of the concepts covered in this chapter. You can find the answers in Appendix A.

1. The following chart lists host IP addresses and the associated CIDR mask or prefix. For each one, enter the dotted-decimal mask, the subnet that the host address is on, and the total number of CIDR addresses that the subnet can support. Calculate the subnet number using the ANDing process.

Host IP Address	CIDR Prefix	Dotted-Decimal Mask	Network/Subnet Number	Total Number of CIDR Host Addresses on This Network/Subnet
172.27.130.53	/22			
192.168.117.40	/27			
10.5.93.226	/24			
172.18.21.138	/20			
192.168.117.5	/30			

2. A small business network uses PAT between its internal private network and the ISP. Host-A on the internal network has IP address 192.168.1.27. A remote server on the Internet has IP address 209.165.200.229. The router interface for the internal network is Fa0/0, which has an IP address of 192.168.1.1. The router's external interface is S0/0/0, which has an IP address of 209.165.202.65.

Host-A sends a packet to the server on the remote network. Based on the preceding information, answer the following questions:

A. When the packet leaves Serial 0/0/0 destined for the remote server, what is the source IP address?

B. What NAT term refers to the public IP address of the external interface of S0/0/0?

C. When the packet from the internal host reaches the Fa0/0 interface, destined for the remote server, what is the source IP address?

D. What NAT term refers to the private IP address of the internal host?

E. When the packet is sent from the internal host to the server, what is the destination IP address?

F. What NAT term refers to the IP address of the remote server?

G. When the packet is sent back from the server to the internal host, what is the source IP address as it leaves the server?

H. When the packet is sent back from the server to the internal host, what is the destination IP address before it reaches the small business router S0/0/0 interface?

I. When the packet is sent back from the server to the internal host and it passes through the router Fa0/0 interface, what is the destination IP address?

3. IP addressing/NAT/PAT information-gathering activity (optional).

In this activity you will investigate the IP addressing of a PC that is connected to the Internet and determine if address translation is being used. You may investigate a PC at your institution, a home/business PC attached directly to the Internet, or one attached to a home network ISR device. This activity will help you better understand IP addressing and the use of NAT/PAT in a production network. You may contact your instructor or a member of your institution's network support staff, if appropriate, to obtain some help with these questions.

Use the **ipconfig /all** command to determine the PC's IP configuration:

A. Institution/organization:

B. What is the PC IP address?

C. What is the PC subnet mask?

D. Based on the IP address and subnet mask, what network or subnet is the PC on?

E. How many IP addresses are supported by this network/mask combination?

F. What is the PC default gateway?

G. How was the PC IP configuration obtained?

H. Is the PC IP address private or public?

I. Is NAT or PAT being used?

J. What is the IP address of the DNS server(s)?

K. Are the IP addresses of the DNS servers private or public?

Compare your notes with those of the other students.

_____

_____

_____

## CHAPTER 5

Configuring Network Devices

Objectives

After completing this chapter, you should be able to answer the following questions:

- What is an ISR?

- What methods are available for configuring an ISR?

- How does in-band configuration differ from out-of-band configuration?

- When is it appropriate to use SDM or SDM Express to configure a Cisco device?

- What is the difference between the startup configuration and the running configuration?

- What commands are required to perform basic configuration on a Cisco 1841 ISR?

- What commands are required to configure an ISR to function as a DHCP server?

- What commands are necessary to configure static NAT on an ISR?

- What commands are required to perform basic configuration on a Cisco 2960 switch?

- What is switch port security, and how is it configured?

- What is CDP, and how does it function?

- What types of WAN connections are available, and how do they compare in terms of cost and speed?

Key Terms

This chapter uses the following key terms. You can find the definitions in the Glossary.

nonvolatile random-access memory (NVRAM)   page 114

startup configuration   page 114

running configuration   page 115

ROMmon mode   page 116

out-of-band management   page 117

in-band management   page 117

command-line interface (CLI)   page 118

Cisco Router and Security Device Manager (SDM)   page 118

graphical user interface (GUI)   page 118

telecommunications service provider (TSP)   page 124

authentication   page 124

context-sensitive   page 129

virtual terminal   page 138

Data Communications Equipment (DCE)   page 139

Data Terminal Equipment (DTE)   page 139

default route   page 141

hop   page 141

internal interface   page 144

external interface   page 144

TFTP server   page 146

Synchronous Optical Network (SONET)   page 153

Asynchronous Transfer Mode (ATM)   page 153

digital subscriber line (DSL)   page 153

cable   page 153

Channel Service Unit/Data Service Unit (CSU/DSU)   page 154

Cisco Network Assistant   page 156

half-duplex   page 158

full-duplex   page 158

autonegotiation   page 159

power-on self-test (POST)   page 159

virtual local-area network (VLAN)   page 161

In the past, different networks were used to move voice, video and data, allowing each to be optimized for the traffic it carried. Now, one network infrastructure must carry all types of traffic for more users than ever before. The underlying routing and switching technologies must provide the foundation for a wide range of business applications. Network technicians and engineers set up and configure routers and switches to provide LAN and WAN connectivity and services.

Part II of this book includes the corresponding labs for this chapter.

Initial ISR Configuration

The Cisco Integrated Services Router (ISR) is one of the most popular series of networking devices to support growing business needs. The ISR combines features such as routing and switching functions, security, voice, and LAN and WAN connectivity into a single device. This makes the ISR ideal for small- to medium-sized businesses and for ISP managed customers. Many different series of ISRs exist, as shown in Figure 5-1 and Table 5-1, each designed to support a specific market segment.

Figure 5-1   Cisco ISRs

Cisco 800 Series ISR   Cisco 3800 Series ISR

Cisco 1800 Series ISR   Cisco 2800 Series ISR

Table 5-1   Cisco ISR Series

ISR Series	Features
800 series	Designed for small offices and home-based users
	Supports one WAN connection (routed port)
	Supports four 10/100-Mbps switch ports
	Combines data, security, and wireless services
	Provides services at broadband speeds
1800 series	Designed for small-to-medium businesses
	Contains modular slots that support both LAN and WAN interfaces
	Supports up to two 10/100-Mbps routed ports
	Supports up to eight 10/100-Mbps switch ports
	Combines data, security, and wireless services
	Provides services ranging from broadband to T1/E1 speeds

ISR Series	Features
2800 series	Designed for small-to-medium businesses
	Contains modular slots that supports both LAN and WAN interfaces
	Supports up to two 10/100/1000-Mbps routed ports
	Supports up to 64 10/100-Mbps switch ports
	Supports 96 Cisco IP phone users
	Combines data, security, voice, video, and wireless services
	Provides services at broadband speeds using multiple T1/E1 connections
3800 series	Designed for medium-to-large businesses and enterprise branch offices
	Contains modular slots that support both LAN and WAN interfaces
	Supports up to two 10/100/1000-Mbps router ports
	Supports up to 112 10/100-Mbps switch ports
	Supports 240 Cisco IP phone users
	Combines data, security, voice, video, and wireless service
	Provides services at broadband speeds using multiple T3/E3 connections

Interactive Activity 5-1: Photozoom of an 1800 ISR (5.1.1)

This interactive activity is a photozoom of the Cisco 1800 series ISR. Use file d2ia-511 on the CD-ROM that accompanies this book to perform this interactive activity.

Internetworking devices are merely a collection of electronic parts similar to a computer. An internetworking device such as an ISR requires an operating system to allow it to function. The Cisco IOS software provides features that enable a Cisco device to send and receive network traffic using a wired or wireless network. IOS software is offered to customers in modules called images. These images support various features for businesses of every size. The IOS is built in a modular format that allows end users to obtain an image that has the specific feature set they require.

> **Note**
>
> The ability to upgrade and manage Cisco IOS files is an important skill set to have. Reasons for upgrading the IOS include access to new and enhanced functionality or correcting faults in an older IOS. Appendix B, "Router Boot and Password Recovery Labs," provides additional information on the Cisco IOS and labs related to password recovery, IOS upgrading, and management.

The entry-level Cisco IOS software image is called the IP Base image. The Cisco IOS IP Base software supports small to medium-sized businesses and supports routing between networks. Other Cisco IOS software images add services to the IP Base image. For example, for you to use advanced security features, the Advanced Security image must be installed on the device. This gives the added functionality necessary to configure advanced security capabilities, private networking, and firewalls. Figure 5-2 shows the various levels of Cisco IOS available.

Figure 5-2   Cisco IOS Capabilities

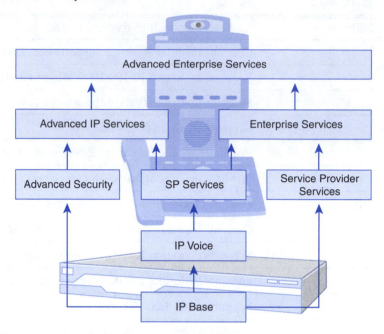

Many different IOS images are available, as well as different versions of each image. These images are designed to operate on specific models of routers, switches, and ISRs. It is important to know what image and version are loaded on a device before you begin the configuration process, because this dictates which features and commands are available.

Physical Setup of the ISR

Each ISR ships with the cables and documentation needed to power on the device and begin the installation. When you receive a new device, unpack it and verify that all necessary hardware and equipment are included. The standard items shipped with a new Cisco 1841 ISR are

- RJ-45-to-DB9 console cable

- DB9-to-DB25 modem adapter

- Power cord

- Product registration card, called the Cisco.com card

- Regulatory Compliance and Safety Information for Cisco 1840 Routers

- Router and Security Device Manager (SDM) Quick Start Guide

- Cisco 1800 Series Integrated Services Routers (Modular) Quick Start Guide

A new Cisco 1841 ISR does not come with all the tools and equipment needed to physically install the device. The necessary tools usually are stocked at the ISP or in the network technician's lab. Additional specific equipment needed depends on the model of the device and any optional equipment ordered. Some of the tools typically required to install a new device are shown in Figure 5-3:

- A PC with a terminal emulation program, such as the HyperTerminal program

- Cable ties

- A number 2 Phillips screwdriver

- Cables for WAN interfaces, LAN interfaces, and USB interfaces

Figure 5-3   Tools Required to Install an ISR

PC with Terminal
Emulation Program

Cable Ties and
Number 2 Phillips
Screwdriver

WAN Interface Cable

LAN Interface Cable

USB Interface Cable

Ethernet Switch

Modem

It is also necessary to have any equipment or devices required for connection to WAN or broadband communication services, such as hubs or modems, available before starting the installation.

Before beginning any equipment installation, be sure to read the Quick Start guide and other documentation that is included with the device. Important safety and procedural information is contained in the documentation that will prevent the equipment from being accidentally damaged during installation.

Here are the steps to perform a power-up procedure on an 1841 ISR:

Step 1.   Securely mount and ground the device chassis, or case. Cisco routers and ISRs can be wall-mounted, set on a shelf or desktop, or installed in a rack.

Step 2.   Seat the external compact flash card. Be certain that it is firmly seated, and verify that the eject button is fully extended. The eject button usually is located to the left of the slot.

Step 3.   Connect the power cable. Routers and networking devices usually are connected to an uninterruptible power supply that contains a battery. This ensures that the device does not fail if the main's electricity goes off unexpectedly.

Step 4.   Configure terminal emulating software on the PC, and connect the PC to the console port. Use the console cable that came with the device to connect the appropriate serial port of the PC to the console port on the ISR.

Step 5.   Turn on the router.

Step 6.   Observe the start-up messages on the PC to check for any errors.

After these steps are completed, the device is ready to be configured to participate in the network.

Bootup Process

The router bootup process has three stages, as shown in Figure 5-4:

- Perform a power-on self-test (POST).

- Locate and load the Cisco IOS software.

- Locate and execute the startup configuration file, or enter setup mode.

Figure 5-4   Router Bootup Process

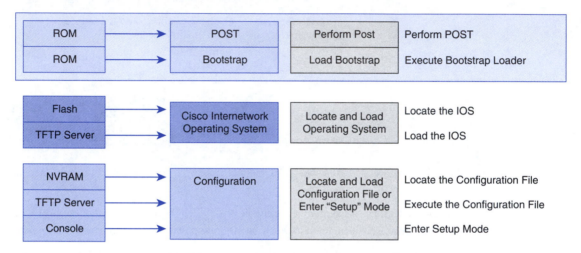

POST is a process that occurs on almost every computer when it boots up. POST is used to test the router hardware. After POST, the bootstrap program is loaded.

The bootstrap program locates the Cisco IOS software and loads it into RAM. Cisco IOS files can be located in one of three places: flash memory, a TFTP server, or another location indicated in the startup configuration file. By default, the Cisco IOS software loads from flash memory. The configuration settings must be changed to load from one of the other locations.

After the Cisco IOS software is loaded, the bootstrap program searches for the startup configuration file in *nonvolatile random-access memory (NVRAM)*. This file contains the previously saved configuration commands and parameters, including interface addresses, routing information, passwords, and other configuration parameters.

To avoid the loss of data, it is important to have a clear understanding of the difference between the startup configuration file and the running configuration file.

Startup Configuration File

The *startup configuration* file is the saved configuration file that sets the device's properties each time the device is powered up. This file is stored in NVRAM, meaning that it is saved even when power to the device is turned off.

When a Cisco router is first powered up, it loads the Cisco IOS software to working memory, or RAM. Next, the startup configuration file is copied from NVRAM to RAM. When the startup configuration file is loaded into RAM, the file becomes the initial running configuration.

Running Configuration File

The term *running configuration* refers to the current configuration running in RAM on the device. This file contains the commands used to determine how the device operates on the network.

The running configuration file is stored in the device's working memory. Changes to the configuration can be made and various device parameters can be chosen when the file is in working memory. However, the running configuration is lost each time the device is shut down, unless the running configuration is saved to the startup configuration file. Changes to the running configuration are not automatically saved to the startup configuration file. You must manually copy the running configuration to the startup configuration file.

Caution

Making a spelling mistake when entering **startup-config** in the **copy** command could lead to the loss of the IOS on a router.

When configuring a device using the Cisco command-line interface (CLI), the command **copy running-config startup-config**, or the abbreviated version, **copy run start**, saves the running configuration to the startup configuration file. When configuring a device using the Cisco SDM GUI, you have an option to save the router running configuration to the startup configuration file each time a command is completed.

After the startup configuration file is loaded and the router boots successfully, you can use the **show version** command to verify and troubleshoot some of the basic hardware and software components used during the bootup process. The output from the **show version** command is shown in Example 5-1. It includes the following:

- The Cisco IOS software version being used.

- The ROM Bootstrap Program—the version of the system bootstrap software, stored in ROM memory, that was initially used to boot the router.

- The complete filename of the Cisco IOS image and where the bootstrap program located it.

- The type of CPU on the router and the amount of RAM. You might need to upgrade the amount of RAM when upgrading the Cisco IOS software.

- The number and type of physical interfaces on the router.

- The amount of NVRAM. NVRAM is used to store the startup-config file.

- The amount of flash memory on the router. Flash is used to permanently store the Cisco IOS image. You might need to upgrade the amount of flash when upgrading the Cisco IOS software.

- The current configured value of the software configuration register in hexadecimal.

Example 5-1 show version Command Output

```
R1> show version
Cisco Internetwork Operating System Software
IOS (tm) C2600 Software (C2600-JK8S-M), Version 12.2(12c), RELEASE SOFTWARE (fc1)
Copyright (c) 1986-2003 by cisco Systems, Inc.
Compiled Wed 05-Feb-03 16:36 by kellythw
Image text-base: 0x8000808C, data-base: 0x8156F2AC

ROM: System Bootstrap, Version 12.2(7r) [cmong 7r], RELEASE SOFTWARE (fc1)
```

```
R1 uptime is 0 minutes
System returned to ROM by power-on
System image file is "flash:c2600-jk8s-mz.122-12c.bin"

cisco 2620XM (MPC860P) processor (revision 0x100) with 59392K/6144K bytes of memory.
Processor board ID JAD07070U10 (959323849)
M860 processor: part number 5, mask 2
Bridging software.
X.25 software, Version 3.0.0.
SuperLAT software (copyright 1990 by Meridian Technology Corp).
TN3270 Emulation software.
1 FastEthernet/IEEE 802.3 interface(s)
2 Low-speed serial(sync/async) network interface(s)
32K bytes of non-volatile configuration memory.
16384K bytes of processor board System flash (Read/Write)

Configuration register is 0x2102
```

The configuration register tells the router how to boot up. For example, the factory default setting for the configuration register is 0x2102. This value indicates that the router attempts to load a Cisco IOS software image from flash and loads the startup configuration file from NVRAM. It is possible to change the configuration register and therefore change where the router looks for the Cisco IOS image and the startup configuration file during the bootup process. If a second value is in parentheses, it denotes the configuration register value to be used during the next reload of the router.

Caution

Anyone who can gain physical access to a device can bypass the password on that device and modify the configuration files. The first line of network security is physical security. Always secure all networking devices and restrict access to those who are responsible for maintaining the device. Appendix B provides a password recovery lab.

Note

The most common settings for the configuration register are as follows:

- **Ox2102**: The factory default setting for Cisco routers. It tells the router to load the IOS image from flash and load the startup configuration file from NVRAM.
- **0x2142**: The router does not load the startup configuration file from NVRAM.
- **0x2120**: The router boots into ROMmon mode.

Sometimes the router does not boot successfully. This failure can be caused by a number of factors, including a corrupt or missing Cisco IOS file, an incorrect location for the Cisco IOS image specified by the configuration register, or inadequate memory to load a new Cisco IOS image. If the router fails to boot the IOS, it then boots in ROM monitor (ROMmon) mode. ROMmon software is a simple command set stored in read-only memory (ROM) that can be used to troubleshoot boot errors and recover the router when the IOS is not present.

When the router boots to *ROMmon mode*, one of the first steps in troubleshooting is to look in flash memory for a valid image using the **dir flash:** command. If an image is located, attempt to boot the image with the **boot flash:** command.

```
rommon 1> boot flash:c2600-is-mz.121-5
```

If the router boots properly with this command, there are two possible reasons why the Cisco IOS image did not load from flash initially. First, use the **show version** command to check the configuration register to ensure that it is configured for the default boot sequence. If the configuration register value is correct, use the **show startup-config** command to see if there is a **bootsystem** command that instructs the router to use a different location for the Cisco IOS image.

Lab 5-1: Powering Up an Integrated Services Router (5.1.3)

In this lab, you start up a Cisco 1841 ISR. Refer to the lab in Part II of this book. You may perform this lab now or wait until the end of the chapter.

In-Band and Out-of-Band Router Configuration

As soon as the ISR is physically installed and cabled, it must be properly configured to participate in the network. There are two possible methods to connect a PC to a network device for configuration and monitoring tasks: in-band and out-of-band management. These are shown in Figure 5-5.

Figure 5-5   In-Band and Out-of-Band Management

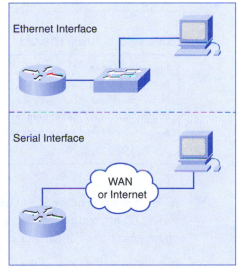

Out-of-Band Management

Out-of-band management requires a computer to be directly connected to the console port or the auxiliary port (AUX) of the network device being configured. This type of connection does not require the local network connections on the device to be active. Out-of-band management normally is used to do the initial configuration on a network device, because until it is properly configured, the device cannot participate in the network. Out-of-band management is also useful when the network connectivity is not functioning correctly and the device cannot be reached over the network. A terminal emulation client is required on the PC to do out-of-band management tasks.

In-Band Management

In-band management is used to monitor and make configuration changes to a network device over a network connection. For a computer to connect to the device and do in-band management tasks, at least one network interface on the device must be connected to the network and must be operational. Two common TCP/IP protocols normally are used to access a Cisco device for in-band management: Telnet and HTTP. A web browser or Telnet client program is required to connect to and monitor the network device or make configuration changes. The secure form of these protocols should be used when connecting to a device to reduce the possibility that passwords can be compromised.

Cisco IOS Programs

The Cisco IOS *command-line interface (CLI)* is a text-based program that lets you enter and execute Cisco IOS commands to configure, monitor, and maintain Cisco devices. CLI commands alter the configurations of the devices and display the current status of processes on the router. For experienced users, it offers many time-saving features for simple and complex configurations. Almost all Cisco networking devices use a similar CLI. The CLI is ready to accept Cisco IOS commands when the router has completed its power-up sequence and the **Router>** command prompt appears. Example 5-2 shows the initial CLI interface on a Cisco device.

Tip

When an internetworking device is first powered up, it does a number of diagnostic tests to verify that the hardware is operating properly and then loads the IOS into RAM. As soon as the IOS is loaded, a configuration file may be automatically applied, or the end user can manually enter commands to configure the device to participate on the network.

Example 5-2 Cisco IOS CLI

```
Router> enable
Router# configure terminal
Enter configuration commands, one per line.  End with CNTL/Z.
Router(config)# interface serial 0/1/0
Router(config-if)# ip address 10.20.30.1 255.255.255.0
Router(config-if)#
```

As soon as the commands and operation of the CLI are familiar, it is easy to monitor and configure a variety of different networking devices. The Cisco CLI can be used with either in-band or out-of-band management tasks. It has an extensive help system that helps you set up and monitor devices.

In addition to the Cisco IOS CLI, other tools are available to assist in configuring a Cisco router or ISR. *Cisco Router and Security Device Manager (SDM)* is a *graphical user interface (GUI)* device management tool. Unlike CLI, SDM can be used only for in-band management tasks.

SDM Express simplifies initial router configuration. It uses a step-by-step approach to configure a basic router configuration quickly and easily. If more advanced configurations are necessary, the full SDM package must be used. The full SDM package allows advanced configurations such as

- Configuration of additional LAN and WAN connections
- Creation of firewalls
- Configuration of VPN connections
- Security tasks

SDM supports a wide range of Cisco IOS software releases and is available free of charge on many Cisco routers. SDM is preinstalled on the flash memory of the Cisco 1800 series ISR. If the router comes with the SDM installed, Cisco recommends that SDM be used to perform the initial router configuration. This is done by connecting to the router via a preset network port. Figure 5-6 shows the initial SDM and SDM Express screens.

Figure 5-6   SDM and SDM Express

Not all Cisco devices support SDM. Furthermore, SDM does not support all the commands that are available through the CLI. Consequently, it is sometimes necessary to use CLI to complete a device configuration that is started using SDM. Familiarity with both methods is critical to successful support of Cisco devices. Table 5-2 briefly compares the Cisco IOS CLI and SDM.

Table 5-2   IOS CLI Versus SDM

	CLI	SDM
User Interface	Terminal emulation software	Web-based browser
	Telnet session	
Router Configuration Method	Text-based Cisco commands	GUI buttons and text boxes
Expertise in Cisco Device Configuration	Depends on the configuration task	Do not need knowledge of the Cisco CLI commands
Help Features	Command prompt-based	GUI based online help and tutorials
Flash Memory Requirements	Covered by IOS requirements	6 MB of free memory
Availability	All Cisco devices	Cisco 830 series through Cisco 7301
When It's Used	When the Cisco device does not support SDM	To perform the initial configuration of an SDM equipped device
	When the configuration task is not supported by SDM	To step through configuration of devices without needing knowledge of CLI

Interactive Activity 5-2: CLI or SDM? (5.1.4)

In this activity, you determine if SDM or the IOS CLI is being described. Use file d2ia-514 on the CD-ROM that accompanies this book to perform this interactive activity.

Configuring an ISR with SDM

When a new device is added to a network, it is critical that the device function correctly. Configuring a networking device, such as a router, can be a complex task no matter which tool is used to enter the configuration. Sometimes the addition of one poorly configured device can cause the entire network to fail.

When installing a new device, it is important to follow best practices to ensure that the device is properly installed, configured, and documented. Table 5-3 summarizes some of the best practices that you should follow.

Table 5-3   Configuration Best Practices

Best Practice	Details
Obtain and document all information before beginning the configuration.	Document these details: Name assigned to the device
	Location where it will be installed
	Usernames and passwords
	Types of connections required (LAN and WAN)
	IP address information for all interfaces, including IP address, subnet mask, and default gateway
	DHCP server settings
	Network Address Translation (NAT) settings
	Firewall settings
Create a network diagram showing how all cables are connected.	Label the diagram with the interface designations and addressing information.
Create a checklist of configuration steps.	Mark off each step as it is successfully completed.
Verify the configuration using a network simulator.	Test it before it is placed on a running network.
Update the network documentation, and keep a copy in a safe place.	Save it on the server. Print it and keep it in a cabinet.

Graphical tools such as SDM are designed to simplify the installation of a new ISR. They are provided as an option and the network technician can choose to either use the tool or the standard IOS CLI to complete the configuration.

SDM Express

Cisco SDM Express is a tool bundled within the Cisco Router and Security Device Manager that makes it easy to create a basic router configuration. The SDM Express windows provide step-by-step guidance for creating the router's initial configuration. After the initial configuration is completed, the router is available on the LAN. The router also can have a WAN connection, a firewall, and up to 30 security enhancements configured.

SDM Express uses eight configuration screens to assist in creating a basic router configuration:

- Overview
- Basic configuration
- LAN IP address
- DHCP
- Internet (WAN)
- Firewall
- Security settings
- Summary

The following sections outline the main steps involved in creating a basic configuration for a new ISR. A more detailed explanation of the configuration screens and the procedure can be found in the labs that accompany this chapter.

Basic Configuration

The Basic Configuration screen, shown in Figure 5-7, is used to configure the router name and the company's domain name. It also controls access to SDM Express, Cisco Router and Security Device Manager, and the CLI. This page of the SDM Express configuration wizard requires the information listed in Table 5-4.

Figure 5-7   SDM Express Wizard: Basic Configuration

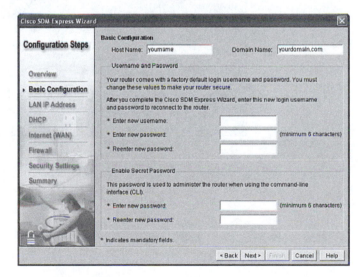

Table 5-4   SDM Express Basic Configuration Information

Field	Description
Host Name	The router's name.
Domain Name	The organization's domain name. (An example of a domain name is cisco.com, but domain names can end with a different suffix, such as .org or .net.)
SDM Username and Password	The username and password used to access SDM Express to configure and monitor the router. The password must be at least six characters long.
Enable Secret Password	The password that controls user access to the router, which affects your ability to make configuration changes using CLI, Telnet, or the console ports. The password must be at least six characters long.

LAN IP Address

The LAN IP address page, as shown in Figure 5-8, is used to configure the router LAN interfaces to participate on the connected local network. Different fields are visible on this page, depending on the LAN interfaces installed. The WLAN section appears only if the router has a wireless interface and **Yes** was clicked in the Wireless Interface Configuration window. Table 5-5 lists some of the information required to complete this page.

Figure 5-8   SDM Express Configuration Wizard: LAN IP Address

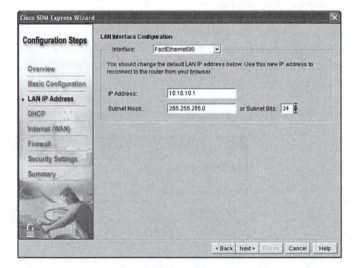

Table 5-5   SDM Express LAN IP Address Information

Field	Description
Interface	Used to select the LAN interface to configure.
IP Address	The IP address for the LAN interface in dotted-decimal format.
	Can be a private IP address if the device is installed in a network that uses NAT or Port Address Translation (PAT).
	Make a note of this address. When the router is restarted, this address is the one used to run SDM Express, not the address that was provided in the Quick Start Guide.
Subnet Mask	The subnet mask for the network. Identifies the network portion of the IP address.
Subnet Bits	The number of bits used to define the network portion of the IP address. Can be used instead of the subnet mask.
Wireless Parameters	Used to specify the SSID of the wireless network if the router is equipped with a wireless interface.

DHCP

Dynamic Host Configuration Protocol (DHCP) is a simple way to assign IP addresses to host devices. DHCP dynamically allocates an IP address to a network host when the host is powered on, and it reclaims the address when the host is powered off. In this way, addresses can be reused when hosts no longer need them. Using SDM Express, a router can be configured as a DHCP server to assign addresses to devices, such as PCs, on the internal local network. Figure 5-9 shows the SDM Express DHCP configuration page. To configure the router as a DHCP server using SDM Express, use the information shown in Table 5-6.

Figure 5-9   SDM Express Configuration Wizard: DHCP

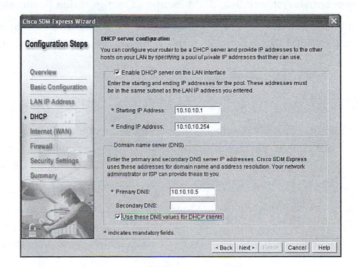

Table 5-6   SDM Express DHCP Configuration

Item	Description
Enable DHCP server on the LAN interface	When checked, this checkbox enables the router to assign private IP addresses to devices on the LAN.
	IP addresses are leased to hosts for one day.
Starting IP Address	The lowest address in the IP address range, based by default on the IP address and subnet mask entered for the LAN interface.
	Can be changed to a different starting IP address, if necessary, but should be the same network or subnet as a configured LAN interface.
Ending IP Address	The highest valid address in the IP address range, based by default on the IP address and subnet mask assigned to the LAN interface.
	Can be changed to decrease the pool size.
	Must be in the same network as the IP address in the starting IP address field.
Primary DNS	The IP address of the primary DNS server host that is used to resolve URLs and names on the network.
Secondary DNS	The IP address of a secondary DNS, if available. Used if the primary DNS server does not respond.
Use these DNS values for DHCP clients	If checked, this checkbox enables the DHCP server to assign DHCP clients with the configured DNS settings.
	Available if a DHCP server has been enabled on the LAN interface.

Interactive Activity 5-3: SDM Express Configuration Parameters (5.2.2)

In this activity, you identify the configuration parameters used by SDM Express. Use file d2ia-522 on the CD-ROM that accompanies this book to perform this interactive activity.

Configuring a Serial WAN Connection

In addition to LAN interfaces, many routers are equipped with serial interfaces that normally are used to connect networks that are separated by large geographic distances. These WAN network interconnections require that the serial connection be made through a *telecommunications service provider (TSP)*.

Serial connections usually are lower-speed links, compared to Ethernet links, which typically run at 10/100/100 Mbps, and they require additional configuration information. The type of connection and protocol encapsulation must be determined before the connection is set up.

The protocol encapsulation must be the same at both ends of a serial connection. Some encapsulation types support *authentication* parameters, such as username and password, to be configured; others do not support authentication. Table 5-7 lists some of the more common serial line encapsulations. Figure 5-10 shows the corresponding SDM Express configuration screen for each type of encapsulation.

Table 5-7   Common Serial Line Encapsulations

Encapsulation	Description
High-Level Data Link Control (HDLC)	A bit-oriented data link layer protocol developed by the International Organization for Standardization (ISO).
	The default encapsulation on Cisco serial interfaces.
Frame Relay	A switched data link layer protocol that handles multiple virtual circuits, meaning that the circuit connections are temporarily built up and broken down based on need.
	Each virtual circuit uses HDLC encapsulation between connected devices.
Point-to-Point Protocol (PPP)	Commonly used to establish a direct connection between two devices.
	PPP can connect computers using serial cable, phone line, trunk line, cellular telephone, specialized radio links, or fiber-optic links.
	Most Internet service providers use PPP for customer dialup access to the Internet.
	Features of PPP allow authentication before a connection is made. PPP usernames and passwords can be set up using the SDM.

Figure 5-10   Configuring WAN Connections with SDM Express

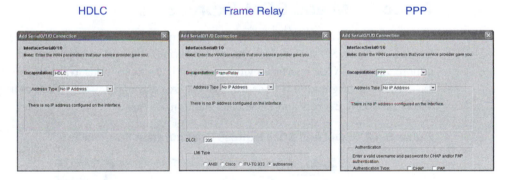

After you select the type of encapsulation, different methods are available to obtain an IP address for the serial interface. These include static IP, IP Unnumbered, and IP Negotiated, as shown in Figure 5-11. You assign an IP address statically by setting an IP address and a subnet mask on an interface. IP Unnumbered sets the serial interface address to match the IP address on one of the router's other functional interfaces. Both static assignment of an address and IP Unnumbered can be used with Frame Relay, PPP, and HDLC encapsulations. PPP encapsulation additionally offers IP Negotiated as an option. When this setting is selected, the router automatically obtains an IP address through PPP.

Figure 5-11   IP Unnumbered

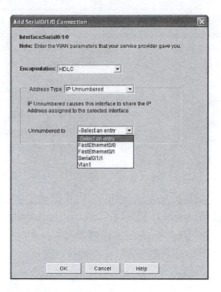

Lab 5-2: Configuring an ISR with SDM Express (5.2.3)

In this lab, you use the Cisco SDM Express configuration Wizard to configure a basic configuration, LAN, and Internet connectivity on a Cisco 1841 ISR. Refer to the lab in Part II of this book. You may perform this lab now or wait until the end of the chapter.

Cisco SDM and SDM Express

The standard configuration of the router can be performed and modified with either Cisco SDM Express or Cisco SDM. Although many of the same features are supported in SDM Express, SDM has a more advanced GUI interface, with more configuration options available. For this reason, after a basic router configuration is done using SDM Express, many users switch to using SDM. Figure 5-12 shows the SDM Express and SDM configuration screens.

Figure 5-12   SDM and SDM Express Configuration Screens

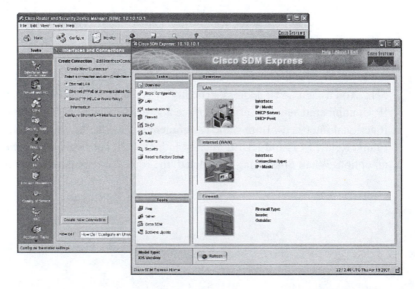

Configuring Dynamic NAT Using Cisco SDM

Dynamic NAT is configured by default when the Cisco SDM Basic NAT Wizard is used. Dynamic NAT enables the hosts on the internal local network to share the registered IP address assigned to the WAN interface. In this manner, hosts with internal private addresses can have access to the Internet. Only the hosts with an internal address in the ranges specified in the SDM configuration are translated. It is important to verify that all address ranges that need access to the Internet are included.

The steps for configuring NAT are as follows (see Figure 5-13):

Step 1.   Enable NAT configuration using SDM.

Step 2.   Navigate through the NAT Wizard.

Step 3.   Select the interface, and set IP ranges.

Step 4.   Review the configuration.

Figure 5-13   Using SDM to Configure Dynamic NAT

Step 1

Step 2

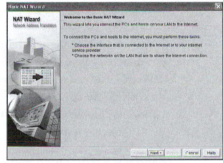

Step 3

Step 4

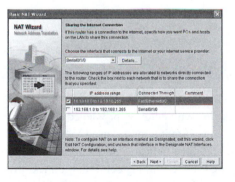

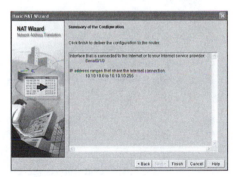

Lab 5-3: Configuring Dynamic NAT with SDM (5.2.4)

In this lab, you use the Cisco SDM Basic NAT Wizard to configure dynamic NAT on a Cisco 1841 ISR. Refer to the lab in Part II of this book. You may perform this lab now or wait until the end of the chapter.

Configuring a Router Using IOS CLI

SDM and SDM Express provide a graphical interface to configure Cisco devices. As mentioned, all Cisco devices that run an IOS use a standard CLI. Many experienced users prefer to carry out configurations using this CLI. The IOS CLI can often be faster and provide access to more commands than are available with the graphical configuration tools.

Command-Line Interface and Modes

Using the Cisco IOS CLI to configure and monitor a device is very different than using the SDM. The CLI does not provide step-by-step configuration assistance. Therefore, it requires more planning and expertise to complete.

The Cisco IOS is designed for two levels of access to the command-line interface: user access and privileged access. When a router or other IOS device is powered on, the access level defaults to user access. This is referred to as the device's being in user EXEC mode. User mode is indicated by a command-line prompt, **Router>**.

Commands that can be executed in user mode are limited to those that give you information about how the device is operating and troubleshooting commands such as **ping** and **traceroute.** To enter commands that can alter the device's operation, you need privileged level access. Enable privileged EXEC mode by entering **enable** at the command prompt and pressing **Enter**. The command-line prompt changes to **Router#** to reflect the mode change. To disable privileged mode and return the device to user mode, enter **disable** or **exit** at the command prompt, as shown in Example 5-3. Both user EXEC mode and privileged EXEC mode can be protected with a password, or a username-and-password combination. To display a list of which commands are available in each mode, enter a **?** at the command prompt.

Example 5-3 Entering and Leaving Privileged EXEC Mode

```
Router>
Router> enable
Router#
Router# disable
Router>
```

Configuring a Cisco IOS device begins with entering privileged EXEC mode. Within privileged mode, it is possible to access the various configuration modes used to set up the device. To obtain access to the configuration commands, first you must indicate which mode will be used to enter commands. In most cases, commands are configured to the running configuration file from the terminal. To inform the router that you will be configuring the device from the terminal, enter **configure terminal** at the privileged mode configuration prompt. This changes the prompt to global configuration mode, which is indicated by the command-line prompt **Router(config)#**, as shown in Example 5-4. It is important to remember that any commands entered in this mode immediately take effect and can alter the device's operation. Within the global configuration mode are other submodes, which contain commands that apply only to specific configuration tasks.

Example 5-4 Entering Global Configuration Mode

```
Router>
Router> enable
Router# configure terminal
Enter configuration commands, one per line.  End with CNTL/Z.
Router(config)#
```

From global configuration mode, the administrator can enter other submodes. Interface configuration mode is used to configure LAN and WAN interfaces. To access interface configuration mode, from global configuration mode enter the command **interface** [*type*] [*number*]. Interface configuration mode is indicated by this prompt:

```
Router(config-if)#
```

Another commonly used submode is the router configuration submode, represented by this prompt:

```
Router(config-router)#
```

This mode is used to configure routing parameters. You access it by entering **router** followed by the name of a routing protocol at the global configuration prompt.

Interactive Activity 5-4: Entering Command Modes (5.3.1)

In this activity, you use some of the most common router configuration modes. Use file d2ia-531 on the CD-ROM that accompanies this book to perform this interactive activity.

Using the Cisco IOS CLI

The Cisco IOS CLI is full of features that help you recall commands needed to configure a device. These features are one reason why network technicians prefer to use the Cisco IOS CLI to configure routers. The *context-sensitive* help feature is especially useful when you're configuring a device. Entering **help** or **?** at the command prompt displays a brief description of the help system, as shown in Example 5-5.

Example 5-5 CLI Help

```
Router# help
Help may be requested at any point in a command by entering
a question mark '?'.  If nothing matches, the help list will
be empty and you must backup until entering a '?' shows the
available options.
Two styles of help are provided:
1. Full help is available when you are ready to enter a
   command argument (e.g. 'show ?') and describes each possible
   argument.
2. Partial help is provided when an abbreviated argument is entered
   and you want to know what arguments match the input
   (e.g. 'show pr?'.)
```

Context-sensitive help can provide suggestions for completing a command. If you know only the first few characters of a command, enter as much of the command as possible, followed by **?**. Note that there is no space between the command characters and the **?**.

Additionally, you may request help at any point to determine additional parameters that complete a command. You enter part of the command, followed by a space and then the **?**. For example, if you enter the command **configure** at the command prompt followed by a space and a **?**, you see a list of possible variations of the **configure** command. Choose one of these to complete the command string. Example 5-6 shows examples of using context-sensitive help.

Example 5-6 Using Context-Sensitive Help

```
Router(config)# interface fa
% Incomplete command.


Router(config)# interface fa?
FastEthernet


Router(config)# interface fastethernet
% Incomplete command.


Router(config)# interface fastethernet ?
  <0-0>  FastEthernet interface number


Router(config)# interface fastethernet 0/0
Router(config-if)# ip address
% Incomplete command.


Router(config-if)# ip address ?
  A.B.C.D  IP address
  dhcp     IP Address negotiated via DHCP
  pool     IP Address autoconfigured from a local DHCP pool


Router(config-if)# ip address 10.20.20.40
% Incomplete command.


Router(config-if)# ip address 10.20.20.40 ?
  A.B.C.D  IP subnet mask


Router(config-if)# ip address 10.20.20.40 255.255.255.0
Router(config-if)#
```

If <cr> appears, this indicates that the command is complete, and pressing the **Enter** key is all that is required. If you enter a **?** and nothing matches, the help list is empty. This indicates that the command string is not a supported command.

When you enter commands, it is possible to make a mistake. CLI provides output indicating when a command is unrecognized or incomplete. Error marker messages are indicated by the % symbol. For example, if the command interface is entered with no other parameters, the output shows that it is an incomplete command (**% Incomplete command.**). Use the **?** to see additional parameters. If you enter an incorrect command, the error message would read **%Invalid input detected**.

It is sometimes hard to see the mistake within an incorrectly entered command. Fortunately, the CLI provides error isolation in the form of an error indicator, a caret symbol (^). The ^ appears at the point in the command string where there is an incorrect or unrecognized character. This enables the user to return to the point where the error was made and use the help function to determine the correct command to use, as shown in Example 5-7.

Example 5-7 Detecting and Correcting Incorrect Commands

```
Router> enable
Router# configure terminal
Enter configuration commands, one per line.  End with CNTL/Z.
Router(config)# interface
% Incomplete command.

Router(config)# interface ethernet
                         ^
% Invalid input detected at '^' marker.

Router(config)# interface ?
  Async             Async interface
  BVI               Bridge-Group Virtual Interface
  CDMA-Ix           CDMA Ix interface
  CTunnel           CTunnel interface
  Dialer            Dialer interface
  FastEthernet      FastEthernet IEEE 802.3
  Group-Async       Async Group interface
  Lex               Lex interface
  Loopback          Loopback interface
  MFR               Multilink Frame Relay bundle interface
  Multilink         Multilink-group interface
  Null              Null interface
  Serial            Serial
  Tunnel            Tunnel interface
  Vif               PGM Multicast Host interface
  Virtual-PPP       Virtual PPP interface
  Virtual-Template  Virtual Template interface
  Virtual-TokenRing Virtual TokenRing
  Vlan              Catalyst Vlans
  range             interface range command

Router(config)# interface fastethernet 0/0
Router(config-if)#
```

Another feature of the Cisco IOS CLI is the ability to recall previously entered commands. This feature is particularly useful for recalling long or complex commands or entries. The command history is enabled by default, and the system records ten command lines in the history buffer. To change the number of command lines the system records during a terminal session, use the **terminal history size** or **history size** command. The maximum number of commands is 256. Example 5-8 shows the output of the **show history** command.

Example 5-8 show history Command

```
Router# show history
  ena
  show running-config
  show ip route
  show ip interface brief
  configure terminal
  show history
Router#
```

To recall the most recent command in the history buffer, press **Ctrl-P** or the **up arrow** key. Repeat this process to recall successively older commands. To return to a more recent command in the history buffer, press **Ctrl-N** or the **down arrow** key. Repeat this process to recall successively more recent commands.

When you enter commands, the CLI recognizes shortcuts. The command characters must be entered only up to the unique characters within that command. For example, **int** can be used in place of **interface**. Press the **Tab** key, and the CLI automatically completes the command entry. The **Tab** key simply acknowledges visually that the router has understood the specific command you intended.

The terminal program used to connect to and configure the router also provides some additional editing capabilities. On most computers, copy and paste functions are available. A previous command string may be copied and then pasted or inserted as the current command entry.

Tip

Using a terminal program such as HyperTerminal allows the device configuration to be captured to a text file for backup and archival purposes. It also allows a configuration file to be created or edited offline and then pasted into the device. This provides a quick method of reconfiguring network devices.

Interactive Activity 5-5: History Navigation Commands (5.3.2)

In this activity, you match the commands to the effect they have on the command history file. Use file d2ia-532 on the CD-ROM that accompanies this book to perform this interactive activity.

Exploring the Cisco IOS CLI (5.3.2)

In this Packet Tracer activity, you explore some of these features and perhaps discover why network technicians prefer the Cisco IOS CLI. Use file d2-532.pka on the CD-ROM that accompanies this book to perform this activity using Packet Tracer.

Using show Commands

The Cisco IOS CLI enables a user to display relevant information about the configuration and operation of the device. To obtain this information, various **show** commands are used. The Cisco IOS CLI **show** commands are used extensively by network technicians. These commands are used to view configuration files, to see the status of the device interfaces and processes, and to verify the device's operational status. **show** commands are available whether the device is configured using the CLI or the SDM configuration tool.

The status of nearly every process or function of the router can be displayed using a **show** command. Here are some of the more popular **show** commands:

- **show running-config**: Displays the current operating configuration.

- **show interfaces**: Displays interface status and configuration.

- **show arp**: Displays the ARP table.

- **show ip route**: Displays the IP routing table.

- **show protocols**: Displays information about configured protocols.

- **show version**: Displays system hardware and software status.

Example 5-9 shows sample output from the **show running-configuration** command. This can be used to check the active configuration.

Example 5-9 Sample Output from the show running-config Command

```
R1# show running-config
< Some output omitted >
Building configuration...
Current configuration : 1063 bytes
!
version 12.4
service timestamps debug datetime msec
service timestamps log datetime msec
no service password-encryption
hostname R1
enable secret 5 $1$i6w9$dvdpVM6zV10E6tSyLdkR5/
no ip domain lookup
!
interface FastEthernet0/0
 description LAN 192.168.1.0 default gateway
 ip address 192.168.1.1 255.255.255.0
 duplex auto
 speed auto
!
interface FastEthernet0/1
 no ip address
 shutdown
 duplex auto
 speed auto
!
interface Serial0/0/0
 description WAN link to R2
 ip address 192.168.2.1 255.255.255.0
 encapsulation ppp
 clock rate 64000
 no fair-queue
!
interface Serial0/0/1
 no ip address
 shutdown
!
```

```
interface Vlan1
 no ip address
!
router rip
 version 2
 network 192.168.1.0
 network 192.168.2.0
!
banner motd ^CUnauthorized Access Prohibited^C
!
ip http server
!
line con 0
 password cisco
 login
line aux 0
line vty 0 4
 password cisco
 login
```

The **show interfaces** command output, as shown in Example 5-10, can be used to see the status of each interface.

Example 5-10   Sample Output from the show interfaces Command

```
R1# show interfaces
< Some output omitted >
FastEthernet0/0 is up, line protocol is up
  Hardware is Gt96k FE, address is 001b.5325.256e (bia 001b.5325.256e)
  Internet address is 192.168.1.1/24
  MTU 1500 bytes, BW 100000 Kbit, DLY 100 usec,
      reliability 255/255, txload 1/255, rxload 1/255
  Encapsulation ARPA, loopback not set
  Keepalive set (10 sec)
  Full-duplex, 100Mb/s, 100BaseTX/FX
  ARP type: ARPA, ARP Timeout 04:00:00
  Last input 00:00:17, output 00:00:01, output hang never
  Last clearing of "show interface" counters never
  Input queue: 0/75/0/0 (size/max/drops/flushes); Total output drops: 0
  Queueing strategy: fifo
  Output queue: 0/40 (size/max)
  5 minute input rate 0 bits/sec, 0 packets/sec
  5 minute output rate 0 bits/sec, 0 packets/sec
     196 packets input, 31850 bytes
     Received 181 broadcasts, 0 runts, 0 giants, 0 throttles
     0 input errors, 0 CRC, 0 frame, 0 overrun, 0 ignored
     0 watchdog
     0 input packets with dribble condition detected
     392 packets output, 35239 bytes, 0 underruns
     0 output errors, 0 collisions, 3 interface resets
     0 babbles, 0 late collision, 0 deferred
```

```
       0 lost carrier, 0 no carrier
       0 output buffer failures, 0 output buffers swapped out

FastEthernet0/1 is administratively down, line protocol is down

Serial0/0/0 is up, line protocol is up
  Hardware is GT96K Serial
  Internet address is 192.168.2.1/24
  MTU 1500 bytes, BW 1544 Kbit, DLY 20000 usec,
      reliability 255/255, txload 1/255, rxload 1/255
  Encapsulation PPP, LCP Listen, loopback not set
  Keepalive set (10 sec)
  Last input 00:00:02, output 00:00:03, output hang never
  Last clearing of "show interface" counters 00:51:52
  Input queue: 0/75/0/0 (size/max/drops/flushes); Total output drops: 0
  Queueing strategy: fifo
  Output queue: 0/40 (size/max)
  5 minute input rate 0 bits/sec, 0 packets/sec
  5 minute output rate 0 bits/sec, 0 packets/sec
      401 packets input, 27437 bytes, 0 no buffer
      Received 293 broadcasts, 0 runts, 0 giants, 0 throttles
      0 input errors, 0 CRC, 0 frame, 0 overrun, 0 ignored, 0 abort
      389 packets output, 26940 bytes, 0 underruns
      0 output errors, 0 collisions, 2 interface resets
      0 output buffer failures, 0 output buffers swapped out
      6 carrier transitions
      DCD=up  DSR=up  DTR=up  RTS=up  CTS=up

Serial0/0/1 is administratively down, line protocol is down
```

Example 5-11 shows the output of the **show arp** command. This command displays the contents of the router's ARP table.

Example 5-11   Sample Output from the show arp Command

```
R1# show arp
Protocol  Address        Age (min)  Hardware Addr   Type   Interface
Internet  172.17.0.1             -  001b.5325.256e  ARPA   FastEthernet0/0
Internet  172.17.0.2            12  000b.db04.a5cd  ARPA   FastEthernet0/0
```

The **show ip route** command displays the contents of the router's IP routing table. Sample output is shown in Example 5-12.

Example 5-12   Sample Output from the show ip route Command

```
R1# show ip route
Codes: C - connected, S - static, R - RIP, M - mobile, B - BGP
       D - EIGRP, EX - EIGRP external, O - OSPF, IA - OSPF inter area
       N1 - OSPF NSSA external type 1, N2 - OSPF NSSA external type 2
       E1 - OSPF external type 1, E2 - OSPF external type 2
       i - IS-IS, su - IS-IS summary, L1 - IS-IS level-1, L2 - IS-IS level-2
```

```
        ia - IS-IS inter area, * - candidate default, U - per-user static route
        o - ODR, P - periodic downloaded static route

Gateway of last resort is not set
C    192.168.1.0/24 is directly connected, FastEthernet0/0
C    192.168.2.0/24 is directly connected, Serial0/0/0
R    192.168.3.0/24 [120/1] via 192.168.2.2, 00:00:24, Serial0/0/0
```

Example 5-13 shows sample output from the **show protocols** command. This command displays information about any configured protocols running on the router.

Example 5-13   Sample Output from the show protocols Command

```
R1# show protocols
Global values:
  Internet Protocol routing is enabled
FastEthernet0/0 is up, line protocol is up
  Internet address is 192.168.1.1/24
FastEthernet0/1 is administratively down, line protocol is down
FastEthernet0/1/0 is up, line protocol is down
FastEthernet0/1/1 is up, line protocol is down
FastEthernet0/1/2 is up, line protocol is down
FastEthernet0/1/3 is up, line protocol is down
Serial0/0/0 is up, line protocol is up
  Internet address is 192.168.2.1/24
Serial0/0/1 is administratively down, line protocol is down
Vlan1 is up, line protocol is down
```

The **show version** command displays system hardware and software information, including the value of the configuration register. Sample output is shown in Example 5-14.

Example 5-14   Sample Output from the show version Command

```
R1# show version
< Some output omitted >
Cisco IOS Software, 1841 Software (C1841-ADVIPSERVICESK9-M), Version 12.4(10b),
RELEASE SOFTWARE (fc3)
Technical Support: http://www.cisco.com/techsupport
Copyright (c) 1986-2007 by Cisco Systems, Inc.
Compiled Fri 19-Jan-07 15:15 by prod_rel_team

ROM: System Bootstrap, Version 12.4(13r)T, RELEASE SOFTWARE (fc1)
R1 uptime is 43 minutes
System returned to ROM by reload at 22:05:12 UTC Sat Jan 5 2008
System image file is "flash:c1841-advipservicesk9-mz.124-10b.bin"

Cisco 1841 (revision 6.0) with 174080K/22528K bytes of memory.
Processor board ID FTX1111W0QF
6 FastEthernet interfaces
2 Serial(sync/async) interfaces
1 Virtual Private Network (VPN) Module
```

```
DRAM configuration is 64 bits wide with parity disabled.
191K bytes of NVRAM.
62720K bytes of ATA CompactFlash (Read/Write)

Configuration register is 0x2102
```

Interactive Activity 5-6: Viewing the Router Interface Configuration (5.3.3)

In this activity, you view the router default settings and enter the commands to view interface information. Use file d2ia-533 on the CD-ROM that accompanies this book to perform this interactive activity.

Using the Cisco IOS show Commands (5.3.3)

In this Packet Tracer activity, you use the **show** commands on a router that is located at an ISP. Use file d2-533.pka on the CD-ROM that accompanies this book to perform this activity using Packet Tracer.

Basic Configuration

The initial configuration of an IOS device involves configuring a device name and then the passwords that are used to control access to the device's various functions. A device should be given a unique name as one of the first configuration tasks. This task is accomplished in global configuration mode with the following command:

```
Router(config)# hostname [name]
```

When the **Enter** key is pressed, the prompt changes from the default hostname, which is Router, to the newly configured hostname. As soon as a hostname is configured on a device, the next configuration step should be configuring passwords to prevent access to the device by unauthorized individuals. The **enable password** and **enable secret** commands are used to restrict access to privileged EXEC mode, preventing unauthorized users from making configuration changes to the router. The following commands are used to set the passwords:

```
Router(config)# enable password [password]
Router(config)# enable secret [password]
```

The difference between the enable password and the enable secret is that the **enable password** command is not encrypted in the configuration file. If the enable password is set, followed by the enable secret, the enable secret overrides the enable password.

Caution

Always use the **enable secret** command to provide security. If the **enable password** command is used and the router's integrity is compromised, the password can be read in clear text. If this password is used on multiple devices in the network, all these devices are now at risk.

Other basic router configurations include configuring a banner, enabling synchronous logging, and disabling domain lookup.

A banner is text that a user sees when initially logging on to the router. Configuring an appropriate banner is part of a good security plan. At the very minimum, a banner should warn against unauthorized access. Never configure a banner that welcomes an unauthorized user. The two types of banners are message-of-the-day (MOTD) and login information. The purpose of having two separate banners is to be able to change one without affecting the entire banner message.

To configure the banners, the commands are **banner motd** and **banner login**. For both types, a delimiting character, such as a #, is used at the beginning and end of the message. The delimiter allows the user to configure a multiline banner. If both banners are configured, the login banner appears after the MOTD but before the login credentials.

The Cisco IOS software often sends unsolicited messages, such as a change in the state of a configured interface. Sometimes these messages occur when you're in the middle of entering a command. The message does not affect the command, but it can cause you confusion when typing. To keep the unsolicited output separate from the typed input, the **logging synchronous** command can be entered in global configuration mode.

By default, when a hostname is entered in enable mode, the router assumes that the user is attempting to telnet to a device. The router tries to resolve unknown names entered in enable mode by sending them to the DNS server. This process includes any words entered that the router does not recognize, including mistyped commands. If you don't want this capability, use the **no ip domain lookup** command to turn off this default feature.

There are multiple ways to access a device to perform configuration tasks. One of these ways is to use a PC attached to the console port on the device. This type of configuration usually is done during initial configuration. Example 5-15 shows the sequence of commands necessary to configure the console port with a password and accept login requests. This prevents unauthorized users from accessing user mode from the console port.

Example 5-15   Configuring the Console Port

```
Router(config)# line console 0
Router(config-line)# password [password]
Router(config-line)# login
```

As soon as the device is connected to the network, it can be accessed over the network connection. When the device is accessed through the network, it is considered a *virtual terminal* connection. The password must be configured on the virtual port. Example 5-16 shows the commands necessary to configure passwords on the five virtual terminal lines.

Example 5-16   Configuring the Virtual Terminal Lines

```
Router(config)# line vty 0 4
Router(config-line)# password [password]
Router(config-line)# login
```

To verify that the passwords are set correctly, use the **show running-configuration** command. These passwords are stored in the running configuration in clear text. It is possible to set encryption on all passwords stored within the router so that they are not easily seen by unauthorized individuals. The command **service password encryption** ensures that passwords are encrypted.

Remember, if the running configuration is changed, it must be copied to the startup configuration file, or the changes are lost when the device is powered down. To copy the changes made to the running configuration back to the stored startup configuration file, use the **copy run start** command.

Performing an Initial Router Configuration (5.3.4)

In this Packet Tracer activity, you use Cisco IOS CLI commands to perform an initial router configuration. Use file d2-534.pka on the CD-ROM that accompanies this book to perform this activity using Packet Tracer.

Configuring an Interface

For a router to direct traffic from one network to another, the interfaces on the router are configured to participate in each of the networks. A router interface connects to a network and has an IP address and subnet mask assigned to it that are appropriate for that network. Many different types of interfaces are available. Serial and Ethernet interfaces are the most common. Most local network connections use Ethernet interfaces.

Most WAN connections require the use of a serial connection through an ISP. When a router connects to the ISP network using a serial connection, a CSU/DSU is required if the WAN is digital. A modem is required if the WAN is analog. These devices convert the data from the router into a form acceptable for crossing the WAN. They also convert data from the WAN into an acceptable format for the router. Unlike Ethernet interfaces, serial interfaces require a clock signal to control the timing of the communications; this is known as a clock rate. In most environments, *Data Communications Equipment (DCE)* devices such as a modem, or CSU/DSU, provide the clock rate. By default, Cisco routers are *Data Terminal Equipment (DTE)* devices. This means that they accept the clock rate from the DCE device. Such an arrangement is shown in Figure 5-14.

Figure 5-14   DTE and DCE Interfaces

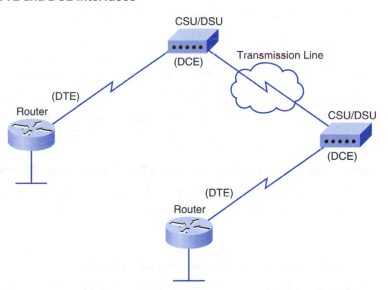

Though uncommon, it is possible to connect two routers directly using a serial connection. In this instance, no CSU/DSU or modem is used, and one of the routers must be configured as a DCE device to provide clocking. If the router is connected as the DCE device, a clock rate must be set on the router interface to control the timing of the DCE/DTE connection.

To configure any interface on the router, you must be in global configuration mode. Configuring a serial interface is very similar to configuring an Ethernet interface. One of the main differences is that a serial interface must have a clock rate set if it is acting as a DCE device.

Several steps are necessary to configure the interface and ensure that enough information is available to allow the technician to configure and maintain the interface:

Step 1. Specify the type of interface and the interface port number.

Step 2. Enter a description for the interface.

Step 3. Configure the interface IP address and subnet mask.

Step 4. Set the clock rate if you're configuring a serial interface as a DCE.

Step 5. Enable the interface.

These steps are shown in Example 5-17.

Example 5-17   Configuring the Serial Interface

```
Router> enable
Router# configure terminal
Enter configuration commands, one per line.  End with CNTL/Z.
Router(config)# interface serial 0/1/0
Router(config-if)# description Connection to Router 2
Router(config-if)# ip address 192.168.1.125 255.255.255.0
Router(config-if)# clock rate 64000
Router(config-if)# no shutdown
Router(config-if)#
```

As soon as an interface is enabled, it may be necessary to turn off the interface for maintenance or troubleshooting. In this case, use the **shutdown** command.

Note

On serial links that are directly interconnected, as in a lab environment, one side must be considered a DCE and provide a clocking signal. The clock is enabled and speed is specified with the **clock rate** command. The available clock rates in bits per second are 1200, 2400, 9600, 19,200, 38,400, 56,000, 64,000, 72,000, 125,000, 148,000, 500,000, 800,000, 1,000,000, 1,300,000, 2,000,000, or 4,000,000. Some bit rates might not be available on certain serial interfaces. This depends on the capacity of each interface.

Interactive Activity 5-7: Configuring a Serial Interface on Routers for Communication (5.3.5)

In this activity, you configure the serial interface on a router to participate in network communications. Use file d2ia-535 on the CD-ROM that accompanies this book to perform this interactive activity.

Configuring Serial and Ethernet Interfaces (5.3.5)

In this Packet Tracer activity, you configure the Ethernet LAN and serial WAN interfaces on a customer router. Use file d2-535.pka on the CD-ROM that accompanies this book to perform this activity using Packet Tracer.

Lab 5-4: Configuring Basic Router Settings with the Cisco IOS CLI (5.3.5)

In this lab, you configure basic settings on a router using the IOS command-line interface (CLI). Refer to the lab in Part II of this book. You may perform this lab now or wait until the end of the chapter.

Configuring a Default Route

A router forwards packets from one network to another based on the destination IP address specified in the packet. It examines the routing table to determine where to forward the packet to reach the destination network. If the router does not have a route to a specific network in its routing table, a *default route* can be configured to tell the router how to forward the packet. The default route is used on a router only if the router does not know where to send a packet.

Usually the default route points to the next-*hop* router on the path to the Internet. The information needed to configure the default route is the IP address of the next-hop router, or the interface that the router uses to forward traffic with an unknown destination network. Figure 5-15 shows an example of configuring a default route. The command required is

```
Router(config)#ip route 0.0.0.0 0.0.0.0 <next-hop IP address>
```

or

```
Router(config)#ip route 0.0.0.0 0.0.0.0 <interface> <port number>
```

Figure 5-15   Default Route Configuration

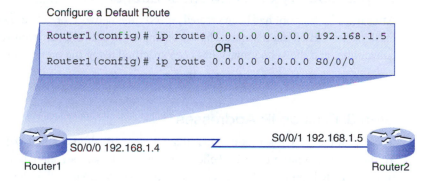

Configure a Default Route

```
Router1(config)# ip route 0.0.0.0 0.0.0.0 192.168.1.5
                            OR
Router1(config)# ip route 0.0.0.0 0.0.0.0 S0/0/0
```

S0/0/1 192.168.1.5

S0/0/0 192.168.1.4

Router1   Router2

Configuring a Default Route (5.3.6)

In this Packet Tracer activity, you configure a default route on a customer router. Use file d2-536.pka on the CD-ROM that accompanies this book to perform this activity using Packet Tracer.

Configuring DHCP Services

It is possible to configure a router with the Cisco IOS CLI to function as a DHCP server. Using a router configured with DHCP simplifies the management of IP addresses on a network. The administrator only needs to update a single, central router when IP configuration parameters change. Configuring DHCP on a router using CLI is a little more complex than configuring it using SDM, because global configuration mode must first be activated. Configuring a router as a DHCP server involves eight steps:

Step 1.   Create the DHCP address pool.

Step 2.   Specify the network or subnet.

Step 3.   Exclude IP addresses.

Step 4.   Specify the domain name.

Step 5.   Specify the DNS server IP address.

Step 6.   Set the default gateway.

Step 7.   Set the lease duration.

Step 8.   Verify the configuration.

The following sections describe each step.

Step 1: Create the DHCP Address Pool

Navigate to privileged EXEC mode, enter the password if prompted, and then enter global configuration mode. Now create a name for the DHCP server address pool. More than one address pool can exist on a router. The Cisco IOS CLI enters DHCP pool configuration mode. For example, the following commands create a DHCP address pool named LAN-addresses:

```
Router> enable
Router# configure terminal
Router(config)# ip dhcp pool LAN-addresses
```

Step 2: Specify the Network or Subnet

After the address pool has been created, specify the network or subnet network number and the subnet mask of the DHCP address pool. In this example the network has been specified using the dot number convention, and the subnet mask has been specified using the prefix convention:

```
Router(dhcp-config)# network 172.16.0.0 /16
```

Step 3: Exclude IP Addresses

Recall that the DHCP server assumes that all other IP addresses in a DHCP address pool subnet are available for assigning to DHCP clients. If some addresses are already in use, they must be excluded from the DHCP pool. Addresses are excluded from the pool so that the DHCP server does not allocate those IP addresses. If a range of addresses is to be excluded, only the starting address and ending address need to be entered. Addresses are excluded in global configuration mode. The example shown excludes the addresses 172.16.1.100, 172.16.1.101, 172.16.1.102, and 172.16.1.103 from being given out to hosts by DHCP. These addresses can be statically assigned by the administrator.

```
Router(config)# ip dhcp excluded-address 172.16.1.100 172.16.1.103
```

Step 4: Specify the Domain Name

If required, the domain name that will be handed out with the IP address should be configured. This is done in DHCP configuration mode. For example, if the domain name cisco.com were to be handed out as part of the DHCP configuration, the following command would be used:

```
Router(dhcp-config)# domain-name cisco.com
```

The domain name is an optional DHCP configuration parameter and is not necessary for DHCP to function. The network administrator can provide information about whether a domain name is necessary.

Step 5: Specify the DNS Server IP Address

Specify the IP address of a DNS server that is available to a DHCP client. One IP address is required. If up to eight IP addresses are specified on one command line, list the servers in order of importance. In this example, clients can use two DNS servers—a primary server and a secondary server. At least one DNS server must be configured for hosts to resolve hostnames and URLs to access services on the network.

```
Router(dhcp-config)# dns server 172.16.1.103 172.16.2.103
```

Step 6: Set the Default Gateway

The IP address of the default router for the DHCP clients on the network must be configured. Typically, this is the router's LAN IP. This command sets the default gateway for the client devices on the network that will use DHCP. After a DHCP client has booted, the client begins sending packets to its default router. The IP address must be on the same subnet as the client IP addresses given out by the router. One IP address is required. In this example, DHCP clients use the router interface 172.16.1.100 as their default gateway:

```
Router(dhcp-config)# default-router 172.16.1.100
```

Step 7: Set the Lease Duration

DHCP gives out IP address information each time a host powers on and connects to the network. The default time that a client IP address is reserved for a specific host is one day. If the host does not renew its address, the reservation ends, and the IP address is again available to be given out through DHCP. It is possible to change the lease timer to a longer period of time if necessary. This is the last step in configuring a DHCP service on a router. Use the **end** command to finish the DHCP configuration and return to global configuration mode.

```
Router(dhcp-config)# lease {days [hours] [minutes]| infinite}
Router(dhcp-config)# end
```

Step 8: Verify the Configuration

The final step of configuring DHCP on a router is verifying all parameters entered. You can do this by examining the relevant parts of the running configuration. The configuration output for our example is shown in Example 5-18.

Example 5-18   DHCP Configuration Lines in the Running Configuration

```
!
ip dhcp pool LAN-addresses
 domain-name cisco.com
 network 172.16.0.0 /16
 ip dhcp excluded-address 172.16.1.100 172.16.1.103
 dns-server 172.16.1.103 172.16.2.103
 default-router 172.16.1.100
 lease infinite
!
```

When the configuration is correct, copy the running configuration to the startup configuration.

Packet Tracer
☐ Activity

Configuring a Cisco Router as a DHCP Server (5.3.7)

In this Packet Tracer activity, you configure a router to act as a DHCP server. Use file d2-537.pka on the CD-ROM that accompanies this book to perform this activity using Packet Tracer.

Lab 5-5: Configuring DHCP with SDM and Cisco IOS CLI (5.3.7)

In this lab, you configure DHCP using both SDM and the IOS CLI. Refer to the lab in Part II of this book. You may perform this lab now or wait until the end of the chapter.

Configuring Static NAT Using Cisco IOS CLI

NAT is used on a network to prevent internal network addresses from being sent across the Internet. When you configure NAT, at least one interface must be configured as the *internal interface*, meaning that it is connected to the internal, protected network. Another interface must be configured as the *external interface*. When devices on the internal network communicate out the external interface, all addresses are translated into a single, specified, registered IP address.

Sometimes a server located on an internal network must be accessible from the Internet. This requires that the server have a specific registered address that external users can specify. One way to provide an Internet-accessible address to an internal server is to provide static NAT translation. Static NAT ensures that addresses assigned to hosts on the internal network are always translated to the same registered IP address.

Configuring NAT and static NAT using the Cisco IOS CLI requires a number of steps:

Step 1.   Specify the interface.

To begin configuring NAT services on a Cisco router, navigate to privileged EXEC mode, enter the password if prompted to, and then enter global configuration mode. Specify which interface is connected to the inside local network. Doing this takes you to interface configuration mode.

```
Router> enable
Router# configure terminal
Router(config)# interface fastethernet 0/0
```

Step 2.   Set the primary IP address.

Set the primary IP address and subnet mask for the inside interface.

```
Router(config-if)# ip address 172.31.232.182 255.255.255.0
```

Step 3.   Identify the inside interface.

Identify this interface as the interface connected to the inside of the network. Then exit the configuration of the inside interface and return to configuration mode.

```
Router(config-if)# ip nat inside
Router(config-if)# exit
```

Step 4.   Configure the outside interface.

Specify the interface connecting to the ISP, and return to interface configuration mode.

```
Router(config)# interface serial 0/0
```

Step 5.   Set the primary IP address.

Configure a primary IP address for the outside interface.

```
Router(config-if)# ip address 10.114.11.39 255.255.255.0
```

Step 6.   Identify the outside interface.

Identify this interface as the interface connected to the outside of the network. Then exit the configuration of the outside interface and return to configuration mode.

```
Router(config-if)# ip nat outside
Router(config-if)# exit
```

Step 7.   Define the address translation for the server.

Create a static translation. The general command is

```
Router(config)# ip nat inside source static <inside-address> <outside-address>
```

In our ongoing example, the command would be

```
Router(config)# ip nat inside source static 172.31.232.14 10.114.11.14
```

This creates a static translation by which a server with the inside address 172.31.232.14 is always translated to the external address 10.114.11.14.

Step 8.   Verify the configuration.

Verify the static NAT configuration by examining the running configuration. Example 5-19 shows the results of the example used.

Example 5-19   NAT Configuration Lines in the Running Configuration

```
!
interface fastethernet 0/0
 ip address 172.31.232.182 255.255.255.0
 ip nat inside
!
interface serial 0/0
 ip address 10.114.11.39 255.255.255.0
 ip nat outside

ip nat inside source static 172.31.232.14 10.114.11.14
```

After verification, copy the running configuration into the startup configuration.

You can use several router CLI commands to view NAT operations for verification and troubleshooting. One of the most useful commands is **show ip nat translations**. The output, as shown in Example 5-20, displays the detailed NAT assignments. The command shows all static translations that have been configured and any dynamic translations that have been created by traffic. Each translation is identified by protocol and its inside and outside local and global addresses.

Example 5-20   Sample Output from the show ip nat translations Command

```
R1# show ip nat translations
Pro    Inside global          Inside local       Outside local      Outside global
---    209.165.202.130        172.31.232.14      ------
icmp   209.165.202.131:512    172.31.232.1:512   209.165.200:512    209.165.200.1:512
udp    209.165.202.131:1067   172.31.232.2:1067  209.165.200:53     209.165.200.1:53
tcp    209.165.202.131:1028   172.31.232.2:1028  209.165.200:80     209.165.200.1:80
```

The **show ip nat statistics** command displays information about the total number of active translations, NAT configuration parameters, how many addresses are in the pool, and how many have been allocated. Additionally, use the **show run** command to view NAT configurations.

By default, if dynamic NAT is configured, translation entries time out after 24 hours. It is sometimes useful to clear the dynamic entries sooner than 24 hours. This is especially true when testing the NAT configuration. To clear dynamic entries before the timeout has expired, use the **clear ip nat translation *** command in enable mode. Only the dynamic translations are removed from the table. Static translations cannot be cleared from the translation table.

Configuring Static NAT on a Cisco Router (5.3.8)

In this Packet Tracer activity, you configure a static NAT translation on a router. Use file d2-538.pka on the CD-ROM that accompanies this book to perform this activity using Packet Tracer.

Lab 5-6: Configuring PAT with SDM and Static NAT Using Cisco IOS (5.3.8)

In this lab, you configure NAT and DHCP on a router using the IOS CLI. Refer to the lab in Part II of this book. You may perform this lab now or wait until the end of the chapter.

Backing Up a Cisco Router Configuration to a TFTP Server

After a router is configured, the running configuration should be saved to the startup configuration file. It is also a good idea to save the configuration file in another location, such as a network server. If the NVRAM fails or becomes corrupt and the router cannot load the startup configuration file, another copy is available.

Configuration files can be saved to a network server using the TFTP protocol, as shown in Example 5-21. The TFTP enabled server must be accessible to the router via a network connection. As soon as the running configuration is saved to the startup configuration file, save the startup configuration to the TFTP server following these steps:

Step 1.   Enter the **copy startup-config tftp** command.

Step 2.   Enter the IP address of the host where the configuration file will be stored.

Step 3.   Enter the name to assign to the configuration file, or accept the default.

Step 4.   If prompted, answer **yes** to confirm that you want to write the file to the TFTP server.

Example 5-21   Saving the Configuration File to a TFTP Server

```
Router# copy startup-config tftp
Address or name of remote host []? 10.10.10.1
Destination filename  [router-confg]? tokyo.2
Write file tokyo.2 to 10.10.10.1 [confirm]
Writing tokyo.2 !!!!!!!! [OK]
```

A current copy of the running configuration can also be stored on a *TFTP server* using the **copy running-config tftp** command.

To restore the backup configuration file, be sure the router has at least one interface configured and can access the TFTP server over the network. The following steps and Example 5-22 show the process of restoring a configuration file from a TFTP server:

Step 1.   Enter the **copy tftp running-config** command.

Step 2.   Enter the IP address of the remote host where the TFTP server is located.

Step 3.   Enter the name of the source configuration file, or press **Enter** to accept the default name.

Step 4.   Enter the name of the destination configuration file, or press **Enter** to accept the default.

Example 5-22   Restoring the Configuration File from a TFTP Server

```
Router# copy tftp running-config
Address or name of remote host []? 10.10.10.1
Source filename  [router-confg]? tokyo.2
Destination filename [running-config]?
Accessing tftp://10.10.10.1/tokyo.2 ...
```

Another way to create a backup copy of the configuration is to capture the output of the **show running-config** command. To do this from the terminal session, copy the output, paste it into a text file, and then save the text file. The following steps are used to capture the configuration from a HyperTerminal screen:

Step 1.   Click **Transfer**.

Step 2.   Click **Capture Text**.

Step 3.   Specify a name for the text file in which to capture the configuration.

Step 4.   Click **Start** to start capturing text.

Step 5.   Use the **show running-config** command to display the configuration on the screen.

Step 6.   Press the spacebar when each "-More -" prompt appears.

After the complete configuration has been displayed, the following steps stop the capture:

Step 1.   Click **Transfer**.

Step 2.   Click **Capture Text**.

Step 3.   Click **Stop**.

After the capture is complete, the configuration file must be edited to remove extra text, such as the "building configuration" Cisco IOS message. Also, the **no shutdown** command must be added to the end of each interface section. Choose **File > Save** to save the configuration. The configuration file can be edited from a text editor such as Notepad.

The backup configuration can be restored from a HyperTerminal session. Before the configuration is restored, any other configurations should be removed from the router using the **erase startup-config** command at the privileged EXEC prompt. The router is then restarted using the **reload** command. After the router is restarted, follow these steps to copy the backup configuration to the router:

Step 1.   Enter router global configuration mode.

Step 2.   Choose **Transfer > Send Text File** in HyperTerminal.

Step 3. Select the name of the file in which to store the saved backup configuration.

Step 4. Restore the startup configuration with the **copy run start** command.

Backing Up a Cisco Router Configuration to a TFTP Server (5.3.9)

In this Packet Tracer activity, you save the running configuration to the startup configuration and then back up the startup configuration to a TFTP server. Use file d2-539.pka on the CD-ROM that accompanies this book to perform this activity using Packet Tracer.

Lab 5-7: Managing Router Configuration Files Using HyperTerminal (5.3.9a)

In this lab, you manage router configuration files using HyperTerminal. Refer to the lab in Part II of this book. You may perform this lab now or wait until the end of the chapter.

Lab 5-8: Managing Router Configuration Files Using TFTP (5.3.9b)

In this lab, you manage router configuration files using a TFTP. Refer to the lab in Part II of this book. You may perform this lab now or wait until the end of the chapter.

Connecting the CPE to the ISP

One of the main responsibilities of an onsite network technician is to install and upgrade equipment located at the customer's home or business. Network devices installed at the customer location are called customer premises equipment (CPE). They include such devices as routers, modems, and switches.

Installing the CPE

Installing or upgrading a router can be disruptive for a business. Many businesses rely on the Internet for their correspondence and have e-commerce services that must be accessed during the day. Planning the installation or upgrade is a critical step in ensuring successful operation. Additionally, planning lets you explore options on paper, where it is easy and inexpensive to correct errors.

The ISP technical staff usually meets with business customers for planning. During planning sessions, the technician determines the router's configuration to meet customer needs and the network software that may be affected by the new installation or upgrade.

The technician works with the customer's IT personnel to decide which router configuration to use and to develop the procedure that verifies the router configuration. From this information, the technician completes a configuration checklist.

The configuration checklist includes the most commonly configured components. It typically includes a description of each component and the configuration setting. This list is a tool for ensuring that everything is configured correctly on new router installations. It is also helpful for troubleshooting previously configured routers.

Many different formats exist for configuration checklists, including some that are quite complex. ISPs should ensure that support technicians have, and know how to use, router configuration checklists. Table 5-8 shows some of the information that is commonly contained on the checklist.

Table 5-8   Router Configuration Checklist

Field	Description
Date and Work Order	Used to record the date that the configuration checklist is issued. Used to record a number used to track the contract work.
ISP Contact	The name and telephone number of the ISP representative if any questions or concerns arise.
Customer and Customer Contact	The name and telephone number of the person at the customer site responsible for the project.
Router Serial Number	The router serial number.
Configured Basic Parameters	Check here to confirm that basic router parameters are configured. Cisco SDM can be used to configure basic parameters if supported by the device.
Configured Global Parameters	Check here to confirm that the global parameters are configured. Includes the router's hostname, a privileged mode password, and disabling the router from recognizing typing mistakes as commands.
Configured Fast Ethernet LAN Interfaces	Check here to confirm that the Fast Ethernet LAN interfaces have been configured.
Configured WAN Interfaces	Check here to confirm that the WAN interfaces have been configured.
Configured Command-Line Access to the Router	Check here to confirm that the parameters used to control Cisco IOS CLI access to the router have been configured. This includes the interval of time that the EXEC command interpreter waits until user input is detected.
Configured Static Routes	Check here to confirm that the static routes are configured. An ISP may use a separate sheet to detail each static route configured. Static routes are manually configured on the router and must be changed manually if new routes are required.
Configured Dynamic Routes	Check here to confirm that the dynamic routing protocols are configured. In dynamic routing, the network protocol adjusts the path automatically, based on network traffic or topology. Changes in dynamic routes are shared with other routers in the network.
Configured Security Features	Check here to confirm that security features on the router are configured. The Cisco SDM configuration tool makes it easy to configure the basic security features. Configuring security features using the Cisco IOS CLI requires in-depth knowledge of the Cisco IOS security commands.

Before any equipment is installed at the customer site, the devices are configured and tested at the ISP site. Anything that is not functioning as expected can be replaced or fixed immediately. The network technician makes sure the router is fully configured and that the router configuration is verified. The router is then repackaged for shipment or delivery to the customer. As soon as the router is known to be configured correctly, all network cables, power cables, management cables, manufacturer documentation, manufacturer software, configuration documentation, and the special tools needed for router installation are assembled.

An inventory checklist is used to verify that all necessary equipment needed to install the router is present. Usually the network technician signs the checklist, indicating that everything has been verified. The signed and dated inventory checklist is included with the router when it is packaged for shipping to the customer premises.

The installation of a new router can be disruptive for a business. Many businesses rely on the Internet for their business correspondence and often have e-commerce services that must be accessed during the day. It may be impossible to install or upgrade network equipment during normal business hours. If the installation of the new equipment will cause the network to be down, the network technician, the ISP salesperson, and a representative of the company prepare a router installation plan. This plan ensures that the customer will experience a minimum disruption in service while the new equipment is installed.

The onsite network technician installs the router at the customer premises, following a router installation plan. This often means the router must be installed after normal working hours or on the weekend. The router installation plan identifies who the customer contact is and what the arrangements are for after-hours access.

When installing customer equipment, it is important to complete the job in a professional manner. This means that all network cables are labeled and fastened together or run through proper cable management equipment. Excess lengths of cable should be coiled and secured out of the way. The documentation should be updated to include the router's current configuration. In addition, update the network diagrams to show the location of the equipment and cables that are installed.

After the router is successfully installed and tested, the network technician completes the installation checklist. The completed checklist is verified by the customer representative. Verifying the router installation often involves demonstrating that the router is correctly configured and that services that depend on the router also work.

When the customer representative is satisfied that the router has been correctly installed and is operational, that person signs and dates the checklist. Sometimes there is a formal acceptance document in addition to the checklist. This procedure is often called the sign-off phase. It is critical that the customer representative sign off on the job, because then the ISP can bill the customer for the work.

When customer equipment is configured and installed on the customer premises, it is important to document the entire process. Documentation includes all aspects of how the equipment is configured, diagrams of how the equipment is installed, and checklists to validate the correct installation. If a new configuration is needed, compare the documentation with the previous router configuration to determine if and how the new configuration has changed.

Start documenting the work during the installation of the router. All cables and equipment should be correctly labeled and indicated on a diagram to simplify future identification. Follow an installation and verification checklist when installing a router. This checklist lists the tasks that need to be completed at the customer's premises. An installation and verification checklist helps a network technician avoid errors and ensures that the installation is done efficiently and correctly.

Activity logs are used to track modifications to configuration and access to equipment. Properly maintained activity logs help with troubleshooting. Use activity logs to document when modifications are made so that they can be used to determine if a configuration activity has contributed to a network problem. A copy of the final documentation should be left with the customer.

Many IT jobs require site visits to customer premises on a regular basis to install and troubleshoot equipment. In the eyes of customers, the network technician is a professional who has the responsibility to support their network. A professional knows how to make the customer feel at ease and confident in the technician's skills. Network technicians can do some things to ensure that they represent their organization in the most professional manner possible.

On the first visit to a customer location, it is important for the technician to make a good first impression. How the technician is dressed and his or her personal grooming are the first things the customer notices. If the technician makes a bad first impression, it may be difficult to change that impression and gain the customer's confidence. Many employers provide a uniform or have a dress code for their onsite technicians.

Remember that the network technician is at the customer location to provide a service. The technician's language and attitude reflect on the organization that the technician represents. A customer may be anxious or concerned about how the new equipment will operate. When speaking with a customer, be polite and respectful, and answer all customer questions. If additional information is required, be sure to write down the customer inquiry and follow up on it as soon as possible.

Customer Connections over a WAN

New equipment at the customer site must be connected back to the ISP to provide Internet services. When customer equipment is upgraded, it is sometimes necessary to also upgrade the type of connectivity provided by the ISP. When a company or organization has locations that are separated by large geographic distances, it may be necessary to use the telecommunications service provider (TSP) to interconnect the LANs at the different locations.

TSPs operate large regional networks that can span long distances. Traditionally, TSPs transported voice and data communications on separate networks. Increasingly, these providers are offering converged information network services to their subscribers.

Individual organizations usually lease connections through the telecommunications service provider network. These networks that connect LANs in geographically separated locations are called wide-area networks (WAN). Although the organization maintains all the policies and administers the LANs at both ends of the connection, the ISP controls the policies within the communications service provider network.

WAN connections come in a variety of different types. WAN connections vary in the type of connector used, in bandwidth, and in cost. As small businesses grow, they begin to require the increased bandwidth offered by some of the more expensive WAN connections. An ISP sells these various types of WAN connections to its clients. One of the jobs at an ISP or medium-sized business is to assess the needs for a WAN connection. The three types of serial WAN connections are point-to-point, circuit-switched, and packet-switched.

Point-to-Point

A point-to-point WAN connection, as shown in Figure 5-16, is a predefined communications path from the customer premises through a TSP network. Point-to-point lines usually are leased from a TSP. These lines often are called leased lines. Point-to-point connections typically are the most expensive of the WAN connection types and are priced based on bandwidth required and distance between the two connected points.

Figure 5-16   Point-to-Point Connection

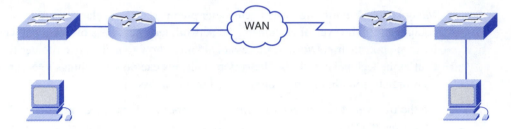

Circuit-Switched

A circuit-switched connection, as shown in Figure 5-17, functions similarly to how a phone call is made over a telephone network. When you make a call, you pick up the phone, open the circuit, and dial the number. You hang up the phone when you're finished and close the circuit. An example of a circuit-switched WAN connection is an ISDN or dialup connection.

Figure 5-17   Circuit-Switched Network

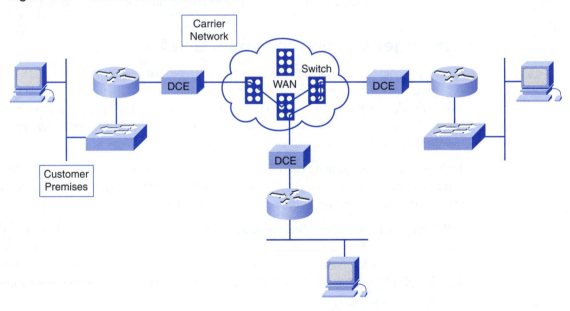

Packet-Switched

In a packet-switched WAN connection, networks have connections into the TSP switched network, as shown in Figure 5-18. Many customers share this TSP network. Instead of the circuit being physically reserved from source to destination, as in a circuit-switched network, each customer has his or her own virtual circuit. A virtual circuit is a logical path between the sender and receiver, not a physical path. An example of a packet-switched network is Frame Relay.

Figure 5-18   Packet-Switched Network

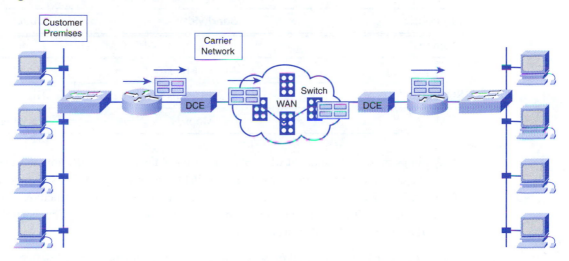

Choosing a WAN Connection

A business has many choices when choosing a WAN. The choice made largely depends on the bandwidth and cost of the WAN connection. Smaller businesses cannot afford some of the more expensive WAN connection options, such as *Synchronous Optical Network (SONET)* and *Asynchronous Transfer Mode (ATM)* WAN connections. They usually install the less-expensive *digital subscriber line (DSL)*, *cable*, or T1 connections. Availability of higher-bandwidth WAN connections can be limited in geographically isolated locations. If the offices supported are close to an urban center, there are more WAN choices.

Another factor that affects the decision of which WAN to choose is how the business plans to use the new WAN connection. If the business provides services over the Internet, it may require higher upstream bandwidth than a business that uses services hosted by ISPs on the Internet. For example, if a business hosts web servers for e-commerce, the business needs enough upstream bandwidth to accommodate the number of external customers who visit its site. On the other hand, if the business's e-commerce site is managed by an ISP, it does not require as much upstream bandwidth.

For some businesses, the ability to get a service-level agreement (SLA) attached to their WAN connection also affects their decision. Less-expensive WAN connections such as dialup, DSL, and cable connections typically do not come with an SLA, whereas more expensive connections do. Table 5-9 compares some of the options available for connecting to a WAN.

Table 5-9   Some Possible WAN Connectivity Options

Connection	Bandwidth	Cost
Dialup	Up to 56 Kbps	Low
Frame Relay	128 Kbps	Low to medium
DSL (upstream speed may be slower)	28 Kbps to 6+ Mbps	Low
Cable (upstream speed may be slower)	128 Kbps to 10+ Mbps	Low
Fractional T1	64 Kbps to 1.544 Mbps	Low to medium
T1	1.544 Mbps	Medium

continues

Table 5-9   Some Possible WAN Connectivity Options   *continued*

Connection	Bandwidth	Cost
Fractional T3	1.544 Mbps to 44.736 Mbps	Medium to high
T3	44.736 Mbps	High
SONET	51.840 Mbps to 9953.280 Mbps	High to very high
ATM	622 Mbps	Very high

Many things must be considered when planning a WAN upgrade. The ISP initiates the process by analyzing the customer needs and reviewing the available options. A proposal is then generated for the customer. Included in the proposal is an explanation of the existing infrastructure. This explanation is necessary because it helps the customer understand how the existing WAN connection provides services to the customer's home or business.

The next section of the proposal discusses the customer requirements and describes why a WAN upgrade is necessary for the business. It outlines where the current WAN connection does not meet the customer needs. It also includes a list of requirements that the new WAN connection must meet to satisfy the current and future customer requirements.

The proposal also lists all the available WAN choices, with the corresponding bandwidth, cost, and other features that are applicable for the business. The recommended choice is indicated, including other possible options.

The WAN upgrade proposal is presented to the business decision-makers. They review the document and consider the options. When they have made their decision, the ISP works with the customer to develop a schedule and coordinate the WAN upgrade process.

Lab 5-9: Planning a WAN Upgrade (5.4.3)

In this lab, you complete a WAN upgrade plan based on the business scenario presented. Refer to the lab in Part II of this book. You may perform this lab now or wait until the end of the chapter.

Configuring WAN Connections

When a WAN connection is configured, the configuration approach depends on what type of WAN connection is required. Some WAN connections support Ethernet interfaces. Other WAN connections support serial interfaces.

Leased-line WAN connections typically use a serial connection and require a ***Channel Service Unit/Data Service Unit (CSU/DSU)*** to attach to the ISP's network. The ISP equipment needs to be configured so that it can communicate through the CSU/DSU with the customer's premises. For a serial connection, it is important to have a preconfigured clock rate that is the same on both ends of the connection. The clock rate is set by the DCE device, which typically is the CSU/DSU. The Data Terminal Equipment (DTE) device, typically the router, accepts the clock rate set by the DCE. The Cisco default serial encapsulation is HDLC. It can be changed to PPP, which provides a more flexible encapsulation and supports authentication by the remote device.

Figure 5-19 and Example 5-23 show an example in which the serial WAN interfaces are configured to use PPP encapsulation.

Figure 5-19   PPP WAN Encapsulation

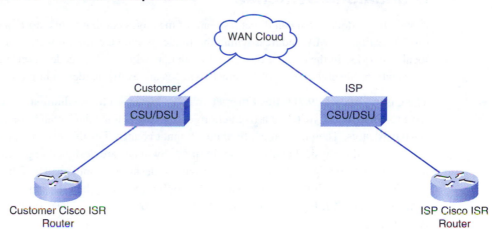

Example 5-23   Router Configurations for PPP Encapsulation

```
Customer Router:
CustomerRouter> enable
CustomerRouter# configure terminal
Enter configuration commands, one per line.  End with CNTL/Z.
CustomerRouter(config)# interface serial 0/1/0
CustomerRouter(config-if)# ip address 192.168.1.125 255.255.255.0
CustomerRouter(config-if)# encapsulation ppp
CustomerRouter(config-if)# no shutdown

ISP Router:
ISPRouter> enable
ISPRouter# configure terminal
Enter configuration commands, one per line.  End with CNTL/Z.
ISPRouter(config)# interface serial 0/1/0
ISPRouter(config-if)# ip address 192.168.1.126 255.255.255.0
ISPRouter(config-if)# encapsulation ppp
ISPRouter(config-if)# no shutdown
```

Configuring a PPP Connection Between a Customer and an ISP (5.4.4)

In this Packet Tracer activity, you configure the IP addressing on the serial WAN interface and change the encapsulation from HDLC to PPP. Use file d2-544.pka on the CD-ROM that accompanies this book to perform this activity using Packet Tracer.

Initial Cisco 2960 Switch Configuration

Routers normally are used to interconnect remote networks. LANs normally deploy access layer switches to allow end users to connect to network resources. As customer networks grow, it is often necessary to add larger, more capable switches to support additional users.

Standalone Switches

A switch is a device that can direct a stream of messages coming in one port, out of another port based on the destination MAC address within the frame. A switch cannot route traffic between two different local networks. In the context of the OSI model, a switch makes its decisions based on the Layer 2 information. Several models of Ethernet switches are available, depending on user requirements.

The Cisco Catalyst 2960 series Ethernet switch is designed for medium-sized and branch office networks. This type of switch is a fixed-configuration standalone device and does not use modules or flash card slots. The physical configuration cannot change. For this reason, the switch must be purchased with the physical configuration in mind. Switches are designed to provide 10/100 Fast Ethernet and 10/100/1000 Gigabit Ethernet connectivity to desktop computers. The 2960 series Ethernet switches use Cisco IOS software and can be configured using the GUI-based *Cisco Network Assistant* or through the CLI. Figure 5-20 shows the Cisco 2960 series switches. Table 5-10 briefly describes each switch.

Figure 5-20   Cisco 2960 Family of Switches

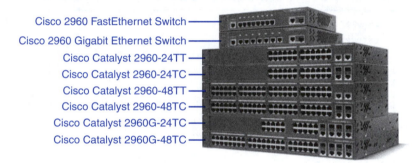

Table 5-10   Cisco 2960 Family of Switches

Switch	Description
Cisco 2960 Gigabit Ethernet Switch	Seven Gigabit Ethernet ports and one dual-purpose gigabit Ethernet uplink port.
	The Ethernet uplink port can support a 10/100/1000 copper cable or a fiber-based small form factor pluggable (SFP) connector.
	This switch does not have a fan.
Cisco 2960 Fast Ethernet Switch	Eight FastEthernet ports and one dual-purpose gigabit Ethernet uplink port.
	The gigabit Ethernet uplink port can support a 10/100/1000 copper cable or a fiber-based SFP connector.
	This switch does not have a fan.
Cisco Catalyst 2960G-24TC	Twenty 10/100/1000 ports.
	Four dual-purpose uplink ports.
Cisco Catalyst 2960-24TC	Twenty-four 10/100 ports.
	Two dual-purpose uplink ports.

Switch	Description
Cisco Catalyst 2960-24TT	Twenty-four 10/100 ports
	Two 10/100/1000 uplink ports
Cisco Catalyst 2960G-48TC	Forty-four 10/100/1000 ports.
	Four dual-purpose uplink ports.
Cisco Catalyst 2960-48TC	Forty-eight 10/100 ports.
	Two dual-purpose uplink ports.
Cisco Catalyst 2960-48TT	Forty-eight 10/100 ports.
	Two 10/100/1000 uplink ports.

Figure 5-21 shows the front and rear views of a Cisco 2960 series switch. Most switch ports are designed to connect to end devices. These access ports can have speeds of 10/100 Mbps or even 10/100/1000 Mbps, depending on the model of switch. SFP ports can support Gigabit Ethernet and can support both fiber and copper transceiver modules. Fiber transceivers support fiber-optic cables, and copper transceivers support Category 5 cables with RJ-45 connectors. The ability to plug into the Gigabit Ethernet SFP ports allows the fiber and copper transceivers to be easily replaced in the field should a connection go bad.

Figure 5-21   Cisco 2960 Switch

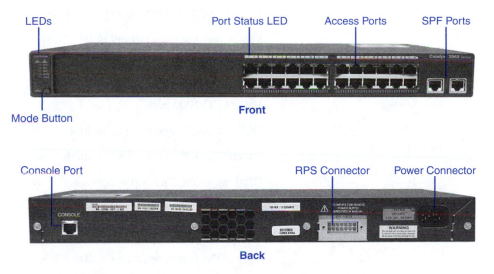

LEDs are used on switches to indicate many different things. The system (SYST) LED shows whether the system is receiving power and functioning properly. If this LED is green, the system is working normally. If the indicator turns amber, the switch is receiving power but is not working properly. The redundant power supply (RPS) LED shows the status of the redundant power supply. If this indicator is green, the RPS is connected and ready to provide backup power if required. If the indicator is blinking green, the RPS is connected but unavailable, because it is providing power to another device. An amber color indicates that the RPS is in standby mode or that a fault condition has occurred. A blinking amber LED signifies that the switch's internal power supply has failed and that the RPS is providing power to the switch.

Also located on the front of the switch are a mode button and a port LED associated with each individual port. The mode button is used to select one of the port modes: status mode, duplex mode, or speed mode. To select or change a mode, press the mode button until the desired mode is selected. The purpose of the LED depends on the port mode setting, as described in Table 5-11.

Table 5-11   Switch Port Modes

Mode	Description
Port Status (STAT)	The default mode.
	Off: No link, or the port was administratively shut down.
	Green: A link is present.
	Blinking green: Activity. The port is transmitting or receiving data.
	Alternating green and amber: Link fault. Error frames can affect connectivity, and errors such as excessive collisions, CRC errors, and alignment and jabber errors are monitored for a link-fault indication.
	Amber: The port is blocked by Spanning Tree Protocol (STP) and is not forwarding data.
	Blinking amber: The port is blocked by STP and is transmitting or receiving packets.
Port Duplex (DUPLX)	Either full or half duplex.
	Off: The port is operating in half duplex.
	Green: The port is operating in full duplex.
Speed (SPEED)	Speed mode: The 10/100 ports, 10/100/1000 ports, and SPF module ports operating speeds.
	For 10/100/1000 ports
	Off: The port is operating at 10 Mbps.
	Green: The port is operating at 100 Mbps.
	Blinking green: The port is operating at 1000 Mbps.
	For SFP module ports:
	Off: The port is operating at 10 Mbps.
	Green: The port is operating at 100 Mbps.
	Blinking green: The port is operating at 1000 Mbps.

The reverse side of the switch contains the console port and the power connectors for the main's voltage and the redundant power supply. The console port is used for out-of-band management of the device. An RJ-45-to-DB9 cable is required to connect the switch to a PC.

Each switch port can operate in either half-duplex or full-duplex mode, as shown in Figure 5-22. When a port is in *half-duplex* mode, at any given time it can either send or receive data, but not both. When a port is in *full-duplex* mode, it can simultaneously send and receive data, doubling the throughput. Both the port and the connected device must be set to the same duplex mode. If they are not the same, this creates a duplex mismatch that can lead to excessive collisions and degrade communication.

Figure 5-22   Full-Duplex and Half-Duplex Communication

Half-Duplex Communication

Full-Duplex Communication

Send

Server

Switch

Send

Receive

Server

Switch

Receive

Server

Switch

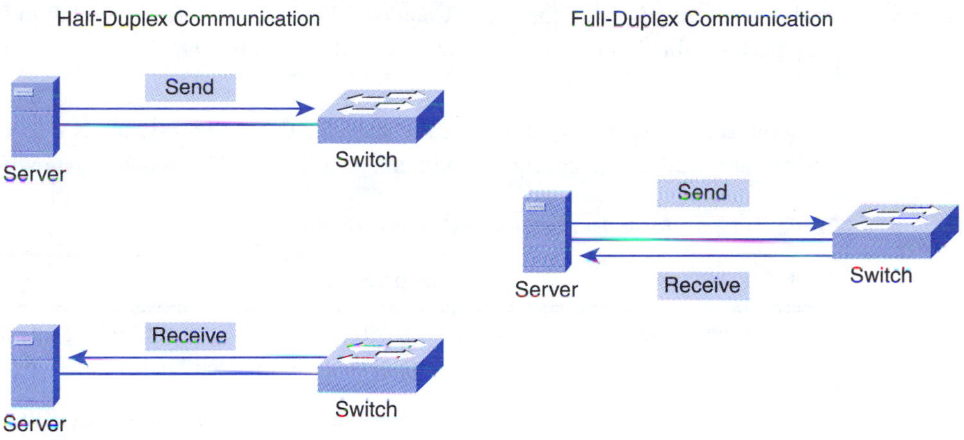

Switch ports can have the speed and duplex set manually or can use autonegotiation. *Autonegotiation* occurs when the port can autodetect the speed and duplex of the device that is connected to the port. Autonegotiation is enabled by default on many Cisco switches. For autonegotiation to be successful, both connected devices must support it. If the switch is in autonegotiation mode and the connected device does not support autonegotiation, the switch uses the speed of the port on the other device and defaults to half-duplex mode. This can create issues if the nonautonegotiating device is set to full-duplex mode, because the switch defaults to half duplex. If the connected device does not autonegotiate, manually configure the duplex settings on the switch to match the duplex settings on the connected device. The speed parameter can adjust itself even if the connected port does not autonegotiate.

The Cisco Catalyst 2960 switch is supported by Cisco IOS switch software. The Cisco Catalyst 2960 switch IOS image choices are similar to software images available for the Cisco 1841 ISR router. The IP-based software image is supplied with the switch and provides the switch with basic switching capabilities. Other Cisco IOS software images supply additional services.

Power Up the Cisco 2960 Switch

Powering up a Cisco 2960 switch is similar to powering up a Cisco 1841 ISR:

Step 1.   Check the components.

Ensure that all the components that came with the Cisco 2960 switch are available. These include the console cable, power cord, Ethernet cable, and switch documentation.

Step 2.   Connect the cables to the switch.

Connect the PC to the switch with a console cable, and start a HyperTerminal session. Connect the AC power cord to the switch and to a grounded AC outlet.

Step 3.   Turn on the switch.

Some Cisco switch models do not have an on/off switch. They power up as soon as the power cord is connected to the electrical power.

When the switch is on, the *power-on self-test (POST)* begins. During the POST, the LEDs blink while a series of tests determine that the switch is functioning properly. The POST is finished when the SYST LED rapidly blinks green. If the switch fails the POST, the SYST LED turns amber. When a switch fails the POST, you must return the switch for repairs.

Lab 5-10: Powering Up a Switch (5.5.2)

In this lab, you power up the Cisco Catalyst 2960 switch. Refer to the lab in Part II of this book. You may perform this lab now or wait until the end of the chapter.

As soon as all startup procedures are finished, the Cisco 2960 switch is ready to configure. Several options are available to configure and manage a Cisco LAN switch, as shown in Table 5-12.

Table 5-12   Tools to Manage a Cisco LAN Switch

Tool	Description
Cisco Network Assistant	PC-based network management GUI application optimized for LANs of small and medium-sized businesses.
	Offers centralized management of Cisco switches through a user-friendly GUI.
	Used to configure and manage groups of switches or standalone switches.
	Available at no cost and can be downloaded from the Cisco website.
Device Manager	Web browser-based software that is stored in the switch memory.
	A web interface that offers quick configuration and monitoring.
	Used to manage individual and standalone switches.
	Accessed through a web browser.
Cisco IOS CLI	Based on Cisco IOS software and enhanced to support desktop-switching features.
	Used to fully configure and monitor the switch.
	Accessed by connecting the PC directly to the switch console port or by using Telnet or SSH from a remote PC.
CiscoView Application	Displays the switch image used to set configuration parameters and to view switch status and performance information.
	Purchased separately. Can be a standalone application or part of a Simple Network Management Protocol (SNMP) platform.
SNMP Network Management	Managed from an SNMP management station.
	Examples of SNMP-compatible management stations are HP OpenView and SunNet Manager.
	Typically carried out at large companies.

Some of these options use IP connectivity or a web browser to connect to the switch. This requires the use of an IP address. Unlike router interfaces, switch ports are not assigned IP addresses. To use an IP-based management product or Telnet session to manage a Cisco switch, you must configure a management IP address on the switch. As soon as the management IP address is assigned, these tools can use that IP address to access the switch. Until this address is assigned, it is necessary to connect directly to the console port and use a terminal emulation program to perform configuration tasks.

The Cisco Catalyst 2960 switch comes preconfigured and only needs to be assigned basic security information before being connected to the network. The commands to configure hostname and passwords on the switch are the same commands used to configure the ISR. To use an IP-based management product or Telnet with a Cisco switch, configure a management IP address. One *virtual local-area network*, *VLAN* 1, is preconfigured in the switch to provide access to management functions. To configure the IP address assigned to the management interface on VLAN 1, enter global configuration mode:

```
Switch> enable
Switch# configure terminal
```

Next, enter interface configuration mode for VLAN 1:

```
Switch(config)# interface vlan 1
```

Set the IP address, subnet mask, and default gateway for the management interface. The IP address must be valid for the local network where the switch is installed.

```
Switch(config-if)# ip address 192.168.1.2 255.255.255.0
Switch(config-if)# no shutdown
Switch(config-if)# exit
Switch(config)# ip default-gateway 192.168.1.1
Switch(config)# end
```

Save the configuration by using the **copy running-config startup-config** command.

Interactive Activity 5-8: Configuring a 2960 Switch (5.5.3)

In this activity, you configure the basic settings on a Cisco 2960 switch. Use file d2ia-553 on the CD-ROM that accompanies this book to perform this interactive activity.

Performing an Initial Switch Configuration (5.5.3)

In this Packet Tracer activity, you configure basic parameters on a Cisco 2960 switch. Use file d2-553.pka on the CD-ROM that accompanies this book to perform this activity using Packet Tracer.

Connecting the LAN Switch to the Router

To connect the switch to a router, use a straight-through cable. Illuminated LED lights on the switch port and the router interface indicate that the connection is successful. After the switch and router are connected, determine whether the two devices can exchange messages. You can do this by pinging between the management VLAN IP address on the switch and the router interface. Use the **show running-config** command to verify that the IP address of the management interface on the switch VLAN 1, and the IP address of the directly connected router interface, are on the same local network.

From the command-line interface on the switch, ping the IP address of the directly connected router interface. Repeat the process from the command-line interface on the router by pinging the management interface IP address assigned to the switch VLAN 1. If the ping is unsuccessful, verify the connections and configurations again. Check to ensure that all cables are correct and that connections are seated. After the switch and router are successfully communicating, connect the individual PCs to the switch using straight-through cables.

Switch ports can be an entry point to the network by unauthorized users. To prevent this, switches provide a feature called port security. Port security limits the number of valid MAC addresses allowed per port. The port does not forward packets with source MAC addresses that are outside the group of defined addresses. Before port security can be activated, the port must be set to access mode using the **switchport mode access** command. There are three ways to configure port security: static, dynamic, and sticky.

With static port security, as shown in Example 5-24, MAC addresses are manually assigned using the **switchport port-security mac-address** *mac-address* interface configuration command. Static MAC addresses are stored in the address table and are added to the running configuration. With dynamic port security, as shown in Example 5-25, MAC addresses are dynamically learned and stored in the address table. The number of addresses learned can be controlled. By default, the maximum number of MAC addresses learned per port is one. Addresses that are learned are cleared from the table if the port is shut down or if the switch is restarted. Sticky port security, as shown in Example 5-26, is similar to dynamic, except that the addresses are also saved to the running configuration.

Example 5-24   Static Switch Port Security

```
S1# configure terminal
S1(config)# interface fastethernet 0/20
S1(config-if)# switchport mode access
S1(config-if)# switchport port-security mac-address 1000.2000.3000
S1(config-if)# end
```

Example 5-25   Dynamic Switch Port Security

```
S1# configure terminal
S1(config)# interface fastethernet 0/20
S1(config-if)# switchport mode access
S1(config-if)# switchport port-security
S1(config-if)# end
```

Example 5-26   Sticky Switch Port Security

```
S1# configure terminal
S1(config)# interface fastethernet 0/20
S1(config-if)# switchport mode access
S1(config-if)# switchport port-security
S1(config-if)# switchport port-security maximum 50
S1(config-if)# switchport port-security  mac-address sticky
S1(config-if)# end
```

Port security is disabled by default. If port security is enabled, a violation causes the port to be shut down. For example, if dynamic port security is enabled and the maximum number of MAC addresses per port is one, the first address learned becomes the secure address. If another workstation attempts to access the port with a different MAC address, a security violation occurs.

A security violation occurs when either of these situations happens:

- The maximum number of secure MAC addresses has been added to the address table, and a device with a MAC address that is not in the address table attempts to access the interface.

- An address learned or configured on one secure interface is seen on another secure interface in the same VLAN.

Note

Port security is similar to MAC address filtering on the Linksys device. Only secure MAC addresses that are learned dynamically or manually configured are permitted to send and receive messages over the network.

To verify port security settings for the switch or the specified interface, use the **show port-security interface** *interface-id* command. Example 5-27 shows sample output from this command. The output displays the following:

- The maximum allowed number of secure MAC addresses for each interface

- The number of secure MAC addresses on the interface

- How many security violations have occurred

- Violation mode

Example 5-27   Verifying Port Security Settings

```
Switch# show port-security interface fa0/20
Port Security                 : Enabled
Port Status                   : Secure-down
Violation Mode                : Shutdown
Aging Time                    : 0 mins
Aging Type                    : Absolute
SecureStatic Address Aging    : Disabled
Maximum MAC Addresses         : 1
Total MAC Addresses           : 1
Configured MAC Addresses      : 0
Sticky MAC Addresses          : 0
Last Source Addess:VLAN       : 0000.0000.0000:0
Security Violation Count      : 0
```

Additionally, the **show port-security address** command displays the secure MAC addresses for all ports, and the **show port-security** command displays the switch's port security settings. Example 5-28 provides sample output for the **show port-security address** command.

Example 5-28   Verifying Secure MAC Addresses

```
Switch# show port-security address
        Secure Mac Address Table
-------------------------------------------------------------------
Vlan    Mac Address      Type             Ports    Remaing Age (mins)
99      0050.BAA6.06CE   SecureConfigured Fa0/20   -
-------------------------------------------------------------------
Total Address in System (excluding one mac per port)         : 0
Max Addresses limit in System (excluding one mac per port)   : 8320
```

If static port security or sticky port security is enabled, the **show running-config** command can be used to view the MAC address associated with a specific port. There are three ways to clear a learned MAC address that is saved in the running configuration:

- Use the **clear port-security sticky interface** *port#* access to clear any learned addresses. Next, shut down the port using the **shutdown** command. Finally, re-enable the port using the **no shutdown** command.

- Disable port security using the **no switchport port-security** interface command. After it is disabled, re-enable port security.

- Reboot the switch.

Rebooting the switch works only if the running configuration is not saved to the startup configuration file. If the running configuration is saved to the startup configuration file, this eliminates the need for the switch to relearn addresses when the system reboots. However, the learned MAC address is always associated with a particular port unless the port is cleared using the **clear port-security** command or by disabling port security. If this is done, be sure to resave the running configuration to the startup configuration file to prevent the switch from reverting to the original associated MAC address upon reboot.

If any ports on a switch are unused, best practice is to disable them. It is simple to disable ports on a switch. Navigate to each unused port, and issue the **shutdown** command. If a port needs to be activated, enter the **no shutdown** command on that interface.

In addition to enabling port security and shutting down unused ports, other security configurations on a switch include setting passwords on vty ports, enabling login banners, and encrypting passwords with the **service password encryption** command. For these configurations, use the same Cisco IOS CLI commands as those used to configure a router.

Connecting a Switch (5.5.4)

In this Packet Tracer activity, you verify basic switch configuration and connect the switch to the company LAN. Use file d2-554.pka on the CD-ROM that accompanies this book to perform this activity using Packet Tracer.

Lab 5-11: Configuring the Cisco 2960 Switch (5.5.4)

In this lab, you configure and connect the Cisco Catalyst 2960 switch. Refer to the lab in Part II of this book. You may perform this lab now or wait until the end of the chapter.

CDP

Cisco Discovery Protocol (CDP) is an information-gathering tool used on a switch, ISR, or router to share information with other directly connected Cisco devices. By default, CDP begins running when the device boots up. It then sends periodic messages, known as CDP advertisements, to its directly connected networks.

CDP operates at Layer 2 only and can be used on many different types of local networks, including Ethernet and serial networks. Because it is a Layer 2 protocol, it can be used to determine the status of a directly connected link when no IP address has been configured, or if the IP address is incorrect.

Two Cisco devices that are directly connected on the same local network are referred to as being neighbors. The concept of neighbor devices is important to understand when interpreting the output of CDP commands. CDP gathers the following information:

- Device identifiers: Configured hostname

- Address list: Layer 3 address, if configured

- Port identifier: Directly connected port, such as serial 0/0/0

- Capabilities list: Function or functions provided by the device

- Platform: The device's hardware platform, such as Cisco 1841

You can display the information that CDP collects using the commands **show cdp neighbors** and **show cdp neighbors detail**. Examples 5-29 and 5-30 show sample output from these commands. Viewing CDP information does not require the user to log into the remote devices. Because CDP collects and displays a lot of information about directly connected neighbors, without requiring a login to those neighbors, it usually is disabled in production networks.

Example 5-29   CDP Neighbors

```
FC-CPE-2# show cdp neighbors
Capability Codes: R - Router, T - Trans Bridge, B - Source Route Bridge
                  S - Switch, H - Host, I - IGMP, r - Repeater

Device ID        Local Intrfce    Holdtme    Capability  Platform  Port ID
Switch           Fas 0/1          175          S I       WS-C2950- Fas 0/1
ISP              Ser 0/1/0        134          R S I     1841      Ser 0/1/0
FC-CPE-1         Ser 0/1/1        127          R S I     1841      Ser 0/1/1
FC-CPE-2#
```

Example 5-30   CDP Neighbors Detail

```
FC-CPE-2# show cdp neighbors detail
-------------------------
Device ID: Switch
Entry address(es):
Platform: cisco WS-C2950-24,  Capabilities: Switch IGMP
Interface: FastEthernet0/1,  Port ID (outgoing port): FastEthernet0/1
Holdtime : 167 sec

Version :
Cisco Internetwork Operating System Software
IOS (tm) C2950 Software (C2950-I6Q4L2-M), Version 12.1(13)EA1, RELEASE SOFTWARE (fc1)
Copyright (c) 1986-2003 by Cisco Systems, Inc.
Compiled Tue 04-Mar-03 02:14 by yenanh

advertisement version: 2
Protocol Hello:  OUI=0x00000C, Protocol ID=0x0112; payload len=27,
  value=00000000FFFFFFFF010231FF000000000000000D65630580FF0000
VTP Management Domain: 'Toronto'
Duplex: full


-------------------------
Device ID: ISP
Entry address(es):
IP address: 10.10.10.2
Platform: Cisco 1841,  Capabilities: Router Switch IGMP
Interface: Serial0/1/0,  Port ID (outgoing port): Serial0/1/0
Holdtime : 124 sec

Version :
Cisco IOS Software, 1841 Software (C1841-ADVIPSERVICESK9-M), Version 12.4(10b),
```

```
   RELEASE SOFTWARE (fc3)
Technical Support: http://www.cisco.com/techsupport
Copyright (c) 1986-2007 by Cisco Systems, Inc.
Compiled Fri 19-Jan-07 15:15 by prod_rel_team

advertisement version: 2
VTP Management Domain: ''

-----------------------
Device ID: FC-CPE-1
Entry address(es):
  IP address: 10.60.30.4
Platform: Cisco 1841,  Capabilities: Router Switch IGMP
Interface: Serial0/1/1,  Port ID (outgoing port): Serial0/1/1
Holdtime : 178 sec

Version :
Cisco IOS Software, 1841 Software (C1841-ADVIPSERVICESK9-M), Version 12.4(10b),
  RELEASE SOFTWARE (fc3)
Technical Support: http://www.cisco.com/techsupport
Copyright (c) 1986-2007 by Cisco Systems, Inc.
Compiled Fri 19-Jan-07 15:15 by prod_rel_team

advertisement version: 2
VTP Management Domain: ''

FC-CPE-2#
```

CDP can be disabled on the device or on a specific interface. To disable CDP on the device, enter **no cdp run** from global configuration mode. To disable CDP on a specific interface, enter **no cdp enable** in interface configuration mode.

Using CDP as a Network Discovery Tool (5.5.5)

In this Packet Tracer activity, you examine CDP configuration and **show** commands. Use file d2-555.pka on the CD-ROM that accompanies this book to perform this activity using Packet Tracer.

Summary

The Integrated Services Router (ISR) combines many of the common networking functions into a single unit. The Cisco 1841 ISR is designed for small to medium-sized businesses and small enterprise branch offices. The main components of this router include

- HWIC slots
- Compact flash module
- USB port
- Dual 10/100 Fast Ethernet ports
- Console and auxiliary ports
- Cisco IOS software image

This device, like most Cisco internetworking devices, can be configured by either in-band or out-of-band techniques. In-band tools include Telnet, SSH, HTTP, SDM, and SDM Express. Out-of-band techniques involve a connection to the console port.

Cisco Router and Security Device Manager (SDM) is a graphical user interface (GUI) tool that can be used to configure, monitor, and maintain Cisco devices. This is the recommended way to configure a new ISR. SDM Express is a tool bundled with SDM that has a simplified interface. It offers a subset of the commands found in the full SDM.

The IOS command-line interface (CLI) is a text-based tool that lets you monitor and configure Cisco devices. The CLI is recommended for advanced configurations that are not possible with the GUI and for older equipment that does not support SDM.

Unlike the GUI interface, which provides extensive help and tutorials, the CLI does not provide step-by-step configuration assistance. It relies more on the skills and knowledge of the networking technician. Context-sensitive help available in the CLI can help you complete commands or determine which parameters must be supplied.

The CLI consists of many different modes. The first mode you encounter when logging into a device is user mode; it offers only a subset of the available commands. A user can examine some of the basic network configurations in this mode but cannot alter any router parameters or view configuration files. Privileged EXEC mode lets you examine and alter device configurations. A number of additional modes exist for configuring specific portions and functions of the router.

The startup configuration is stored in NVRAM and is copied into RAM when the device first starts. In RAM, this file becomes the running configuration. All changes made to a device's configuration are made to the running configuration. The running configuration must be copied back to the startup configuration to ensure that these changes are not lost.

Network devices installed at a customer site are known as customer premises equipment (CPE). When equipment is installed at the customer site, it is important to document the entire process, including the final configuration, network diagrams, and installation checklists. A copy of this documentation should be provided to the customer upon completion of the installation. When working at a customer site, it is important to keep in mind the culture of the workplace and also adhere to all safety requirements.

WAN connections are used to send signals across long distances. Many different types of WAN connections are available. These can be broken into three main categories: point-to-point, circuit-switched, and packet-switched. Some technologies support Ethernet connections, but most WAN connections rely on serial interfaces. Configuring a network device across a WAN connection requires a

Telnet or SSH connection. SSH is the preferred technique, because it encrypts the transmitted data, making it difficult to obtain usernames and passwords.

The Cisco 2960 family of access layer switches provides network connectivity for end users. These switches come in various configurations to suit any business environment and are powered by a Cisco IOS. Because they operate with a Cisco IOS, configuration is similar to the 1841 ISR.

To use in-band management with a switch, an IP address must be configured on the management VLAN. By default, this is VLAN 1 on a Cisco switch.

Switch port security is used to ensure that only valid devices connect to the switch port. Static switch port security requires the administrator to program the switch with the acceptable MAC address. Dynamic and sticky modes allow the switch to detect the MAC address.

Cisco Discovery Protocol (CDP) is an information-gathering tool used on a switch, ISR, or router to share information with other directly connected Cisco devices. CDP operates at Layer 2 and can discover linked devices without their being configured with a Layer 3 address.

Activities and Labs

This summary outlines the activities you can perform to help reinforce important concepts described in this chapter. You can find the activity and Packet Tracer files on the CD-ROM accompanying this book.

Interactive Activities on the CD:

Activity 5-1: Photozoom of an 1800 ISR (5.1.1)

Activity 5-2: CLI or SDM? (5.1.4)

Activity 5-3: SDM Express Configuration Parameters (5.2.2)

Activity 5-4: Entering Command Modes (5.3.1)

Activity 5-5: History Navigation Commands (5.3.2)

Activity 5-6: Viewing the Router Interface Configuration (5.3.3)

Activity 5-7: Configuring a Serial Interface on Routers for Communication (5.3.5)

Activity 5-8: Configuring a 2960 Switch (5.5.3)

Packet Tracer Activities on the CD:

Exploring the Cisco IOS CLI (5.3.2)

Using the Cisco IOS **show** Commands (5.3.3)

Performing an Initial Router Configuration (5.3.4)

Configuring Serial and Ethernet Interfaces (5.3.5)

Configuring a Default Route (5.3.6)

Configuring a Cisco Router as a DHCP Server (5.3.7)

Configuring Static NAT on a Cisco Router (5.3.8)

Backing Up a Cisco Router Configuration to a TFTP Server (5.3.9)

Configuring a PPP Connection Between a Customer and an ISP (5.4.4)

Performing an Initial Switch Configuration (5.5.3)

Connecting a Switch (5.5.4)

Using CDP as a Network Discovery Tool (5.5.5)

Hands-on Labs in Part II of this book:

Lab 5-1: Powering Up an Integrated Services Router (5.1.3)

Lab 5-2: Configuring an ISR with SDM Express (5.2.3)

Lab 5-3: Configuring Dynamic NAT with SDM (5.2.4)

Lab 5-4: Configuring Basic Router Settings with the Cisco IOS CLI (5.3.5)

Lab 5-5: Configuring DHCP with SDM and Cisco IOS CLI (5.3.7)

Lab 5-6: Configuring PAT with SDM and Static NAT Using Cisco IOS (5.3.8)

Lab 5-7: Managing Router Configuration Files Using HyperTerminal (5.3.9a)

Lab 5-8: Managing Router Configuration Files Using TFTP (5.3.9b)

Lab 5-9: Planning a WAN Upgrade (5.4.3)

Lab 5-10: Powering Up a Switch (5.5.2)

Lab 5-11: Configuring the Cisco 2960 Switch (5.5.4)

Appendix B contains additional labs on IOS management and password recovery.

Check Your Understanding

Complete all the review questions listed here to check your understanding of the topics and concepts in this chapter. Answers are listed in Appendix A, "Check Your Understanding and Challenge Questions Answer Key."

1. Why is the Cisco IOS built in a modular format?

   A. Most ISRs cannot handle a large IOS, so the modular format allows them to use a smaller image.

   B. It allows businesses to select the feature set that matches their requirements.

   C. It prevents end users from having advanced functionality that they do not require.

   D. It allows end users to mix and match modules to gain functionality.

2. What is the preferred method of configuring a new ISR?

   A. In-band with SDM

   B. In-band with the IOS CLI

   C. Out-of-band with SDM

   D. Out-of-band with the IOS CLI

3. Where is the startup configuration file stored on a router?

4. Which items are required to complete the SDM Express Basic Configuration page? (Choose all that apply.)

   A. Domain name

   B. DHCP range

   C. SDM username and password

   D. Enable password

   E. WAN interface IP address

   F. Type of WAN connection

5. What is the default Cisco serial line encapsulation technology?

   A. Ethernet

   B. Frame Relay

   C. HDLC

   D. PPP

6. What is IP Unnumbered, and when is it used?

7. What type of NAT is configured when using the Cisco SDM Basic NAT Wizard?

   A. Static

   B. Dynamic

   C. Overloaded

   D. Overlapping

8. Which CLI prompt do you see when excluding addresses from a DHCP pool?

   A. Router>

   B. Router#

   C. Router(config)#

   D. Router(config-if)#

   E. Router(dhcp-config)#

9. What is the result of issuing the following command? Assume that the Ethernet interface has been identified as the inside interface and the serial interface has been identified as the outside interface.

   ```
   Router(config)# ip nat inside source static 172.31.232.14 10.114.11.14
   ```

10. Which **show** command can be used to display the amount of NVRAM in an ISR?

    A. **show running-config**

    B. **show interfaces**

    C. **show arp**

    D. **show ip route**

    E. **show version**

11. What is the difference between the following two commands?

```
Router(config)#enable password [password]
Router(config)#enable secret [password]
```

12. The following is a portion of a running-config file. What is the first IP address that the DHCP server will hand out?

```
!
ip dhcp pool LAN-addresses
 domain-name cisco.com
 network 172.16.0.0 /16
 ip dhcp excluded-address 172.16.1.100 172.16.1.103
 dns-server 172.16.1.103 172.16.2.103
 default-router 172.16.1.100
 lease infinite
!
```

A. 172.16.0.1

B. 172.16.1.100

C. 172.16.1.102

D. 172.16.1.103

E. 172.16.1.104

13. What is the normal condition of a Port Status LED on a 2960 switch when the port is actively transmitting and receiving data?

A. Off

B. Steady green

C. Flashing green

D. Steady amber

E. Flashing amber

F. Red

14. What keystroke is used to recall the most recent command in the history file?

A. Crtl-A

B. Ctrl-E

C. Ctrl-N

D. Ctrl-P

15. What is a default route, and why is it necessary?

Challenge Questions and Activities

These questions require a deeper application of the concepts covered in this chapter. You can find the answers in Appendix A.

1. As the senior network administrator at AnyCompany, you have been asked to train a new networking technician. The technician asks you if she should use SDM or the CLI to configure a new company ISR. What do you tell her? Justify your position.

2. You have just been hired by AnyCompany as a network administrator. During your review of the current network, you notice that CDP is enabled on all devices, so you instruct the junior network technician to immediately disable CDP on all devices. The technician asks you how to disable CDP and why it is necessary to do so. What do you tell her?

## CHAPTER 6

Routing

Objectives

After completing this chapter, you should be able to answer the following questions:

- What are the purpose and function of dynamic routing?

- What are the characteristics of directly connected static and dynamic routes?

- What are the main interior gateway protocols and their key features?

- How is RIPv2 dynamic routing configured using the Cisco IOS?

- What are exterior gateway routing protocols, and how are they used across the Internet?

- What is required to enable BGP on a customer site router?

Key Terms

This chapter uses the following key terms. You can find the definitions in the glossary.

algorithm page 180

convergence page 180

Routing Information Protocol (RIP) page 183

Enhanced Interior Gateway Routing Protocol (EIGRP) page 184

Diffusing Update Algorithm (DUAL) page 185

Open Shortest Path First (OSPF) page 185

link-state advertisement (LSA) page 186

topological database page 186

Shortest Path First (SPF) algorithm page 186

SPF tree page 186

autonomous system (AS) page 193

AS number (ASN) page 193

interior gateway protocol (IGP) page 195

exterior gateway protocol (EGP) page 195

border gateway page 195

Border Gateway Protocol (BGP) page 195

reachability page 196

transit traffic page 198

Small-business networks rely on routing to connect their users with the Internet. As these networks grow, routing also becomes an integral piece of the LAN infrastructure. Dynamic routing protocols enable routers to react quickly when links fail or when previously used routes become unavailable. Network engineers and technicians select, configure, and troubleshoot routing operation within the LAN and WAN.

Part II of this book includes the corresponding labs for this chapter.

Enabling Routing Protocols

Routers are the primary devices used to interconnect networks within a single building, across town, or around the world. Router tables contain static and dynamic network destination entries. Dynamic entries are created by a routing protocol running on the router. A routing protocol is software loaded onto the router that enables it to communicate with other routers and learn what networks can be reached and how to get to them. This section provides an overview of routing and discusses common interior routing protocols such as RIP, EIGRP, and OSPF. It also provides RIP configuration and verification procedures.

Routing Basics

As the internal network of an organization grows, it might be necessary to break up the network into multiple smaller networks for security or organizational purposes. This division is often accomplished by subnetting the network. Subnetting requires a router to pass traffic from one subnet to another.

In addition, the organization might expand to include multiple sites in different locations. This also requires the use of routing to connect the geographically separate networks.

Routing is the process by which network devices direct messages across networks to arrive at the correct destination. All routers must make routing decisions. They do this by looking up information stored in their routing tables. Every router contains a table of all locally connected networks and the interfaces that connect to them. These routing tables also contain information about the routes, or paths, that the router uses to reach other remote networks that are not locally attached.

These routes can be statically assigned to the router by an administrator, or they can be dynamically given to the router by another router via a program called a *routing protocol*.

Figure 6-1 shows a packet traveling from Host H1 on Network 1 to Host H3 on Network 3. The path it takes is highlighted. Each router in the path contains an entry in its routing table that lists the network number and the next-hop router along the way to the destination. Each router the packet passes through on its way to the destination is called a *hop*. In Figure 6-1, R3 has an entry in its routing table for Network 3 that indicates it must send the packet to R4 and that Network 3 is three hops away.

Every router uses a routing table to decide where to send packets. The routing table contains a set of routes, where each route describes which gateway or interface the router needs to use to reach a specified network.

A route has four main components:

- Destination value
- Mask
- Gateway or interface address
- Metric

To direct a message to the correct destination, the router looks at the destination IP address in an incoming packet and then looks for a matching route in the routing table.

The destination values in a routing table refer to destination network addresses. For the router to determine if it has a route to the destination IP address in its table, it must first find out which bits represent the destination network address.

Figure 6-1   Routers Directing Packets

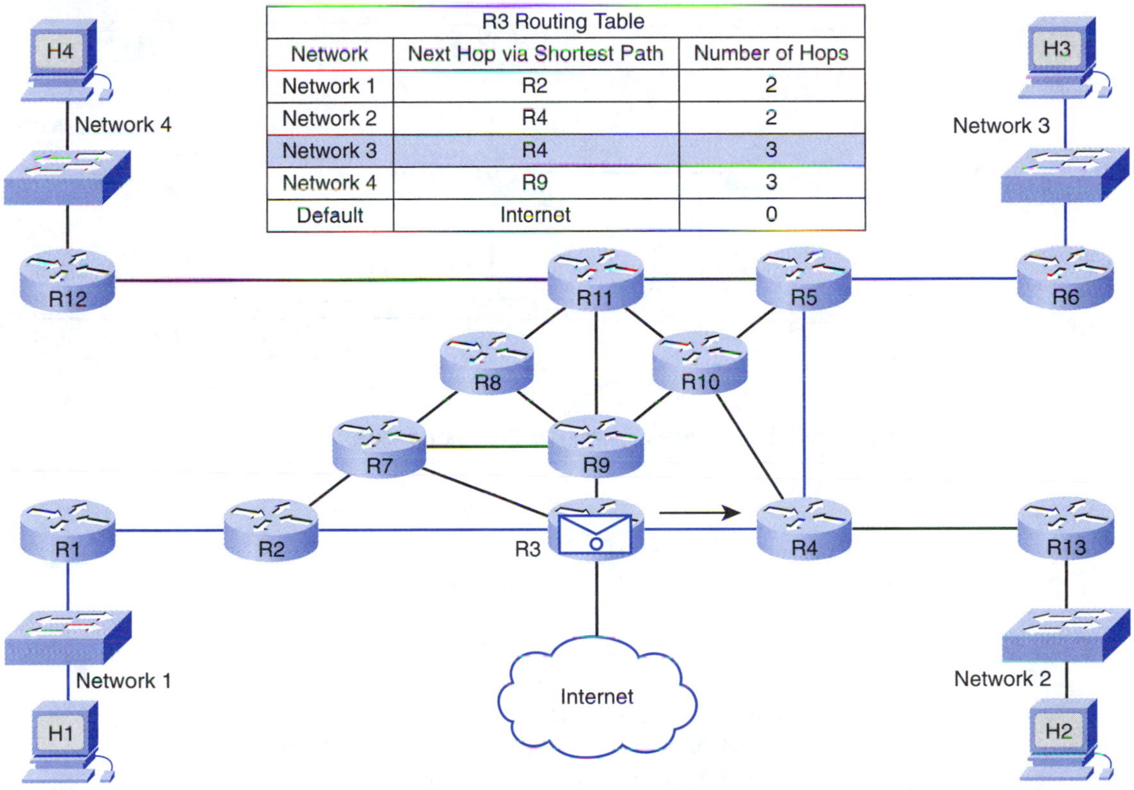

R3 Routing Table		
Network	Next Hop via Shortest Path	Number of Hops
Network 1	R2	2
Network 2	R4	2
Network 3	R4	3
Network 4	R9	3
Default	Internet	0

Each potential route in the table has a subnet mask assigned. The router applies each subnet mask to the destination IP address in the packet. The resulting network address is then compared to the network address of the route in the table.

- If a match is found, the packet is forwarded out the correct interface or to the appropriate gateway.

- When the network address matches more than one route in the routing table, the router uses the route that has the most specific, or longest, network address match from its routing table.

- Sometimes there is more than one equal-cost route to the same destination network. Routing protocol rules determine which route the router will use.

- If none of the route entries match, the router directs the message to the gateway specified by the default route if it has been configured.

Figure 6-2 shows how a router matches the network portion of the destination IP address of a packet to determine where to send the packet. Example 6-1 shows the routing table for the R1 router.

Figure 6-2   Route Matching

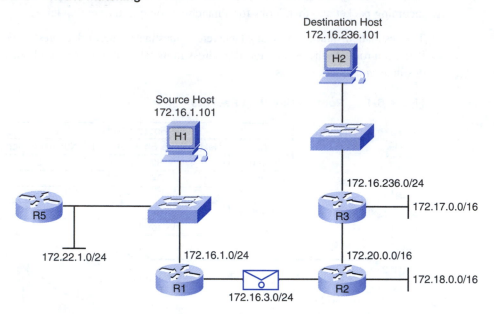

Example 6-1 R1 show ip route Command Output

```
R1 show ip route

(*** output omitted ***)
Gateway of last resort is 172.16.3.1 to network 0.0.0.0
S       172.17.0.0/16 [1/0] via 172.16.3.1
        172.16.0.0/16 is variably subnetted, 4 subnets, 2 masks
S       172.16.236.0/24 [1/0] via 172.16.3.1
S       172.16.0.0/16 [1/0] via 172.16.3.1
C       172.16.1.0/24 is directly connected, FastEthernet0/0
C       172.16.3.0/24 is directly connected, FastEthernet0/1
S       172.18.0.0/16 [1/0] via 172.16.3.1
S       172.20.0.0/16 [1/0] via 172.16.3.1
        172.22.0.0/24 is subnetted, 1 subnets
S       172.22.1.0/24 [1/0] via 172.16.1.1
S*      0.0.0.0/0 [1/0] via 172.16.3.1
```

In the figure, source host H1 is sending a packet to destination host H2 with IP address 172.16.236.101.
Because H2 is not on H1's local network, the packet is first sent to H1's default gateway, which is router
R1. When the packet is received at router R1, the router applies each subnet mask to the destination
IP address to find the network address with the longest match or the greatest number of subnet bits.
For destination address 172.16.236.101, the longest match is 172.16.236.0/24 (24 bits is subnet mask
255.255.255.0).

Next the router compares the resulting network address to the routing table entries and finds the following
route:

```
S       172.16.236.0/24 [1/0] via 172.16.3.1
```

172.16.3.1 is the IP address of the next-hop R2 interface.

Router R1 looks up the 172.16.3.0 network in its routing table and finds that the 172.16.3.0 network is directly connected on its FastEthernet 0/1 interface:

```
C    172.16.3.0/24 is directly connected, FastEthernet 0/1
```

R1 then sends the packet out the correct interface to reach the next-hop address toward the destination network.

Note that routing tables do not contain end-to-end information about the entire path from a source network to a destination network. They contain only information about the next hop along that path. The next hop typically is a directly connected gateway on the same subnet. In the case of a static route, the next hop could be any IP address, as long as it can be resolved in the routing table or can be reached by that router. Eventually the message gets passed to a router that is directly connected to the destination host, and the message is delivered. In Figure 6-2, this is router R3.

Routing information between all the intermediate routers on a path is in the form of network addresses, not specific hosts. Only in the final router does the destination address in the routing table point specifically to a host computer rather than a network.

For a Cisco router, the IOS command **show ip route** displays the routes in the routing table. As shown in Example 6-2 and described in the following sections, several types of routes can appear in the routing table:

- Directly connected routes
- Dynamically updated routes (also called dynamic routes)
- Default route
- Static routes

Example 6-2 shows the routing table for the R1 router, with various types of routes identified.

Example 6-2 R1 show ip route Command Output with Different Route Types

```
R1 show ip route

Codes: C - connected, S - static, R - RIP, M - mobile, B - BGP
       D - EIGRP, EX - EIGRP external, O - OSPF, IA - OSPF inter area
       N1 - OSPF NSSA external type 1, N2 - OSPF NSSA external type 2
       E1 - OSPF external type 1, E2 - OSPF external type 2
       i - IS-IS, su - IS-IS summary, L1 - IS-IS level-1, L2 - IS-IS level-2
       ia - IS-IS inter area, * - candidate default, U - per-user static route
       o - ODR, P - periodic downloaded static route
! The following is the gateway as set by the default static route entry (S*)
Gateway of last resort is 192.168.1.2 to network 0.0.0.0
! The following is a directly connected network
C    172.16.0.0/16 is directly connected, FastEthernet0/0
     10.0.0.0/24 is subnetted, 1 subnets
! The following is a normal static route
S    10.10.10.0 [1/0] via 192.168.1.2
C    192.168.0.0/24 is directly connected, Serial0/1
C    192.168.1.0/24 is directly connected, Serial0/0
! The following is a dynamically updated route via RIP
R    192.168.2.0/24 [120/1] via 192.168.1.2, 00:00:23
! The following is a default static route that sets the gateway above
S*   0.0.0.0/0 [1/0] via 192.168.1.2
```

Directly Connected Routes

When the router powers up, the configured interfaces are enabled. As they become operational, the router stores the directly attached local network addresses as connected routes in the routing table. For Cisco routers, these routes are identified in the routing table with the prefix C (for Connected). These routes are automatically updated whenever the interface is reconfigured or shut down.

Dynamically Updated Routes (Dynamic Routes)

Dynamic routes are automatically created and maintained by routing protocols. Routing protocols are implemented in programs that run on routers and that exchange routing information with other routers in the network. Dynamically updated routes are identified in the routing table with the prefix that corresponds to the type of routing protocol that created the route. For example, R is used for Routing Information Protocol (RIP).

Default Route

The default route is a type of static route that specifies a gateway to use when the routing table does not contain a path to use to reach the destination network. It is common for default routes to point to the next router in the path to the ISP. If a subnet connects to only one router, that router is automatically the default gateway, because all network traffic to and from that local network has no option but to travel through that router.

> **Note**
>
> For a route to appear in a routing table, the status of the associated interface must be up/up. If the interface is shut down or the other end of the link is down, even directly connected networks and static routes will not appear in the routing table because the packet cannot be directed to a network if an interface or a link is down.

Static Routes

A network administrator can manually configure a static route to a specific network. A static route does not change until the administrator manually reconfigures it. These routes are identified in the routing table with the prefix S.

Figure 6-3 shows two routers, each with its own local network attached. The router R1 local network is 192.168.14.0, and the router R2 local network is 192.168.16.0. These routers share a common link between them on network 192.168.15.0. Without a dynamic routing protocol, R1 has no knowledge of R2's 192.168.16.0 local network, and R2 has no knowledge of R1's 192.168.14.0 local network. With a simple two-router network like this, you can use static routes to manually inform each router of the other router's local network.

Figure 6-3   Static Route Configuration

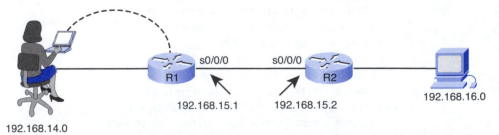

192.168.14.0

The steps to configure a static route on a Cisco router are as follows:

Step 1.   Connect to the router using a console cable.

Step 2.   Open a HyperTerminal window to connect with the first router that you want to configure.

Step 3.   Enter privileged mode by entering **enable** at the R1> prompt. Note how the > symbol changes to a # to indicate that privileged mode is operative.

```
R1> enable
R1#
```

Step 4.   Enter global configuration mode:

```
R1#config terminal
R1(config)#
```

Step 5.   Use the **ip route** IOS command to configure the static route, using the following format:

```
ip route [destination_network] [subnet_mask] [gateway_address or exit_interface]
```

For example, to enable a host on R1's local network to reach a host on R2's local network 192.168.16.0, the administrator configures a static route on R1 with the following IOS command in global configuration mode:

```
R1(config)#ip route 192.168.16.0 255.255.255.0 192.168.15.2
```

This command specifies the network to be reached, its subnet mask, and the next-hop router interface IP address. The command syntax also allows you to specify the R1 router exit interface instead of the IP address of the next hop:

```
R1(config)#ip route 192.168.16.0 255.255.255.0 s0/0/0
```

To enable two-way communication with a host on network 192.168.16.0, the administrator also configures a static route on R2 so that return packets can find their way back to the R1 host:

```
R2(config)#ip route 192.168.14.0 255.255.255.0 192.168.15.1
```

or

```
R2(config)#ip route 192.168.14.0 255.255.255.0 s0/0/0
```

Because static routes are configured manually, network administrators must add and delete static routes to reflect any changes in network topology. On small networks with few possible changes, static routes require very little maintenance. In a large network, the manual maintenance of routing tables could require significant administrative time. For this reason, larger networks generally use dynamic routing rather than static routes.

Configuring Static Routes (6.1.1)

In this Packet Tracer activity, you manually configure and reconfigure static routes. Use file d2-611.pka on the CD-ROM that accompanies this book to perform this activity using Packet Tracer.

Routing Protocols

Routes can change very quickly. Problems with cables and hardware failures can make destinations unreachable through the designated interface. Routers need a way to quickly update routes that does not depend on the administrator to make changes.

Routers use routing protocols to dynamically manage information received from their own interfaces and from other routers. Routing protocols can also be configured to manage manually entered routes.

Dynamic routing makes it possible to avoid the time-consuming and exacting process of configuring static routes. Dynamic routing enables routers to react to changes in the network and to adjust their routing tables accordingly, without the intervention of the network administrator. A dynamic routing protocol learns all available routes, places the best routes into the routing table, and removes routes when they are no longer valid.

The method that a routing protocol uses to determine the best route to a destination network is called a routing *algorithm*. The two main classes of routing algorithms are distance vector and link-state. Each type uses a different method to determine the best route to a destination network.

The routing algorithm is very important to dynamic routing. Whenever the topology of a network changes because of reconfiguration or failure, the routing tables in all the routers must also change to reflect an accurate view of the new topology. When all the routers in a network have updated their tables to reflect the new route, the routers are said to have converged. The *convergence* process can take considerable time, depending on the network design and the routing protocol being used. During this time routers may have incorrect routes to networks, and portions of the network may be unreachable.

For two routers to exchange routes, they must be using the same routing protocol and therefore the same routing algorithm. Figure 6-4 shows a router sending an update to another router so that it can learn about networks.

Figure 6-4   Exchanging Route Information Using a Routing Protocol

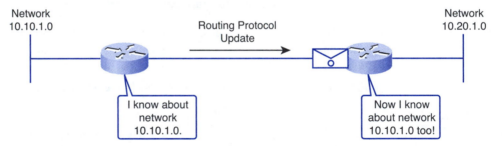

The distance vector routing algorithm passes periodic copies of a routing table from router to router. These regular updates between routers communicate topology changes.

> **Note**
>
> A topology change can result from the addition or removal of a router on the network, a change to the network IP addressing scheme, or the failure of a device or communications link.

The distance vector algorithm evaluates the route information it receives from other routers in terms of two basic criteria:

- **Distance**: How far is the network from this router?

- **Vector**: In what direction should the packet be sent to reach this network?

The distance component of a route is expressed in terms of a route cost, or metric, that can represent the following:

- Number of hops

- Administrative cost

- Bandwidth

- Transmission speed

- Likelihood of delays

- Reliability

The vector or direction component of a route is the address of the next hop along the path to the network named in the route.

An analogy for distance vectors is a highway sign, as shown in Figure 6-5. A sign points toward a destination and indicates the distance that must be traveled to reach that destination. Farther down the highway, another sign points toward the same destination, but now the distance remaining to that destination is shorter. As long as the distance is shorter, the traffic is on the best path.

Figure 6-5   Distance Vector Routing Protocol Characteristics

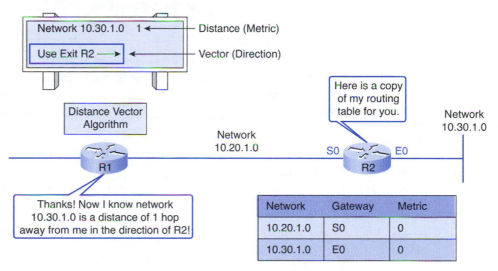

Each router that uses distance vector routing communicates its routing information to its neighbors. Neighbor routers share a directly connected network. The interface that leads to each directly connected network has a distance of 0.

Each router receives a routing table from its directly connected neighbor routers. For example, in Figure 6-6, router R2 receives information from Router R1. Router R2 adds to the metric—in this case, hop count—to show that there is now one more hop to get to the destination network. Then Router R2 sends this new routing table to its neighbors, including Routers R3 and R4. These routers then add another hop to the metric to show that they must go through R2 to get to the network being advertised. This same step-by-step process occurs in all directions between neighbor routers. R2 also sends a routing update back to R1 but it does not include any networks in the update that were learned from R1. This is because R1 is closer to those networks and knows more about their status than R2 does.

Figure 6-6   Distance Vector Routing Protocol Operation

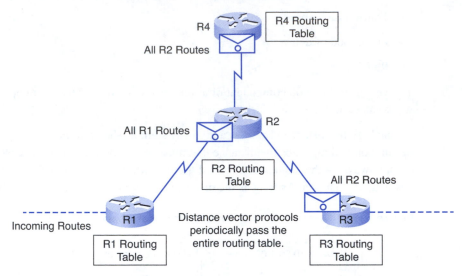

Eventually, each router learns about other, more remote networks based on the information it receives from its neighbors. Each of the network entries in the routing table has an accumulated distance vector to show how far away that network is in a given direction.

As the distance vector discovery process proceeds, routers discover the best path to destination networks based on the information they receive from each neighbor. The best path is the path with the shortest distance or smallest metric.

Routing table updates also occur when the topology changes, such as when a new network is added or when a router fails. This causes a network to no longer be reachable. As with the network discovery process, topology change updates proceed step by step by sending copies of routing tables from router to router.

Interactive Activity 6-1: Selecting the Shortest Path Through the Network (6.1.2)

In this interactive activity, for each router, you select the shortest path, based on the number of hops, to the destination Ethernet networks. If the network is directly connected, specify the exit interface; otherwise, specify the next-hop router. Use file d2ia-612 on the CD-ROM that accompanies this book to perform this interactive activity.

Lab 6-1: Creating a Network Diagram from Routing Tables (6.1.2)

In this lab you create a network topology diagram based on the output of the **show ip route** command. Refer to the lab in Part II of this book. You may perform this lab now or wait until the end of the chapter.

Common Interior Routing Protocols

This section describes the characteristics of three common interior routing protocols: Routing Information Protocol (RIP), Enhanced Interior Gateway Routing Protocol (EIGRP), and Open Shortest Path First (OSPF).

RIP

Routing Information Protocol (RIP) is a distance vector routing protocol that is used in thousands of networks throughout the world.

The key characteristics of RIP include the following:

- It was initially specified in RFC 1058.

- It is a distance vector routing protocol.

- It uses hop count as the metric for path selection.

- It defines a hop count greater than 15 as an unreachable route.

- It sends routing table contents every 30 seconds by default.

When a router receives a routing update that includes a new or changed route, the router updates its routing table to reflect this new route. At each router, the hop count value is increased by 1. The router uses the network address of the directly connected router that sent the update as the next-hop address.

After updating its routing table, the router immediately begins transmitting routing updates to inform other network routers of the change. These updates, called *triggered updates*, are sent independently of the regularly scheduled updates that RIP routers forward.

Figure 6-7 shows a network topology with three routers and four networks. Table 6-1 shows the routing tables of routers R1, R2, and R3 before updates are sent. Initially all the routers' tables contain only directly connected networks, each with a hop count of 0. When RIP is configured on each of the routers, they send updates to each other. After they have converged, each router's table shows the networks from the other routers. Table 6-2 shows the routing table of each router after updates are sent. For example, in Table 6-2, after all routers have convergence, router R1 contains an entry for network 10.4.0.0 that is attached to R3 (R3's Ethernet LAN). R1 learned about this network through its own S0/0/0 interface and the network is two hops away from R1. There is also an entry for network 10.4.0.0 in R2's routing table but it was learned through R2's S0/0/1 interface and is only one hop away.

Figure 6-7   Network Topology

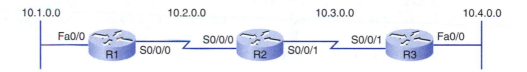

Table 6-1   RIP Router Routing Tables Before Updates Are Sent

R1 Network	Interface	Hop	R2 Network	Interface	Hop	R3 Network	Interface	Hop
10.1.0.0	Fa0/0	0	10.2.0.0	S0/0/0	0	10.3.0.0	S0/0/1	0
10.2.0.0	S0/0/0	0	10.3.0.0	S0/0/1	0	10.4.0.0	Fa0/0	0

Table 6-2   RIP Router Routing Tables After Updates Are Sent

R1 Network	Interface	Hop	R2 Network	Interface	Hop	R3 Network	Interface	Hop
10.1.0.0	Fa0/0	0	10.2.0.0	S0/0/0	0	10.3.0.0	S0/0/1	0
10.2.0.0	S0/0/0	0	10.3.0.0	S0/0/1	0	10.4.0.0	Fa0/0	0
10.3.0.0	S0/0/0	1	10.1.0.0	S0/0/0	1	10.2.0.0	S0/0/1	1
10.4.0.0	S0/0/0	2	10.4.0.0	S0/0/1	1	10.1.0.0	S0/0/1	2

The RIP protocol is simple, is easy to implement, and comes free with most routers. These advantages make RIP a widely used and popular routing protocol.

However, RIP has several disadvantages:

- It allows a maximum of 15 hops, as shown in Figure 6-8, so it can be used only for networks that connect no more than 16 routers in series.

- It periodically sends complete copies of the entire routing table to directly connected neighbors. In a large network, a periodic update can cause a significant amount of network traffic.

- It converges slowly on larger networks when the network changes.

Figure 6-8   RIP Hop Count Limitation

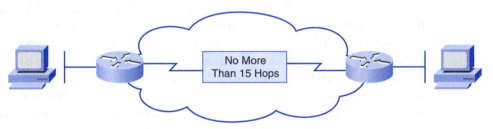

Currently, two versions of RIP are available—RIPv1 and RIPv2. RIPv2 has many advantages over RIPv1 and usually is used unless the equipment cannot support RIPv2. The most significant difference between RIP versions 1 and 2 is that RIPv2 can support classless routing, because it includes the subnet mask information in routing updates. RIPv1 does not send subnet mask information in the updates, so it must rely on the classful default subnet masks.

EIGRP

Enhanced Interior Gateway Routing Protocol (EIGRP) is a Cisco-proprietary enhanced distance vector routing protocol. EIGRP was developed to address some of the limitations of other distance vector routing protocols, such as RIP. These limitations include the use of the hop count metric and the maximum network size of 15 hops.

Instead of hop count, EIGRP uses a number of metrics, including a configured bandwidth value, and the delay encountered when a packet travels a particular route.

The key characteristics of EIGRP are as follows:

- It uses a variety of metrics to calculate the cost of a route.

- It combines the next-hop and metric features of distance vector protocols with additional database and update features.

- Its maximum hop count is 224 hops.

Unlike RIP, EIGRP does not rely on only the routing table in the router to hold all the information it needs to operate. EIGRP creates two additional database tables: the neighbor table and the topology table.

The neighbor table stores data about the neighboring routers that are on directly connected local networks. This neighbor table includes information such as the interface IP addresses, interface type, and bandwidth.

EIGRP builds the topology table from the advertisements of its neighbors. The topology table contains all the routes advertised by the neighbor routers. EIGRP depends on a routing algorithm called *Diffusing Update Algorithm (DUAL)* to calculate the shortest path to a destination within a network and to install this route into the routing table. The topology table enables a router running EIGRP to find the best alternative path quickly when a network change occurs. If no alternative route exists in the topology table, EIGRP queries its neighbors to find a new path to the destination.

Unlike RIP, which is limited to small, simple networks of less than 16 hops, EIGRP is ideal for larger, more complex networks up to 224 hops in size that require fast convergence. Figure 6-9 shows communications between EIGRP routers. After the initial exchange between neighbors, routing tables are sent only when a route metric changes. When all routers know of the change, they have converged.

Figure 6-9   EIGRP Routing Protocol Updates

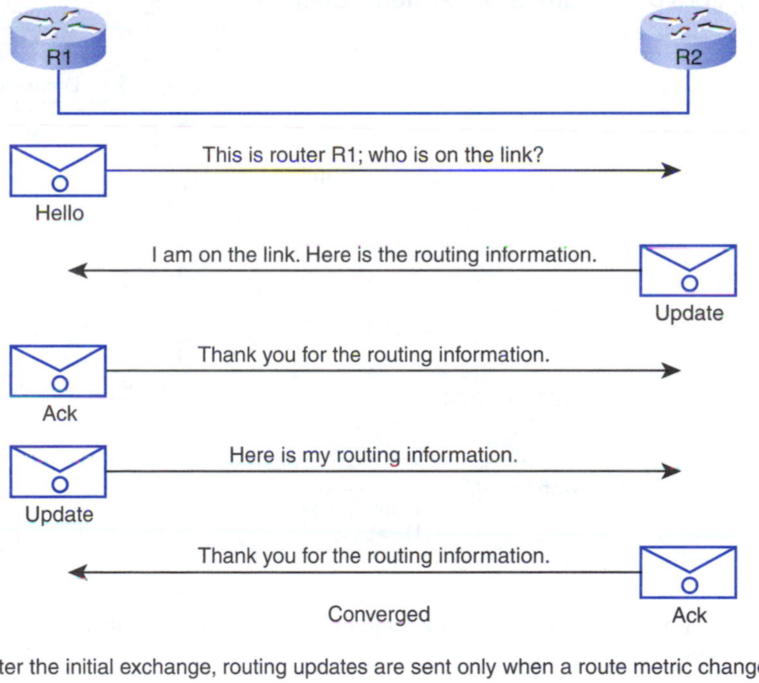

After the initial exchange, routing updates are sent only when a route metric changes.

The disadvantages of using EIGRP are that it requires more knowledgeable support staff and, because it is a Cisco-proprietary protocol, it is not supported by other router manufacturers. In addition, it requires more router resources, such as CPU and RAM, because of its sophisticated routing algorithm and maintenance of multiple tables.

Link-State Protocols: OSPF

Routers that use the distance vector routing algorithm have little information about distant networks and none about distant routers. Link-state routing protocols such as *Open Shortest Path First (OSPF)* use a link-state routing algorithm that maintains a full database of distant routers and how they interconnect. The other major link-state protocol in use is OSI Intermediate System-to-Intermediate System (IS-IS), which is much less common than OSPF.

Link-state routing uses the following features:

- **Routing table**: A list of the known paths and interfaces.

- *Link-state advertisement (LSA)*: A small packet of routing information that is sent between routers. LSAs describe the state of a router's interfaces (links), as well as other information, such as the IP address of each link.

- *Topological database*: A collection of information gathered from all the LSAs received by the router.

- *Shortest Path First (SPF) algorithm*: A calculation performed on the database that results in the SPF tree. The *SPF tree* is a map of the network as seen from the router's point of view. The information in this tree is used to build the routing table.

When LSAs are received from other routers, the SPF algorithm analyzes the information in the database to construct the SPF tree. Based on the SPF tree, the SPF algorithm then calculates the shortest paths to other networks. Each time a new LSA packet causes a change in the link-state database, SPF recalculates the best paths and updates the routing table. Link-state protocols pass updates when a link's state changes. As shown in Figure 6-10, when the link to network 172.16.3.0 goes down, R1 sends a link update to R2, which then forwards it to R3 and R4.

Figure 6-10   Link-State Protocol Updates

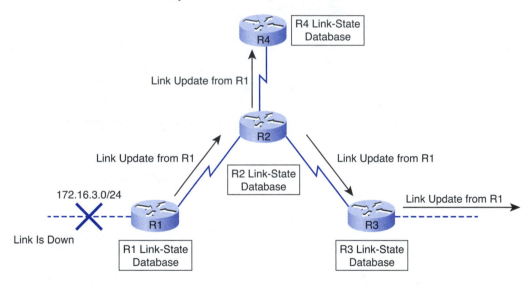

OSPF is a nonproprietary link-state routing protocol described in RFC 2328. The key characteristics of OSPF are as follows:

- It uses the SPF algorithm to calculate the lowest cost to a destination.

- It sends routing updates only when the topology changes. It does not send periodic updates of the entire routing table.

- It provides fast convergence.

- It supports VLSM and discontiguous subnets.

- It provides route authentication.

In OSPF-enabled networks, routers send link-state advertisements to each other when a change occurs, such as the following:

- A new neighbor is added

- A link fails

- A link is restored

If the network topology changes—for example, if a link goes down or a new router is added—the routers affected by the change send update LSAs to the rest of the network. All routers update their topology databases accordingly, regenerate their SPF trees to find new shortest paths to each network, and update their routing tables with the changed routes.

In Figure 6-11, OSPF router R1 sends LSAs to R2 and R3 to begin the convergence process as follows:

1. Each router receives the LSA.

2. The link-state databases are updated.

3. The SPF algorithm is performed.

4. The SPF tree is created.

5. The best routes are installed into the routing table.

Figure 6-11   OSPF Link-State Routing Protocol Operation

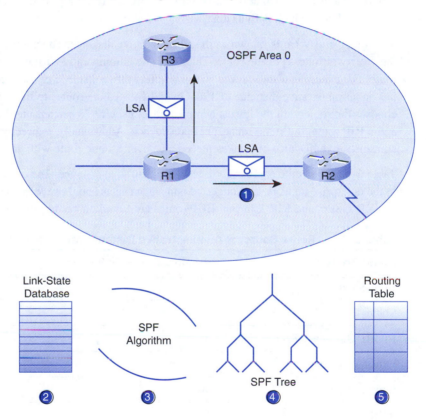

As with EIGRP, OSPF and link-state protocols in general require more knowledgeable support staff and more router resources, such as CPU and RAM, because of the sophisticated routing algorithm and maintenance of multiple tables.

Routing Within an Organization

Each routing protocol uses different metrics. The metric used by one routing protocol is not comparable to the metric used by another routing protocol. Two routing protocols might choose different paths to the same destination because they use different metrics. For example, RIP chooses the path with the fewest number of hops, whereas EIGRP chooses the path based on the highest bandwidth and least delay.

Metrics used in IP routing protocols include

- **Hop count:** The number of routers a packet must traverse
- **Bandwidth:** The bandwidth of a specific link.
- **Load:** The traffic utilization of a specific link.
- **Delay:** The time a packet takes to traverse a path.
- **Reliability:** The probability of a link failure, based on the interface error count or previous link failures.
- **Cost:** Determined by either the Cisco IOS application or the network administrator to indicate preference for a route. Cost can represent a metric, a combination of metrics, or a policy.

It is possible to have more than one routing protocol enabled on a single router. Additionally, a network administrator may choose to configure static routes to a specific destination. If a router has two different paths to a destination based on two different routing protocols and their metrics, how does the router know which path to use?

The router uses what is known as the administrative distance. The administrative distance represents the "trustworthiness" of the route. The lower the administrative distance, the more trustworthy the route. For example, a static route has an administrative distance of 1, whereas a RIP-discovered route has an administrative distance of 120. Given two separate routes to the same destination, the router chooses the route with the lowest administrative distance. When a router has the choice of a static route and a RIP route, the static route takes precedence. Additionally, a directly connected route with an administrative distance of 0 takes precedence over a static route with an administrative distance of 1.

Table 6-3 shows route sources sorted by administrative distance. The ones most commonly encountered in the enterprise network are connected and static routes and those learned via internal routing protocols EIGRP, OSPF, and RIP. External BGP routes are found on border routers and ISP routers.

Table 6-3   Route Sources, Administrative Distance, and Metrics

Route Source	Administrative Distance	Default Metric(s)
Connected	0	0
Static	1	0
EIGRP Summary Route	5	N/A
External BGP	20	Value assigned by Admin
Internal EIGRP	90	Bandwidth, Delay
IGRP	100	Bandwidth, Delay
OSPF	110	Link cost (bandwidth)
IS-IS	115	Link cost (bandwidth)
RIP	120	Hop count
External EIGRP	170	N/A
Internal BGP	200	Value assigned by Admin

Choosing one routing protocol over another can be difficult even for expert network designers. The following guidelines may help when designing a network.

Small networks with only one gateway to the Internet can probably use static routes (see Figure 6-12). Such a topology rarely needs dynamic routing. Small offices may not use routing at all. An Internet connection may be all the routing that takes place. For a small to medium-sized business, static routing may be used.

Figure 6-12   Small-Office Routing

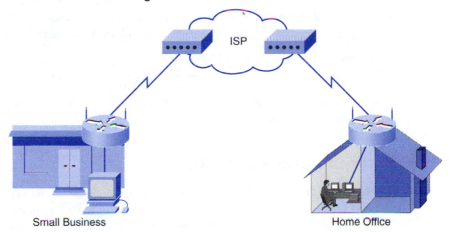

As an organization grows and adds routers to its network topology, RIPv2 and some static routing can be used. RIP is easy to configure, and it can work well in small networks. When the number of routers in a network begins to approach 15, RIP becomes a less desirable choice, because it takes longer to converge and has a maximum hop count of 15.

Large businesses may switch over to EIGRP or OSPF. Organizations with multivendor equipment use OSPF. EIGRP is a Cisco-proprietary protocol. Worldwide enterprises, such as the one shown in Figure 6-13, may have hundreds of routers. They might adopt a routing solution similar to the one used by ISPs.

Figure 6-13   Worldwide Enterprise Routing

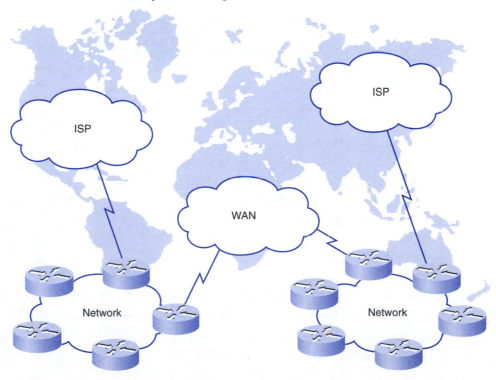

Although both EIGRP and OSPF are quite common for larger networks, no simple principle makes it obvious to choose one over the other. Each network has to be considered independently. Four main criteria can help you choose a protocol:

- **Ease of management**: What information does the protocol keep about itself? What **show** commands are available?

- **Ease of configuration**: How many commands will the average configuration require? Is it possible to configure several routers in your network with the same configuration?

- **Efficiency**: How much bandwidth does the routing protocol take up while in steady state? How much could it take up when converging in response to a major network event?

- **Knowledge level**: What network support staff and level of knowledge are available to maintain the network protocol?

Configure and Verify RIP

RIP is a popular distance vector protocol supported by most routers. It is an appropriate choice for small networks containing multiple routers. Before configuring RIP on a router, think about the networks a router serves, and the interfaces on the router that connect to these networks.

Figure 6-14 shows three routers. Each router serves a separate private local network, so there are three LANs. The routers are connected by separate networks as well, so a total of six networks are shown.

Figure 6-14   RIP Router Configuration

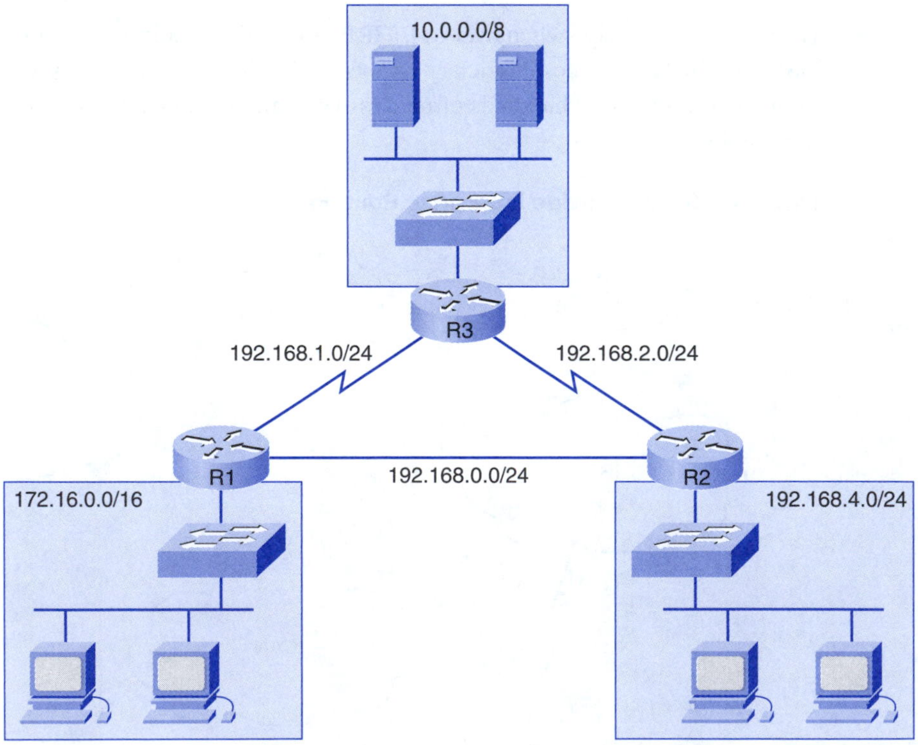

With a topology like this, be careful not to assume that R1 links directly to 10.0.0.0/8 and 172.16.0.0/16. R1 will be able to reach those networks after RIP routing is properly configured.

Before configuring RIP, assign an IP address and enable all the physical interfaces that will participate in routing. After this is done, configure RIP.

For the most basic RIP configuration, you must remember three commands:

- Router(config)#**router rip**

- Router (config-router)#**version 2**

- Router(config-router)#**network** [*network-number*]

Enter the **router rip** command in global configuration mode to enable RIP on the router. Enter the **network** command from router configuration mode to tell the router which networks will be part of the RIP routing process. The routing process associates specific interfaces with the network numbers and begins to send and receive RIP updates on these interfaces.

In Figure 6-14, R1 is connected to R3 using a serial link to R2 using a FastEthernet link. Example 6-3 shows how to configure R1. Begin by configuring the R1 serial interfaces and then the FastEthernet interfaces.

Example 6-3 Configuring Interfaces on R1

```
R1> enable
R1#configure terminal
R1(config)#interface serial 0/0/0
R1(config-if)#ip address 192.168.1.2 255.255.255.0
R1(config-if)#no shutdown
R1(config-if)#interface fastethernet 0/0
R1(config-if)#ip address 192.168.0.1 255.255.255.0
R1(config-if)#no shutdown
R1(config-if)#interface fastethernet 0/1
R1(config-if)#ip address 172.16.245.254 255.255.0.0
R1(config-if)#no shutdown
```

After the interfaces have been configured with the proper IP addresses and subnet masks, configure the RIP routing protocol, as shown in Example 6-4.

Example 6-4 Configuring RIP on R1

```
R1(config)#router rip
R1(config-router)#version 2
R1(config-router)#network 192.168.1.0
R1(config-router)#network 192.168.0.0
R1(config-router)#network 172.16.0.0
```

As soon as a configuration is done, it is a good idea to compare the running configuration with an accurate topology diagram to verify network numbers and interface IP addresses. This is a good practice, because sometimes it is easy to make a simple data entry error.

There are several ways to verify that RIP is functioning properly in the network, including the following:

- If the configuration is correct, you should be able to ping devices on remote networks. If a ping is successful, it is likely that routing is working.

- Run the IP routing verification commands **show ip protocols** and **show ip route** at the CLI command prompt:

  The **show ip protocols** command verifies that RIP routing is configured, that the correct interfaces are sending and receiving RIP updates, and that the router is advertising the correct networks. Example 6-5 shows the output from the **show ip protocols** command.

  The **show ip route** command shows the routing table, which verifies that routes received by RIP neighbors are installed in the routing table. Example 6-6 shows the output from the **show ip route** command.

- Use the **debug ip rip** command to observe the networks advertised in the routing updates as they are sent and received. **debug** commands display router activity in real time. Because debug activity uses router processor resources, **debug** should be used with care in a production network; it can affect network operation. Example 6-7 shows the output from the **debug ip rip** command.

Example 6-5 show ip protocols Command Output

```
R1#show ip protocols

Routing Protocol is "rip"
  Outgoing update filter list for all interfaces is not set
  Incoming update filter list for all interfaces is not set
  Sending updates every 30 seconds, next due in 27 seconds
  Invalid after 180 seconds, hold down 180, flushed after 240
  Redistributing: rip
  Default version control: send version 2, receive version 2
    Interface           Send  Recv  Triggered RIP  Key-chain
    FastEthernet0/0       2     2
    FastEthernet0/1       2     2
    Serial0/0/0           2     2
  Automatic network summarization is in effect
  Maximum path: 4
  Routing for Networks:
    172.16.0.0
    192.168.0.0
    192.168.1.0
  Routing Information Sources:
    Gateway         Distance      Last Update
  Distance: (default is 120)
```

Example 6-6 show ip route Command Output

```
R1#show ip route

Codes: C - connected, S - static, R - RIP, M - mobile, B - BGP
       D - EIGRP, EX - EIGRP external, O - OSPF, IA - OSPF inter area
       N1 - OSPF NSSA external type 1, N2 - OSPF NSSA external type 2
       E1 - OSPF external type 1, E2 - OSPF external type 2
       i - IS-IS, su - IS-IS summary, L1 - IS-IS level-1, L2 - IS-IS level-2
       ia - IS-IS inter area, * - candidate default, U - per-user static route
       o - ODR, P - periodic downloaded static route

Gateway of last resort is not set
```

```
R       10.0.0.0/8 [120/1] via 192.168.1.1, 00:00:17, Serial0/0/0
C     172.16.0.0/16 is directly connected, FastEthernet0/1
C     192.168.0.0/24 is directly connected, FastEthernet0/0
C     192.168.1.0/24 is directly connected, Serial0/0/0
R       192.168.2.0/16 [120/1] via 192.168.0.2, 00:00:20, FastEthernet0/0
R       192.168.4.0/24 [120/1] via 192.168.0.2, 00:00:23, FastEthernet0/0
```

Example 6-7 debug ip rip Command Output

```
R1#debug ip rip

RIP protocol debugging is on
R1#
00:13:31.819: RIP: sending v2 update to 224.0.0.9 via FastEthernet0/1 (172.16.245.254)
00:13:31.819: RIP: build update entries
00:13:31.819:    192.168.0.0/24 via 0.0.0.0, metric 1, tag 0
00:13:41.407: RIP: sending v2 update to 224.0.0.9 via FastEthernet0/0 (192.168.0.1)
```

Configuring and Verifying RIP (6.1.5)

In this Packet Tracer activity, you configure and verify RIP. Use file d2-615.pka on the CD-ROM that accompanies this book to perform this activity using Packet Tracer.

Lab 6-2: Configuring and Verifying RIP (6.1.5)

In this lab you configure and verify RIP. Refer to the lab in Part II of this book. You may perform this lab now or wait until the end of the chapter.

Exterior Routing Protocols

Interior routing protocols direct packets between routers that are within an organization and under the control of that organization. Exterior routing protocols control packet routing between organizations and ISPs on the Internet. This section describes autonomous systems and BGP, the primary exterior routing protocol used between ISPs and major networks on the Internet.

Autonomous Systems

Internet routing architecture has evolved over the years into a distributed system of interconnected networks. The Internet is now so vast and involves so many networks that it would be impossible for a single organization to manage all the routing information needed to reach every destination around the world.

Instead, the Internet is divided into collections of networks called *autonomous systems (AS)* that are independently controlled by different organizations and companies. An AS is a set of networks controlled by a single administrative authority using the same internal routing policy throughout. Each AS is identified by a unique *AS number (ASN)*. ASNs are controlled and registered on the Internet. Figure 6-15 shows a group of routers under one AS number.

Figure 6-15   Autonomous System: Networks Under a Single Administration

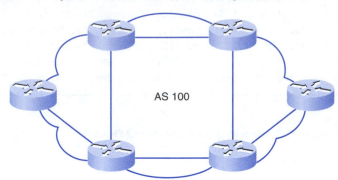

The most common example of an AS is the ISP. Most businesses connect to the Internet through an ISP and therefore become part of the routing domain of that ISP. The AS is administered by the ISP. Therefore, not only does it include its own network routes, but it also manages the routes to all the business and other customer networks that are connected to it.

The same ASN applies to all network devices within the AS routing domain. In Figure 6-16, ISP A is an AS whose routing domain includes a local business that directly connects to that ISP for Internet access. That business does not have a separate ASN. Instead, it uses the AS number of ISP A (ASN 100) in its routing information.

Figure 6-16   Interconnected Autonomous Systems

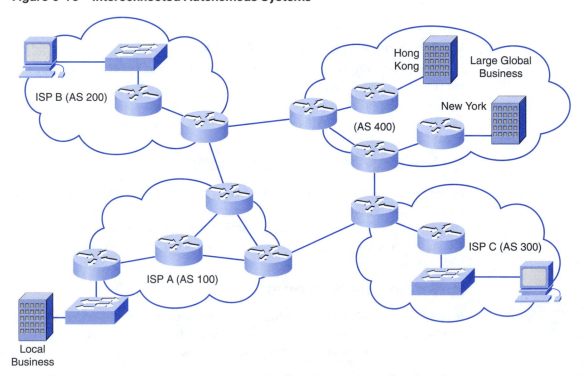

Also shown is a large global business with corporate offices located in Hong Kong and New York. Because they are located in different countries, each office connects to a different local ISP for Internet access. This means that the business is connected to two ISPs.

Because the company communicates through both ISP B and ISP C, this causes routing confusion in terms of connectivity. Traffic from the Internet does not know which AS to use to reach the large global business. To solve the problem, the business registers as an AS in its own right and is assigned an ASN of 400.

Interactive Activity 6-2: Autonomous Systems (6.2.1)

In this interactive activity, you identify which networks require shared or private AS numbers. Use file d2ia-621 on the CD-ROM that accompanies this book to perform this interactive activity.

Routing Between Autonomous Systems

Interior gateway protocols (IGP) are used to exchange routing information within an autonomous system or individual organization. The purpose of an interior routing protocol is to find the best path through the internal network. IGPs run on the interior routers—that is, the routers inside an organization. Examples of interior gateway protocols are RIP, EIGRP, and OSPF.

By contrast, *exterior gateway protocols (EGP)* are designed to exchange routing information between different autonomous systems. Because each AS is managed by a different administration and may use different interior protocols, networks must use a protocol that can communicate between diverse systems. The EGP serves as a translator for ensuring that external routing information is successfully interpreted in each AS network.

EGP protocols run on the exterior routers—that is, the routers that are located at the border of an AS. Exterior routers are also called *border gateways*. Figure 6-17 shows three border gateway routers interconnecting three different autonomous systems using the BGP exterior gateway routing protocol.

Unlike interior routers, which exchange individual routes with each other using IGPs, exterior routers exchange information about how to reach various networks using exterior protocols. Exterior routing protocols seek the best path through the Internet as a sequence of autonomous systems.

The most common exterior routing protocol on the Internet today is *Border Gateway Protocol (BGP)*. BGP functions like a distance vector protocol. It builds a database of networks and autonomous systems. From this database, direction and distance to a destination network are determined. It is estimated that 95 percent of autonomous systems use BGP. The most current version of BGP is version 4 (BGP-4), for which the latest description is provided in RFC 4271.

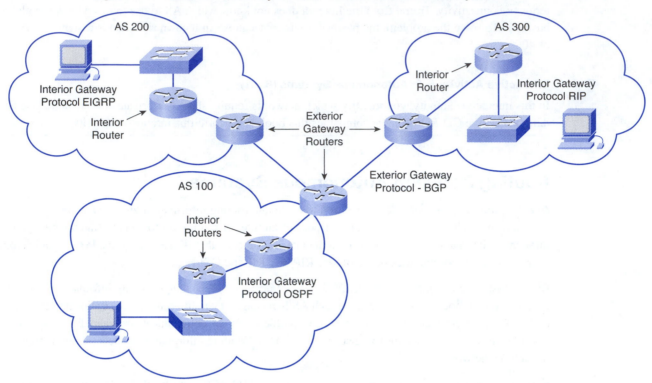

Figure 6-17   Exterior Gateway Routers Connect Autonomous Systems

Routing Across the Internet

Each AS is responsible for informing other autonomous systems about which networks they can reach through that AS. Autonomous systems exchange this *reachability* information with each other through exterior routing protocols that run on dedicated routers, called border gateways.

Packets are routed across the Internet in several steps. Refer to Figure 6-18 and follow the steps listed here to learn how a packet moves through the Internet between autonomous systems:

1. The source host in AS 200 sends a packet destined for 192.168.32.1, a remote host located in another AS.

2. Because the packet's destination IP address is not a local network, the interior routers keep passing the packet along their default routes, until eventually it arrives at an exterior router at the edge of the local AS.

3. The exterior border router maintains a database for all the autonomous systems with which it connects. This reachability database tells the router the following:

   - The 192.168.32.0 network is located within AS 400.

   - The path to the destination network passes through several autonomous systems.

   - The next hop on the path is through a directly connected exterior router on a neighboring AS.

4. The exterior router directs the packet to its next hop on the path, which is the exterior router at the neighboring AS 400.

5. The packet arrives at the neighboring AS, where the exterior router checks its own reachability database and forwards the packet to the next AS on the path.

6. The process is repeated at each AS until the exterior router at the destination AS recognizes the packet's destination IP address as an internal network in that AS.

7. The final exterior router directs the packet to the next-hop interior router listed in its routing table. From then on, the packet is treated just like any local packet. It is directed through interior routing protocols using a series of internal next hops until it arrives at the destination host, 192.168.32.1.

Figure 6-18   Packets Routed Across the Internet from Source Host to Destination Host

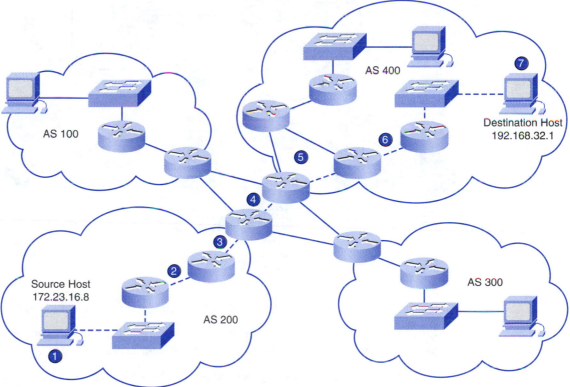

Exterior Routing Protocols and the ISP

Exterior gateway protocols provide many useful features for ISPs. Not only do exterior protocols allow traffic to be routed across the Internet to remote destinations, but they also provide the method by which ISPs can set and enforce policies and local preferences so that the traffic flow through the ISP is efficient and that none of the internal routes are overloaded with transit traffic.

Business customers insist on reliability for their Internet service, so ISPs must make sure that the Internet connection for those customers is always available. They do this by providing backup routes and routers in case the regular route fails. During normal conditions, the ISP advertises the regular route to other autonomous systems. If that regular route fails, the ISP sends an exterior protocol update message to advertise the backup route instead.

Figure 6-19 shows several business customers connected to an ISP. These business customers use various IGPs internally and typically use static default routes to the ISP, but they may communicate with the ISP using BGP. The ISP can use various IGPs, such as OSPF, internally.

Figure 6-19   ISP Provides Multiple Backup Routes

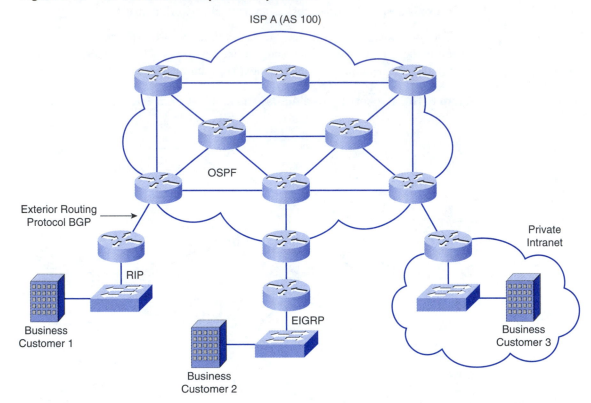

The flow of messages in the Internet is called *traffic*. Internet traffic can be categorized in one of two ways:

- **Local traffic**: Traffic carried within an AS that either originated in that same AS or is intended to be delivered within that AS. This is like local traffic on a street.

- *Transit traffic*: Traffic that was generated outside that AS and that can travel through the internal AS network en route to being delivered to destinations outside the AS. This is like through traffic on a street.

The flow of traffic between autonomous systems is carefully controlled. It is important to be able to limit or even prohibit certain types of messages from going to or from an AS, for security reasons or to prevent overloading.

Many autonomous systems are unwilling to carry transit traffic. Transit traffic can cause routers to overload and fail, if those routers do not have the capacity to handle large amounts of traffic. Figure 6-20 shows an example in which traffic from AS 100 is allowed to transit through AS 300 but not AS 200.

Figure 6-20   Transit Traffic

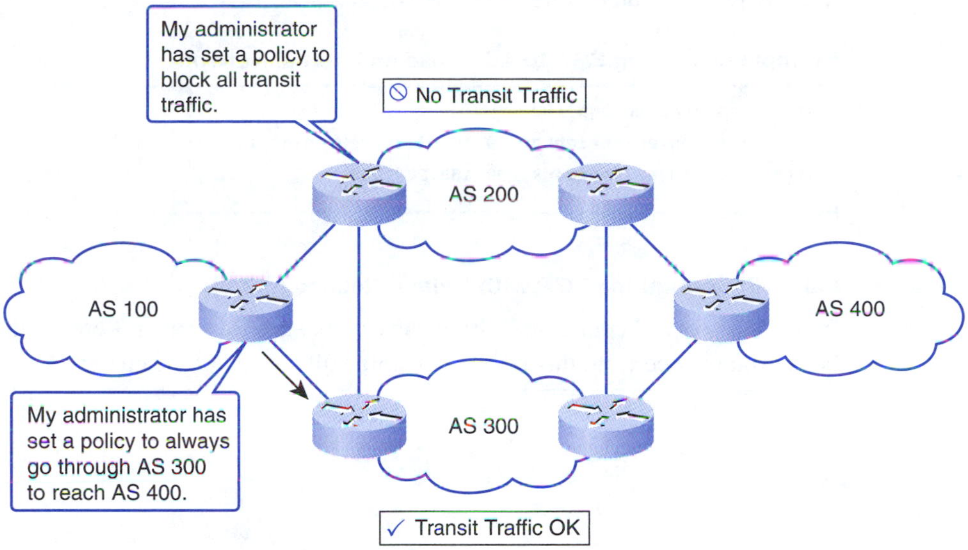

My administrator
has set a policy to
block all transit
traffic.

⊘ No Transit Traffic

AS 200

AS 100

AS 400

My administrator has
set a policy to always
go through AS 300
to reach AS 400.

AS 300

✓ Transit Traffic OK

Configure and Verify BGP

When an ISP puts a border router at a customer location, it usually configures the router with a default static route to the ISP. Sometimes, though, an ISP may want the router to be included in its AS and to participate in BGP. In these cases, it is necessary to configure the customer premises router with the commands necessary to enable BGP.

The first step in enabling BGP on a router is to configure the AS number using the command **router bgp** [*AS number*].

The next step is to identify the ISP router that is the BGP neighbor with which the customer premises equipment (CPE) router exchanges information. The command to identify the neighbor router is **neighbor** [*IP address*] **remote-as** [*AS number*].

When an ISP customer has its own registered IP address block, it may want the routes to some of its internal networks to be known on the Internet. To use BGP to advertise an internal route, a network command is needed. The format of the **network** command is **network** [*network address*].

As soon as all the CPE is installed and the routing protocols are configured, the customer has both local and Internet connectivity. Now the customer can fully participate in other services the ISP may offer.

The IP addresses used for BGP normally are registered, routable addresses that identify unique organizations. In very large organizations, private addresses may be used in the BGP process. On the Internet, BGP should never be used to advertise a private network address. Figure 6-21 shows a business customer using BGP to advertise an internal network to the ISP.

Figure 6-21   Configuring BGP

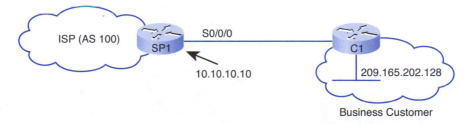

ISP (AS 100)

SP1   S0/0/0

10.10.10.10

C1   209.165.202.128

Business Customer

Example 6-8 configures BGP on a router to communicate with the neighboring ISP router in AS 100 while advertising internal network 209.165.202.128.

Example 6-8 Using BGP to Advertise an Internal Network

```
R1(config)#router bgp 100
R1(config-router)#neighbor 10.10.10.10 remote-as 100
R1(config-router)#network 209.165.202.128
```

Lab 6-3: Configuring BGP with Default Routing (6.2.4)

In this lab you will configure BGP on the external gateway router. Refer to the lab in Part II of this book. You may perform this lab now or wait until the end of the chapter.

Summary

Routing is used to forward messages to the correct destination and can be dynamic or static.

Dynamic routing requires the use of routing protocols to exchange route information between routers. Examples of dynamic routing include distance vector routing protocols and link-state routing protocols.

Distance vector routing protocols calculate the direction and distance to any network. Routing tables and updates are sent to neighbors periodically. Link-state protocols update nodes with information on the state of the link. These routing protocols reduce routing loops and network traffic.

Choose the routing protocol for an organization based on ease of management, ease of configuration, and efficiency.

The Internet is divided into collections of networks called autonomous systems. Within an autonomous system, interior gateway routing protocols are used, such as RIP, EIGRP, and OSPF.

Between autonomous systems, exterior gateway routing functions are required. Exterior Gateway Protocols (EGP) run on exterior routers, or border gateways, that are located at the border of an AS. The most common EGP is Border Gateway Protocol (BGP), which functions like a distance vector protocol.

Exterior protocols enable traffic to be routed across the Internet to remote destinations. They provide the method by which ISPs can set and enforce policies and local preferences for traffic flow efficiency.

Activities and Labs

This summary outlines the activities you can perform to help reinforce important concepts described in this chapter. You can find the activity and Packet Tracer files on the CD-ROM accompanying this book.

Interactive Activities on the CD-ROM:

Interactive Activity 6-1: Selecting the Shortest Path Through the Network (6.1.2)

Interactive Activity 6-2: Autonomous Systems (6.2.1)

Packet Tracer
□ Activity

Packet Tracer Activities on the CD-ROM:

Configuring Static Routes (6.1.1)

Configuring and Verifying RIP (6.1.5)

Labs in Part II of this book:

Lab 6-1: Creating a Network Diagram from Routing Tables (6.1.2)

Lab 6-2: Configuring and Verifying RIP (6.1.4)

Lab 6-3: Configuring BGP with Default Routing (6.2.4)

Check Your Understanding

Complete the review questions to check your understanding of the topics and concepts in this chapter. Answers are listed in Appendix A, "Check Your Understanding and Challenge Questions Answer Key."

1. Which two of the following are characteristics of interior routers?

    A. They use BGP routing protocols.

    B. They use IGP routing protocols.

    C. They are known as border gateways.

    D. They exchange local routes.

    E. They route between autonomous systems.

2. What two methods are used to allow remote networks to be added to a routing table?

    A. Entered by an administrator

    B. Learned through a routing protocol

    C. Exported from the MAC address table

    D. Imported from flash memory on the router

    E. Learned through address translation

    F. Learned by NICs broadcasting their network number

3. Where does the router get information about the best path on which to send a packet destined for a host located on a remote network?

    A. From the IOS stored in flash memory

    B. From the routing table stored in RAM

    C. From the configuration file stored in RAM

    D. From the IP packet being transmitted

4. Which two of the following statements are true about transit traffic?

    A. All ISPs must allow transit traffic.

    B. Transit traffic can overload an Internet router.

    C. Transit traffic is destined for a network contained in the same AS.

    D. ISPs cannot allow transit traffic from one AS to another.

    E. Transit traffic travels through an AS to reach a remote AS.

5. A customer router is configured to use BGP to exchange routes with a directly connected neighbor router. What is identified by the remote AS number in the command **neighbor 209.165.201.1 remote-as 200**?

6. Match the term on the left to its definition on the right.

    AS   An example is BGP

    ASN   A provider of Internet access

    ISP   A registered number that identifies a particular set of networks

    IGP   A group of networks administered by a single entity

    EGP   Examples include RIP, EIGRP, and OSPF

7. A new network is to be configured on a router. Which of the following tasks must be completed to configure this interface and implement dynamic IP routing for the new network? (Choose three.)

A. Select the routing protocol to be configured.

B. Assign an IP address and subnet mask to the interface.

C. Update the **ip host** configuration information with the device name and new interface IP address.

D. Configure the routing protocol with the new network IP address.

E. Configure the routing protocol with the new interface IP address and subnet mask.

F. Configure the routing protocol in use on all other enterprise routers with the new network information.

8. What is the purpose of the **network** command, used to configure the RIP routing protocol?

A. It specifies RIPv2 as the routing protocol.

B. It enables the use of VLSM.

C. It specifies the fastest path to the destination route.

D. It specifies which interfaces will exchange RIP routing updates.

E. It activates RIP for all routes that exist within the enterprise network.

9. To ensure proper routing in a network, the network administrator should always check the router configuration to verify that appropriate routes are available. The commands on the left allow the network administrator to view the router configuration for the information needed. Match each command to its result on the right.

debug ip rip	Verifies that routes received are installed in the routing table.
show ip protocols	Displays current configuration information for configured routing protocols and interfaces.
show running-config	Verifies the routing protocol process running and that the correct networks are advertised.
show ip route	Checks to see that the interfaces are up and operational.
show interfaces	Displays the networks advertised in the updates as the updates are sent and received.

10. Which IOS command displays the routes a router has learned via a dynamic routing protocol?

11. Which of the following static route commands use the correct syntax? (Choose three.)

A. **ip route 192.168.1.0 255.255.255.0 S0/0/0**

B. **ip route 192.168.3.0 S0/0/0 255.255.255.0**

C. **ip route 172.18.0.0 255.255.0.0 Fa0/0**

D. **ip route 172.18.0.0 255.255.0.0 192.168.8.2**

E. **ip route 192.168.3.0 192.168.2.1 255.255.255.0**

12. A network engineer is configuring a new router. The interfaces have been configured with IP addresses, but no routing protocols or static routes have been configured yet. What routes are present in the routing table?

A. Default routes

B. Broadcast routes

C. Direct connections

D. No routes; the routing table is empty.

13. Which of the following tasks are completed by routing protocols? (Choose three.)

A. Learning the available routes to all destinations

B. Providing an addressing scheme for identifying networks

C. Informing LAN hosts of new default gateway addresses

D. Placing the best route in the routing table

E. Removing routes from the routing table when they are no longer valid

F. Carrying user data to the destination network

14. What is the router called that is used in the Internet to route traffic between autonomous systems?

15. What is an example of a routing protocol used to exchange information between autonomous systems?

16. When a dynamic routing protocol is being used and a network topology change takes place, the routers must pass the information among themselves so that their routing tables reflect the changes in the network. What is it called when the routing tables in all routers reflect the changes in the network?

17. When the EIGRP interior routing protocol is implemented, what two metrics are used by default?

A. Delay

B. Interface type

C. Bandwidth

D. Hop count

E. Cost

18. Which command is used to show real-time exchanges of RIP routing advertisements?

19. A network administrator configures a static route on a router that specifies a next-hop IP address that uses FastEthernet 0/0 as the exit interface. Given the following output from the **show ip interface brief** command, will this route appear in the routing table?

```
R1#show ip interface brief

Interface        IP-Address      OK? Method   Status    Protocol
FastEthernet0/0  192.168.0.1     YES manual   up        down
FastEthernet0/1  172.16.8.1      YES manual   up        up
Serial0/0/0      192.168.1.2     YES manual   up        down
Serial0/0/0      192.168.0.2     YES manual   up        up
```

Objectives

After completing this chapter, you should be able to answer the following questions:

- What types of network services does an ISP provide?

- What protocols support the services offered by an ISP, and how do they work?

- How does UDP differ from TCP?

- What type of traffic uses UDP, and what type uses TCP?

- What are some of the more common application layer protocols, and what is their purpose?

- What is the purpose of the Domain Name System (DNS), and how does it function?

- How do common protocols such as HTTP, HTTPS, FTP, SMTP, IMAP, and POP3 function?

Key Terms

This chapter uses the following key terms. You can find the definitions in the glossary.

reliability   page 207

mean time between failure (MTBF)   page 207

mean time to repair (MTTR)   page 207

availability   page 208

redundancy   page 208

converged IP network   page 208

Transmission Control Protocol (TCP)   page 212

User Datagram Protocol (UDP)   page 212

encapsulation   page 213

three-way handshake   page 213

acknowledgment   page 214

sequencing   page 214

flow control   page 214

port   page 215

socket   page 217

resource record   page 220

zone database   page 220

domain namespace   page 220

resolver   page 220

fully qualified domain name (FQDN)   page 221

forward lookup zone   page 224

reverse lookup zone   page 224

primary DNS zone   page 225

secondary DNS zone   page 225

Hypertext Transfer Protocol (HTTP)   page 227

Secure HTTP (HTTPS)   page 227

uniform resource locator (URL)   page 227

proxy server   page 228

File Transfer Protocol (FTP)   page 229

protocol interpreter (PI)   page 229

data transfer process (DTP)   page 229

Simple Mail Transfer Protocol (SMTP)   page 231

Post Office Protocol version 3 (POP3)   page 233

Internet Message Access Protocol (IMAP4)   page 234

An ISP offers its customers many different services. Often ISP help desk technicians and network support technicians must help customers resolve issues with these services. To do this, technicians must understand the underlying protocols and functions of the services that the ISP provides.

Part II of this book includes the corresponding labs for this chapter.

Introducing ISP Services

As soon as the connection is made to the ISP, the business or customer must decide which services it requires from the ISP and which services it will provide in-house. ISPs serve several different markets. Individuals in homes make up the consumer market. Large multinational companies make up the enterprise market. In between are smaller markets, such as small-to-medium-sized businesses, or larger nonprofit organizations. Each of these customers has different service requirements, and most ISPs try to cater to all these markets.

ISP Services

Escalating customer expectations and increasingly competitive markets are forcing service providers to offer new services at competitive prices. These services enable ISPs to increase revenue and differentiate themselves from their competitors.

E-mail, web hosting, media streaming, IP telephony, and file transfer are key services that ISPs can provide to all customers. These services are important for the ISP consumer market and for the small-to-medium-sized business that does not have the expertise to maintain its own services.

Many organizations, both large and small, find it expensive to keep up with new technologies, or they simply prefer to devote resources to other parts of the business. ISPs offer managed services that enable these organizations to have access to the leading network technologies and applications without having to make large investments in equipment and support. When a company subscribes to a managed service, the service provider manages the network equipment and applications according to the terms of a service-level agreement (SLA). Some managed services are also hosted, meaning that the service provider hosts the applications in its facility instead of at the customer site.

Every individual, company, or organization requires different levels of service and support from the ISP. Figure 7-1 illustrates three possible relationships that could exist between an ISP and an end user.

In scenario 1, the customer owns and manages all its own network equipment and services. These customers require only a reliable Internet connection from the ISP. This type of arrangement is common in larger companies with dedicated support teams and highly skilled individuals.

Most home and small-business users purchase a connection service from an ISP that includes a device installed at the customer site. The ISP owns and manages this equipment and is responsible for setting up, maintaining, and administering the equipment for the customer. The customer is responsible for monitoring the status of the network and the applications and receives regular reports on the network's performance. This arrangement is shown in scenario 2.

Some customers have their network equipment located at the ISP facilities, as shown in scenario 3. The customer owns the network equipment, but the applications that the business relies on are hosted by the ISP. In this scenario, the actual servers that run the applications are located at the ISP facility. These servers may be owned by the customer or the ISP, although the ISP maintains both the servers and the applications. Servers normally are kept in server farms in the ISP network operations center (NOC) and are connected to the ISP's network with a high-speed switch. This provides the customer with a level of service and reliability that could be cost-prohibitive if the customer had to host its own applications.

Figure 7-1   ISP Customer Relationships

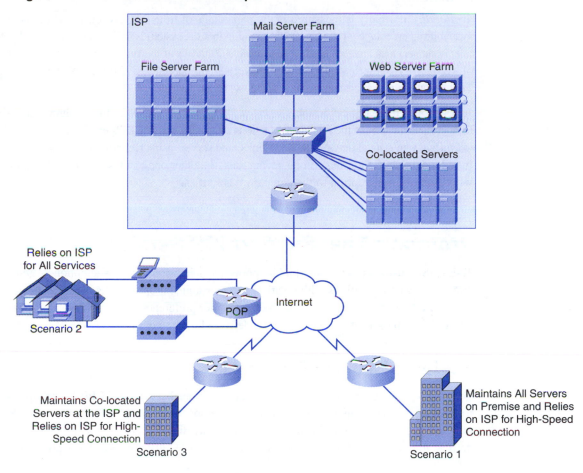

Reliability and Availability

Creating new services can be challenging. Not only must ISPs have a strong understanding of what their end customers want, but they also must have the ability and resources to provide them. As business and Internet applications become more complex, an increasing number of ISP customers rely on the services provided or managed by the ISP.

ISPs provide services to customers for a fee and guarantee a level of service in the SLA. To meet this expectation, ISPs' service offerings have to be reliable and available.

Reliability

Reliability can be thought of in terms of two measures: *mean time between failure (MTBF)* and *mean time to repair (MTTR)*. Equipment manufacturers specify MTBF from tests they perform as part of manufacturing. The measure of equipment robustness is fault tolerance: the longer the MTBF, the greater the fault tolerance. The mean time to repair is established by warranty or service agreements.

When an equipment failure occurs and the network or service becomes unavailable, it impacts the ability of the ISP to meet the terms of the SLA. To prevent this, an ISP may purchase expensive service agreements for critical hardware to ensure rapid manufacturer or vendor response. An ISP may also choose to purchase redundant hardware and keep spare parts onsite.

Availability

Availability normally is measured in the percentage of time that a resource is accessible. A perfect availability percentage would be 100%, meaning that the system is never down or unreachable. Traditionally, telephone services are expected to be available 99.999% of the time. This is called the "five 9s" standard of availability. With this standard, only a very small percentage, 0.001%, of downtime is acceptable. This equates to less than six minutes of downtime in a year.

As ISPs offer more critical business services, such as IP telephony, or high-volume retail sale transactions, ISP services must meet the higher expectations of their customers. ISPs ensure accessibility by incorporating *redundancy* in critical network devices, links, and servers using technologies designed for high availability. In redundant configurations, if one device fails, the other one can take over the functions automatically with little or no disruption to the company's activities.

Protocols That Support ISP Services

Today, ISP customers are using mobile phones as televisions, PCs as telephones, and televisions as interactive gaming stations with a variety of entertainment options. As network services become more advanced, ISPs must accommodate these customer preferences. The development of *converged IP networks* enables all these services to be delivered over a common network.

Review of TCP/IP Protocols

To provide support for the many end-user applications that rely on TCP/IP for delivery, it is important for ISP support personnel to be familiar with the operation of all TCP/IP protocols. ISP servers need to be able to support multiple applications for many different customers, as shown in Figure 7-2. To do this, they must use functions provided by the two TCP/IP transport layer protocols, TCP and UDP.

Figure 7-2   Hosts Accessing Multiple Services

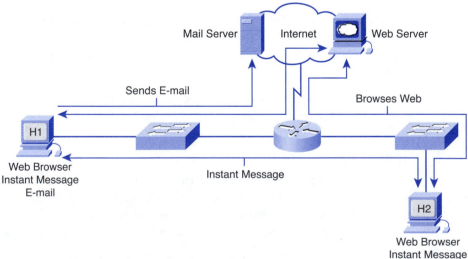

Common hosted applications, such as web serving and e-mail, also depend on underlying TCP/IP protocols to ensure reliability. In addition, all the IP services rely on domain name servers, usually hosted by the ISPs, to provide the link between the IP addressing structure and the URLs that customers use to access these services.

Clients and servers use specific IP protocols and standards in the process of exchanging information. The TCP/IP protocols can be represented using a four-layer model. Some of the TCP/IP protocols and the layer with which they are associated are shown in Figure 7-3. Table 7-1 describes the purpose of each protocol. Many of the key services provided to ISP customers depend on protocols that reside at the application and transport layers of the TCP/IP model.

Figure 7-3   TCP/IP Protocols

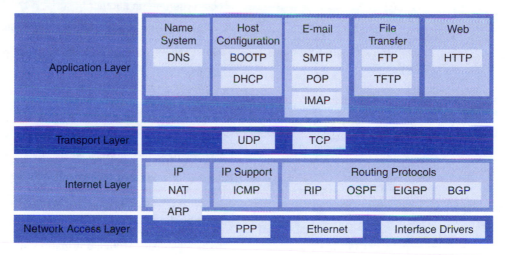

Table 7-1   Common TCP/IP Protocols

Protocol	Description
Domain Name System (or Service)	Translates domain names, such as cisco.com, into IP addresses.
Bootstrap Protocol	Enables a diskless workstation to discover its own IP address, the IP address of a BOOTP server on the network, and a file to be loaded into memory to boot the machine.
	BOOTP is being replaced by DHCP.
Dynamic Host Configuration Protocol (DHCP)	Dynamically assigns IP addresses to client stations at startup. Allows the addresses to be reused when no longer needed.
Simple Mail Transfer Protocol (SMTP)	Enables clients to send e-mail to a mail server. Enables servers to send e-mail to other servers.
Post Office Protocol version 3 (POP3)	Enables clients to retrieve e-mail from a mail server. Downloads e-mail from the mail server to the desktop.
Internet Message Access Protocol (IMAP)	Enables clients to access e-mail stored on a mail server. Maintains e-mail on the server.
File Transfer Protocol (FTP)	Sets rules that enable a user on one host to access and transfer files to and from another host over a network.
	Is a reliable, connection-oriented, acknowledged file delivery protocol.
Trivial File Transfer Protocol (TFTP)	Is a simple, connectionless file transfer protocol. Is a best-effort, unacknowledged file delivery protocol.
	Uses less overhead than FTP.

continues

Table 7-1   Common TCP/IP Protocols   continued

Protocol	Description
Hypertext Transfer Protocol (HTTP)	Is a set of rules for exchanging text, graphic images, sound, video, and other multimedia files on the World Wide Web.
User Datagram Protocol (UDP)	Enables a process running on one host to send packets to a process running on another host. Does not confirm successful datagram transmission.
Transmission Control Protocol (TCP)	Enables reliable communication between processes running on separate hosts. Provides reliable, acknowledged transmissions that confirm successful delivery.
Internet Protocol (IP)	Receives message segments from the transport layer. Packages messages into packets. Addresses packets for end-to-end delivery over an internetwork.
Network Address Translation (NAT)	Translates IP addresses from a private network into globally unique public IP addresses.
Internet Control Message Protocol (ICMP)	Provides feedback from a destination host to a source host about errors in packet delivery or a successful connection.
Routing protocols	Enables exchange of routing information between routers. Determines route selection for packet-forwarding decisions.
Address Resolution Protocol (ARP)	Provides dynamic address mapping between an IP address and a hardware address.
Point-to-Point Protocol (PPP)	Provides a means of encapsulating packets for transmission over a serial link.
Ethernet	Defines the rules for wiring and signaling standards of the network access layer.
Interface driver	Provides instruction to a machine for the control of a specific interface on a network device.

User applications such as e-mail programs and web browsers communicate with application layer protocols. These application layer protocols in turn rely on transport layer protocols to deliver the message.

Application Layer Protocols

Application layer protocols specify the format and control information necessary for many of the common Internet communication functions. Here are some of the more common TCP/IP application layer protocols:

- DNS protocol is used to resolve Internet names to IP addresses.
- HTTP is used to transfer files that make up the web pages of the World Wide Web.
- SMTP is used for the transfer of mail messages and attachments.
- Telnet, a terminal emulation protocol, is used to provide remote access to servers and networking devices.
- FTP is used for interactive file transfer between systems.

Transport Layer Protocols

Different types of data can have unique requirements. For some applications, communication segments must arrive in a very specific sequence to be processed successfully. In other cases, all the data must be received for any of it to be of use. Sometimes an application can tolerate the loss of a small amount of data during transmission over the network.

In today's converged networks, applications with very different transport needs may be communicating on the same network. Different transport layer protocols have different rules to enable devices to handle these diverse data requirements.

The lower layers of the TCP/IP model are unaware that multiple applications are sending data on the network. Their responsibility is to get the data to the device. It is the job of the transport layer to deliver the data to the appropriate application. The two primary transport layer protocols are TCP and UDP.

The TCP/IP model is very similar to the OSI model. The TCP/IP model is based on actual protocols and standards developed, whereas the OSI model is a theoretical guide for how protocols interact.

Similarities between the TCP/IP model and OSI model include the following:

- Both use layers to visualize the interaction of protocols and services.

- The transport and network layers are comparable.

- The networking field uses both models when referring to protocol interaction.

Differences between the TCP/IP model and OSI model include the following:

- The OSI model breaks the function of the TCP/IP application layer into separate, distinct layers. The upper three layers of the OSI model specify the same functionality as the application layer of the TCP/IP model.

- The TCP/IP protocol suite does not specify protocols for the physical network interconnection. The two lower layers of the OSI model are concerned with access to the physical network and the delivery of bits between hosts on a local network.

Figure 7-4 shows the relationship between the OSI and TCP/IP models.

Figure 7-4   TCP/IP and OSI Models

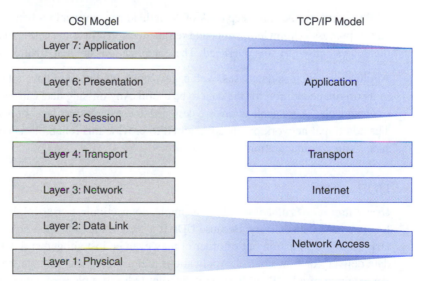

TCP and UDP

Different applications have different transport needs. The two TCP/IP protocols at the transport layer are TCP and UDP, as shown in Figure 7-5. These protocols accept information from the application layer and control transport across the network. Both of these offer distinct advantages to different types of network traffic.

Figure 7-5   TCP and UDP at the Transport Layer

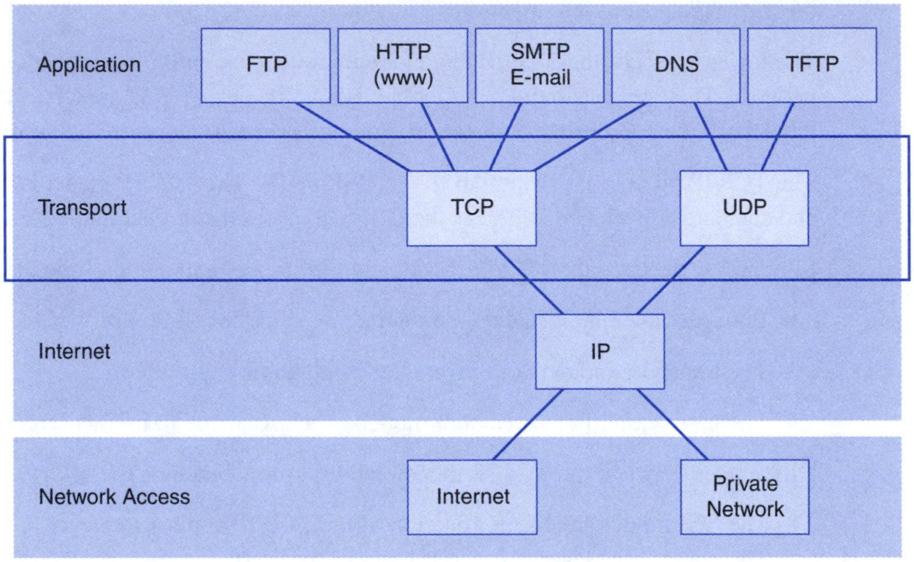

TCP

Transmission Control Protocol (TCP) is a reliable, guaranteed-delivery protocol. TCP specifies the methods hosts use to acknowledge the receipt of packets and requires the source host to resend packets that are not acknowledged. TCP protocols also govern the exchange of messages between the source and destination hosts to create a communication session. TCP is often compared to a pipeline, or a persistent connection, between hosts. Because of this, TCP is called a *connection-oriented protocol*.

TCP requires overhead to keep track of the individual conversations between source and destination hosts and to process acknowledgments and retransmissions. In some cases, the application cannot tolerate the delays caused by this overhead. These applications are better suited to UDP.

Applications such as databases, web pages, and e-mail need to have all data arrive at the destination in its original condition for the data to be useful. Any missing data can cause the messages to be corrupt or unreadable. These applications are designed to use a transport layer protocol that implements reliability. The additional network overhead required to provide this reliability is considered a reasonable cost of successful communication.

UDP

User Datagram Protocol (UDP) is a simple, connectionless protocol. It has the advantage of providing low-overhead data delivery. Because UDP is a "best-effort" transport layer protocol, UDP datagrams may arrive at the destination out of order or may even be lost altogether. UDP does not provide guaranteed data delivery or flow control. Applications that use UDP can tolerate small amounts of missing data. An example of a UDP application is Internet radio. If a piece of data is not delivered, there may be only a minor effect on the quality of the broadcast.

The transport layer protocol is determined based on the type of application data being sent. For example, an e-mail message requires acknowledged delivery and therefore would use TCP. An e-mail client, using SMTP, sends an e-mail message as a stream of bytes to the transport layer. At the transport layer, the TCP functionality divides the stream into segments.

Within each segment TCP identifies each byte, or octet, with a sequence number. These segments are passed to the internetwork protocol layer, which places each segment in a packet. These packets then are passed to the network access layer, where they are converted in frames. Packets contain the logical IP address of both the sending and receiving device; frames add on the physical address associated with both devices. Frames are transported across the physical media in the form of bits. This process is known as *encapsulation*. At the destination, the process is reversed, and the packets are de-encapsulated. The enclosed segments are sent through the TCP process, which converts the segments back into a stream of bytes to be passed to the e-mail server application. Figure 7-6 shows the process of encapsulation at the source and de-encapsulation at the destination.

Figure 7-6   Encapsulation

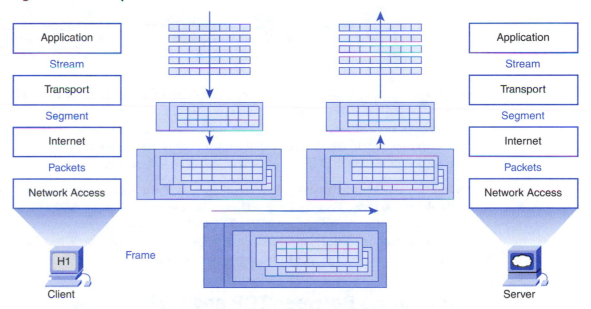

Before a TCP session can be used, the source and destination hosts exchange messages to set up the connection over which data segments can be sent. To do this, the two hosts use a three-step process:

1. The source host sends a type of message called a SYN to begin the TCP session establishment process. The message serves two purposes:

    - It indicates the intention of the source host to establish a connection with the destination host over which to send the data.

    - It synchronizes the TCP sequence numbers between the two hosts so that each host can keep track of the segments sent and received during the conversation.

2. The destination host replies to a SYN message with a synchronization acknowledgment, or SYN-ACK message.

3. The sending host receives the SYN-ACK, and it sends an ACK message back to complete the connection setup. Data segments can now be reliably sent.

This SYN, SYN-ACK, ACK activity between the TCP processes on the two hosts is called a *three-way handshake*. As soon as the three-way handshake is complete, a source-to-destination connection is established, as shown in Figure 7-7.

Figure 7-7   Source-to-Destination Connection

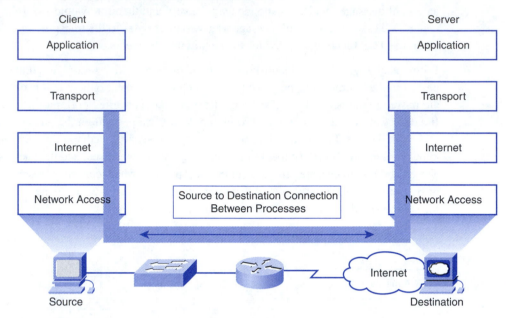

When a source host sends message segments to a destination host using TCP, the TCP process on the source host starts a timer. The timer allows sufficient time for the message to reach the destination host and for an *acknowledgment* to return. If the source host does not receive an acknowledgment from the destination within the allotted time, the timer expires, and the source assumes the message is lost. The portion of the message that was not acknowledged is then re-sent.

In addition to acknowledgment and retransmission, TCP also specifies how messages are reassembled at the destination host. Each TCP segment contains a sequence number. At the destination host, the TCP process stores received segments in a TCP buffer. By evaluating the segment sequence numbers, the TCP process can confirm that there are no gaps in the received data. When data is received out of order, the TCP process can reorder the segments as necessary.

Differences Between TCP and UDP

UDP is a very simple protocol. Because it is not connection-oriented and does not provide the sophisticated retransmission, *sequencing*, and *flow control* mechanisms of TCP, UDP has a much lower overhead. UDP is often called an unreliable delivery protocol because there is no guarantee that a message has been received by the destination host. This does not mean that applications that use UDP are unreliable. It simply means that these functions are not provided by the transport layer protocol and must be implemented elsewhere if required.

Although the total amount of UDP traffic found on a typical network is often relatively low, many key application layer protocols and applications use UDP:

- DNS
- SNMP
- DHCP
- Routing Information Protocol (RIP)
- TFTP
- Online games

- Voice over Internet Protocol (VoIP)

- Streaming technologies (audio and video)

The main differences between TCP and UDP are the specific functions that each protocol implements and the amount of overhead incurred. Viewing the headers of both protocols is an easy way to see the differences between them.

Each TCP segment has 20 bytes of overhead in the header that encapsulates the application layer data. This overhead is incurred because of the error-checking mechanisms supported by TCP. The pieces of communication in UDP are called datagrams. These datagrams are sent as "best effort" and, therefore, require only 8 bytes of overhead. Figure 7-8 shows these headers.

Figure 7-8   TCP and UDP Headers

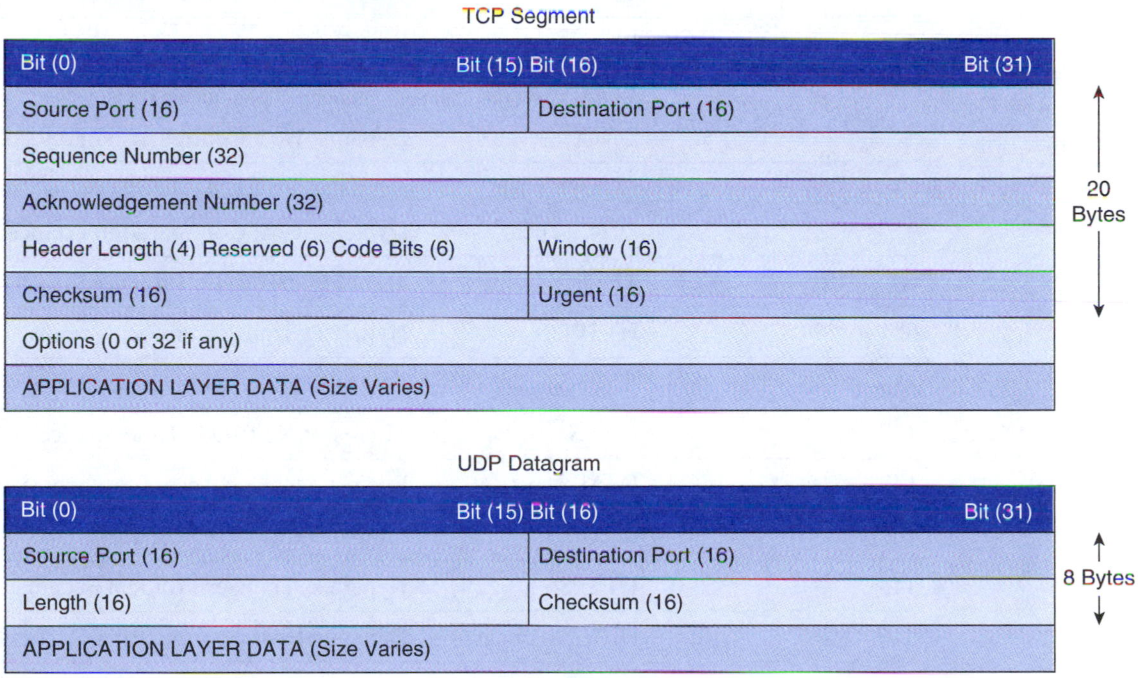

TCP Segment

Bit (0)	Bit (15) Bit (16)	Bit (31)	
Source Port (16)	Destination Port (16)		
Sequence Number (32)			20 Bytes
Acknowledgement Number (32)			
Header Length (4) Reserved (6) Code Bits (6)	Window (16)		
Checksum (16)	Urgent (16)		
Options (0 or 32 if any)			
APPLICATION LAYER DATA (Size Varies)			

UDP Datagram

Bit (0)	Bit (15) Bit (16)	Bit (31)	
Source Port (16)	Destination Port (16)		8 Bytes
Length (16)	Checksum (16)		
APPLICATION LAYER DATA (Size Varies)			

Interactive Activity 7-1: TCP and UDP Characteristics (7.2.3)

In this activity, you classify characteristics as describing either TCP or UDP. Use file d2ia-723 on the CD-ROM that accompanies this book to perform this interactive activity.

Supporting Multiple Services

The transport layer manages multiple simultaneous communication processes. The TCP and UDP services keep track of the various applications that are communicating over the network. To differentiate the segments and datagrams for each application, both TCP and UDP have header fields that can uniquely identify these applications for data communication purposes.

The header of each segment or datagram has a source and destination *port*. Port numbers are assigned in various ways, depending on whether the message is a request or a response. When a client application sends a request to a server application, the destination port contained in the header is the port number that is assigned to the specific application running on the server. For example, when a web browser application makes a request to a web server, the browser uses TCP and port number 80. This is because

TCP port 80 is the default port assigned to web-serving applications. Many common applications have default port assignments. E-mail servers, using SMTP, are usually assigned to TCP port 25. Table 7-2 lists some of the more common TCP and UDP port numbers.

Table 7-2   TCP and UDP Port Numbers

Destination Port Number	Name	Definition
20	FTP data	File Transfer Protocol (for data transfer)
21	FTP control	File Transfer Protocol (to establish a connection)
23	Telnet	Teletype network
25	SMTP	Simple Mail Transfer Protocol
53	DNS	Domain Name System
67	BOOTP server	Bootstrap Protocol (server)
	DHCP server	Dynamic Host Configuration Protocol (server)
68	BOOTP client	Bootstrap Protocol (client)
	DHCP client	Dynamic Host Configuration Protocol (client)
69	TFTP	Trivial File Transfer Protocol
80	HTTP	Hypertext Transfer Protocol
110	POP3	Post Office Protocol (version 3)
137	NBNS	Microsoft NetBIOS Name Service
143	IMAP4	Internet Message Access Protocol (version 4)
161	SNMP	Simple Network Management Protocol
443	HTTPS	Hypertext Transfer Protocol Secure
546	DHCPv6 client	Dynamic Host Configuration Protocol (client)
547	DHCPv6 server	Dynamic Host Configuration Protocol (server)

As segments are received for a specific port, TCP or UDP places the incoming segments in the appropriate queue. For instance, if the application request is for HTTP, the TCP process running on a web server places incoming segments in the web server queue. These segments are then passed up to the HTTP application as quickly as HTTP can accept them. Segments with port 25 specified are placed in a separate queue that is directed toward e-mail services. In this manner, transport layer protocols enable servers at the ISP to host many different applications and services simultaneously. This is illustrated in Figure 7-9 with two incoming streams—one on port 80 for HTTP and one on port 25 for SMTP.

Figure 7-9   Keeping Track of Data Streams

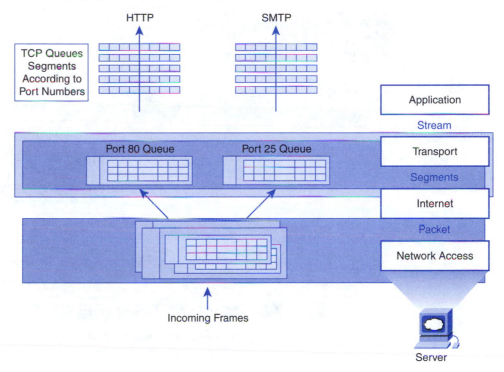

Every Internet transaction has a source host and a destination host, normally a client and a server, respectively. The TCP processes on the sending and receiving hosts are slightly different. Clients are active and request connections, whereas servers are passive and listen for and accept connections. Server processes are usually statically assigned well-known port numbers from 0 to 1023. Well-known port numbers enable a client application to assign the correct destination port when generating a request for services.

Clients also require port numbers to identify the requesting client application. Source ports are dynamically assigned from the port range 1024 to 65535. This port assignment acts like a return address for the requesting application. The transport layer keeps track of the source port and the application that initiated the request so that when a response is returned, it can be forwarded to the correct application.

The combination of the transport layer port number and the host's network layer IP address uniquely identifies a particular application process running on an individual host device. This combination is called a *socket*. A socket pair, consisting of the source and destination IP addresses and port numbers, is also unique and identifies the specific conversation between the two hosts. A client socket would look similar to 192.168.1.1:7151, where 192.168.1.1 is the IP address and 7151 is the source port number. The socket on a destination web server might be 10.10.10.10:80, with the 80 specifically identifying the web service on the destination machine. Together these two sockets combine to form a socket pair: 192.168.1.1:7151, 10.10.10.101:80.

With the creation of sockets, communication endpoints are known so that data can move from an application on one host to an application on another, as shown in Figure 7-10. Sockets enable multiple processes running on a client to distinguish themselves from each other, and also multiple connections to a server process to be distinguished from each other.

Figure 7-10   Socket Pair

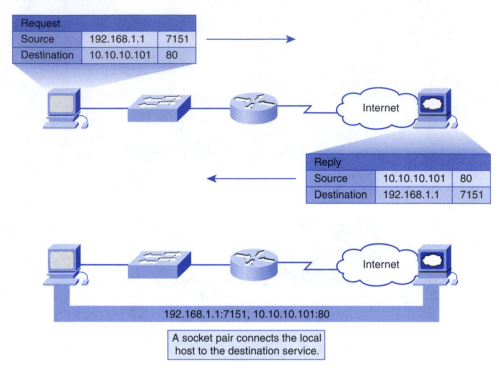

A socket pair connects the local host to the destination service.

Domain Name Service

Communication between source and destination hosts over the Internet requires a valid IP address for each host. However, numeric IP addresses, especially the hundreds of thousands of addresses assigned to servers available over the Internet, are difficult for humans to remember. Human-readable domain names, such as cisco.com, are easier for people to use. Network naming systems are designed to translate human-readable names into the machine-readable IP addresses that can be used to communicate over the network.

Humans use network naming systems every day when surfing the web or sending e-mail messages, and they may not even realize it. Naming systems work as a hidden but integral part of network communication. For example, to browse to the Cisco website, open a browser and enter http://www.cisco.com in the address field. www.cisco.com is a network name that is associated with a specific IP address. Entering the server IP address into the browser brings up the same web page.

TCP/IP Hosts File

Network naming systems are a human convenience to help users reach the resource they need without having to remember the complex IP address. In the early days of the Internet, hostnames and IP addresses of computers on the network were managed through the use of a single HOSTS file located on a centrally administered server.

The central HOSTS file contained the mapping of hostname and IP address for every device connected to the early Internet. Each site could download the HOSTS file and use it to resolve hostnames on the network. When a hostname was entered, the sending host would check the downloaded HOSTS file to obtain the IP address of the destination device.

At first, the HOSTS file was acceptable for the limited number of computer systems participating in the Internet. As the network grew, so did the number of hosts needing name-to-IP translations. It became impossible to keep the HOSTS files up to date. As a result, a new method to resolve hostnames to IP addresses was developed. DNS was created for domain name-to-address resolution. DNS uses a distributed set of servers to resolve the names associated with these numbered addresses. The single, centrally administered HOSTS file is no longer needed.

However, the HOSTS file is still used by virtually all computer systems. A local HOSTS file is created when TCP/IP is loaded on a host device. As part of the name resolution process on a computer system, the HOSTS file is scanned even before the more robust DNS service is queried. A local HOSTS file can be used for troubleshooting or to override records found in a DNS server. Example 7-1 shows a typical HOSTS file.

Example 7-1 Sample HOSTS File

```
# Copyright (c) 1993-1999 Microsoft Corp.
#
# This is a sample HOSTS file used by Microsoft TCP/IP for Windows.
#
# This file contains the mappings of IP addresses to host names. Each
# entry should be kept on an individual line. The IP address should
# be placed in the first column followed by the corresponding host name.
# The IP address and the host name should be separated by at least one
# space.
#
# Additionally, comments (such as these) may be inserted on individual
# lines or following the machine name denoted by a '#' symbol.
#
# For example:
#
#      102.54.94.97     rhino.acme.com        # source server
#      38.25.63.10      x.acme.com            # x client host


127.0.0.1       localhost
::1             localhost
192.168.1.50    wkst1
```

Lab 1-1: Editing the HOSTS File in Windows (7.3.1)

In this lab, you modify the Windows HOSTS file to provide name resolution to a host system. Refer to the lab in Part II of this *Learning Guide*. You may perform this lab now or wait until the end of the chapter.

DNS

Domain Name System (DNS) is a hostname resolution system that solves the shortcomings of the HOSTS file. The structure of DNS is hierarchical, with a distributed database of hostname-to-IP mappings spread across many DNS servers all over the world. This is unlike the HOSTS files, which required all mappings to be maintained on one server. When one host wants to communicate with another host, a DNS query is issued to the DNS server for the correct IP address of the destination host (see Figure 7-11).

Figure 7-11   DNS Query

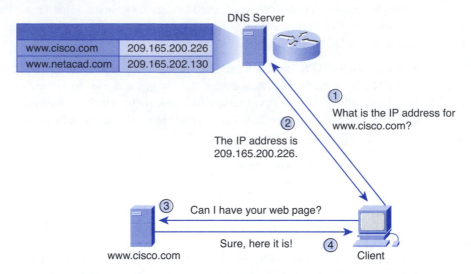

DNS uses domain names to form the hierarchy. The naming structure is broken into small, manageable zones. Each DNS server maintains a specific zone database file and is only responsible for managing name-to-IP mappings for that small portion of the entire DNS structure. When a DNS server receives a request for a name translation that is not within that DNS zone, the DNS server forwards the request to another DNS server within the proper zone for translation. This creates a highly scalable system.

DNS is made up of three components:

- Resource records and domain namespace
- Domain name servers
- Resolvers

Resource Records and Domain Namespace

A *resource record* is a data record in the DNS *zone database* file. It is used to identify a type of host, a host's IP address, or a parameter of the DNS database. The *domain namespace* is the hierarchical naming structure for organizing resource records. The domain namespace is made up of various domains, or groups, and the resource records within each group.

Domain Name Servers

These servers maintain the databases that store resource records and information about the domain namespace structure. DNS servers attempt to resolve client queries using the domain namespace and resource records it maintains in its zone database files. If the name server does not have the requested information in its DNS zone database, the name server uses additional predefined name servers to help resolve the name-to-IP query.

Resolvers

Resolvers are applications or operating system functions that run on DNS clients and DNS servers. When a domain name is used, the resolver queries the DNS server to translate that name to an IP address. A resolver is loaded onto a DNS client and is used to create the DNS name query that is sent to a DNS server. Resolvers are also loaded onto DNS servers. If the DNS server does not have the name-to-IP mapping requested, it uses the resolver to forward the request to another DNS server.

DNS uses a hierarchical system to provide name resolution. The hierarchy looks like an inverted tree, with the root at the top and branches below. At the top of the hierarchy, the root servers maintain records about how to reach the top-level domain servers, which in turn have records that point to the secondary-level domain servers.

The different top-level domains represent either the type of organization or the country of origin. Here are some examples of top-level domains:

- .au: Australia

- .co: Colombia

- .com: A business or industry

- .jp: Japan

- .org: A nonprofit organization

After top-level domains are second-level domain names, and below them are other lower-level domains (see Figure 7-12).

Figure 7-12   DNS Hierarchy

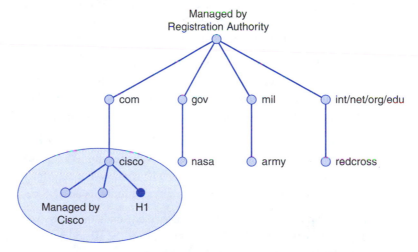

In Figure 7-12, the root DNS server may not know exactly where the final host **H1.cisco.com** is located, but it does have a record for the **.com** top-level domain. Likewise, the servers within the **.com** domain may not have a record for **H1.cisco.com** either, but they do have a record for the **cisco.com** domain. The DNS servers within the **cisco.com** domain do have the record for **H1.cisco.com** and can resolve the address.

DNS relies on this hierarchy of decentralized servers to store and maintain these resource records. The resource records contain domain names that the server can resolve and alternative servers that can also process requests.

The name **H1.cisco.com** is called a *fully qualified domain name (FQDN)* or DNS name, because it defines the exact location of the computer within the hierarchical DNS namespace.

DNS Name Resolution

When a host needs to resolve a DNS name, it uses the resolver to contact a DNS server within its domain. The resolver knows the IP address of the DNS server to contact because it is preconfigured as part of the host's IP configuration. When the DNS server receives the request from the client resolver, it first checks the local DNS records it has cached in its memory. If it is unable to resolve the IP address locally, the server uses its resolver to forward the request to another preconfigured DNS server. This process continues until the IP address is resolved. The name resolution information is then sent back to the original DNS server, which caches the information and responds to the initial query.

During the process of resolving a DNS name, each DNS server caches, or stores, the information it receives as replies to the queries. The cached information enables the DNS server to reply more quickly to subsequent resolver requests, because the server checks the cache records before querying other DNS servers. DNS servers cache information for only a limited amount of time. DNS servers should not cache information for too long, because hostname records change periodically. If a DNS server has old information cached, it may give out the wrong IP address for a computer.

The DNS resolution process, shown in Figure 7-13, works as follows:

1. **Local recursive query**: The resolver sends a recursive DNS query to the local DNS server, asking for the IP address of webserver.cisco.com, the fully qualified domain name of the remote host it wants to connect to. The local DNS server looks in its DNS zone database and its DNS cache to see if it has that name mapping recorded. It does not find it.

2. **Root domain iterative query**: The local DNS server then sends an iterative DNS query to one of the preconfigured root servers, asking for the DNS servers that maintain the .com top-level domain. The root DNS server replies with the list of .com top-level domain DNS servers. The local DNS server then caches the location of the .com DNS servers in its DNS cache.

3. **Top-level domain iterative query**: The local DNS server then sends an iterative DNS query to one of the .com servers, asking for the DNS servers that manage the cisco.com second-level domains. The .com server replies with the list of DNS servers that maintain the cisco.com second-level domain. The local DNS server then caches the location of the cisco.com DNS servers in its DNS cache.

4. **Second-level domain iterative query**: The local DNS server then sends an iterative DNS query to one of the cisco.com DNS servers, asking for the IP address of webserver.cisco.com. The cisco.com DNS server replies with the IP address mapping for webserver.cisco.com. The local DNS server then caches the resource record in its local DNS cache.

5. **Local response**: The local DNS server then sends the reply back to the client with the IP address of webserver.cisco.com. The client then uses the IP address to connect to the remote web server and request the web page it was looking for.

Figure 7-13   DNS Resolution Process

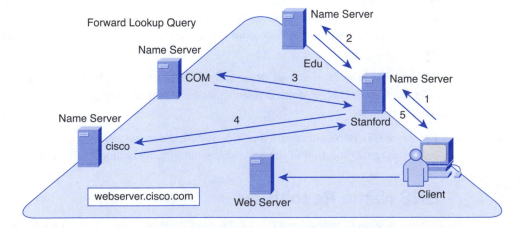

Lab 1-2: Examining Cached DNS Information on a Windows DNS Server (7.3.3)

In this lab, you examine the interface of a Windows DNS server to view the cached DNS information from a DNS lookup. Refer to the lab in Part II of this *Learning Guide*. You may perform this lab now or wait until the end of the chapter.

In the early implementations of DNS, resource records for hosts were all added and updated manually. However, as networks grew and the number of host records needing to be managed increased, it became very inefficient to maintain the resource records manually. Furthermore, when DHCP is used, the resource records within the DNS zone have to be updated even more frequently. To make updating the DNS zone information easier, the DNS protocol was changed to allow computer systems to update their own record in the DNS zone through dynamic updates.

Dynamic updates enable DNS client computers to register and dynamically update their resource records with a DNS server whenever changes occur. To use dynamic updates, the DNS server and the DNS clients, or DHCP server, must support the dynamic update feature. Dynamic updates on the DNS server are not enabled by default and must be explicitly enabled. Most current operating systems support the use of dynamic updates.

Figure 7-14 shows the process a DHCP client uses to update its DNS record. The steps are as follows:

1. The client requests an address from a DHCP server.

2. The DHCP server assigns an IP address to the client.

3. The client registers its DNS host record with the configured DNS server.

4. The DHCP server updates the pointer name on the DNS server.

Figure 7-14   Client Update of DNS Record

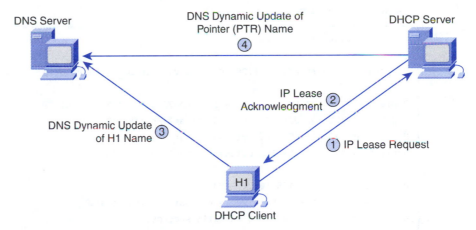

Some older operating systems do not support dynamic updating DNS. For these operating systems, you can configure some DHCP servers to dynamically update DNS on behalf of the client. Figure 7-15 shows the process of using DHCP to update DNS for the client. The steps are as follows:

1. The client requests an address from a DHCP server.

2. The DHCP server assigns an IP address to the client.

3. The DHCP server registers a DNS host record with the configured DNS server on behalf of the client.

4. The DHCP server updates the pointer name on the DNS server.

Figure 7-15   DHCP Update of DNS Record

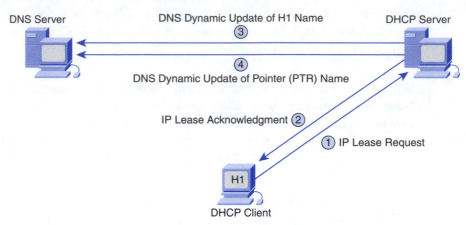

DNS servers maintain the zone database for a given portion of the overall DNS hierarchy. Resource records are stored within that DNS zone. DNS zones can be either forward lookup or reverse lookup zones. They can also be either a primary or secondary forward or reverse lookup zone. Each zone type has a specific role within the overall DNS infrastructure.

Forward Lookup Zones

A *forward lookup zone* is a standard DNS zone that resolves fully qualified domain names to IP addresses, as shown in Example 7-2. This zone type is most commonly found when surfing the Internet. When you enter a website address, such as www.cisco.com, a recursive query is sent to the local DNS server to resolve that name to an IP address to connect to the remote web server.

Example 7-2   DNS Forward Lookup

```
C:\> ping cisco.netacad.net

Pinging cisco.netacad.net [128.107.229.50] with 32 bytes of data:

Reply from 128.107.229.50: bytes=32 time=73ms TTL=113
Reply from 128.107.229.50: bytes=32 time=71ms TTL=113
Reply from 128.107.229.50: bytes=32 time=72ms TTL=113
Reply from 128.107.229.50: bytes=32 time=71ms TTL=113

Ping statistics for 128.107.229.50:
    Packets: Sent = 4, Received = 4, Lost = 0 (0% loss),
Approximate round trip times in milli-seconds:
    Minimum = 71ms, Maximum = 73ms, Average = 71ms
```

Reverse Lookup Zones

A *reverse lookup zone* is a special zone type that allows you to resolve an IP address to a fully qualified domain name, as shown in Example 7-3. Some applications use reverse lookups to identify computer systems that are actively communicating with them. An entire reverse-lookup DNS hierarchy on the Internet enables any publicly registered IP address to be resolved. Many private networks choose to implement their own local reverse lookup zones to help identify computer systems within their network. You can find reverse lookups on IP addresses using the **ping -a** *ip address* command.

Example 7-3 DNS Reverse Lookup

```
C:\> ping -a 128.107.229.50

Pinging cna-prod-nv.cisco.com [128.107.229.50] with 32 bytes of data:

Reply from 128.107.229.50: bytes=32 time=158ms TTL=121
Reply from 128.107.229.50: bytes=32 time=95ms TTL=121
Reply from 128.107.229.50: bytes=32 time=73ms TTL=121
Reply from 128.107.229.50: bytes=32 time=73ms TTL=121

Ping statistics for 128.107.229.50:
    Packets: Sent = 4, Received = 4, Lost = 0 (0% loss),
Approximate round trip times in milli-seconds:
    Minimum = 73ms, Maximum = 158ms, Average = 99ms

C:\>
```

Primary Zones

A *primary DNS zone* is a zone that can be modified as needed. When a new resource record needs to be added or an existing record needs to be updated or deleted, you would make the changes on a primary DNS zone. You can have primary forward and reverse lookup zones. When you have a primary zone on a DNS server, that server is said to be authoritative for that DNS zone, because it has the answer for DNS queries for records within that zone. Any given DNS domain can have only one primary DNS zone.

Secondary Zones

A *secondary DNS zone* is a read-only backup zone maintained on a DNS server separate from the primary zone. The secondary zone is a copy of the primary zone. It receives updates to the zone information from the primary server through zone transfers. Because the secondary zone is a read-only copy of the zone, all updates to the records need to be done on the corresponding primary zone. You can also have secondary zones for both forward and reverse lookup zones. Depending on the availability requirements for a DNS zone, you may have many secondary DNS zones spread across many DNS servers.

Lab 1-3: Creating Primary and Secondary Forward Lookup Zones (7.3.3)

In this lab, you create resource records and primary and secondary DNS zones on a Windows server. Refer to the lab in Part II of this *Learning Guide*. You may perform this lab now or wait until the end of the chapter.

Provisioning DNS Servers

You can implement DNS either by using the services of an ISP or by locally configuring and maintaining DNS servers.

Using ISP DNS Servers

ISPs typically maintain caching-only DNS servers. These servers are configured to forward all name resolution requests to the root servers on the Internet. Results are cached and used to reply to any future requests. Because ISPs typically have many customers, the number of cached DNS lookups is high. The large cache reduces network bandwidth by reducing the frequency at which DNS queries are forwarded to the root servers. Caching-only servers do not maintain any authoritative zone information, meaning that they do not store any name-to-IP mappings directly within their database.

Using Local DNS Servers

A business may run its own DNS server. The client computers on that network are configured to point to the local DNS server rather than the ISP DNS server. The local DNS server may maintain some authoritative entries for that zone, so it has name-to-IP mappings of any host within the zone. Requests that the DNS server receives that it cannot resolve are forwarded. The cache required on a local server is relatively small compared to the ISP DNS server because of the smaller number of requests hitting the local DNS server.

It is possible to configure local DNS servers to forward requests directly to the root DNS server. However, some administrators configure local DNS servers to forward all DNS requests to an upstream DNS server, such as the ISP's DNS server. That way, the local DNS server benefits from the large number of cached DNS entries of the ISP, rather than having to go through the entire lookup process, starting from the root server. This process is shown in Figure 7-16.

Figure 7-16   DNS Configuration

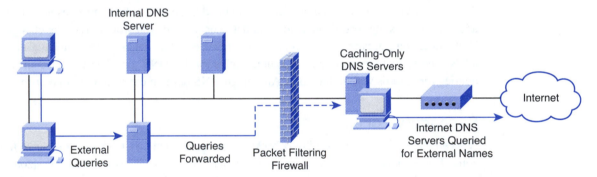

Losing access to DNS servers affects the visibility of public resources. If a user enters a domain name that cannot be resolved, he or she cannot access the resource. For this reason, when an organization registers a domain name on the Internet, a minimum of two DNS servers must be provided with the registration. These servers are the ones that will hold the DNS zone database. Redundant DNS servers ensure that if one fails, the other will still be available for name resolution. This practice provides fault tolerance. Two are required, if hardware resources permit, but even more DNS servers within a zone can provide additional protection and organization.

It is also a good idea to make sure that the multiple DNS servers that host the zone information are located on different physical networks. For example, the primary DNS zone information can be stored on a DNS server on the local business premises. Usually a customer's ISP hosts an additional secondary DNS server to ensure fault tolerance.

DNS is a critical network service. As such, DNS servers must be protected through the use of firewalls and other security measures. If DNS fails, other web services are not accessible.

Services and Protocols

In addition to providing private and business customers with connectivity and DNS services, ISPs provide many business-oriented services to customers. These services are enabled by software installed on servers. Among the different services provided by ISPs are

- E-mail hosting

- Website hosting

- E-commerce sites

- File storage and transfer

- Message boards and blogs

- Streaming video and audio services

TCP/IP application layer protocols enable many of these ISP services and applications. The most common TCP/IP application layer protocols are HTTP, FTP, SMTP, POP3, and IMAP4. Application layer protocols also include secure versions such as FTPS and HTTPS.

Interactive Activity 7-2: Which Protocols Are Required? (7.4.1)

In this activity, you determine which protocols are required for various servers. Use file d2ia-741 on the CD-ROM that accompanies this book to perform this interactive activity.

Supporting HTTP and HTTPS

Hypertext Transfer Protocol (HTTP) is one of the protocols in the TCP/IP suite. It was originally developed to enable the retrieval of HTML formatted web pages. It is now used for distributed, collaborative information sharing. The HTTP protocol has evolved through multiple versions. Most ISPs currently use HTTP version 1.1 to provide web-hosting services. Unlike earlier versions, this version enables a single web server to host multiple websites. It also permits persistent connections so that multiple request and response messages can use the same connection, reducing the time it takes to initiate new TCP sessions.

HTTP specifies a request/response protocol, as shown in Figure 7-17. When a client, typically a web browser, sends a request message to a server, the HTTP protocol defines the message types that the client uses to request the web page. The HTTP protocol also defines the message types the server uses to respond.

Figure 7-17   HTTP Request/Response

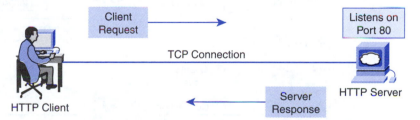

Although it is remarkably flexible, HTTP is an insecure protocol. The request messages send information to the server in plain text that can be intercepted and read. Similarly, the server responses, typically HTML pages, are also sent unencrypted. For secure communication across the Internet, the *Secure HTTP (HTTPS)* protocol is used to access or post web server information. HTTPS can use authentication and encryption to secure data as it travels between the client and server. HTTPS specifies additional rules for passing data between the application layer and the transport layer.

When an HTTP server is contacted to download a web page, a *uniform resource locator (URL)* is used to locate the server and a specific resource. The URL identifies the protocol being used, the domain name being accessed, and the specific location of the resource on the server. For example, http://example.com/example1/index.htm specifies that the HTTP protocol is to be used to retrieve a document named index.htm, which is in the example1 directory on the web server at example.com.

Many web server applications allow short URLs. Short URLs are popular because they are easier to write down, remember, and share. With a short URL, a default resource page is assumed when a specific URL is entered. When a user enters a shortened URL, such as http://example.com, the default page is sent to the client. The actual location of the default web page can be configured on the web server itself.

HTTP supports proxy services. A *proxy server* allows clients to make indirect network connections to other network services. A proxy is a device in the communications stream that acts as a server to the client and as a client to a server. The client connects to the proxy server and requests from the proxy a resource on a different server. The proxy connects to the specified server and retrieves the requested resource. It then forwards the resource back to the client.

The proxy server can cache the resulting page or resource for a configurable amount of time. This enables future clients to access the web page quickly, without having to access the actual server where the page is stored, as shown in Figure 7-18. Proxies are used for three reasons:

- **Speed**: Caching allows resources requested by one user to be available to subsequent users without their having to access the actual server where the page is stored.

- **Security**: Proxy servers can be used to intercept computer viruses and other malicious content and prevent them from being forwarded to clients.

- **Filtering**: Proxy servers can view incoming HTTP messages and filter unsuitable and offensive web content.

Figure 7-18   Caching Proxy Server

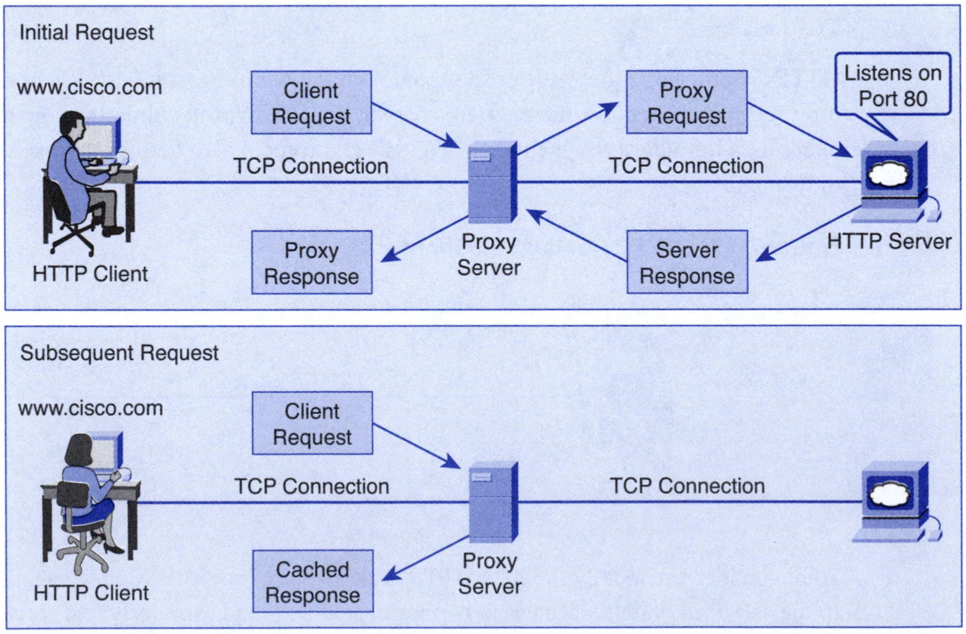

HTTP sends clear-text messages back and forth between a client and a server. These text messages can be easily intercepted and read by unauthorized users. To safeguard data, especially confidential information, some ISPs provide secure web services. To support secure web services, ISPs use HTTPS (HTTP over

Secure Socket Layer [SSL]). HTTPS uses the same client request-server response process as HTTP, but the data stream is encrypted with SSL before being transported across the network. When the HTTP data stream arrives at the server, the TCP layer passes it up to SSL in the server's application layer, where it is decrypted.

The maximum number of simultaneous connections that a server can support for HTTPS is less than that for HTTP. HTTPS creates additional load and processing time on the server because of the encryption and decryption of traffic. To keep up server performance, HTTPS should be used only when necessary, such as when exchanging confidential information.

Interactive Activity 7-3: HTTP and HTTPS Characteristics (7.4.2)

In this activity, you determine the characteristics of HTTP and HTTPS. Use file d2ia-742 on the CD-ROM that accompanies this book to perform this interactive activity.

Supporting FTP

File Transfer Protocol (FTP) is a connection-oriented protocol that uses TCP to communicate between a client FTP process and an FTP process on a server. FTP implementations include the functions of a *protocol interpreter (PI)* and a *data transfer-process (DTP)*. PI and DTP define two separate processes that work together to transfer files. As a result, FTP requires two connections to exist between the client and server—one to send control information and commands, and a second one for the actual file data transfer.

Protocol Interpreter (PI)

The PI function is the main control connection between the FTP client and the FTP server. It establishes the TCP connection and passes control information to the server. Control information includes things such as commands to navigate through a file hierarchy, as well as renaming or moving files. The control connection, or control stream, stays open until the user closes it. When a user wants to connect to an FTP server, the following process occurs:

1. The user-PI sends a connection request to the server-PI on well-known port 21.

2. The server-PI replies, and the connection is established.

3. With the TCP control connection open, the server-PI process begins the login sequence.

4. The user enters credentials through the user interface and completes authentication.

5. The data transfer process can begin.

Data Transfer Process (DTP)

DTP is a separate data transfer function. This function is enabled only when the user wants to actually transfer files to or from the FTP server. Unlike the PI connection, which remains open, the DTP connection closes automatically when the file transfer is complete.

Figure 7-19 shows the complete FTP process.

Figure 7-19   Establishing an FTP Session

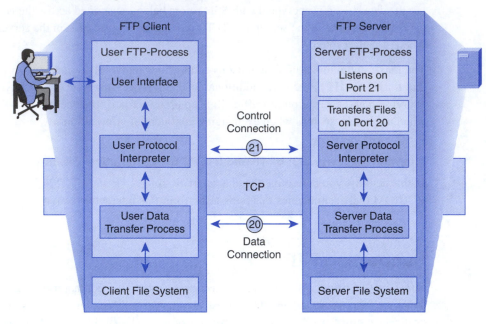

The two types of data transfer connections supported by FTP are active data connections and passive data connections.

Active Data Connections

In an active data connection, a client initiates a request to the server and opens a port for the expected data. The server then connects to the client on that port, and the data transfer begins. The server initiates the data transfer connection. A user requests data transfer. The server-PI instructs the server-DTP to connect to the user-DTP. The user-DTP listens for the connection from the server-DTP.

Passive Data Connections

In a passive data connection, the FTP server opens a random source port (greater than 1023). The server forwards its IP address and this random port to the FTP client over the control stream. The server then waits for a connection from the FTP client to begin the data file transfer. The client initiates the data transfer connection. The user-PI connects to the server-PI and instructs the server-DTP to be passive. The server-PI responds with an IP address and a dynamic port number for the client to use for data transfer. The server-DTP then listens for the connection from the user-DTP.

ISPs typically support passive data connections to their FTP servers. Firewalls often do not permit active FTP connections to hosts located on the inside network.

Supporting SMTP, POP3, and IMAP

One of the primary services that an ISP offers is e-mail hosting. E-mail is a store-and-forward method of sending, storing, and retrieving electronic messages across a network. E-mail messages are stored in databases on mail servers. ISPs often maintain mail servers that support many different customer accounts.

E-mail clients communicate with mail servers to send and receive e-mail. Mail servers communicate with other mail servers to transport messages from one domain to another. In other words, an e-mail client does not communicate directly with another e-mail client when sending e-mail. Both clients must rely on the mail server to transport the messages. This is true even when both users are in the same domain.

E-mail clients send messages to the e-mail server configured in the application settings. When the server receives the message, it checks to see if the recipient domain is located on its local database. If it is not, it sends a DNS request to determine the mail server for the destination domain. As soon as the IP address of the destination mail server is known, the e-mail is sent to the appropriate server.

E-mail supports three separate protocols for operation: SMTP, POP3, and IMAP4. The application layer process that sends mail, either from a client to a server or between servers, implements SMTP. A client retrieves e-mail using either POP3 or IMAP4.

Simple Mail Transfer Protocol (SMTP)

The functions specified by *Simple Mail Transfer Protocol (SMTP)* enable the transfer of mail reliably and efficiently. For SMTP applications to do this, two conditions must be met:

- The mail message must be formatted properly.
- SMTP processes must be running on both client and server.

SMTP message formats require a message header and a message body. Although the message body can contain any amount of text, the message header must have a properly formatted recipient e-mail address and a sender address. Any other header information is optional.

When a client sends e-mail, the client SMTP process connects with a server SMTP process on well-known port 25. As soon as the connection is made, the client attempts to send mail to the server across the connection. After the server receives the message, it either places the message in a local account or forwards the message using the same SMTP connection process to another mail server, as shown in Figure 7-20.

Figure 7-20   SMTP

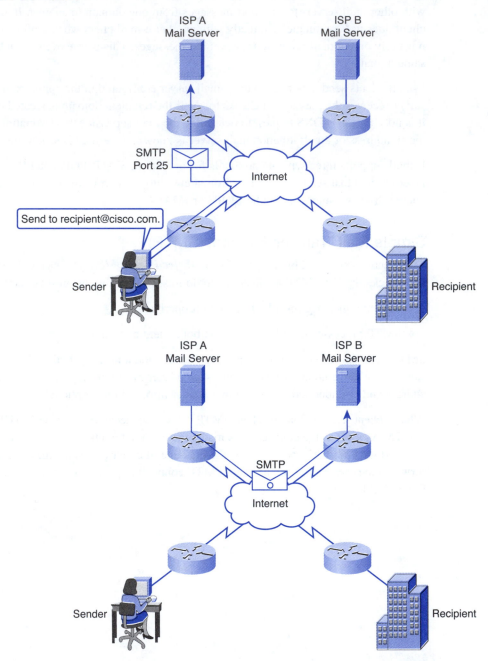

The destination e-mail server may not be online, or may be busy, when e-mail messages are sent. Therefore, SMTP provides for the spooling of messages to be sent later. Periodically, the server checks the queue for messages and attempts to send them again. After a predetermined expiration time, if the message is still undelivered, it is returned to the sender as undeliverable.

One of the required fields in an e-mail message header is the recipient e-mail address. The structure of an e-mail address includes the e-mail account name or an alias, as well as the domain name of the mail server. An example of an e-mail address is recipient@cisco.com. The @ symbol separates the account and the server's domain name.

When a message is sent to recipient@cisco.com, the domain name is sent to the DNS server to obtain the IP address of the domain mail server. Mail servers are identified in DNS by an MX record indicator. When the destination mail server receives the message, it stores the message in the appropriate mailbox. The mailbox location is determined based on the account specified in the first part of the e-mail address—in this case, the recipient account. The message remains in the mailbox until the recipient connects to the server to retrieve the e-mail. If the mail server receives an e-mail message that references an account that does not exist, the e-mail is returned to the sender as undeliverable.

Post Office Protocol Version 3 (POP3)

Post Office Protocol version 3 (POP3) is used to enable a workstation to retrieve mail from a mail server. With POP3, mail is downloaded from the server to the client and then is deleted on the server, as shown in Figure 7-21.

The server starts the POP3 service by passively listening on TCP port 110 for client connection requests. When a client wants to use the service, it sends a request to establish a TCP connection with the server. After the connection is established, the POP3 server sends a greeting. The client and POP3 server then exchange commands and responses until the connection is closed or aborted.

With POP3, e-mail messages are downloaded to the client and are removed from the server. This means that there is no centralized location where e-mail messages are kept. This makes the POP3 protocol undesirable in a centralized backup solution for a small business. The POP3 protocol is desirable for an ISP because it alleviates the ISP's responsibility of managing large amounts of storage for their e-mail servers.

Figure 7-21   POP3

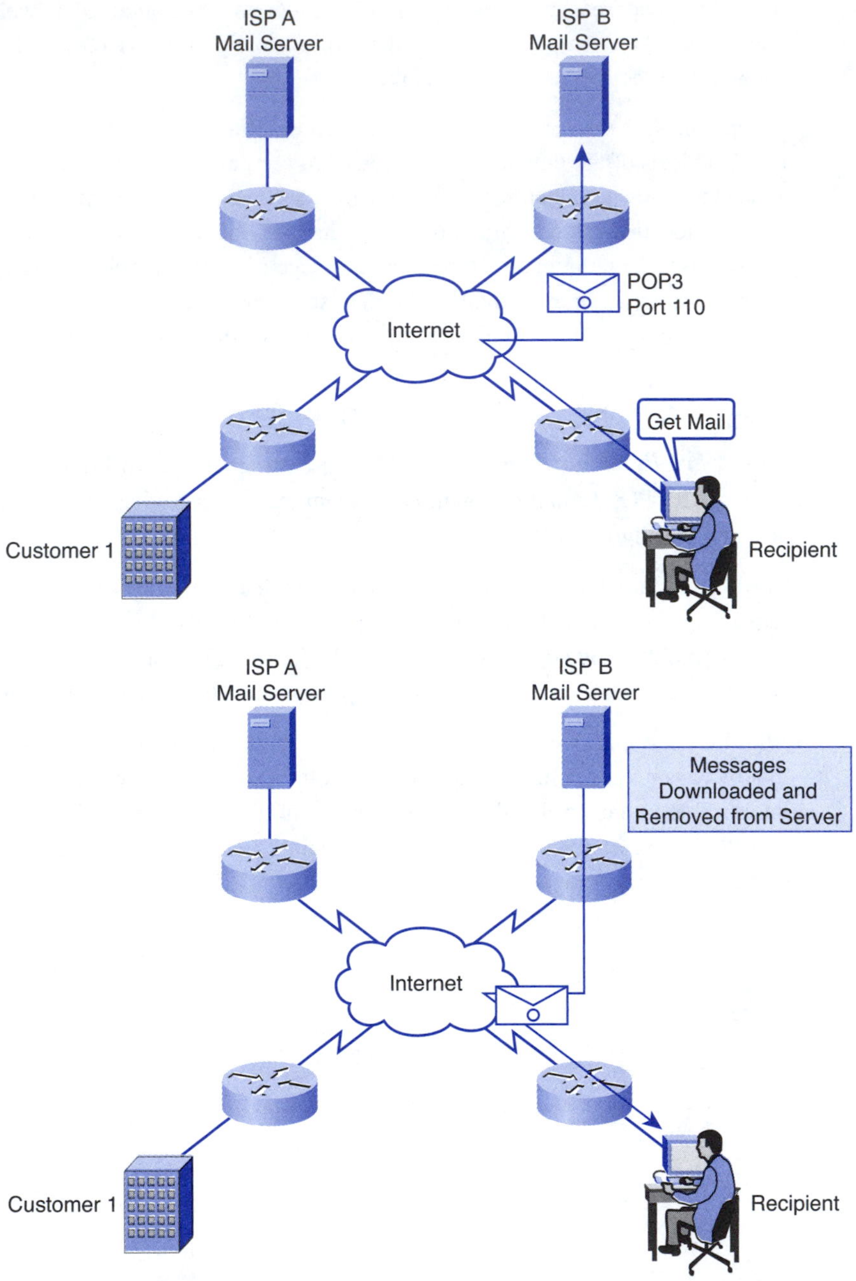

Internet Message Access Protocol (IMAP4)

Internet Message Access Protocol (IMAP4) is another protocol that describes a method to retrieve e-mail messages. However, unlike POP3, when the user connects to an IMAP-capable server, copies of the messages are downloaded to the client application. The original messages are kept on the server until they are manually deleted. Users view copies of the messages in their e-mail client software. This process is shown in Figure 7-22.

Figure 7-22   IMAP4

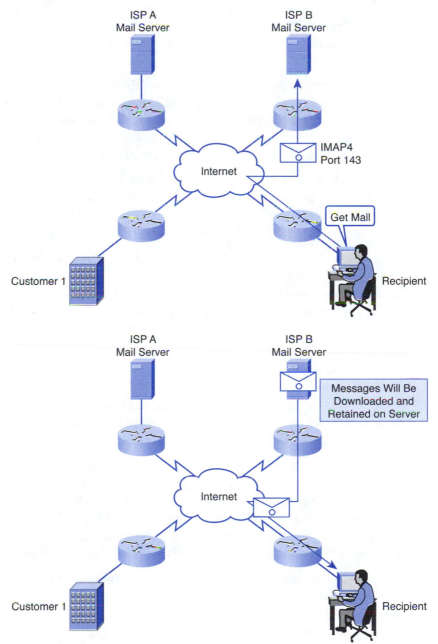

Users can create a file hierarchy on the server to organize and store mail. That file structure is duplicated on the e-mail client as well. When a user decides to delete a message, the server synchronizes that action and deletes the message from the server.

For small-to-medium-sized businesses, the IMAP protocol offers many advantages. IMAP can lead to long-term storage of e-mail messages on mail servers and allow for centralized backup. It also enables employees to access e-mail messages from multiple locations, using different devices or client software. The mailbox folder structure that a user establishes is available for viewing, regardless of how the user accesses the mailbox.

For an ISP, IMAP may not be the protocol of choice. It can be expensive to purchase and maintain the disk space to support the large number of stored e-mails. Additionally, if customers expect their mailboxes to be backed up routinely, that can further increase the costs to the ISP.

Summary

Many different application layer protocols exist and provide services for home and business users alike. All these protocols depend on the transport layer protocols, TCP and UDP, to move the information across the network.

TCP is considered a connection-oriented, reliable delivery protocol. It segments and sequences the data before sending across the network. On the receiving end, TCP stores the incoming segments in a buffer until it receives all the necessary information. At this point it reassembles the data stream and passes it to the correct application layer protocol. If any packets are lost in transmission, TCP requests that they be re-sent through a system of acknowledgments.

UDP is a connectionless protocol and does not use acknowledgments to ensure that the information has been successfully transmitted across the network. It is a best-effort delivery mechanism and relies on higher-layer protocols to ensure that the data is successfully received. By eliminating the overhead associated with TCP, UDP can move information much quicker.

TCP is used when it is important that all the information is received and any data loss cannot be tolerated. A good example of this is e-mail. UDP is used when the loss of small amounts of information can be tolerated and the delay associated with TCP overhead would be detrimental. Common examples of this are streaming audio and video. Both TCP and UDP use port numbers to keep track of communications and to direct the information to the correct application layer protocol.

Communication on an IP network relies on the structure of the IP address. IP addresses are difficult for humans to remember and manipulate, so a system of naming has been developed. Device names must be converted to IP addresses before network communications can occur. This conversion was originally done using a HOSTS file on each machine that contained a database of device names and IP addresses. As networks grew, this system became unmanageable, so a hierarchical database system known as DNS was developed. The entries were distributed among the root, top-level domains, second-level domains, and subdomains.

Dynamic updates allow client machines to automatically update their DNS information every time change occurs. This is especially important in networks that use DHCP. Most ISPs provide caching-only name servers, which store DNS information for a specific period of time. Customers can use the domain service of the ISP or run their own DNS servers, depending on technical and financial resources. Customer DNS servers can point either to the ISP DNS servers or directly to the root servers.

Some of the most common services used on the Internet are HTTP, HTTPS, SMTP, FTP, and FTPS. HTTPS is a secure form of HTTP, and FTPS is a secure form of FTP. Because secure protocols encrypt and decrypt information, the servers that support these protocols must be high-performance to support the demands of the encryption technology.

FTP can be either active or passive. Active connections require the server to initiate the connection, whereas the host initiates passive connections. E-mail uses three protocols. SMTP is used to send mail, and POP3 and IMAP4 are used to retrieve e-mail from mail servers.

Activities and Labs

This summary outlines the activities and labs you can perform to help reinforce important concepts described in this chapter. You can find the activity files on the CD-ROM accompanying this book. The complete hands-on labs appear in Part II.

Interactive Activities on the CD:

Activity 1-1: TCP and UDP Characteristics (7.2.3)

Activity 1-2: Which Protocols Are Required? (7.4.1)

Activity 1-3: HTTP and HTTPS Characteristics (7.4.2)

Packet Tracer Activities on the CD:

This chapter has no Packet Tracer Activities.

Hands-on Labs in Part II of this book:

Lab 1-1: Editing the HOSTS File in Windows (7.3.1)

Lab 1-2: Examining Cached DNS Information on a Windows DNS Server (7.3.3)

Lab 1-3: Creating Primary and Secondary Forward Lookup Zones (7.3.3)

Check Your Understanding

Complete all the review questions listed here to check your understanding of the topics and concepts in this chapter. Answers are listed in Appendix A, "Check Your Understanding and Challenge Questions Answer Key."

1. What allows a company to have current networking technology and services without incurring unexpected costs and expensive upgrades?

   A. High MTBF

   B. Managed services

   C. Service-level agreement

   D. In-house system design and management

2. What is the "five 9s" standard of system availability, and how is it achieved?

3. Which protocols function at the transport layer of the TCP/IP model? (Choose all that apply.)

   A. DNS

   B. HTTPS

   C. IP

   D. TCP

   E. UDP

4. Which OSI model layers correspond to the TCP/IP model application layer? (Choose all that apply.)

   A. Application

   B. Presentation

   C. Session

   D. Transport

   E. Network

   F. Data link

   G. Physical

5. What is the last step in the TCP three-way handshake process?

   A. The source host sends a SYN to the destination host.

   B. The destination host sends a SYN to the source host.

   C. The source host sends a SYN-ACK message to the destination host.

   D. The destination host sends a SYN-ACK message to the source host.

   E. The source host sends an ACK message to the destination host.

   F. The destination host sends an ACK message to the source host.

6. What does UDP do when a portion of a message is lost during transit?

   A. It retransmits the lost portion.

   B. It retransmits the entire message.

   C. It retransmits only the lost octet.

   D. It does not retransmit the lost portion.

7. What types of network traffic typically use UDP? (Choose all that apply.)

   A. Domain Name System (DNS)

   B. File Transfer Protocol (FTP)

   C. E-mail (POP3, IMAP4)

   D. Trivial File Transfer Protocol (TFTP)

   E. Voice over Internet Protocol (VoIP)

   F. Streaming technologies (audio and video)

8. What is used to uniquely identify a particular application process running on an individual host device?

   A. Source IP address

   B. Destination IP address

   C. Source port

   D. Destination port

   E. Socket

9. If the **ping** command specifies an FQDN rather than an IP address, what type of DNS lookup must be done?

   A. DNS forward lookup

   B. DNS reverse lookup

   C. Primary zone lookup

   D. Secondary zone lookup

10. Which application layer protocol is used to retrieve e-mail in a company that uses centralized backup and storage?

    A. SMTP

    B. POP3

    C. HTTPS

    D. IMAP4

11. Briefly differentiate between an active and a passive FTP data connection.

Challenge Questions and Activities

These questions require a deeper application of the concepts covered in this chapter. You can find the answers in Appendix A.

1. You have been hired by a company to troubleshoot its network connectivity problems. The client claims that it can no longer browse to the company website using the URL that worked previously. You know that the IP address of this website was just changed. What could be a reason that the URL no longer works, how would you prove this, and what measures would you take to remedy the problem?

2. To protect the information being transferred to a company web server, the previous system administrator implemented HTTPS. The transaction volume has recently increased, and the server is having difficulty handling the increased volume. What two remedies can you suggest for this problem, and which would you implement? Justify your choice.

## CHAPTER 8

ISP Responsibility

Objectives

After completing this chapter, you should be able to answer the following questions:

- What security policies and procedures do ISPs employ?

- What tools are used to implement security at the ISP?

- How is the ISP monitored and managed?

- What are the ISP's responsibilities for maintenance and recovery?

Key Terms

This chapter uses the following key terms. You can find the definitions in the Glossary.

malware   page 242

Microsoft Baseline Security Analyzer (MBSA)   page 244

Nessus Vulnerability Scanner   page 244

authentication, authorization, and accounting (AAA)   page 246

encryption   page 247

Secure Socket Layer (SSL)   page 248

IP security (IPsec)   page 249

denial-of-service (DoS) attack   page 249

SYN flood   page 249

LAND attack   page 249

distributed denial-of-service (DDoS) attack   page 249

distributed reflected denial-of-service (DRDoS) attack   page 250

stateful packet inspection (SPI)   page 252

demilitarized zone (DMZ)   page 252

intrusion detection system (IDS)   page 254

intrusion prevention system (IPS)   page 255

preshared key (PSK)   page 257

Extensible Authentication Protocol (EAP)   page 257

phishing   page 259

Trojan   page 260

Wireshark   page 262

Simple Network Management Protocol (SNMP)   page 265

CiscoWorks   page 265

management information base (MIB)   page 265

trap   page 266

syslog   page 267

optical media   page 270

direct-attached storage (DAS)   page 270

network-attached storage (NAS)   page 270

storage-area network (SAN)   page 270

solid-state media   page 271

full backup   page 271

differential backup   page 272

incremental backup   page 273

As reliance on network services increases, the ISP must provide, maintain, secure, and recover critical business services. The ISP develops and maintains security policies and procedures for its customers, along with disaster recovery plans for its network hardware and data.

Part II of this book includes the corresponding labs for this chapter.

ISP Security Considerations

ISPs have a responsibility to help protect user computers and data from malicious attacks. They provide a variety of services to users and must employ best practices to ensure security. They use data encryption techniques to secure data transmitted to and from their servers. This section examines the role of the ISP in protecting user data and network resources.

ISP Security

Any active Internet connection for a computer can make that computer a target for malicious activity. *Malware*—malicious software such as a computer virus, worm, or spyware—can arrive in an e-mail or be downloaded from a website. Problems that cause large-scale failures in service provider networks often originate from unsecured desktop systems at the ISP customer locations.

If the ISP is hosting any web or e-commerce sites, it may have confidential files with financial data or bank account information stored on its servers. The ISP is required to maintain the customer data in a secure way.

ISPs play a big role in helping protect the home and business users who use their services. The security services that they provide also protect the servers that are located at the service provider premises. Service providers may also help their customers secure their local networks and workstations to reduce the risk of compromise.

System administrators at both the local site and the ISP can take many actions to secure operating systems, any data stored on computers, and any data transmitted between computer systems. ISPs have a responsibility to help protect users from hackers who might intercept user login information, as shown in Figure 8-1. The ISP can use secure protocols such as HTTPS and encrypt passwords to improve security.

Figure 8-1   Hacker Intercepting a Username and Password

Username
Password

If an ISP provides web hosting or e-mail services for a customer, it is important that the ISP protect that information from malicious attack. This can be complicated, because often an ISP uses a single server, or cluster of servers, to maintain data that belongs to more than one customer. If the server is being shared by multiple customers, it is important to provide security measures to make sure that they cannot access each other's data.

To help prevent attacks on these vulnerabilities, many ISPs provide managed desktop security services for their customers. An important part of an onsite support technician's job is to implement security best practices on client computers. Some of the security services that an ISP support technician can provide include the following:

- Helping clients create secure passwords for devices
- Removing unnecessary applications and services that can create vulnerabilities
- Securing applications using patch management and software upgrades
- Ensuring that applications and services are available to the users who need them and no one else
- Configuring desktop firewalls and virus-checking software
- Performing security scans on software and services to determine vulnerabilities that the technician must protect from attack

Security methods can be categorized into the following specific areas:

- Password security
- Extraneous services
- Patch management
- Application security
- User rights
- Security scanning

The following sections describe each method.

Password Security

Choose a complex password. A complex password consists of a mix of uppercase characters, lowercase characters, numbers, and symbols. A complex password should be at least eight characters long and never should be based on a dictionary word or personal information that someone may be able to guess. It is also recommended that passwords be changed periodically. Software exists that can allow a hacker to crack passwords by trying every possible combination of letters, numbers, and symbols to figure out passwords. If you change your password periodically, brute-force password cracking is less of an issue, because by the time the hacker cracks the password, the password should already be changed to something different.

Extraneous Services

One of the most common ways in which a computer system is compromised is through unconfigured or misconfigured services that are installed. The nature of a service is that it listens for requests for the service it provides from external computer systems. If that service has a known exploitable flaw because it isn't configured or is configured incorrectly, a hacker or worm can compromise that service and gain access to the computer system that the service is running on. As a best practice, remove or disable all unnecessary services. For services that are necessary or cannot be uninstalled, make sure that you follow the best practices in any configuration guide for that particular service.

Patch Management

New security exploits are identified for operating systems almost every day. All it takes is a simple online search. You may be able to find sites that list various exploitable vulnerabilities for virtually every operating system that is available today. Operating system developers release updates regularly—daily in some cases. It is important to regularly review and install security updates for your operating systems. Patching the operating system regularly can prevent most intrusions by a hacker or infections from worms and viruses.

Application Security

Unpatched and unnecessary applications installed on an operating system can also increase the risk of being compromised. Just as the operating system needs to be patched regularly, so do installed applications. Internet-based applications, such as Internet browsers and e-mail applications, are the most important applications to patch regularly, because they are the most frequently targeted.

User Rights

A typical modern operating system has multiple levels of access. When a user account has administrative access to the operating system, malware can more easily infect the computer system. This is because of the unrestricted access to the file system and system services. Normal user accounts cannot install new applications, because the accounts do not have access to areas of the file system and system files that are necessary to install most applications. As a result, normal users are not as susceptible to malware infections that try to install or access certain areas of the file system. As a best practice, users should have limited access to the computer system to perform their normal daily work. Administrative access should be used only when it is necessary to perform functions that are not permitted for a normal user.

Security Scanning

Many tools can help you secure your operating system. Most security scanning tools review many key system security weaknesses and report back on how to rectify the problems the software found. Some of the more advanced scanning software packages go beyond the typical operating system security scans. These advanced packages look at the software and services running on a computer and suggest ways to protect the entire computer system from attack.

Microsoft has a free downloadable tool called the *Microsoft Baseline Security Analyzer (MBSA)*. It examines everything from user account security to installed Windows services and even checks to see what patch level an operating system is at. Another popular utility created to scan for vulnerabilities is the *Nessus Vulnerability Scanner*. This security scanning tool is not specific to Windows; it scans for vulnerabilities on a variety of platforms. Many other tools are available online. Usually, it is best to use more than one tool to examine your system's security to get the best overall results.

Figure 8-2 shows the Windows login screen, requiring a valid username and secure password, as well as the Automatic Update options windows. These are two built-in Windows XP security features. When activated, Automatic Updates can automatically download and install OS patches that can correct known security vulnerabilities.

Figure 8-2   Windows Login and Automatic Updates Screens

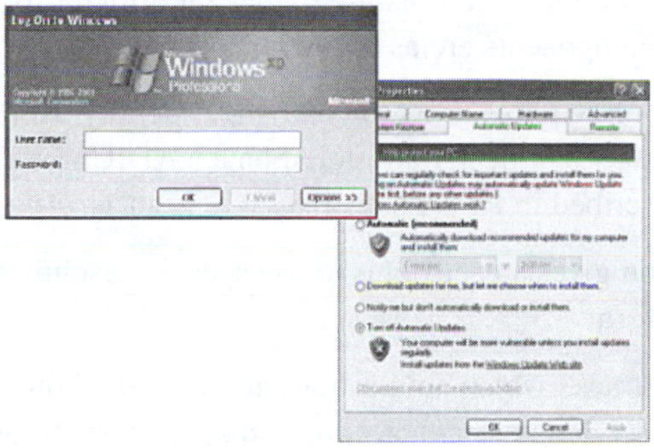

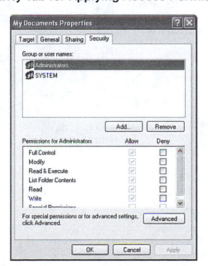

Best Practices for Security

If an ISP provides web hosting services or e-mail services for a customer, it is important that the ISP protect that information from malicious attack. Common data security features and procedures include

- Encrypting data stored on server hard drives

- Using permissions to secure access to files and folders

- Permitting or denying access based on the user account or group membership

- If access is permitted, assigning various levels of access permissions based on the user account or on group memberships

When you're assigning permissions to files and folders, a security best practice is to apply permissions based on the principle of least privilege. This means giving a user access to only those resources that are required for the user to be able to do his job. It also means giving the appropriate level of permission, such as read-only access or write access. Additional permissions that the user does not require should not be assigned. For example, a user might only need to view files in a folder. Giving him write access to the folder increases the chance that he could accidentally or intentionally modify or erase files. Figure 8-3 shows the Windows XP folder Properties Security tab that allows permissions to be applied to the My Documents folder for specific users or groups of users.

Figure 8-3   Properties Security Tab for Applying Access Permissions to Folders

Authentication, authorization, and accounting (AAA) is a set of protocols, normally installed on a server, that network administrators use to make it difficult for attackers to gain access to a network. The three main components are as follows:

- Authentication requires users to prove their identity using a username and password. User authentication databases typically are stored on a RADIUS or TACACS server. RADIUS is an Internet standard described in RFC 2865. TACACS is a Cisco-proprietary security protocol.

- Authorization gives a user rights to use specific resources and controls which specific tasks he or she can perform.

- Accounting tracks which applications are used and how long they are used. For example, authentication acknowledges that a user named student exists and can log in. Authorization services specify that user student can access host serverXYZ using Telnet. Accounting tracks that user student accessed host serverXYZ using Telnet on a specific day for 15 minutes.

AAA can be used on various types of network connections. AAA requires a database to keep track of user credentials, permissions, and account statistics. Local authentication is the simplest form of AAA and keeps a local database on the gateway router. If an organization has more than a handful of users authenticating with AAA, the organization typically uses a database on a separate server.

Figure 8-4 shows the use of a standalone RADIUS server to provide AAA services. Unauthorized users may attempt to access network resources from inside or outside of the network. All clients attempting to log in are challenged by the AAA authentication service on the RADIUS server. The authentication service verifies the username and password using a database of valid users. An authenticated user is authorized to use specific services in the network. When a user logs out, the accounting service records where she has been, what she has done, and how long she used a network service.

Figure 8-4   AAA RADIUS Server Controls User Access

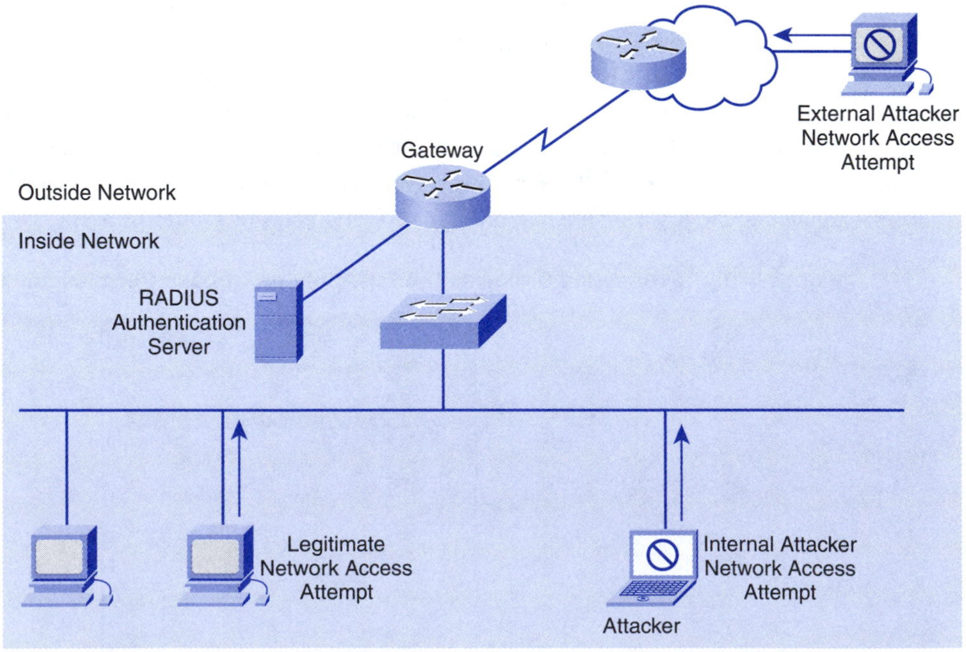

Data Encryption

ISPs must also be concerned with securing data that is transmitted to and from their servers. By default, data sent over the network is unsecured and transmitted in clear text. Unauthorized individuals can intercept unsecured data as it is being transmitted. Capturing data in transit bypasses all file system security that is set on the data. Methods are available to protect against this security issue.

Encryption is the process of encoding all transmitted data between the client and the server. Many of the protocols used to transmit data offer a secure version that uses digital encryption. As a best practice, use the secure version of a protocol whenever the data being exchanged between two computers is confidential.

For example, if a user must submit a username and password to log in to an e-commerce website, a secure protocol is required. This protects the username and password information from being captured, as shown in Figure 8-5. Another example of the use of a secure protocol is any time a user must submit a credit card number or bank account information. This information must be encrypted whenever it is transmitted.

Figure 8-5   Clear-Text and Encrypted Login Information

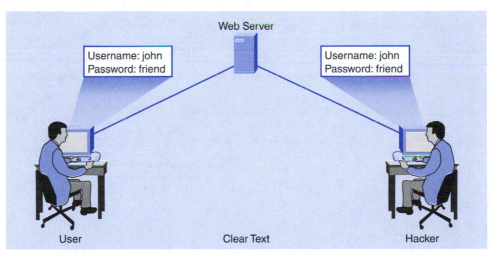

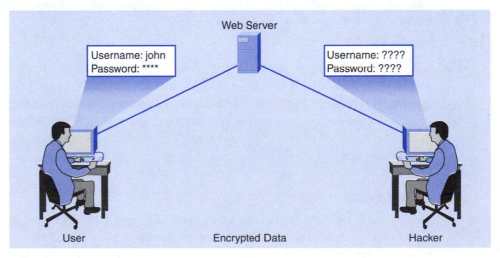

When you're surfing the Internet and viewing publicly accessible websites, securing the transmitted data is not necessary. Using a secure protocol in this situation can lead to slower response times and additional computational overheads.

Applications use many network protocols. Some offer secure versions, and some do not. Figure 8-6 shows several of the standard network applications, such as HTTP, Telnet, and FTP, and their secure versions. Also shown are some independent protocols that can be used to provide encryption for e-mail and other applications. The next sections describe how various servers use secure protocols.

Figure 8-6   Secure and Unsecure Network Protocols

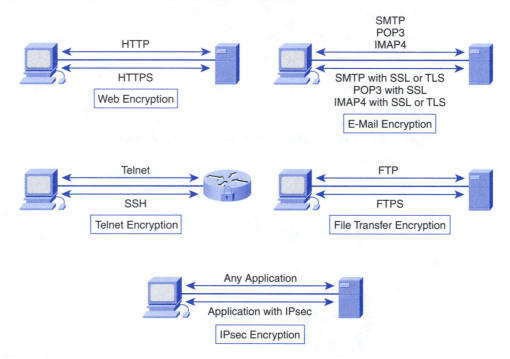

Web Servers

Web servers use the HTTP protocol by default. This is not a secure protocol. Switching to HTTPS enables the exchange of data to be done securely.

E-mail Servers

E-mail servers use several different protocols, including SMTP, POP3, and IMAP. When a user logs on to an e-mail server, POP3 and IMAP require a username and password for authentication. By default, this submission is sent without security and can be captured. POP3 can be secured by using *Secure Socket Layer (SSL)*. SMTP and IMAP can use either SSL or Transport Layer Security (TLS) as a security protocol.

Telnet Servers

Using Telnet to remotely log in to a Cisco router or Cisco switch creates an unsecure connection. Telnet sends authentication information, as well as any commands a user enters, across the network in basic clear text. Use SSH to authenticate and work with the router or switch securely.

FTP Servers

FTP is also an unsecure protocol. When you log into an FTP server, authentication information is sent in clear text. FTP can use SSL to securely exchange authentication and data. Some versions of FTP can also use SSH.

File Servers

File servers can use many different protocols to exchange data, depending on the computer's operating system. In most cases, file server protocols do not offer a secure version.

IP security (IPsec) is a network layer security protocol that can be used to secure any application layer protocol used for communication. This includes file server protocols that do not offer any other security protocol version.

Lab 8-1: Securing Local Data and Transmitted Data (8.1.3)

In this lab you perform the data security tasks needed to analyze and secure local data and transmitted data. Refer to the hands-on lab in Part II of this book. You may perform this lab now or wait until the end of the chapter.

Security Tools

A number of tools, both local and network, are available to help protect computers and networks from attack. These include access lists, port filters, firewalls, intrusion detection and prevention systems, wireless access control, and local host security software. This section first explains different types of denial-of-service (DoS) attacks and then explores these tools and their application.

Denial-of-Service Attacks

In spite of AAA and the use of encryption, an ISP must protect against many different types of attacks. ISPs are especially vulnerable to denial-of-service (DoS) attacks, because the ISP may host sites for many different registered domain names that may or may not require authentication. Currently there are three key types of denial-of-service attacks: DoS, distributed denial of service (DDoS), and distributed reflected denial of service (DRDoS). The next sections describe these types of attacks.

DoS

A standard *denial-of-service (DoS) attack* prevents legitimate access to a server or service. Some examples of standard DoS attacks are *SYN-flood*, ping flood, *LAND attack*, bandwidth consumption attack, and buffer overflow attack.

DDoS

A *distributed denial-of-service (DDoS) attack* occurs when multiple computers are used to attack a specific target. In DDoS attacks, the attacker has access to many compromised computer systems, usually on the Internet. Because of this, the attacker can remotely launch the attack. DDoS attacks usually are the same kinds of attacks as standard DoS attacks, except that DDoS attacks are run from many computer systems simultaneously.

Figure 8-7 shows a DDoS attack in which the attacker's remote computer has compromised a number of other computers on the network. When a controlled command is issued to the compromised computers, they all attack a specific target computer and deny service to legitimate users.

Figure 8-7   DDoS Attack Method

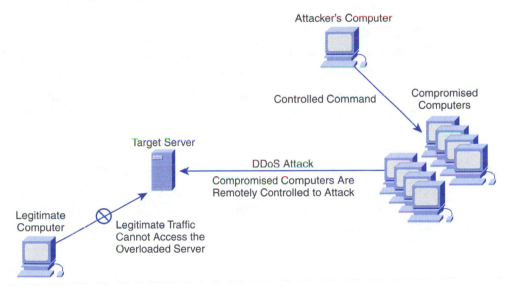

DRDoS

A *distributed reflected denial-of-service (DRDoS) attack* occurs when an attacker sends a spoofed, or mock, request to many computer systems on the Internet, with the source address modified to be the targeted computer system. The computer systems that receive the request respond, and all the requests are directed at the target computer system. Because of the attack's reflection, it is very difficult to determine the originator of the attack.

Access Lists and Port Filtering

The ISP must be able to filter out network traffic, such as DoS attacks, that can be harmful to the operation of the ISP network or servers. This can be done using port filtering and access lists to control traffic to servers and networking equipment.

Port Filtering

Port filtering is the ability to control the flow of traffic based on a specific TCP or UDP port. Many server operating systems provide options to restrict access using port filtering. In this way, the server can provide the needed services while still being protected. Port filtering is also used by network routers and switches to help control traffic flow and to secure access to the device.

Figure 8-8 illustrates how a port filter can be implemented that prevents access to all other ports on the server except TCP port 80. This allows web access to the server. If a user tries to connect to the server using any other port, such as Telnet on TCP port 23 or SSH on port 22, the user is denied access. This protects the server from being compromised.

Figure 8-8   Port Filtering

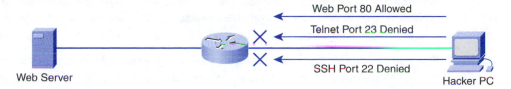

Access Lists

Access lists are used to define traffic that is permitted or denied through the network based on the source and destination IP addresses. Access lists can also permit or deny traffic on the source and/or destination port of the protocol being used to transport packets. Additionally, ICMP and routing update traffic can be controlled using ACLs. Administrators create access lists on network devices, such as routers, to control whether traffic is forwarded or blocked.

Access lists are only the first line of defense and are not enough to secure a network. Access lists can prevent access to a network but do not protect the network from all types of malicious attacks.

Figure 8-9 illustrates the use of an access list on a router to control traffic. With the access list in place, all computers on Network A are denied access to all computers on Network B. The access list specifies the IP address of Network A as the source network and the IP address of Network B as the destination network. Traffic is denied if it meets those conditions. This still allows the computers on Network A to communicate with the server on Network C.

Figure 8-9   Access List Controlling Traffic

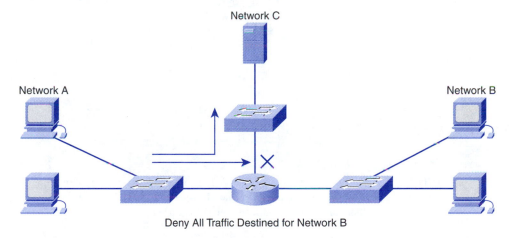

 Lab 8-2: Planning for Access Control Lists and Port Filters (8.2.1)

In this lab you determine where to implement access control lists and port filters to help protect the network. Refer to the hands-on lab in Part II of this book. You may perform this lab now or wait until the end of the chapter.

Firewalls

A firewall is network hardware or software that defines what traffic can come into and go out of sections of the network, as well as how traffic is handled.

Access lists are one of the tools used by firewalls. Access lists help control the type of traffic that is allowed to pass through the firewall. The direction in which the traffic is allowed to travel is also controlled. In a medium-sized network, the amount of traffic and number of networking protocols that need to be controlled can be quite large, and firewall access lists can become very complicated.

Firewalls use access lists to control which traffic is passed or blocked. They are constantly evolving as new capabilities are developed and new threats are discovered. The greater the firewall's functionality, the more time it takes for packets to be processed.

Different firewalls offer different types of features. For example, a dynamic packet filter firewall or stateful firewall keeps track of the actual communication process occurring between the source and destination devices. This is also known as *stateful packet inspection (SPI)*. The firewall does this by using a state table. As soon as a communication stream is approved, only traffic that belongs to one of these communication streams is permitted through the firewall.

In Figure 8-10, when host H1 sends a file to the FTP server, the router records in a database the initiation of the conversation between H1 and the server. The router inspects the packet returning from the server and allows it to pass to H1, because the conversation with the FTP server is in its database. If a packet is sent from H2 to H1, the router blocks it because no record exists of a conversation initiated by H1 to H2.

Figure 8-10   Dynamic or Stateful Packet Inspection

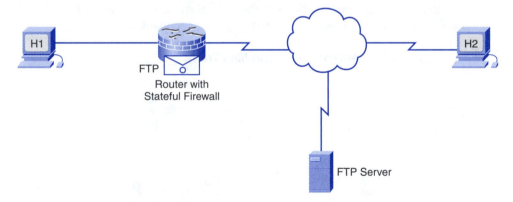

FTP
Router with
Stateful Firewall

FTP Server

Note

The Cisco IOS Firewall software is embedded in Cisco IOS software. It allows the user to turn a router into a network layer firewall with dynamic or stateful inspection. The IOS Firewall is configured using IOS commands and is optional, based on the network administrator's needs.

Firewalls can provide perimeter security for the entire network, controlling access from external sources. They also can be applied to internal local network segments, such as server farms or other high-security areas of the network, to control access from internal sources.

Within an ISP network or a medium-sized business, firewalls typically are implemented in multiple layers. Traffic that comes in from an untrusted network first encounters a packet filter on the border router, as shown in Figure 8-11. Permitted traffic goes through the border router to an internal firewall to route traffic to a *demilitarized zone (DMZ)*. A DMZ contains servers that users from the Internet are allowed to access. Only traffic that is intended for these servers is permitted into the DMZ. Firewalls also control what kind of traffic is permitted into the protected local network itself. The traffic that is allowed into the internal network usually is traffic that is being sent because of a specific request by an internal device. For example, if an internal device requests a web page from an external server, the firewall permits the web page to enter the internal network.

Figure 8-11   Trusted and Untrusted Networks and the DMZ

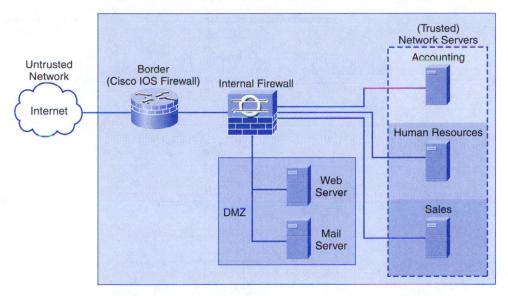

Some organizations can choose to implement additional internal firewalls to protect sensitive areas. Internal firewalls are used to restrict access to areas of the network that need to have additional protection. Internal firewalls separate and protect business resources on servers from users inside the organization. Internal firewalls can prevent external and internal hackers, as well as unintentional internal attacks and malware.

Planning Network-Based Firewalls (8.2.2)

In this activity, you position firewalls on a network diagram for a medium-sized business. Use file d2-822.pka on the CD-ROM that accompanies this book to perform this activity.

IDS and IPS

ISPs also have a responsibility to prevent, when possible, intrusions into their networks and the networks of customers who purchase managed services. ISPs and customers often use two tools to accomplish this: IDS and IPS.

IDS and IPS technologies are deployed as sensors. An IDS or IPS sensor can be any of the following:

- A router configured with Cisco IOS version IPS
- An appliance (hardware) specifically designed to provide dedicated IDS or IPS services
- A network module installed in an adaptive security appliance (ASA), switch, or router

IDS and IPS sensors respond differently to incidents detected on the network, but both have roles within a network. Figure 8-12 compares the operation of an IDS and IPS. The IDS sensor cannot deny the attack but seeks to detect it and alert the Management system. The IPS sensor seeks to detect and deny the attack before it reaches the intended target.

Figure 8-12   Comparing the IDS and IPS

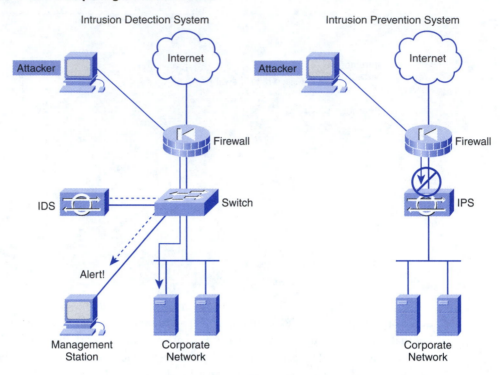

IDS

An *intrusion detection system (IDS)* is a software- or hardware-based solution that passively listens to network traffic. Network traffic does not pass through an IDS device. Instead, the IDS device monitors traffic through a network interface. When the IDS detects malicious traffic, it sends an alert to a pre-configured management station.

IDS solutions are reactive when it comes to detecting intrusions. They detect intrusions based on a signature for network traffic or computer activity. They do not stop the initial traffic from passing through to the destination, but react to the detected activity.

When properly configured, the IDS can block further malicious traffic by actively reconfiguring network devices such as security appliances or routers, in response to malicious traffic detection. It is important to realize that the original malicious traffic has already passed through the network to the intended destination and cannot be blocked. Only subsequent traffic is blocked. In this regard, IDS devices cannot prevent some intrusions from succeeding.

IDS solutions are often used on a network's untrusted perimeter, outside the firewall. Here the IDS can analyze the type of traffic that is hitting the firewall and determine how attacks are executed. The firewall can be used to block most malicious traffic. An IDS can also be placed inside the firewall to detect firewall misconfigurations. When the IDS sensor is placed here, any alarms that go off indicate that malicious traffic has been allowed through the firewall. These alarms mean that the firewall has been configured incorrectly.

Figure 8-13 shows packets passing into the network and reaching the target computer. The IDS sensor detects the attack and sends an alert to the management station. The external firewall may need to be reconfigured. It is possible for an IDS to detect what it thinks is an attack that is not really one. This is known as a false positive. Because the IDS does not seek to actively block the attack, this kind of problem is not as much of a concern with the IDS. With an IPS, false positive traffic that should be permitted may be blocked if it is identified as a threat.

Figure 8-13   IDS Functionality

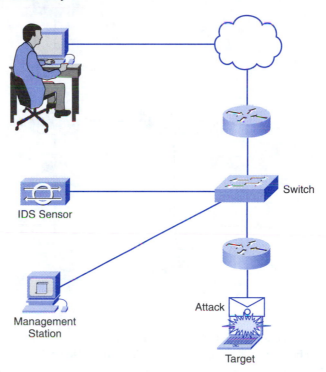

IPS

An *intrusion prevention system (IPS)* is an active physical device or software feature. Traffic travels in one interface of the IPS and out the other. The IPS examines the actual data packets that are in the network traffic and works in real time to permit or deny packets that want access into the network.

Unlike IDS solutions, which are reactive, IPS solutions are proactive. They block all suspicious activity in real time. An IPS can examine almost the entire data packet from Layer 2 to Layer 7 of the OSI model. When the IPS detects malicious traffic, it can block the malicious traffic immediately. The IPS is then configured to send an alert to a management station about the intrusion, as shown in Figure 8-14. The original and subsequent malicious traffic is blocked as the IPS proactively prevents attacks.

Figure 8-14   IPS Functionality

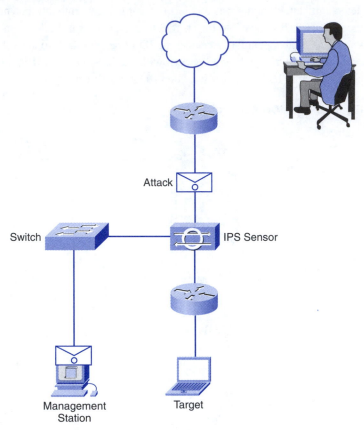

An IPS is an intrusion detection appliance, not software. It is most often placed inside the firewall. This is because the IPS can examine the entire data packet and therefore can be used to protect server applications. The firewall typically does not examine the entire data packet, whereas the IPS does. The firewall drops most of the packets that are not allowed, but it may still allow some malicious packets through. The IPS has a smaller number of packets to examine, but it examines the entire packet. This allows the IPS to immediately drop new attacks that the firewall cannot stop or could not be configured to stop. One potential disadvantage with an IPS is that false positive traffic that should be permitted may be blocked if it is identified as a threat.

Interactive Activity 8-1: IDS and IPS (8.2.3)

In this interactive activity, you identify characteristics and features of IPS and IDS. Use file d2ia-823 on the CD-ROM that accompanies this book to perform this interactive activity.

Wireless Security

Some ISPs offer services to create wireless hotspots for customers to log in to wireless local-area networks (WLAN). A wireless network is easy to implement but is vulnerable when not properly configured. Because the wireless signal travels through walls, it can be accessed from outside the business premises. A wireless network can be secured by changing the default settings, enabling authentication, or enabling MAC address filtering.

Changing Default Settings

The default values for the SSID, usernames, and passwords on a wireless access point should be changed. Additionally, broadcasting of the SSID should be disabled.

Enabling Authentication

Authentication is the process of permitting entry to a network based on a set of credentials. It is used to verify that the device attempting to connect to the network is trusted. Three types of authentication methods can be used:

- **Open authentication**: Any and all clients can have access, regardless of who they are. Open authentication is most often used on public wireless networks.

- *Preshared key (PSK)*: Requires a matching, preconfigured key on both the server access point and the client. When you connect, the access point sends a random string of bytes to the client. The client accepts the string, encrypts it (or scrambles it) based on the key, and sends it back to the access point. The access point gets the encrypted string and uses its key to decrypt (or unscramble) it. If they match, authentication is successful.

- *Extensible Authentication Protocol (EAP)*: Provides mutual, or two-way, authentication and user authentication. A client with EAP software communicates with a backend authentication server, such as RADIUS.

The following methods are used to secure a wireless network:

- MAC address filtering

- Wired Equivalent Privacy (WEP)

- WiFi Protected Access (WPA)

- WiFi Protected Access 2 (WPA2)

MAC Address Filtering

MAC address filtering prevents unwanted computers from connecting to your network by restricting MAC addresses, as shown in Figure 8-15. It is possible, however, to clone a MAC address; therefore, other security measures should be implemented along with MAC address filtering.

Figure 8-15   Wireless MAC Filtering

WEP

Wired Equivalent Privacy (WEP) provides data security by encrypting data that is sent between wireless nodes, as shown in Figure 8-16. WEP uses a 64-, 128-, or 256-bit preshared hexadecimal key to encrypt the data. A major weakness of WEP is its use of static encryption keys. The same key is used by every device to encrypt every packet transmitted. Many WEP cracking tools are available on the Internet. WEP should be used only with older equipment that does not support newer wireless security protocols.

Figure 8-16   Using WEP Encryption

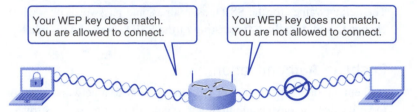

WPA

WiFi Protected Access (WPA) is a newer wireless encryption protocol that uses an improved encryption algorithm called Temporal Key Integrity Protocol (TKIP). TKIP generates a unique key for each client and rotates the security keys at a configurable interval. WPA provides a mechanism for mutual authentication, and because both the client and the access point have the key, the key is never transmitted.

WPA2

WiFi Protected Access 2 (WPA2), shown in Figure 8-17, is a new, improved version of WPA. WPA2 uses the more secure Advanced Encryption Standard (AES) encryption technology.

Figure 8-17   Using WPA/WPA2 Encryption

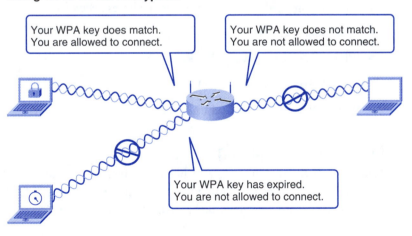

Configuring WEP on a Wireless Router (8.2.4)

In this activity, you configure WEP security between a computer and a wireless router. Use file d2-824.pka on the CD-ROM that accompanies this book to perform this activity.

Host Security

Regardless of the layers of defense that exist on the network, all servers are still susceptible to attack if they are not properly secured. ISP servers are especially vulnerable, because they generally are accessible from the Internet. New vulnerabilities for servers are discovered every day, so it is critical for an ISP to protect its servers from known and unknown vulnerabilities whenever possible. One way they accomplish this is through the use of host-based firewalls.

A host-based firewall is software that runs directly on a host operating system. It protects the host from malicious attacks that might have made it through all other layers of defense. Host-based firewalls control inbound and outbound network traffic. These firewalls allow filtering based on a computer's IP address and port, thereby offering additional protection over regular port filtering.

Host-based firewalls typically come with predefined rules that block all incoming network traffic. Exceptions are added to the firewall rule set to permit the correct mixture of inbound and outbound network traffic. When enabling host-based firewalls, it is important to balance the need to allow access to network resources required to complete job tasks with the need to prevent applications from being left vulnerable to malicious attacks. Many server operating systems are preconfigured with a simple host-based firewall with limited options. More-advanced third-party packages are available.

ISPs use host-based firewalls to restrict access to the specific services a server offers. By using a host-based firewall, the ISP protects its servers and its customers' data by blocking access to the extraneous ports that are available. Figure 8-18 shows the use of host-based firewalls, as well as a secure switch and router.

Figure 8-18   Host-Based Firewalls

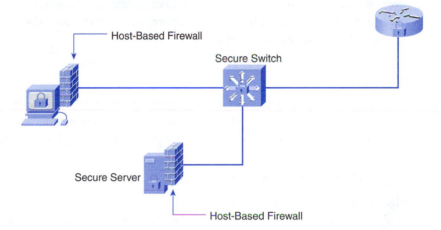

In addition to host-based firewalls, Anti-X software can be installed on the host. Anti-X software protects computer systems from viruses, worms, spyware, malware, *phishing*, and even spam. Many ISPs offer customers Anti-X software as part of their comprehensive security services. Not all Anti-X software protects against the same threats. The ISP should constantly review what threats the Anti-X software actually protects against and make recommendations based on a threat analysis of the company.

Many Anti-X software packages allow for remote management. This includes a notification system that can alert the administrator or support technician about an infection, via e-mail or pager. Immediate notification to the proper individual can drastically reduce the impact of the infection. Using Anti-X software does not diminish the number of threats to the network but reduces the risk of being infected.

ISP servers that use host-based firewalls are protected from a variety of different types of attacks and vulnerabilities, as discussed in the following sections.

Known Attacks

Host-based firewalls recognize malicious activity based on updatable signatures or patterns. They detect a known attack and block traffic on the port used by the attack. They monitor ports known to be associated with malicious activity, as shown in Figure 8-19.

Figure 8-19   Blocking a Known Attack

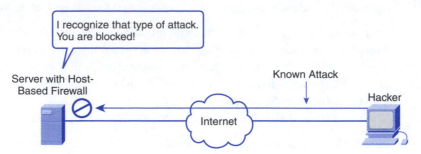

Exploitable Services

Host-based firewalls protect exploitable services running on servers by preventing access to the ports that the service is using. Some host-based firewalls can also inspect the contents of a packet to see if it contains malicious code. Web and e-mail servers are common targets for service exploits. They can be protected if the host-based firewall can perform packet inspection. This inspection confirms whether the packet contains malicious code.

Worms and Viruses

Worms and viruses propagate by exploiting vulnerabilities in services and other weaknesses in operating systems. Host-based firewalls prevent this malware from gaining access to servers. They can also help prevent the spread of worms and viruses by controlling outbound traffic originating from a server.

Back Doors and Trojans

Back doors or Trojans allow hackers to remotely gain access to servers on a network. The software typically works by sending a message to let the hacker know of a successful infection. It then provides a service that the hacker can use to gain access to the system. Host-based firewalls can prevent a *Trojan* from sending a message by limiting outbound network access. They can also prevent the attacker from connecting to any services.

Occasionally infections and attacks still occur and can be very destructive. It is important to have an incident management process to track all incidents and the corresponding resolutions, to help prevent that infection from occurring again. Incident management is required by ISPs that manage and maintain customer data, because the ISP has committed to the protection and integrity of the data it hosts for its customers. For example, suppose the ISP network were the target of a hacker and, as a result, thousands of credit card numbers that were stored in a database that the ISP manages were stolen. The customer would need to be notified so that it could tell the cardholders.

 Lab 8-3: Researching Anti-X Software Products (8.2.5)

In this lab, you recommend an Anti-X software package for a small business. Refer to the hands-on lab in Part II of this book. You may perform this lab now or wait until the end of the chapter.

Monitoring and Managing the ISP

The ISP monitors and manages network resources to help protect them and ensure optimal performance. The ISP often negotiates agreements with customers, mainly businesses, to ensure uptime and adequate bandwidth and to define issue-resolution processes. As part of its responsibilities, the ISP manages network performance using both in-band and out-of-band tools. This section reviews service-level agreements and tools used to monitor network performance.

Service-Level Agreements

An ISP and a business customer typically have a contract known as a service-level agreement (SLA). It clearly documents the expectations and obligations of both parties. The SLA is an important document that clearly outlines network management, monitoring, and maintenance.

The parts of a typical SLA include the following:

- **Service description**: Defines the range of services that an ISP provides. Includes the service amount or service volume and the times when the service is and is not covered by the SLA.

- **Availability, performance, and reliability**: Defines the following:

  - **Availability**: The hours and days per month per year that service is available.

  - **Performance**: A measure of service capability expectations during peak data volumes.

  - **Reliability**: The percentage of time that the system should be up and operating normally. An example of this is the rule of "five 9s," which states that the system should be operational 99.999% of the time.

- **Tracking and reporting**: Defines how often reports, such as performance reports, are provided to the customer. Includes a written explanation of what level of network service users are experiencing.

- **Problem management**: Defines the process used to handle and resolve unplanned incidents. Defines the different levels of a problem and who should be called for each problem level. Also includes the ISP response time, which is a measure of how fast an ISP can respond to unexpected events that cause the service to stop.

- **Security**: Defines security measures that are the ISP's responsibility versus the customer's responsibility. Determines how network services that the ISP offers fit within the customer's and ISP's security policies.

- **Termination**: Defines the termination agreement and costs if services are terminated early. Typically SLAs are renegotiated annually and coincide with the customer's budget cycle.

- **Penalties for service outages**: Describe the penalties for a network service failure. This is especially important if the ISP is providing services critical for business operation.

- **Costs**: Describes the charges to the customer by defining services rather than equipment. The ISP can cost out the services needed, and the customer pays for only the services used.

Lab 8-4: Interpreting a Service-Level Agreement (8.3.1)

In this lab, you examine an SLA and practice interpreting the key sections of the SLA. Refer to the hands-on lab in Part II of this book. You may perform this lab now or wait until the end of the chapter.

Monitoring Network Link Performance

The ISP is responsible for monitoring and checking device connectivity. This includes any equipment that belongs to the ISP, as well as equipment at the customer end that the ISP agreed to monitor in the SLA. Monitoring and configuration can be performed either out-of-band or in-band. Out-of-band refers to techniques that do not require a network connection and do not use network bandwidth. These include direct console or dial-in modem connections. In-band uses a network connection such as Ethernet or WAN technology, and the management traffic between devices shares the bandwidth with normal network traffic.

Out-of-band management is useful for initial configurations, if the device is not accessible via the network, or if a visual inspection of the device is necessary. For example, a server or network device may be experiencing network accessibility problems, and it is not possible to telnet to the device over the existing network infrastructure. In this case, the technician may be able to travel to the device and access the user interface either directly or using a console connection. This may not be possible, depending on the location of the device. If a modem is connected to the server or network device, it may be possible to dial in remotely to investigate and possibly correct the problem using out-of-band management.

Most ISPs cannot visually inspect or have physical access to all devices. An in-band management tool allows for easier administration, because the technician does not require a physical connection. For this reason, in-band management is preferred over out-of-band management for managing servers and network devices that are accessible on the network. Additionally, conventional in-band tools can provide more management functionality than may be possible with out-of-band management, such as an overall view of the network design. Traditional in-band management protocols include Telnet, SSH, HTTP, and Simple Network Management Protocol (SNMP).

Many embedded tools, commercial tools, and shareware tools use these management protocols. For example, HTTP access is through a web browser. Some applications, such as Cisco Security Device Manager (SDM), use this access for in-band management. In addition, in-band network monitoring software is available, such as *Wireshark* and others.

Figure 8-20 illustrates out-of-band management, where the management station may be directly connected locally to a device or dialed in from a remote location using a modem. Figure 8-21 illustrates in-band management, where the management station is attached to the same Ethernet switch as other hosts.

Figure 8-20   Out-of-Band Management

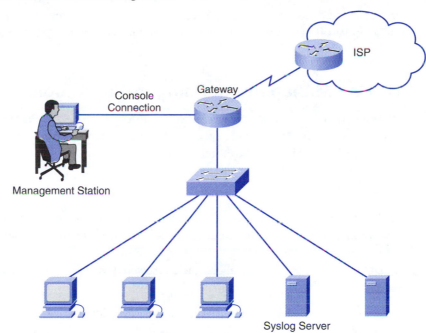

Figure 8-21   In-Band Management

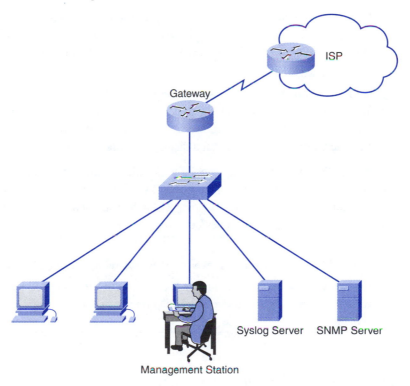

Lab 8-5: Conducting a Network Capture with Wireshark (8.3.2)

In this lab you download, install, and conduct a network capture with Wireshark. Refer to the hands-on lab in Part II of this book. You may perform this lab now or wait until the end of the chapter.

Device Management Using In-Band Tools

After a new network device is installed at the customer premises, it must be monitored from the remote ISP location. Sometimes minor configuration changes need to be made without the physical presence of a technician at the customer site.

Telnet

A Telnet client can be used over an IP network connection to connect to a device in-band for the purpose of monitoring and administering it. A connection using Telnet is called a Virtual Terminal (VTY) session or connection. Telnet is a client/server protocol. The connecting device runs the Telnet client. To support Telnet client connections, the connected device, or server, runs a service called a Telnet daemon.

Most operating systems include an Application Layer Telnet client. On a Microsoft Windows PC, Telnet can be run from the command prompt. Other common terminal emulation applications that run as Telnet clients are HyperTerminal, Minicom, and TeraTerm. Devices such as routers run both the Telnet client and the Telnet daemon and can act as either the client or server.

After a Telnet connection is established, users can perform any authorized function on the server, just as if they were using a command-line session on the server itself. If authorized, users can start and stop processes, configure the device, and even shut down the system.

A Telnet session can be initiated using the router's command-line interface (CLI) with the **telnet** command followed by the IP address or domain name. A Telnet client can connect to multiple servers simultaneously. On a Cisco router, the keystroke sequence Ctrl-Shift-6 X toggles between Telnet sessions. Additionally, a Telnet server can support multiple client connections. On a router acting as a server, the **show sessions** command displays all client connections.

Although the Telnet protocol supports user authentication, it does not support the transport of encrypted data. All data exchanged during a Telnet session is transported as plain text across the network. This means that the data can be intercepted and easily understood, including the username and password used to authenticate the device.

Lab 8-6: Managing Remote Network Devices with Telnet (8.3.3a)

In this lab you use Telnet to remotely manage multiple routers and a switch from a PC and a router. Refer to the hands-on lab in Part II of this book. You may perform this lab now or wait until the end of the chapter.

Secure Shell (SSH)

If security is a concern, the Secure Shell (SSH) protocol offers an alternative and secure method for server access. SSH provides secure remote login and other network services. It also provides stronger authentication than Telnet and supports the transport of session data using encryption. As a best practice, network professionals should always use SSH in place of Telnet whenever possible.

Cisco IOS includes an integrated SSH client and server. Two versions of the SSH server service exist. Which SSH version is supported depends on the Cisco IOS image loaded on the device. Many different GUI-based SSH client software packages, such as PuTTY, are available for PCs. An SSH client must support the SSH version configured on the server.

Lab 8-7: Configuring a Remote Router Using SSH (8.3.3b)

In this lab you use SDM and the CLI to configure a router to accept SSH connections from a PC client. Refer to the hands-on lab in Part II of this book. You may perform this lab now or wait until the end of the chapter.

Using SNMP and Syslog

Network administrators use industry-standard utilities to manage servers and network devices. These include SNMP for in-band device management and syslog for monitoring device status.

SNMP

Simple Network Management Protocol (SNMP) is a network management protocol that enables network administrators to gather data about the network and corresponding devices. SNMP management system software is available in tools such as *CiscoWorks*. Free versions of CiscoWorks are available for download on the Internet. SNMP management agent software is often embedded in operating systems on servers, routers, and switches.

SNMP is made up of four main components:

- **Management station**: The administrator uses a computer with the SNMP management application loaded to monitor and configure the network.

- **Management agent**: Software installed on a device managed by SNMP.

- *Management information base (MIB)*: A database that a device keeps about itself concerning network performance parameters.

- **Network management protocol**: The communication protocol used between the management station and the management agent.

The management station contains the SNMP management applications that the administrator uses to configure devices on the network. It also stores data about those devices. The management station collects information by polling the devices. A poll occurs when the management station requests specific information from an agent. Figure 8-22 shows a router and a switch, each with its own MIB, and an SNMP management station that can be used to configure the devices and query the device MIBs.

Figure 8-22   SNMP Agents, Management Station, and Central MIB

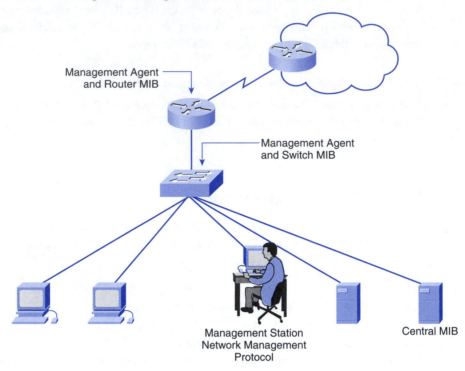

The agent's task is to report to the management station by responding to the polls. When the management station polls an agent, the agent calls on statistics that have accumulated in the MIB. Particular parameters or variables from each agent may be processed by the management station for storage in a central MIB in a database.

Agents can also be configured with traps. A *trap* is an alarm-triggering event on an agent. Certain areas of the agent are configured with thresholds, or maximums, that must be maintained, such as the amount of traffic that can access a specific port. If the threshold is exceeded, the agent sends an alert message to the management station. This frees the management station from continuously polling network devices.

Management stations and managed devices are identified by a community ID, called a *community string*, that permits access to the devices. The community string on the SNMP agent must match the community string on the SNMP management station. When an agent is required to send information to a management station because of a poll or trap event, first it verifies the management station using the community string.

Figure 8-23 shows a scenario in which a customer calls the network administrator to report that its server is very slow. The administrator at the management station wants to find out how many users are on the server. He accesses the SNMP management application and sends a request to the server agent to determine connection statistics. This request includes a community string. The server agent verifies the community string and the management station's IP address. It also tells the management station that thousands of users are on the server, which could be the reason that it is slow.

Figure 8-23   SNMP in Action

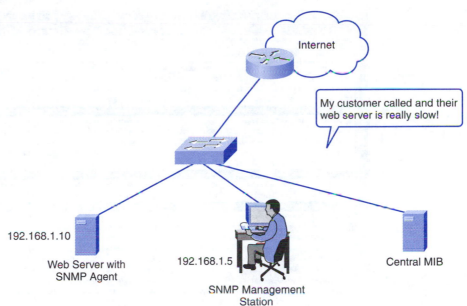

Syslog

Storing device logs and reviewing them periodically is an important part of network monitoring. *Syslog* is the standard for logging system events. Like SNMP, syslog is an application layer protocol that enables devices to send information to a syslog daemon that is installed and running on a management station.

A syslog system is composed of syslog servers and syslog clients. A number of freeware syslog servers are available for download from the Internet. The server software normally is installed on a computer and accepts and processes log messages from one or more syslog clients. Clients typically are network devices to be monitored. A syslog client generates and forwards log messages to syslog servers. An example of a syslog client is a Cisco router configured using IOS to send console messages to a computer running the syslog server.

Log messages normally consist of a log message ID, the type of message, a time stamp (date, time), which device sent the message, and the message text. Depending on which network equipment is sending the syslog messages, a syslog message can contain more items than those listed. A network technician uses a management station to view syslog messages on a syslog server. Figure 8-24 shows the output from a GUI-based syslog server application.

Figure 8-24   Syslog Application Output

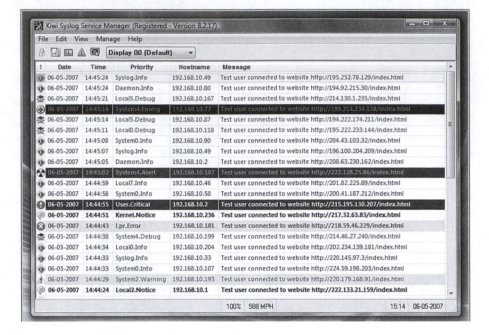

Backups and Disaster Recovery

As part of their responsibilities to their customers, ISPs provide backup data services. Those that host websites and e-mail for customers have disaster recovery plans to prevent loss of data and keep business continuity. This section investigates various types of backup media and the primary methods used to back up data. Best practices for disaster recovery are discussed.

Causes of Data Loss

Network management and monitoring help ISPs and businesses identify and correct network issues. This software can also help correct the causes of network failures. This includes failures caused by malware and malicious activity, network functionality, and other issues, such as failed devices.

Data loss can be caused by a number of issues, including those described in this section:

- Hardware failure
- User error
- Theft
- Malicious activity
- Operating system failure

Hardware Failure

As hardware ages, the probability of hardware failure and data loss increases. Hardware failure usually means a lot of lost data. Recovering from hardware failure requires replacing the failed hardware and restoring all the data from a current backup.

User Error

User error includes accidentally overwriting a file, deleting an important file, editing a file incorrectly, or deleting important information within the file. Although this type of data loss is relatively low-impact for the business, it is critical to the user who needs the data. With user error, generally a specific file or folder must be retrieved from a backup source.

Theft

Thieves target laptops, memory sticks, CDs and DVDs, tapes, and other data storage devices. When taking company data offsite, create backup copies of all data. Keep careful track of portable data sources. It is also a good idea to encrypt all data on portable devices so that it is of no use to the thief.

Malicious Activity

Viruses and hackers can destroy data. Some viruses target specific types of files to corrupt. Some viruses can affect the hard drive that the data is stored on and can cause the drive to be inaccessible. Additionally, hackers can manipulate data, such as defacing a website to gain exposure.

Operating System Failure

A bad patch or driver update could result in serious operating system failure, preventing access to needed data. With backed-up operating system files, the operating system can often be restored at a functional level. However, a reinstallation may be necessary, or even a full restore of all the missing data.

Regardless of the cause of failure, an ISP that hosts websites or e-mail for customers must protect the web and e-mail content from being lost. Losing the data stored on a website could mean hundreds, or even thousands, of hours re-creating the content, not to mention the lost business that results from the downtime while the content is being re-created.

Losing e-mail messages that were stored on the ISP's e-mail server could potentially be crippling for a business that relies on the data within the e-mails. Some businesses are legally required to maintain records of all e-mail correspondence, so losing those e-mails would be unacceptable.

Data backup is essential. An IT professional's job is to try to reduce the risks of data loss and provide mechanisms for quick recovery of any data that is lost.

Backup Media

When an ISP needs to back up its data, the cost of a backup solution and its effectiveness must be balanced. The choice of backup media can be complex, because many factors affect the choice:

- The amount of data
- The media's cost
- The media's performance
- The media's reliability
- Ease of offsite storage

Many types of backup media are available, including magnetic tape media, optical media, hard disk media, and solid-state media.

Tape Media

Tape remains one of the most common types of backup media available. Tapes have large capacities and remain the most cost-effective media on the market. Tape is also very fast if large quantities of data are to be recorded and retrieved sequentially. If data is to be retrieved randomly, a random-access device such as a hard disk or optical drive would be able to access the data much more rapidly.

For data volumes that have more than a single tape, tape autoloaders and libraries can swap tapes during the backup procedure, allowing the data to be stored on as many tapes as required. These devices can be expensive and typically are not found in small- to medium-sized businesses. However, depending on the volume of data, there may be no alternative other than an autoloader or library.

Tape media is prone to failure, and tape drives require regular cleaning to maintain functionality. Tapes also have a high failure rate as they wear out. Tapes should be used for only a fixed amount of time before they are removed from circulation. Some of the different types of tapes are

- Digital data storage (DDS)
- Digital audio tape (DAT)
- Digital linear tape (DLT)
- Linear tape open (LTO)

These all have different capacities and performance characteristics.

Optical Media

Optical media is a common choice for smaller amounts of data. CDs have a storage capacity of 700 MB, DVDs can support up to 8.5 GB on a single-sided dual-layer disk, and HD-DVD and Blu-ray disks can have capacities in excess of 25 GB per disk. ISPs may use optical media to transfer web content data to their customers. Customers may also use this medium to transfer website content to the ISP web hosting site. Optical media can easily be accessed by any computer system that has a CD or DVD drive built in. Figure 8-25 shows examples of digital tape and optical backup recording media.

Figure 8-25   Digital Tape and Optical Backup Media

Tape   Optical

Hard Disk Media

Hard disk-based backup systems are becoming increasingly popular because of the low cost of high-capacity drives. However, hard disk-based backup systems make offsite storage difficult. Large disk arrays such as *direct-attached storage (DAS)*, *network-attached storage (NAS)*, and *storage-area networks (SAN)* are not transportable.

Many implementations of hard disk-based backup systems work in conjunction with tape backup systems for offsite storage. Using both hard disks and tapes in a tiered backup solution can give you a quick restore time, with the data available locally on the hard disks, as well as a long-term archival solution.

Solid-State Media

Solid-state media refers to all nonvolatile storage media that do not have any moving parts. Examples of solid-state media range from small postage-stamp-sized drives holding 1 GB of data to router-sized devices that can store 1000 GB (1 TB) of data.

Solid-state media are ideal for storing data when fast storage and retrieval are important. Applications of solid-state data storage systems include database acceleration, high-definition video access and editing, data retrieval, and SANs. High-capacity solid-state storage devices can be extremely expensive, but as the technology matures, the prices will come down. Solid-state storage is the least prone to failure, because it is all electronic and has no moving parts. Figure 8-26 shows an example of a solid-state backup medium.

Figure 8-26　Solid-State Backup Medium

Methods of File Backup

After you choose a backup solution, you must decide how to perform the backups. You have three methods to choose from:

- Normal (full)
- Differential
- Incremental

Normal (Full)

A normal (or full) backup copies all selected files and marks each file as having been backed up. With normal backups, only the most recent backup is required to restore all files, speeding up and simplifying the restore process. However, because all data is being backed up, a *full backup* takes the longest. Figure 8-27 shows how a normal or full backup works over the course of a week.

Figure 8-27 Normal or Full Backup

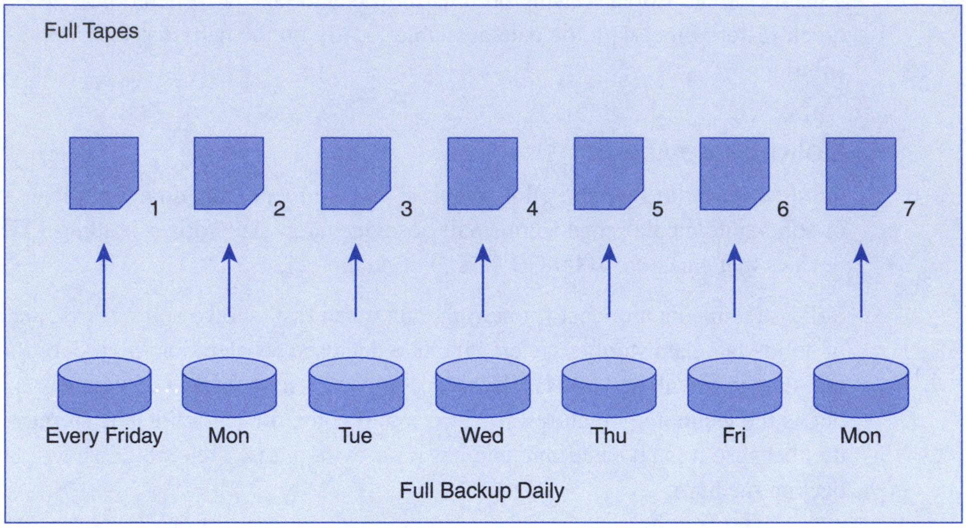

Full Tapes
1
2
3
4
5
6
7
Every Friday
Mon
Tue
Wed
Thu
Fri
Mon
Full Backup Daily

Normal Backup

Differential

A ***differential backup*** copies only the files that have been changed since the last full backup. With differential backups, a normal full backup on the first day of the backup cycle is necessary. Only the files that have been created or changed since the time of the last full backup are saved. The differential backup process continues until another full backup is run. This reduces the amount of time required to perform the backup. When it is time to restore data, the last normal backup is restored, and the latest differential backup restores all files that have changed since the last full backup. Figure 8-28 shows how a differential backup works over the course of a week.

Figure 8-28 Differential Backup

Full Tapes
Differential Tapes
1
8
2
3
4
5
6
7
9
Every Friday
Mon
Tue
Wed
Thu
Fri
Mon
Only Files Changed Since Last Full Backup

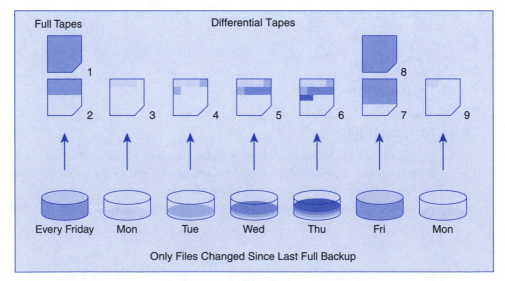

Differential Backup

Incremental

An *incremental backup* differs from a differential backup on one important point. Whereas a differential backup saves files that were changed since the last full backup, an incremental backup saves only files that were created or changed since the last incremental backup. This means that if an incremental backup is run every day, the backup media would contain only files created or changed on that day. Incremental backups are the quickest kind of backup. However, they take the longest to restore, because the last normal backup and every incremental backup since the last full backup must be restored. Figure 8-29 shows how an incremental backup works over the course of a week.

Figure 8-29   Incremental Backup

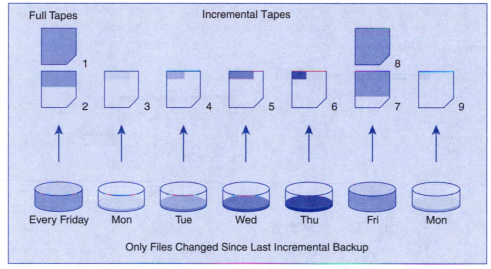

Incremental Backup

Backup System Maintenance

Backup systems require regular maintenance to keep them running properly. Some steps to ensure the successful completion of backups include the following:

- Swap media
- Review backup logs
- Perform trial restores
- Perform drive maintenance

This section describes each of these maintenance steps.

Swap Media

Many backup scenarios require daily swapping of media to maintain a history of backed-up data. Data loss could occur if the tape or disk is not swapped daily. Because swapping the tapes is a manual task, it is prone to failure. Users need to use a notification method, such as calendar or task scheduling. Figure 8-30 shows a large backup system with swap media.

Figure 8-30   Swap Media

Review Backup Logs

Virtually all backup software produces backup logs. Regularly review backup logs. These logs report on the success of the backup, specifying where it failed. Regular monitoring of backup logs allows for quick identification of any backup issues that require attention. Figure 8-31 shows GUI-based backup utility logs.

Figure 8-31   Backup Logs

Perform Trial Restores

Monitoring backup logs regularly does not mean that the procedure was successful. To verify that backup data is usable and that the restore procedure works, periodically perform a trial restore of data. This ensures that the backup procedures work. Figure 8-32 shows doing a test restore using Windows Backup.

Figure 8-32   Perform Trial Restores

Perform Drive Maintenance

Many backup systems require special hardware to perform the backups. Tape backup systems use a tape backup drive to read and write to the tapes. Tape drives can become dirty from use and can lead to mechanical failure. Perform routine cleaning of the tape drive using designated cleaning tapes. Hard drive-based backup systems can benefit from an occasional defragmentation to improve the system's overall performance. Figure 8-33 shows some of the key backup operations required to maintain a dependable backup system.

Figure 8-33   Perform Drive Maintenance

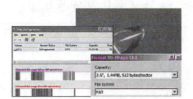

 Lab 8-8: Planning a Backup Solution (8.4.2)

In this lab you plan a backup solution for a small business. Refer to the hands-on lab in Part II of this book. You may perform this lab now or wait until the end of the chapter.

Backing Up and Restoring Cisco IOS Image Files

In addition to backing up server files, it is also necessary for the ISP to protect configurations and the Cisco IOS software used on networking devices owned by the ISP.

Using TFTP to Update the IOS Image

The Cisco networking device software and configuration files can be saved to a network server using TFTP and variations of the **copy** command. The command to save the IOS file is very similar to the command to back up and save a running configuration file.

Backing up Cisco IOS software involves three basic steps:

 Step 1.   Ping the TFTP server where the file should be saved. This verifies connectivity to the TFTP server.

Step 2.   On the router, verify the IOS image in flash. Use the **show flash** command to view the filename of the IOS image and file size. Confirm that the TFTP server has enough disk space to store the file. Example 8-1 shows output for the **show flash** command.

Example 8-1   R1 show flash Command Output

```
R1# show flash
-#- --length-- -----date/time------ path
1      22063220 Feb 22 1907 17:31:44 +00:00 c1841-advipservicesk9-mz.124-10b.bin
41947136 bytes available (22065152 bytes used)
```

Step 3.   Copy the IOS image to the TFTP server using the command **copy tftp flash**. Example 8-2 shows output for the **copy tftp flash** command.

Example 8-2   R1 copy tftp flash Command Output

```
R1# copy flash tftp
Source filename []? c1841-advipservicesk9-mz.124-10b.bin
Address or name of remote host []? 172.17.0.2
Destination filename [c1841-advipservicesk9-mz.124-10b.bin]?
!!!!!!!!!!!!!!!!!!!!!!!!!!!!!!!!!!!!!!!!!!!!!!!!!!!!!!!!!!!!!!!!!!!!!!!!!!!!!!!!!!!!!!
22063220 bytes copied in 58.264 secs (378677 bytes/sec)
```

When you use the **copy** command, the router prompts the user for the source filename, the IP address of the TFTP server, and the destination filename.

Images stored on the TFTP server can be used to restore or upgrade the Cisco IOS software on routers and switches in a network.

Lab 8-9: Managing Cisco IOS Images with TFTP (8.4.3a)

In this lab you use a TFTP server to back up and restore a Cisco router IOS image file. Refer to the hands-on lab in Part II of this book. You may perform this lab now or wait until the end of the chapter.

Using ROMmon to Recover the IOS Image

If the router is set to boot from flash, but the Cisco IOS image in flash is erased, corrupted, or inaccessible because of lack of memory, the image may need to be restored. The quickest way to restore a Cisco IOS image to the router is by using TFTP in ROM monitor (ROMmon) mode.

The ROMmon TFTP transfer works on a specified LAN port and defaults to the first available LAN interface. To use TFTP in ROMmon mode, the user must first set a few environmental variables, including the IP address, and then use the **tftpdnld** command to restore the image.

To set a ROMmon environment variable, enter the variable name, an equals sign (=), and the value for the variable. For example, to set the IP address to 10.0.0.1, enter IP_ADDRESS=10.0.0.1.

The required environment variables are as follows:

- IP_ADDRESS: IP address on the LAN interface
- IP_SUBNET_MASK: Subnet mask for the LAN interface
- DEFAULT_GATEWAY: Default gateway for the LAN interface
- TFTP_SERVER: IP address of the TFTP server
- TFTP_FILE: Cisco IOS filename on the server

Example 8-3 shows how to set the ROMmon variable to prepare for running **tftpdnld** and then the results of running **tftpdnld**.

Caution

The **tftpdnld** utility erases flash memory completely before copying the new IOS image. In addition to the IOS image, you should back up all other files in router flash memory to a TFTP server so they can be copied back to flash after the IOS image is restored.

Example 8-3 Setting ROMmon Variables and Running tftpdnld

```
rommon 7 > IP_ADDRESS=172.17.0.1
rommon 8 > IP_SUBNET_MASK=255.255.0.0
rommon 9 > DEFAULT_GATEWAY=172.17.0.1
rommon 10 > TFTP_SERVER=172.17.0.2
rommon 11 > TFTP_FILE=c1841-advipservicesk9-mz.124-10b.bin

rommon 12 > tftpdnld
          IP_ADDRESS: 172.17.0.1
      IP_SUBNET_MASK: 255.255.0.0
     DEFAULT_GATEWAY: 172.17.0.1
         TFTP_SERVER: 172.17.0.2
```

```
           TFTP_FILE: c1841-advipservicesk9-mz.124-10b.bin
        TFTP_MACADDR: 00:1b:53:25:25:6e
        TFTP_VERBOSE: Progress
    TFTP_RETRY_COUNT: 18
        TFTP_TIMEOUT: 7200
       TFTP_CHECKSUM: Yes
             FE_PORT: 0
        FE_SPEED_MODE: Auto Detect
Invoke this command for disaster recovery only.
WARNING: all existing data in all partitions on flash: will be lost!
Do you wish to continue? y/n:  [n]:  y
.
Receiving c1841-advipservicesk9-mz.124-10b.bin from 172.17.0.2
!!!!!!!!!!!!!!!!!!!!!!!!!!!!!!!!!!!!!!!!!!!!!!!!!!!!!!!!!!!!!!!!!!!!!!!!!!!!
<output omitted>
!!!!!!!!!!!!!!!!!!!!!!!!!!!!!!!!!!!!!!!!!!!!!!!!!!!!!!!!!!!!!!!!!!!!!!!!!!!!!!
File reception completed.
Validating checksum.
Copying file c1841-advipservicesk9-mz.124-10b.bin to flash:.
program load complete, entry point: 0x8000f000, size: 0xcb80

Format: Drive communication & 1st Sector Write OK...
Writing Monlib sectors.

Format: All system sectors written. OK...
Format: Operation completed successfully.

Format of flash: complete
program load complete, entry point: 0x8000f000, size: 0xcb80
```

Lab 8-10: Managing Cisco IOS Images with ROMmon and TFTP (8.4.3b)

In this lab you use ROMmon and **tftpdnld** to restore a Cisco router IOS image file from a TFTP server. Refer to the hands-on lab in Part II of this book. You may perform this lab now or wait until the end of the chapter.

Best Practices for Disaster Recovery

Data backup is an important part of any disaster recovery plan. A disaster recovery plan is a comprehensive document that describes how to restore operation quickly and keep a business running during or after a disaster occurs. The objective of the disaster recovery plan is to ensure that the business can smoothly adapt to the physical and social changes that a disaster causes. Disasters can include anything from natural disasters that affect the network structure to malicious attacks on the network itself.

The disaster recovery plan can include information such as offsite locations where services can be moved, information on switching out network devices and servers, and backup connectivity options. It is important when building a disaster recovery plan to fully understand the services that are critical to maintaining operation. Services that might need to be available during a disaster include

- Database
- Application servers

■ System management servers

■ Web

■ Data stores

■ Directory

Figure 8-34 shows a main headquarters site with a remote backup site. The data from the main site is backed up to the backup site on a regular basis. If a disaster strikes the main site, the backup site can continue processing.

Figure 8-34   Headquarters and the Backup Site

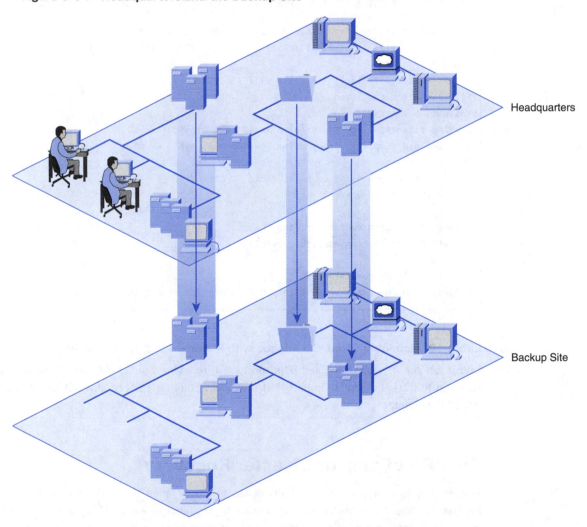

When designing a disaster recovery plan, it is important to understand the organization's needs. It is also important to gain the support necessary for a disaster recovery plan. The steps to accomplish this include the following:

■ **Vulnerability assessment**: Conduct a study that assesses how vulnerable the critical business processes and associated applications are to common disasters, such as fire and tornados.

■ **Risk assessment**: Analyze the risk of a disaster occurring and the associated effects and costs to the business. Part of risk assessment is creating a top ten potential disasters and effects list, including the scenario of the business being destroyed.

- **Management awareness**: Get senior management approval on the disaster recovery project. Maintaining equipment and locations in the event of a possible disaster recovery could be expensive. Senior management must understand the possible effect of any disaster situation.

- **Establish a planning group**: Establish a planning group to manage the development and implementation of the disaster recovery strategy and plan. When a disaster occurs, be it small or large, it is important that individuals understand their roles and responsibilities.

- **Prioritize**: For each disaster scenario, assign a priority of mission-critical, important, or minor for the business network, applications, and systems.

The disaster recovery planning process should first engage the top managers, and then eventually include all personnel who work with critical business processes. Everyone must be involved and support the plan for it to be successful.

As soon as the need for a disaster recovery plan is agreed on, along with the services and applications that are most critical, it is time to actually create the plan. Doing so involves these steps:

- **Network design recovery strategy**: Analyze the network design. Here are some aspects of the network design that you should include in the disaster recovery:

  - Whether the network is designed to survive a major disaster. This includes the use of backup connectivity options and redundancy in the network design.

  - Availability of offsite servers that can support applications such as e-mail and database services.

  - Availability of backup routers, switches, and other network devices should they fail.

  - Location of services and resources the network needs. Are they spread over a wide geography?

- **Inventory and documentation**: An inventory should be done of all locations, devices, vendors, used services, and contact names. Verify cost estimates that are created during risk assessment.

- **Verification**: Create a verification process to prove that the disaster recover strategy works. Practice disaster recovery exercises to ensure that the plan is up-to-date and workable.

- **Approval and implementation**: Obtain senior management approval, and create a budget to implement the disaster recovery plan.

- **Review**: After the disaster recovery plan has been implemented for a year, review the plan.

Interactive Activity 8-2: Best Practices for Disaster Recovery (8.4.4)

In this interactive activity, you match the disaster recovery planning phases to the correct disaster recovery procedure. Use file d2ia-844 on the CD-ROM that accompanies this book to perform this interactive activity.

Summary

Desktop security services for customers include creating secure passwords, securing applications with patches and upgrades, removing unnecessary applications, performing security scans, and setting appropriate permissions on resources.

When you assign permissions to files and folders, a security best practice is to apply permissions based on the principle of least privilege.

Authentication, authorization, and accounting (AAA) is a three-step process used to monitor and control access on a network. It requires a database to keep track of user credentials, permissions, and account statistics.

Digital encryption is the process of encrypting transmitted data between the clients and servers. Many protocols offer secure versions. As a best practice, use the secure version of a protocol whenever the data exchanged is meant to be confidential.

Security threats include DoS, DDoS, and DRDoS attacks. In addition, they can include data destruction and alteration by internal and external attackers.

You can use a variety of tools to help protect your network from security threats. Port filtering can restrict or allow traffic based on the TCP or UDP port. Access lists define traffic that is permitted or denied based on IP addresses as well as TCP or UDP ports. A firewall is network hardware or software that defines what traffic can come into and go out of sections of the network. IDS is a software- or hardware-based solution that passively listens to network traffic. It does not stop the initial traffic from passing through to the destination. IPS is an active physical device or software feature. Traffic actually passes through IPS interfaces, and the IPS can block all suspicious activity in real time. A host-based firewall and Anti-X software runs directly on a host operating system and protects the host from malicious attacks that might have made it through all other layers of defense.

A service-level agreement (SLA) is an agreement between a service provider and a service user that clearly documents the expectations and obligations.

ISPs monitor and check devices' connectivity. They accomplish this through in-band or out-of-band management. In-band management is preferred for managing servers that are accessible on the network.

Several backup media options are available, including tape, optical, hard disk, and solid-state media. There are also three methods of backing up data, including full backup, differential backup, and incremental backup. A combination of all three backup methods generally is recommended.

In addition to user data backups, ISPs also must be able to back up and restore device configurations and Cisco IOS software used on networking devices. TFTP servers and ROMmon are tools that can assist with this process.

A disaster recovery plan is a comprehensive document that describes how to restore operation quickly and keep a business running during or after a disaster occurs. Assess the vulnerabilities, assess the risk, ensure management awareness, establish a planning group, and prioritize needs when creating a disaster recovery plan.

Activities and Labs

This summary outlines the activities and labs you can perform to help reinforce important concepts described in this chapter. You can find the activity and Packet Tracer files on the CD-ROM that accompanies this book. The complete hands-on labs appear in Part II.

Interactive Activities on the CD-ROM:

Interactive Activity 8-1: IDS and IPS (8.2.3)

Interactive Activity 8-2: Best Practices for Disaster Recovery (8.4.4)

Packet Tracer Activities on the CD-ROM:

Planning Network-Based Firewalls (8.2.2)

Configuring WEP on a Wireless Router (8.2.4)

Labs in Part II of this book:

Lab 8-1: Securing Local Data and Transmitted Data (8.1.3)

Lab 8-2: Planning for Access Control Lists and Port Filters (8.2.1)

Lab 8-3: Researching Anti-X Software Products (8.2.5)

Lab 8-4: Interpreting a Service-Level Agreement (8.3.1)

Lab 8-5: Conducting a Network Capture with Wireshark (8.3.2)

Lab 8-6: Managing Remote Network Devices with Telnet (8.3.3a)

Lab 8-7: Configuring a Remote Router Using SSH (8.3.3b)

Lab 8-8: Planning a Backup Solution (8.4.2)

Lab 8-9: Managing Cisco IOS Images with TFTP (8.4.3a)

Lab 8-10: Managing Cisco IOS Images with ROMmon and TFTP (8.4.3b)

Check Your Understanding

Complete all the review questions listed here to check your understanding of the topics and concepts in this chapter. Answers are listed in Appendix A, "Check Your Understanding and Challenge Questions Answer Key."

1. Which term describes the ability of a web server to keep a log of the users who access the server, as well as how long they use it?

   A. Authentication

   B. Authorization

   C. Accounting

   D. Assigning permissions

2. Which two statements describe out-of-band network management?

   A. It does not require a physical connection.

   B. It is preferred over in-band management for managing services.

   C. It is used for initial device configuration.

   D. It uses a direct console or dial-in connection.

   E. It provides greater functionality than in-band management.

3. What two are duties of an SNMP management agent?

   A. It collects information for the management station by polling devices.

   B. It permits access to devices by assigning each a community ID.

   C. It reports to the management station by responding to polls.

   D. It runs the applications that the administrator uses to configure devices on the network.

   E. It sends an alert message to the management station if a threshold is exceeded.

4. What is the principle of least privilege?

   A. The use of only a single server to store shared data for a local network.

   B. Give each user access to only those resources needed to do his or her job.

   C. All local users should have open access to shared data.

   D. When more than one user needs access to the same data, access should be first come, first served.

5. Match the AAA term on the left to its definition on the right. Not all terms will be used.

Accounting	Permissions to a specific network resource
Authorization	Username and password
Authentication	Who used what network resource

6. What is the main reason that magnetic tape is used to back up data?

   A. Cost

   B. Random-access speed

   C. To easily locate data

   D. The tape never needs replacing

7. The CEO of a company decides that the company's backup process needs to allow for a very quick restoration of lost data. He is willing to accept a lengthier time for the backup process and wants to be able to access all the data available for a backup on any given day. Which type of backup should be implemented?

8. The IT manager performs a full backup on Monday and differential backups on Tuesday, Wednesday, and Thursday. On Friday morning, the server crashes, and all the data must be restored. In which sequence should the backup tapes be restored?

   A. The full backup tape from Monday, and then differential tapes from Thursday, Wednesday, and Tuesday

   B. The differential tape from Thursday, and then the full backup tape from Monday

   C. The full backup tape from Monday, and then the differential tape from Thursday

   D. Only the full backup tape from Monday

   E. Only the differential tape from Thursday

9. Where is the safest place to store backups?

   A. Portable lockbox

   B. Locked telecommunications room

   C. Locked server room

   D. Offsite secure facility

10. Which firewall filtering technology keeps track of the actual communication process occurring between the source and destination devices and stores it in a table?

   A. Access list filtering

   B. Stateful filtering

   C. URL filtering

   D. Content filtering

11. Why is risk assessment critical to disaster recovery planning?

   A. It includes management approval to implement the plan.

   B. It identifies the high-priority applications that must be restored quickly.

   C. It outlines the roles of each member of the disaster recovery team.

   D. It identifies the likely disasters that could occur and their effect on the business.

12. Why would a business choose an IPS instead of an IDS? (Choose two.)

   A. An IPS identifies and blocks malicious activity.

   B. An IPS is installed out-of-band and does not affect network traffic throughput.

   C. An IDS cannot stop some malicious traffic from getting through.

   D. An IDS is an in-band device that can affect network traffic.

   E. An IDS device must be installed outside the firewall to monitor traffic.

13. List two protocols that typically are used for in-band network management.

14. Which of the following protocols provide for encrypted data transfer? (Choose three.)

A. SSL

B. SIP

C. DHCP

D. HTTP

E. HTTPS

F. IPsec

15. What type of standard server is frequently used to record informational and error messages, sent by various networking devices, for analysis by a network technician?

16. A network administrator configures a server to allow access to the web service but deny access to all other services. What type of security measure is this?

A. Access list

B. Encryption

C. Anti-X software

D. Port filtering

E. Authentication

17. Which of the following terms is not directly related to SNMP?

A. MIB

B. IDS

C. Trap

D. Agent

E. Community ID

18. Which wireless security protocol provides the strongest data encryption?

A. WLAN

B. WEP2

C. WPA

D. WEP

E. WPA2

19. What type of server can help a network administrator back up, recover, and update Cisco configuration and IOS images files?

20. When the IOS image file is missing or corrupted, and the router will not boot to the IOS, what tools can be used to clear the flash memory and load a new IOS image?

21. Which of the following are methods of wireless authentication? (Choose three.)

A. Open

B. WEP

C. PSK

D. WPA

E. EAP

## CHAPTER 9

Troubleshooting

Objectives

After completing this chapter, you should be able to answer the following questions:

- How is the OSI model used as a framework for troubleshooting network problems?

- How are problems with hardware and the operation of Layer 1 and Layer 2 identified and corrected?

- What is the procedure for troubleshooting IP addressing problems, including subnet mask, host range errors, DHCP, and NAT issues?

- How are problems with RIPv2 configuration and implementation identified and corrected?

- What are some possible causes of problems occurring with user applications, and how can symptoms of DNS failure be recognized?

- What must be done to create a plan to prepare to take the ICND1 examination to obtain a CCENT certification?

This chapter is a review of previous chapters and does not introduce any new terms.

Troubleshooting configuration or operation problems requires the application of networking knowledge and skills. Employers value networkers who can troubleshoot in an organized manner to identify symptoms, isolate the causes, and fix the problems quickly. Cisco Career Certifications bring valuable, measureable rewards to network professionals and the organizations that employ them. Practicing troubleshooting can help you prepare to obtain a Cisco Certified Entry Networking Technician (CCENT) certification.

Troubleshooting Methodologies and Tools

When used with a structured troubleshooting approach, the OSI model can help speed the diagnostics process and reduce network downtime. This section provides a review of the OSI model as it relates to troubleshooting and describes various troubleshooting tools.

The OSI Model and Troubleshooting

One of the most important abilities for a network professional to develop is to efficiently troubleshoot network problems. Good network troubleshooters are always in high demand. For this reason, Cisco certification exams measure the ability to identify and correct network problems.

When troubleshooting, many technicians use the OSI and TCP/IP networking models to help isolate the cause of a problem. Logical networking models separate network functionality into modular layers. Each layer of the OSI or TCP/IP model has specific functions and protocols. Knowledge of the features, functions, and devices of each layer, and how each layer relates to the layers around it, help a network technician troubleshoot more efficiently. Figure 9-1 show the seven-layer OSI model as it relates to the four-layer TCP/IP model. The OSI model is a more conceptual model, whereas the TCP/IP model is built around specific IP-based protocols that operate at each layer. The TCP/IP application layer corresponds to the top three layers of the OSI model and includes the same functions. The OSI transport layer corresponds directly with the TCP/IP transport layer, and the OSI network layer corresponds directly with the TCP/IP internet layer. The TCP/IP network access layer combines the functions of the OSI data link and physical layers, although a revised version of the TCP/IP model breaks out the last two layers the same as the OSI.

The following describes the functions of each OSI layer in greater detail:

- **Applications Layer**:
    - Defines interfaces between application software and network communications functions.
    - Provides standardized services, such as file transfer between systems.
- **Presentation Layer**:
    - Standardizes user data formats for use between different types of systems.
    - Encodes and decodes user data; encrypts and decrypts data; compresses and depresses data.
- **Session Layer**:
    - Manages user sessions and dialogues.
    - Manages links between applications.

- **Transport Layer**:
  - Manages end-to end message delivery over the network.
  - Can provide reliable and sequential packet delivery through error recovery and flow control mechanisms.
- **Network Layer**:
  - Defines logical network addressing assigned to hosts.
  - Routes packets between networks based on logical addressing.
- **Data Link Layer**:
  - Defines procedures for operating the communication links.
  - Detects and corrects frame transmit errors.
  - Adds physical addresses to frame.
- **Physical Layer**:
  - Defines physical means of sending data over network devices.
  - Interfaces between network medium and devices.
  - Defines optical, electrical, and mechanical characteristics.
  - Includes all forms of electromagnetic transmission such as light, electricity, infrared, and radio waves.

Figure 9-1 compares the OSI model and TCP/IP model.

Figure 9-1   Comparing the OSI Model and TCP/IP Model

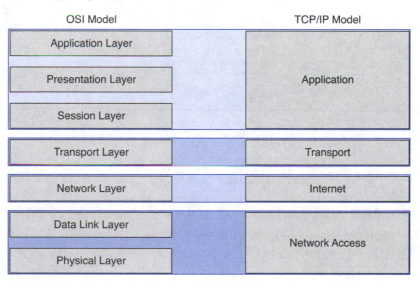

The OSI reference model provides a common language for network technicians and engineers. It is important to understand the functions that occur and the networking devices that operate at each layer of the OSI model.

The upper layers of the OSI model (Layers 5 through 7) deal with specific application functionality and generally are implemented only in software. Problems isolated with these layers can frequently be caused by end-system software configuration errors on clients and servers. The lower layers of the OSI model (Layers 1 through 4) handle data-transport functions.

The network layer (Layer 3) and the transport layer (Layer 4) are generally implemented only in software. In addition to software errors on end systems, software configuration errors on routers and firewalls account for many problems isolated to these layers. IP addressing and routing errors occur at Layer 3.

The physical layer (Layer 1) and data link layer (Layer 2) are implemented in both hardware and software. The physical layer is closest to the physical network medium, such as the network cabling, and is responsible for actually placing information on the medium. Hardware problems and incompatibilities cause most Layer 1 and Layer 2 problems.

Refer to the icons that represent physical devices (and software installed) and the OSI layers shown in Figure 9-2. Hubs are dumb devices that simply repeat electrical signals and operate only at OSI Layer 1. A standard Ethernet LAN switch repeats electrical signals like a hub but also works with Layer 2 MAC addresses to direct frames to their destination. Standard switches operate at OSI Layers 1 and 2. Routers and firewalls work with Layers 1 and 2 but also with IP addresses at Layer 3 and TCP/UDP port numbers at Layer 4. End systems run applications software and must be able to operate at all seven layers of the OSI model.

Figure 9-2   Network and Transport Layers

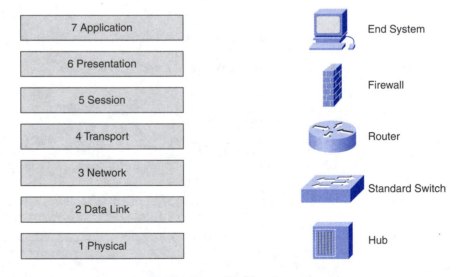

Interactive Activity 9-1: The OSI Model and Troubleshooting (9.1.1)

In this interactive activity, you identify the layer to which the protocol or technology belongs. Use file d2ia-911 on the CD-ROM that accompanies this book to perform this interactive activity.

Lab 9-1: Organizing CCENT Objectives by OSI Layer (9.1.1)

In this lab, using the worksheet provided, you organize the CCENT objectives by which layer or layers they address. Refer to the lab in Part II of this book. You may perform this lab now or wait until the end of the chapter.

Troubleshooting Methodologies

There are three main troubleshooting approaches when using network models:

- Top-down
- Bottom-up
- Divide-and-conquer

Each method assumes a layered concept of networking. Using one of these troubleshooting methods, a troubleshooter can verify all functionality at each layer until the problem is located and isolated.

Top-Down

Top-down troubleshooting starts with the application layer and works down. It looks at the problem from the point of view of the user and the application. Is only one application not functioning, or do all applications fail? For example, can the user access various web pages on the Internet but not e-mail? Do other workstations have similar issues?

It is most suited for simpler problems or those that are suspected to be related to applications/user or upper layers. A disadvantage of the top-down approach is that if the problem turns out to be related to lower layers, you have spent a lot of time and effort at the upper-layer applications.

Bottom-Up

Bottom-up troubleshooting starts with the physical layer and works up. The physical layer is concerned with hardware and wire connections: Have cables been pulled out of their sockets? If the equipment has indicator lights, are they on or off?

It is most suited for complex cases where a very structured approach is required. It is a slow but solid approach. When the problem is upper-layer or application related, this approach can take a long time.

Divide-and-Conquer

Divide-and-conquer troubleshooting typically begins at one of the middle layers, such as data link, network, or transport and works up or down from there. For example, the troubleshooter might begin at the network layer by verifying IP configuration information.

This approach is most suitable when you are experienced and the problem has precise symptoms. It targets the problem layer faster than the other approaches.

The structure of these approaches makes them ideally suited for the novice troubleshooter. More experienced individuals often bypass structured approaches and rely on instinct and experience.

Interactive Activity 9-2: Troubleshooting Methodologies (9.1.2)

In this interactive activity, you place the actions taken by the technician into the correct troubleshooting method category. Use file d2ia-912 on the CD-ROM that accompanies this book to perform this interactive activity.

Troubleshooting Tools

It is very difficult to troubleshoot any type of network connectivity issue without a network diagram that depicts the IP addresses, IP routes, and devices, such as firewalls and switches. Logical and physical topologies are extremely useful in troubleshooting.

In addition to using network topologies in troubleshooting, you also will need a variety of software and hardware troubleshooting tools.

Network Topologies

This section describes how physical and logical network topologies are helpful in troubleshooting.

Physical Network Topologies

A physical network topology shows the physical layout of the devices connected to the network, as can be seen in Figure 9-3. Knowing how devices are physically connected is necessary for troubleshooting problems at the physical layer, such as cabling or hardware problems. Physical network topologies typically include

- Device types
- Models and manufacturers of devices
- Locations
- Operating system versions
- Cable types and identifiers
- Cabling endpoints

Figure 9-3   Physical Topology

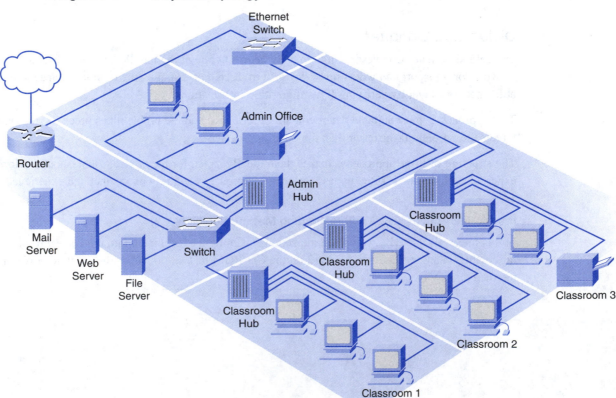

Logical Network Topologies

Figure 9-4 shows the same network in a logical view. A logical network topology shows how data is transferred on the network. Symbols are used to represent network elements such as routers, servers, hubs, hosts, and security devices. Logical network topologies typically include

- Device identifiers
- IP addresses and subnet masks
- Interface identifiers
- Routing protocols
- Static and default routes
- Data-link protocols
- WAN technologies

Figure 9-4   Logical Topology

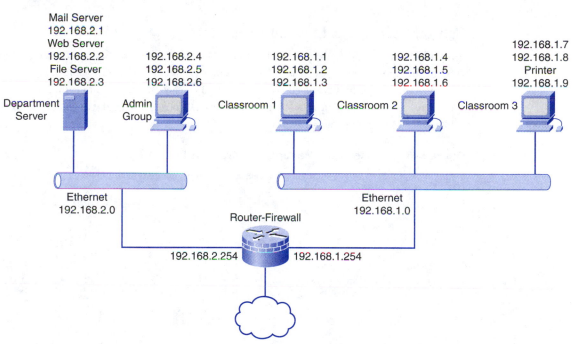

Software Troubleshooting Tools

In addition to network diagrams, other tools are needed to effectively troubleshoot network performance issues and failures.

Network Documentation and Baseline Tools

Network documentation and baseline tools are available for Windows, Linux, and UNIX operating systems. Cisco Works can be used to draw network diagrams, keep network software and hardware documentation up to date, and help cost-effectively measure baseline network bandwidth use. These software tools often provide monitoring and reporting functions for establishing the network baseline. Figure 9-5 shows the SolarWinds LANsurveyor automated network mapping tool and the CyberGauge bandwidth monitoring tool

Figure 9-5   Baseline Tools

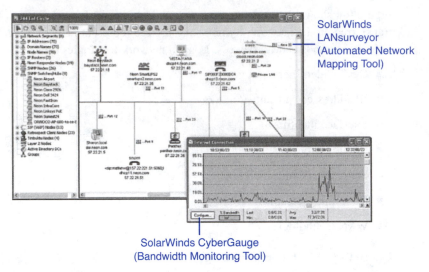

SolarWinds
LANsurveyor
(Automated Network
Mapping Tool)

SolarWinds CyberGauge
(Bandwidth Monitoring Tool)

Network Management System Tools

Network management system tools monitor network performance. They graphically display a physical view of the network devices. If a failure occurs, the tool can locate the source, such as whether it was caused by malware, malicious activity, or a failed device. Examples of commonly used network management tools are CiscoView, HP Openview, SolarWinds, and WhatsUp Gold. Figure 9-6 shows the WhatsUP Gold device status display.

Figure 9-6   Network Management System Tool

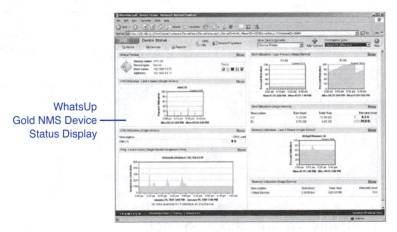

WhatsUp
Gold NMS Device
Status Display

Knowledge Bases

Network device vendor knowledge bases have become indispensable sources of information. When online knowledge bases are combined with Internet search engines, a network administrator has access to a vast pool of experience-based information. Figure 9-7 shows the Cisco website support tools and resources available.

Figure 9-7   Knowledge Base Tool

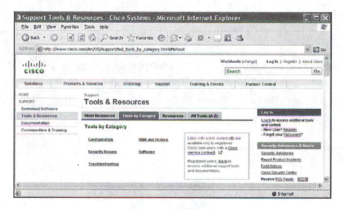

Protocol Analyzers

A protocol analyzer decodes the various protocol layers in a recorded frame and presents this information in a relatively easy-to-use format. Protocol analyzers can capture network traffic for analysis. The captured output can be filtered to view specific traffic or types of traffic based on certain criteria; for example, all traffic to and from a particular device. Protocol analyzers, such as Wireshark, provide detailed troubleshooting information about the data being communicated on the network. An example of the types of information that can be viewed using a protocol analyzer is the setup and termination of a TCP session between two hosts. Figure 9-8 shows the WireShark protocol analyzer.

Figure 9-8   Protocol Analyzer Tool

Wireshark
Protocol
Analyzer

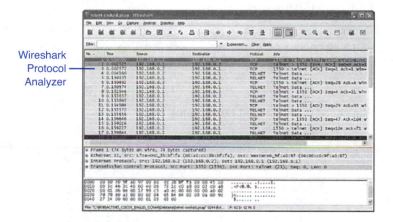

Lab 9-2: Using Wireshark to Observe the TCP Three-Way Handshake (9.1.3)

In this lab you use Wireshark to observe the TCP/IP three-way handshake. Refer to the lab in Part II of this book. You may perform this lab now or wait until the end of the chapter.

Hardware Troubleshooting Tools

Sometimes failures in the lower layers of the OSI model cannot be easily identified with software tools. In these cases, it might be necessary to use hardware troubleshooting tools, such as cable testers, multimeters, and network analyzers.

Cable Testers

Cable testers are specialized, handheld devices designed for testing the various types of data communication cabling. Cable testers can be used to detect broken wires, crossed-over wiring, shorted connections, and improperly paired connections. More sophisticated testers, such as a time-domain reflectometer (TDR), can pinpoint the distance to a break in a cable. Cable testers can also determine the length of a cable. Figure 9-9 shows two models of Fluke cable testers. These are relatively sophisticated cable testers. Less expensive basic cable testers are available that can verify the functionality of most common Ethernet network cables.

Figure 9-9　Cable Testers

Fluke Networks LinkRunner Pro Tester　　Fluke Networks CableIQ
Qualification Tester

Digital Multimeters

Digital multimeters (DMM) are test instruments that directly measure electrical values of voltage, current, and resistance. In network troubleshooting, most of the multimeter tests involve checking power-supply voltage levels and verifying that network devices are receiving power. Figure 9-10 shows a Fluke digital multimeter.

Figure 9-10　Digital Multimeter

Fluke 179 Digital Multimeter

Portable Network Analyzers

By plugging in a network analyzer to a switch anywhere on the network, a network engineer can see the average and peak utilization of the segment. The analyzer can also be used to identify the devices producing the most network traffic, analyze network traffic by protocol, and view interface details. Network analyzers are useful when troubleshooting problems caused by malware or denial-of-service attacks. Figure 9-11 shows the Fluke OptiView network analyzer.

Figure 9-11   Network Analyzers

Fluke Networks OptiView Series III Integrated Network Analyzer

CCENT Study Guide 1: Troubleshooting Methodologies and Tools (9.1.4)

See the CCENT Study Guide 1 on the CD-ROM accompanying this book.

Troubleshooting Layer 1 and Layer 2 Issues

The OSI physical Layer 1 and data link Layer 2 are the foundation of network communication. Problems at these layers can prevent any of the upper layers from receiving any information on which to act. This section covers device hardware and boot errors, cabling problems, and LAN/WAN connectivity issues.

Layer 1 and 2 Problems

The physical and data link layers encompass both hardware and software functions. All network communications rely on the technologies at these layers to function. A network technician must be able to quickly isolate and correct problems occurring at these layers.

The physical layer, or Layer 1, is responsible for the physical and electric specifications for the transmission of bits from one host to another over the physical medium, either wired or wireless. Network problems occurring at Layer 1 can cause the loss of network connectivity, or just cause network performance to degrade.

The types of problems that occur at Layer 1 are directly related to the type of technology used. For example, Ethernet is a multiaccess technology. Ethernet protocols use an algorithm to sense when there are no other signals on the wire to begin a transmission. However, it is possible for two devices to begin sending at the exact same time, causing a collision. When a collision occurs, all devices stop transmitting and wait a random amount of time before transmitting again. Basic shared Ethernet technology uses Carrier Sense Multiple Access with Collision Detection (CSMA/CD). This means that multiple Ethernet hosts (multiple access) listen to the wire (sense the carrier) and can detect collisions. If a collision is detected, each host can recover by retransmitting. CSMA/CD is necessary only when the medium is shared and only one host can transmit or receive at a time, as with the early Ethernet technologies such as hubs. Newer switched Ethernet technologies have dedicated send and receive circuits and operate in full-duplex mode. This allows hosts to send and receive simultaneously. Although modern switched technologies retain CSMA/CD for backward compatibility, there are virtually no collisions to deal with.

Excessive collisions can degrade network performance and can be a significant problem on shared media, such as a hub network, which is one big collision domain. A switched network breaks down a collision domain to one per port, effectively eliminating collisions.

The following are other common symptoms of network problems at the physical layer:

- Performance lower than baseline

  - Inadequate cable or poor terminations can result in errors that increase the rate of retransmissions.

  - Electrical interference can cause poor performance over copper links.

  - Cabling that exceeds the recommended standard distance limitations can cause attenuation problems.

  - In a wireless network, interference or a significant increase in traffic can degrade network responses.

- Loss of connectivity

  - Intermittent loss can be caused by power-related problems, such as a failing UPS or power supply, resulting in a device reboot or temporary link or device failure.

  - Loose connections and tension on the connectors and wires can also cause intermittent loss.

  - For wireless coverage areas, intermittent connectivity can be caused by overlapping wireless channels.

  - Complete loss can be caused by a cable connection failure or a failed device or interface.

- High collision counts

  - Average collision counts on shared media should generally be below 1 percent of total traffic.

  - Collision-based problems are often traced to a single source, such as a bad uplink cable on a hub or switch port, or a link that is exposed to external electrical noise. A faulty NIC can also cause excessive collisions on a wired network.

  - Too many hosts on a single shared segment can contribute to high collision rates.

  - Duplex mismatches between devices can cause collisions to be recorded on a switch link.

  - A full-duplex switch port should have no collisions.

- Network bottlenecks or congestion

  - When congestion occurs, frames can be dropped.

  - Unexpected high rates of traffic on devices or cables not designed to handle the load can cause congestion.

- Malware, such as Trojans and worms, can cause Layer 1 devices and cabling to become congested.

- A protocol analyzer can assist in finding the source of high traffic–related problems.

- High CPU utilization rates

  - High CPU utilization indicates that a device is operating at or exceeding its design limits.

  - CPU overloading can cause a device to shut down or fail.

- Console error message (messages displayed on the computer connected to Line console 0)

  - Error messages reported on the device console can indicate a physical layer problem.

  - Messages indicating that a device or protocol is down indicate interface or cabling problems. Protocol problems are typically associated with Layer 2 whereas interface and cabling are normally Layer 1.

The data link layer, or Layer 2, specifies how the data is formatted for transmission over the network media. It also regulates how access to the network is granted. Layer 2 provides the link between the network layer software functions and the Layer 1 hardware for both LAN and WAN applications. To effectively troubleshoot Layer 1 and Layer 2 problems, technicians must be familiar with cabling standards, as well as encapsulation and framing.

After a technician verifies that Layer 1 is functioning, he or she must determine whether the problem resides in Layer 2 or one of the higher layers. For example, if a host can ping the local loopback address 127.0.0.1 but cannot access any services over the network, the problem might be isolated to Layer 2 framing issues or a misconfigured interface card. Network analyzers and other online tools can be used to locate the source of a Layer 2 issue. In some instances, a networking device, such as a router, recognizes that a Layer 2 problem occurred and sends alert messages to the console.

The following are some common symptoms of Layer 2 problems:

- No functionality or connectivity at the network layer or above

  - Misconfigured network cards or faulty NIC drivers can stop the exchange of frames across a link.

  - Encapsulation errors on serial or WAN links can also cause connectivity to fail over operational circuits.

- Network operating below baseline performance levels

  - Interfaces dropping frames that exceed the capacity of the interface or have CRC or framing errors can cause poor network performance. These problems can be identified through error counter statistics and console error messages on the switch or router.

  - Faulty NICs, interface errors, and electric noise are common Layer 1 hardware issues that can create Layer 2 framing errors in the network.

- Excessive broadcasts

  - Large Layer 2 network segments can contribute to excessive broadcasts.

  - Viruses and worms can add excessive broadcast traffic to the network.

- Console error messages

  - Console messages typically occur when the device detects a problem with interpreting incoming frames because of encapsulation or framing problems.

- Messages also occur when keepalives are expected but do not arrive.

- The most common console message that indicates a Layer 2 problem is a line protocol down message.

Interactive Activity 9-3: Matching Layer 1 and 2 Problems with Symptoms (9.2.1)

In this interactive activity, you match the Layer 1 or Layer 2 problem with a possible symptom. Use file d2ia-921 on the CD-ROM that accompanies this book to perform this interactive activity.

Troubleshooting Device Hardware and Boot Errors

Network problems often occur after a device is restarted. Restarts can happen intentionally after an upgrade or unexpectedly after a power failure. To troubleshoot device hardware failures and boot errors, it is first necessary to review the process that Cisco IOS devices use during startup. The bootup process has three stages:

1. Performing the POST and loading the bootstrap program.

2. Locating and loading the Cisco IOS Software.

3. Locating and loading the startup configuration file or entering setup mode.

Figure 9-12 shows the three stages of router bootup. In the first stage, the POST and Bootstrap are executed from read-only memory (ROM). In stage two, the Cisco IOS image software is commonly loaded from flash memory into RAM, but the router can be configured to retrieve the IOS image from a TFTP server. In stage three, the router looks for a configuration file that will define the router name, enable interfaces, and assign IP addresses, routing protocols, and other parameters. This configuration file normally comes from NVRAM, but can come from a TFTP server or the configuration can be entered from the console using setup mode if the configuration file is not available from either of the previous sources.

Figure 9-12   Router Bootup Stages

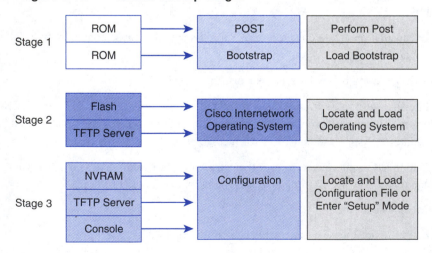

When booting any Cisco networking device, it is helpful to observe the console messages that appear during the boot sequence. After the Cisco IOS Software is loaded, the technician can use commands to verify that the hardware and software are fully operational. Example 9-1 shows output for a router as it boots up.

Example 9-1   Router Bootup Process Output

```
<some output omitted>
System Bootstrap, Version 12.4(13r)T, RELEASE SOFTWARE (fc1)
Technical Support: http://www.cisco.com/techsupport
Copyright (c) 2006 by Cisco Systems, Inc.
c1841 platform with 196608 Kbytes of main memory
Main memory is configured to 64 bit mode with parity disabled
Upgrade ROMMON initialized
program load complete, entry point: 0x8000f000, size: 0x150a6d4
Self decompressing the image : #################################################
######################################################## [OK]

Cisco IOS Software, 1841 Software (C1841-ADVIPSERVICESK9-M), Version 12.4(10b),
RELEASE SOFTWARE (fc3)

Cisco 1841 (revision 6.0) with 174080K/22528K bytes of memory.
Processor board ID FTX1111W0QF
6 FastEthernet interfaces
2 Serial(sync/async) interfaces
1 Virtual Private Network (VPN) Module
DRAM configuration is 64 bits wide with parity disabled.
191K bytes of NVRAM.
62720K bytes of ATA CompactFlash (Read/Write)

Press RETURN to get started!
```

The **show version** command displays the version of the operating system and whether all interface hardware is recognized. Example 9-2 shows output for the **show version** command.

Example 9-2   R1 show version Output

```
<some output omitted>
R1# show version
Cisco IOS Software, 1841 Software (C1841-ADVIPSERVICESK9-M), Version 12.4(10b),
RELEASE SOFTWARE (fc3)
Technical Support: http://www.cisco.com/techsupport
Copyright (c) 1986-2007 by Cisco Systems, Inc.
Compiled Fri 19-Jan-07 15:15 by prod_rel_team

ROM: System Bootstrap, Version 12.4(13r)T, RELEASE SOFTWARE (fc1)

R1 uptime is 23 minutes
System returned to ROM by power-on
System image file is "flash:c1841-advipservicesk9-mz.124-10b.bin"

Cisco 1841 (revision 6.0) with 174080K/22528K bytes of memory.
```

```
Processor board ID FTX1111W0QF
6 FastEthernet interfaces
2 Serial(sync/async) interfaces
1 Virtual Private Network (VPN) Module
DRAM configuration is 64 bits wide with parity disabled.
191K bytes of NVRAM.
62720K bytes of ATA CompactFlash (Read/Write)


Configuration register is 0x2102
```

The **show flash** command displays the contents of the Flash memory, including the Cisco IOS image file. It also displays the amount of Flash memory currently being used and the amount of memory available. Example 9-3 shows output for the **show flash** command.

Example 9-3   R1 show flash Output

```
R3# show flash:
-#- —length— — —-date/time— — — path
1      22063220 Mar 15 2007 07:17:16 +00:00 c1841-advipservicesk9-mz.124-10b.bin
2          1821 Mar 15 2007 07:33:34 +00:00 sdmconfig-18xx.cfg
3       4734464 Mar 15 2007 07:34:14 +00:00 sdm.tar
4        833024 Mar 15 2007 07:34:36 +00:00 es.tar
5       1052160 Mar 15 2007 07:35:00 +00:00 common.tar
6          1038 Mar 15 2007 07:35:22 +00:00 home.shtml
7        102400 Mar 15 2007 07:35:42 +00:00 home.tar
8        491213 Mar 15 2007 07:36:06 +00:00 128MB.sdf
9       1684577 Mar 15 2007 07:36:40 +00:00 securedesktop-ios-3.1.1.27-k9.pkg
10       398305 Mar 15 2007 07:37:08 +00:00 sslclient-win-1.1.0.154.pkg
32616448 bytes available (31379456 bytes used)
```

The **show ip interfaces brief** command shows the operational status of the device interfaces and IP addresses assigned.

The **show running-configuration** and **show startup-configuration** commands verify whether all the configuration commands were recognized during the reload.

When a device fails to boot correctly and creates a network outage, replace the device with a known good device to restore services to end users. Replace the device before beginning to troubleshoot and repair the failed device.

After a router boots successfully, the green LED indicators will display. The following describes the LED indicators for an 1841 router upon successful bootup:

- **SYS PWR LED:** Should be green indicating the router has successfully booted up and the software is functional. Slow, steady blinking when the system is booting or if it in the ROM monitor mode.

- **SYS ACT LED:** Blinking green when packets are transmitted on a WAN or LAN interface or when monitoring system activity.

- **CF (Compact Flash):** Off or blinking green if Flash memory is busy. Do not remove the Compact Flash memory card when this light is on. If you issue the **show flash** command, the LED will blink for a short time.

When errors occur during the bootup process, Cisco devices execute default actions to recover from the errors, such as loading into ROMmon mode. These default actions can cause network operations to fail or to perform erratically. The following are some common bootup errors and troubleshooting strategies:

- **Device fails POST:** When a device fails POST, no output appears on the console screen. In addition, system LEDs may change color or blink, depending on the device type. For a description of LED operation, check the documentation provided with the device. If the POST fails, turn off the power, unplug the device, and remove all interface modules. Then reboot the device. If the POST still fails, the device requires service. If it completes the POST successfully without the interface modules installed, an interface module might have failed. Disconnect the power and reinstall each module individually, rebooting each time, to determine which module has failed. When the failed module is identified, replace it with a known good module and restart the device.

- **Cisco IOS image in flash is corrupt:** If the image file in flash is corrupt or missing, the bootloader cannot find a valid Cisco IOS file to load. Some Cisco IOS devices have an image with limited functionality that is loaded and run if no image exists in flash or another specified location. This image is called a boothelper. Boothelper images might not have enough functionality to successfully execute the necessary configuration commands to bring the device back into operation. If there is no boothelper, the device enters ROMmon mode. Use ROMmon commands to reload the correct Cisco IOS image from a TFTP server.

- **Memory is not recognized or fails:** If there is not enough memory to decompress the image, the device scrolls error messages rapidly or constantly reboots. The device might be able to boot into ROMmon mode by issuing a Ctrl break command during startup. In ROMmon mode, commands can be issued to determine the status of the memory. The memory might have to be replaced or increased for the device to function normally.

- **Interface modules are not recognized:** Faulty or improperly seated interface modules might not be recognized during the POST and Cisco IOS load. When this occurs, the list of available interfaces displayed by the **show version** command does not match the physically installed modules. If an interface module is new, check that the module is supported by the Cisco IOS version installed and that enough memory exists to support the module. Always power down the device, disconnect the power, and reseat the module into the device to determine whether there is a hardware problem. After reseating, if the module is not recognized during reboot, replace it with a known good module.

- **Configuration file is corrupt or missing:** If a valid startup configuration file cannot be found, some Cisco devices execute an autoinstall utility. This utility broadcasts a TFTP request for a configuration file. Other devices immediately enter an initial configuration dialog, known as the setup utility or setup mode. Devices that have the autoinstall utility also enter setup mode if no TFTP server responds after five inquiries. Use either TFTP or manual configuration to reload or re-create the configuration. Devices do not forward traffic until a valid configuration is loaded.

Troubleshooting Cable and Device Port Errors

Router interface errors are often the first symptom of Layer 1 and Layer 2 cabling or connectivity errors. To troubleshoot, begin by examining the statistics recorded on the problematic interface using the **show interfaces** command and the status of interfaces using the **show ip interface brief** command.

The output for the **show ip interface brief** command includes a summary of the device interfaces, including the IP address and interface status.

- Up/up status indicates normal operation and that both the media and the Layer 2 protocol are functional.

- Down/down status indicates that a connectivity or media problem exists.

- Up/down status indicates that the media is connected properly, but the Layer 2 protocol is not functioning or is misconfigured.

Common cable or media issues that can cause a down/down output include

- Loose cable or too much tension on the cable. If all the pins cannot make a good connection, the circuit is down.

- Incorrect termination. Ensure that the correct cabling standard is followed and that all pins are correctly terminated in the connector.

- Damaged serial interface connector. Pins on the interface connection are bent or missing.

- Break or short in the cable. If there are problems along the circuit, the interface cannot sense the correct signals.

Common Layer 2 issues that can cause an up/down output include

- Improperly configured encapsulation

- No keepalives received on the interface

Example 9-4 shows output from the **show ip interface brief** command.

Example 9-4   R1 show ip interface brief Output

```
<some output omitted>
System Bootstrap, Version 12.4(13r)T, RELEASE SOFTWARE (fc1)
R1# show ip interface brief
Interface          IP-Address      OK? Method Status                 Protocol
FastEthernet0/0    192.168.1.1     YES NVRAM  up                     up
FastEthernet0/1    unassigned      YES NVRAM  administratively down  down
Serial0/0/0        10.10.10.1      YES NVRAM  up                     down
Serial0/0/1        unassigned      YES NVRAM  administratively down  down
```

Occasionally, media errors are not severe enough to cause the circuit to fail, but do cause network performance issues. The **show interfaces** command provides additional troubleshooting information to help identify these media errors.

Output for the **show interfaces** command includes

- Excessive noise
- Excessive collisions
- Excessive runt frames
- Late collisions

The next sections describe how to troubleshoot each of these issues.

Excessive Noise

On Ethernet and serial interfaces, the presence of many CRC errors but not many collisions is an indication of excessive noise. CRC errors usually indicate a media or cable error. Common causes include electrical interference, loose or damaged connections, or using the incorrect cabling type.

To determine whether your network is experiencing excessive noise, follow these steps:

How To

Step 1. Use the **show interface** command to determine the status of the Ethernet interfaces. The presence of many CRC errors but not many collisions is an indication of excessive noise.

Step 2. Inspect the cables for damage or sources of interference.

Step 3. Verify that the correct cable and termination standard is in use for the speed of the interface.

Step 4. If using 1000BASE-TX, make sure that Category 5e or above cabling is being used.

Excessive Collisions

Collisions usually occur on only half-duplex or shared-media Ethernet connections. Damaged cables can cause excessive collisions.

To troubleshoot for excessive collisions, follow these steps:

How To

Step 1. Use the **show interface** command to check the rate of collisions. The total number of collisions with respect to the total number of output packets should be 1 percent or less.

Step 2. Use a Time Domain Reflectometer (TDR) to find any damaged cables.

Excessive Runt Frames

Malfunctioning NICs are the usual cause of runt frames, but they can be caused by the same issues as excessive collisions. To troubleshoot for excessive runt frames, follow these steps:

How To

Step 1. In a shared Ethernet environment, runt frames are almost always caused by collisions. If the collision rate is high, see the "Excessive Collisions" problem.

Step 2. If runt frames occur when collision rates are not high or in a switched Ethernet environment, they are the result of bad software on a NIC.

Step 3. Use a protocol analyzer to try to determine the source address of the runt frames.

Late Collisions

A properly designed and configured network should never have late collisions. Excessive cable lengths are the most common cause. Duplex mismatches can also be responsible. To troubleshoot late collisions, follow these steps:

How To

Step 1. Use a protocol analyzer to check for late collisions. Late collisions should never occur in a properly designed Ethernet network. They usually occur when Ethernet cables are too long or when a duplex mismatch occurs.

Step 2. Verify that the diameter of the network is within specification. This can be determined by checking cable lengths from the center (MDF or IDF) switching devices to the furthest host.

Lab 9-3: Identifying Cabling and Media Errors (9.2.3)

In this lab you use the **show ip interface brief** and **show interfaces** commands to identify possible cable or media errors. Refer to the lab in Part II of this book. You may perform this lab now or wait until the end of the chapter.

Troubleshooting LAN Connectivity Issues

LAN troubleshooting usually centers on switches because the majority of LAN users connect to the network via switch ports. Many of the same Cisco IOS **show** commands can be used on switches to gather troubleshooting information. In addition, each port on a switch has an LED indicator that provides valuable troubleshooting information.

The first step in troubleshooting LAN connectivity issues is to verify that the switch port connected to the user is active and that the appropriate LED indicators are lit. If there is physical access to the switch, you can save time by looking at the port LEDs, which give the link status or indicate an error condition (if red or orange). Check to see that both sides of the connection have a link.

If no link light is present, ensure that the cable is connected at both ends and that it is connected to the correct port. Make sure that both devices are powered up, and that there are no bootup errors on either device. Swap out any patch cables with known good cables and verify that the cable terminations are correct for the type of connectivity desired. If there is still no link light, verify that the port is not administratively shut down. Use the **show running-config interface** command to determine the status of a switch port as displayed in Example 9-5.

Example 9-5   R1 show running-config interface Output

```
Switch# show running-config interface fastEthernet 4/2
Current configuration : 96 bytes
!
interface FastEthernet4/2
 shutdown
 duplex full
 speed 100
end
```

Tip

The **show running-config interface fastEthernet 4/2** command can be abbreviated:

```
Switch# sh run int f4/2
```

Figure 9-13 shows the LEDs on the front of a Catalyst 2960 switch.

Figure 9-13   Cisco Catalyst 2960 Switch LEDs

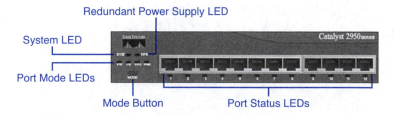

Even if a link light is present, it does not guarantee that the cable is fully functional. The cable can be damaged, causing intermittent performance problems. Normally, this situation is identified by using Cisco IOS **show** commands to determine whether the port has many packet errors or the port constantly flaps (loses and regains a link).

The **show version** and **show interfaces** commands executed on a switch provide similar information to the same commands executed on a router. To get a quick view of switch port error statistics, use the **show interface** [*port type/number*] **counters errors** command. Replace [*port*] with the actual port number, such as Fa0/6.

Duplex mismatches are more common on switches than on routers. Many devices are set to autonegotiate speed and duplex settings. If one device on a link is configured to autonegotiate and the other side is manually configured with speed and duplex settings, mismatches can occur, leading to collisions and dropped packets.

To view the speed and duplex settings on a port and whether manual or autonegotiation features were used, use the **show interface** [*port type/number*] **status** command.

If the mismatch occurs between two Cisco devices with the Cisco Discovery Protocol (CDP) enabled, there are CDP error messages on the console or in the logging buffer of both devices. CDP is useful to detect errors and port and system statistics on nearby Cisco devices.

To correct duplex mismatch errors, set both devices to autonegotiate speed and duplex. If the negotiation does not produce the desired results, manually configure matching speed and duplex settings on each device.

The following shows an error message generated by CDP from a duplex mismatch:

```
Jun 2 11:01;15 %CDP-4-DUPLEX_MISMATCH: duplex mismatch discivered on FastEthernet6/2 (not half
    duplex), with TBA04251366 3/2 (half duplex).
```

Example 9-6 shows the output from **show interface port status** command.

Example 9-6   R1 show interface port status Output

```
Switch# show interfaces FastEthernet 6/1 status
Port Name         Status        Vlan      Duplex      Speed        Type
Fa6/1             notconnect    1         auto        auto         10/10BaseTX
```

Configuring and Troubleshooting a Switched Network (9.2.4)

In this Packet Tracer activity, you configure a switched network and troubleshoot duplex mismatches. Use file d2-924.pka on the CD-ROM that accompanies this book to perform this activity using Packet Tracer.

Lab 9-4: Troubleshooting LAN Connectivity (9.2.4)

In this lab you troubleshoot LAN connectivity using LEDs and **show** commands. Refer to the lab in Part II of this book. You may perform this lab now or wait until the end of the chapter.

Troubleshooting WAN Connectivity Issues

Troubleshooting a serial WAN connection is different from troubleshooting Ethernet LAN connections. Typically, WAN connectivity relies on equipment and media that is owned and managed by a telecommunications service provider (TSP). Because of this, it is important for technicians to know how to troubleshoot the customer premises equipment (CPE) and to communicate the results to the TSP.

Most serial interface and line problems can be identified and corrected using information gathered from the **show interfaces serial** command. In addition to the error counters, serial connections may experience problems caused by errors or mismatches in encapsulation and timing. Because serial WAN connections usually rely on a CSU/DSU or modem for timing, these devices must be considered when troubleshooting serial lines. In prototype networks, a router can be configured to provide DCE clocking functions, eliminating the CSU or modem.

To successfully troubleshoot serial WAN connectivity problems, it is important to know the type of modem or CSU/DSU that is installed and how to place the device in a loopback state for testing. Figure 9-14 shows various types of WAN devices and interconnection technologies.

Figure 9-14   WAN Devices and Interconnection Technologies

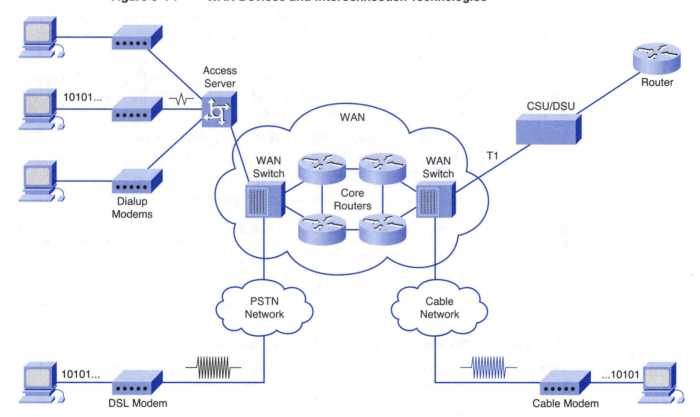

The interface status line of the **show interfaces serial** command can display six possible states:

- **Serial x is down, line protocol is down (DTE mode):** When the router serial interface cannot detect any signal on the line, it reports both the line and the Layer 2 protocol down.

- **Serial x is up, line protocol is down (DTE mode):** If the serial interface does not receive keepalives, or if there is an encapsulation error, the Layer 2 protocol is reported down.

- **Serial x is up, line protocol is down (DCE mode):** When the router is providing the clock signal and a DCE cable is attached but no clock rate is configured, the Layer 2 protocol is reported down.

- **Serial x is up, line protocol is up (looped):** It is common practice to place a circuit in a loopback condition to test connectivity. If the serial interface receives its own signals back on the circuit, it reports the line as looped.

- **Serial x is up, line protocol is down (disabled):** High error rates cause the router to place the line in a protocol disabled mode. This type of problem is usually hardware related.

- **Serial x is administratively down, line protocol is down:** An administratively down interface is configured with the **shutdown** command. Usually all that is needed to fix this condition is to enter the **no shutdown** command on the interface. If the interface does not come up using the **no shutdown** command, check the console messages for a duplicate IP address message. If a duplicate IP address exists, correct the problem and reissue the **no shutdown** command.

- **Serial x is up, line protocol is up:** The interface is operating as expected.

Each of these possible conditions for the serial link is described in greater detail in the next sections. For each condition, some possible problems are listed along with steps that can be used to troubleshoot the problems.

Serial x Is Down, Line Protocol Is Down (DTE)

This problem indicates that the router is not sensing a carrier detect signal. Possible causes of the problem include the following:

- Telephone company problem. Line is down or not connected to CSU/DSU.

- Faulty or incorrect cabling.

- Hardware failure (CSU/DSU).

To troubleshoot, follow these steps:

How To

Step 1. Check the LEDs on the CSU/DSU to see whether the light is active.

Step 2. Verify that you are using the proper cable and interface.

Step 3. Contact your leased-line or other carrier service to see whether there is a problem.

Step 4. Replace the serial interface module with a known good module.

Step 5. Replace the CSU/DSU with a known good device.

Serial x Is Up, Line Protocol Is Down (DTE)

Possible causes of the problem include the following:

- Local or remote router is misconfigured.

- Keepalives are not being sent by the remote router.

- Failed remote CSU or DSU.

- Failed local or remote CSU/DSU.

To troubleshoot, follow these steps:

How To

Step 1. Put the modem, CSU, or DSU in local loopback mode, and use the **show interface serial** command to determine whether the line protocol comes up. If the line protocol comes up, a telephone company problem or a failed remote router is probably the cause.

Step 2. If the problem appears to be on the remote end, repeat Step 1 on the remote modem, CSU, or DSU.

Step 3. Verify all cabling. Make certain that the cable is attached to the correct interface, the correct CSU/DSU, and the correct telephone company network termination point.

Step 4.   Verify that the encapsulation is correct on both ends of the circuit.

Step 5.   If the line protocol does not come up in local loopback mode and there is no encapsulation mismatch, replace failed hardware.

Serial x Is Up, Line Protocol Is Down (DCE)

Possible causes of the problem include the following:

- Missing **clockrate** interface configuration command for an interface with a DCE cable attached.
- Failed local or remote CSU/DSU.
- Failed or incorrect cable.
- Router hardware failure.

To troubleshoot, follow these steps:

Step 1.   Add the **clockrate** interface configuration command on the serial interface if it is DCE.

Step 2.   Verify that the correct cable is being used.

Step 3.   If the line protocol is still down, there is a possible hardware failure or cabling problem.

Step 4.   Replace faulty parts as necessary with known good equipment.

Serial x Is Up, Line Protocol Is Up (Looped)

A possible problem could be that a loop exists in the circuit. The sequence number in the keepalive packet changes to a random number when a loop is detected initially. If the same random number is returned over the link, a loop exists.

To troubleshoot, follow these steps:

Step 1.   Use the **show running-config** privileged EXEC command. This will enable you to look for any physical interfaces that have been configured for internal loopback using the interface configuration command **loopback**. This is not the same as a virtual Loopback interface created for simulation, such as Loopback 0 (Lo0).

Step 2.   If you find an interface that has been place in loopback mode, use the **no loopback** interface configuration command to remove the loop.

Step 3.   If you do not find the **loopback** interface configuration command, examine the CSU/DSU to determine whether it is configured in manual loopback mode. If it is, disable manual loopback.

Step 4.   Reset the CSU/DSU and inspect the line status. If the line protocol comes up, no other action is needed.

Step 5.   If the CSU/DSU is not configured in manual loopback mode, contact the leased line of your carrier service for line troubleshooting assistance.

Serial x Is Up, Line Protocol Is Down (Disabled)

Possible causes of the problem include the following:

- High error rate because of telecommunications service problem.
- CSU/DSU hardware problem.
- Bad router hardware.

To troubleshoot, follow these steps:

Step 1.   Contact the telecommunications service provider.

Step 2.   Loop CSU/DSU (DTE loop). If the problem continues, there is likely a hardware problem. If the problem does not continue, the problem is likely with the telephone company.

Step 3.   Swap out bad hardware as required (CSU/DSU, switch, interface module, or remote router).

Serial x Is Administratively Down, Line Protocol Is Down

Possible causes of the problem include the following:

- Router configuration includes the **shutdown** interface configuration command.

- Duplicate IP address.

To troubleshoot, follow these steps:

Step 1.   Check the configuration for the **shutdown** command. Using the **show running-config** privileged EXEC command or the **show interface** EXEC command will verify that interfaces being used do not display shutdown.

Step 2.   Use the **no shutdown** interface configuration command to remove the **shutdown** command.

Step 3.   Verify that there are no identical IP addresses using the **show running-config** privileged EXEC command or the **show interface** EXEC command.

Step 4.   If there are duplicate addresses, resolve the conflict by changing one of the IP addresses.

WAN Encapsulation Mismatches (9.2.5)

In this Packet Tracer activity, you troubleshoot WAN encapsulation mismatches. Use file d2-925.pka on the CD-ROM that accompanies this book to perform this activity using Packet Tracer.

Lab 9-5: Troubleshooting WAN Connectivity (9.2.5)

In this lab you troubleshoot WAN connectivity using LEDs and **show** commands. Refer to the lab in Part II of this book. You may perform this lab now or wait until the end of the chapter.

CCENT Study Guide 2: Troubleshooting Layer 1 and Layer 2 Issues (9.2.6)

See the CCENT Study Guide 2 on the CD-ROM accompanying this book.

Troubleshooting Layer 3 IP Addressing Issues

All communication on the Internet is based on the Internet protocol (IP). Many network connectivity problems arise from misconfigured IP addressing and routing issues. This section provides a review of Layer 3 addressing. It describes IP design, configuration, planning, and allocation and focuses on issues associated with IP addressing, DHCP, and NAT.

Review of Layer 3 Functionality and IP Addressing

Layer 1 networks are created by interconnecting devices using physical media. Layer 2 network protocols are hardware dependent. Ethernet cannot operate over a serial link, nor can serial communications occur using an Ethernet NIC.

Layer 3 (the network layer) protocols are not bound to a specific type of media or Layer 2 framing protocol. The same Layer 3 protocols can operate on Ethernet, wireless, serial, or other Layer 2 networks. Figure 9-15 shows two hosts connected by several different network technologies. At each hop along the path, an intermediary device accepts frames from one medium, deencapsulates the frames, and then forwards the packets in a new frame, based on the media for the next link. The headers of each frame are formatted for the specific medium that it will cross.

Figure 9-15   Multiple Layer 2 Protocols Interconnect Different Links

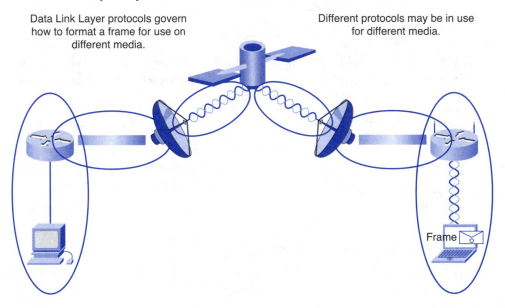

Layer 3 networks can contain hosts that are connected using different Layer 1 and 2 technologies. The primary functions implemented at Layer 3 of the OSI model are network addressing and routing. Layer 3 networks are referred to as logical networks because they are created only in software.

In Figure 9-16, the Layer 3 protocol—in this case IP—is not aware of the different Layer 2 protocols required to move from one communications link technology to the next. Although the frame format may change every time the physical media changes, the format of the network layer packet remains the same.

Figure 9-16   A Single Layer 3 Protocol from End-to-End

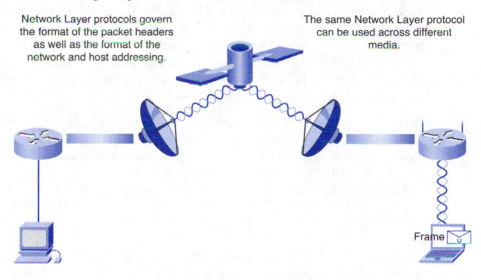

Network Layer protocols govern the format of the packet headers as well as the format of the network and host addressing.

The same Network Layer protocol can be used across different media.

Frame

This is similar to sending a letter from a person in one part of the world to someone in another part of the world. The letter may travel by automobile to the post office, by truck to the airport, by airplane to another airport, by another truck to a local post office, and, finally, to the recipient by automobile. Even though the letter is transported in several different vehicles, the "from" address and "to" address on the letter never change.

Today most networks implement the TCP/IP protocol to exchange information between hosts. As a result, much of the focus of troubleshooting Layer 3 problems is concentrated on IP addressing errors and on routing protocol operation.

Troubleshooting Layer 3 problems requires a thorough understanding of network boundaries and IP addressing. Poorly designed and configured IP addressing schemes account for a large number of network performance problems.

At Layer 3, each packet must be identified with the source and destination addresses of the two end systems. With IPv4, each packet has a 32-bit source address and a 32-bit destination address in the Layer 3 header.

The IP address identifies not only the individual host, but also the Layer 3 local network on which the host can communicate. A simple IP network can be created by configuring two interconnected hosts with unique addresses that share the same network prefix and subnet mask.

A device must be configured with an IP address to exchange messages using TCP/IP. Individual Layer 3 IP networks encompass a range of IP addresses. These boundaries are determined by the number of bits contained in the network prefix portion of the address. A simple rule is the longer the network prefix, the smaller the range of IP addresses that can be configured on hosts in that IP network.

To troubleshoot Layer 3 problems, an administrator must be able to determine the range of host addresses that belong to each individual IP network. The range of addresses is determined by the number and position of host bits. Figure 9-17 shows an example that starts with the 192.168.1.0/24 network and then borrows three bits for subnetting. This leaves 5 bits for host addresses. This creates 8 subnets ($2^3 = 8$) and 32 host addresses per subnet. Only 30 of the host addresses on each subnet are usable ($2^5 - 2 = 30$). For each subnet, the first address is reserved for the subnet number itself and the last address is reserved as a broadcast address.

Note

Remember that the local router interface, usually FastEthernet, is considered a host and must be assigned an IP address within the range of allowable addresses for a given subnet. Be sure to include router interfaces when determining the number of addresses required for a subnet.

If the local router interface is not assigned an address on the local subnet, hosts on the subnet will be able to communicate with each other but not with other hosts outside the subnet. Each host also must be configured with the IP address of the local router interface (the default gateway).

In Figure 9-17, if you look at subnet number 3, 192.168.1.96/27 (actually the fourth subnet), the first usable host address on the subnet is 192.168.1.97, and the last usable host address is 192.168.1.126. The broadcast address for this subnet is 192.168.1.127. This can be seen by looking at the binary of the last octet:

(011 subnet) 96 + (00001 first host) 1 = (01100001) 97 in decimal

(011 subnet) 96 + (11110 last host) 30 = (01111110) 126

(011 subnet) 96 + (11111 broadcast) 31 = (01111111) 127

This example uses a Class C address. This same technique can be applied to Class A and Class B addresses. Remember that the location of host bits can extend into more than one octet.

Interactive Activity 9-4: Determining Host Range, Broadcast Address and Next Network (9.3.1)

In this interactive activity, you are given a network address and subnet mask and must determine the host range, broadcast address, and the next network address. Use file d2ia-931 on the CD-ROM that accompanies this book to perform this interactive activity.

Troubleshoot a Small IP Network (9.3.1)

In this Packet Tracer activity, you troubleshoot a small network. Use file d2-931.pka on the CD-ROM that accompanies this book to perform this activity using Packet Tracer.

Figure 9-17   **Creating Eight Subnets from a Single Class C Address**

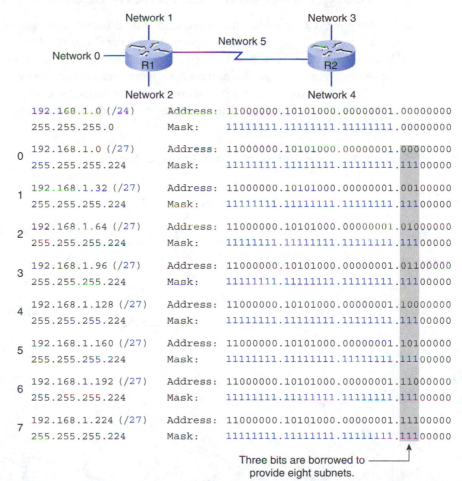

	192.168.1.0 (/24)	Address:	11000000.10101000.00000001.00000000
	255.255.255.0	Mask:	11111111.11111111.11111111.00000000
0	192.168.1.0 (/27)	Address:	11000000.10101000.00000001.00000000
	255.255.255.224	Mask:	11111111.11111111.11111111.11100000
1	192.168.1.32 (/27)	Address:	11000000.10101000.00000001.00100000
	255.255.255.224	Mask:	11111111.11111111.11111111.11100000
2	192.168.1.64 (/27)	Address:	11000000.10101000.00000001.01000000
	255.255.255.224	Mask:	11111111.11111111.11111111.11100000
3	192.168.1.96 (/27)	Address:	11000000.10101000.00000001.01100000
	255.255.255.224	Mask:	11111111.11111111.11111111.11100000
4	192.168.1.128 (/27)	Address:	11000000.10101000.00000001.10000000
	255.255.255.224	Mask:	11111111.11111111.11111111.11100000
5	192.168.1.160 (/27)	Address:	11000000.10101000.00000001.10100000
	255.255.255.224	Mask:	11111111.11111111.11111111.11100000
6	192.168.1.192 (/27)	Address:	11000000.10101000.00000001.11000000
	255.255.255.224	Mask:	11111111.11111111.11111111.11100000
7	192.168.1.224 (/27)	Address:	11000000.10101000.00000001.11100000
	255.255.255.224	Mask:	11111111.11111111.11111111.11100000

Three bits are borrowed to
provide eight subnets.

Addressing Scheme: Example of Eight Networks

Subnet	Network Address	Host Range	Broadcast Address
0	192.168.1.0/27	192.168.1.1 - 192.168.1.30	192.168.1.31
1	192.168.1.32/27	192.168.1.33 - 192.168.1.62	192.168.1.63
2	192.168.1.64/27	192.168.1.65 - 192.168.1.94	192.168.1.95
3	192.168.1.96/27	192.168.1.97 - 192.168.1.126	192.168.1.127
4	192.168.1.128/27	192.168.1.129 - 192.168.1.158	192.168.1.159
5	192.168.1.160/27	192.168.1.161 - 192.168.1.190	192.168.1.191
6	192.168.1.192/27	192.168.1.193 - 192.168.1.222	192.168.1.223
7	192.168.1.224/27	192.168.1.225 - 192.168.1.254	192.168.1.255

IP Design and Configuration Issues

If IP addressing is assigned in a random manner, it is difficult to determine where a source or destination address is located. Today, most networks employ a hierarchical IP addressing scheme. Hierarchical IP addressing schemes offer many advantages, including smaller routing tables that require less processing power. Hierarchical IP addressing also creates a more structured environment that is easier to document, troubleshoot, and expand. Figure 9-18 shows the use of hierarchical addressing, where multiple 172.16.X.0/24 and 172.16.X.0/22 networks can be summarized into a single 172.16.0.0/16 network for advertising to another network.

Figure 9-18   Hierarchical IP Addressing Scheme

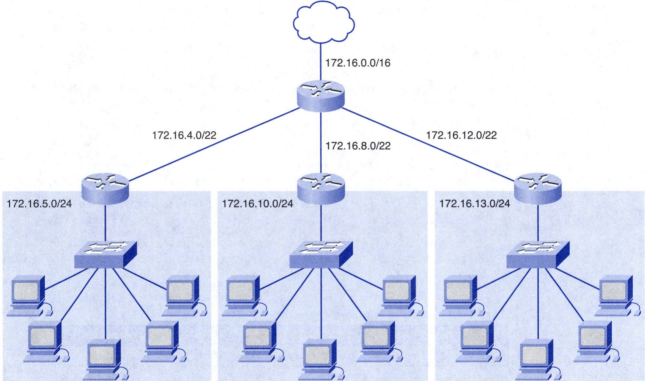

However, a poorly planned hierarchical network or a badly documented plan can create problems, such as overlapping subnets or incorrectly configured subnet masks on devices. These two conditions account for many IP addressing and routing issues within networks.

An overlapping subnet occurs when the address range of two separate subnets includes some of the same host or broadcast addresses. Overlapping is usually a result of poor network documentation or accidentally entering the incorrect subnet mask or network prefix. Overlapping subnets do not always cause a complete network outage. They may affect only a few hosts, depending on where the miscon-figured subnet mask is placed.

Cisco IOS Software does permit you to configure an IP address from overlapping subnets on two different interfaces for a router. However, the second interface will be administratively shut down.

For example, the router R1 interface Fast Ethernet 0/0 is configured with an IP address and subnet mask on the 192.168.1.0/24 network. If Fast Ethernet 0/1 is configured with an IP address on the 192.168.1.0/30 network, an overlapping error message appears. If there is an attempt to enable the interface with the **no shutdown** command, a second error message appears. No traffic is forwarded through the interface. The output from the **show ip interface brief** command shows that the second interface configured for the 192.168.1.0/24 network, FastEthernet 0/1, is down.

It is important to verify the status of the interfaces after making configuration changes. An interface that remains administratively down after the **no shutdown** command is issued can indicate an IP addressing problem.

Example 9-7 shows the configuration of interface FastEthernet 0/1 with an IP address that overlaps with the one on FastEthernet 0/0 and the resulting error message generated.

Example 9-7   IP Address Configuration Error and Output

```
R1(config)# interface FastEthernet0/1
R1(config-if)#ip address 192.168.1.2 255.255.255.252
192.168.1.0 overlaps with FastEthernet0/

R1(config-if)# no shutdown
192.168.1.0 overlaps with FastEthernet0/0
FastEthernet0/1: incorrect IP address assignment
2nd button output:

R1# show ip interface brief
<output omitted>
FastEthernet0/0/1 192.168.1.2 YES manual administratively down down
```

Although Cisco IOS Software has safeguards to ensure that overlapping subnets are not configured on multiple interfaces of the same device, it does not prevent overlapping subnets from being configured on different devices or on hosts within the network.

A poorly configured subnet mask can cause some hosts on a network to not have access to network services. Subnet mask configuration errors can also present a variety of symptoms that might not be easily identified. Figure 9-19 shows an issue where a server is accessible only by hosts on the same subnet.

Figure 9-19   Issue 1: A Server Is Accessible Only by Hosts on the Same Subnet

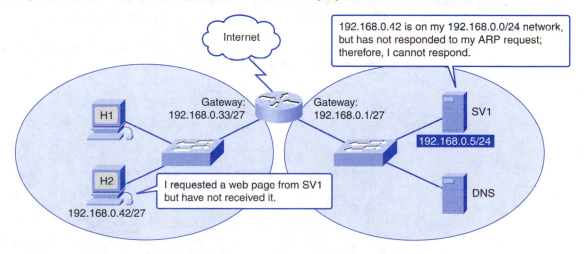

In Figure 9-19, a server on one of the subnets is manually configured using the default /24 network prefix instead of the /27. This misconfiguration causes the server to determine that all hosts on the various subnets are on the same Layer 3 network that the server is on. The server does not send any traffic to the default gateway for any hosts on the /27 subnets. Check server configurations if this symptom occurs.

In Figure 9-20, a host or group of hosts is configured with a /24 subnet mask that causes an overlap with the server network subnet addresses. Each host correctly determines that Internet addresses are not on their local Layer 3 network, and sends the traffic to the default gateway. The hosts incorrectly determine that internal server addresses are on their local network, and use ARP to attempt to get the server MAC addresses. Check DHCP server configurations and host configurations when this symptom is evident. A network sniffer can be used to show the ARP frames.

Figure 9-20   Issue 2: Hosts Get Responses from Internet Servers but Not Servers on Another Subnet

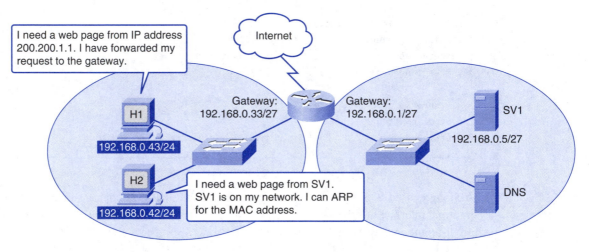

In Figure 9-21, a host or group of hosts is configured with a /24 subnet mask that causes an overlap with the server network subnet addresses, including the DNS server. Subnet mask errors on hosts do not usually affect Internet connectivity; however, if the subnet mask error causes the host subnet to overlap the subnet containing the DNS server, the host(s) will not be able to contact the DNS server. Without DNS, no IP addresses can be resolved and no services that rely on DNS can be accessed. Check host and DNS configurations if you're unable to access the Internet.

Figure 9-21   Issue 3: Hosts Are Unable to Get Responses from Internet Servers or Servers on Another Subnet, Using Hostnames

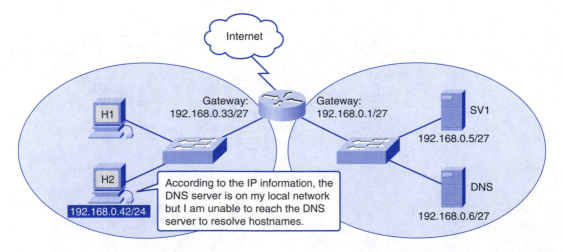

In Figure 9-22, the subnet mask configuration error occurs on a router interface that serves as a default gateway for one of the /27 subnets. If the router interface is incorrectly configured with a /28 subnet mask, the route entered in the routing table will not include all hosts on the /27 subnet. Hosts with addresses on the lower portion of range that are within the /28 subnet IP address boundaries will be able to send and receive through the router. Those with addresses in the top half of the range can send packets to remote destinations, but when the responses return, the router does not have a route to the destination IP addresses. Always verify all connected routes in the routing table using the **show ip route** command.

Figure 9-22   Issue 4: Some Hosts Are Able to Get Responses from Internet Servers or Servers on Another Subnet, but Others Cannot

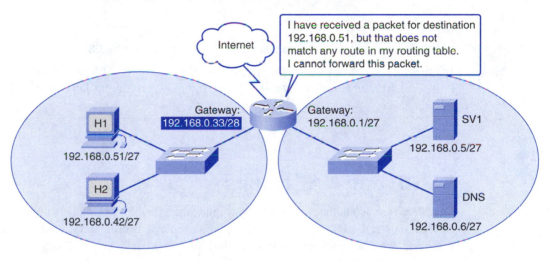

IP Address Planning and Allocation Issues

Poor address allocation planning can cause other problems. Often, an administrator underestimates the potential for growth when designing subnets. As a result, the IP subnetting scheme does not allow for enough host addresses in each subnet. One indication of a subnet having too many hosts is when some hosts are unable to receive an IP address from the DHCP server.

When a host running Microsoft Windows does not receive an address from a DHCP server, it automatically assigns itself an address on the 169.254.0.0 network. If this occurs, use the **show ip dhcp binding** command to check whether the DHCP server has available addresses.

Example 9-8 shows the output from the **show ip dhcp binding** command.

Example 9-8   R1 show ip dhcp binding Command Output

```
R1# show ip dhcp binding
Bindings from all pools not associated with VRF:
IP address      Client-ID/            Lease expiration    Type
                Hardware address
                User name
192.168.10.10   0100.e018.5bdd.35     Mar 26 2008  06:15 PM    Automatic
192.168.10.11   0100.e0b6.b77f.26     Mar 26 2008  06:18 PM    Automatic
```

Another indication of not enough IP addresses is an error message on a host stating that duplicate IP addresses exist. If a host device is turned off when the DHCP lease expires, the address is returned to the DHCP pool and can be issued to another host. When the original lease holder is turned back on, it requests a renewal of its previous IP address. In a Microsoft Windows network, both hosts report a duplicate IP address error.

Interactive Activity 9-5: Determining the Number of Hosts for a Network (9.3.3)

In this interactive activity, you are given a network address and subnet mask and must determine number of host addresses available. Use file d2ia-933 on the CD-ROM that accompanies this book to perform this interactive activity.

Lab 9-6: Designing an IP Subnetting Scheme for Growth (9.3.3)

In this lab, you create an IP addressing scheme that allows for 20% growth in the number of attached hosts. Refer to the lab in Part II of this book. You may perform this lab now or wait until the end of the chapter.

DHCP and NAT Issues

DHCP can create another level of complication when troubleshooting network issues. If hosts are configured to use DHCP and are not able to connect to the network, verify that IP addressing is assigned using the Windows command, **ipconfig /all**. If hosts are not receiving IP addressing assignments, it is necessary to troubleshoot the DHCP configuration.

Regardless of whether the DHCP service is configured on a dedicated server or on the router, the first step in troubleshooting is to check the physical connectivity. If a separate server is used, check that the server is receiving network traffic. If the DHCP service is configured on a router, use the **show interfaces** command on the router to confirm that the interface is operational. If the interface connected to the host network is down, the port does not pass traffic, including DHCP requests.

Next, verify that the DHCP server is correctly configured and has available IP addresses to lease. After this is confirmed, check for any address conflicts. Address conflicts can occur, even if there are available addresses within the DHCP pool. This can happen if a host is statically configured with an address that is also contained in the range of the DHCP pool.

Use the **show ip dhcp conflict** command to display all address conflicts recorded by the DHCP server. If an address conflict is detected, the address is removed from the pool and not assigned until an administrator resolves the conflict.

If none of these steps diagnoses the problem, test to ensure that the issue is actually with DHCP. Configure a host with a static IP address, subnet mask, and default gateway. If the workstation is unable to reach network resources with a statically configured IP address, the root cause of the problem is not DHCP. At this point, network connectivity troubleshooting is required. Example 9-9 shows the **ipconfig /all** output from a Windows PC that has access to a DHCP server.

Example 9-9   **Windows PC ipconfig /all Output**

```
C:\> ipconfig /all
Windows IP Configuration
    Host Name . . . . . . . . . . . . : PC1
    Primary Dns Suffix  . . . . . . . :
    Node Type . . . . . . . . . . . . : Hybrid
    IP Routing Enabled. . . . . . . . : No
    WINS Proxy Enabled. . . . . . . . : No
    DNS Suffix Search List. . . . . . : cisco.com

Ethernet adapter Local Area Connection:
    Connection-specific DNS Suffix  . : cisco.com
    Description . . . . . . . . . . . : Broadcom 440x 10/100 Integrated Controller
    Physical Address. . . . . . . . . : 00-18-8B-8A-42-4F
    DHCP Enabled. . . . . . . . . . . : Yes
    Autoconfiguration Enabled . . . . : Yes
    IP Address. . . . . . . . . . . . : 192.168.1.102
    Subnet Mask . . . . . . . . . . . : 255.255.255.0
    Default Gateway . . . . . . . . . : 192.168.1.1
    DHCP Server . . . . . . . . . . . : 192.168.1.1
    Lease Obtained. . . . . . . . . . : Wednesday, March 26, 2008 5:15:07 PM
    Lease Expires . . . . . . . . . . : Monday, March 31, 2008 5:15:08 AM
```

DHCP is a broadcast protocol, which means the DHCP server must be reachable through a broadcast message. Because routers normally do not forward broadcasts, either the DHCP server must be on the same local network as the hosts or the router must be configured to relay the broadcast messages. Figure 9-23 shows a DHCP server that is not accessible by host PC1. This is because the router does not normally forward DHCP request broadcasts.

Figure 9-23   **DHCP Relay Problem**

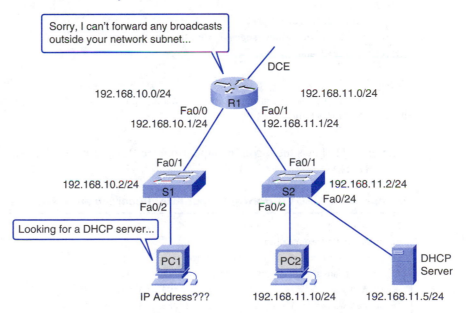

A router can be configured to forward all broadcast packets, including DHCP requests, to a specific server using the **ip helper address** command. This command allows a router to change the destination broadcast addresses within a packet to a specified unicast address:

```
Router(config-if)# ip helper-address A.B.C.D
```

After this command is configured, all broadcast packets will be forwarded to the server IP address specified in the command, including DHCP requests.

When a router forwards address requests, it is acting as a DHCP relay agent. If DHCP relay is not operational, no hosts can obtain an IP address. When no hosts can obtain an IP address from a DHCP server located on another network, verify that the helper address is configured correctly on the router.

Example 9-10 shows the **ipconfig /release** and **ipconfig /renew** output and the resulting error message when the host is unable to obtain an IP address from a DHCP server.

Example 9-10   PC1 Errors Resulting from DHCP Server Being Unavailable

```
C:\> ipconfig /release
Windows IP Configuration
Ethernet adapter Local Area Connection:
   Connection-specific DNS Suffix  . :
   IP Address. . . . . . . . . . . : 0.0.0.0
   Subnet Mask . . . . . . . . . . : 0.0.0.0
   Default Gateway . . . . . . . . :
C:\>ipconfig /renew
Windows IP Configuration
An error occurred while renewing interface Local Area Connection : unable to contact your
  DHCP server. Request has timed out.
```

In Figure 9-23, if R1 is configure using the following commands, it will forward DHCP requests from the 192.168.10.0 network to the DHCP server 192.168.11.5 on the 192.168.11.0 network.

```
R1# config t
R1(config)# interface Fa0/0
R1(config-if)# ip helper-address 192.168.11.5
R1(config-if)# end
```

Note

The DHCP server must be configured with two address pools to provide addresses for both the 192.168.10.0 and the 192.168.11.0 networks.

Example 9-11 shows the **ipconfig** output from the PC after it has received an IP address from the remote DHCP server.

Example 9-11   PC1 ipconfig Output After Receiving an IP Address

```
C:\> ipconfig
Windows IP Configuration
Ethernet adapter Local Area Connection:
   Connection-specific DNS Suffix  . :
   IP Address. . . . . . . . . . . : 192.168.10.11
   Subnet Mask . . . . . . . . . . : 255.255.255.0
   Default Gateway . . . . . . . . : 192.168.10.1
```

If the hosts on the internal network are assigned private addresses, NAT is required to communicate with the public network. Usually the first indication that there is a NAT problem is that users cannot reach sites located on the Internet. There are three types of address translation: static, dynamic, and PAT. Two common types of configuration errors affect all three translation methods:

- **Incorrect Designation of Inside and Outside Interfaces:** It is critical that the correct interfaces are designated as the inside or outside interface for NAT. In most NAT implementations, the inside interface connects to the local network, which uses private IP address space. The outside interface connects to the public network, usually the ISP. Verify this configuration using the **show running-config interface** command.

- **Incorrect Assignment of Interface IP Address or Pool Addresses:** In most NAT implementations, the IP address pool and static NAT translation entries must use IP addresses that are on the same local IP network as the outside interface. If not, addresses are translated but no route to the translated addresses are found. Check the configuration to verify that all the translated addresses are reachable. When the address translation is configured to use the outside interface address in PAT, make sure the interface address is on the correct network and is configured with the proper subnet mask.

Another common issue is that when dynamic NAT or PAT is enabled, external users are no longer able to connect to internal devices. If external users must be able to reach specific servers on the internal network, be sure that static translations are configured.

Example 9-12 shows the configuration of NAT. Comments are embedded in the running-config output.

Example 9-12   Configuring Dynamic NAT on R1

```
R1(config)# Access-list 1 permit 192.168.0.0 0.0.255.255
! Defines which addresses are eligible to be translated
R1(config)# ip nat pool NAT-1 209.165.200.226 209.165.200.240
! Defines a pool of addresses named NAT-1 to be used for NAT translation
R1(config)# ip nat inside source list 1 pool NAT-1 overload
! Binds the NAT pool with ACL 1
R1(config)# interface s0/0/0
R1(config-if)# ip nat inside
! Identifies serial 0/0/0 as the inside NAT interface
R1(config)# interface s0/0/1
R1(config-if)# ip nat outside
! Identifies serial 0/0/1 as the outside NAT interface
```

If you are certain that NAT is configured correctly, it is important to verify that NAT is operational.

One of the most useful commands when verifying NAT operation is the **show ip nat translations** command. After viewing the existing translations, clear them using the **clear ip nat translation ***command. Be aware that clearing all IP translations on a router may disrupt user services. Then use the **show ip nat translations** command again. If new translations appear, another problem might be causing the loss of Internet connectivity.

Verify that there is a route to the Internet for the translated addresses. Use **traceroute** to determine the path the translated packets are taking and verify that the route is correct. Also, if possible, trace the route to a translated address from a remote device on the outside network. This can help isolate the next troubleshooting target. There might be a routing problem on the router where the trace output stops. Figure 9-24 shows a network topology that uses port address translation (PAT). Example 9-13 shows the configuration of NAT overload on R2.

Figure 9-24   NAT Configurations and Output

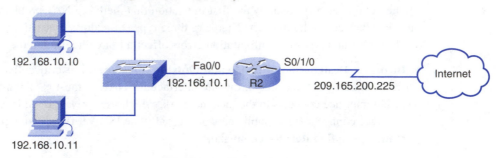

Example 9-13   Configuring NAT Overload (PAT) on R2

```
R2(config)# access-list 1 permit 192.168.10.0 0.0.0.255
R2(config)# ip nat inside source list 1 interface serial 0/1/0 overload
R2(config)# interface fastethernet0/0
R2(config-if)# ip nat inside
R2(config-if)# interface serial 0/1/0
R2(config-if)# ip nat outside
```

Example 9-14 shows the output of the **show ip nat translation** command.

Example 9-14   The show ip nat translation and show ip nat translation verbose Command Output

```
R2# show ip nat translations
Pro Inside global        Inside local       Outside local      Outside global
tcp 209.165.200.225:16642   192.168.10.10:16642   209.165.200.254:80   209.165.200.254:80
tcp 209.165.200.225:62452   192.168.10.11:62452   209.165.200.254:80   209.165.200.254:80


R2# show ip nat translations verbose
Pro Inside global
tcp 209.165.200.225:16642   192.168.10.10:16642   209.165.200.254:80   209.165.200.254:80
   create 00:01:45, use 00:01:1:43 timeout:86400000, left 23:58:16, Map-Id(In): 1,
   flags:
extended, use_count: 0, entry-id: 4, lc_entries:0
tcp 209.165.200.225:62452   192.168.10.11:62452   209.165.200.254:80   209.165.200.254:80
   create 00:00:37, use 00:00:35 trimeout:86400000, left 23:59:24, Map-Id(In): 1,
   flags:
extended, use_count: 0, entry-id: 5, lc_entries:0
R2#
```

Example 9-15 shows using the **clear ip nat translations** command and the resulting **show ip nat translation**.

Example 9-15   Using the clear ip nat translation Command

```
R2# clear ip nat translation *
R2# show ip nat translations
R2#
```

Troubleshooting DHCP and NAT (9.3.4)

In this Packet Tracer activity, you use **show** commands to troubleshoot DHCP and NAT. Use file d2-934.pka on the CD-ROM that accompanies this book to perform this activity using Packet Tracer.

CCENT Study Guide 3: Troubleshooting Layer 3 IP Addressing Issues (9.3.5)

See the CCENT Study Guide 3 on the CD-ROM accompanying this book.

Troubleshooting Layer 3 Routing Issues

One of the most important aspects of network Layer 3 is routing, which moves packets from one network to another. This section describes Layer 3 routing issues and dynamic routing errors.

Layer 3 Routing Issues

Layer 3 encompasses the addressing of networks and hosts and the protocols that route packets between networks.

Most networks have several different types of routes, including a combination of static, dynamic, and default routes. Problems with routing can cause network failures or adversely affect network performance. These problems can be the result of manual route entry errors, routing protocol configuration and operation errors, or failures at lower layers of the OSI model.

To troubleshoot Layer 3 problems, it is important to understand how routing works, including how each type of route functions and is configured.

You might want to review the materials and activities in Discovery 1 and Discovery 2 on routing and routing protocols before continuing with this chapter. Symptoms of Layer 3 routing problems can include network failure and network performance below baseline.

The status of a network can change frequently for a variety of reasons:

- An interface fails
- A service provider drops a connection
- The available bandwidth is overloaded
- An administrator enters an incorrect configuration

When there is a change in the network status, routes can be lost, or an incorrect route can be installed into the routing table.

The primary tool to use when troubleshooting Layer 3 routing problems is the **show ip route** command. This command displays all the routes the router uses to forward traffic. The routing table consists of route entries from the following sources:

- Directly connected networks
- Static routes
- Dynamic routing protocols

Routing protocols choose which routes are preferred based on route metrics. Directly connected networks have a metric of 0, static routes also have a default metric of 0, and dynamic routes have various routing metrics, depending on the routing protocol used.

If there is more than one route to a specific destination network, the route with the lowest administrative distance is installed into the routing table. Table 9-1 shows various routing sources sorted by administrative distance.

Any time a routing problem is suspected, use the **show ip route** command to ensure that all the expected routes are installed in the routing table.

Table 9-1   Route Sources, Administrative Distance, and Metrics

Route Source	Administrative Distance	Default Metric(s)
Connected	0	0
Static	1	0
EIGRP Summary Route	5	—
External BGP	20	Value assigned by admin
Internal EIGRP	90	Bandwidth, delay
IGRP	100	Bandwidth, delay
OSPF	110	Link cost (bandwidth)
IS-IS	115	Link cost (bandwidth)
RIP	120	Hop count
External EIGRP	170	—
Internal BGP	200	Value assigned by admin

Connected Route Problems

Directly connected routes are automatically installed in the routing table when an IP address is configured on an interface, and the interface is enabled using the **no shutdown** command. If a directly connected route does not appear in the table, use the **show interfaces** or **show ip interface brief** command to verify that an address is assigned and that the interface is in an up/up state.

Static and Default Route Problems

When a static or default route does not appear in the routing table, the problem is most likely a configuration error. Static and default routes must use either an exit interface or the IP address of a next hop router. Static routing errors sometimes occur because the next hop address is not in the correct IP address range of any directly connected network. Verify that the configuration statements are correct and that the exit interfaces used by the routes are in an up/up state.

Dynamic Route Problems

Many different types of problems can cause dynamic routes to not appear in the routing table. Because dynamic routing protocols exchange route tables with all other routers in the network, a missing route could be caused by a misconfiguration on one or more of the routers on the path to the destination.

Example 9-16 shows the routing table for the R1 router, with various types of routes identified.

Example 9-16   R1 show ip route Command Output with Different Route Types

```
R1# show ip route

Codes: C - connected, S - static, R - RIP, M - mobile, B - BGP
       D - EIGRP, EX - EIGRP external, O - OSPF, IA - OSPF inter area
       N1 - OSPF NSSA external type 1, N2 - OSPF NSSA external type 2
       E1 - OSPF external type 1, E2 - OSPF external type 2
       i - IS-IS, su - IS-IS summary, L1 - IS-IS level-1, L2 - IS-IS level-2
       ia - IS-IS inter area, * - candidate default, U - per-user static route
       o - ODR, P - periodic downloaded static route
! The following is the gateway as set by the default static route entry (S*)
Gateway of last resort is 192.168.1.2 to network 0.0.0.0
! The following is a directly connected network
C       172.16.0.0/16 is directly connected, FastEthernet0/0
        10.0.0.0/24 is subnetted, 1 subnets
! The following is a normal static route
S       10.10.10.0 [1/0] via 192.168.1.2
C       192.168.0.0/24 is directly connected, Serial0/1
C       192.168.1.0/24 is directly connected, Serial0/0
! The following is a dynamically updated route via RIP
R       192.168.2.0/24 [120/1] via 192.168.1.2, 00:00:23
! The following is a default static route that sets the gateway above
S*      0.0.0.0/0 [1/0] via 192.168.1.2
```

Applying Routing Table Principles (9.4.1)

In this Packet Tracer activity, you use routing table principles to solve a routing problem. Use file d2-941.pka on the CD-ROM that accompanies this book to perform this activity using Packet Tracer.

Dynamic Routing Errors

Routing table updates usually occur when a new network is configured or an already configured network becomes unreachable.

If directly connected routes appear in the router table, the routing table is accessed and changed only if the directly connected interface changes states. If static or default routes are configured, the routing table changes only if new routes are specified or if the exit interface specified in the static or default route changes states.

Dynamic routing protocols automatically send updates to other routers in the network. If dynamic routing is enabled, a router accesses and changes its own routing table any time a change is reported in an update from a neighboring router.

RIP is a dynamic routing protocol used in small- to medium-sized LANs. When troubleshooting issues specific to RIP, check the versioning and configuration statements.

It is always best to use the same version of the routing protocol on all routers. Although RIPv1 and RIPv2 are compatible, RIPv1 does not support classless routing or variable length subnet masks (VLSM). This can create issues if both RIPv1 and RIPv2 are configured to run on the same network. Additionally, while RIPv2 automatically listens for both RIPv1 and RIPv2 updates from neighbors, RIPv1 does not listen for RIPv2 updates.

Routing problems also occur if there are incorrect or missing network statements. The network statement does two things:

- It enables the routing protocol to send and receive updates on any local interfaces that belong to that network.

- It includes that network in its routing updates to its neighboring routers.

A missing or incorrect network statement results in inaccurate routing updates and can prevent an interface from sending or receiving routing updates.

Refer to Figure 9-25 for a sample RIP network topology. Example 9-17 shows the commands used to configure the router for RIP. The commands specify RIP version 2 and advertise networks 172.30.0.0 and 209.165.200.0. The **no summary** command prevents RIP from automatically summarizing subnets of a Classful network.

Figure 9-25   RIP Network Topology

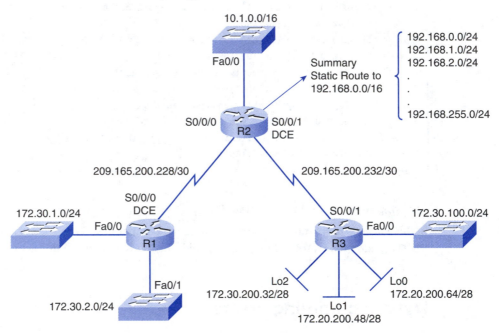

Example 9-17   R1 show running-config Command Output

```
R1# show running-config
Building configuration…
!
Hostname R1
!
Interface FastEthernet 0/0
 ip address 172.30.1.1 255.255.255.0
!
Interface FastEthernet0/1
 ip address 172.30.2.1 255.255.255.0
!
Interface Serial0/0/0
 ip address 209.165.200.230 255.255.255.252
 clock rate 64000
!
```

```
Router rip
 version 2
 network 172.30.0.0
 network 209.165.200.0
 no auto-summary
!
<some output omitted for brevity>
!
End
```

Many tools exist for troubleshooting dynamic routing issues.

TCP/IP utilities, such as ping and traceroute, are used to verify connectivity. Telnet can be used to verify connectivity and make configuration changes. Cisco IOS **show** commands display a snapshot of a configuration or the status of a particular component. Figure 9-26 shows another basic RIP network, and Examples 9-18 through 9-22 show output from several of the more commonly used Cisco IOS **show** commands and highlights the RIP related commands.

Figure 9-26   The show Command Network Topology

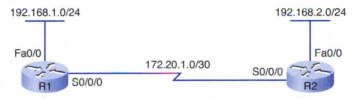

Example 9-18   R1 show ip protocols Command Output

```
R1# show ip protocols
Routing Protocol is "rip"
 Outgoing update filter list for all interfaces is not set
 Incoming update filter list for all interfaces is not set
 Sending updates every 30 seconds, next due in 22 seconds
 Invalid after 180 seconds, hold down 180, flushed after 240
 Redistributing: rip
 Default version control: send version 2, receive version 2
 Interface  Send Recv Triggered RIP Key-chain
 Serial0/0/0  2 2
 Automatic network summarization is in effect
 Maximum path: 4
 Routing for Networks:
 172.20.0.0
 192.168.1.0
 Passive Interface(s):
 FastEthernet0/0
 Routing Information Sources:
 Gateway  Distance Last Update
 172.20.1.2  120 00:00:15
 Distance: (default is 120)
```

Example 9-19   R1 show running-config Command Output

```
R1# show running-config
Building configuration...
< *** Some output omitted *** >
Current configuration : 1120 bytes
!
version 12.4
!
hostname R1
!
enable secret 5 $1$kbVM$rqp03lY42AhaHURL9BXTl0
enable password cisco
!
interface FastEthernet0/0
 description LAN gateway for 192.168.1.0
 ip address 192.168.1.1 255.255.255.0
 duplex auto
 speed auto
!
interface FastEthernet0/1
 no ip address
 shutdown
 duplex auto
 speed auto
!
interface Serial0/0/0
 description WAN link to R2
 ip address 172.20.1.1 255.255.255.252
 no fair-queue
!
interface Serial0/0/1
 no ip address
 shutdown
!
interface Vlan1
 no ip address
!
router rip
 version 2
 passive-interface FastEthernet0/0
 network 172.20.0.0
 network 192.168.1.0
 no auto-summary

!
banner motd #Unauthorized use prohibited#
!
line con 0
 password cisco
 login
line aux 0
```

```
 line vty 0 4
  password cisco
  login
 !
 end
```

Example 9-20   R1 show interfaces Command Output

```
R1# show interfaces
< *** Some output omitted *** >
FastEthernet0/0 is up, line protocol is up
 Hardware is Gt96k FE, address is 001b.5325.256e (bia 001b.5325.256e)
 Description: LAN gateway for 192.168.1.0
 Internet address is 192.168.1.1/24
 MTU 1500 bytes, BW 100000 Kbit, DLY 100 usec,
 reliability 255/255, txload 1/255, rxload 1/255
 Encapsulation ARPA, loopback not set
 Keepalive set (10 sec)
 Auto-duplex, Auto Speed, 100BaseTX/FX

Serial0/0/0 is up, line protocol is up
 Hardware is GT96K Serial
 Description: WAN link to R2
 Internet address is 172.20.1.1/30
 MTU 1500 bytes, BW 1544 Kbit, DLY 20000 usec,
 reliability 255/255, txload 1/255, rxload 1/255
 Encapsulation HDLC, loopback not set
 Keepalive set (10 sec)
```

Example 9-21   R1 show ip interface Command Output

```
R1# show ip interface
< *** Some output omitted *** >
FastEthernet0/0 is up, line protocol is up
 Internet address is 192.168.1.1/24
 Broadcast address is 255.255.255.255
 Address determined by setup command
 MTU is 1500 bytes
 Helper address is not set
 Directed broadcast forwarding is disabled
 Multicast reserved groups joined: 224.0.0.9

Serial0/0/0 is up, line protocol is up
 Internet address is 172.20.1.1/30
 Broadcast address is 255.255.255.255
 Address determined by setup command
 MTU is 1500 bytes
 Helper address is not set
 Directed broadcast forwarding is disabled
 Multicast reserved groups joined: 224.0.0.9
```

Example 9-22   R1 show ip route Command Output

```
R1# show ip route
Codes: C - connected, S - static, R - RIP, M - mobile, B - BGP
 D - EIGRP, EX - EIGRP external, O - OSPF, IA - OSPF inter area
 N1 - OSPF NSSA external type 1, N2 - OSPF NSSA external type 2
 E1 - OSPF external type 1, E2 - OSPF external type 2
 i - IS-IS, su - IS-IS summary, L1 - IS-IS level-1, L2 - IS-IS level-2
 ia - IS-IS inter area, * - candidate default, U - per-user static route
 o - ODR, P - periodic downloaded static route

Gateway of last resort is not set

 172.20.0.0/30 is subnetted, 1 subnets
C 172.20.1.0 is directly connected, Serial0/0/0
C 192.168.1.0/24 is directly connected, FastEthernet0/0
R 192.168.2.0/24 [120/1] via 172.20.1.2, 00:00:04, Serial0/0/0
```

The Cisco IOS command set also includes various debug commands. Debug commands are dynamic and provide real-time information on traffic movement and the interaction of protocols. For example, the **debug ip rip** command displays the exchange of RIP routing updates and packets as they occur. A sample debug output is provided in Example 9-23 for the network in Figure 9-26.

Example 9-23   R1 debug ip rip Command Output

```
R1# debug ip rip
RIP protocol debugging is on
R1#
*Sep 12 21:08:51.959: RIP: build update entries
*Sep 12 21:08:51.959: 192.168.1.0/24 via 0.0.0.0, metric 1, tag 0
*Sep 12 21:09:16.399: RIP: received v2 update from 172.20.1.2 on Serial0/0/0
*Sep 12 21:09:16.399: 192.168.2.0/24 via 0.0.0.0 in 1 hops
*Sep 12 21:09:18.575: RIP: sending v2 update to 224.0.0.9 via Serial0/0/0 (172.20.1.1)
```

Debug functions use a significant portion of CPU resources and can slow or stop normal router operations. For this reason, use debug commands to isolate problems, not to monitor normal network operation. Before using the **debug** command, narrow the problems to a likely subset of causes. Use debug commands to isolate problems, not to monitor normal network operation.

RIPv2 Configuring RIPv2 Challenge (9.4.2)

In this Packet Tracer activity, you subnet an address space, configure devices, and use a combination of RIPv2 and static routing to provide connectivity between remote hosts. Use file d2-942.pka on the CD-ROM that accompanies this book to perform this activity using Packet Tracer.

Lab 9-7: Correcting RIPv2 Routing Problems (9.4.2)

In this lab, you will troubleshoot a RIP router network configured with errors. Refer to the lab in Part II of this book. You may perform this lab now or wait until the end of the chapter.

CCENT Study Guide 4: Troubleshooting Layer 3 Routing Issues (9.4.3)
See the CCENT Study Guide 4 on the CD-ROM accompanying this book.

Troubleshooting Layer 4 and Upper Layer Issues

If Layers 1 through 3 are functioning correctly, transport Layer 4 TCP and UDP protocols may present problems. Firewalls are often configured to deny specific types of traffic based on TCP or UDP port numbers. This section covers troubleshooting upper-layer issues and the use of Telnet and SSH to verify application layer connectivity.

Layer 4 Traffic Filtering Errors

Layer 4, the transport layer, is considered a transition between the upper and lower layers of the OSI model. Layer 4 is responsible for transporting data packets and specifies the port number used to reach specific applications. Layer 4 network problems can arise at the edge of the network where security technologies are examining and modifying the traffic. Many problems are caused by firewalls that are configured to deny traffic based on port numbers, even though this traffic should be forwarded.

Layer 4 supports both UDP and TCP traffic. Some applications use TCP, some use UDP, and some use both. When denying traffic based on the port number, it is necessary to specify the transport protocol used. Some engineers are unsure of which transport protocol is used by specific applications and therefore deny the port number for both TCP and UDP traffic. This practice may unexpectedly deny traffic that should be allowed.

Firewalls are also often configured to deny everything except the applications specified in the permit statements. If traffic that should be permitted is not included in the firewall statements, or if a new application is added to the network without a corresponding permission being added to the firewall, filtering problems occur. Table 9-2 shows some of the more common Layer 4 TCP and UDP ports that firewalls deal with. These are called well-known ports.

A common indication of Layer 4 problems is users reporting that some web services, especially video or audio, are not reachable.

Verify that the ports being permitted and denied by the firewall are the correct ones for the applications. For a better understanding of which ports correspond to specific applications, review the information on TCP, UDP, and ports in Discovery 1 and Discovery 2.

Transport layer problems often exhibit the following symptoms:

- Intermittent network problems
- Security problems
- Trouble reaching some websites or other network-based applications and services

Table 9-2   Well-Known Ports

Destination Port Number	Abbreviation	Definition
20	FTP Data	File Transfer Protocol (for data transfer)
21	FTP Control	File Transfer Protocol (to establish connection)
23	TELNET	TELetype NETwork
25	SMTP	Simple Mail Transfer Protocol
53	DNS	Domain Name Service
67	DHCP v4 Client	Dynamic Host Configuration Protocol (Client)
68	DHCP v4 Server	Dynamic Host Configuration Protocol (Server)
69	TFTP	Trivial File Transfer Protocol
80	HTTP	Hypertext Transfer Protocol
110	POP3	Post Office Protocol (version 3)
137	NBNS	Microsoft NetBIOS Name Service
143	IMAP4	Internet Message Access Protocol (version 4)
161	SNMP	Simple Network Management Protocol
443	HTTPS	Hypertext Transfer Protocol Secure

Interactive Activity 9-6: Matching Port Numbers to Protocol Names (9.5.1)

In this interactive activity, you match the protocol name to the port number. Use file d2ia-951 on the CD-ROM that accompanies this book to perform this interactive activity.

Troubleshooting Upper-Layer Problems

Most of the upper-layer protocols provide user services that are typically used for network management, file transfer, distributed file services, terminal emulation, and e-mail. Protocols at these layers are often referred to as TCP/IP application layer protocols because the TCP/IP model application layer encompasses the upper three layers of the OSI model.

The most widely known and implemented TCP/IP Application Layer protocols include

- **Telnet:** Enables users to establish unsecure terminal session connections with remote hosts.

- **HTTP:** Supports the exchange of text, graphic images, sound, video, and other multimedia files on the Web.

- **FTP:** Performs interactive file transfers between hosts, using TCP.

- **TFTP:** Performs basic interactive file transfers typically between hosts and networking devices, using UDP.

- **SMTP:** Supports basic e-mail message delivery services.

- **POP3:** Connects to mail servers and downloads e-mail to a client application.

- **IMAP4:** Enables e-mail clients to retrieve messages and store e-mail on servers.

- **SNMP:** Collects information from managed devices.

- **NTP:** Provides updated time to hosts and network devices.

- **DNS:** Maps IP addresses to the names assigned to hosts.

- **SSL:** Provides encryption and security for HTTP transactions.

- **SSH:** Provides secure remote terminal access to servers and networking devices.

Isolating problems to the upper layers can be difficult, especially if the client configuration does not reveal any obvious problems. To determine that a network problem is with an upper-layer function, start by eliminating basic connectivity as the source of the problem.

Using the "divide and conquer" method of troubleshooting, begin by verifying Layer 3 connectivity:

Step 1.   Ping the host default gateway.

Step 2.   Verify end-to-end connectivity.

Step 3.   Verify the routing configuration.

Step 4.   Ensure that NAT is working correctly.

Step 5.   Check for firewall filter rules.

If the problem exists on a remote network, end-to-end connectivity cannot be verified because there is no control over all the connections. For this reason, it is possible that even though the configurations on the local devices are correct, there is still a problem with the remote network. Be sure to check with the ISP to ensure that their network connection is up and operational.

If all these steps are completed successfully, and it is verified that the end-to-end connectivity is not the issue but the end device is still not operating as expected, the problem has been isolated to the upper layers.

The five steps are described in greater details as follows.

Step 1: Ping the Default Gateway

If both the host and the server can successfully ping their default gateways, Layer 1 and Layer 2 services are functioning properly and Layer 3 local network connectivity exists. If the ping to the local default gateway address fails, troubleshoot Layers 3, 2, and 1 to locate the source of the problem.

Step 2: Verify End-to-End Connectivity

Ping or telnet from the host to a remote server or networking device. If successful, Layer 3 routing is operating correctly. When Layers 1, 2, and 3 are functioning properly, the issue must exist at a higher layer.

If this ping is unsuccessful, it is necessary to troubleshoot the routing, NAT, and firewall configurations to ensure proper packet delivery.

Step 3: Verify Routing Configuration

Ensure that the routing configuration is correct and that routes are updating as expected. If the routing table does not contain expected routes, troubleshoot and fix the routing configuration and attempt Step 2 again. If still unable to ping, check the NAT configuration.

Step 4: Verify NAT Operation

When there is a problem reaching services on a remote network such as over the Internet, NAT might not be functioning correctly. Use the **show ip nat translations** command to verify that translations are occurring. Clear the NAT translations with the **clear ip nat translation *** command and try to access the external resource again. If still not successful, check the configuration of the inside and outside interfaces. When the NAT configuration has been verified, attempt Step 2 again. If still unable to ping, check for firewall filter rules.

Step 5: Verify Firewall Filtering Rules

Even though there is IP connectivity between a source and a destination, problems may still exist for a specific upper-layer protocol, such as FTP, HTTP, or Telnet. These protocols ride on top of the basic IP transport but are subject to protocol-specific problems relating to packet filters and firewalls. Verify that the necessary ports are permitted on all firewalls.

Upper-layer problems prevent services from being provided to application programs. A problem at the upper layers can result in unreachable or unusable resources, even when the lower layers are functional. It is possible to have full network connectivity but the application cannot provide data.

Problems with upper-layer functions usually affect just a few applications, perhaps even only one. It is not unusual for a help desk technician to get a call from a user who cannot receive e-mail, although all other applications are functioning correctly.

Misconfigured client applications account for the majority of upper-layer network problems. When an incorrect e-mail or FTP server is specified, the client cannot find and retrieve information. When more than one application is affected, the upper-layer problem may be attributed to a DNS server issue.

To verify that DNS is functioning correctly and can resolve server addresses, use the Windows command **nslookup**. If DNS is not working as expected, ensure that the correct DNS server address is configured on the host. When hosts receive DNS server information from a DHCP server, verify that the DHCP server has the correct IP address for the DNS server.

If the DNS server is operational and reachable, check for DNS zone configuration errors. Look for a typographical error in an address or name within the files.

The following are upper-layer problem symptoms:

- User complains about slow application performance
- Application error message
- Unable to access application services, such as FTP
- Unable to access Web services

The upper layers are responsible for encryption and compression. A mismatch between the way a client encrypts or compresses the data and the way the server interprets it can cause applications to not function or to function poorly.

When a problem occurs on a single host or workstation, it might be a problem with the way the information is being interpreted in the host software. Browser plug-in programs, such as Flash, often perform upper-layer functions. These programs must be kept updated for web pages to display correctly.

Using an incorrect protocol to request data can cause a web page to be unreachable. For example, it might be necessary to specify **https://** on the browser address line, rather than **http://**, to retrieve an SSL-protected web page. Figure 9-27 shows an example of an error that results from upper-layer issues.

Figure 9-27   Server Not Found Error

Using Telnet to Check Upper-Layer Connectivity

Telnet is an excellent tool to use when troubleshooting problems with upper-layer functions. Using Telnet to access the networking devices enables the technician to enter commands on each device as if they were locally attached. In addition, the ability to reach devices using Telnet indicates that the lower-layer connectivity exists between the devices.

However, Telnet is an insecure protocol, which means that all data communicated can be captured and read. If there is a possibility that communications can be intercepted by unauthorized users, Secure Shell (SSH) protocol should be used instead. SSH is a more secure method for remote device access. Figure 9-28 shows a Telnet client accessing a remote server.

Figure 9-28   Telnet Client and Server

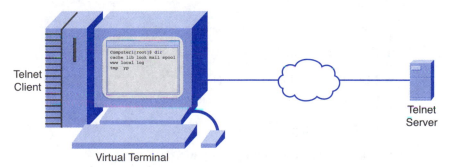

Most newer versions of the Cisco IOS software contain an SSH server. In some devices, this service is enabled by default. Other devices require the SSH server to be manually enabled.

Cisco IOS devices also include an SSH client that can be used to establish SSH sessions with other devices. Similarly, a remote computer with an SSH client can be used to start a secure CLI session. SSH client software is not provided by default on all computer operating systems. The technician may need to acquire, install, and configure SSH client software on the computer.

Review the material in Discovery 2 on configuring and using SSH.

Lab 9-8: Using Telnet and SSH to Access Networking Devices (9.5.3)

In this lab, you will access networking devices using Telnet and SSH. Refer to the lab in Part II of this book. You may perform this lab now or wait until the end of the chapter.

CCENT Study Guide 5: Troubleshooting Layer 4 and Upper Layer Services (9.5.4)

See the CCENT Study Guide 5 on the CD-ROM accompanying this book.

Preparing for Cisco Certification

Cisco certification is a valuable asset in the world of networking. This section describes the process of creating a plan and getting ready to take a certification exam. It also explores the Cisco CCNA Exam Prep website.

Knowledge, Skills, and Abilities

The Cisco Certified Entry Networking Technician (CCENT) certification validates the skills required for entry-level network support positions, the starting point for many successful careers in networking. CCENT certification is the first step toward achieving CCNA certification (Cisco Certified Network Associate), which covers medium-size enterprise branch networks that have more complex connections. To obtain CCENT certification, a candidate must pass the ICND1 examination at a Cisco Certified Testing Center.

The ICND1 exam (640-822) tests the ability to install, operate, and troubleshoot a small branch office network. The exam includes topics on networking fundamentals:

- Connecting to a WAN
- Basic security and wireless concepts
- Routing and switching
- TCP/IP and OSI models
- IP addressing
- WAN technologies
- Operating and configuring Cisco IOS devices
- Configuring RIPv2, static, and default routing
- Implementing NAT and DHCP
- Configuring simple networks

Mastering a Cisco certification exam is not an easy task. Some candidates pass the exam the first time; many pass it after multiple attempts, while other do not pass it. Good preparation is the best way to ensure that you pass the exam the first time. Figure 9-29 shows taking the ICND1 exam to become CCENT certified. By also taking the ICND2 exam, you can become CCNA certified.

Figure 9-29   CCENT/CCNA Certification Exam Process

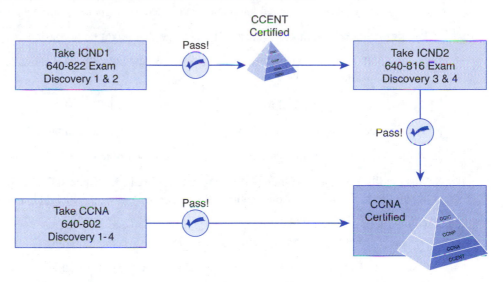

Before preparing for any certification examination, it is important to understand the purpose of the exam. Cisco certification examinations are designed to measure the knowledge, skills, and abilities of an individual in a defined area of expertise.

- **Knowledge:** Knowledge statements are typically factual or procedural in nature. They relate directly to the performance of a function.

- **Skills:** Skill statements refer to the capacity to manually, verbally, or mentally manipulate data or things to achieve a desired result. Skills can be measured by a performance test where quantity and quality of performance are tested, usually within an established time limit. Examples of skill-related tasks include skill in typing or skill in operating a vehicle.

- **Abilities:** Ability statements refer to the power to perform an observable activity at the present time. This means that abilities have been proven through activities or behaviors that are similar to those required on the job. An example is the ability to plan and organize work.

The exams use a combination of techniques to enable a candidate to demonstrate readiness to perform various networking tasks. The exam can contain multiple-choice questions, various exercises, and simulated network configuration tasks. Each question or task is designed to address a specific objective. The Cisco certification website lists the objectives for the ICND1 exam.

http://www.cisco.com/web/learning/le3/current_exams/640-822.html

Networking Knowledge, Skills, and Abilities

To perform most networking tasks, some knowledge must be recalled from memory. This type of knowledge is made up of facts. When studying for a certification exam, identify the pertinent facts associated with each exam objective. Some individuals find it useful to create flashcards to help memorize these facts. While there may be a few questions on the exam that require the basic factual answers, more often the factual knowledge is needed to diagnose or solve a networking problem.

The following are examples of facts or knowledge that might be on flash cards:

1. In a RIP network, what is the maximum number of hops a packet can take before a destination becomes unreachable?

2. Which routing protocol uses a distance vector algorithm?

3. How does a switch determine which port to use to reach a destination?

4. Where is the startup configuration stored in a Cisco router?

Many skills are required when performing networking tasks. Some skills are fairly easy, such as creating and terminating a crossover cable. Other skills are more difficult, such as mastering IP subnetting.

The mastery of networking skills requires practice. Lab and Packet Tracer activities are designed to provide a structured practice environment for learners.

Cisco certifications measure and validate the networking skills of an individual based on how they interact with Cisco networking devices. Because of this, it is very important to practice with Cisco IOS Software. Many exam tasks require the interpretation of Cisco IOS command output, especially the output of the various **show** commands.

The question will instruct you to refer to the exhibit, such as the topology shown in Figure 9-30, and then ask: Which Cisco IOS command will assign the first usable IP address in the subnetwork to FastEthernet 0/1 of RTA?

A. RTA(config-if)# **ip address 172.18.13.1 255.255.254.0**

B. RTA(config-if)# **ip address 172.18.14.1 255.255.252.0**

C. RTA(config-if)# **ip address 172.18.14.1 255.255.255.252**

D. RTA(config-if)# **ip address 172.18.16.1 255.255.252.0**

E. RTA(config-if)# **ip address 172.18.16.1 255.255.255.252**

F. RTA(config-if)# **ip address 172.18.16.229 255.255.255.252**

The question is designed to test the IP addressing skills of the candidate. It also requires the candidate to be familiar with configuring Cisco IOS software.

The answer to the question is choice D. The IP address of RTA Fa0/1 is the default gateway for the LAN and must be compatible with the IP address of Host A. The Host A IP address is 172.18.16.230/22. The prefix /22 translates to a subnet mask of 255.255.252.0. Only two of the six answers have a subnet mask of 255.255.252.0, so the possible answers are narrowed to B or D. In answer B, the IP address is 172.18.14.1 and the first three octets do not match the IP address assigned to Host A. By process of elimination, only Answer D has the same first three octets as Host A.

You can also use the more precise ANDing process to determine the answer. By comparing the Host A subnet mask bits to its IP address you can determine the network or subnet the host is on, the range of allowable host IP addresses, and the broadcast address for the subnetwork. A decimal mask of 255.255.252.0 is binary 11111111.11111111.11111100.0000000.

Host A IP Address decimal:	172	.18	.16	.230
Host A IP address binary:	10101100.00010010.00010000.11100110			
Host A subnet mask binary:	11111111.11111111.11111100.00000000			
Host A network binary:	10101100.00010010.00010000.00000000			
Host A network decimal:	172	.18	.16	.0

First host address binary:	10101100.00010010.00010000.00000001			
First host address decimal:	172	.18	.16	.1
Last host address binary:	10101100.00010010.00010011.11111110			
Last host address decimal:	172	.18	.19	.254
Broadcast address binary:	10101100.00010010.00010011.11111111			
Broadcast address binary:	172	.18	.19	.255

Figure 9-30   Sample Certification Question Topology

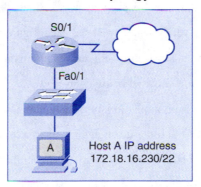

The ability to plan, organize, execute, and problem solve is critical to the success of an entry-level network technician. In a certification exam environment, these abilities are usually measured using configuration and troubleshooting tasks. Effort is made when designing the exams to simulate conditions that an individual would encounter when performing an actual networking job. These conditions can be presented on the exam using scenarios or simulations.

Preparing for a scenario-based or simulation task is not as simple as memorizing a fact or practicing a specific skill. These types of tasks require an individual to apply both the facts and skills to solve a problem or meet a stated requirement.

The best way to analyze what information is needed to perform a specific networking task is to envision what would happen if the information was not known. Make a list of the possible outcomes and determine what skills could be used to identify and correct any problem that would be created. That sounds difficult, but here are a few examples to consider:

- What would happen if a network technician did not know the correct number of host addresses available using a specific subnet mask? How could the problems be identified and corrected?

- What problems might arise in a RIPv2 network that has more than 15 hops from a source to a destination address? What would be a symptom of this problem? How could the problem be corrected?

Task: Configure RIPv2 to route network traffic.

Information needed:

- Steps to configure RIPv2 routing:

Step 1.   Log in to the router.

Step 2.   Enter privileged mode.

Step 3.   Enter configuration mode.

Step 4.   Enable RIP.

Step 5.   Enable version 2.

Step 6.   Configure a network statement for each connected network that participates in RIP.

- Cisco IOS commands to enable RIPv2 routing:

   1. **config t**
   2. **router rip**
   3. **version 2**
   4. **network** [*address*]
   5. **copy running-config startup-config**

- Network addresses for each connected network

- Methods to verify whether RIPv2 is configured correctly and functioning:

Step 1.   Use the **show running-config** command.

Step 2.   Use the **show ip route** command.

Step 3.   Ping from a host to a remote IP address on another network.

Step 4.   Trace the route through a router to a remote IP address.

Step 5.   Use **debug** to verify that RIPv2 routing updates are being sent and received.

Possible incorrect outcomes (if I do not possess the necessary knowledge):

- I cannot enter configuration mode to begin the configuration.

- I forget to configure version 2 or add the network statements.

- I do not configure all the networks.

- I enter the wrong IP address information.

- I cannot verify if RIPv2 is operating correctly.

Possible symptoms of problems:

- Cannot ping hosts on other networks

- Cannot traceroute through the router

- No routes appear in routing table of router

Interactive Activity 9-7: Identifying Knowledge, Skills, and Abilities Tasks (9.6.2)

In this interactive activity, you identify knowledge tasks, skills related tasks, and abilities. Use file d2ia-962 on the CD-ROM that accompanies this book to perform this interactive activity.

Lab 9-9: Identifying Necessary Knowledge, Skills, and Abilities (9.6.2)

In this lab, you will identify the knowledge, skills, and abilities needed to perform the lab tasks. Refer to the lab in Part II of this book. You may perform this lab now or wait until the end of the chapter.

Making the Commitment

Getting ready to take a certification exam can be an overwhelming task. There is much information to review, many skills to practice, and pressure to succeed. Just like installing a network for a customer, exam preparation is more successful if it is broken down into a series of smaller steps:

1. Making the commitment.

2. Creating a plan.

3. Practicing test taking.

After you complete these steps, you are ready to begin the exam preparation.

The first step to obtaining a Cisco certification is making the commitment to devote the time and effort necessary to prepare for the examination. This commitment must be assigned a top priority, because it will take time that was previously used for other activities.

In addition to taking time, preparing for a certification exam requires concentration. Find a place at home or at school where you can study for long periods of time uninterrupted. Trying to learn and practice networking skills can be extremely difficult if other distractions are present.

Having the right equipment and resources is also important. Make sure you have access to a computer, the online course materials, and Packet Tracer software. Discuss with your instructor how to schedule lab time to practice your skills on actual equipment. Find out if remote lab access over the Internet is available in your area.

Inform friends and family of your commitment to obtaining the CCENT certification. Explain to them that their assistance and support are needed during the exam preparation. Even if they have no understanding of networking, they can help you study with flashcards or ask practice questions. At a minimum, they can help by respecting your need for uninterrupted study time. If others in your class are preparing for the exam at the same time, it might be helpful to organize a study group.

Creating a Plan

After you have made the commitment to dedicate the time necessary to prepare to take the ICND1 examination, the next step is creating a plan. A certification preparation plan includes information on how you intend to prepare, a schedule of dates and times, and a list of the resources.

There are two ways to approach studying for a certification exam: individually or in a group. Many people find that creating a study group helps them focus better on the material and keep to a schedule.

When studying with a partner or in a group, it is critical for all participants to know how to contact each other, the schedule and place for meetings, and other pertinent information. It might be necessary to assign members of the group different responsibilities, such as

- Obtaining and distributing study materials

- Scheduling lab time

- Ensuring all necessary supplies are available

- Keeping track of the group progress

- Finding answers to problems

Studying alone might make the coordination of resources easier, but it does not diminish the importance of a good plan.

Use the following checklist:

☐ Set a realistic target date for taking the exam based on the amount of time available each week to dedicate to the preparation.

☐ Use smaller amounts of time for fact memorization, and larger blocks of time for practicing skills. It can be frustrating to begin a lab or skill practice exercise and not have sufficient time scheduled to complete it.

The Cisco Press CCENT exam review guide titled *31 Days Before Your CCENT Certification* can be used to structure a schedule. The book takes each exam objective and highlights the important information to study. It contains references to the sections and topics in the first and second courses of the Discovery curriculum that need to be reviewed and practiced.

A good way to create a schedule is to record all the available time on a calendar. Then assign each block of time to a specific task, such as "learn OSI model layers and their functions" or "practice IP subnetting." When all tasks are entered, determine when to schedule the exam.

☐ Investigate all the tools and resources available to help you study. The ICND1 exam tests the knowledge and skills obtained during this course, in addition to all the content from the first course in the Discovery curriculum. Access to the online curriculum, labs, and Packet Tracer activities is critical to successful preparation.

In addition to these tools, many other study aids exist on the Cisco CCNA certification preparation website. The link for the CCNA Prep Center is

http://forums.cisco.com/eforum/servlet/PrepCenter?page=main

Figure 9-31 shows the CCNA Prep Center website.

Figure 9-31   CCNA Prep Center Website

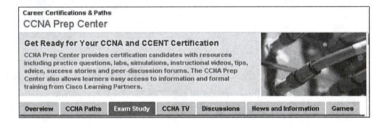

Cisco Press publishes a number of books that cover the CCENT exam objectives. These books can be purchased through the Cisco Marketplace Bookstore or through Cisco Press:

http://www.cisco.com/pcgi-bin/marketplace/welcome.pl?STORE_ID=CISCO_
BOOKSTORE&KEYCODE=Certifications

http://www.ciscopress.com

After the necessary materials have been gathered, it is important to organize them. Reviewing and practicing the CCENT knowledge and skills can be difficult if it is approached in a haphazard manner. It is easier to recall and use information if it is learned and practiced in an organized framework.

Practicing Test Taking

Recalling and performing networking skills in a formal testing environment is different from doing the same functions in a classroom or at home. It is important to understand the format of the exam and how it is administered.

Visit the Testing Center

Before taking the exam, visit the testing center and see how the exam is administered. Ask questions about what to expect. Some testing centers provide each examinee with a separate testing room; others have larger areas where a number of people are taking exams at the same time. Find out what is permitted to bring into the room and, more importantly, what items are not permitted. Visit the Cisco certification website to find the nearest testing center.

Format of the Examination

Certification exams are given online, similar to the manner in which Networking Academy assessments are delivered. There are, however, some differences:

- Survey questions may be presented before the actual examination begins. It is important to answer these questions truthfully. The survey questions have no impact on the content of the examination or on your final score.

- Certification exams are timed. The time remaining is displayed on the screen so that you can decide how long to spend on each question or task.

- There may be many different types of questions or tasks on the same examination.

- You cannot go back to a previous question after moving to the next one.

There is no way to skip a question or mark a question for review. If you do not know an answer, it is best to guess the answer and move on to the next question.

Cisco certification exams include the following test formats:

- Multiple-choice single answer
- Multiple-choice multiple answer
- Drag-and-drop
- Fill-in-the-blank
- Testlet
- Simlet
- Simulations

Before taking the exam, become familiar with how all question types function, especially the testlet, simlet, and simulation tool. This practice enables you to focus on the exam questions rather than on how to correctly use the tools. Practice the exam tutorial found on the Cisco CCNA prep website until you are comfortable with the format and operation of each type of question and task.

Lab 9-10: Exploring the CCNA Prep Center (9.6.5)

In this lab, you will use the Cisco CCNA Prep Center website to find study materials and tools to help prepare for the CCENT exam. Refer to the lab in Part II of this book. You may perform this lab now or wait until the end of the chapter.

Although nothing substitutes for the experience of taking the actual exam, it is often helpful to take practice exams. The CCNA Prep Center provides sample tests for the ICND1 exam that include multiple-choice questions. If you're studying for the exam with other students, create practice questions and share them. In addition, there are commercially available practice exams that can be purchased and downloaded from the Internet.

Cisco certifications include tasks that simulate the operation of Cisco routers and switches. It is recommended that you repeat all Packet Tracers and Labs in this course in preparation for the ICND1 exam. However, just reading the curriculum and practicing the labs might not be adequate preparation for the types of integrated tasks that appear on a certification exam. It is important to investigate what might happen if there is an error in the setup or configuration of a device. Much can be learned by creating error situations and observing the changes in command output and device operation. Many of the scenario questions and tasks on the ICND1 exam are based on troubleshooting network problems.

Figure 9-32 shows a sample exam simulation question. The simulation contains three windows. The Instructions window provides instructions on how to complete the simulation. The Topology window displays the topology of the network and provides additional context for the simulation. The Router window displays a terminal emulation screen. It is used to enter CLI commands to make changes to device configuration and to display output.

Figure 9-32   Sample Simulation Exam Question

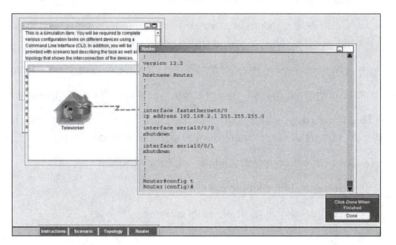

CCENT Troubleshooting Challenge (9.6.5)

In this Packet Tracer activity, you use Telnet and other tools to troubleshoot problems in a small network. Use file d2-965.pka on the CD-ROM that accompanies this book to perform this activity using Packet Tracer.

CCENT Study Guide 9-6: WLANs (9.6.6)

See the CCENT Study Guide 6 on the CD-ROM accompanying this book.

CCENT Preparation Guide (9.6.6)

See the CCENT Preparation Guide on the CD-ROM accompanying this book.

Summary

Each layer of the OSI or TCP/IP model has specific functions and protocols. Knowledge of the features, functions, and devices of each layer, and how each layer relates to the layers around it, help a network technician to troubleshoot more efficiently.

The upper layers (5 through 7) of the OSI model deal with specific application functionality and are generally implemented only in software. The lower layers (1 through 4) of the OSI model handle data transport and physical networking functions.

There are three main troubleshooting approaches when using network models:

- Top-down
- Bottom-up
- Divide-and-conquer

Tools that assist with network troubleshooting include

- Network diagrams and documentation
- Network documentation and baseline tools
- Network management systems
- Knowledge bases
- Protocol analyzers

Sometimes failures in the lower layers of the OSI model cannot be easily identified with software tools. In these instances, it might be necessary to use hardware troubleshooting tools, such as cable testers, multimeters, and network analyzers.

The physical and data link layers encompass both hardware and software functions. The physical layer, or Layer 1, is responsible for the physical and electrical specifications for the transmission of bits from one host to another over the physical medium, either wired or wireless.

Layer 1 problems include

- Cable type, length, and termination problems
- Duplex mismatches
- Interference and noise that disrupts transmissions
- Device hardware and boot errors

Router interface errors are often the first symptom of Layer 1 and Layer 2 cabling or connectivity errors. Device LEDs provide valuable troubleshooting information that can be used to identify the causes of connectivity issues.

The data link layer, or Layer 2, specifies how the data is formatted for transmission over the network media. It also regulates how access to the network is granted. Layer 2 provides the link between the network layer software functions and the Layer 1 hardware for both LAN and WAN applications. Layer 2 problems include

- Encapsulation mismatches
- No keepalives generated or received
- Timing problems on WAN connections

The **show version**, **show interfaces**, and **show interface brief** commands provide troubleshooting information to isolate and identify Layer 1 and Layer 2.

The primary functions implemented at Layer 3 of the OSI model are network addressing and routing.

Poorly designed and configured IP addressing schemes, especially overlapping subnet addresses, account for a large number of network performance problems. Overlapping subnets can be caused by careless address assignment or by improperly configured subnet masks on devices.

Problems obtaining an IP address from a DHCP server can cause PC clients to automatically configure an address on the 169.254.0.0 network. NAT configuration and operation issues can cause Internet sites to be unreachable from the privately addressed LAN.

Most networks have several different types of routes, including a combination of static, dynamic, and default routes. Problems with routing can be the result of manual route entry errors, routing protocol configuration and operation errors, or failures at lower layers of the OSI model.

The primary tool to use when troubleshooting Layer 3 routing problems is the **show ip route** command. The routing table consists of route entries from the following sources:

- Directly connected networks
- Static routes
- Dynamic routing protocols

Problems that occur with RIPv2 routing include

- Version not specified, causing version mismatch between routers
- Misconfigured or missing network statements
- Improperly configured interface IP addresses

Layer 4 is responsible for transporting data packets and specifies the port number used to reach specific applications. Firewall and port filtering rules that permit or deny the incorrect ports can cause needed services to be unreachable from client computers.

Upper-layer services include DNS name resolution, encryption, and compression. Errors occurring with these functions can make end-user applications unusable. The Windows command **nslookup** can provide information to assist with troubleshooting DNA failures.

The Cisco Certified Entry Networking Technician (CCENT) certification validates the skills required for entry-level network support positions, the starting point for many successful careers in networking. To obtain CCENT certification a candidate must pass the ICND1 (640-822) examination, which tests the ability to install, operate, and troubleshoot a small branch office network.

Cisco certifications measure and validate the networking skills of an individual based on how they interact with Cisco networking devices. Many exam tasks require the interpretation of Cisco IOS command output, especially the output of the various **show** commands.

Just like installing a network for a customer, exam preparation is more successful if it is broken down into a series of smaller steps:

1. Making the commitment.
2. Creating a plan.
3. Practicing test taking.

Activities and Labs

This summary outlines the activities you can perform to help reinforce important concepts described in this chapter. You can find the activity, study guide, and Packet Tracer files on the CD-ROM accompanying this book. You can find the labs in Part II.

Interactive Activities on the CD-ROM:

Interactive Activity 9-1: The OSI Model and Troubleshooting (9.1.1)

Interactive Activity 9-2: Troubleshooting Methodologies (9.1.2)

Interactive Activity 9-3: Matching Layer 1 and 2 Problems with Symptoms (9.2.1)

Interactive Activity 9-4: Determining Host Range, Broadcast Address and Next Network (9.3.1)

Interactive Activity 9-5: Determining the Number of Hosts for a Network (9.3.3)

Interactive Activity 9-6: Matching Port Numbers to Protocol Names (9.5.1)

Interactive Activity 9-7: Identifying Knowledge, Skills and Abilities Tasks (9.6.2)

CCENT Study Guides on the CD-ROM:

CCENT Study Guide 9-1: Troubleshooting Methodologies and Tools (9.1.4)

CCENT Study Guide 9-2: Troubleshooting Layer 1 and Layer 2 Issues (9.2.6)

CCENT Study Guide 9-3: Troubleshooting Layer 3 IP Addressing Issues (9.3.5)

CCENT Study Guide 9-4: Troubleshooting Layer 3 Routing Issues (9.4.3)

CCENT Study Guide 9-5: Troubleshooting Layer 4 and Upper Layer Services (9.5.4)

CCENT Study Guide 9-6: WLANs (9.6.6)

CCENT Preparation Guide (9.6.6)

Packet Tracer Activities on the CD-ROM:

Configuring and Troubleshooting a Switched Network (9.2.4)

WAN Encapsulation Mismatches (9.2.5)

Troubleshoot a Small IP Network (9.3.1)

Troubleshooting DHCP and NAT (9.3.4)

Applying Routing Table Principles (9.4.1)

RIPv2 Configuring RIPv2 Challenge (9.4.2)

CCENT Troubleshooting Challenge (9.6.5)

Labs in Part II of this book:

Lab 9-1: Organizing CCENT Objectives by OSI Layer (9.1.1)

Lab 9-2: Using Wireshark to Observe the TCP Three-Way Handshake (9.1.3)

Lab 9-3: Identifying Cabling and Media Errors (9.2.3)

Lab 9-4: Troubleshooting LAN Connectivity(9.2.4)

Lab 9-5: Troubleshooting WAN Connectivity (9.2.5)

Lab 9-6: Designing an IP Subnetting Scheme for Growth (9.3.3)

Lab 9-7: Correcting RIPv2 Routing Problems (9.4.2)

Lab 9-8: Using Telnet and SSH to Access Networking Devices (9.5.3)

Lab 9-9: Identifying Necessary Knowledge, Skills, and Abilities (9.6.2)

Lab 9-10: Exploring the CCNA Prep Center (9.6.5)

Check Your Understanding

Complete the review questions to check your understanding of the topics and concepts in this chapter. Answers are listed in Appendix A, "Check Your Understanding and Challenge Questions Answer Key."

1. Draw a line from the networking tool on the left to its correct testing description on the right.

Networking Tool	Description
Cable tester	Checks power-supply voltage levels and verifies that network devices are receiving power.
Digital multimeter	Graphically displays a physical view of network devices and can locate the source of a failed device.
Network analyzer	Identifies devices producing the most network traffic, analyzes network traffic by protocol, and views interface details.
Network management system	Detects broken wires, crossed-over wiring, shorted connections, and improperly paired connections.
Protocol analyzer	Filters traffic that meets certain criteria so that all traffic between two devices can be captured.

2. A network administrator is troubleshooting connectivity issues with a router and finds that the S0/0/0 interface IP address has been improperly configured. At what layer of the OSI model is this problem occurring?

   A. Layer 1

   B. Layer 3

   C. Layer 4

   D. Layer 7

3. In the Cable Type column, enter an "S" for Straight-through cable and a "C" for Crossover cable to identify the correct cable to connect each pair of devices.

Device Pair	Cable Type (S or C)
Host to switch	
Hub to switch	
Router to switch	
Routers Fa0/0 to host	
Hub to router	
Switch to switch	

4. In the Layer column, enter a "1" for physical Layer 1 or a "2" for data link Layer 2 to identify the correct layer the issue is associated with.

Network Situation	Layer (1 or 2)
Excessive broadcasts	
Encapsulated error	
Loose cable connection	
Fluctuating power supply	
Serial 0/0/0 is up, protocol is down	
Misconfigured NIC	
Incorrect cable type	
Damaged serial interface connector	

5. Refer to Figure 9-33. A network administrator is troubleshooting the connectivity between the headquarters and the branch office. Which important troubleshooting information can the administrator get from the output of the **show interface serial 0/0/0** command?

Figure 9-33   Question 5 Network Topology

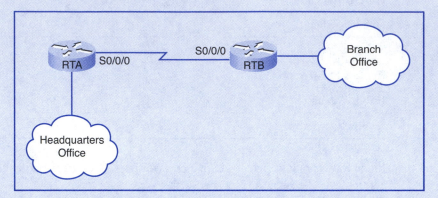

A. Encapsulated type

B. CSU/DSU type

C. CSU/DSU timing

D. Routing protocol type

6. Which interface status indicates a high error rate?

A. Serial 0/0/0 is down, line protocol is down.

B. Serial 0/0/0 is up, line protocol is down.

C. Serial 0/0/0 is up, line protocol is down (looped).

D. Serial 0/0/0 is up, line protocol is down (disabled).

E. Serial 0/0/0 is administratively down, line protocol is down.

7. Refer to the following set of commands and the resulting output from the **show ip dhcp binding** command. Hosts on the LAN are able to communicate with hosts on the same LAN, but are unable to connect outside the network. What is the possible problem?

```
RouterA(config)# ip dhcp pool LANpool
RouterA(dhcp-config)# network 192.168.1.0 255.255.255.240
RouterA(dhcp-config)# default-router 192.168.1.30
RouterA(dhcp-config)# dns-server 192.168.1.2
RouterA(dhcp-config)# end
#SYS-5-CONFIG_I: Configured from console by console
RouterA# show ip dhcp binding
IP address          Client-ID/            Lease expiration         Type
                    Hardware address
192.168.1.4         00D0.BCBD.993B        Feb 01 2008 8:15 AM      Automatic
192.168.1.5         00D0.D30B.C23E        Feb 01 2008 9:25 AM      Automatic
192.168.1.7         0001.C91C.D0EC        Feb 01 2008 10:21 AM     Automatic
```

A. The **pool** command is not applied to an interface.

B. The DNS address is misconfigured.

C. The DHCP address is missing.

D. The default gateway address is on a different network.

8. Refer to the output from the **debug ip rip** command. What can be concluded from the output? (Choose two.)

```
R1# debug ip rip
RIP protocol debugging is on
R1#
8d05h: RIP: sending v1 update to 255.255.255.255. via FastEthernet0/0 (172.16.1.1)
8d05h: RIP: build update entries
8d05h: network 10.0.0.0 metric 1
8d05h: network 192.168.1.0 metric 2
8d05h: RIP: sending v1 update to 255.255.255.255 via Serial0/0/0 (10.0.8.1)
8d05h: RIP: build update entries
8d05h: network 172.16.0.0 metric 1
R1#
8d05h: RIP: received v1 update from 10.0.15.2 on Serial0/0/0
8d05h: 192.168.1.0 in 1 hops
8d05h: 192.168.168.0 in 16 hops (inaccessible)
```

A. The 10.0.0.0 network is two hops from R1.

B. A ping to 192.168.168.10 will be successful.

C. R1 sent information about five destinations in the update.

D. R1 sent a RIP broadcast on Fa0/0 that advertises two networks.

E. R1 has received updates from one router at source address 10.0.15.2.

9. Refer to Figure 9-34. What is the result of the following commands issued on R1?

```
R1(config)# interface fa0/0
R1(config-if)# ip helper-address 192.168.2.3
```

Figure 9-34   Question 9 Network Topology

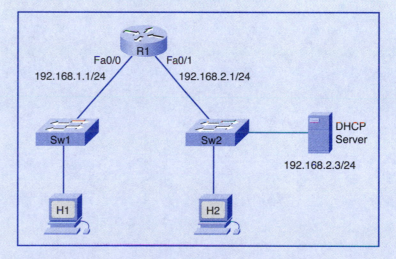

A. The 192.168.1.0 network will not receive any DHCP requests.

B. DHCP acknowledgments will be issued from the 192.168.1.0 network.

C. Switch SW2 is acting as a DHCP relay agent for the 192.168.1.0 network.

D. DHCP requests are forwarded to 192.168.2.3.

10. Refer Figure 9-35. Based on the results from the following troubleshooting commands, what is one possible problem?

```
Pings from 192.168.1.20 to 192.168.1.1 are successful
Pings from 192.168.1.20 to 192.168.3.16 are successful
Telnet from 192.168.1.20 to 192.168.3.16 are not successful
```

Figure 9-35   Question 10 Network Topology

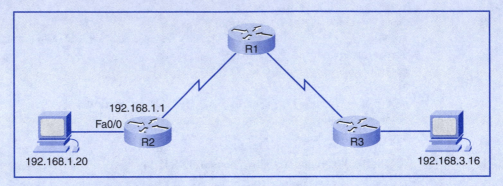

A. An incorrect IP address was assigned.

B. The packets were blocked by a firewall.

C. The routing protocol was not configured correctly.

D. There is a Layer 2 capsulation error.

## CHAPTER 10

Putting It All Together

A network is essential to any successful organization, and it must deliver vital services without disruption. Network support technicians, whether working at an ISP company help desk or at the customer location, are the first point of contact for most business users when they have a problem. ISPs, like all good businesses, never stop looking for a competitive advantage. By competently performing your duties in a professional manner, you can become a valuable member of a support team.

Throughout this course, you have learned about the Internet, ISP responsibilities, help desk support, network upgrades, routing, IP addressing, and network device configuration. This course has provided the skills and information you need to understand the role of a network support technician at a small-to-medium business or ISP.

Summary Activity

By successfully completing this course, you have gained the knowledge and skills you need for a career as an entry-level network support technician. The Packet Tracer activity and the hands-on lab that culminate this course are designed to give you an opportunity to demonstrate your new abilities.

In the summary activities, you use the knowledge and skills presented in this course to perform a simulated network upgrade. You will use a customer work order to create an IP addressing plan, configure the network, and verify device configurations and network connectivity.

Putting It All Together (10.0.1)

In this activity, you use the knowledge and skills presented in this course to perform a simulated network upgrade. You create an IP addressing plan for a small network, implement a network equipment upgrade, verify device configurations and network connectivity, and configure switch port security.

Activities and Labs

This chapter does not include interactive activities.

Packet Tracer Activities on the CD:

Putting It All Together (10.0.1)

Hands-on Lab in Part II of this book:

Capstone Project: Putting It All Together

PART II
Labs

Chapter 1   **Lab: The Internet and Its Uses**   page 357

Chapter 2   **Lab: Help Desk**   page 367

Chapter 3   **Lab: Planning a Network Upgrade**   page 369

Chapter 4   **Lab: Planning the Addressing Structure**   page 373

Chapter 5   **Lab: Configuring Network Devices**   page 383

Chapter 6   **Lab: Routing**   page 487

Chapter 7   **Lab: ISP Services**   page 505

Chapter 8   **Lab: ISP Responsibility**   page 521

Chapter 9   **Lab: Troubleshooting**   page 589

Chapter 10   **Capstone Project: Putting It All Together**   page 679

Appendix A   **Check Your Understanding and Challenge Questions Answer Key**   page 693

Appendix B   **Router Boot and Password Recovery Labs**   page 709

Appendix C   **Lab Equipment Interfaces and Initial Configuration Restoration**   page 721

Glossary   page 725

## CHAPTER 1

Lab: The Internet and Its Uses

The lab exercise included in this chapter covers the Chapter 1 online curriculum lab. It ensures that you have mastered the practical, hands-on skills needed to understand the structure of the Internet. As you work through this lab, use Chapter 1 in Part I of this book, or use the corresponding Chapter 1 in the *Working at a Small-to-Medium Business or ISP* course of the *CCNA Discovery* online curriculum, for assistance.

Lab 1-1: Mapping ISP Connectivity Using traceroute (1.2.3)

Objectives

- Use the Windows **tracert** utility to trace the path that packets take from a local host computer to a website on a different continent.

- Interpret the **traceroute** output to determine which ISPs the packets passed through on their way from the local host to the destination website.

- Draw a diagram of the **traceroute** path, showing the routers and ISP clouds passed through from the local host to the destination website, including IP addresses for each device.

Background/Preparation

In this activity, you will use the Windows **tracert** utility to map Internet connectivity between your local ISP and the other ISPs that it uses to provide global Internet access. You will also map connectivity to the following major Regional Internet Registries (RIR). However, your instructor may choose different destination websites:

- AfriNIC (African Network Information Centre): Africa Region

- APNIC (Asia Pacific Network Information Centre): Asia/Pacific Region

- ARIN (American Registry for Internet Numbers): North America Region

- LACNIC (Regional Latin-American and Caribbean IP Address Registry): Latin America and some Caribbean islands

- RIPE NCC (Réseaux IP Européens): Europe, the Middle East, and Central Asia

The following resources are required:

- Host computer with the Windows operating system

- Access to the command prompt

- Internet connection

- Routes Traced worksheet for each destination URL

- Global Connectivity Map, which is shown later in Figure 1-1.

Task 1: Run the tracert Utility from a Host Computer

Step 1.   Verify that the host computer has a connection to the Internet.

Step 2.   Open a command prompt window by choosing **Start > Run** and entering **cmd**. Alternatively, you may choose **Start > All Programs > Accessories > Command Prompt**.

Step 3.   At the prompt, enter **tracert** and your first destination website. The output should look similar to that shown in Example 1-1, which is a **tracert** to http://www.ripe.net.

Example 1-1   Sample tracert Output

```
C:\> tracert www.ripe.net


Tracing route to kite-www.ripe.net [193.0.0.214]

over a maximum of 30 hops:


  1     1 ms    <1 ms    <1 ms   192.168.1.1

  2    10 ms    12 ms     11 ms   d64-180-160-254.bchsia.telus.net
  [64.180.160.254]

  3     7 ms     7 ms     6 ms   VANCBC01DR04.bb.telus.com [208.181.240.94]

  4     6 ms     6 ms     6 ms   nwmrbc01gr01.bb.telus.com [154.11.4.98]

  5     7 ms     6 ms     7 ms   204.225.243.25

  6    17 ms    17 ms    16 ms   so-3-3-2.cr1.sea1.us.above.net [208.185.175.69]

  7    17 ms    17 ms    17 ms   so-0-0-0.cr2.sea1.us.above.net [64.125.28.186]

  8    27 ms    28 ms    27 ms   so-2-0-0.cr2.ord2.us.above.net [64.125.30.222]

  9    33 ms    33 ms    33 ms   so-1-1-0.mpr2.1ga5.us.above.net [64.125.27.34]

 10    33 ms    32 ms    32 ms   so-0-0-0.mpr1.1ga5.us.above.net [64.125.27.237]

 11   101 ms   102 ms   102 ms   so-7-0-0.mpr3.ams1.n1.above.net [64.125.27.186]

 12   111 ms   110 ms   111 ms   cogent-1101.xe-0-0-0.jun1.kelvin.network.bit.nl
  [149.6.128.58]

 13   126 ms   130 ms   131 ms   kite.ripe.net [193.0.0.214]


Trace complete.
```

Step 4.   Save the **tracert** output in a text file as follows:

a.   Right-click the title bar of the Command Prompt window and choose **Edit > Select All**.

b.   Right-click the title bar of the Command Prompt window and choose **Edit > Copy**.

c.   Open the Windows Notepad program by choosing **Start > All Programs > Accessories > Notepad**.

d.   To paste the output into Notepad, choose **Edit > Paste**.

e.   Choose **File > Save As** and save the Notepad file to your desktop as tracert1.txt.

Step 5.   Run **tracert** for each destination website, and save the output in sequentially numbered files.

Step 6.   Run **tracert** from a different computer network, such as at the public library or on a friend's computer that accesses the Internet using a different ISP (for instance, cable instead of DSL). Save a copy of that output in Notepad, and print it for later reference.

Task 2: Interpret tracert Outputs to Determine ISP Connectivity

Routes traced may go through many hops and a number of different ISPs, depending on the size of your ISP and the location of the source and destination hosts. In the sample output shown in Example 1-1, the **tracert** packets travel from the source PC to the local router default gateway to the ISP's point of presence (POP) router. From there the packets travel through four Tier 2 routers before reaching the IXP. They then pass through several Tier 1 ISP routers as they move across the Internet backbone. When they leave the Tier 1 ISP's backbone, they move through another Tier 2 ISP on the way to the destination server at http://www.ripe.net.

The lines in Example 1-1 can be interpreted as follows:

Local router:

```
1     1 ms     <1 ms     <1 ms   192.168.1.1
```

POP router:

```
2     10 ms    12 ms      11 ms  d64-180-160-254.bchsia.telus.net [64.180.160.254]
```

Source Tier 2 network:

```
3     7 ms     7 ms      6 ms   VANCBC01DR04.bb.telus.com [208.181.240.94]
4     6 ms     6 ms      6 ms   nwmrbc01gr01.bb.telus.com [154.11.4.98]
```

IXP:

```
5     7 ms     6 ms      7 ms   204.225.243.25
```

Tier 1 ISP network:

```
6    17 ms    17 ms     16 ms   so-3-3-2.cr1.sea1.us.above.net [208.185.175.69]
7    17 ms    17 ms     17 ms   so-0-0-0.cr2.sea1.us.above.net ]64.125.28.186]
8    27 ms    28 ms     27 ms   so-2-0-0.cr2.ord2.us.above.net [64.125.30.222]
9    33 ms    33 ms     33 ms   so-1-1-0.mpr2.1ga5.us.above.net [64.125.27.34]
10    33 ms    32 ms     32 ms   so-0-0-0.mpr1.1ga5.us.above.net [64.125.27.237]
11    101 ms   102 ms    102 ms  so-7-0-0.mpr3.ams1.n1.above.net [64.125.27.186]
```

Destination tier 2 ISP network:

```
12    111 ms   110 ms    111 ms  cogent-1101.xe-0-0-0.jun1.kelvin.network.bit.nl
[149.6.128.58]
```

Destination web server:

```
13    126 ms   130 ms    131 ms  kite.ripe.net [193.0.0.214]
```

Step 1.   Open the first **traceroute** output file, and answer the following questions:

    a. What is the IP address of your local POP router?

    _____

    b. How many hops did the **traceroute** packet take on its journey from the host computer to the destination?

    _____

    c. How many different ISPs did the **traceroute** packet pass through on its journey from the host computer to the destination?

    _____

    d. Using the Routes Traced worksheet at the end of this chapter, list the IP addresses and URLs of all the devices in the **traceroute** output in the order in which they appear.

    _____

    e. In the Network Owner column of the worksheet, identify which ISP owns each router. If the router belongs to your LAN, write "LAN." The last two parts of the URL indicate the ISP name. For example, a router that has sprint.net in its URL belongs to the network of an ISP called Sprint.

    _____

    f. Did the **traceroute** pass through an unidentified router between two ISPs? This might be an IXP. Run the **whois** command utility or **whois** function of a visual **traceroute** program to identify ownership of that router. Alternatively, go to http://www.arin.net/whois to determine to whom the IP is assigned.

Step 2.   Complete the worksheet using the **traceroute** output file for each of the other destination URLs.

Step 3.   Compare your results from the different **traceroute** output files. Did your ISP connect to different ISPs to reach different destinations?

    _____

Step 4.   If you ran a **traceroute** from a different computer network, check the output for that **traceroute** file as well. Was the number of hops different to reach the same destination from different local ISPs? Which ISP was able to reach the destination in fewer hops?

    _____

Task 3: Map the Connectivity of Your ISP

Step 1.   For each **traceroute** output, draw a diagram on a separate sheet of paper showing how your local ISP interconnects with other ISPs to reach the destination URL, as follows:

- Show all the devices in sequence from the LAN router to the destination website server. Label all the devices with their IP addresses.

- Draw a box around the local POP router you identified, and label it "POP."

- Draw an ISP cloud around all the routers that belong to each ISP, and label it with the ISP name.

- Draw a box around any IXP routers you identified, and label it "IXP."

Step 2.   Use the global connectivity map shown in Figure 1-1 to create a combined drawing showing only ISP clouds and IXP boxes.

Figure 1-1   Global Connectivity Map

Routes Traced Worksheet

Destination URL: _____

Total number of hops _____

Router IP Address	Router URL (if Any)	Network Owner (LAN, Name of ISP or IXP)

Destination URL: _____

Total number of hops: _____

Router IP Address	Router URL (if Any)	Network Owner (LAN, Name of ISP or IXP)

Destination URL: _____

Total number of hops: _____

Router IP Address	Router URL (if Any)	Network Owner (LAN, Name of ISP or IXP)

Lab: Help Desk

Chapter 2 in the *Working at a Small-to-Medium Business or ISP* course of the *CCNA Discovery* online curriculum does not include hands-on labs.

## CHAPTER 3

Lab: Planning a Network Upgrade

The lab exercise included in this chapter covers the Chapter 3 online curriculum lab. It ensures that you have mastered the practical, hands-on skills needed to understand a cable upgrade plan. As you work through this lab, use Chapter 3 in Part I of this book, or use the corresponding Chapter 3 in the *Working at a Small-to-Medium Business or ISP* course of the *CCNA Discovery* online curriculum, for assistance.

 ## Lab 3-1: Evaluating a Cabling Upgrade Plan (3.2.4)

Objectives

- Examine the customer's existing floor plan to determine existing cabling.
- Propose a cable upgrade plan to accommodate extra floor space.

Background/Preparation

A medium-sized company has existing space on the second floor of an office tower and has just acquired the rest of the second floor. The company has asked you to examine its existing floor plan and help with the placement of a new intermediate distribution facility (IDF), placement of cables to support all the new office space, and determining if any new devices are required.

This lab can be done individually or in groups.

This lab requires the existing floor plan, which is provided as Figure 3-1 at the end of this lab.

Task 1: Examine the Existing Floor Plan

On the existing floor plan (Figure 3-1), label the following items:

- Point of presence (POP)
- Main distribution facility (MDF)
- Intermediate distribution facility (IDF)
- Vertical/backbone cabling
- Horizontal cabling

What type of cabling could be used for the vertical/backbone cabling? Explain your answer.

_____

_____

Task 2: Evaluate the Plan for the New Floor Space

AnyCompany has just merged with a small web design group and has acquired the remaining space on the second floor to accommodate the web design team. This new space is represented in Figure 3-1 as the floor space on the right side of the floor plan. It has been decided to add a second IDF to support the workstations in the new area.

Suggest a possible location for the new IDF. What room or location did you choose? Explain why you think it is suitable.

_____

_____

What type of cable would you suggest for the vertical cabling required to connect the new IDF to the existing MDF? Explain your reasons.

_____

_____

_____

The new space contains mostly offices. Assume that each office will be provisioned with two network connections. Also plan for two drops in the auditorium to support Internet access for presentations and training sessions. How many additional data drops need to be ordered?

_____

You have been asked to determine how many new 24-port switches will be required for the new IDF. Remember to plan on approximately 25% growth. How many new switches will AnyCompany need to purchase?

_____

How many horizontal cables will terminate on patch panels in the new IDF?

_____

_____

Task 3: Examine the Floor Space and Wiring Plan

What equipment other than switches would you expect to find in the IDF?

_____

What equipment other than switches would you expect to find in the MDF?

_____

Using existing cable runs, could you use UTP to connect the devices in room 2.20 or 2.30 directly to a switch in the MDF?

_____

Task 4: Reflection

With one or two classmates, discuss the following:

1. Is it better to have an IDF in this floor space, or should the company run the horizontal cables for each device directly back to the existing MDF?

_____

_____

_____

_____

_____

_____

_____

2. How many cables will be required from the MDF to the IDF to support the switches? Explain your answer.

_____

_____

_____

Figure 3-1   AnyCompany Floor Plan

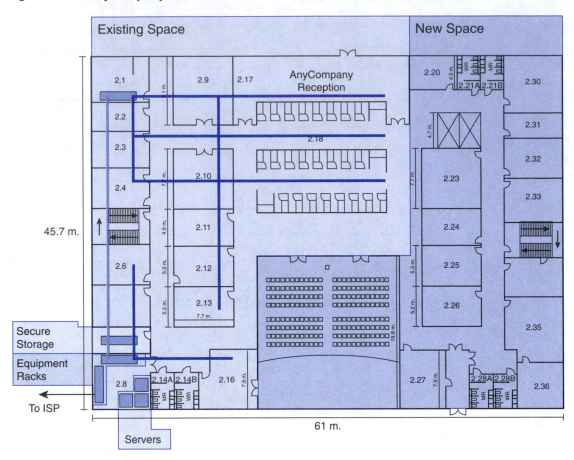

## CHAPTER 4

Lab: Planning the Addressing Structure

The lab exercises included in this chapter cover the Chapter 4 online curriculum labs. They ensure that you have mastered the practical, hands-on skills needed to work with subnets. As you work through these labs, use Chapter 4 in Part I of this book, or use the corresponding Chapter 4 in the *Working at a Small-to-Medium Business or ISP* course of the *CCNA Discovery* online curriculum, for assistance.

Lab 4-1: Subnetting a Network (4.1.5)

Objective

- Create an IP addressing plan for a small network.

Background/Preparation

In this activity, you will play the role of an onsite installation and support technician from an ISP.

A customer has called the ISP, complaining of e-mail problems and occasional poor Internet performance. On an earlier site visit, the technician drew a diagram of the customer's existing network, as shown in Figure 4-1.

Figure 4-1   Existing Network Model

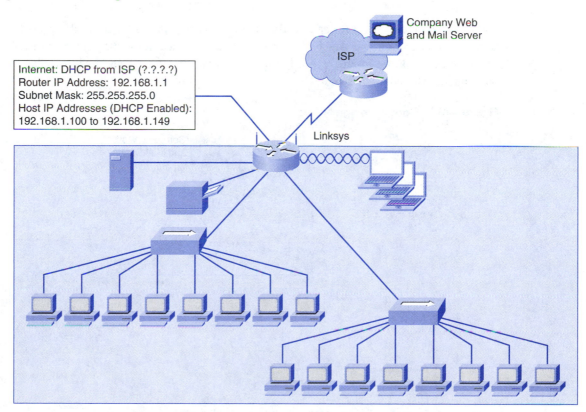

The ISP is preparing a design for a network upgrade. The interim topology diagram for the proposed network is shown in Figure 4-2.

Figure 4-2   Proposed Network Model

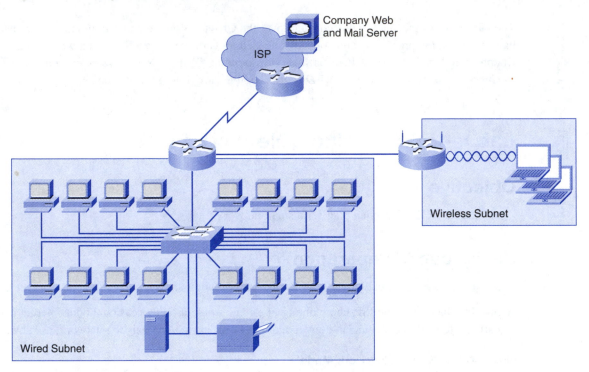

There is still a requirement for an IP addressing plan. One of the ISP network designers has made some notes on a simplified sketch of the proposed network and has written down some requirements. These notes are shown in Figure 4-3. The designer asks you to create an IP address plan for the network upgrade based on these notes.

Figure 4-3   Rough Design Notes

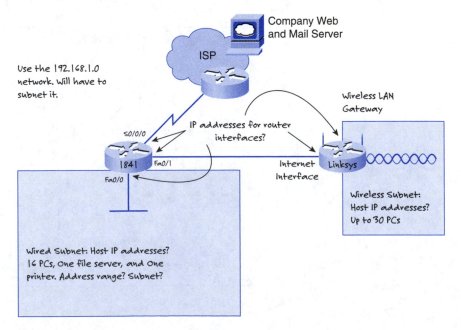

Task 1: Analyze the Network

Step 1.   Referring to the rough design notes shown in Figure 4-3, determine the minimum number of hosts that a subnet needs to support the new network design.

The largest subnet must be able to support _____ hosts.

To support that many hosts, the number of host bits required is _____.

Step 2.   What is the minimum number of subnets required for the new network design?

_____

Step 3.   Can this network be subnetted according to the requirements?

_____

For example, if four subnets are required and the largest subnet has to support 128 hosts, this is a problem, because a subnet in a Class C network that has been partitioned four ways can support only 62 hosts.

Step 4.   Fill in the blanks to summarize the subnetting requirements of this new network design:

This network requires _____ major subnets, each supporting 30 host—one for the wireless users and one for the wired users. In addition, a subnet is required for the link between the two routers. Although this link requires only two IP addresses, one of the 30-host subnets can be assigned to it. Therefore, _____ host ID bits are reserved for the subnet ID. With those values, this network supports _____ subnets, and each subnet has _____ hosts.

Task 2: Calculate the Custom Subnet Mask

Now that you know the number of subnet ID bits, you can calculate the subnet mask. A Class C network has a default subnet mask of 24 bits, or 255.255.255.0. What will the custom subnet mask be?

The custom subnet mask for this network will be _____ as a dotted-decimal mask or _____ as a CIDR prefix mask.

Task 3: Specify the Host IP Addresses

Now that the subnet mask has been identified, the network addressing scheme can be created. The addressing scheme includes the subnet number, the subnet broadcast address, and the range of IP addresses that can be assigned to hosts.

Step 1.   Complete the following table, showing all the possible subnets for the 192.168.1.0 network:

Subnet	Subnet Address	Host IP Address Range	Broadcast Address

Step 2.   The following table was found along with the rough design notes diagram, with a message asking for it to be completed. Hosts will be assigned IP addresses as follows (fill in the table):

Device	Interface	IP Address	What It Connects To	IP Address
1841	Serial 0/0/0	10.11.11.100	ISP router	10.11.11.1
	Fa 0/0	_____	Wired hosts	Wired host range: _____ to _____
	Fa 0/1	_____	Linksys Internet	_____
Linksys	Internet	_____	1841 Fa 0/1	_____
	LAN gateway	_____	Wireless hosts	Wireless host range: _____ to _____

Task 4: Consider Other Subnetting Options

What if more than 30 hosts needed to be supported on either the wired or wireless portion of the network? You could borrow fewer bits, which would create fewer subnets, but each one would support more hosts per subnet.

1.   How many bits would be borrowed to create four subnets?

2. How many bits would be left for hosts on each subnet?

   _____

3. What is the maximum number of hosts each subnet could support?

   _____

   _____

4. What would the subnet mask be in dotted-decimal and slash-number (/#) format?

   _____

5. If you start with the same 192.168.1.0 network as before and subnet it into four subnets, what would the subnet numbers be?

   _____

Task 5: Reflection

1. Does subnetting help reduce the problem of IP address depletion? Explain your answer.

   _____

   _____

2. Figure 4-3 noted that the wireless subnet would have up to 30 PCs connecting. In pairs or in small groups, discuss whether that creates a situation in which IP addresses might get wasted. Does it matter? Why or why not?

   _____

   _____

3. Alternative methods of subnetting using CIDR and VLSM exist. Would VLSM be a worthwhile option for subnetting this network? Discuss in small groups.

   _____

   _____

   _____

   _____

Lab 4-2: Determining PAT Translations (4.2.4)

Figure 4-4 shows the basic process of network translation. The following steps describe the sequence numbers shown in the figure:

1. The client on a private network sends a request to a web server on the public Internet.

2. The NAT router translates the client (local) source address in each packet to the global address assigned to the router external interface and forwards the request to the web server.

3. The web server responds to the client's translated request, sending packets back to the destination address of the router external interface.

4. The NAT router translates the destination address back to the original client private address and delivers the packet to the client.

Figure 4-4   NAT Requests and Responses

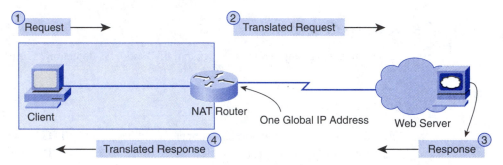

Objectives

- Explain the active network connections that are open on a computer when you view a particular web page.

- Determine what an internal IP address and port number are translated into using Port Address Translation (PAT).

Background/Preparation

Port Address Translation (PAT) is a form of Network Address Translation (NAT). With PAT, the router translates multiple internal (usually private) addresses to a single public IP address on an interface that is connected to the Internet. Port numbers are used, in combination with IP addresses, to keep track of individual connections. In this lab, you use the **ipconfig** and **netstat** commands to view open ports on a computer. You will be able to see the initial IP address and port combination and determine the translated IP address and port combination.

The following resources are required:

- A computer running Windows XP Professional

- A connection to a gateway router or an ISR using PAT

- An Internet connection

- Access to the PC command prompt

Task 1: Determine the IP Address of the Computer

1. Open the Command Prompt window by choosing **Start > Run** and entering **cmd**. Alternatively, you can choose **Start > All Programs > Accessories > Command Prompt**. At the prompt, enter the **ipconfig** command to display the computer's IP address.

2. What is the computer's IP address?

    _____

3. Is a port number shown? Why or why not?

    _____

    _____

Task 2: Determine the IP Addresses of the Gateway Router or ISR

Check with your instructor to get the IP addresses for the ISR NAT router gateway. These will be used later in the lab to analyze NAT translations.

Internal Ethernet address:

_____

_____

_____

External Internet address:

_____

_____

Task 3: Display Baseline netstat Results

1. At the command prompt, enter **netstat -n**.

2. What type of information does the **netstat -n** command return?

    _____

    _____

3. Where does the IP address found in Task 1 appear? Is a port number associated with it? Why or why not?

    _____

    _____

    _____

    _____

    _____

Task 4: Display Active Network Connections

Step 1.   Ping http://www.cisco.com and record the address.

_____

Step 2.   Open a web browser, and enter **www.cisco.com** in the address bar.

Step 3.   Go back to the Command Prompt window. Enter the **netstat -n** command again, and then enter the command without the **-n** option. The output will vary, depending on what other network applications and connections were open when you issued the command.

Step 4.   What is the difference in the output between the **netstat** and **netstat -n** commands?

_____

_____

Step 5.   Write down the connection entries for the client IP address and the IP address of the http://www.cisco.com web server.

Local client IP address and port number:

_____

Foreign IP address and port number:

_____

Step 6.   Are there more **netstat** entries the second time?

_____

_____

Task 5: Determine Translated Addresses

Use the information you recorded in Tasks 2 and 4 and the topology diagram shown in Figure 4-4 to fill in the Address:Port columns of Figure 4-5.

Figure 4-5   Translating NAT Addresses

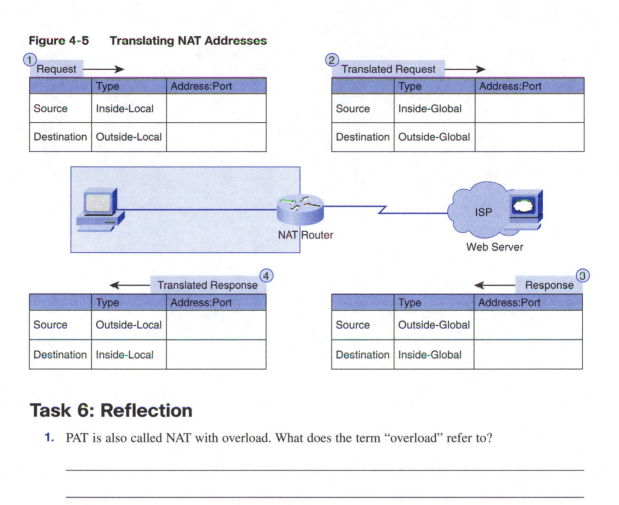

Task 6: Reflection

1. PAT is also called NAT with overload. What does the term "overload" refer to?

   _____

   _____

2. The NAT terminology used in this lab includes four types of addresses: inside local, inside global, outside local, and outside global. In many connections that pass through NAT routers, two of these addresses are often the same. Which two of these four addresses normally remain unchanged, and why do you think that is the case?

   _____

   _____

   _____

## CHAPTER 5

Lab: Configuring Network Devices

The lab exercises included in this chapter cover the Chapter 5 online curriculum labs. They ensure that you have mastered the practical, hands-on skills needed to perform basic configurations on Cisco routers and switches. As you work through this lab, use Chapter 5 in Part I of this book, or use the corresponding Chapter 5 in the *Working at a Small-to-Medium Business or ISP* course of the *CCNA Discovery* online curriculum, for assistance.

Additional labs on password recovery and IOS management can be found in Appendix B, "Router Boot and Password Recovery Labs." You also need to bookmark Appendix C, "Lab Equipment Interfaces and Initial Configuration Restoration," which this chapter references frequently. Appendix C provides a reference for router interface designations and instructions for restoring routers and switches to their default configurations.

Lab 5-1: Powering Up an Integrated Services Router (5.1.3)

Objectives

- Set up a new Cisco 1841 Integrated Services Router (ISR).

- Connect a computer to the router console interface.

- Configure HyperTerminal so that the computer can communicate with the router.

- Display router configuration information using the **show running-config** and **show startup-config** commands.

- Restart the router using the **reload** command.

- Display router system, IOS, and configuration register information using the **show version** command.

Background/Preparation

This is a two-part lab that uses a Cisco 1841 ISR. If a Cisco 1841 ISR is not available, you can use another router model. The information in this lab applies to other routers. A Cisco ISR combines routing and switching functions, security, voice, and LAN and WAN connectivity into a single device, which makes it appropriate for small to medium-sized businesses and for ISP-managed customers.

Some steps in this lab normally are performed only once, during initial setup. These steps are indicated as optional.

The following resources are required:

- Cisco 1841 ISR or a comparable router

- Power cable

- Windows PC with terminal emulation program

- RJ-45-to-DB9 connector console cable

Part 1: Initial Router Setup and Startup

Part 1 of this lab focuses on the initial setup of the Cisco 1841 ISR.

Task 1: Position the Router and Connect the Ground Wire (Optional)

This task is optional and is required only if the router is being set up for the first time. Read through this task to become familiar with the process.

Step 1.   Position the router chassis to allow unrestricted airflow for chassis cooling. Keep at least 1 inch (2.54 cm) of clear space beside the cooling inlet and exhaust vents.

Caution: Do not place any items that weigh more than 10 pounds (4.5 kilograms) on top of the chassis, and do not stack routers on top of each other.

Step 2.   Connect the chassis to a reliable earth ground, as shown in Figure 5-1. This is done using a ring terminal and size 14 AWG (2 mm) wire using these steps:

   a.   Strip one end of the ground wire to expose approximately 3/4 inch (20 mm) of conductor.

   b.   Crimp the 14 AWG (2 mm) green ground wire to a UL Listed/CSA certified ring terminal using a crimping tool that is recommended by the ring terminal manufacturer. The ring terminal provided on the back panel of the Cisco 1841 ISR is suitable for a number 6 grounding screw.

   c.   Attach the ring terminal to the chassis, as shown in Figure 5-1. Use a number 2 Phillips screwdriver and the screw that is supplied with the ring terminal, and tighten the screw.

   d.   Connect the other end of the ground wire to a suitable earth ground that your instructor indicates.

Note: Your instructor should inform you where a reliable earth ground is.

Figure 5-1   Connecting the ISR Chassis to Ground

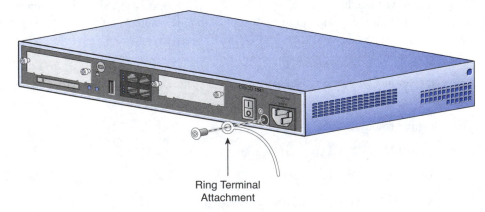

Ring Terminal
Attachment

Task 2: Install the Compact Flash Memory Card (Optional)

This task is optional and is required only if the router is being set up for the first time. To avoid wear on the memory card and ejector mechanism, do not actually perform this step. Read through this task to become familiar with the process.

Step 1.   Attach a grounding strap to your wrist to avoid electrostatic damage to the card. Seat the external Compact Flash memory card properly into the slot. This task depends on the type of router. Not all routers have flash cards.

Step 2.   If the router has a Compact Flash memory card, check that the ejector mechanism is fully seated. The ejector button is next to the Compact Flash memory card.

Step 3.   Connect the power cable to the ISR and to the power outlet.

Task 3: Connect the PC and Configure the Terminal Emulation Program

Step 1.   Connect the PC to the ISR using an RJ-45-to-DB9 connector console cable, as shown in the Figure 5-2. Using the light blue RJ-45-to-DB9 console cable (2), connect the RJ-45 end to the console port (1) of the ISR, and then connect the DB9 end (3) to the serial port of the PC. To view the router startup messages, connect the PC to the ISR, power up the PC, and start the terminal emulation program before powering up the router.

Figure 5-2   Connecting a PC to the ISR

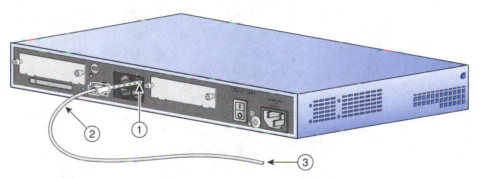

Caution: To ensure adequate cooling, never operate the router unless the cover and all modules and cover plates are installed.

Step 2.   Load a terminal emulation program, such as HyperTerminal, on the PC.

Step 3.   Select a COM port that matches the port where the RJ-45-to-DB9 connector is connected to the PC. The COM port is usually COM1 or COM2.

Step 4.   Configure the terminal emulation parameters as follows:

- 9600 baud

- 8 data bits

- No parity

- 1 stop bit

- No flow control

Task 4: Power Up the ISR

Step 1. Move the power switch on the back of the ISR to the ON position. During this task, the LEDs on the chassis turn on and off, not necessarily at the same time. The LED activity depends on what is installed in the ISR.

Step 2. Observe the startup messages as they appear in the terminal emulation program window. While these messages appear, do not press any keys on the keyboard. Pressing a key interrupts the router startup process. Some examples of startup messages displayed are the amount of main memory installed and the image type of the Cisco IOS software that the computer is using. Can you find these sample startup messages in Example 5-1?

Example 5-1   ISR Startup Screen

```
Allocating additional 13357964 bytes to IO Memory.


PMem allocated: 178257920 bytes; IOMem allocated: 23068672 bytes


            Restricted Rights Legend


Use, duplication, or disclosure by the Government is

subject to restrictions as set forth in subparagraph

(c) of the Commercial Computer Software - Restricted

Rights clause at FAR sec. 52.227-19 and subparagraph

(c) (1) (ii) of the Rights in Technical Data and Computer

Software clause at DFARS sec. 252.227-7013.


        Cisco Systems, Inc.

        170 West Tasman Drive

        San Jose, California 95134-1706



Cisco IOS Software, 1841 Software (C1841-ADVIPSERVICESK9-M), Version 12.4(10b),

  RELEASE SOFTWARE (fc3)

Technical Support: http://www.cisco.com/techsupport

Copyright (c) 1986-2007 by Cisco Systems, Inc.

Compiled Fri 19-Jan-07 15:15 by prod_rel_team

Image text-base: 0x600792C4, data-base: 0x61C00000
```

Example 5-1 shows that 178 MB of memory is installed on this router, and the Cisco IOS image type is C1841-ADVIPSERVICESK9-M. Startup messages are generated by the router's operating system. The messages vary depending on the software installed on the router. These messages scroll by quickly and take a few minutes to stop.

When the Cisco 1841 ISR is correctly powered up, the SYS PWR LED is a steady green light, and the fans operate. When the router is finished starting up, the following system message appears in the terminal emulation window:

```
          --- System Configuration Dialog ---
Would you like to enter the initial configuration dialog? [yes/no]: no
Would you like to terminate autoinstall? [yes]:

Press RETURN to get started!
```

Step 3.   After pressing **Enter** to get started, you see several system messages about interface and line status. If the router is in its default configuration, the user mode prompt Router> is displayed.

Note: You might need to press **Enter** after the interface status messages are displayed.

Task 5: Troubleshoot a Nonworking Router

If the SYS PWR LED does not blink green, the fans do not operate, and the correct system message does not appear in the terminal emulation window, turn off the router and verify that the power cable is securely attached to the router and plugged into the power source. If the router does not power on, ask the instructor for assistance.

Part 2: Displaying Router Information Using show Commands

Part 2 focuses on the use of basic **show** commands to display internal router system, IOS, and configuration information.

Task 1: Display the Router Running Configuration

Step 1.   From the router user prompt, enter privileged mode using the **enable** command, and then issue the **show running-config** command to see the current router configuration in RAM. Sample output from this command is given in Example 5-2.

If the router is in the default configuration, the output is similar to that shown in Example 5-2. The default hostname is Router, and none of the interfaces have IP addresses. This 1841 router has two built-in FastEthernet interfaces (0/0 and 0/1) and two serial interfaces (Serial0/0/0 and Serial0/0/1) if the serial card is installed in Slot 0. If the serial card is installed in Slot 1, the serial interfaces are listed as Serial0/1/0 and Serial0/1/1. This router also has a FastEthernet switch module installed with four ports (FastEthernet 0/1/0, 0/1/1, 0/1/2, and 0/1/3). In the default configuration, all interfaces are shut down. In addition, no passwords are set.

Example 5-2   Sample ISR Running Configuration

```
Router> enable
Router# show running-config
Building configuration...

Current configuration : 809 bytes
!
version 12.4
service timestamps debug datetime msec
```

```
service timestamps log datetime msec
no service password-encryption
!
hostname Router
!
boot-start-marker
boot-end-marker
!
no aaa new-model
ip cef
!
interface FastEthernet0/0
 no ip address
 shutdown
 duplex auto
 speed auto
!
interface FastEthernet0/1
 no ip address
 shutdown
 duplex auto
 speed auto
!
interface FastEthernet0/1/0
interface FastEthernet0/1/1
interface FastEthernet0/1/2
interface FastEthernet0/1/3
!
interface Serial0/0/0
 no ip address
 shutdown
!
interface Serial0/0/1
 no ip address
 shutdown
!
interface Vlan1
 no ip address
!
ip http server
no ip http secure-server
!
line con 0
```

```
line aux 0
line vty 0 4
 login
!
end
```

Step 2.   From the router privileged mode prompt, issue the **configure terminal** command to enter global configuration mode. Change the router name to Netacad using the **hostname** command, and then end configuration mode with the **end** command.

```
Router# configure terminal
Enter configuration commands, one per line.  End with CNTL/Z.
Router(config)# hostname Netacad
Netacad(config)# end
Netacad#
*Feb  8 01:13:00.999: %SYS-5-CONFIG_I: Configured from console by console
Netacad#
```

What is the router prompt now?

_____

Step 3.   From the router privileged mode prompt, issue the **show running-config** command again. How does the output differ from the first time you issued this command?

_____

Task 2: Display the Router Startup Configuration

From the router privileged mode prompt, issue the **show startup-config** command to see the startup file stored in nonvolatile RAM (NVRAM). Is the output from this command the same as that from the **show running-config** command issued in Task 1 Step 1?

_____

```
Router# show startup-config
```

Task 3: Save the Running-Config to the Startup-Config

When the router is booted, the startup-config file is loaded into router RAM and becomes the running-config file. Changes made to the running-config take effect immediately but do not affect the startup-config. To make running-config changes permanent, you must copy them to the startup-config using the command **copy running-config startup-config**.

Step 1.   From the router privileged mode prompt, issue the **copy running-config startup-config** command to make the changes permanent. When prompted for the Destination filename, press **Enter** to accept the default name of startup-config.

```
Netacad# copy running-config startup-config
Destination filename [startup-config]?
Building configuration...
[OK]
Netacad#
```

Step 2.   From the router privileged mode prompt, issue the **show startup-config** command again. Is the output from this command the same as that from the **show running-config** command issued in Task 1 Step 1?

_____

Step 3.   To restart the router, from the router privileged mode prompt, issue the **reload** command (warm boot). This performs a software restart and loads the startup-config file from NVRAM. What is the router prompt now?

_____

Task 4: Display the Router System Information Using the **show version** Command

The **show version** command displays useful information about the router's internal components, including the amount of RAM, the IOS version, the number and type of interfaces installed, and the configuration register, which controls how the router boots up. By default the config register is set to hexadecimal 2102 (0x2102), which causes the router to load the operating system (IOS) from flash memory.

This information displayed by the **show version** command is displayed as part of router bootup. The output from the 1841 router is shown in Example 5-3. Your output will vary depending on the router model, IOS version, and internal components installed.

From the router privileged mode prompt, issue the **show version** command, as shown in Example 5-3.

Example 5-3   Sample Output from the show version Command

```
Netacad# show version
Cisco IOS Software, 1841 Software (C1841-ADVIPSERVICESK9-M), Version 12.4(10b),
RELEASE SOFTWARE (fc3)
Technical Support: http://www.cisco.com/techsupport
Copyright (c) 1986-2007 by Cisco Systems, Inc.
Compiled Fri 19-Jan-07 15:15 by prod_rel_team


ROM: System Bootstrap, Version 12.4(13r)T, RELEASE SOFTWARE (fc1)


Netacad uptime is 55 minutes
System returned to ROM by reload at 00:35:23 UTC Fri Feb 8 2008
System image file is "flash:c1841-advipservicesk9-mz.124-10b.bin"


This product contains cryptographic features and is subject to United
States and local country laws governing import, export, transfer and
use. Delivery of Cisco cryptographic products does not imply
third-party authority to import, export, distribute or use encryption.
Importers, exporters, distributors and users are responsible for
compliance with U.S. and local country laws. By using this product you
agree to comply with applicable laws and regulations. If you are unable
to comply with U.S. and local laws, return this product immediately.
```

```
A summary of U.S. laws governing Cisco cryptographic products may be found at:
http://www.cisco.com/wwl/export/crypto/tool/stqrg.html


If you require further assistance please contact us by sending email to
export@cisco.com.


Cisco 1841 (revision 6.0) with 174080K/22528K bytes of memory.
Processor board ID FTX1111W0QF
6 FastEthernet interfaces
2 Serial(sync/async) interfaces
1 Virtual Private Network (VPN) Module
DRAM configuration is 64 bits wide with parity disabled.
191K bytes of NVRAM.
62720K bytes of ATA CompactFlash (Read/Write)


Configuration register is 0x2102
```

Using the output from the show **version command**, answer the following questions.

What is the IOS software version number?

_____

How long has the router been up (uptime)?

_____

What is the name of the System image file?

_____

How many and what types of interfaces does this router have?

_____

_____

How many bytes of NVRAM does the router have?

_____

How many bytes of flash (RAM) memory does the router have?

_____

What is the configuration register setting?

_____

Task 5: Reflection

Is anything about this procedure risky?

_____

_____

_____

Why do the router cover, all modules, and cover plates need to be installed?

_____

_____

How many routers can you safely stack on top of each other?

    A. 0

    B. 1

    C. 2

    D. 3

Lab 5-2: Configuring an ISR with SDM Express (5.2.3)

Objectives

- Configure basic router global settings —router name, users, and login passwords—using Cisco SDM Express.

- Configure LAN and Internet connections on a Cisco ISR using Cisco SDM Express.

Background/Preparation

Cisco Router and Security Device Manager (SDM) is a Java-based web application and a device-management tool for Cisco IOS software-based routers. The Cisco SDM simplifies router and security configuration through the use of smart wizards. This allows you to deploy, configure, and monitor a Cisco router without needing knowledge of the command-line interface (CLI). The Cisco SDM is supported on a wide range of Cisco routers and Cisco IOS software releases. Many newer Cisco routers come with SDM preinstalled. If you are using an 1841 router, SDM (and SDM Express) is preinstalled.

This lab assumes the use of a Cisco 1841 router. You can use another router model as long as it can support SDM. If you are using a supported router that does not have SDM installed, you can download the latest version from http://www.cisco.com/pcgi-bin/tablebuild.pl/sdm.

From this URL, view or download the document "Downloading and Installing Cisco Router and Security Device Manager." This document provides instructions for installing SDM on your router. It lists specific model numbers and IOS versions that can support SDM, and the amount of memory required.

Cisco SDM Express is a component of SDM. SDM Express automatically runs a GUI wizard that allows you to perform an initial basic configuration of a Cisco router using a browser and the router's web interface. SDM Express is activated only when the router is in its factory-default state. In this lab, you will use Cisco SDM Express to configure LAN and Internet connections on a Cisco ISR.

Figure 5-3 shows the topology for this lab.

Figure 5-3   Topology Diagram for Lab 5-2

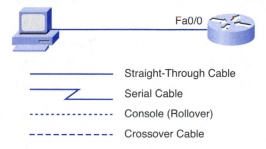

The following resources are required:

- Cisco 1841 ISR with SDM version 2.4 installed (This is critical. See Task 1.)

- Cisco 1841 ISR configured with factory default settings and with a serial port add-in module (This is critical. See the Notes in Task 1.)

- Another Cisco router model with SDM installed (optional)

- Windows XP computer with Internet Explorer 5.5 or higher and Sun Java Runtime Environment (JRE) version 1.4.2_05 or later (or Java Virtual Machine [JVM] 5.0.0.3810) (see Task 1)

- Straight-through or crossover Category 5 Ethernet cable

- Access to PC network TCP/IP configuration

Task 1: Configure the PC to Connect to the Router, and Then Launch Cisco SDM

Step 1.   Power up the router.

Step 2.   Power up the PC.

Step 3.   Disable any popup blocker programs. Popup blockers prevent SDM Express windows from appearing.

Step 4.   Connect the PC NIC to the FastEthernet 0/0 port on the Cisco 1841 ISR with the Ethernet cable.

Note: An SDM router other than the 1841 may require connection to a different port to access SDM.

Step 5.   Configure the IP address of the PC to be 10.10.10.2, with a subnet mask of 255.255.255.248.

Step 6.   SDM does not load automatically on the router. You must open the web browser to reach the SDM. Open the web browser on the PC and connect to http://10.10.10.1.

Note: If you cannot connect and see the login screen, check your cabling and connections and make sure that the PC's IP configuration is correct. The router may have been previously configured to an address of 192.168.1.1 or even a different address on the Fa0/0 interface. Try setting the IP address of the PC to 192.168.1.2, with a subnet mask of 255.255.255.0, and connect to http://192.168.1.1 using the browser. If you have difficulty with this procedure, contact your instructor for assistance.

If the startup-config is erased in an SDM router, SDM will no longer come up by default when the router is restarted. You will need to build a basic router configuration using IOS commands. Refer to the procedure in Appendix C or contact your instructor.

Step 7.   In the **Connect to** dialog box, shown in Figure 5-4, enter **cisco** for the username and **cisco** for the password. Click **OK**. The main SDM web application starts, and you are prompted to use HTTPS. Click **Cancel**. In the Security Warning window, click **Yes** to trust the Cisco application.

Figure 5-4   Connecting to SDM

Step 8.   In the Welcome to the Cisco SDM Express Wizard window, shown in Figure 5-5, read the message, and then click **Next**.

Figure 5-5   SDM Express Wizard

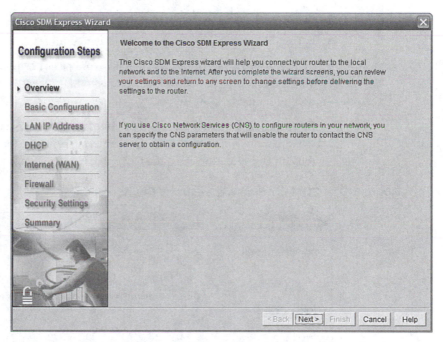

Step 9.   Verify that you are using the latest version of SDM. The initial SDM screen that appears immediately after the login shows the current version number. It is also displayed on the main SDM screen, along with the IOS version.

Note: If the current version is not 2.4 or higher, notify your instructor before continuing with this lab. You will need to download the latest zip file from http://www.cisco.com/pcgi-bin/tablebuild.pl/sdm and save it to the PC. From the SDM GUI, choose **Tools > Update SDM** to specify the location of the zip file and start the update.

Note: If you connect to the router and SDM Express starts but the SDM Express Setup Wizard does not start automatically, the router may be partially configured; it needs to be reset to its factory defaults. If the SDM Express main screen is displayed, choose the **Reset to Factory Defaults** option, repeat Steps 1 through 5, and log in again. If the full SDM application starts (not SDM Express), on the main SDM screen choose **File > Reset to Factory Defaults**. Repeat Steps 1 through 5, and log in again. If you have difficulty with this procedure, contact your instructor for assistance.

Also note that the Windows XP computer you are using must have Internet Explorer 5.5 or higher and Sun Java Runtime Environment (JRE) version 1.4.2_05 or later (or Java Virtual Machine [JVM] 5.0.0.3810). If it does not, SDM will not start. You will need to download and install JRE on the PC before continuing with the lab.

Task 2: Perform Initial Basic Configuration

Step 1.   In the Basic Configuration window, shown in Figure 5-6, enter the following information. When you complete the basic configuration, click **Next** to continue.

- In the Host Name field, enter **CustomerRouter**.

- In the Domain Name field, enter **customer.com**.

- Enter the username **admin** and the password **cisco123** for SDM Express users and Telnet users. This password gives access to SDM locally, through the console connection, or remotely using Telnet.

- Enter the enable secret password of **cisco123**. This entry creates an encrypted password that prevents casual users from entering privileged mode and modifying the router's configuration using the CLI.

Figure 5-6   SDM Express Wizard: Basic Configuration

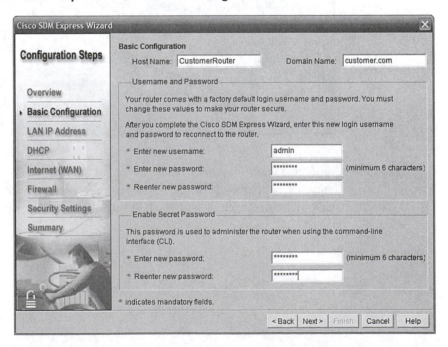

Step 2.   From the Router Provisioning screen, shown in Figure 5-7, click the radio button next to **SDM Express**, and then click **Next**.

Figure 5-7   SDM Express Wizard: Router Provisioning Screen

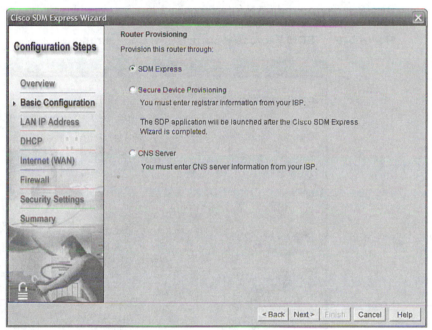

Task 3: Configure the LAN IP Address

In the LAN Interface Configuration window, shown in Figure 5-8, choose **FastEthernet0/0** from the Interface list. For interface FastEthernet 0/0, enter the IP address of **192.168.1.1** and subnet mask of **255.255.255.0**. You can also enter the subnet mask information in a different format. You can enter a count of the number of binary digits or bits in the subnet mask, such as **255.255.255.0** or 24 subnet bits. When finished, click **Next** to continue.

Figure 5-8   SDM Express Wizard: LAN Interface Configuration

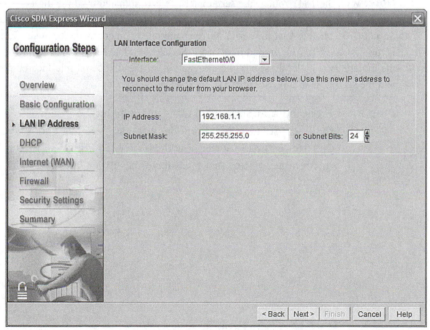

Task 4: Deselect the DHCP Server

At this point, do not enable the DHCP server. This procedure is covered in a later section of this course. In the DHCP server configuration window, shown in Figure 5-9, ensure that the **Enable DHCP server on the LAN interface** check box is cleared before proceeding. Click **Next** to continue.

Figure 5-9   SDM Express Wizard: DHCP Configuration

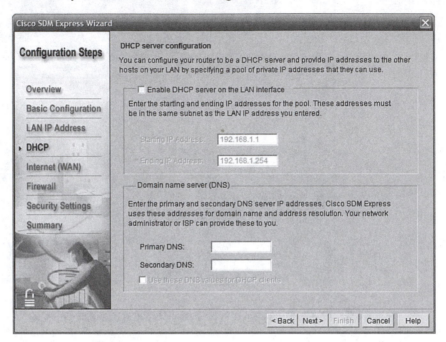

Task 5: Configure the WAN Interface

Step 1.   In the WAN Configuration window, shown in Figure 5-10, choose the **Serial0/1/0** interface from the list and click the **Add Connection** button. The Add Connection window appears.

Note: With the 1841 router, the serial interface is designated by three digits—C/S/P—where C is the controller number, S is the slot number, and P is the port number. The 1841 has two modular slots. The designation Serial0/1/0 indicates that the serial interface module is on controller 0, in slot 1, and that the interface to be used is the first one (0). The second interface is Serial0/1/1. The serial module may be installed in slot 0 or slot 1. If the module is installed in slot 0, the designation for the first serial interface on the module would be Serial0/0/0, and the second would be Serial0/0/1.

Step 2.   From the Add Serial0/1/0 Connection dialog box, shown in Figure 5-11, choose **PPP** from the Encapsulation list. From the Address Type list, choose **Static IP Address**. Enter **209.165.200.225** for the IP address and **255.255.255.224** for the Subnet mask. Click **OK** to continue. Notice that this subnet mask translates to a /27, or 27 bits for the mask.

Figure 5-10   SDM Express Wizard: WAN Configuration

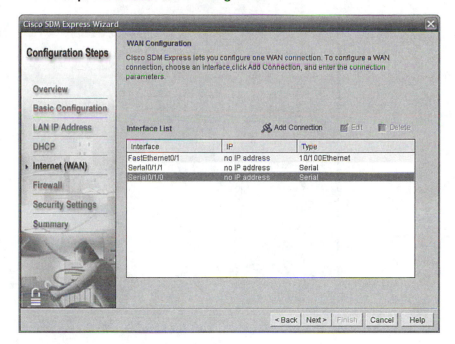

Figure 5-11   SDM Express Wizard: Serial Interface Configuration

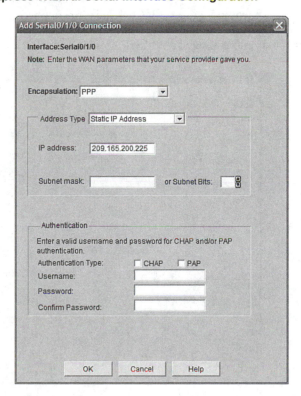

Step 3.   Verify that the IP address that you just set for the serial WAN interface now appears in the Interface List, as shown in Figure 5-12. Click **Next** to continue.

Figure 5-12   SDM Express Wizard: Configured Serial Interface

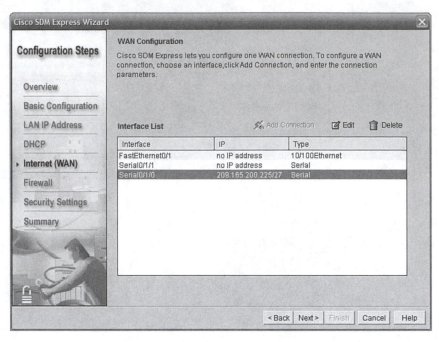

Step 4.   Enter the IP address **209.165.200.226** as the Next Hop IP Address for the default route, as shown in Figure 5-13. Click **Next** to continue.

Figure 5-13   SDM Express Wizard: Configuring the Next Hop

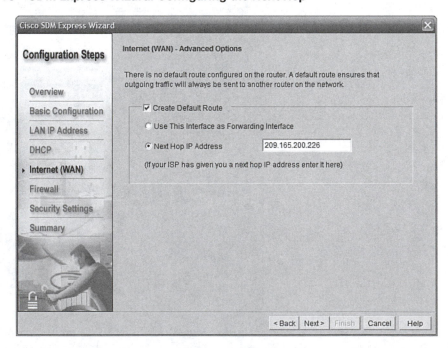

Step 5.   On the Internet (WAN) - Private IP Address screen, shown in Figure 5-14, ensure that the check box next to **Enable NAT** is cleared. This procedure is covered in a later section of this course. Click **Next** to continue.

Figure 5-14   SDM Express Wizard: NAT

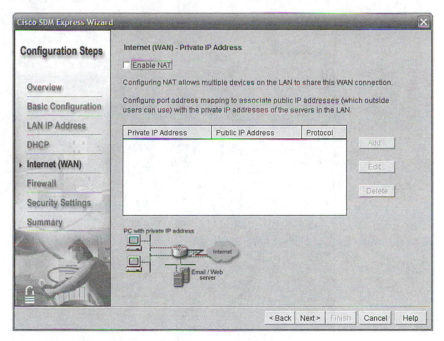

Task 6: Enable the Firewall and Security Settings

Depending on the router IOS version, the next task may be firewall configuration, as shown in Figure 5-15. In the Firewall Configuration window, click the radio button that enables the firewall, and then click **Next**. The Security Configuration window appears, as shown in Figure 5-16. Leave all the default security options checked, and then click **Next**.

Figure 5-15   SDM Express Wizard: Firewall Configuration

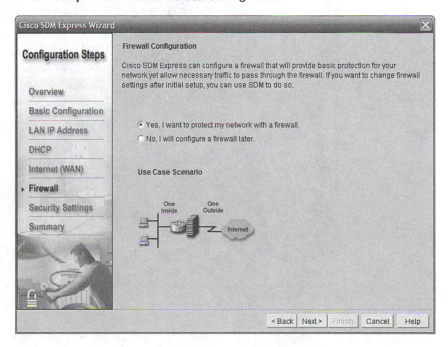

Figure 5-16   SDM Express Wizard: Security Configuration

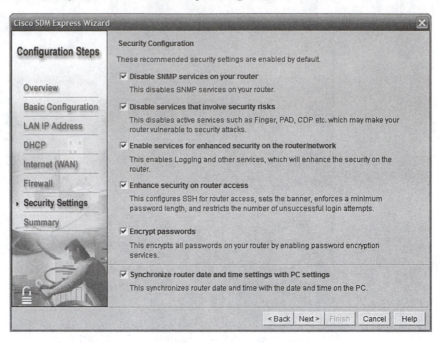

Task 7: Review and Complete the Configuration

Step 1.   If you are not satisfied with the Cisco SDM Express Summary, shown in Figure 5-17, click **Back** to fix any changes, and then click **Finish** to commit the changes to the router.

Figure 5-17   SDM Express Wizard: Summary

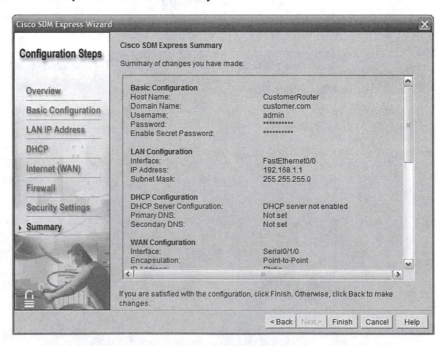

Step 2.   Reconnection Instructions, as shown in Figure 5-18, are displayed. Click **OK** after reading the Reconnection Instructions. Save these instructions to a file for future reference, if desired.

Note: Before the next time you connect, you need to change the PC's IP address to be compatible with the new address that you configured on FastEthernet 0/0.

Figure 5-18   SDM Express Wizard: Reconnection Instructions

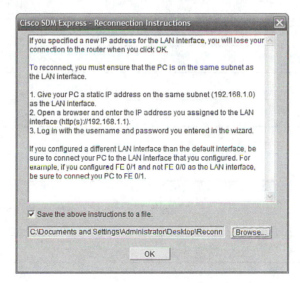

Step 3.   A message appears to inform you that the configuration is being delivered to the router, as shown in Figure 5-19. When the delivery of the configuration to the router is complete, the **OK** button will be clickable. Click **OK** to close Cisco SDM Express.

Figure 5-19   SDM Express Wizard: Configuration Delivery

Task 8: Reflection

What feature makes configuring the router easy?

_____

_____

Summarize the tasks that are configured by the Cisco SDM Express.

_____

_____

_____

_____

_____

_____

_____

_____

_____

_____

_____

Lab 5-3: Configuring Dynamic NAT with SDM (5.2.4)

Objective

- Configure Network Address Translation (NAT) using Port Address Translation (PAT) on a Cisco ISR with the Cisco SDM Basic NAT Wizard.

Background/Preparation

Cisco Router and Security Device Manager (SDM) is a Java-based web application and a device-management tool for Cisco IOS software-based routers. The Cisco SDM simplifies router and security configuration through the use of smart wizards. This allows you to deploy, configure, and monitor a Cisco router without needing knowledge of the CLI. The Cisco SDM is supported on a wide range of Cisco routers and Cisco IOS software releases. Many newer Cisco routers come with SDM prein-stalled. If you are using an 1841 router, SDM (and SDM Express) is preinstalled.

This lab assumes the use of a Cisco 1841 router. You can use another router model as long as it can support SDM. If you are using a supported router that does not have SDM installed, you can down-load the latest version free of charge from http://www.cisco.com/pcgi-bin/tablebuild.pl/sdm.

From this URL, view or download the document "Downloading and Installing Cisco Router and Security Device Manager." This document provides instructions for installing SDM on your router. It lists specific model numbers and IOS versions that can support SDM, and the amount of memory required.

Cisco SDM is the full SDM product, and SMD Express is a subset. SDM is activated automatically when the router has been previously configured and is not in its factory default state. In this lab, you will use the Cisco SDM Basic NAT Wizard to configure NAT using a single external global IP address. This address can support connections to the Internet from many internal private addresses.

You must complete Lab 5-2, "Configuring an ISR with SDM Express (5.2.3)," on the router to be used before performing this lab. This lab assumes that the router was previously configured with basic settings using SDM Express.

Figure 5-20 shows the topology for this lab.

Figure 5-20 Topology Diagram for Lab 5-3

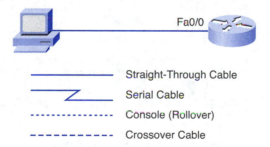

The following resources are required:

- Cisco 1841 ISR with SDM version 2.4 installed and with basic configuration completed (This is critical. See Task 1.)

- Another Cisco router model with SDM installed (optional)

- Windows XP computer with Internet Explorer 5.5 or higher and Sun Java Runtime Environment (JRE) version 1.4.2_05 or later (or Java Virtual Machine [JVM] 5.0.0.3810)

- Straight-through or crossover Category 5 Ethernet cable

- Access to PC network TCP/IP configuration

Task 1: Establish a Connection from the PC to the Router

Step 1. Power up the router.

Step 2. Power up the PC.

Step 3. Disable any popup blocker programs. Popup blockers prevent SDM windows from appearing.

Step 4. Connect the PC NIC to the FastEthernet 0/0 (Fa0/0) port on the Cisco 1841 ISR with the Ethernet cable.

Note: An SDM router other than the 1841 may require connection to a different port to access SDM.

Step 5. Configure the IP address of the PC to be **192.168.1.2**, with a subnet mask of **255.255.255.0**.

Step 6. SDM does not load automatically on the router. You must open the web browser to reach the SDM. Open the web browser on the PC, and connect to http://192.168.1.1. The SDM configuration screen should appear, as shown in Figure 5-21.

Figure 5-21   SDM

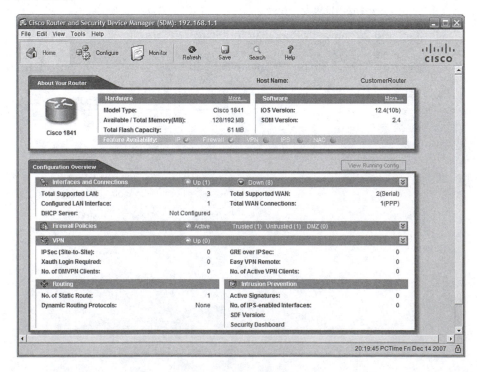

Note: If you cannot connect and see the login screen, check your cabling and connections, and make sure that the PC's IP configuration is correct. If the router was not previously configured, it may still be in the default state, with an IP address of 10.10.10.1 on the Fa0/0 interface. Try setting the IP address of the PC to **10.10.10.2**, with a subnet mask of **255.255.255.248**, and connect to http://10.10.10.1 using the browser. If you have difficulty with this procedure, contact your instructor for assistance.

Note: If the startup-config is erased in an SDM router, SDM will no longer come up by default when the router is restarted. You will need to build a basic router configuration using IOS commands. Refer to the section "SDM Router Basic IOS Configuration" in Appendix C or contact your instructor.

Step 7.   In the **Connect to** dialog box, enter **admin** for the username and **cisco123** for the password. These were configured in Lab 5-2. Click **OK**. The main SDM web application starts, and you are prompted to use HTTPS. Click **Cancel**. In the Security Warning window, click **Yes** to trust the Cisco application.

Step 8.   Verify that you are using the latest version of SDM. The initial SDM screen that appears immediately after the login shows the current version number. It is also displayed on the main SDM screen, along with the IOS version.

Note: If the current version is not 2.4 or higher, notify your instructor before continuing with this lab. You will need to download the latest zip file from http://www.cisco.com/pcgi-bin/tablebuild.pl/sdm and save it to the PC. From the SDM GUI, choose **Tools > Update SDM** to specify the location of the zip file and install the update.

Task 2: Configure SDM to Show Cisco IOS CLI Commands

Step 1.   In the main SDM window, choose **Edit > Preferences**. The User Preferences dialog box appears, as shown in Figure 5-22.

Figure 5-22   SDM User Preferences

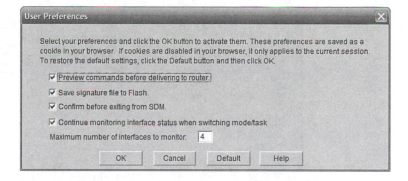

Step 2.   Check the **Preview commands before delivering to router** check box, and then click **OK**. With this check box checked, you can see the Cisco IOS CLI commands that you will use to perform a configuration function on the router before they are sent to the router. You can learn about Cisco IOS CLI commands this way.

Task 3: Launch the Basic NAT Wizard

Step 1.   On the **Configure** menu, click the **NAT** button to view the NAT configuration page, as shown in Figure 5-23. Click the **Basic NAT** radio button, and then click **Launch the selected task**.

Figure 5-23   SDM NAT Configuration

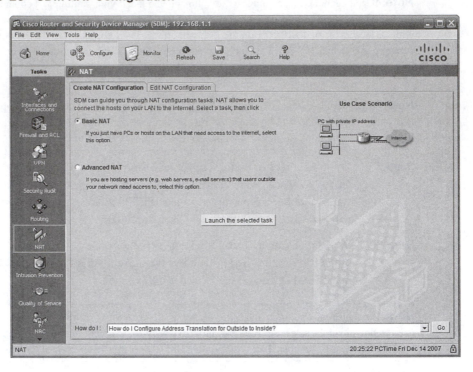

Step 2.   In the Welcome to the Basic NAT Wizard window, shown in Figure 5-24, click **Next**.

Figure 5-24   SDM Basic NAT Wizard

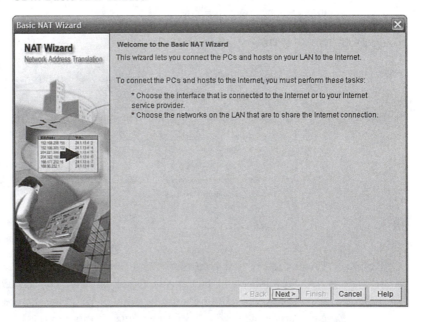

Task 4: Select the WAN Interface for NAT

Step 1.   From the screen shown in Figure 5-25, choose the WAN interface **Serial0/1/0** from the list. Check the box for the IP address range that represents the internal network of **192.168.1.0** to **192.168.1.255**. This is the range that requires conversion using the NAT process.

Figure 5-25   SDM Basic NAT Wizard: Sharing the Internet Connection

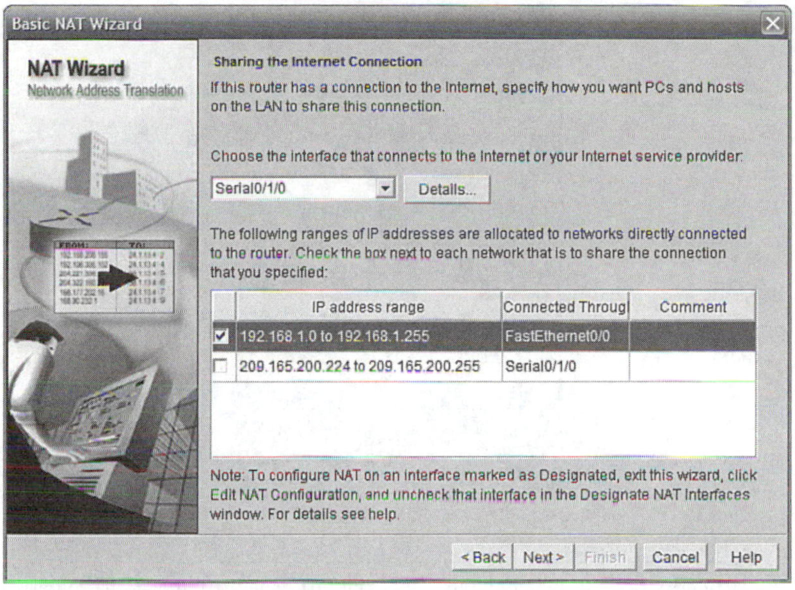

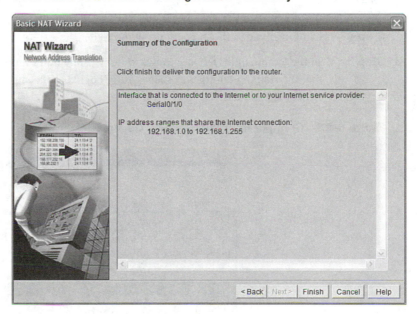

Step 2.   Click **Next**. After you have read the Summary of the Configuration, as shown in Figure 5-26, click **Finish.**

Figure 5-26   SDM Basic NAT Wizard: Configuration Summary

Step 3.   In the Deliver Configuration to Router window, shown in Figure 5-27, review the CLI commands that were generated by the Cisco SDM. These are the commands that will be delivered to the router to configure NAT. The commands can also be manually entered from the CLI to accomplish the same task. Check the box for **Save running config. to router's startup config.**

Figure 5-27   Configuration Delivery

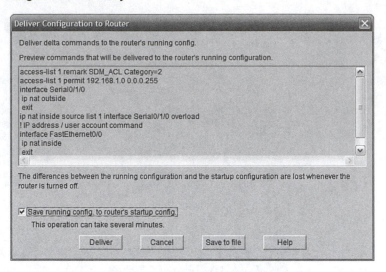

Note: By default, the commands that you just generated update the router's running configuration file only when delivered. If the router is restarted, the changes you made will be lost. Checking this box updates the startup config file as well and, when the router is restarted, it loads the new commands into the running config.

If you choose not to save the commands to the startup config at this time, in SDM choose **File > Write to Startup config**, or use the **copy running-config startup-config** command from the CLI using a terminal or Telnet session.

Step 4.   Click **Deliver** to finish configuring the router.

Step 5.   In the Commands Delivery Status window, shown in Figure 5-28, note the text that says that the running config was successfully copied to the startup config. Click **OK** to exit the Basic NAT wizard.

Figure 5-28   Configuration Successfully Delivered

Step 6.   The final NAT screen, shown in Figure 5-29, shows that the inside interface is Fa0/0 and the outside interface is S0/1/0. The internal private (Original) addresses will be translated dynamically to the external public address.

Figure 5-29   Final NAT Configuration

Task 5: Reflection

If a PC or a LAN within your organization does not require Internet access, what do you think would be one way to stop the PC from gaining access to the Internet?

_____

_____

Consider the skills that you need to configure NAT using Cisco IOS CLI commands. What do you think are the benefits and disadvantages of using the Cisco SDM?

_____

_____

_____

_____

Why do you think that the default, after the commands have been generated, is to update the router's running configuration file only when delivered? Why not always update the startup config file as well? What are the advantages and disadvantages of one over the other?

_____

_____

_____

_____

_____

_____

Lab 5-4: Configuring Basic Router Settings with the Cisco IOS CLI (5.3.5)

Objectives

- Configure the device hostname for a router.

- Configure console, privileged EXEC mode, and virtual terminal passwords.

- Configure FastEthernet and serial interfaces, including a description.

- Configure a message-of-the-day (MOTD) banner.

- Configure the routers to not perform domain lookup of hostnames.

- Configure synchronous console logging.

- Verify connectivity between hosts and routers.

Background/Preparation

In this lab you will build a multirouter network and configure the routers to communicate using the most common Cisco router IOS configuration commands.

Set up a network similar to the one shown in Figure 5-30 using the information shown in Table 5-1. Any router that meets the interface requirements displayed in Figure 5-30—such as 800, 1600, 1700, 1800, 2500, 2600, and 2800 routers, or a combination—may be used.

Figure 5-30   Topology Diagram for Lab 5-4

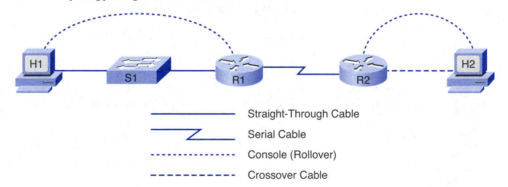

Straight-Through Cable
Serial Cable
Console (Rollover)
Crossover Cable

Table 5-1   Device Configuration Information for Lab 5-4

Router Designation	Router Name	Fast Ethernet 0/0 Address	Serial 0/0/0 Address	Interface Type	Subnet Mask for Both Interfaces
Router 1	R1	172.16.0.1	172.17.0.1	DCE	255.255.0.0
Router 2	R2	172.18.0.1	172.17.0.2	DTE	255.255.0.0

The Router Interface Summary table (Table C-1) in Appendix C will help you determine the interface identifiers to be used, based on the equipment in the lab. Depending on the router model, output may vary somewhat from that shown in this lab. The tasks in this lab are intended to be executed on each router unless you are specifically instructed otherwise.

The following resources are required:

- Two routers, each with a FastEthernet and serial interface. These should be non-SDM routers, if possible, because the required SDM startup configuration is deleted when the startup-config is erased.

- One Cisco 2960 switch or equivalent

- Two Windows XP computers with HyperTerminal installed

- Two straight-through Category 5 Ethernet cables (H1 to S1 and S1 to R2)

- Crossover Category 5 Ethernet cable (H2 to router R2)

- Null serial cable (R1 to R2)

- Console cable(s) (H1 to R1 and H2 to R2)

- Access to the host H1 and H2 command prompt

- Access to the host H1 and H2 network TCP/IP configuration

From each PC, start a HyperTerminal session to the attached router.

Note: Go to the "Erasing and Reloading the Router" instructions in Appendix C. Perform those tasks on all routers used in this lab assignment before continuing.

If the startup-config is erased in an SDM router, SDM will no longer come up by default when the router is restarted. You will need to build a basic router configuration using IOS commands. Refer to the procedure in Appendix C or contact your instructor.

Task 1: Configure Host IP Settings

Step 1.   Connect all devices as shown in Figure 5-30.

Step 2.   Configure static IP addresses on the PCs as follows:

PC attached to the R1 switch:

- IP address: 172.16.0.2

- Subnet mask: 255.255.0.0

- Default gateway: 172.16.0.1

PC attached to R2 directly:

- IP address: 172.18.0.2

- Subnet mask: 255.255.0.0

- Default gateway: 172.18.0.1

Task 2: Log In to Each Router, and Configure a Hostname and Password

Step 1.   Configure a hostname for each of the two routers:

```
Router> enable
Router# configure terminal
Router(config)# hostname R1
```

Repeat this process for router R2 (use **R2** for the name of the second router).

Step 2.   Configure a console password, and enable login for each of the two routers:

```
R1(config)# line console 0
R1(config-line)# password cisco
R1(config-line)# login
R1(config-line)# exit
R1(config)#
```

Repeat this process for router R2.

Step 3.   Configure the password on the virtual terminal lines for each of the two routers:

```
R1(config)# line vty 0 4
R1(config-line)# password cisco
R1(config-line)# login
R1(config-line)# exit
R1(config)#
```

Repeat this process for router R2.

Step 4.   Configure the enable and enable secret passwords for each of the two routers:

```
R1(config)# enable password cisco
R1(config)# enable secret class
R1(config)# exit
```

Repeat this process for router R2.

Note: Remember that the enable secret password is encrypted from the configuration view. Also, do not enter **enable secret password class**. If you do, the secret password will be **password**, not **class**. The enable secret password takes precedence over the enable password. After an enable secret password is entered, the enable password no longer is accepted.

Step 5.   Configure a message-of-the-day (MOTD) banner using the **banner motd** command. When a user connects to the router, the MOTD banner appears before the login prompt. In this example, the number sign (#) is used to start and end the message. The # is converted to ^C when the running-config is displayed.

```
R1(config)# banner motd #Unauthorized Use Prohibited#
```

Step 6.   Configure the router to not attempt to resolve hostnames using a DNS server. If this is not configured, the router assumes that any mistyped command is a hostname and attempts to resolve it by looking for a DNS server. On some routers, it can take considerable time before the prompt returns.

```
R1(config)# no ip domain lookup
```

Step 7.   Configure the router so that console messages do not interfere with command input. This is helpful when exiting configuration mode, because it returns you to the command prompt and prevents messages from breaking into the command line.

```
R1(config)# line console 0
R1(config-line)# logging synchronous
```

Task 3: Show the Router Running Configuration

From the privileged EXEC prompt, issue the **show running-config** command. This command can be abbreviated as **sh run**. The output of this command is shown in Example 5-4.

Example 5-4   Router Configuration

```
R1# show running-config


*** Some output omitted ***


Building configuration...
Current configuration : 605 bytes
!
hostname R1
!
enable secret 5 $1$eJB4$SH2vZ.aiT7/tczUJP2zwT1
enable password cisco
!
no ip domain lookup
!
interface FastEthernet0/0
 no ip address
 shutdown
 duplex auto
 speed auto
!
interface Serial0/0/0
 no ip address
 shutdown
!
interface Serial0/0/1
 no ip address
```

```
  shutdown
!
banner motd ^CUnauthorized Use Prohibited^C
!
line con 0
 password cisco
 logging synchronous
 login
line aux 0
line vty 0 4
 password cisco
 login
!
end
```

Is there an encrypted password?

_____

Are there any other passwords?

_____

Are any of the other passwords encrypted?

_____

Task 4: Configure the Serial Interface on R1

In global configuration mode, configure interface Serial 0/0/0 on router R1. See the Router Interface Summary table in Appendix C for the proper designation for the serial interface on the router you are using. Because the R1 Serial 0/0/0 interface is acting as the DCE for the WAN link, you must config-ure the clock rate. When configuring an interface, always use the **no shutdown** command to enable it.

```
R1(config)# interface serial 0/0/0
R1(config-if)# ip address 172.17.0.1 255.255.0.0
R1(config-if)# description WAN link to R2
R1(config-if)# clock rate 64000
R1(config-if)# no shutdown
R1(config-if)# exit
R1(config)# exit
```

Note: Enter the clock rate only on the router serial interface to which the DCE interface end of the cable is attached. The cable type (DTE or DCE) is printed on the outside of each end of the null serial cable. When in doubt, enter the **clock rate** command on both router serial interfaces. The command is ignored on the router to which the DTE end is attached. The command **no shutdown** turns on the interface. The command **shutdown** turns off the interface.

Task 5: Display Information About the Serial Interface on R1

Enter the **show interfaces** command on R1 for the specific serial interface you have just configured. Refer to the Router Interface Summary table in Appendix C. Sample output is provided in Example 5-5.

Example 5-5   Router 1 Serial Interface Configuration

```
R1# show interfaces serial 0/0/0

Serial0/0/0 is down, line protocol is down
  Hardware is PowerQUICC Serial
  Description: WAN link to R2
  Internet address is 172.17.0.1/16
  MTU 1500 bytes, BW 128 Kbit, DLY 20000 usec,
      reliability 255/255, txload 1/255, rxload 1/255
  Encapsulation HDLC, loopback not set
  Keepalive set (10 sec)
  Last input never, output never, output hang never
  Last clearing of "show interface" counters 00:01:55
  Input queue: 0/75/0/0 (size/max/drops/flushes); Total output drops: 0
  Queueing strategy: fifo
  Output queue :0/40 (size/max)
  5 minute input rate 0 bits/sec, 0 packets/sec
  5 minute output rate 0 bits/sec, 0 packets/sec
     0 packets input, 0 bytes, 0 no buffer
     Received 0 broadcasts, 0 runts, 0 giants, 0 throttles
     0 input errors, 0 CRC, 0 frame, 0 overrun, 0 ignored, 0 abort
     6 packets output, 906 bytes, 0 underruns
     0 output errors, 0 collisions, 3 interface resets
     0 output buffer failures, 0 output buffers swapped out
     0 carrier transitions
     DCD=down  DSR=down  DTR=up  RTS=up  CTS=down
```

What do you discover by issuing the **show interfaces** command?

Serial 0/0/0 status is

_____

Line protocol is

_____

Internet address is

_____

Encapsulation:

_____

To what OSI layer does the Encapsulation refer?

_____

If the serial interface was configured, why does the **show interfaces serial 0/0/0** say that the interface is down?

_____

Task 6: Configure the Serial Interface on R2

In global configuration mode, configure the serial interface Serial 0/0/0 on router R2. See the Router Interface Summary table in Appendix C for the proper designation for the serial interface on the router that you are using.

```
R2(config)# interface serial 0/0/0
R2(config-if)# description WAN link to R1
R2(config-if)# ip address 172.17.0.2 255.255.0.0
R2(config-if)# no shutdown
R2(config-if)# exit
R2(config)# exit
```

Note: Enter the clock rate only on the router serial interface to which the DCE interface end of the cable is attached. The cable type (DTE or DCE) is printed on the outside of each end of the null serial cable. When in doubt, enter the **clock rate** command on both router serial interfaces. This command is ignored on the router to which the DTE end is attached. The command **no shutdown** turns on the interface. The command **shutdown** turns off the interface.

Task 7: Display Information About the Serial Interface on R2

Enter the **show interfaces** command on R2 for the specific serial interface you have just configured. Refer to the Router Interface Summary table in Appendix C. Sample output is shown in Example 5-6.

Example 5-6   Router 2 Serial Interface Configuration

```
R2# show interfaces serial 0/0/0

Serial0/0/0 is up, line protocol is up
  Hardware is PowerQUICC Serial
  Description: WAN link to R1
  Internet address is 172.17.0.2/16
  MTU 1500 bytes, BW 128 Kbit, DLY 20000 usec,
     reliability 255/255, txload 1/255, rxload 1/255
  Encapsulation HDLC, loopback not set
  Keepalive set (10 sec)
  Last input 00:00:08, output 00:00:08, output hang never
  Last clearing of "show interface" counters 00:04:54
  Input queue: 0/75/0/0 (size/max/drops/flushes); Total output drops: 0
  Queueing strategy: fifo
  Output queue :0/40 (size/max)
```

```
5 minute input rate 0 bits/sec, 0 packets/sec
5 minute output rate 0 bits/sec, 0 packets/sec
   3 packets input, 72 bytes, 0 no buffer
   Received 3 broadcasts, 0 runts, 0 giants, 0 throttles
   0 input errors, 0 CRC, 0 frame, 0 overrun, 0 ignored, 0 abort
   6 packets output, 933 bytes, 0 underruns
   0 output errors, 0 collisions, 2 interface resets
   0 output buffer failures, 0 output buffers swapped out
   0 carrier transitions
   DCD=up  DSR=up  DTR=up  RTS=up  CTS=up
```

What do you discover by issuing the **show interfaces** command?

Serial 0/0/0 is

_____

Line protocol is

_____

Internet address is

_____

Encapsulation:

_____

To what OSI layer does the Encapsulation refer?

_____

Why does the **show interfaces serial 0/0/0** say that the interface is up?

_____

Task 8: Verify That the Serial Connection Is Functioning

Step 1.   Use the **ping** command to test connectivity to the serial interface of the other router. From R1, ping the R2 router serial interface:

```
R1# ping 172.17.0.2
```

Does the ping work?

_____

Step 2.   From R2, ping the R1 router serial interface:

```
R2# ping 172.17.0.1
```

Does the ping work?

_____

If the answer to either question is no, troubleshoot the router configurations to find the error. Then ping the interfaces again until the answer to both questions is yes.

Task 9: Configure the FastEthernet Interface on R1

From global configuration mode, configure the FastEthernet interface on router R1. Refer to the Router Interface Summary chart in Appendix C for the proper designation for the Ethernet interface on the router that you are using for this lab.

```
R1(config)# interface FastEthernet 0/0
R1(config-if)# description R1 LAN Default Gateway
R1(config-if)# ip address 172.16.0.1 255.255.0.0
R1(config-if)# no shutdown
R1(config-if)# exit
R1(config)# exit
```

Note: Ethernet interfaces do not have a DTE or DCE distinction; therefore, you do not need to enter the **clock rate** command.

Task 10: Display Information About the FastEthernet Interface on R1

Enter the **show interfaces** command on R1 for the specific FastEthernet interface you have just configured. Refer to the Router Interface Summary table in Appendix C. Sample output is provided in Example 5-7.

Example 5-7   Router 1 Ethernet Interface Configuration

```
R1# show interfaces FastEthernet 0/0

FastEthernet0/0 is up, line protocol is up
  Hardware is AmdFE, address is 000c.3076.8460 (bia 000c.3076.8460)
  Internet address is 172.16.0.1/16
  MTU 1500 bytes, BW 100000 Kbit, DLY 100 usec,
     reliability 255/255, txload 1/255, rxload 1/255
  Encapsulation ARPA, loopback not set
  Keepalive set (10 sec)
  Auto-duplex, Auto Speed, 100BaseTX/FX
  ARP type: ARPA, ARP Timeout 04:00:00
  Last input never, output 00:00:18, output hang never
  Last clearing of "show interface" counters never
  Input queue: 0/75/0/0 (size/max/drops/flushes); Total output drops: 0
  Queueing strategy: fifo
  Output queue :0/40 (size/max)
  5 minute input rate 0 bits/sec, 0 packets/sec
  5 minute output rate 0 bits/sec, 0 packets/sec
```

```
     0 packets input, 0 bytes
     Received 0 broadcasts, 0 runts, 0 giants, 0 throttles
     0 input errors, 0 CRC, 0 frame, 0 overrun, 0 ignored
     0 watchdog
     0 input packets with dribble condition detected
     52 packets output, 5737 bytes, 0 underruns
     0 output errors, 0 collisions, 1 interface resets
     0 babbles, 0 late collision, 0 deferred
     52 lost carrier, 0 no carrier
     0 output buffer failures, 0 output buffers swapped out
```

What do you discover by issuing the **show interfaces** command?

FastEthernet 0/0 is

Line protocol is

Internet address is

Encapsulation:

To what OSI layer does the Encapsulation refer?

Why does the **show interfaces FastEthernet 0/0** say that the interface is up?

Task 11: Configure the FastEthernet Interface on R2

From global configuration mode, configure the FastEthernet interface on Router R2. Refer to the Router Interface Summary chart in Appendix C for the proper designation for the Ethernet interface on the router that you are using for this lab.

```
R2(config)# interface FastEthernet 0/0
R2(config-if)# description R2 LAN Default Gateway
R2(config-if)# ip address 172.18.0.1 255.255.0.0
R2(config-if)# no shutdown
R2(config-if)# exit
R2(config)# exit
```

Note: Ethernet interfaces do not have a DTE or DCE distinction; therefore, you do not need to enter the **clock rate** command.

Task 12: Display Information About the FastEthernet Interface on R2

Enter the **show interfaces FastEthernet 0/0** command on R2. Refer to the Router Interface Summary chart in Appendix C. Sample output is shown in Example 5-8.

Example 5-8   Router 2 Ethernet Interface Configuration

```
R2# show interfaces FastEthernet 0/0

FastEthernet0/0 is up, line protocol is up
  Hardware is AmdFE, address is 000c.3076.8460 (bia 000c.3076.8460)
  Internet address is 172.16.0.1/16
  MTU 1500 bytes, BW 100000 Kbit, DLY 100 usec,
     reliability 255/255, txload 1/255, rxload 1/255
  Encapsulation ARPA, loopback not set
  Keepalive set (10 sec)
  Auto-duplex, Auto Speed, 100BaseTX/FX
  ARP type: ARPA, ARP Timeout 04:00:00
  Last input never, output 00:00:05, output hang never
  Last clearing of "show interface" counters never
  Input queue: 0/75/0/0 (size/max/drops/flushes); Total output drops: 0
  Queueing strategy: fifo
  Output queue :0/40 (size/max)
  5 minute input rate 0 bits/sec, 0 packets/sec
  5 minute output rate 0 bits/sec, 0 packets/sec
     0 packets input, 0 bytes
     Received 0 broadcasts, 0 runts, 0 giants, 0 throttles
     0 input errors, 0 CRC, 0 frame, 0 overrun, 0 ignored
     0 watchdog
     0 input packets with dribble condition detected
     14 packets output, 1620 bytes, 0 underruns
     0 output errors, 0 collisions, 1 interface resets
     0 babbles, 0 late collision, 0 deferred
     14 lost carrier, 0 no carrier
     0 output buffer failures, 0 output buffers swapped out
```

What do you discover by issuing the **show interfaces** command?

FastEthernet 0/0 is

_____

Line protocol is

_____

Internet address is

Encapsulation:

To what OSI layer does the Encapsulation refer?

Why does the **show interfaces FastEthernet 0/0** say that the interface is up?

Task 13: Save the Configuration on Both Routers

Save the running configuration to the startup configuration in privileged EXEC mode:

```
R1# copy running-config startup-config
R2# copy running-config startup-config
```

Note: Save the running configuration for the next time the router is restarted. The router can be restarted by either a software **reload** command or a power shutdown. The running configuration will be lost if it is not saved. The router uses the startup configuration when the router is started.

Task 14: Check Both Router Configurations

Issue the **show running-config** command from privileged EXEC mode on both routers, and verify all the configuration commands you have entered so far. Note that this command can be abbreviated as **sh run**.

```
R1# show running-config
R2# show running-config
```

Task 15: Verify That the FastEthernet Connection to Each Router Is Functioning

On host H1, open a Command Prompt window by choosing **Start > Run** and entering **cmd**. Alternatively, you may choose **Start > All Programs > Accessories > Command Prompt**.

Step 1. Use the **ping** command to test connectivity to the FastEthernet interface of each router from its associated PC. From H1, ping the R1 router FastEthernet interface:

```
C:\> ping 172.16.0.1
```

Was the ping successful?

Step 2.   From H2, ping the R2 router FastEthernet interface:

C:\> **ping 172.18.0.1**

Was the ping successful?

_____

Step 3.   If the answer is no to either question, troubleshoot the router configurations to find the error. Then ping the interfaces again until the answer to both questions is yes.

Task 16: Test Connectivity (Optional Challenge)

In previous tasks you tested network connectivity by pinging from R1 to the serial interface of R2. You also pinged from each host to its respective default gateway. These pings were successful because, in each case, the source and destination IP addresses were on the same network. Now you will ping from router R1 to the router R2 FastEthernet interface and then from H1 to H2. The source and destination IP addresses for these pings are not on the same network.

Step 1.   From R1, ping the R2 FastEthernet interface:

C:\> **ping 172.18.0.1**

Was the ping successful?

_____

Step 2.   From host H1, use the **ping** command to test end-to-end connectivity from H1 (172.16.0.2) to H2 (172.18.0.2):

C:\> **ping 172.18.0.2**

Does the ping work?

_____

The pings from R1 to the R2 FastEthernet interface and from H1 to H2 do not work because router R1 has no knowledge of how to get to the R2 Ethernet network (172.18.0.0). In addition, R2 has no knowledge of the Ethernet network on R1 (172.16.0.0). The pings cannot get from R1 or H1 to the R2 Ethernet network. Even if they could, they could not return. For the pings to work from one host computer to the other, a default route and a static route must be configured on each router, or a dynamic routing protocol must be set up between them.

Lab 5-5: Configuring DHCP with SDM and the Cisco IOS CLI (5.3.7)

Objectives

- Configure a customer router for DHCP using SDM.
- Configure a customer router for DHCP using Cisco IOS.
- Configure a DHCP client.
- Verify DHCP functionality.

Background/Preparation

In this lab you will set up a customer router to act as a DHCP server for internal client computers. DHCP assigns an address, subnet mask, and default gateway to hosts dynamically from a defined pool of addresses.

Set up a network similar to the one shown in Figure 5-31 and described in Table 5-2. Other routers may be used but they must meet the interface requirements displayed in that figure and be capable of supporting SDM. Refer to the Router Interface Summary table in Appendix C to determine the interface identifiers to be used, based on the equipment in the lab. Depending on the router model, the output may vary somewhat from that shown in this lab.

Figure 5-31   Topology Diagram for Lab 5-5

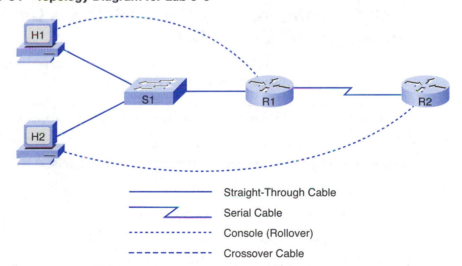

Table 5-2   Device Configuration Information for Lab 5-5

Router Designation	Router Name	Fast Ethernet 0/0 Address and Subnet Mask	Serial 0/0/0 Address and Subnet Mask	Interface Type	Loopback Address
R1	Customer	192.168.1.1 255.255.255.0	209.165.200.225 255.255.255.224	DCE	—
R2	ISP	—	209.165.200.226 255.255.255.224	DTE	209.165.200.1 255.255.255.224

The following resources are required:

- Cisco 1841 ISR with SDM version 2.4 installed to act as the customer router

- Cisco 1841 router (or another router) to act as the ISP router

- Cisco 2960 switch (or another switch/hub) to connect hosts H1 and H2 and the customer router

- Windows XP computer (host H1) with Internet Explorer 5.5 or higher and Sun Java Runtime Environment (JRE) version 1.4.2_05 or later (or Java Virtual Machine [JVM] 5.0.0.3810)

- Windows XP computer (host H2)

- Straight-through Category 5 Ethernet cables

- Null serial cable (R1 to R2)

- Console cables (H1 to R1 and H2 to R2)

- Access to the host H1 and H2 command prompt

- Access to the host H1 and H2 network TCP/IP configuration

From hosts H1 and H2, start a HyperTerminal session with each router.

Note: Be sure that the routers and switch have been erased and have no startup configurations. Instructions for erasing both the switch and router are provided in Appendix C. Check with your instructor if you are unsure how to do this.

Task 1: Configure Basic Router Settings Using IOS, and Configure PAT Using SDM

Step 1.   Build the network and configure host computer IP settings. Make sure that the host computers are connected according to Figure 5-31.

Note: An SDM router other than the 1841 may require a connection to a port other than FastEthernet 0/0 to access SDM.

Step 2.   Configure host H1 with the following static IP information:

- IP address: 192.168.1.101

- Subnet mask: 255.255.255.0

- Default gateway: 192.168.1.1

Step 3.   Configure host H2 as a DHCP client.

Choose **Start > Settings > Control Panel > Network Connections > Local Area Connection**. Click the **Properties** button and then **Internet Protocol (TCP/IP) Properties** and click the **Properties** button. Select **Obtain an IP address automatically** and **Obtain a DNS server address automatically**.

Step 4.   On hosts H1 and H2, open a command prompt. Choose **Start > Run,** and then enter **cmd** and press **Enter**. Alternatively, choose **Start > All Programs > Accessories > Command Prompt**. Issue the **ipconfig /all** command. Record the MAC addresses for H1 and H2.

Host H1 MAC address:

Host H2 MAC address:

Step 5.   Configure the Customer router basic settings with the IOS CLI. Configure the hostname, passwords, interfaces, and HTTP service in preparation for the use of SDM. Also configure a default route to the ISP.

```
Router> enable
Router# config t
Router(config)# hostname Customer
Customer(config)# enable secret class
Customer(config)# username admin privilege 15 secret cisco123
Customer(config)# no ip domain-lookup
Customer(config)# line console 0
Customer(config-line)# password cisco
Customer(config-line)# logging synchronous
Customer(config-line)# login
Customer(config-line)# line vty 0 4
Customer(config-line)# password cisco
Customer(config-line)# login
Customer(config-line)# exit
Customer(config)# interface FastEthernet0/0
Customer(config-if)# description LAN Default Gateway
Customer(config-if)# ip address 192.168.1.1 255.255.255.0
Customer(config-if)# no shutdown
Customer(config-if)# interface Serial0/0/0
Customer(config-if)# ip address 209.165.200.225 255.255.255.224
Customer(config-if)# description WAN link to ISP
Customer(config-if)# no shutdown
Customer(config-if)# exit
Customer(config)# ip http server
Customer(config)# ip http authentication local
Customer(config)# ip route 0.0.0.0 0.0.0.0 209.165.200.226
```

Step 6.   Configure ISP router basic settings with the IOS CLI.

Configure the hostname, passwords, and interfaces.

```
Router> enable
Router# configure terminal
Router(config)# hostname ISP
ISP(config)# enable secret class
ISP(config)# line console 0
ISP(config-line)# password cisco
ISP(config-line)# login
ISP(config)# line vty 0 4
ISP(config-line)# password cisco
ISP(config-line)# login
```

```
ISP(config-line)# exit
ISP(config)# exit
ISP(config)# interface serial 0/0/0
ISP(config-if)# description WAN link to Customer
ISP(config-if)# ip address 209.165.200.226 255.255.255.224
ISP(config-if)# clock rate 64000
ISP(config-if)# no shutdown
ISP(config-if)# exit
ISP(config)# ip http server
ISP(config)# exit
```

Step 7.   Save the router configurations.

Save the running configuration to the startup configuration in privileged EXEC mode.

```
Customer# copy running-config startup-config
ISP# copy running-config startup-config
```

Step 8.   Connect to Customer with host H1 using SDM.

On host H1, disable any popup blocker programs. Popup blockers prevent SDM windows from appearing.

The SDM GUI does not load automatically on the router. You must open the web browser to reach the SDM. Open the web browser on the PC, and connect to http://192.168.1.1 (the IP address of the Customer FastEthernet 0/0 interface—the H1 default gateway). A screen similar to that shown in Figure 5-32 should appear.

Note: If you cannot connect and see the login screen, as shown in Figure 5-32, check your cabling and connections, and make sure that the PC's IP configuration is correct.

Figure 5-32   SDM Login

Step 9.   In the dialog box, enter **admin** for the username and **cisco123** for the password. These were configured in Step 2. Click **OK**. The main SDM web application starts. If you are prompted to use HTTPS, click **Cancel**. If a Security Warning window appears, click **Yes** to trust the Cisco application.

Step 10.   Verify that you are using the latest version of SDM. The initial SDM screen that appears immediately after the login shows the current version number. It is also displayed on the main SDM screen shown in Figure 5-33, along with the IOS version.

Note: If the current version is not 2.4 or higher, notify your instructor before continuing with this lab. You will need the latest zip file on the host H1 PC for use in updating the router SDM application. If you need to update SDM, from the SDM GUI, choose **Tools > Update SDM** to specify the location of the zip file and install the update.

Figure 5-33   SDM Main Screen

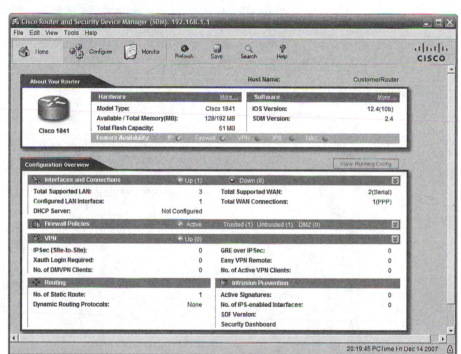

Step 11.   Configure SDM to show Cisco IOS CLI commands.

In the main SDM window, choose **Edit > Preferences**. You see a screen similar to that shown in Figure 5-34.

Check the **Preview commands before delivering to router** check box. With this check box checked, you can see the Cisco IOS CLI configuration commands that SDM generates before they are sent to the router. You can learn about Cisco IOS CLI commands this way. Click **OK** when you're finished.

Figure 5-34   SDM User Preferences Dialog Box

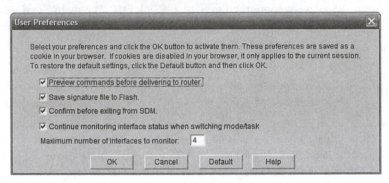

Step 12.   Choose **Configure > Additional Tasks**.

Click the **Configure** button at the top of the SDM window and select **Additional Tasks** from the **Tasks** menu at the left of the screen. This opens a screen similar to that shown in Figure 5-35. A menu window of Additional Tasks appears. Click the plus sign (+) next to DHCP in the Additional Tasks window to expand the menu, and then click **DHCP Pools**.

Figure 5-35   SDM Additional Tasks Screen

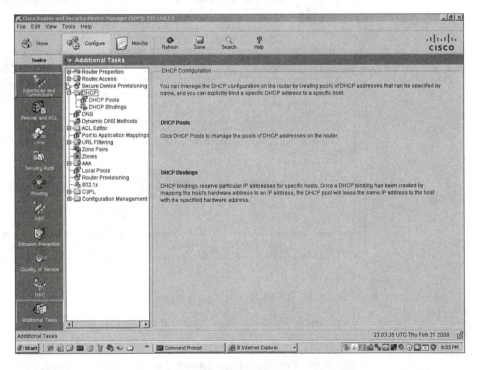

Step 13.   From the DHCP Pools screen, click the **Add** button to display the dialog box shown in Figure 5-36 and create a new DHCP pool. Enter the values shown in this dialog box to define the DHCP pool name, network, subnet mask, start and end of the IP address range, DNS server address, domain name, and default gateway router. Click **OK** when you have entered all the values.

Figure 5-36   SDM Add DHCP Pool Dialog Box

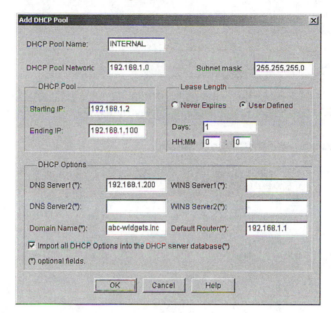

Why is the Starting IP address set to 192.168.1.2 instead of 192.168.1?

_____

_____

Step 14.   In the **Deliver Configuration to Router** window, shown in Figure 5-37, review the CLI commands that were generated by the Cisco SDM. These are the commands that will be delivered to the router to configure DHCP. The commands can also be manually entered from the CLI to accomplish the same task, which you will do in Task 2 of this lab. Do *not* check the box for **Save running config. to router's startup config.** Click **Deliver** to finish configuring the router.

Note: By default, the commands that you just generated will update only the running configuration file of the router when it is delivered. When you're finished configuring the router for DHCP with SDM, you will configure DHCP using Cisco IOS. When you restart the router, you want it to revert to the configuration that you saved in Step 2.

Figure 5-37   Delivering the Configuration to the Router

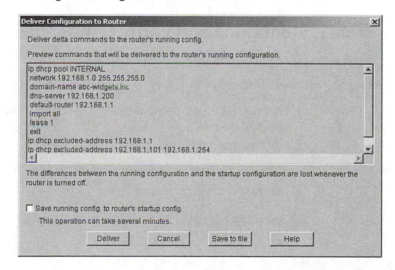

What do you think is the purpose of the last two commands in this configuration?

_____

_____

_____

After the commands are delivered, the final DHCP screen showing the details of the DHCP Pool is displayed, as shown in Figure 5-38.

Figure 5-38   DHCP Configuration

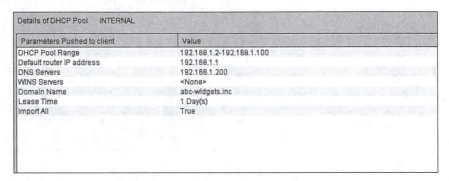

Details of DHCP Pool   INTERNAL

Parameters Pushed to client	Value
DHCP Pool Range	192.168.1.2-192.168.1.100
Default router IP address	192.168.1.1
DNS Servers	192.168.1.200
WINS Servers	<None>
Domain Name	abc-widgets.inc
Lease Time	1 Day(s)
Import All	True

Choose **File > Exit** from SDM to end the SDM session. Click **Yes** to confirm exiting SDM.

Step 15.   Test the DHCP pool configured with SDM.

On the customer host H2, open a command prompt. Choose **Start > Run,** and then enter **cmd** and press **Enter**. Alternatively, choose **Start > All Programs > Accessories > Command Prompt**. Issue the **ipconfig** command.

What IP address is issued to H2?

_____

From host H1, ping the default gateway (the router Ethernet interface). Does the ping succeed?

_____

Troubleshoot as necessary, and do not proceed until the ping is successful.

Task 2: Configure and Verify DHCP Using IOS

In this task you will configure the router as a DHCP server from the IOS CLI.

Step 1.   Restart the Customer router to remove the DHCP commands added by SDM.

a.   Because you did not save the DHCP configuration created using SDM to NVRAM on the Customer router, restarting the router will restore the basic configuration created in Step 2. On the Customer router, issue the **reload** command.

b.   When the following prompt appears, respond with **no**:

```
System configuration has been modified. Save? [yes/no]:
```

c.   When the following prompt appears, press **Enter**:

```
Proceed with reload? [confirm]
```

      d.   At the following prompt, press **Enter**:

```
Press RETURN to get started!
```

         You should now see the Customer> prompt.

Step 2.   Check the host DHCP client H2 IP configuration.

      a.   Open a command prompt on H2, and issue the **ipconfig /release** and **ipconfig /renew** commands. Because no DHCP server is currently configured, it may take a while to time out.

      b.   On host H2, open a command prompt. Choose **Start > Run**, and then enter **cmd** and press **Enter**. Alternatively, choose **Start > All Programs > Accessories > Command Prompt** and issue the **ipconfig** command.

         What are the IP address and subnet mask for H2?

         _____

         _____

         _____

Step 3.   Configure the DHCP server excluded addresses on the Customer router.

To prevent certain addresses from being assigned, you must exclude them from the pool. This includes the IP address of the router FastEthernet 0/0 interface (the default gateway). In this lab you will also exclude addresses from 192.168.1.101 through 192.168.1.254 to reserve them for other purposes, such as servers and printers, which need to have a fixed IP address.

On the customer router, exclude addresses from the pool DHCP using the **ip dhcp excluded-address** command:

```
Customer(config)# ip dhcp excluded-address 192.168.1.1
Customer(config)# ip dhcp excluded-address 192.168.1.101 192.168.1.254
```

Why would you want to exclude addresses before the DHCP pool is even created?

_____

_____

Step 4.   Configure the DHCP pool.

On the customer router, configure a DHCP pool for the internal clients:

```
Customer(config)# ip dhcp pool INTERNAL
Customer(dhcp-config)# network 192.168.1.0 255.255.255.0
Customer(dhcp-config)# domain-name abc-widgets.inc
Customer(dhcp-config)# default-router 192.168.1.1
Customer(dhcp-config)# dns-server 192.168.1.200
```

Step 5.   Test the DHCP pool for H2.

On the customer host H2, open a command prompt and issue the **ipconfig /release** and **ipconfig /renew** commands. On the host H2, issue the **ipconfig /all** command.

What IP address is issued to H2?

_____

What is the subnet mask of host H2?

_____

What is the default gateway for host H2?

_____

What is the connection-specific DNS suffix (domain name) of host H2?

_____

What is the DHCP server IP address?

_____

What is the DNS server IP address?

_____

_____

What is the MAC address of host H2?

_____

From host H2, ping the default gateway (the router FastEthernet interface). Does the ping succeed?

_____

Troubleshoot as necessary, and do not proceed until the ping is successful.

Step 6.   Test the DHCP pool for H1.

On host H1, choose **Start > Settings > Control Panel > Network Connections > Local Area Connection**. Change the IP configuration from static to dynamic to make host H1 a DHCP client like host H2. Click the **Properties** button, and then select **Internet Protocol (TCP/IP)** and click the **Properties** button. Select **Obtain an IP address automatically** and **Obtain a DNS server address automatically**. Click OK to exit the configuration window.

Open a command prompt on H1, and issue the **ipconfig /release** and **ipconfig /renew** commands.

On host H1, open a command prompt. Choose **Start > Run**, and then enter **cmd** and press **Enter**. Alternatively, choose **Start > All Programs > Accessories > Command Prompt** and enter the **ipconfig** command.

What IP address is issued to H1?

_____

Step 7.   Display DHCP binding on the customer router.

To see the IP address and host hardware (MAC) address combination assigned by the DHCP server in the router, issue the **show ip dhcp binding** command on the Customer router:

```
Customer# show ip dhcp binding
IP address    Client-ID/           Lease expiration        Type
                    Hardware address
192.168.1.2  0100.0bdb.04a5.cd  Feb 22 2008 11:19 AM    Automatic
192.168.1.3  0100.07e9.63ce.53  Feb 22 2008 11:27 AM    Automatic
```

Do the hardware addresses displayed match those recorded for hosts H1 and H2 in Step 1?

_____

_____

Step 8.   On the Customer router, display the characteristics of the DHCP pool using the **show ip dhcp pool** command:

```
Customer# show ip dhcp pool
Pool INTERNAL :
 Utilization mark (high/low)    : 100 / 0
 Subnet size (first/next)       : 0 / 0
 Total addresses                : 254
 Leased addresses               : 2
 Pending event                  : none
 1 subnet is currently in the pool :
 Current index      IP address range                Leased addresses
 192.168.1.4        192.168.1.1 - 192.168.1.254     2
```

How many addresses have been leased?

_____

In the output from the command, what do you think Current index means?

_____

Task 3: Reflection

What are some advantages and disadvantages of using DHCP?

_____

_____

_____

_____

What are some advantages and disadvantages of using SDM to configure DHCP on a router as compared to the IOS CLI?

_____

_____

_____

_____

Lab 5-6: Configuring PAT with SDM and Static NAT Using Cisco IOS (5.3.8)

Objectives

- Configure basic router settings using the IOS CLI.

- Configure NAT Port Address Translation (PAT) with the Cisco SDM Basic NAT Wizard.

- Verify NAT translations using IOS commands.

- Configure and verify static NAT using IOS.

Background/Preparation

In Task 1 of this lab, you will use the Cisco SDM Basic NAT Wizard to configure Network Address Translation (NAT) using a single external global IP address. This address can support connections to the Internet from many internal private addresses. This is also referred to as NAT Overload or Port Address Translation (PAT).

You will use IOS show commands to view the PAT translations. In Task 2 you will use IOS to configure the customer router for static NAT to permanently map a public address to an internal server private address.

Cisco SDM is a web-based GUI application that supports HTTP connections to the router. If the router has SDM installed and it is configured for HTTP server access (the default for most Cisco routers), SDM is activated automatically when you connect to the router using a browser.

This lab assumes the use of a Cisco 1841 router. You can use another router model as long as it can support SDM. If you are using a supported router that does not have SDM installed, you can download the latest version free of charge from http://www.cisco.com/pcgi-bin/tablebuild.pl/sdm.

From this URL, view or download the document "Downloading and Installing Cisco Router and Security Device Manager." This document provides instructions for installing SDM on your router. It lists specific model numbers and IOS versions that can support SDM, and the amount of memory required.

Figure 5-39 shows the topology for this lab, and Table 5-3 includes the device configuration information.

Figure 5-39   Topology Diagram for Lab 5-6

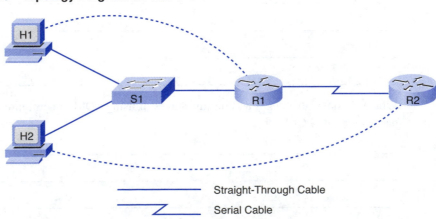

Table 5-3   Device Configuration Information for Lab 5-6

Device	Hostname	Fast Ethernet 0/0 Address and Subnet Mask	Serial 0/0/0 Address and Subnet Mask	Interface Type
R1	CustomerRouter	192.168.1.1	209.165.200.225 255.255.255.0	DTE 255.255.255.224
R2	ISP	—	209.165.200.225 255.255.255.224	DCE

The following resources are required:

- Cisco 1841 ISR with SDM version 2.4 installed to act as the customer router
- Cisco 1841 router (or another router) to act as the ISP router
- Cisco 2960 switch (or another switch/hub) to connect hosts H1 and H2 and the customer router
- Windows XP computer (host H1) with Internet Explorer 5.5 or higher and Sun Java Runtime Environment (JRE) version 1.4.2_05 or later (or Java Virtual Machine [JVM] 5.0.0.3810)
- Windows XP computer (host H2)
- Straight-through Category 5 Ethernet cables
- Null serial cable (R1 to R2)
- Console cables (H1 to R1 and H2 to R2)
- Access to the host H1 and H2 command prompt
- Access to the host H1 and H2 network TCP/IP configuration

From each host computer, start a HyperTerminal session to the attached router.

Note: Make sure that the routers and switches have been erased and have no startup configurations. Instructions for erasing both switch and router are provided in Appendix C. Check with your instructor if you are unsure how to do this.

Task 1: Configure Basic Router Settings Using IOS, and Configure PAT Using SDM

Step 1.   Build the network and configure host computer IP settings.

a.   Make sure that the host computers are connected according to Figure 5-39.

Note: An SDM router other than the 1841 may require a host connection to a port other than FastEthernet 0/0 on CustomerRouter to access SDM.

b.   Configure the hosts with static IP addresses using the following settings:

Host H1:

IP address: 192.168.1.5

Subnet mask: 255.255.255.0

Default gateway: 192.168.1.1

Host H2:

IP address: 192.168.1.9

Subnet mask: 255.255.255.0

Default gateway: 192.168.1.1

Step 2.   Configure CustomerRouter basic settings with the IOS CLI.

Configure the hostname, passwords, and interfaces in preparation for the use of SDM:

```
Router> enable
Router# config t
Router(config)# hostname CustomerRouter
CustomerRouter(config)# enable secret class
CustomerRouter(config)# username admin privilege 15 secret cisco123
CustomerRouter(config)# line console 0
CustomerRouter(config-line)# password cisco
CustomerRouter(config-line)# login
CustomerRouter(config-line)# line vty 0 4
CustomerRouter(config-line)# password cisco
CustomerRouter(config-line)# login
CustomerRouter(config-line)# exit
CustomerRouter(config)# interface FastEthernet0/0
CustomerRouter(config-if)# description LAN Default Gateway
CustomerRouter(config-if)# ip address 192.168.1.1 255.255.255.0
CustomerRouter(config-if)# no shutdown
CustomerRouter(config-if)# interface Serial0/0/0
CustomerRouter(config-if)# ip address 209.165.200.225 255.255.255.224
CustomerRouter(config-if)# description WAN link to ISP
CustomerRouter(config-if)# no shutdown
CustomerRouter(config-if)# exit
CustomerRouter(config)# ip http server
CustomerRouter(config)# ip http authentication local
```

Step 3.   Configure ISP router basic settings with the IOS CLI.

Configure the hostname, passwords, and interfaces:

```
Router> enable
Router# configure terminal
Router(config)# hostname ISP
ISP(config)# enable secret class
ISP(config)# line console 0
ISP(config-line)# password cisco
ISP(config-line)# login
ISP(config)# line vty 0 4
ISP(config-line)# password cisco
ISP(config-line)# login
```

```
ISP(config-line)# exit
ISP(config)# exit
ISP(config)# interface serial 0/0/0
ISP(config-if)# description WAN link to CustomerRouter
ISP(config-if)# ip address 209.165.200.226 255.255.255.224
ISP(config-if)# clock rate 64000
ISP(config-if)# no shutdown
ISP(config-if)# exit
ISP(config)# ip http server
ISP(config)# exit
```

Step 4.   Connect to CustomerRouter using SDM.

    a.   On host H1, disable any popup blocker programs. Popup blockers prevent SDM windows from appearing.

    b.   The SDM GUI does not load automatically on the router. You must open the web browser to reach the SDM. Open the web browser on the PC, and connect to http://192.168.1.1 (the IP address of the CustomerRouter FastEthernet 0/0 interface—the H1 default gateway).

Note: If you cannot connect and see the login screen, check your cabling and connections, and make sure that the PC's IP configuration is correct.

    c.   In the **Connect to** dialog box, enter **admin** for the username and **cisco123** for the password. These were configured in Step 2. Click **OK**. The main SDM web application starts. If you are prompted to use HTTPS, click **Cancel**. If a Security Warning window appears, click **Yes** to trust the Cisco application.

    d.   Verify that you are using the latest version of SDM. The initial SDM screen that appears immediately after the login shows the current version number. It is also displayed on the main SDM screen, along with the IOS version.

Note: If the current SDM version is not 2.4 or higher, notify your instructor before continuing with this lab. You will need the latest zip file on the host H1 PC for use in updating the router SDM application. If you need to update SDM, in the SDM GUI, choose **Tools > Update SDM** to specify the location of the zip file and install the update.

Step 5.   Configure SDM to show Cisco IOS CLI commands.

    a.   In the main SDM window, choose **Edit > Preferences**.

    b.   Check the **Preview commands before delivering to router** check box. With this check box checked, you can see the Cisco IOS CLI configuration commands that SDM generates before they are sent to the router. You can learn about Cisco IOS CLI commands this way.

Step 6.   Launch the Basic NAT Wizard.

    a.   With the Basic NAT Wizard, shown in Figure 5-40, you are configuring overloaded NAT or Port Address Translation (PAT). From the **Configure** menu, click the **NAT** button to view the NAT configuration page. Click the **Basic NAT** radio button, and then click **Launch the selected task**.

Figure 5-40   SDM NAT Configuration

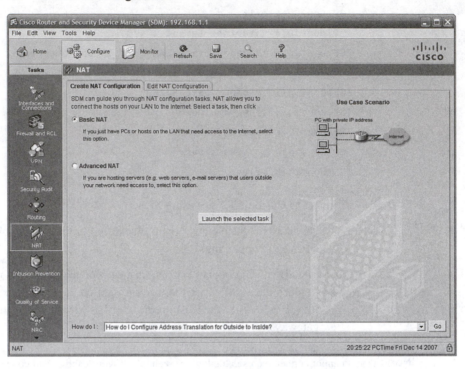

b.   In the Welcome to the Basic NAT Wizard window, shown in Figure 5-41, click **Next**.

Figure 5-41   SDM NAT Wizard

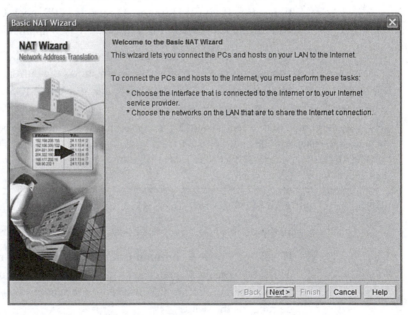

Step 7.   Select the WAN interface for NAT.

a.   In the screen shown in Figure 5-42, choose the WAN interface Serial0/0/0 from the list. Check the box for the IP address range that represents the internal network of 192.168.1.0 to 192.168.1.255. This is the range that requires conversion using the NAT process.

Figure 5-42   Selecting the WAN Interface

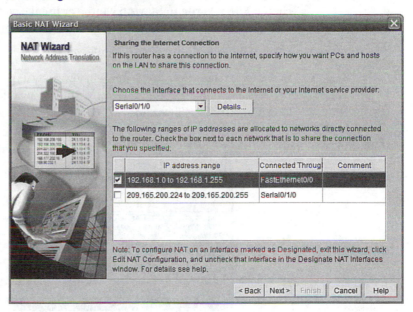

b. Click **Next**. After you have read the Summary of the Configuration, click **Finish**.

c. In the Deliver Configuration to Router window, shown in Figure 5-43, review the CLI commands that were generated by the Cisco SDM. These are the commands that will be delivered to the router to configure NAT. The commands can also be manually entered from the CLI to accomplish the same task. Check the box for **Save running config. to router's startup config.**

Figure 5-43   Delivering the Configuration to the Router

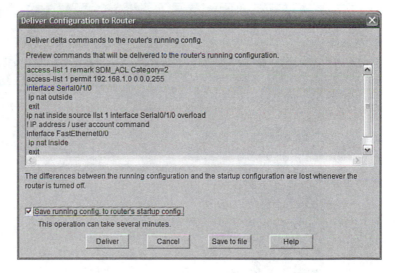

Note: By default, the commands that you just generated update the router's running configuration file only when delivered. If the router is restarted, the changes you made will be lost. Checking this box updates the startup config file as well and, when the router is restarted, it loads the new commands into the running config.

If you choose to not save the commands to the startup config at this time, in SDM choose **File > Write to Startup config**, or use the **copy running-config startup-config** command from the CLI using a terminal or Telnet session.

d. Click **Deliver** to finish configuring the router.

e. In the Commands Delivery Status window, shown in Figure 5-44, notice the text that says that the running config was successfully copied to the startup config. Click **OK** to exit the Basic NAT wizard.

Figure 5-44   SDM Commands Delivery Status

The final NAT screen, shown in Figure 5-45, shows that the inside interface is the FastEthernet interface and the outside interface the serial interface. The internal private (Original) addresses will be translated dynamically to the external public address.

Figure 5-45   Final NAT Configuration

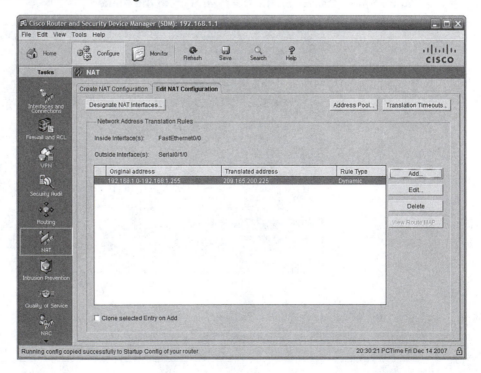

From SDM, choose **File > Exit** to end the SDM session. Click **Yes** to confirm exiting SDM.

Step 8.   Verify NAT functionality.

a.   On host H1, open a Command Prompt window by choosing **Start > Run** and entering **cmd**. Alternatively, you may choose **Start > All Programs > Accessories > Command Prompt**.

From H1, ping the ISP router serial interface at 209.165.200.226. Are the pings successful?

_____

b.   From the CustomerRouter terminal window, use the command **show ip nat translations** to see the H1 internal private address being translated to the Serial 0/0/0 external public address:

```
CustomerRouter# show ip nat translations
Pro  Inside global      Inside local     Outside local      Outside global
icmp 209.165.200.225:512 192.168.1.2:512  209.165.200.226:512 209.165.200.226:512
```

What type of NAT address is the host H1 IP address?

_____

What type of NAT address is the CustomerRouter Serial 0/0/0 public IP address?

_____

What type of NAT address is the ISP router Serial 0/0/0 public IP address?

_____

Ping first from H1 and then from H2, in quick succession, to the ISP router serial interface at 209.165.200.226. Are the pings successful?

_____

c.   Use the command **show ip nat translations** to see the H1 internal private address being translated to the Serial 0/0/0 external public address:

```
CustomerRouter# show ip nat translation
Pro  Inside global      Inside local     Outside local      Outside global
icmp 209.165.200.225:512 192.168.1.2:512  209.165.200.226:512 209.165.200.226:512
icmp 209.165.200.225:513 192.168.1.9:512  209.165.200.226:512 209.165.200.226:513
```

What is the difference between the H1 and H2 translations?

_____

_____

_____

_____

d. Use the command **clear ip nat translations** * to clear the router NAT translation table, and issue the **show ip nat translations** command again to verify they are gone:

```
CustomerRouter# clear ip nat translations *
CustomerRouter# show ip nat translations
```

e. From H1, ping the CustomerRouter Serial interface at 209.165.200.225. Are the pings successful?

_____

f. From the CustomerRouter terminal window, use the command **show ip nat translations** again to see address translations.

Were there any translations this time? Why or why not?

_____

_____

_____

g. On host H1, open a browser such as Internet Explorer, and enter the IP address of the ISP router serial interface at http://209.165.200.226 in the address area. What is the result?

_____

_____

h. Display the NAT translation table using the **show ip nat translations** command. Does the translation appear in the NAT table?

_____

```
CustomerRouter# show ip nat translations
Pro  Inside global        Inside local      Outside local      Outside global
tcp  209.165.200.225:1059 192.168.1.2:1059  209.165.200.226:80 209.165.200.226:80
---  209.165.200.229      192.168.1.9
```

For the translation of the H1 IP inside local address, what are the protocol and the *IP address:port number* for the outside local and outside global (destination) addresses? What does the outside port number represent?

_____

_____

Task 2: Configure and Verify Static NAT Using IOS

Step 1. Configure a static mapping for the server.

Host H2, with IP address 192.168.1.9/24, has been designated as the public web server. Thus, it needs a permanently assigned public IP address. This mapping is defined using a static NAT mapping.

a. To configure a static IP NAT mapping, use the **ip nat inside source static** command:

```
CustomerRouter(config)# ip nat inside source static 192.168.1.9
  209.165.200.229
```

This permanently maps public address 209.165.201.229 to 192.168.1.9, the inside address of the web server. Any attempt to access public address 209.165.200.229 will be passed by the router to host H2 at private address 192.168.1.9.

b. Display the NAT translation table using the **show ip nat translations** command. Does the static mapping appear in the output of the command?

```
CustomerRouter# show ip nat translations
Pro Inside global     Inside local    Outside local    Outside global
--- 209.165.200.229   192.168.1.9     ---              ---
```

Step 2.   Test static NAT functionality.

a. Ping from host H1 to the public static NAT address mapped to host H2. Are the pings successful?

---

b. Display the NAT translation table using the **show ip nat translations** command. Does the translation appear in the NAT table?

```
CustomerRouter# show ip nat translations
Pro  Inside global        Inside local     Outside local        Outside global
icmp 209.165.200.225:512 192.168.1.2:512 209.165.200.229:512 209.165.200.229:512
---  209.165.200.229      192.168.1.9      ---                  ---
```

What is the outside local and outside global address used in the translation?

---

c. From the ISP router HyperTerminal window, ping the H2 host with the static NAT translation by entering **ping 192.168.1.9**. Are the pings successful?

---

d. From the ISP router, ping the public static addresses mapped to the H2 internal server at 209.165.201.229. Are the pings successful? Why or why not?

What is the translation of the inside global address to inside local host address?

```
CustomerRouter# show ip nat translations
Pro  Inside global      Inside local    Outside local    Outside global
icmp 209.165.200.229:5  192.168.1.9:5   209.165.200.226:5  209.165.200.226:5
---  209.165.200.229    192.168.1.9     ---              ---
```

Step 3.   Save the router configurations.

Save the running configuration to the startup configuration in privileged EXEC mode.

```
CustomerRouter# copy running-config startup-config
ISP# copy running-config startup-config
```

Task 3: Reflection

Consider the skills that you need to configure NAT using Cisco IOS CLI commands. What do you think the benefits and disadvantages are of using the Cisco SDM?

_____

_____

_____

_____

Why do you think that the default, after the commands have been generated, is to update the router's running configuration file only when delivered? Why not always update the startup config file as well? What are the advantages and disadvantages of one over the other?

_____

_____

_____

_____

_____

Lab 5-7: Managing Router Configuration Files Using HyperTerminal (5.3.9a)

Objectives

- Establish a HyperTerminal session with a router, and use it to capture and save the running configuration as a text file for use as a backup.

- Edit the file using the Notepad text editor, and use HyperTerminal to restore the backup configuration to the router.

- Modify the file using Notepad, and use HyperTerminal to transfer the file and configure a different router.

- Verify network connectivity.

Background/Preparation

In this lab you will build a multirouter network and configure one of the routers. You will capture the running-config to a text file using HyperTerminal. You will edit the file using the Notepad text editor so that it can be used as a backup for the first router. You will then modify the file so that it can be used to configure the second router. The HyperTerminal capture option can be very useful not only for configuration files but also for capturing command output and for documentation purposes. It is a simple way to save whatever is displayed on the screen of the PC acting as a console to the router.

Set up a network similar to the one shown in Figure 5-46 and described in Table 5-4. Any router that meets the interface requirements displayed in the figure—such as 800, 1600, 1700, 1800, 2500, 2600, or 2800 routers, or a combination of these—can be used. See the Router Interface Summary table in Appendix C to determine which interface identifiers to use based on the equipment in the lab. Depending on the model of router, output may vary from what is shown in this lab.

Figure 5-46   Topology Diagram for Lab 5-7

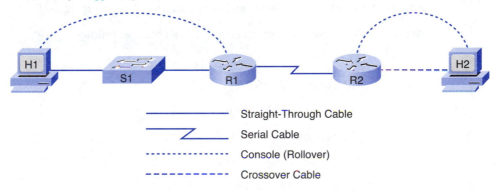

Table 5-4   Device Configuration Information for Lab 5-7

Device	Hostname	Interface	IP Address	Subnet Mask
R1	R1	Serial 0/0/0 (DCE)	172.17.0.1	255.255.0.0
		FastEthernet 0/0	172.16.0.1	255.255.0.0
R2	R2	Serial 0/0/0 (DTE)	172.17.0.2	255.255.0.0
		FastEthernet 0/0	172.18.0.1	255.255.0.0

The following resources are required:

- Two routers, each with an Ethernet and serial interface
- Two Windows XP computers
- Two straight-through Category 5 Ethernet cables (H1 to switch and switch to R1)
- Crossover Category 5 Ethernet cable (H2 to router R2)
- Null serial cable
- Console cables (from H1 and H2 to routers R1 and R2)
- Access to the computer host command prompt
- Access to the computer host network TCP/IP configuration

From each computer, start a HyperTerminal session to the attached router.

Note: Be sure that the routers and switches have been erased and have no startup configurations. Instructions for erasing both switch and router are provided in Appendix C. Check with your instructor if you are unsure how to do this.

Task 1: Configure Host IP Settings

Step 1.   Be sure that the hosts are connected according to Figure 5-46.

Step 2.   Configure static IP addresses on both hosts as follows:

Host H1:

IP address: 172.16.0.2

Subnet mask: 255.255.0.0

Default gateway: 172.16.0.1

Host H2:

IP address: 172.18.0.2

Subnet mask: 255.255.0.0

Default gateway: 172.18.0.1

Task 2: Log In to Router R1, and Configure the Basic Settings

Step 1.   Configure the hostname for R1:

```
Router> enable
Router# configure terminal
Router(config)# hostname R1
```

Step 2.   Configure console, vty, and enable secret passwords. Configure logging synchronous for the console line:

```
R1(config)# line console 0
R1(config-line)# password cisco
R1(config-line)# login
R1(config-line)# logging synchronous
R1(config-line)# line vty 0 4
R1(config-line)# password cisco
R1(config-line)# login
R1(config-line)# exit
R1(config)# enable secret class
R1(config)# exit
```

Step 3.   Configure a message-of-the-day (MOTD) banner and **no ip domain lookup**:

```
R1(config)# banner motd #Unauthorized Use Prohibited#
R1(config)# no ip domain lookup
```

Step 4.   Configure the R1 FastEthernet and Serial interfaces:

```
R1(config)# interface serial 0/0/0
R1(config-if)# description WAN link to R2
R1(config-if)# ip address 172.17.0.1 255.255.0.0
R1(config-if)# clock rate 64000
R1(config-if)# no shutdown
R1(config-if)# exit
R1(config)# interface FastEthernet 0/0
R1(config-if)# description R1 LAN Default Gateway
R1(config-if)# ip address 172.16.0.1 255.255.0.0
R1(config-if)# no shutdown
R1(config-if)# end
```

Task 3: Display the R1 Router Configuration

Issue the **show running-config** command in privileged EXEC mode, and verify all the configuration commands you have entered so far. Note that this command can be abbreviated as **sh run**.

```
R1# show running-config
```

Task 4: Save the Configuration on R1

Save the running configuration to the startup configuration from the privileged EXEC prompt:

```
R1# copy running-config startup-config
```

Note: Save the running configuration for the next time the router is restarted. The router can be restarted by either a software **reload** command or a power cycle. The running configuration will be lost if it is not saved. The router uses the startup configuration when it is started.

Task 5: Start Capturing the Running Configuration File

Step 1.   From HyperTerminal, clear the screen by choosing **Edit > Clear Screen** and **Edit > Clear Backscroll**. This is not required to capture the file but makes it easier to see what you are doing.

Step 2.   Use HyperTerminal to capture all text displayed on its screen to a text file by choosing **Transfer > Capture Text**.

Step 3.   Specify the name of the router plus your initials for the filename, and use .txt for the extension. An example is R1-XYZ.txt, where XYZ are your initials. Browse to find the desired location to store the text file on the computer. This file will be edited and used in later steps of this lab. Click the **Start** button to start capturing text.

Step 4.   Write down the name and location where you saved this file:

Step 5.   Enter the **show running-config** command from privileged EXEC mode to begin capturing the output. Press the **Spacebar** when the "- More -" prompt appears. The **show running-config** command is used to display the active configuration file for the router that is stored in RAM.

Task 6: Stop Capturing the Configuration File

Discontinue capturing the output of the router configuration to a text file. From HyperTerminal, choose **Transfer > Capture Text > Stop**.

Task 7: Clean Up the Captured Configuration File

Step 1.   Start Notepad. From the Windows Desktop, choose **Start > Run**. Enter **Notepad** and press the **Enter** key.

Step 2.   From Notepad, choose **File > Open**. Navigate to the file you captured, select it, and click **Open**. Alternatively, navigate to the saved .txt file and double-click to open the file in Notepad.

Note: The captured text file has information not required for configuring a router. For example, the "- More -" prompts are not required to configure a router. To put this in a form to be "pasted" back into the router, remove any unnecessary information from the captured configuration. Be careful not to delete any part of the commands.

To add comments to the configuration to explain its various parts, use the exclamation mark (!). The router will ignore any comment in a router configuration that starts with an exclamation mark. Therefore, write any kind of comment that helps you understand the configuration.

Step 3.   At the end of each of the interface sections for configured interfaces, add the command **no shutdown**:

```
interface serial 0/0/0
description WAN link to R2
ip address 172.17.0.1 255.255.0.0
clock rate 64000
no shutdown
```

Step 4.   Edit the line **enable secret 5 $1$8SfN$BFKkGdAdqowyyoKm8WSmn/**. Delete the number 5 and the encrypted string, and replace them with the password **class**.

Step 5.   Edit the line **banner motd ^CUnauthorized Use Prohibited^C**. Replace each ^C character with a number sign (#).

Step 6.   Delete the lines that contain the following:

Show running-config

Building configuration

Current configuration:

- More -

Lines that appear after the word End

Example 5-9 shows an unedited captured running configuration from an 1841 router. This router has a four-port integrated FastEthernet switch. The lines that need to be kept are highlighted.

Note: The router IOS inserts a number of commands by default. These can be removed if you want, in most cases, because the IOS automatically reinserts them. Generally, the commands you want to keep are the ones you configure yourself.

Example 5-9   Unedited Configuration File

```
Building configuration...
Current configuration : 1073 bytes
!
version 12.4
service timestamps debug datetime msec
service timestamps log datetime msec
no service password-encryption
!
hostname R1
!
boot-start-marker
boot-end-marker
!
enable secret 5 $1$8SfN$BFKkGdAdqowyyoKm8WSmn/
!
no aaa new-model
```

```
ip cef
!
no ip domain lookup
!
interface FastEthernet0/0
 description R1 LAN Default Gateway
 ip address 172.16.0.1 255.255.0.0
 duplex auto
 speed auto
!
interface FastEthernet0/1
 no ip address
 shutdown
 duplex auto
 speed auto
!
interface FastEthernet0/1/0
!
interface FastEthernet0/1/1
!
interface FastEthernet0/1/2
!
interface FastEthernet0/1/3
!
interface Serial0/0/0
 description WAN link to R2
 ip address 172.17.0.1 255.255.0.0
clock rate 64000
 no fair-queue
!
interface Serial0/0/1
 no ip address
 shutdown
!
interface Vlan1
 no ip address
 shutdown
!
!
ip http server
no ip http secure-server
```

```
!
control-plane
!
banner motd ^CUnauthorized Use Prohibited^C
!
line con 0
 password cisco
 logging synchronous
 login
line aux 0
line vty 0 4
 password cisco
 login
!
scheduler allocate 20000 1000
end
```

Step 7.   The edited version of the 1841 running configuration is shown in Example 5-10. You only need to specify the interfaces you want to configure, as long as the startup-config file is erased before you load this file. The other interfaces will be shut down by default.

Caution: If the startup-config is not erased before this file is loaded, these new commands will be comingled with the existing configuration and may produce unpredictable results.

Example 5-10   Edited Configuration File

```
hostname R1
!
enable secret class
!
no ip domain lookup
!
interface FastEthernet0/0
 description R1 LAN Default Gateway
 ip address 172.16.0.1 255.255.0.0
 no shutdown
!
interface Serial0/0/0
 description WAN link to R2
 ip address 172.17.0.1 255.255.0.0
 clock rate 64000
 no shutdown
!
banner motd #Unauthorized Use Prohibited#
```

```
!
line con 0
 password cisco
 logging synchronous
 login
line aux 0
line vty 0 4
 password cisco
 login
!
end
```

Step 8.   When you're finished editing the file in Notepad, be sure to save it.

Task 8: Erase the Current Startup Configuration, and Restart the Router

Any form of backup that has not been tested could be a problem in a failure situation. This includes backup configurations. The backup configuration must be tested. The test should be scheduled during low network usage periods, because the router will have to be taken offline. All users who may be affected should be notified well in advance to ensure that the downtime will not be an inconvenience.

Step 1.   Before testing the backup configuration, erase the startup configuration. From the HyperTerminal session, enter the command **erase startup-config** at the enable router prompt. This deletes the configuration file from NVRAM.

Step 2.   When the following prompt appears, press **Enter** to continue:

```
erasing the nvram filesystem will remove all configuration files!
  Continue? [confirm]
```

Step 3.   Confirm that the startup configuration has been deleted by entering **show startup-config** at the router prompt. What does the router show after this command is entered?

Step 4.   Enter the **reload** command at the privileged EXEC mode prompt to reboot the router. If you're told that the configuration has been modified and are asked whether you want to save, enter **N** and press **Enter**.

Step 5.   When asked to proceed with the reload, press **Enter** to confirm. The router restarts.

Step 6.   When prompted to enter the initial configuration dialog, enter **N** and press **Enter**.

Step 7.   When prompted to terminate autoinstall, enter **Y** and press **Enter**, or press **Enter** to accept the default response ([yes]). Press **Enter** again to go to the router prompt. What is the router prompt now?

Task 9: Reconfigure the R1 Router from the Saved Text File

Use the **send file** command in HyperTerminal to restore the new configuration. The edited version of the router configuration file from the previous task will be copied into the area of memory known as the clipboard.

Step 1. Change to privileged EXEC mode. Why isn't a password required?

_____

Step 2. Enter global configuration mode using the command **configure terminal**.

Step 3. From HyperTerminal, choose **Transfer > Send Text File**.

Step 4. Navigate to the location where you saved the file previously, and select the file.

Each line in the text file will be used to configure the router as it is read from the text file.

Step 5. Observe the file as it loads, and note any errors. These may result from typing errors.

What is the most obvious indication that the router configuration has been restored?

_____

Step 6. Enter **end** and press **Enter** or press **Ctrl-Z** to exit global configuration mode.

Step 7. Save the new configuration file as the startup configuration file in NVRAM. Use the command **copy running-config startup-config** to save the newly created router configuration.

Step 8. Verify that the running configuration is correct by using the **show running-config** command.

Task 10: Modify the R1 Text File, and Use It to Configure the R2 Router

Step 1. Before configuring the R2 router, erase the startup configuration, and issue the **reload** command to reboot the router.

Step 2. Using Windows Explorer or another method, copy the R1-XYZ.txt file and name it R2-XYZ.txt, where XYZ are your initials.

Step 3. Edit the new R2 text file and modify the necessary parameters to match those in the device configuration table for router R2:

- Router hostname.

- Serial 0/0/0 interface address and description. Remove the **clock rate** command, because this is the DTE side of the connection to R1.

- FastEthernet 0/0 interface address and description.

- Be sure to add the **no shutdown** command to the FastEthernet 0/0 and Serial 0/0/0 interfaces.

Step 4. Save the modified R2 text file in Notepad.

Step 5. Enter configuration mode by entering **enable** and then **configure terminal**. Make sure that the router prompt displays **Router(config)#**.

Step 6. From HyperTerminal, choose **Transfer > Send Text File**.

Step 7. Navigate to the location where you saved the R2 text file, and select the file.

Step 8.   Observe the file as it loads, and note any errors. These may result from typing errors. If R2 is a different model router, these can also result from IOS version variations and interface designation inconsistencies (such as entering S0/0/0 when the router interface should be S0/0).

What is the most obvious indication that the router configuration has been restored?

_____

Step 9.   Enter **end** and press **Enter** or press **Ctrl-Z** to exit global configuration mode.

Step 10.   Save the new configuration file as the startup configuration in NVRAM. Use the command **copy running-config startup-config** to save the newly created router configuration.

Step 11.   Verify that the running configuration is correct by using the **show running-config** command.

Task 11: Verify That the Network Is Functioning

Step 1.   From host H1, ping the R1 FastEthernet 0/0 interface IP address at 172.16.0.1. Are the pings successful?

_____

Step 2.   From host H2, ping the R2 FastEthernet 0/0 interface IP address at 172.18.0.1. Are the pings successful?

_____

Step 3.   From R1, ping the R2 Serial 0/0/0 interface IP address at 172.17.0.2. Are the pings successful?

_____

If any of the pings were not successful, troubleshoot the host and router configs until they are.

Note: You will not be able to ping from host H1 to H2, because routing has not been configured.

Lab 5-8: Managing Router Configuration Files Using TFTP (5.3.9b)

Objectives

- Download and install TFTP server software.

- Use TFTP to copy the router running configuration from a router to the TFTP server.

- Edit the file using the Notepad text editor, and copy the new configuration from the TFTP server to the router.

Background/Preparation

In this lab you will download and install TFTP server software and use it to back up the router running configuration to the TFTP server. You will then edit the file using the Notepad text editor and copy the new configuration from the TFTP server to the router.

Set up a network similar to the one shown in Figure 5-47, and use the device configuration information shown in Table 5-5. Any router that meets the interface requirements displayed in Figure 5-47—such as 800, 1600, 1700, 1800, 2500, 2600, or 2800 routers, or a combination of these—can be used. See the Router Interface Summary table in Appendix C to determine which interface identifiers to use based on the equipment in the lab. Depending on the model of router, output may vary from what is shown in this lab.

Figure 5-47   Topology Diagram for Lab 5-8

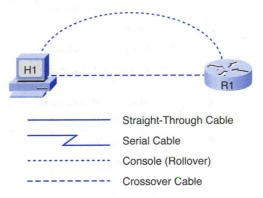

Table 5-5   Device Configuration Information for Lab 5-8

Device	Hostname	Interface	IP Address	Subnet Mask
R1	R1	FastEthernet 0/0	172.17.0.1	255.255.0.0

The following resources are required:

- One router with an Ethernet interface

- One Windows XP computer (or optional Discovery Server)

- Crossover Category 5 Ethernet cable (H1 to router R1)

- Console cable (from H1 to R1)

- Access to the computer host command prompt
- Access to the computer host network TCP/IP configuration

Note: Instead of using a PC and installing TFTP server software, you may use the Discovery server, because it has Linux-based TFTP server software preinstalled. Check with your instructor on the availability of a Discovery Server CD. The Discovery Server can take the place of host H1 shown in Figure 5-47. The IP addresses used to configure host H1 and R1 in this lab are compatible with Discovery Server.

From host H1, start a HyperTerminal session to the attached router.

Note: Be sure that the router has been erased and has no startup configurations. Instructions for erasing the router are provided in Appendix C. Check with your instructor if you are unsure how to do this.

Task 1: Build the Network and Verify Connectivity

Step 1.   Configure the TFTP server host.

Connect the router and host H1 according to Figure 5-47. Configure the host H1 IP address as follows:

IP address: 172.17.0.2

Subnet mask: 255.255.0.0

Default gateway: 172.17.0.1

Step 2.   Log in to router R1, and configure the basic settings.

a.   Configure the hostname for R1:
```
Router> enable
Router# configure terminal
Router(config)# hostname R1
```

b.   Configure console, vty, and enable secret passwords. Configure logging synchronous for the console line:
```
R1(config)# line console 0
R1(config-line)# password cisco
R1(config-line)# login
R1(config-line)# logging synchronous
R1(config-line)# line vty 0 4
R1(config-line)# password cisco
R1(config-line)# login
R1(config-line)# exit
R1(config)# enable secret class
R1(config)# exit
```

c.   Configure a message-of-the-day (MOTD) banner and **no ip domain lookup**:
```
R1(config)# banner motd #Unauthorized Use Prohibited#
R1(config)# no ip domain lookup
```

   d. Configure the R1 FastEthernet interface:

```
R1(config)# interface FastEthernet 0/0
R1(config-if)# description R1 LAN Default Gateway
R1(config-if)# ip address 172.17.0.1 255.255.0.0
R1(config-if)# no shutdown
R1(config-if)# end
```

Step 3.   Display the R1 router configuration.

Issue the **show running-config** command in privileged EXEC mode, and verify all the configuration commands you have entered so far. Note that this command can be abbreviated as **sh run**.

```
R1# show running-config
```

Step 4.   Verify basic connectivity.

Host H1 will be the TFTP server, and router R1 will be the TFTP client. To copy files to and from a TFTP server, you must have IP connectivity between the server and the client.

From host H1, ping the router FastEthernet interface at IP address 172.17.0.1. Are the pings successful?

_____

If the pings were not successful, troubleshoot the host and router configs until they are.

Step 5.   Save the configuration on R1.

Save the running configuration to the startup configuration from the privileged EXEC prompt:

```
R1# copy running-config startup-config
```

Task 2: Use TFTP to Save a Cisco IOS Configuration

Step 1.   Obtain and install the TFTP server application.

Many free TFTP servers are available. A search for "free TFTP server" will identify several you can choose from to download. This lab uses the SolarWinds TFTP Server application. SolarWinds' free TFTP Server is a multithreaded TFTP server commonly used to upload and download executable images and configurations to routers and switches. The free TFTP Server runs on most Microsoft operating systems, including Windows XP, Vista, 2000, and 2003. The SolarWinds software requires the Microsoft .NET 2.0 framework to install. This software can be downloaded free from http://www.solarwinds.com/.

Note: Check with your instructor for a copy of SolarWinds or another TFTP server that you can install.

Go to the SolarWinds website and download the free TFTP server software and save it to your desktop:

http://www.solarwinds.com/downloads/

Double-click the SolarWinds TFTP application to begin installation. Click **Next**. Agree to the license agreement, and accept the default settings. After SolarWinds has finished installing, click **Finish**.

Step 2.   Start the TFTP application.

Start the TFTP server by choosing **Start > Programs > SolarWinds TFTP Server > TFTP Server**. You see the screen shown in Figure 5-48.

Figure 5-48   TFTP Server

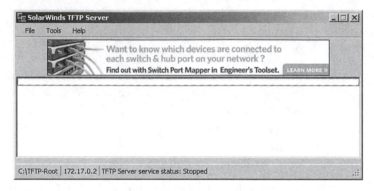

Step 3.   Configure the TFTP server.

a.   To configure the TFTP server, choose **File > Configure**. The screen that appears should be similar to Figure 5-49. On the **General** tab, ensure that the default TFTP Server Root Directory is set to C:\TFTP-Root.

Figure 5-49   TFTP Server Configuration

b.   Click the **Security** tab, shown in Figure 5-50. Ensure that **Permitted Transfer Types** is set to **Send and Receive files**. Set **IP Address Restrictions** to allow transfers from only the router R1 IP address (From 172.17.0.1 To 172.17.0.1).

Figure 5-50   TFTP Security

c. From the **General** tab, click the **Start** button to activate the TFTP server.

When you're finished, click OK. The screen should look similar to that shown in Figure 5-51.

Figure 5-51   TFTP Server Screen

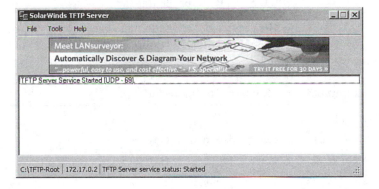

On which well-known UDP port number is the TFTP server operating?

_____

Leave the TFTP Server GUI window open so that you can view the activity as the file is copied.

Step 4.   Save the R1 configuration to the TFTP server.

From the HyperTerminal session on router R1, begin the TFTP upload to the TFTP server using the command **copy running-config tftp**. Respond to the prompts as shown here. The default name of the destination file is the device name (r1), followed by a dash and confg. If you're successful, the output from the router terminal window should look similar to the following:

```
R1# copy running-config tftp
```

```
Address or name of remote host []? 172.17.0.2
```

```
Destination filename [r1-confg]? <ENTER>
!!
1078 bytes copied in 1.188 secs (907 bytes/sec)
R1#
```

Step 5.   Verify the TFTP server activity.

Observe the TFTP Server GUI window, which should show the connection entries for the transfer of the running-config file to the server. The output should look similar to Figure 5-52.

Figure 5-52   TFTP Connection Entries

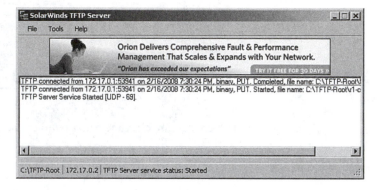

Step 6.   Verify the TFTP server file transfer.

Use Microsoft Word or WordPad to examine the contents of file C:\TFTP-Root\r1-confg on the host H1 TFTP server. The contents should be similar to those shown in Example 5-11.

Example 5-11   Sample Configuration

```
version 12.4
service timestamps debug datetime msec
service timestamps log datetime msec
no service password-encryption
!
hostname R1
!
boot-start-marker
boot-end-marker
!
enable secret 5 $1$ofoK$Ur.oKj60xRxiVk3u1kDBu1
!
no aaa new-model
ip cef
!
no ip domain lookup
!
```

```
interface FastEthernet0/0
 description R1 LAN Default Gateway
 ip address 172.17.0.1 255.255.0.0
 duplex auto
 speed auto
!
interface FastEthernet0/1
 no ip address
 shutdown
 duplex auto
 speed auto
!
interface FastEthernet0/1/0
!
interface FastEthernet0/1/1
!
interface FastEthernet0/1/2
!
interface FastEthernet0/1/3
!
interface Serial0/0/0
 no ip address
 shutdown
!
interface Serial0/0/1
 no ip address
 shutdown
!
interface Vlan1
 no ip address
!
ip http server
no ip http secure-server
!
control-plane
!
banner motd #Unauthorized Use Prohibited#
!
line con 0
 password cisco
 logging synchronous
 login
line aux 0
```

```
line vty 0 4
 password cisco
 login
!
scheduler allocate 20000 1000
```

Task 3: Use TFTP to Restore a Cisco IOS Configuration

Step 1.   Erase the R1 startup-config and restart the router.

Before testing the backup configuration, erase the router startup configuration. From the HyperTerminal session, enter the command **erase startup-config** at the enable router prompt. This deletes the configuration file from NVRAM.

    a.   When you're told that erasing the NVRAM file system will remove all configuration files, and you're asked whether you want to continue, press **Enter**.

    b.   Confirm that the startup configuration has been deleted by entering **show startup-config** at the router prompt.

    c.   Enter the **reload** command at the privileged EXEC mode prompt to reboot the router. If you're told that the configuration has been modified, and you're asked whether you want to save, enter **N** and press **Enter**.

    d.   When you're asked to proceed with the reload, press **Enter** to confirm. The router restarts.

    e.   When prompted to enter the initial configuration dialog, enter **N** and press **Enter**.

    f.   When prompted to terminate autoinstall, enter **Y** and press **Enter**, or press **Enter** to accept the default response ([yes]). Press **Enter** again to go to the router prompt.

Step 2.   Restore the R1 configuration from the TFTP server.

When the startup-config is erased and the router is reloaded, the router interfaces are shut down by default and are no longer configured with IP addresses. This results in loss of connectivity between the router and the TFTP server. To copy the saved config file back to the router, connectivity must be reestablished with the TFTP server.

    a.   Configure R1 FastEthernet 0/0 with an IP address, and enable the interface:

```
Router> enable
Router# conf t
Enter configuration commands, one per line. End with CNTL/Z.
Router(config)# interface fastethernet 0/0
Router(config-if)# ip address 172.17.0.1 255.255.0.0
Router(config-if)# no shutdown
Router(config-if)# exit
```

    b.   Verify connectivity by pinging from host H1 to the R1 FastEthernet 0/0 IP address 172.17.0.1. Are the pings successful?

If the pings were not successful, troubleshoot until they are.

c. Download the R1 configuration file from the TFTP server using the command **copy tftp startup-config**. Respond to the prompts as shown here. If you're successful, the output from the router terminal window should look similar that shown in Example 5-12.

Example 5-12   Sample Router Configuration

```
Router# copy tftp startup-config
Address or name of remote host [172.17.0.2]? <ENTER>
Source filename [r1-confg]? <ENTER>
Destination filename [startup-config]? <ENTER>
Accessing tftp://172.17.0.2/r1-confg...
Loading r1-confg from 172.17.0.2 (via FastEthernet0/0): !
[OK - 1078 bytes]
[OK]
1078 bytes copied in 12.780 secs (84 bytes/sec)
Router#
*Feb 17 02:18:33.551: %SYS-5-CONFIG_NV_I: Nonvolatile storage configured from
  tftp://172.17.0.2/r1-confg by console
Router#
```

d. View the configuration in NVRAM to verify an accurate transfer using the **show startup-config** command. The configuration should be the same as what was configured in Task 1, Step 2.

e. Reload the router, and click **No** at the prompt that says "Configuration has been modified."

The previous configuration should be restored, and the router's hostname should now be R1.

Task 4: Reflection

How do you think TFTP could be used to manage networking device files in an Enterprise network?

_____

_____

_____

Lab 5-9: Planning a WAN Upgrade (5.4.3)

Objective

- Create a business proposal based on a scenario of an organization that requires a WAN upgrade.

Background/Preparation

You are employed at an ISP. A local business has contacted your company to inquire about establishing a WAN connection between its main office and a second office that will be opening in the next few months. You have been assigned to the new business account. Your job is to provide a proposal that outlines what the ISP can offer the business to meet its requirements for a new WAN connection.

You visit the site to examine the existing setup. Currently, only one employee gains access to the head office using dialup access and a 56-Kbps modem. This employee requires access to a database server that stores the data for the company's contact management software application. The new office will initially have ten people who need to access the database server, but the business anticipates that the second office will have 30 employees within a year.

After running some benchmarking tests, you determine that each connection to the database uses 50 Kbps to function optimally. You also discover that if the database server cannot be reached, the application fails to function, and the employee can no longer work. After talking with the customer, you learn that the availability of the new WAN connection is critical to the business and that service disruption needs to be kept to a minimum.

The ISP you work for has a variety of WAN connection options for business customers. Table 5-6 lists available options that you can offer the customer.

Table 5-6　ISP Connectivity Options

WAN Connection	Upstream Bandwidth	Downstream Bandwidth	SLA Availability	Cost
Dialup	33.6 Kbps	53 Kbps	No	$12.95/month
ADSL	1 Mbps	3 Mbps	No	$64.95/month
Fractional T1	768 Kbps	768 Kbps	Yes	$149.95/month
T1	1.544 Mbps	1.544 Mbps	Yes	$299.95/month
Fractional T3	9.264 Mbps	9.264 Mbps	Yes	$1399.95/month
T3	45 Mbps	45 Mbps	Yes	$2499.95/month

Task 1: Identify the Business Requirements for the WAN Upgrade

Outline the business requirements for a WAN connection between the two offices. Document these requirements in the WAN Upgrade Proposal included in this lab.

Task 2: List Available WAN Options for the Business

List the ISP offerings for WAN connections that meet or exceed the requirements for the WAN connection between the two offices. Include this information in your proposal.

Task 3: Identify the Best WAN Connection Option for the Business

Based on the list of suitable WAN connection options, identify the most appropriate WAN connection for the business. Justify your answer.

Task 4: Group Discussion

Assemble in groups of two or more to discuss your answers. Identify any items you missed when filling out the WAN Upgrade Proposal, and correct your proposal as needed.

WAN Upgrade Proposal

Objective

- Establish WAN connectivity between the two offices for a company.

Existing Environment

Main Office

- Presently 45 employees connected over a 100-Mbps Ethernet network

- Main database server that stores data for a contact management application

- Single external user using dialup to connect to the corporate network to access the database server

Second Office

- Opening in a few months

- Across town from the main office

- Initially will have ten people, but is anticipated to grow to 30 people over the next year

Business Requirements

The new WAN connection between the two offices must meet these minimum specifications to satisfy the business requirements:

1.

2.

Available WAN Connection Options

The following WAN connection choices meet the business requirements:

1.

2.

3.

WAN Upgrade Proposal   continued

Recommendation

The following WAN connection is recommended to satisfy the requirements:

_____

_____

_____

_____

Lab 5-10: Powering Up a Switch (5.5.2)

Objectives

- Set up a new Cisco LAN switch.

- Connect a computer to the router console interface.

- Configure HyperTerminal so that the computer can communicate with the switch.

Background/Preparation

This lab focuses on the initial setup of the Cisco 2960 switch. If a Cisco 2960 switch is not available, you can use another switch model. The information in this lab applies to other switches. The Cisco 2960 switch is a fixed-configuration, standalone device that does not use modules or flash card slots. It is appropriate for small to medium-sized businesses and ISP-managed customers.

The following resources are required:

- Cisco 2960 switch or a comparable switch

- Power cable

- Windows PC with terminal emulation program

- Console cable

Task 1: Position and Ground the Switch (Optional)

Note: This task is optional and is required only if the switch is being set up for the first time. Read through this section to become familiar with the process.

Step 1.   Position the switch chassis to allow unrestricted airflow for chassis cooling. Keep at least 3 inches (7.6 cm) of clear space beside the cooling inlet and exhaust vents.

Step 2.   Connect the chassis to a reliable earth ground using a ring terminal and size 14 AWG (2 mm) wire using these tasks:

Note: Your instructor should inform you where a reliable earth ground is.

a.   Strip one end of the ground wire to expose approximately 3/4 inch (20 mm) of conductor.

b.   Crimp the 14 AWG (2 mm) green ground wire to a UL Listed/CSA certified ring terminal using a crimping tool that is recommended by the ring terminal manufacturer.

c.   Attach the ring terminal to the chassis. Use a number 2 Phillips screwdriver and the screw that is supplied with the ring terminal, and tighten the screw.

Task 2: Connect the Computer to the Switch

Connect the PC to the Cisco 2960 switch using an RJ-45-to-DB9 connector console cable, as shown in Figure 5-53. To view the switch startup messages, connect the PC to the switch, power up the PC, and start the terminal emulation program before powering up the switch.

Caution: To ensure adequate cooling, never operate the switch unless the cover is installed.

Figure 5-53   Connecting a PC to the Switch Console Port

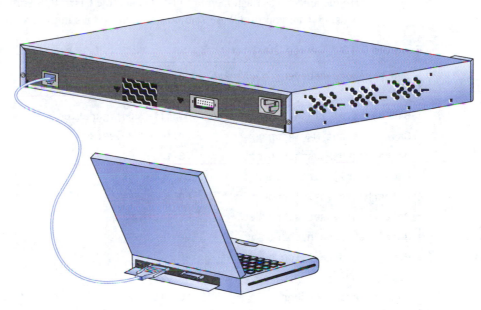

Task 3: Configure the PC Terminal Emulation Program

Step 1.   Load the terminal emulation program on the PC.

Step 2.   Select a COM port that matches the port where the RJ-45-to-DB9 connector is connected to the PC. The COM port is usually COM1 or COM2.

Step 3.   Configure the terminal emulation parameters as follows:

- 9600 baud

- 8 data bits

- No parity

- 1 stop bit

- No flow control and no parity

Task 4: Power Up the Switch

Step 1.   Connect the power cable to the Cisco 2960 switch and to the electrical outlet to power the switch on. The 2960 switch does not have a power switch, but other switches may have one.

As the switch powers on, the power-on self-test (POST) begins. POST is a series of tests that run automatically to ensure that the switch is functioning properly. The POST lasts approximately 1 minute. When the switch begins the POST, the System, Status, Duplex, and Speed LEDs turn green. The System LED blinks green, and the other LEDs remain solid green.

Step 2.   Observe the startup messages as they appear in the terminal emulation program window. While these messages are appearing, do not press any keys on the keyboard. Pressing a key interrupts the switch startup process. Some examples of startup messages displayed are the amount of flash memory installed and the Cisco IOS software version the computer is using. Can you find these sample startup messages in the Example 5-13?

Example 5-13   Switch Start-up

```
The password-recovery mechanism is enabled.


64K bytes of flash-simulated non-volatile configuration memory.
Base ethernet MAC Address         : 00:1D:46:3D:99:80
Motherboard assembly number       : 73-10390-04
Power supply part number          : 341-0097-02
Motherboard serial number         : FOC11285FYV
Power supply serial number        : DCA112784DB
Model revision number             : D0
Motherboard revision number       : A0
Model number                      : WS-C2960-24TT-L
System serial number              : FOC1129X57C
Top Assembly Part Number          : 800-27221-03
Top Assembly Revision Number      : A0
Version ID                        : V03
CLEI Code Number                  : COM3L00BRB
Hardware Board Revision Number    : 0x01



Switch   Ports  Model               SW Version         SW Image
------   -----  -----               ----------         ----------
*   1    26     WS-C2960-24TT-L     12.2(25)SEE3       C2960-LANBASE-M
```

The example shows that 64 KB of flash memory is installed in the switch and that the Cisco IOS software version is 12.2(25)SEE3. Startup messages are generated by the switch's operating system. The messages vary depending on the software installed on the switch. These messages can scroll by quickly and can take a few minutes to stop.

When the POST completes successfully, the System LED remains green. The other LEDs turn off and then reflect the switch operating status.

Step 3.   When the switch is finished starting up, the following system message appears in the terminal emulation window:

```
Would you like to enter the initial configuration dialog? [yes/no]:
```

If this message does not appear, the switch may have been previously configured and needs to be restored to the factory default settings according to the procedure described in Appendix C.

Step 4.   Turn off the switch by disconnecting the power cord from the switch.

Task 5: Troubleshoot a Nonworking Switch

If the switch fails the POST, the System LED turns amber. If your switch fails the POST, unplug the switch and inform your instructor.

Task 6: Reflection

1. Which LED shows after the POST completes successfully, and what color does it show?

   A. Status LED blinks green

   B. Speed LED blinks green

   C. Status LED blinks amber

   D. System LED is solid green

   _____

2. What is the minimum amount of space required around the Cisco 2960 switch ventilation openings?

   A. 1 inch (2.54 cm)

   B. 2 inches (5.08 cm)

   C. 3 inches (7.6 cm)

   _____

3. When the Cisco 2960 switch is finished starting up for the first time, what happens?

   A. You are asked to perform an initial configuration of the switch.

   B. You are not asked to do anything. The switch system prompt appears.

   C. If your switch is configured with Cisco SDM, you are told that con0 is available.

   _____

Lab 5-11: Configuring the Cisco 2960 Switch (5.5.4)

Objectives

- Configure the initial switch global settings.

- Configure the hosts' PCs, and attach them to the switch.

- Configure a router, and attach it to the switch.

- Configure a switch management VLAN IP address.

- Configure basic port security.

- Configure port duplex and speed settings.

Background/Preparation

In this lab, you will connect multiple hosts and a router to the switch and test connectivity. You will configure port security for a switch port, as well as port speed and duplex settings. This lab focuses on the basic configuration of the Cisco 2960 switch using Cisco IOS commands. The Cisco Catalyst 2960 switch comes preconfigured and only needs to be assigned basic security information before being connected to a network. To use an IP-based management product or Telnet with a Cisco switch, you must configure a management IP address. You will configure VLAN 1 to provide IP access to management functions. The information in this lab applies to other switches, but the command syntax may vary.

Figure 5-54 shows the topology for this lab, and Table 5-7 summarizes the device configuration information.

Figure 5-54   Topology Diagram for Lab 5-11

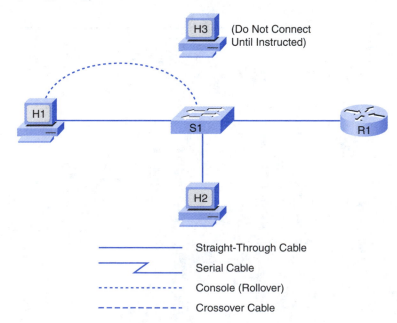

Table 5-7   Device Configuration Information for Lab 5-11

Device	Hostname	Interface	IP Address	Subnet Mask	Default Gateway	Switch Port
S1	CustomerSwitch	VLAN 1	192.168.1.5	255.255.255.0	192.168.1.1	—
R1	CustomerRouter	Fa0/1	192.168.1.1	255.255.255.0	—	Fa0/5
H1	H1	NIC	192.168.1.2	255.255.255.0	192.168.1.1	Fa0/11
H2	H2	NIC	192.168.1.4	255.255.255.0	192.168.1.1	Fa0/18
H3	H3	NIC	192.168.1.6	255.255.255.0	192.168.1.1	None

The following resources are required:

- Cisco 2960 switch or a comparable switch

- Router with an Ethernet interface to connect to the switch

- Three Windows-based PCs, one with a terminal emulation program

- RJ-45-to-DB9 connector console cable

- Three straight-through Ethernet cables

- Access to the PC command prompt

- Access to the PC network TCP/IP configuration

Note: Go to the "Erasing and Reloading the Switch" instructions in Appendix C. Perform those tasks on the switch in this lab assignment before continuing.

If the startup-config is erased in an SDM router, SDM will no longer come up by default when the router is restarted. You will need to build a basic router configuration using IOS commands. Refer to the procedure in Appendix C or contact your instructor.

Task 1: Connect the Hosts to the Switch, and Configure Them

Step 1.   Connect host H1 to Fast Ethernet S1 switch port Fa0/11, and connect H2 to port Fa0/18. Configure the hosts to use the same IP subnet for the address and mask as on the switch, as shown in Figure 5-54 and Table 5-7.

Step 2.   Do *not* connect host H3 to the switch yet.

Task 2: Connect the Router to the Switch, and Configure the Router

Note: If necessary, refer to Lab 5-4, "Configuring Basic Router Settings with the IOS CLI (5.3.5)," for instructions on setting the hostname, passwords, and interface addresses.

Step 1.   Connect the router to Fast Ethernet switch port Fa0/5.

Step 2.   Configure the router with a hostname of **CustomerRouter**.

Step 3.   Configure the console access and password, vty access and password, and enable secret password.

Step 4.   Configure the router Fa0/0 interface as shown in Figure 5-54.

Task 3: Perform an Initial Configuration on the Switch

Step 1.   Configure the hostname of the switch as CustomerSwitch:

```
Switch> enable
Switch# config terminal
Switch(config)# hostname CustomerSwitch
```

Step 2.   Set the privileged EXEC mode password to cisco:

```
CustomerSwitch(config)# enable password cisco
```

Step 3.   Set the privileged EXEC mode secret password to cisco123:

```
CustomerSwitch(config)# enable secret cisco123
```

Step 4.   Set the console password to cisco123:

```
CustomerSwitch(config)# line console 0
CustomerSwitch(config-line)# password cisco123
```

Step 5.   Configure the console line to require a password at login:

```
CustomerSwitch(config-line)# login
```

Step 6.   Set the vty password to cisco123:

```
CustomerSwitch(config-line)# line vty 0 15
CustomerSwitch(config-line)# password cisco123
```

Step 7.   Configure the vty to require a password at login:

```
CustomerSwitch(config-line)# login
CustomerSwitch(config-line)# end
```

Task 4: Configure the Management Interface on VLAN 1

Step 1.   Enter global configuration mode. Remember to use the new password:

```
CustomerSwitch> enable
CustomerSwitch# configure terminal
```

Step 2.   Enter interface configuration mode for VLAN 1:

```
CustomerSwitch(config)# interface vlan 1
```

Step 3.   Set the IP address, subnet mask, and default gateway for the management interface. The IP address must be valid for the local network where the switch is installed.

```
CustomerSwitch(config-if)# ip address 192.168.1.5 255.255.255.0
CustomerSwitch(config-if)# no shutdown
CustomerSwitch(config-if)# exit
CustomerSwitch(config)# ip default-gateway 192.168.1.1
CustomerSwitch(config)# end
```

Task 5: Verify Configuration of the Switch

Step 1. Verify that the IP address of the management interface on switch VLAN 1 and the IP address of host H1 are on the same local network. Use the **show running-configuration** command to check the switch's IP address configuration. You should obtain output similar to that shown in Example 5-14.

Example 5-14   Switch Configuration

```
CustomerSwitch# show running-configuration
Building configuration...

Current configuration : 1283 bytes
!
version 12.2
no service pad
hostname CustomerSwitch
!
enable secret 5 $1$XUe/$ch4WQ/SpcFCDd2iqd9bda/
enable password cisco
!
interface FastEthernet0/1
!
*** Output Omitted ***
!
interface FastEthernet0/24
!
interface Vlan1
 ip address 192.168.1.5 255.255.255.0
 no ip route-cache
!
ip default-gateway 192.168.1.1
ip http server
!
line con 0
 password cisco123
 login
line vty 0 4
 password cisco123
 login
line vty 5 15
 password cisco123
 login
!
end
```

Step 2.   Save the configuration using the following command:

CustomerSwitch# **copy running-configuration startup-configuration**

Task 6: Verify Connectivity Using ping and Telnet

Step 1.   To verify that the switch and router are correctly configured, ping the router Fa0/0 interface (default gateway) IP address from the switch CLI.

Are the pings successful?

_____

Step 2.   To verify that the hosts and switch are correctly configured, ping the switch IP address from H1.

Are the pings successful?

_____

If the pings were not successful, verify the connections and configurations again. Check to ensure that all cables are correct and that connections are seated. Check the host, switch, and router configurations.

Step 3.   Open a command prompt on H2, and enter the **telnet** command followed by the IP address assigned to switch management VLAN 1. Enter the vty password configured in Task 3. What is the result?

_____

Step 4.   At the switch prompt, issue the **show version** command. Example 5-15 shows sample output.

Example 5-15   Sample Output from the show version Command

```
CustomerSwitch# show version
Cisco IOS Software, C2960 Software (C2960-LANBASE-M), Version 12.2(25)SEE3,
  RELEASE SOFTWARE (fc2)
Copyright (c) 1986-2007 by Cisco Systems, Inc.
Compiled Thu 22-Feb-07 13:57 by myl
Image text-base: 0x00003000, data-base: 0x00AA3380


ROM: Bootstrap program is C2960 boot loader
BOOTLDR: C2960 Boot Loader (C2960-HBOOT-M) Version 12.2(25r)SEE1, RELEASE SOFTWARE
  (fc1)


Switch uptime is 11 minutes
System returned to ROM by power-on
System image file is "flash:c2960-lanbase-mz.122-25.SEE3/c2960-lanbase-mz.122-
  25.SEE3.bin"


cisco WS-C2960-24TT-L (PowerPC405) processor (revision D0) with 61440K/4088K bytes
  of memory.
```

```
Processor board ID FOC1129X57C
Last reset from power-on
1 Virtual Ethernet interface
24 FastEthernet interfaces
2 Gigabit Ethernet interfaces
The password-recovery mechanism is enabled.


64K bytes of flash-simulated non-volatile configuration memory.
Base ethernet MAC Address       : 00:1D:46:3D:99:80
Motherboard assembly number     : 73-10390-04
Power supply part number        : 341-0097-02
Motherboard serial number       : FOC11285FYV
Power supply serial number      : DCA112784DB
Model revision number           : D0
Motherboard revision number     : A0
Model number                    : WS-C2960-24TT-L
System serial number            : FOC1129X57C
Top Assembly Part Number        : 800-27221-03
Top Assembly Revision Number    : A0
Version ID                      : V03
CLEI Code Number                : COM3L00BRB
Hardware Board Revision Number  : 0x01



Switch    Ports  Model            SW Version        SW Image
------    -----  -----            ----------        ----------
*    1    26     WS-C2960-24TT-L   12.2(25)SEE3      C2960-LANBASE-M


Configuration register is 0xF
```

What is the Cisco IOS version of this switch?

_____

Step 5.   Enter **quit** at the switch command prompt to terminate the Telnet session.

Task 7: Determine Which MAC Addresses the Switch Has Learned

Step 1.   From the Windows command prompt, determine the Layer 2 addresses of the PC network interface card for each host by using the **ipconfig /all** command.

Host-A: _____

Host-B: _____

Host-C: _____

Step 2.   Determine which MAC addresses the switch has learned by using the **show mac-address-table** command at the privileged EXEC mode prompt. Sample output is given in Example 5-16.

Example 5-16   Switch MAC Address Table

```
CustomerSwitch# show mac-address-table
          Mac Address Table
-----------------------------------------

Vlan    Mac Address        Type         Ports
----    -----------        --------     -----
 All    000b.be7f.ed40     STATIC       CPU
 All    0100.0ccc.cccc     STATIC       CPU
 All    0100.0ccc.cccd     STATIC       CPU
 All    0100.0cdd.dddd     STATIC       CPU
   1       000b.db04.a5cd   DYNAMIC      Fa0/5
   1       000c.3076.8380   DYNAMIC      Fa0/11
   1       000d.1496.36ad   DYNAMIC      Fa0/18
Total Mac Addresses for this criterion: 7
```

How many dynamic addresses are there?

_____

Do the MAC addresses match the host MAC addresses?

_____

Step 3.   Review the options that the **mac-address-table** command has by using the **?** option:

CustomerSwitch(config)# **mac-address-table ?**

```
    address        address keyword
    aging-time     aging-time keyword
    count          count keyword
    dynamic        dynamic entry type
    interface      interface keyword
    multicast      multicast info for selected wildcard
```

```
notification  MAC notification parameters and history table
static        static entry type
vlan          VLAN keyword
|             Output modifiers
<cr>
```

Step 4.   Set up a static MAC address on the Fast Ethernet interface 0/18. Use the address that was recorded for H1 in Step 2. The MAC address XXXX.YYYY.ZZZZ is used in the sample statement only.

```
CustomerSwitch(config)# mac-address-table static XXXX.YYYY.ZZZZ interface
  fastethernet 0/18 vlan 1
```

Step 5.   Verify the MAC address table entries. Sample output is given in Example 5-17.

Example 5-17   Switch MAC Address Table

```
CustomerSwitch# show mac-address-table
        Mac Address Table
-------------------------------------------

Vlan    Mac Address      Type       Ports
----    -----------      --------   -----
 All    000b.be7f.ed40   STATIC     CPU
 All    0100.0ccc.cccc   STATIC     CPU
 All    0100.0ccc.cccd   STATIC     CPU
 All    0100.0cdd.dddd   STATIC     CPU
   1    000b.db04.a5cd   DYNAMIC    Fa0/5
   1    000c.3076.8380   DYNAMIC    Fa0/11
   1    000d.1496.36ad   STATIC     Fa0/18
```

How many total MAC addresses are there now?

_____

What type are they?

_____

_____

Task 8: Configure Basic Port Security

Step 1.   Determine the options for setting port security on Fast Ethernet interface 0/18:

```
CustomerSwitch# configure terminal
CustomerSwitch(config)# interface fastEthernet 0/18
CustomerSwitch(config-if)# switchport port-security ?
aging Port-security aging commands
mac-address Secure mac address
```

```
maximum Max secure addrs
violation Security Violation Mode
```

Step 2. To allow the switch port FastEthernet 0/18 to accept only one device, configure port security as follows:

```
CustomerSwitch(config-if)# switchport mode access
CustomerSwitch(config-if)# switchport port-security
CustomerSwitch(config-if)# switchport port-security mac-address sticky
CustomerSwitch(config-if)# end
```

Step 3. Check the port security settings:

```
CustomerSwitch# show port-security
```

Secure Port	MaxSecureAddr (Count)	CurrentAddr (Count)	SecurityViolation (Count)	Security Action
Fa0/18	1	0	0	Shutdown

What is the security action for port fa0/18?

_____

What is the maximum secure address count?

_____

Step 4. Display the running configuration. Sample output is provided in Example 5-18. Some output is omitted.

Example 5-18   Switch Running Configuration

```
CustomerSwitch# show running-config
Building configuration...
Current configuration : 1452 bytes
version 12.2
hostname CustomerSwitch
!
interface FastEthernet0/1
!
interface FastEthernet0/2
!
interface FastEthernet0/3
<output omitted>
!
interface FastEthernet0/18
 switchport mode access
 switchport port-security
 switchport port-security mac-address sticky
!
```

```
interface FastEthernet0/5
!
*** Output Omitted ***


mac-address-table static 000b.db04.a5cd vlan 1 interface FastEthernet0/18
!
end
```

Are there statements that directly reflect the security implementation in the listing of the running configuration?

Task 9: Connect a Different PC to the Secure Switch Port

If you do not have another PC available (H3) or you cannot disconnect the PC, please go to Alternative Task 9.

Step 1.   Disconnect host H2 from FastEthernet 0/18, and connect host H3 to the port. Host H3 has not yet been attached to the switch. From H3, ping the switch address 192.168.1.5 to generate some traffic.

Step 2.   Record any observations at the PC and the switch terminal session.

```
01:11:12: %PM-4-ERR_DISABLE: psecure-violation error detected on Fa0/18, putting
Fa0/18 in err-disable state
01:11:12: %PORT_SECURITY-2-PSECURE_VIOLATION: Security violation occurred, caused
  by MAC address 000c.3076.8380 on port FastEthernet0/18.
01:11:13: %LINEPROTO-5-UPDOWN: Line protocol on Interface FastEthernet0/18, changed
  state to down
01:11:14: %LINK-3-UPDOWN: Interface FastEthernet0/18, changed state to down
```

Step 3.   To see the configuration information for just FastEthernet port 0/18, enter the following command at the privileged EXEC mode prompt:

CustomerSwitch# **show interface fastethernet 0/18**

Step 4.   What is the state of this interface?

FastEthernet0/18 is

Line protocol is

Alternative Task 9: Change the MAC Address of H2 (Optional)

If you do not have a third PC (host H3), or you are working with a remote lab setup and cannot physically disconnect H2, you may be able to use the following procedure to change the MAC address of H2. The following procedure will work for a wide variety of NICs:

Step 1.   Choose **Start > Settings > Control Panel** and double-click **Network Connections**.

Step 2.   Right-click the NIC whose MAC address you want to change, and click **Properties**.

Step 3.   Under the **General** tab, click the **Configure** button.

Step 4.   Click the **Advanced** tab.

Step 5.   Under the Property section, click **Network Address or Locally Administered Address**.

Step 6.   On the right side, under Value, enter the new MAC address. Use the original MAC address, changing only the last value. For example, if the original MAC address is 000C29C1510A, change it to 000C29C1510B.

Step 7.   Enter **c:\>ipconfig /all** to verify the changes.

Step 8.   From H2, ping the switch VLAN 1 address at 192.168.1.5:

```
c:\> ping 192.168.1.5
```

Record any observations at the PC and the switch terminal session.

_____

_____

```
01:11:12: %PM-4-ERR_DISABLE: psecure-violation error detected on Fa0/18, putting
Fa0/18 in err-disable state
01:11:12: %PORT_SECURITY-2-PSECURE_VIOLATION: Security violation occurred, caused
  by MAC address 000c.3076.8380 on port FastEthernet0/18.
01:11:13: %LINEPROTO-5-UPDOWN: Line protocol on Interface FastEthernet0/18, changed
  state to down
01:11:14: %LINK-3-UPDOWN: Interface FastEthernet0/18, changed state to down
```

Step 9.   To see the configuration information for just FastEthernet port 0/18, enter the following command at the privileged EXEC mode prompt:

```
CustomerSwitch# show interface fastethernet 0/18
```

What is the state of this interface?

FastEthernet0/18 is

_____

Line protocol is

_____

Task 10: Reactivate the Port

Step 1.   If a security violation occurs and the port is shut down, use the **no shutdown** command to reactivate it:

```
CustomerSwitch(config)# interface fastEthernet 0/18
CustomerSwitch(config-if)# no shutdown
```

Step 2.   Try reactivating this port a few times by switching between the original port 0/18 host and the new one. Plug in the original host, enter the **no shutdown** command on the interface, and ping using the command prompt. You must ping multiple times or use the **ping 192.168.1.5 -n 200** command, which sets the number of ping packets to 200, instead of 4.

Step 3.   Switch hosts and repeat Steps 1 and 2.

Task 11: Set Speed and Duplex Options for a Port

Switch port settings default to Auto-duplex and Auto-speed. If a computer with a 100-Mbps NIC is attached to the port, it automatically goes into full-duplex 100-Mbps mode. If a hub is attached to the switch port, it normally goes into half-duplex 10-Mbps mode.

Step 1.   Issue the **show interfaces** command to see the setting for ports Fa0/5, Fa0/11, and Fa0/18. This command generates a large amount of output. Press the **Spacebar** until you can see all the information for these ports. What are the duplex and speed settings for these ports?

Port Fa0/5:

_____

Port Fa0/11:

_____

Port Fa0/18:

_____

Step 2.   It is sometimes necessary to set a port's speed and duplex to ensure that it operates in a particular mode. You can set the speed and duplex with the **duplex** and **speed** commands while in interface configuration mode. To force Fast Ethernet port 5 to operate at half duplex and 10 Mbps, issue the following commands:

```
Switch> enable
Switch# configure terminal
Switch(config-if)# interface fastEthernet 0/5
Switch(config-if)# speed 10
Switch(config-if)# duplex half
Switch(config-if)# end
Switch#
```

Step 3.   Issue the **show interfaces** command again. What are the duplex and speed settings for Fa0/5 now?

Task 12: Exit the Switch

Step 1.   Enter **exit** to leave the switch and return to the welcome screen.

Step 2.   When the tasks are completed, turn off all the devices. Then remove and store the cables and adapter.

Step 3.   Erase and reload the switch.

Task 13: Reflection

Which password needs to be entered to switch from user mode to privileged EXEC mode on the Cisco switch, and why?

_____

_____

Which symbol is used to show a successful ping in the Cisco IOS software?

_____

What is the benefit of using port security?

_____

What other port-related security steps could be taken to further improve switch security?

_____

## CHAPTER 6

Lab: Routing

The lab exercises included in this chapter cover the Chapter 6 online curriculum labs. They ensure that you have mastered the practical, hands-on skills needed to work with basic routing protocols. As you work through these labs, use Chapter 6 in Part I of this book, or use the corresponding Chapter 6 in the *Working at a Small-to-Medium Business or ISP* course of the *CCNA Discovery* online curriculum, for assistance.

Lab 6-1: Creating a Network Diagram from Routing Tables (6.1.2)

Objectives

- Interpret router outputs.
- Identify networks and IP addresses for each router.
- Draw a diagram of the network topology.
- Reflect on and document the network implementation.

Background/Preparation

In this lab you will create a network topology diagram based only on the output of the **show ip route** command from two routers. The **show ip route** command displays the current state of the routing table. Routers R1 and R2 are directly connected over a Serial WAN link, and both are running the RIP dynamic routing protocol. In addition to the WAN link, each router is connected to its own local network.

Note: Some Cisco router IOS images do not support BGP. You must have an IOS image that supports BGP and enough Flash memory and RAM available to load the image. The Discovery lab configuration document lists the Cisco 1841 router with 32 MB of flash, 128 MB of DRAM, and Basic IP IOS as a requirement for this course. An 1841 router with these specifications was used to perform this lab. If you are unsure whether your router can be used for this lab, contact your instructor.

Task 1: Examine the Routing Table Entries for Router R1

Examine the **show ip route** output from router R1:

```
R1# show ip route
Codes: C - connected, S - static, I - IGRP, R - RIP, M - mobile, B - BGP
       D - EIGRP, EX - EIGRP external, O - OSPF, IA - OSPF inter area
       N1 - OSPF NSSA external type 1, N2 - OSPF NSSA external type 2
       E1 - OSPF external type 1, E2 - OSPF external type 2, E - EGP
       i - IS-IS, L1 - IS-IS level-1, L2 - IS-IS level-2, ia - IS-IS inter area
       * - candidate default, U - per-user static route, o - ODR
       P - periodic downloaded static route

Gateway of last resort is not set
```

```
C       172.17.0.0/16 is directly connected, Serial0/0/0
C       192.168.1.0/24 is directly connected, FastEthernet0/0
C       192.168.2.0/24 is directly connected, FastEthernet0/1
R       192.168.3.0/24 [120/1] via 172.17.0.2, 00:00:17, Serial0/0/0
R       192.168.4.0/24 [120/1] via 172.17.0.2, 00:00:17, Serial0/0/0
```

How many networks does router R1 know about?

_____

How many networks are directly connected to this router?

_____

How many networks have been learned from another router?

_____

Using the codes at the beginning of the **show ip route** output, what does the R mean?

_____

_____

In the routes learned via RIP, to which device does the IP address 172.17.0.2 belong?

_____

In the routes learned via RIP, to which device is Serial0/0/0 referring, and what does it mean?

_____

Task 2: Examine the Routing Table Entries for Router R2

Examine the **show ip route** output from router R2:

```
R2# show ip route
Codes: C - connected, S - static, I - IGRP, R - RIP, M - mobile, B - BGP
       D - EIGRP, EX - EIGRP external, O - OSPF, IA - OSPF inter area
       N1 - OSPF NSSA external type 1, N2 - OSPF NSSA external type 2
       E1 - OSPF external type 1, E2 - OSPF external type 2, E - EGP
       i - IS-IS, L1 - IS-IS level-1, L2 - IS-IS level-2, ia - IS-IS inter area
       * - candidate default, U - per-user static route, o - ODR
       P - periodic downloaded static route


Gateway of last resort is not set

C       172.17.0.0/16 is directly connected, Serial0/0/0
R       192.168.1.0/24 [120/1] via 172.17.0.1, 00:00:17, Serial0/0/0
R       192.168.2.0/24 [120/1] via 172.17.0.1, 00:00:17, Serial0/0/0
C       192.168.3.0/24 is directly connected, FastEthernet0/0
C       192.168.4.0/24 is directly connected, FastEthernet0/1
```

How many networks does router R2 know about?

_____

How many networks are directly connected to this router?

_____

How many networks have been learned from another router?

_____

In the routes learned via RIP, to which device does the IP address 172.17.0.1 belong?

_____

Task 3: Document Router Interfaces and IP Addresses

Based on the **show ip route** output from routers R1 and R2, fill in Table 6-1 with the router name, the names of all interfaces in use, and their IP addresses and subnet masks. Use the first available IP address for each of the local network FastEthernet interfaces.

Table 6-1   Router Interface and IP Address Information

Device Name	Interface	IP Address	Subnet Mask (Dotted Decimal and /xx)
R1			
R1			
R1			
R2			
R2			
R2			

In this example, can you determine the exact IP address of all router interfaces by looking at the routing tables?

_____

Which router interface IP addresses can you determine from the routing tables?

_____

Task 4: Create a Network Topology Diagram

Based on the **show ip route** output from routers R1 and R2, and the information you entered in Table 6-1, draw the network topology in the space provided in Figure 6-1. Be sure to include all devices, connections, interfaces, IP addresses, subnet masks, and network numbers.

Figure 6-1   Network Topology Diagram

Task 5: Reflection

What do you think would happen to the entries in the routing table on R1 if one of the Ethernet networks on R2 was disconnected?

_____

_____

What do you think would happen to the entries in the routing tables on R1 and R2 if the Serial interface on R2 was shut down?

_____

_____

_____

_____

Lab 6-2: Configuring and Verifying RIP (6.1.5)

Objective

- Implement RIP routing, and verify that network routes are being exchanged dynamically.

Background/Preparation

The RIP routing protocol is one of the most commonly used and widely supported protocols in the networking industry. Knowledge of RIP and how to configure it using the Cisco IOS CLI is essential to success as a network technician. In this lab you will build a multirouter network and use RIP to automatically propagate routes so hosts on a remote network can communicate.

Set up a network similar to the one shown in Figure 6-2 and as described in Table 6-2. You can use any router or combination of routers that meets the interface requirements in the diagram, such as 800, 1600, 1700, 1800, 2500, or 2600 routers. Refer to the section "Router Interface Summary" in Appendix C, "Lab Equipment Interfaces and Initial Configuration Restoration," to correctly identify the interface identifiers to be used based on the equipment in the lab. Depending on the model of router, your output may vary from the output shown in this lab. The lab steps are intended to be executed on each router, unless you are specifically instructed otherwise.

Figure 6-2   Lab 6-2 Topology Diagram

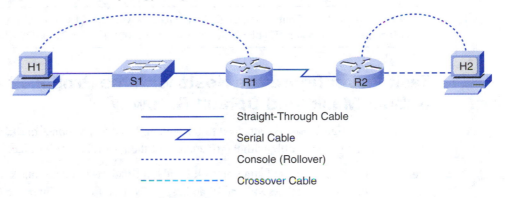

Table 6-2   Router Interface and IP Address Information

Device	Host Name	Interface	IP Address	Subnet Mask
R1	R1	Serial 0/0/0 (DCE)	172.17.0.1	255.255.255.224
		Fast Ethernet 0/0	172.16.0.1	255.255.255.0
R2	R2	Serial 0/0/0 (DTE)	172.17.0.2	255.255.255.224
		Fast Ethernet 0/0	172.18.0.1	255.255.255.0

Note: Before you begin the lab, start a HyperTerminal session, and use the "Erasing and Reloading the Router" and "Erasing and Reloading the Switch" instructions in Appendix C on all routers and switches before continuing.

The following resources are required:

- Two routers, each with an Ethernet and Serial interface. These should be non-SDM routers, if possible, because the required SDM startup configuration is deleted when the startup-config is erased.

- Two Windows XP computers.

- Straight-through Category 5 Ethernet cables (host H1 to switch and switch to router).

- Crossover Category 5 Ethernet cable (host H2 to router R2).

- Null Serial cable.

- Console cable(s) (from hosts H1 and H2 to routers R1 and R2).

- Access to the host H1 and H2 command prompt.

- Access to the host H1 and H2 network TCP/IP configuration.

Task 1: Build the Network and Configure the Routers

Step 1.   Build the network shown in Figure 6-2.

Step 2.   In global configuration mode, configure the hostnames as shown in Table 6-2. Next, configure the interfaces according to Table 6-2.

Note: Refer to Lab 5-4, "Configuring Basic Router Settings with IOS CLI (5.3.5)," if you have difficulty with the basic router configuration. That lab provides instructions for using the Cisco IOS CLI.

Task 2: Configure the Hosts with the Proper IP Address, Subnet Mask, and Default Gateway

Step 1.   Configure host H1 attached to R1 with an IP address, subnet mask, and default gateway that is compatible with the IP address of the Fast Ethernet interface (172.16.0.1).

Step 2.   Configure host H2 attached to R2 with an IP address, subnet mask, and default gateway that is compatible with the IP address of the Fast Ethernet interface (172.18.0.1).

Task 3: Check the Routing Table Entries

View the IP routing table for R1 using the **show ip route** command:

```
R1> show ip route
<output omitted>
Gateway of last resort is not set
C 172.16.0.0/16 is directly connected, FastEthernet0/0
C 172.17.0.0/16 is directly connected, Serial0/0/0
```

What is the significance of the C to the left of the 172.16.0.0 and 172.17.0.0 network entries in the routing table?

Is there a route in the R1 routing table to the R2 Ethernet network 172.18.0.0? Why?

_____

_____

Task 4: Test End-to-end Connectivity

From R1, ping the R2 router Fast Ethernet interface:

`R1#ping 172.18.0.1`

Were the pings successful?

_____

From host H1, ping host H2 (from network 172.16.0.2 to network 172.18.0.2):

`C:\>ping 172.18.0.2`

Were the pings successful?

_____

Why?

_____

_____

_____

_____

_____

_____

Task 5: Configure the Routing Protocol of the Routers

There are two versions of RIP: version 1 and version 2. It is important to specify RIP version 2 (RIPv2) in this configuration, because RIPv2 is the most current version. Some routers default to RIPv2, but it is best not to assume that this is the case.

Step 1.   In global configuration mode, enter the following on R1:

```
R1(config)# router rip
R1(config-router)# version 2
R1(config-router)# network 172.16.0.0
R1(config-router)# network 172.17.0.0
R1(config-router)# exit
R1(config)# exit
```

Step 2.   Save the R1 router configuration:

```
R1# copy running-config startup-config
```

Step 3.   In global configuration mode, enter the following on R2:

```
R2(config)# router rip version 2
R2(config-router)# version 2
R2(config-router)# network 172.17.0.0
R2(config-router)# network 172.18.0.0
R2(config-router)# exit
R2(config)# exit
```

Step 4.   Save the R2 router configuration:

```
R2# copy running-config startup-config
```

Task 6: Show the Routing Tables for Each Router

Step 1.   In enable or privileged EXEC mode, examine the routing table entries using the **show ip route** command on router R1:

```
R1# show ip route
Codes: C - connected, S - static, I - IGRP, R - RIP, M - mobile, B - BGP
       D - EIGRP, EX - EIGRP external, O - OSPF, IA - OSPF inter area
       N1 - OSPF NSSA external type 1, N2 - OSPF NSSA external type 2
       E1 - OSPF external type 1, E2 - OSPF external type 2, E - EGP
       i - IS-IS, L1 - IS-IS level-1, L2 - IS-IS level-2, ia - IS-IS
         inter area
       * - candidate default, U - per-user static route, o - ODR
       P - periodic downloaded static route

Gateway of last resort is not set

C    172.17.0.0/16 is directly connected, Serial0/0/0
C    172.16.0.0/16 is directly connected, FastEthernet0/0
R    172.18.0.0/16 [120/1] via 172.17.0.2, 00:00:17, Serial0/0/0
```

What are the entries in the R1 routing table?

_____

_____

_____

What is the significance of the R to the left of the 172.18.0.0 network entry in the routing table?

_____

What does "via 172.17.0.2" mean for this network route?

_____

_____

What does "Serial0/0/0" mean for this network route?

_____

Step 2.   Examine the routing table entries using the **show ip route** command on router R2:

```
R2# show ip route
Codes: C - connected, S - static, I - IGRP, R - RIP, M - mobile, B - BGP
       D - EIGRP, EX - EIGRP external, O - OSPF, IA - OSPF inter area
       N1 - OSPF NSSA external type 1, N2 - OSPF NSSA external type 2
       E1 - OSPF external type 1, E2 - OSPF external type 2, E - EGP
       i - IS-IS, L1 - IS-IS level-1, L2 - IS-IS level-2, ia - IS-IS
         inter area
       * - candidate default, U - per-user static route, o - ODR
       P - periodic downloaded static route

Gateway of last resort is not set

C    172.17.0.0/16 is directly connected, Serial0/0/0
R    172.16.0.0/16 [120/1] via 172.17.0.1, 00:00:13, Serial0/0/0
C    172.18.0.0/16 is directly connected, FastEthernet0/0
```

What are the entries in the R2 routing table?

_____

_____

_____

Task 7: Test End-to-end Connectivity

From R1, ping the R2 router Fast Ethernet interface:

```
R1#ping 172.18.0.1
```

Were the pings successful?

_____

From host H1, ping host H2 (from 172.16.0.2 to 172.18.0.2):

```
C:\>ping 172.18.0.2
```

Were the pings successful?

_____

If the answer is no for either question, troubleshoot the router configurations to find the error, and then do the pings again until the answer to both questions is yes. Be sure to check physical cabling for problems and bad connections, and make sure you are using the correct cable types.

Why were the pings successful this time?

_____

_____

_____

Task 8: Use debug to Observe RIP Communications

Using the **debug ip rip** command, you can see real-time communication and updates passing between routers that are running RIP.

Note: Running **debug** commands puts a significant load on the router's CPU. Do not use **debug** commands on a production network if possible.

Step 1.   On router R1, enter the **debug ip rip** command from privileged EXEC mode. Examine the exchange of routes between the two routers. The output should look similar to that shown here:

```
R1# debug ip rip
RIP protocol debugging is on
R1#
00:51:28: RIP: sending v2 update to 224.0.0.9 via Serial0/0/0 (172.17.0.1)
00:51:28: RIP: build update entries
00:51:28:        172.16.0.0/16 via 0.0.0.0, metric 1, tag 0
00:51:49: RIP: received v2 update from 172.17.0.2 on Serial0/0/0
00:51:49:        172.18.0.0/16 via 0.0.0.0 in 1 hops
00:51:57: RIP: sending v2 update to 224.0.0.9 via FastEthernet0/0
   (172.16.0.1)
00:51:57: RIP: build update entries
00:51:57:        172.17.0.0/16 via 0.0.0.0, metric 1, tag 0
00:51:57:        172.18.0.0/16 via 0.0.0.0, metric 2, tag 0
```

Step 2.   Enter the command **undebug all** to stop all debugging activity:

```
R1# undebug all
All possible debugging has been turned off
R1#
```

What interface does router R1 send and receive updates through?

_____

_____

Why does the route to 172.17.0.0 have a metric of 1 and the route to 172.18.0.0 have a metric of 2?

_____

_____

Step 3.   Log off by entering **exit**, and turn off the router.

Task 9: Reflection

What do you think would happen to the routing table on router R1 if the Ethernet network on router R2 went down?

_____

_____

What do you think would happen if router R1 was configured to run RIPv1 and R2 was configured to run RIPv2?

_____

_____

Lab 6-3: Configuring BGP with Default Routing (6.2.4)

Objectives

- Configure the customer router with an internal network that will be advertised by ISP1 via Border Gateway Protocol (BGP).

- Configure BGP to exchange routing information between ISP1 in AS 100 and ISP2 in AS 200.

Background/Preparation

A small company needs access to the Internet. It has arranged for services to be provided by its local ISP (ISP1). ISP1 connects to the Internet through ISP2 using an external routing protocol. BGP4 is the most popular routing protocol between ISPs on the Internet. In this lab, the customer router will connect to the ISP using a default route, and ISP1 will connect to ISP2 via BGP4.

Refer to the section "Router Interface Summary" in Appendix C to correctly identify the interface identifiers to be used based on the equipment in the lab.

Figure 6-3 shows the topology for this lab, and Table 6-3 shows the corresponding router interface and IP address information.

Figure 6-3   Lab 6-3 Topology Diagram

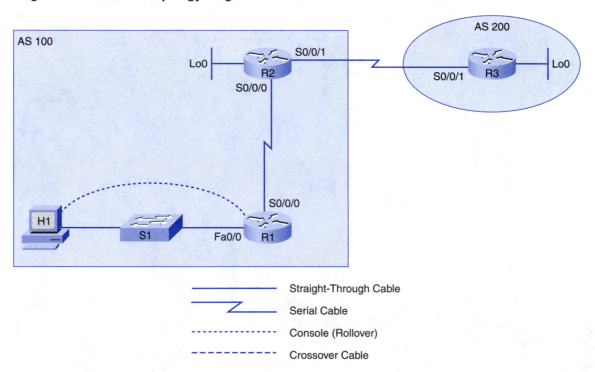

Table 6-3   Router Interface and IP Address Information

Device	Host Name	Interface	IP Address	Subnet Mask
R1	CR	Serial 0/0/0 (DTE)	10.10.10.1	255.255.255.0
		Fast Ethernet 0/0	192.168.1.1	255.255.255.0
R2	ISP1	Serial 0/0/0 (DCE)	10.10.10.2	255.255.255.0
		Serial 0/0/1 (DCE)	172.16.1.1	255.255.255.0
		Loopback 0	192.168.100.1	255.255.255.0
R3	ISP2	Serial 0/0/1 (DTE)	172.16.1.2	255.255.255.0
		Loopback 0	192.168.200.1	255.255.255.0

The following resources are required:

- Customer router (1841 or other)

- Switch (optional if a crossover cable is used between H1 and customer router)

- Two ISP routers (1841 or other routers that support BGP)

- Windows XP computer with a terminal emulation program installed

- Two straight-through category 5 Ethernet cables (H1 to switch and switch to R1)

- Two null serial cables

- Console cable to configure routers

- Access to the H1 command prompt

- Access to the H1 network TCP/IP configuration

Note: Before you begin the lab, start a HyperTerminal session. Use the "Erasing and Reloading the Router" and "Erasing and Reloading the Switch" instructions in Appendix C on all routers and switches before continuing.

Task 1: Configure Basic Information on Each Router

Step 1.   Build and configure the network according to the topology diagram shown in Figure 6-3, but do not configure a routing protocol. If necessary, refer to Lab 5-4, "Configuring Basic Router Settings with IOS CLI (5.3.5)," for instructions on setting hostnames, passwords, and interface addresses.

Step 2.   Configure the host H1 IP address and subnet mask on the customer network to be compatible with the CR router FastEthernet interface with a default gateway of 192.168.1.1.

Step 3.   Use **ping** to test connectivity between the directly connected routers. Could the CR router reach the ISP2 router?

_____

Could the customer host reach ISP1?

_____

Step 4.   Configure a loopback interface with an IP address for the ISP1 and ISP2 routers, as shown in the topology diagram in Figure 6-3. A loopback interface is a virtual interface that simulates a real network for testing purposes. Configure the loopback interface on the ISP1 router:

```
ISP1> enable
ISP1# configure terminal
ISP1(config)# interface loopback0
ISP1(config-if)# ip address 192.168.100.1 255.255.255.0
```

Step 5.   Configure the loopback interface on the ISP2 router:

```
ISP2> enable
ISP2# configure terminal
ISP2(config)# interface loopback0
ISP2(config-if)# ip address 192.168.200.1 255.255.255.0
```

Task 2: Configure the Default and Static Routes

Step 1.   On the CR router, configure the default route so that users will have access to ISP1:

```
CR(config)# ip route 0.0.0.0 0.0.0.0 10.10.10.2
```

Step 2.   On the ISP1 router, configure a static route back to the customer's network:

```
ISP1(config)# ip route 192.168.1.0 255.255.255.0 10.10.10.1
```

Step 3.   Test connectivity by issuing a ping from the host to ISP1 at 10.10.10.2.

Note: If pings are unsuccessful, troubleshoot router and host configurations and connections as necessary.

Task 3: Configure BGP on Both ISP Routers

Step 1.   Configure BGP on the ISP1 router:

```
ISP1(config)# router bgp 100
ISP1(config-router)# neighbor 172.16.1.2 remote-as 200
ISP1(config-router)# network 192.168.1.0
ISP1(config-router)# network 192.168.100.0
ISP1(config-router)# end
ISP1# copy running-config startup-config
```

Note: It is always good practice to save your configuration frequently, especially after completing major configuration steps.

Step 2.   Configure BGP on the ISP2 router:

```
ISP2(config)# router bgp 200
ISP2(config-router)# neighbor 172.16.1.1 remote-as 100
ISP2(config-router)# network 192.168.200.0
ISP2(config-router)# end
ISP2# copy running-config startup-config
```

Task 4: View the Routing Tables

The BGP configuration is complete. Check the routing table for each router.

Note: Output may vary slightly, depending on the model of router used.

Step 1.   View the ISP2 routing table:

```
ISP2# show ip route
Codes: C - connected, S - static, I - IGRP, R - RIP, M - mobile, B - BGP
       D - EIGRP, EX - EIGRP external, O - OSPF, IA - OSPF inter area
       N1 - OSPF NSSA external type 1, N2 - OSPF NSSA external type 2
       E1 - OSPF external type 1, E2 - OSPF external type 2, E - EGP
       i - IS-IS, L1 - IS-IS level-1, L2 - IS-IS level-2, ia - IS-IS
          inter area
       * - candidate default, U - per-user static route, o - ODR
       P - periodic downloaded static route

Gateway of last resort is not set

     172.16.0.0/24 is subnetted, 1 subnets
C       172.16.1.0 is directly connected, Serial0/0/0
C    192.168.200.0/24 is directly connected, Loopback0
B    192.168.1.0/24 [20/0] via 172.16.1.1, 00:40:38
B    192.168.100.0/24 [20/0] via 172.16.1.1, 00:40:38
```

Is network 192.168.1.0 in the routing table of ISP2?

What letter is to the left of the entry for 192.168.1.0?

What does the letter mean?

Is network 192.168.100.0 in the routing table?

Which router advertised network 192.168.1.0?

Step 2.   View the ISP1 routing table:

```
ISP1# show ip route
Codes: C - connected, S - static, I - IGRP, R - RIP, M - mobile, B - BGP
       D - EIGRP, EX - EIGRP external, O - OSPF, IA - OSPF inter area
       N1 - OSPF NSSA external type 1, N2 - OSPF NSSA external type 2
       E1 - OSPF external type 1, E2 - OSPF external type 2, E - EGP
       i - IS-IS, L1 - IS-IS level-1, L2 - IS-IS level-2, ia - IS-IS
          inter area
       * - candidate default, U - per-user static route, o - ODR
       P - periodic downloaded static route
```

```
Gateway of last resort is not set


     172.16.0.0/24 is subnetted, 1 subnets
C    172.16.1.0 is directly connected, Serial0/1
B    192.168.200.0/24 [20/0] via 172.16.1.2, 00:33:45
     10.0.0.0/24 is subnetted, 1 subnets
C    10.10.10.0 is directly connected, Serial0/0/0
S    192.168.1.0/24 [1/0] via 10.10.10.1
C    192.168.100.0/24 is directly connected, Loopback0
```

What network(s) did ISP1 learn from ISP2?

_____

How did ISP1 learn about network 192.168.1.0?

_____

_____

Will ISP1 advertise any networks to the customer router?

_____

Step 3.   View the CR routing table:

```
CR# show ip route

Codes: C - connected, S - static, I - IGRP, R - RIP, M - mobile, B - BGP

       D - EIGRP, EX - EIGRP external, O - OSPF, IA - OSPF inter area

       N1 - OSPF NSSA external type 1, N2 - OSPF NSSA external type 2

       E1 - OSPF external type 1, E2 - OSPF external type 2, E - EGP

       i - IS-IS, L1 - IS-IS level-1, L2 - IS-IS level-2, ia - IS-IS
          inter area

       * - candidate default, U - per-user static route, o - ODR

       P - periodic downloaded static route


Gateway of last resort is 10.10.10.2 to network 0.0.0.0



     10.0.0.0/24 is subnetted, 1 subnets

C    10.10.10.0 is directly connected, Serial0/0/0

C    192.168.1.0/24 is directly connected, FastEthernet0/0

S*   0.0.0.0/0 [1/0] via 10.10.10.2
```

Why are networks 192.168.100.0 and 192.168.200.0 not in CR's routing table?

_____

_____

Task 5: Verify Connectivity

Step 1.   Ping from host H1 on the CR Ethernet network to the loopback interface on ISP2.

Step 2.   Ping from the ISP2 router to the host H1 on the Ethernet network of CR.

Note: If pings are unsuccessful, troubleshoot router and H1 configurations and connections as necessary.

Task 6: View BGP Information on the ISP Routers

Step 1.   On the ISP1 router, view the BGP routing:

```
ISP1# show ip bgp
BGP table version is 4, local router ID is 192.168.100.1
Status codes: s suppressed, d damped, h history, * valid, > best, i -
   internal
Origin codes: i - IGP, e - EGP, ? - incomplete
```

	Network	Next Hop	Metric	LocPrf	Weight	Path
*>	192.168.1.0	10.10.10.1	0		32768	i
*>	192.168.100.0	0.0.0.0	0		32768	i
*>	192.168.200.0	172.16.1.2	0		0	200 i

Step 2.   On the ISP2 router, view the BGP routing:

```
ISP2# show ip bgp
BGP table version is 4, local router ID is 192.168.200.1
Status codes: s suppressed, d damped, h history, * valid, > best, i -
   internal
Origin codes: i - IGP, e - EGP, ? - incomplete
```

	Network	Next Hop	Metric	LocPrf	Weight	Path
*>	192.168.1.0	172.16.1.1	0		0	100 i
*>	192.168.100.0	172.16.1.1	0		0	100 i
*>	192.168.200.0	0.0.0.0	0		32768	i

Task 7: Reflection

Why doesn't ISP1 advertise any networks to the customer router?

_____

_____

## CHAPTER 7

Lab: ISP Services

The lab exercises included in this chapter cover the Chapter 7 online curriculum labs. They ensure that you have mastered the practical, hands-on skills needed to understand DNS. As you work through these labs, use Chapter 7 in Part I of this book, or use the corresponding Chapter 7 in the *Working at a Small-to-Medium Business or ISP* of the *CCNA Discovery* online curriculum, for assistance.

Lab 7-1: Editing the HOSTS File in Windows (7.3.1)

Objective

- Edit the local HOSTS file on a Windows PC to map a name to an IP address for easier identification.

Background/Preparation

You are employed at an ISP. You have been sent to a customer location to troubleshoot an issue with one of the customer's servers. A user on the network constantly needs to access the server to administer a development website that the company is working on. Currently, the customer does not have any local servers that perform the function of associating a name to the server's IP address. However, the website that the customer is working on requires the use of a name in the URL to access the site properly. Because this is the only workstation that needs to access the server based on a name, you decide to use the local HOSTS file on the Windows workstation to resolve the issue with name resolution. Your plan is to edit the local HOSTS file and add a name mapping for the web server. You will test the functionality of the name resolution using the **ping** command from the command prompt.

The following resources are required:

- PC running Windows XP
- Administrator privileges on the PC

Note: The screen layout of your Windows-based operating system may be slightly different from what appears here, but the procedure is the same.

Task 1: Locate the HOSTS File in Windows

Step 1. Click the **Start** button, choose **All Programs > Accessories**, and click the **Notepad** program.

Step 2. In Notepad, choose **File > Open**. Change the **Files of Type** to **All Files** to be able to see files other than text files. Navigate to C:\WINDOWS\system32\drivers\etc.

Step 3. Select the **HOSTS** file and click **Open**. A sample HOSTS file follows:

```
# Copyright (c) 1993-1999 Microsoft Corp.
#
# This is a sample HOSTS file used by Microsoft TCP/IP for Windows.
#
# This file contains the mappings of IP addresses to host names. Each
```

```
# entry should be kept on an individual line. The IP address should
# be placed in the first column followed by the corresponding host name.
# The IP address and the host name should be separated by at least one
# space.
#
# Additionally, comments (such as these) may be inserted on individual
# lines or following the machine name denoted by a '#' symbol.
#
# For example:
#
#      102.54.94.97       rhino.acme.com          # source server
#       38.25.63.10       x.acme.com              # x client host


127.0.0.1       localhost
```

Task 2: Edit the HOSTS File

Step 1.   At the bottom of the HOSTS file is a list of hosts that have already been recorded. Add a new entry for the web server. Enter **10.10.11.1**, press the Tab key, and then enter **webserver1**. Press the Tab key again, and add a comment preceded by a # sign. The # sign is used to signify a comment. The following shows the HOSTS file with the simulated web server mapping:

```
# Copyright (c) 1993-1999 Microsoft Corp.
#
# This is a sample HOSTS file used by Microsoft TCP/IP for Windows.
#
# This file contains the mappings of IP addresses to host names. Each
# entry should be kept on an individual line. The IP address should
# be placed in the first column followed by the corresponding host name.
# The IP address and the host name should be separated by at least one
# space.
#
# Additionally, comments (such as these) may be inserted on individual
# lines or following the machine name denoted by a '#' symbol.
#
# For example:
#
#      102.54.94.97       rhino.acme.com          # source server
#       38.25.63.10       x.acme.com              # x client host


127.0.0.1       localhost
10.10.11.1      webserver1            # simulated web server mapping
```

Step 2.   Save the updated **HOSTS** file.

Task 3: Test the New Name Mapping

Step 1.   To open the command prompt, click the **Start** button and then click **Run**. In the Run dialog box, enter **CMD** and click **OK**. Alternatively, you can choose **Start > All Programs > Accessories > Command Prompt** to open a command window.

Step 2.   In the command prompt window, enter **ping webserver1** and press the **Enter** key.

As shown in the following output, the name webserver1 was resolved to 10.10.11.1 just before the subsequent echo requests were sent out. This indicates that the HOSTS file was modified correctly and is functioning correctly in the name resolution process on this workstation. Because this is a simulation and webserver1 doesn't exist, the destination host is unreachable. If a webserver1 could be reached from this host, it would most likely have replied to the ping.

```
C:\> ping webserver1

Pinging webserver1 [10.10.11.1] with 32 bytes of data:

Request timed out.
Request timed out.
Request timed out.
Request timed out.

Ping statistics for 10.10.11.1:
    Packets: Sent = 4, Received = 0, Lost = 4 (100% loss),
```

Task 4: Reflection

What other files are located in the \etc folder with the HOSTS file?

_____

What character is used to indicate that a line of text in the HOSTS file should be treated as a comment?

_____

Lab 7-2: Examining Cached DNS Information on a Windows DNS Server (7.3.3)

Objective

- View the cached DNS information on a Windows DNS server after making a DNS request that is looked up.

Background/Preparation

In this lab, you will examine the information that is cached in a local DNS server after it has performed a lookup. You will see the configured Root servers on the DNS server. You will also see the cached top-level, second-level, and host records within each level after the lookup is complete. It is important to understand that the entire process of finding the information using the various levels of the DNS hierarchy takes only fractions of a second to complete.

The following resources are required:

- Windows 2003 Server with DNS running

- Administrative access to the server

- Internet connectivity

Note: If you do not have access to a Windows DNS server, the instructor may demonstrate this lab. If the equipment is not available to perform the lab, or if it cannot be demonstrated, read through the steps of the lab to gain a better understanding of DNS and how DNS servers operate.

Task 1: Use the Windows Server DNS Administrative Tool

Step 1.   Choose **Start > All Programs > Administrative Tools**, and then click **DNS**, as shown in Figure 7-1, to launch the DNS administrative tool.

Step 2.   Expand the Cached Lookups folder and all subfolders to see that there are no cached lookups, as shown in Figure 7-2.

Step 3.   To verify that the server has been configured to use the Root servers on the Internet, right-click the DNS server and choose **Properties**.

Step 4.   From the Properties dialog box, select the **Root Hints** tab, as shown in Figure 7-3, and verify the presence of the Root servers. Click **OK** to close the Properties dialog box.

Figure 7-1 **Starting the DNS Administrative Tool**

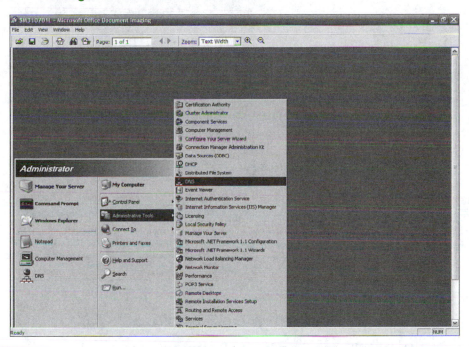

Figure 7-2 **Verifying the Absence of Cached DNS Entries**

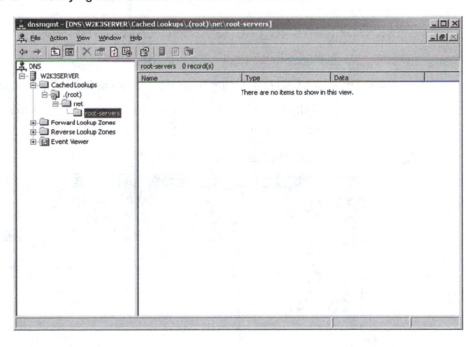

Figure 7-3   Root Hints

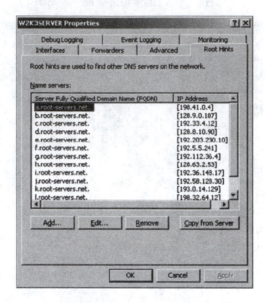

Task 2: Perform a DNS Lookup

On the DNS server, open Internet Explorer and browse to http://www.cisco.com. As soon as the web page opens, close the web browser.

Task 3: Examine the Cached DNS Entries

Step 1.   Switch back to the DNS Administrative tool.

Step 2.   From the Cached Lookups root folder, click the **Refresh** button on the toolbar.

Step 3.   Expand all the subfolders below the Cached Lookups folder to reveal the cached DNS entries, as shown in Figure 7-4.

Figure 7-4   Cached DNS Entries

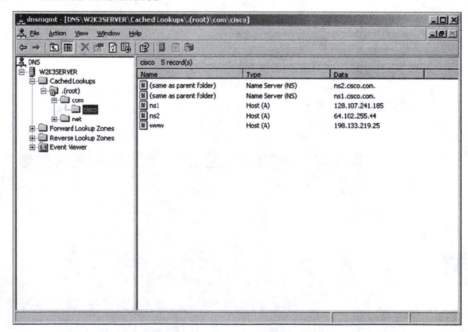

Notice that you now have a folder structure that expands down to Cisco. Within the Cisco folder, notice the two Name Server type records, which identify the two name servers that manage the Cisco.com DNS zone. Also notice the Host record for www that maps to 198.133.219.25.

Task 4: Reflection

The DNS server had to do a query to the cisco.com domain name servers to resolve the server name (www.cisco.com) to an IP address. What do you think would happen if this website is visited again within a few minutes?

_____

_____

What would happen if there are no requests for this website for a longer period of time?

_____

_____

_____

Lab 7-3: Creating Primary and Secondary Forward Lookup Zones (7.3.3)

Objective

- Create primary and secondary forward lookup zones on Windows DNS servers.

Background/Preparation

You have been asked to implement a DNS zone for a customer that has registered a second-level domain on the Internet. The customer would like to host the DNS zone on two spare servers. You go on site to configure the zone on each of the two DNS servers. One server will function as the primary DNS server, and the other will function as the secondary DNS server.

The following resources are required:

- Two Windows 2003 servers with DNS running

- Administrative access to the servers

- Internet connectivity

Note: If you do not have access to the Windows DNS servers, the instructor may demonstrate this lab. If the equipment is not available to perform the lab, or if it cannot be demonstrated, read through the steps of the lab to gain a better understanding of DNS and how DNS servers operate.

Task 1: Create a Primary Forward Lookup Zone on Windows

Step 1.   Choose **Start > All Programs > Administrative Tools**, and then click **DNS** to launch the DNS administrative tool.

Step 2.   Right-click **Forward Lookup Zones**, and then choose **New Zone**, as shown in Figure 7-5.

Figure 7-5   Creating a New DNS Zone

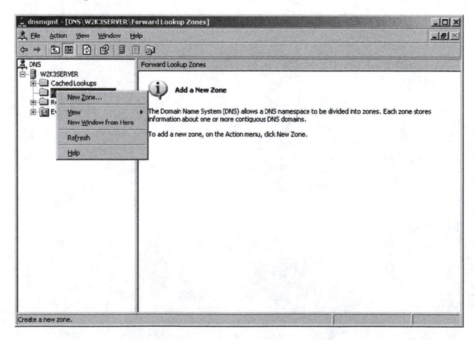

Step 3.   When the New Zone Wizard appears, as shown in Figure 7-6, click **Next**.

Figure 7-6   New Zone Wizard

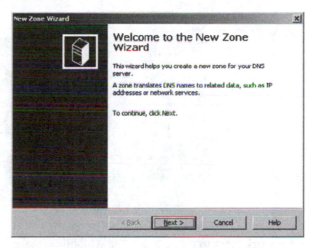

Step 4.   By default, the **Primary zone** radio button is selected, as shown in Figure 7-7. Click **Next** to create a primary zone.

Figure 7-7   Creating a Primary Forward Lookup Zone

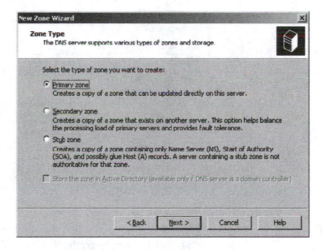

Step 5.   Enter the domain name, **example.com**, into the Zone name field, as shown in Figure 7-8, and click **Next**.

Figure 7-8   Creating an Authoritative Namespace

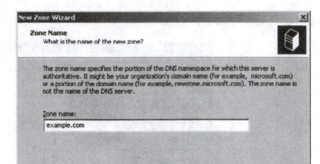

Step 6.   Click **Next** to create a new file with this name, as shown in Figure 7-9.

Figure 7-9   Creating the DNS Zone File

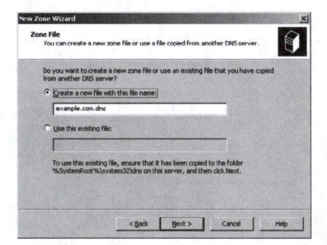

Step 7.   Notice that the option to allow dynamic updates is disabled by default, as shown in Figure 7-10. If this feature isn't properly controlled, it could allow unauthorized computers to impersonate authorized computers and populate the DNS zone file with bad information. For security reasons, you will leave this disabled. Click **Next**.

Figure 7-10   Dynamic Updates

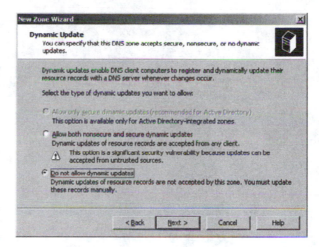

Step 8.   Review the information displayed, as shown in Figure 7-11, and click **Finish** to create the primary forward lookup zone.

Figure 7-11   Creating the Zone

Task 2: Add a Host Record to the Primary Forward Lookup Zone

Step 1.   Right-click the **example.com** forward lookup zone, and choose **New Host (A)** from the menu that appears, as shown in Figure 7-12.

Figure 7-12   Adding a New Host to a Zone

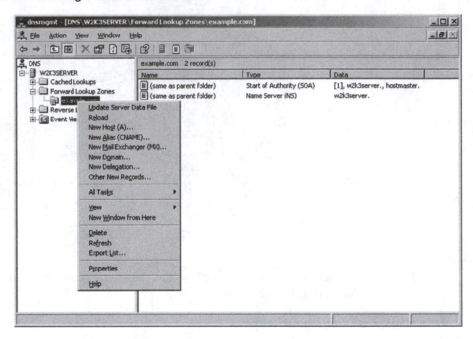

Step 2.   The New Host dialog box appears, as shown in Figure 7-13. In the Name field, enter **www**. In the IP address field, enter **192.168.1.25**. Leave the other settings at their default values. This creates a host named www.example.com, which will resolve to 192.168.1.25. Click the **Add Host** button.

Figure 7-13   Specifying a New Host

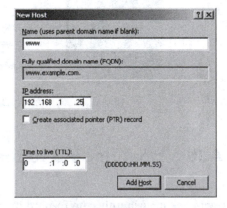

Step 3.   Click **OK**. You should receive a message stating that the host record was successfully created, as shown in Figure 7-14.

Figure 7-14   Host Record Successfully Created

Step 4.   Click **Done**.

The host record is now in your DNS zone, as shown in Figure 7-15.

Figure 7-15   Host Record Created

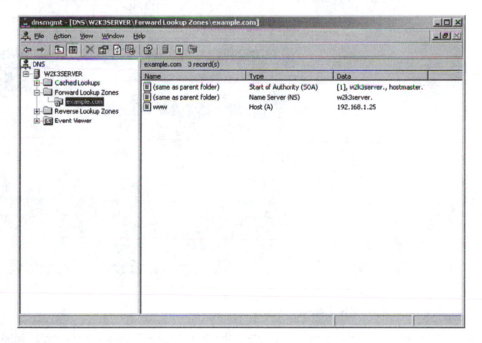

Task 3: Create a Secondary Forward Lookup Zone

Step 1.   On the second Windows DNS server, launch the DNS administrative tool. Follow the instructions in Task 1.

Step 2.   Right-click **Forward Lookup Zones**, and choose **New Zone**.

Step 3.   When the New Zone Wizard appears, click **Next**.

Step 4.   Click the **Secondary zone** radio button, as shown in Figure 7-16, and then click **Next**.

Figure 7-16   Creating a Secondary DNS Zone

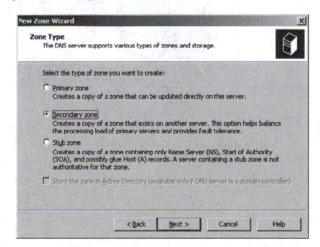

Step 5.   Enter **example.com** in the Zone name field, and then click **Next**.

Step 6.   In the IP address field, shown in Figure 7-17, enter **192.168.1.10**, which is the IP address of the primary server. Then click **Add**. Ask your instructor for the correct IP address to use in your class.

Figure 7-17   Specifying the Location of the Primary DNS Server

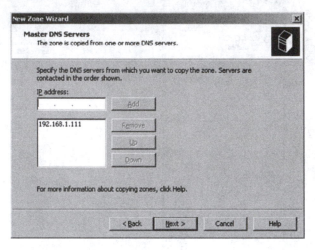

Step 7.   Click **Next**.

Step 8.   Verify the information shown in Figure 7-18, and then click **Finish**.

Figure 7-18   Creating the Secondary Zone

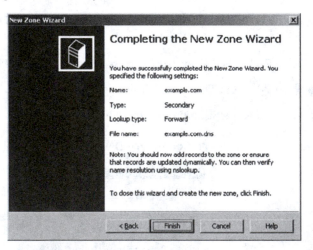

Step 9.   When you view the secondary zone, notice that the www host record created on the primary server has transferred down to the secondary server, as shown in Figure 7-19.

Figure 7-19   DNS Secondary Zone

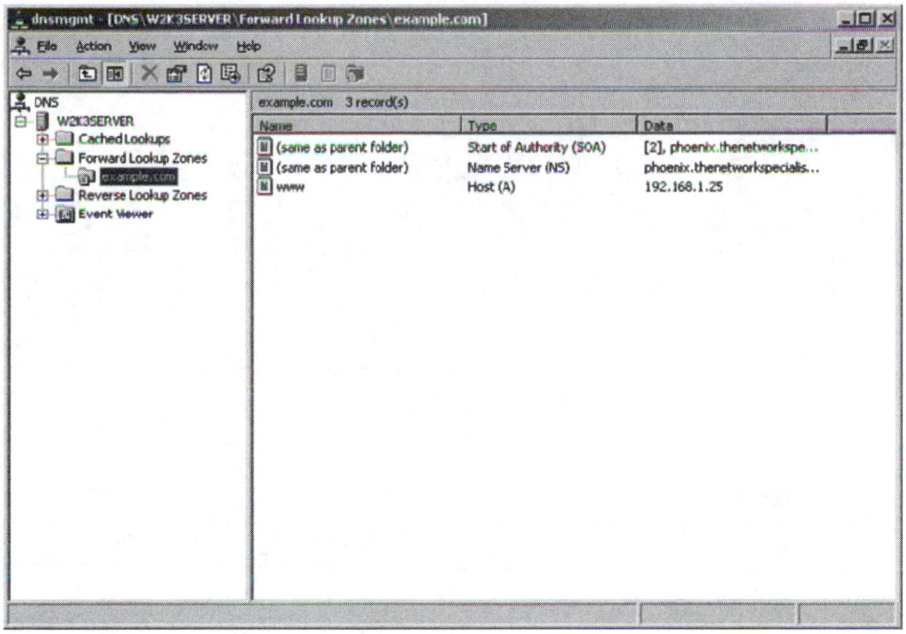

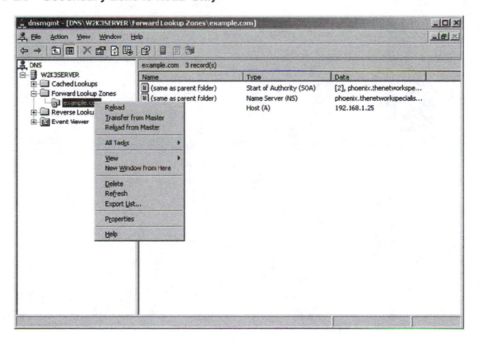

Step 10.   To verify that the zone is a secondary zone and is read-only, right-click the zone and notice that there is not an option to create any records, as shown in Figure 7-20.

Figure 7-20   Secondary Zone Is Read-Only

Task 4: Reflection

What is the major benefit of having a primary and secondary DNS server in a zone?

## CHAPTER 8

Labs: ISP Responsibility

The lab exercises included in this chapter cover all the Chapter 8 online curriculum labs. They ensure that you have mastered the practical, hands-on skills needed to work with security tools. As you work through these labs, use Chapter 8 in Part I of this book, or use the corresponding Chapter 8 in the *Working at a Small-to-Medium Business or ISP* course of the *CCNA Discovery* online curriculum, for assistance.

Lab 8-1: Securing Local Data and Transmitted Data (8.1.3)

Objectives

- Use Windows New Technology Files System (NTFS) permissions to secure local data on a Windows XP Professional Edition computer.

- Use Internet Explorer 7 to access secure websites.

Background/Preparation

This is a two-part lab. The parts can be performed together or independently.

The following resources are required:

- Windows XP Professional computer with administrator access

- NTFS on the computer with **Use Simple File Sharing** turned off (in Windows Explorer, select **Tools > Folder Options > View**)

- User accounts preconfigured for users Bob and Joe

- Internet connectivity

Part 1: Securing Local Data

In part 1 you will secure data on a computer using NTFS.

Scenario: Two users at a small business share a workstation. Confidential data is stored locally on the computer's hard drive. You have been asked to help protect the data and secure it so that only one local user can access the data. Using NTFS permissions, you will secure that local data.

The two local users are Bob and Joe. Bob will require Modify access to a folder called "Bob's Files," located below a folder called "Local Data on the C drive." Joe will not have access to "Bob's Files."

Task 1: Secure Bob's Files Folder

Step 1. Log in to the Windows XP computer as administrator.

Step 2. From the Accessories menu, launch Windows Explorer.

Step 3. Use Windows Explorer to create a folder on Local Disk (C:) called **Local Data**. Choose **File > New > Folder**.

Step 4. Click the **Local Data** folder and then right-click in the open area at the right side of the screen. Choose **New** and then choose **Folder**, and create a folder called **Bob's Files**. Repeat this process to create the folders **Common Files** and **Joe's Files**.

Step 5. Navigate to the Local Data folder, where you can see the **Bob's Files** folder, as shown in Figure 8-1.

Figure 8-1 Local Data Folders

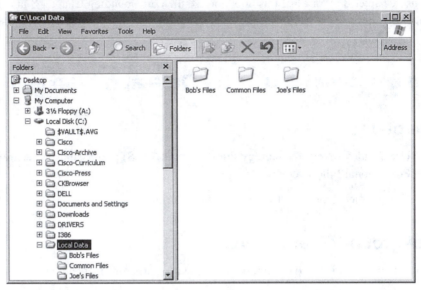

Step 6. Right-click the **Bob's Files** folder, and choose **Properties**.

Step 7. From the Bob's Files Properties dialog box, click the **Security** tab, as shown in Figure 8-2.

Figure 8-2 Bob's Files Properties

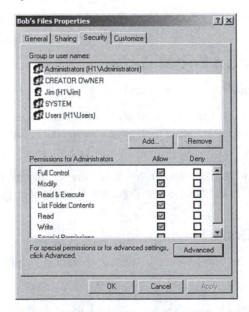

Note: You must be working on a drive that has NTFS installed; otherwise, you will not see the Security tab.

Step 8.   Notice that the permissions are dimmed and not modifiable. This restriction is due to the permissions that were inherited from a parent folder. To secure the folder, you need to disable the inherited permissions. From the **Security** tab, click the **Advanced** button.

Step 9.   Uncheck the check box next to **Inherit from parent the permission entries that apply to child objects**.

Step 10.   Click **Copy** to retain the existing permissions. The screen should look like that shown in Figure 8-3.

Figure 8-3   Advanced Security Settings for Bob's Files

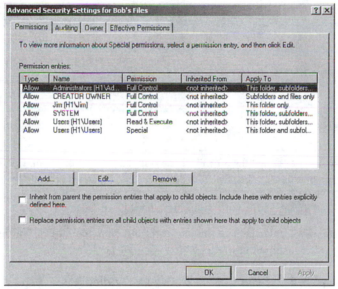

Step 11.   Click **OK**. Now that inheritance is turned off, you can modify the permissions.

Step 12.   Select the **Users** group and click **Remove**, as shown in Figure 8-4. Continue to select the other remaining users and groups, except for Administrators and SYSTEM, and click **Remove**.

Figure 8-4   Removing the Users Group from Permissions

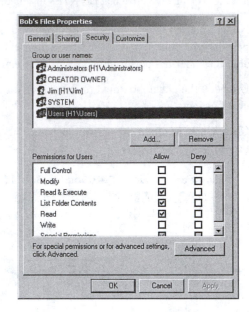

Note: Always grant the SYSTEM and Administrators groups Full Control access to directories and files to ensure that files can be backed up, recovered, and scanned properly by the computer system.

Step 13.   Add Bob to the list by clicking **Add**.

Step 14.   Enter **Bob** in the text box, and click the **Check Names** button to verify his account, as shown in Figure 8-5.

Figure 8-5   Select Users or Groups: Adding Bob

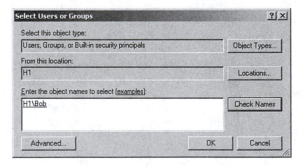

Step 15.   Now that Bob has been verified, click **OK**.

Step 16.   Bob is now added to the list. Notice that he currently has the Read & Execute, List Folder Contents, and Read permissions. Because Bob will need to write new files and delete existing files, grant Bob Modify permission. Check the check box in the **Allow** column next to **Modify**.

Step 17.   Now that Bob has been granted Modify permission, as shown in Figure 8-6, click **OK** to set the security.

Figure 8-6   Bob's Files with New Permissions

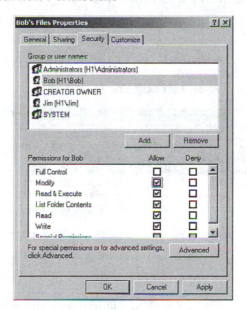

Task 2: Test Joe's Access to Bob's Files

Step 1.   Log in to the local PC as Joe, and try to access the **Bob's Files** directory.

Step 2.   You see a dialog box indicating that Joe does not have permission to access these files, as shown in Figure 8-7. Because Joe does not have Administrative access to the PC, he is prevented from gaining access to Bob's Files.

Figure 8-7   Bob's Files Folder Access Denied

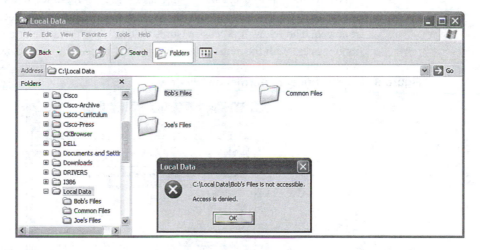

Part 2: Identifying a Secure Communication Channel When Transmitting Data over the Internet

In part 2 you will use Internet Explorer to identify secure and unsecure websites.

Scenario: You are in charge of educating end users in a small business on secure access to websites. You need to teach them how to recognize a legitimate secure website versus an untrusted secure website.

Task 1: Identify a Secure Web Page

Step 1. Launch Internet Explorer and navigate to http://www.microsoft.com/learning. This site is a typical unsecured page. Click the **MCP Members Site** link, under Member Resources. The Microsoft Learning MCP website appears, as shown in Figure 8-8.

Figure 8-8   Microsoft Learning MCP Site

Step 2. Notice that the URL changed from http to https. HTTPS is the secure version of HTTP and uses SSL for its security. Also notice the lock icon to the right of the URL. The presence of the lock icon indicates that the site is secure. Click the lock icon to see more information about the secure site.

Step 3. The popup window displays information about the issuer of the security certificate for this website. It also indicates that the connection to that server is secure. Click the **View certificates** link at the bottom of the popup window.

Step 4. The Certificate window opens. It displays the certificate that has been installed on the web server to allow it to use SSL, as shown in Figure 8-9. Notice the **Valid from** date range at the bottom. Certificates are valid for only a specific period of time, and then they must be renewed. The renewal process ensures that web server administrators continually validate their servers with the certificate authority that issued the certificate.

Figure 8-9   Certificate Information Window

Step 5.   Click the **Details** tab for more information about the certificate, as shown in Figure 8-10.

Figure 8-10   Certificate Details Tab

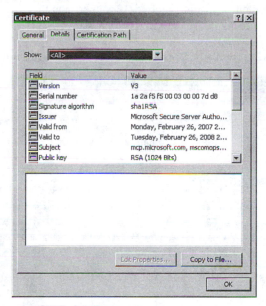

Step 6.   Click the **Certification Path** tab, as shown in Figure 8-11. It displays a hierarchical list of certification authorities that have been authorized to issue the web server certificate. Click **OK** to close the Certificate window.

Figure 8-11   Certification Path Tab

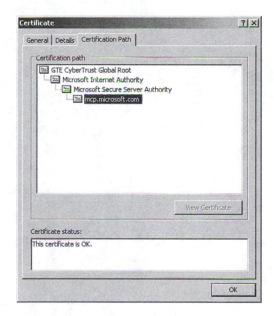

Task 2: Examine Secure Access to an Untrusted Source Warning

If the security certificate presented by a website is not from a trusted authority, Internet Explorer displays the screen shown in Figure 8-12 to alert you that there is a problem. It gives you options for closing the web page or continuing to the website.

Figure 8-12   Security Certificate Error from a Website

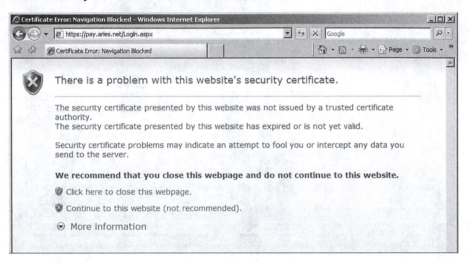

Unless you know the website to be legitimate, you might not be able to trust the server or the content it provides. If you navigate to the certification path, as previously described, you do not see a list of trusted certification authorities. You may be working with a secure (HTTPS) website but one that is self-certified and not certified by approved authorities.

Lab 8-2: Planning for Access Control Lists and Port Filters (8.2.1)

Objective

- Based on the predefined network diagram, determine where to implement access lists and port filters to help protect the network.

Background/Preparation

You are the support technician sent onsite to assess the current network for a business customer that would like to reduce the risk of a security breach on the network. Figure 8-13 shows the network topology.

Figure 8-13   Network Topology Diagram

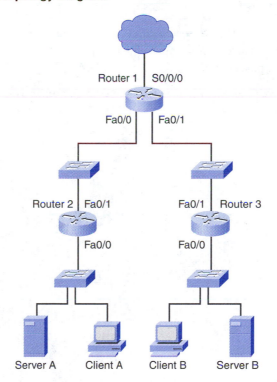

Task 1: Restrict Client A to One Subnet

You are asked to restrict Client A to the subnet to which it is currently attached. Client A needs to be able to access Server A, but it does not need to access the Internet or Server B. Where would you place the access list?

Router	Interface	Permit or Deny?	Input or Output Filter?	Why?
R2	Fa0/0	Deny	Input: Deny Client A IP	Keeps traffic local.

Task 2: Restrict Client B Access to Server A, But Allow Access to Server B and the Internet

You are asked to restrict Client B from accessing Server A, but Client B needs Internet access and access to Server B. Where would you place the access list?

Router	Interface	Permit or Deny?	Input or Output Filter?	Why?
R1	Fa0/0	Deny	Output: Deny Client B IP	Lets traffic go only as far as necessary for Client B to get to the Internet.

Task 3: Allow Only Client A to Access the Routers Using Only SSH

You have been asked to secure access to the routers for only Client A, which will be the management PC for those routers. You want to limit access to SSH from Client A and prevent Telnet access. Where would you place the access list?

Hint: More than one interface on more than one router is needed to control SSH and Telnet access to the routers.

Router(s)	Interface	Input or Output Filter?	Port	Permit or Deny?	Why?

Lab 8-3: Researching Anti-X Software Products (8.2.5)

Objective

- Research an Anti-X software package that meets the requirements for a small business.

Background/Preparation

You have been asked to recommend an Anti-X software package for a small business. The business is concerned about viruses and malware, because both have been a problem in the past. The customer also wants to be able to centrally manage the Anti-X solution. The customer would like to have all Anti-X alerting viewable in one location and would like to receive e-mail alerts when an infection has occurred.

Task 1: Identify Three Products

Using the Internet, research products from three different companies that meet the requirements of the small business. The Anti-X product needs to have the following features:

- Anti-virus
- Anti-spyware
- Anti-malware
- Central management
- E-mail alerts

Company	Product
McAfee	Total Protection for Small Business - Advanced
Symantec (business products)	Endpoint Protection

Task 2: Compare Pricing

Now that you have identified three different products that meet the customer's requirements, compare the pricing. The business has 27 workstations and three servers. Be sure to account for licensing of all the computer systems to generate the overall price. Examine the cost, and show all itemized components that comprise the overall price.

You might want to use a separate spreadsheet to compare these products and their features as well as price.

Company	Product	Price

Lab 8-4: Interpreting a Service-Level Agreement (8.3.1)

Objectives

- Describe the purpose of a service-level agreement (SLA).

- Review general customer SLA requirements.

- Analyze a sample SLA, and answer questions about content and suitability based on customer needs.

Background/Preparation

An SLA is a formal agreement between a customer and a service provider. The SLA defines the types and levels of service that the customer can expect to receive, as well as any penalties that may exist for nonconformance. In this lab, you will review the purpose of an SLA and the types of customer requirements it can cover. You will then analyze a sample SLA between an ISP and a customer of a medium-sized business and answer questions about the provisions of the SLA. You may work alone or in small groups.

Task 1: Review Typical Customer Needs

A typical customer will have the following requirements for an SLA. These requirements should be included in the SLA with the service provider:

- **Service description:** Describes the service volume and the times when the service is needed. It also describes the times when the service does not need to be covered by the SLA. The services described could be those typically found in a small to medium-sized manufacturing company: e-mail service, electronic data interchange, online accounting, secure remote worker support, remote instrumentation and control systems, and backup and recovery services.

- **Availability:** Describes the availability of each service in hours per day and days per month that the service can be available.

- **Performance:** Describes the peak and off-peak distribution of the volume of data the customer expects to generate for each service.

- **Reliability:** Describes the reliability percentage required for each service.

- **Response time tracking and reporting:** Describes the performance need of the users for each service.

- **Security:** Describes the customer's security policies as they pertain to the services to be covered by the SLA.

- **Budget cycle:** Identifies the customer's budget cycle.

- **Penalties for service outages:** Estimates the cost to the customer for a service outage for each of the services the customer wants covered by an SLA.

- **Costs:** Provides a table of costs that the customer has paid in the past for the services provided by other SLAs.

Task 2: Analyze a Sample SLA and Identify Its Key Components

Read the following sample SLA and answer these questions about content, ISP responsibilities, and customer requirements:

1. According to this agreement, can the ISP be held liable for damage to equipment owned by the customer [Client] or data loss that occurs due to accidental actions by ISP vendor staff or other persons?

   _____

2. What are some examples of One-Time Services included in the SLA?

   _____

3. What are some examples of Ongoing Services included in the SLA?

   _____

   _____

4. When will regular downtime maintenance be scheduled, and how many business days' notice must the ISP give before any scheduled downtime?

   _____

   _____

5. What does the ISP's network monitoring system do when an error condition is detected?

   _____

6. What is the stated availability of the systems administrators in the event of a system failure?

   _____

7. What is "usage monitoring," and how does the ISP provide this service?

   _____

   _____

   _____

8. Regarding problem severity and ISP response time, what is the difference in response between "Level 1: normal business hours" and "Level 3: normal business hours"?

   _____

   _____

9. On what factors are the penalties for service outages based?

   _____

(Sample)

Service-Level Agreement

Between

[Client]

and

ISP Services Vendor, Inc.

As of [Date]

I.   General Terms of the Service-Level Agreement

This Service-Level Agreement (SLA) documents the agreement between [Client] and the ISP Services Vendor, Inc. (ISPSV) for delivery of ISP services, including services delivered, levels of service, communications, and pricing. This agreement is in effect from [start_date] to [end_date] unless otherwise modified by an amendment. All terms are in effect until modified by an amendment.

Amendments can be added to the agreement at any time that the parties agree. If there are substantial service changes, some time may be required to implement. The timing of the amendment will be included in the amendment. Changes to the agreement that result in changes in charges may require 30 days to implement.

Either party can terminate this agreement in whole or in part with 30 days' notice. The SLA is reviewed on its anniversary. Billing rates may be adjusted based on service-level changes.

II.   Warranty and Liability

It is the mission of the ISPSV is to provide high-quality, cost-effective ISP services to the surrounding community.

We commit to protecting the equipment and data supported under this SLA from deliberate damage from ISPSV or other persons provided access to the equipment by ISPSV. However, we will not be held liable for any damage to equipment owned by the Client or data loss that occurs due to accidental actions by ISP VENDOR staff or other persons.

III.   Services Provided to [Client]

This table indicates which services are to be included in this SLA. Pricing of services is via the ISPSV pricing model and is attached as an amendment to this SLA.

Service	Comments
One-Time Services	
Rack and Computer Installation	
Backup Implementation	
Firewall Configuration	
Ongoing Services	
Server Hosting	
Backup and Recovery	
UNIX System Administration	
Windows System Administration	
Application Administration	

IV.   System Availability

Systems will be available 24/7 except for regularly scheduled maintenance downtime. The down-time maintenance schedule will be negotiated with each Client and will occur between 7 p.m. and 7 a.m. Clients will be given at least three (3) business days' notice of any scheduled downtime.

The ISP facility is staffed with professional systems administrators from 7 a.m. to 7 p.m. on work-days. The systems administrators are on call 24/7 for system failures.

V.   System Monitoring

Basic operating monitoring, periodically testing systems for proper functioning, is provided for all systems housed in the ISP facilities. The monitoring pages the on-call systems administrator when error conditions are detected.

External operating monitoring can be arranged through a contract with ExternalAlertServices, which provides external monitoring. This can be arranged with the Client paying the fees (approxi-mately $25 per month per URL) for this service.

Usage monitoring provides users with statistics on website "hits." The ISP facility maintains a WebTrends server for this purpose. Data from the WebTrends server is available to Clients on a monthly basis.

VI.   System Notifications

The ISP facilities will provide a set of e-mail lists for each server and application. The membership of these is determined and maintained by the Client. The lists are

- **[system]-info:** Will be notified of system logged messages on the operational status of the system.

- **[system]-announce:** Will receive all ISP facilities messages about planned maintenance, systems outages, or other events.

- **[system]-[application]-info:** Will be notified of system logged messages on the operational status of the application.

- **[system]-[application]-announce:** Will receive all ISP facilities messages about planned main-tenance, systems outages, or other events.

VII.   Change Management Process

All requests for changes to systems or applications, whether originated by the Client or by ISPSV staff, must go through the ISPSV change management process for approval. The process starts with a request submitted via the ISP Management Change Process (MCP). Requests will be logged and then sent via e-mail to the authorized Client for approval. The Client will return the request via e-mail with approval or denial of the request.

With the exception of emergencies, requests will not be done without Client approval. In the case of an emergency, the Client will be contacted as quickly as feasible and informed of the changes.

Communications Methods

- **Standard requests:** All standard requests for account changes or other nonemergency requests must be submitted via ISP MCP. The request must include

  - Client name

  - System name

  - Application name

  - Nature of the request

  - Date the change is needed

  - Problem severity (level 1, 2, 3, or 4)

- **Emergency requests:** Emergency requests must be submitted either in person or via the ISP facilities hotline at (123) 456-7890. If the call transfers to voicemail, leave a message that includes your name and a callback phone number. The on-call systems administrator will be automatically paged within 5 minutes and will return your call.

- **Escalation:** If problems are not resolved to the Client's satisfaction by the above methods, the Client can escalate the response by contacting ISP Vendor management in the following order: 1. Facilities Director, 2. Marketing Director, 3. President.

Systems Request Authority

We will maintain four lists to grant people authority. These lists are in the Client addendum and are as follows:

- **Master authority list:** List of people who can add people to or remove people from the remaining lists.

- **Account changes authority list:** List of people who can request Account changes.

- **Systems changes authority list:** List of people who can request System changes.

- **Application changes authority list:** List of people who can request Application changes.

Problem Severity and Response Time

ISPSV will respond to problems according to the following severity levels:

Problem Severity	Initial Response Time	Follow Up with Client
Level 1: normal business hours	Respond to Client within 30 minutes of notification 100% of the time	Hourly
Level 1: off hours	Respond to Client within 1 hour of notification 95% of the time	Hourly
Level 2: normal business hours	Respond to Client within 4 hours of notification 100% of the time	Daily
Level 3: normal business hours	Respond to Client within 1 working day of notification 100% of the time	Weekly
Level 4: normal business hours	Respond to Client within 3 working days of notification 100% of the time	Monthly

Severity Level 1

Major Business Impact is defined as a problem that causes complete loss of service to the Client production environment, and work cannot reasonably continue. Workarounds to provide the same functionality are not possible and cannot be found in time to minimize the impact on the Client's business. The problem has one or more of the following characteristics:

- A large number of users cannot access the system.

- Critical functionality is unavailable. The application cannot continue because a vital feature is inoperable, data cannot be secured or backed up, etc.

Severity Level 2

Significant Business Impact applies when processing can proceed, but performance is significantly reduced, and/or operation of the system is considered severely limited. No workaround is available, but operation can continue in a restricted fashion. The problem has one or more of the following characteristics:

- Internal software error, causing the system to fail, but restart or recovery is possible.

- Severely degraded performance.

- Some important functionality is unavailable, yet the system can continue to operate in a restricted fashion.

Severity Level 3

Minor Business Impact is a problem that causes minimal loss of service. The impact of the problem is minor or an inconvenience, such as a manual bypass to restore product functionality. The problem has one or more of the following characteristics:

- A software error for which there is a Client-acceptable workaround.

- Minimal performance degradation.

- Software error requiring manual editing of configuration or script files around a problem.

Severity Level 4

No Business Impact is a problem that causes no loss of service and in no way impedes use of the system. The impact of the problem has one or more of the following characteristics:

- A software enhancement for which there is a Client-acceptable workaround.

- Documentation error.

VIII.   Penalties for Service Outages

Problem Severity Level	Service Affected	Penalty Assessed

IX.   ISP Facilities Policies

See the ISPSV Policies document for all policies, including Security, Change Management, Scheduled Maintenance, Backup and Restore Procedure, Appropriate Use Policy, and Hardware Requirements.

X.   Billing

ISPSV bills on a monthly basis, directly charging the appropriate Client account with the agreed-upon charges.

XI.   Signatures

This Service-Level Agreement has been read and accepted by the authorized representatives of ISPSV and [Client].

Signature (ISPSV)	Date	Signature ([Client])	Date
Name		Name	
Title		Title	

Appendix 1: Services and Pricing

System or Application	Services	Price

Appendix 2: System Requests Contact Lists

Name	E-mail	Work	Cell	Home
Master Contact				
Account Change				
System Change				
App Change				

Lab 8-5: Conducting a Network Capture with Wireshark (8.3.2)

Objectives

- Perform a network traffic capture with Wireshark to become familiar with the Wireshark interface and environment.
- Analyze traffic to a web server.
- Create a filter to limit the network capture to ICMP packets.
- Ping a remote host to observe how the ICMP packet filter operates during the network capture.

Background/Preparation

In this lab, you will install Wireshark, a well-known network protocol analyzer and monitoring tool. Wireshark captures all packets sent or received by the computer NIC. It can be installed either in the lab or on a PC at home. You will use it to trace and view various types of network protocols and traffic. Wireshark was formerly known as Ethereal.

Wireshark software is freeware and is available from http://www.wireshark.org. The software installer, wireshark-setup-0.99.5.exe, should be available on the local Networking Academy server.

You can perform this lab individually, in pairs, or in teams.

The following resources are required:

- A Windows XP-based PC with an Ethernet network and at least two hosts
- Wireshark version 0.99.5 software (or the most current version)
- Internet connectivity (optional but desirable)
- Access to the PC command prompt
- Access to PC network TCP/IP configuration

Task 1: Install and Launch Wireshark

Step 1.   Given the local network path to the Wireshark software installer, wireshark-setup-0.99.5.exe, download the installer to the PC desktop.

Step 2.   Double-click the installer, and follow the installation prompts, accepting the defaults.

Step 3.   Click **I Agree**.

Step 4.   When prompted, be sure to install WinPcap on the PC. WinPcap includes a driver to support packet capture. Wireshark uses this library to capture live network data with Windows.

Step 5.   Click **Install** and follow the remaining prompts to the end of the installation process.

Step 6.   After the software is installed, click the checkbox to launch Wireshark.

Task 2: Select an Interface to Use for Capturing Packets (Optional)

Step 1.   Start the Wireshark application.

Step 2.   If you have more than one NIC in the test computer, choose **Capture > Interfaces**.

Step 3.   Click the **Start** button for the Ethernet interface (NIC) that you want to use to capture network traffic. Note that if you click **Start** here you can skip Task 3, because this starts the capture process for the selected interface, as shown in Figure 8-14. Allow the capture to continue for a few minutes so that you can observe the different types of traffic on the network.

Figure 8-14   Wireshark Capture Interfaces Window

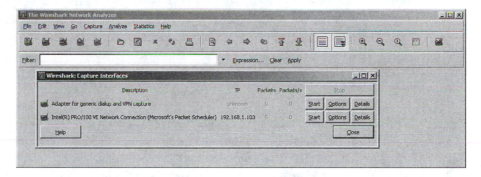

Task 3: Start a Network Capture

Step 1.   Scroll through the menus and view the toolbar on the Wireshark startup interface.

Step 2.   If you did not select a specific interface in Task 2, you may start a capture using the default Ethernet NIC by clicking the **New Live Capture** button, or choose **Capture > Capture**. Allow the capture to continue for a few minutes so that you can observe the different types of traffic on the network.

Task 4: Analyze Web Traffic Information (Optional)

Step 1.   If Internet connectivity is available, open a browser and go to http://www.google.com. Minimize the Google window and return to Wireshark. You should see captured traffic similar to that shown in Figure 8-15. Locate the **Source**, **Destination**, and **Protocol** columns on the Wireshark display screen.

Figure 8-15   Wireshark Capture of a Google Web Request

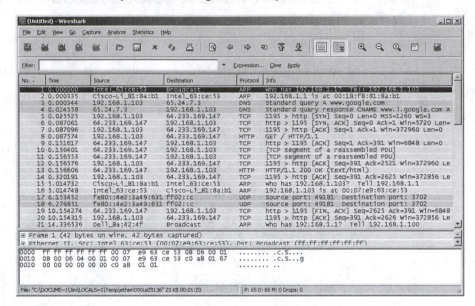

The connection to the Google server may start with an ARP request for the MAC address of the default gateway and then a query to the DNS server to look up the Google server IP address. The destination server IP address will most likely start with 64.*x.x.x*. What are the source address and destination address of the first packet sent to the Google server?

_____

_____

Step 2.   Open another browser window. Go to the ARIN Whois database at http://www.arin.net/whois/, or use another whois lookup tool, and enter the IP address of the destination server. To what organization is this IP address assigned?

_____

What protocols are used to establish the connection to the web server and deliver the web page to your local host?

_____

What color is used to highlight the traffic between your host and the Google web server?

_____

Task 5: Filter a Network Capture

Step 1.   Open a command prompt window by choosing **Start > All Programs > Run** and entering **cmd**. Alternatively, choose **Start > All Programs > Accessories** and select **Command Prompt**.

Step 2.   Ping a host IP address on your local network, and observe the Wireshark capture window. Scroll up and down the window in which the traffic is displayed. What types of protocols are in use?

_____

Step 3.   In the Filter text box, enter **icmp** and click **Apply**. The filtered packet list is displayed, as shown in Figure 8-16. Internet Control Message Protocol (ICMP) is the protocol that **ping** uses to test network connectivity to another host.

Figure 8-16   Filtering Captured Packets for ICMP

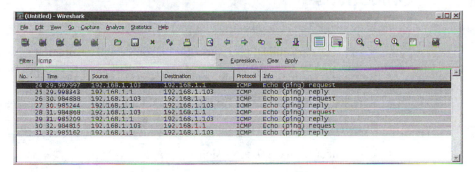

When **icmp** is entered in the Filter text box, what kind of traffic is displayed?

_____

Step 4.   Click the **Expression** button on the Wireshark window (next to the filter name entry area). Scroll down the list and view the filter possibilities there. Are TCP, HTTP, ARP, and other protocols listed?

_____

Task 6: Reflection

Hundreds of filters are listed in the Filter: Expression option. A large network might have enormous amounts and many different types of traffic. Which three filters in the long list do you think might be most useful to a network administrator?

_____

Is Wireshark a tool for out-of-band or in-band network monitoring? Explain your answer.

_____

_____

_____

Lab 8-6: Managing Remote Network Devices with Telnet (8.3.3a)

Objectives

- Establish a Telnet connection to a remote router.

- Verify that the application layer between source and destination is working properly.

- Retrieve information about remote routers using **show** commands.

- Retrieve CDP information from routers that are not directly connected.

- Suspend and reestablish a Telnet session.

- Disconnect from a Telnet session.

- Engage in multiple Telnet sessions.

- Display active Telnet sessions.

Background/Preparation

This lab focuses on the Telnet (remote terminal) utility to access routers remotely. Telnet is used to connect from a local router to another remote router to simulate being at the console on the remote router. The local router acts as a Telnet client, and the remote router acts as a Telnet server. Telnet is a good testing or troubleshooting tool because it is an application layer utility. A successful Telnet demonstrates that the entire TCP/IP protocol stack on both the client and server is functioning properly. You can Telnet from the workstation as a client into any router with IP connectivity on the network. In addition, you can Telnet into an Ethernet switch if an IP address has been assigned.

Set up a network similar to the one shown in the Figure 8-17 using the interface and IP address information in Table 8-1. You can use any router or combination of routers that meets the interface requirements in the figure, such as 800, 1600, 1700, 1800, 2500, or 2600 routers. Refer to Table C-1 in Appendix C, "Lab Equipment Interfaces and Initial Configuration Restoration," to correctly identify the interface identifiers to be used based on the equipment in the lab. Depending on the model of router, your output may vary from the output shown in this lab.

Figure 8-17   Lab 8-6 Topology Diagram

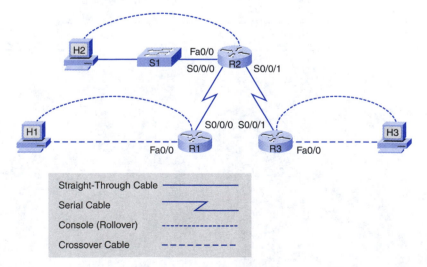

Table 8-1   **Router Interface and IP Address Information**

Device	Hostname	Interface	IP Address	Subnet Mask	RIP v2 Network Statements
R1	R1	Serial 0/0/0 (DTE)	10.10.10.1	255.255.255.0	10.0.0.0
		Fast Ethernet 0/0	192.168.1.1	255.255.255.0	192.168.1.0
R2	R2	Serial 0/0/0 (DCE)	10.10.10.2	255.255.255.0	10.0.0.0
		Serial 0/0/1 (DCE)	172.16.1.1	255.255.255.0	172.16.0.0
		Fast Ethernet 0/0	192.168.2.1	255.255.255.0	192.168.2.0
R3	R3	Serial 0/0/1 (DTE)	172.16.1.2	255.255.255.0	172.16.0.0
		Fast Ethernet 0/0	192.168.3.1	255.255.255.0	192.168.3.0
S1	S1	VLAN 1 (mgmt)	192.168.2.99	255.255.255.0	—

The following resources are required:

- One router with two serial interfaces and one FastEthernet (1841 or other)

- Two routers with one serial interface and one FastEthernet (1841 or other)

- One 2960 switch (or comparable) for the R2 LAN

- Three Windows XP computers (hosts H2 and H3 are mainly for configuring routers R2 and R3)

- Straight-through and crossover Category 5 Ethernet cables as required

- Two null serial cables

- Console cable to configure the routers

- Access to the host H1 command prompt

- Access to the host H1 network TCP/IP configuration

Note: Before you begin the lab, start a HyperTerminal session, and use the "Erasing and Reloading the Router" and "Erasing and Reloading the Switch" instructions in Appendix C on all routers and switches before continuing.

Task 1: Build the Network and Verify Connectivity

Step 1.   Configure basic information on each router and the switch.

a. Build and configure the network according to Figure 8-17 and Table 8-1. If necessary, refer to Lab 5-4, "Configuring Basic Router Settings with the IOS CLI (5.3.5)," for instructions on setting hostname, passwords, and interface addresses.

Be sure to set the vty login and a password of cisco on all routers or you will not be able to Telnet to the router.

b. Configure the RIP version 2 routing protocol on each router, and advertise the networks shown in Table 8-1. If necessary, refer to Lab 6-2, "Configuring and Verifying RIP (6.1.5)," for instructions on configuring the RIP routing protocol.

    c. Configure basic settings on switch S1 to include hostname, passwords and VLAN 1 IP address. If necessary, refer to Lab 5-11, "Configuring the Cisco 2960 Switch (5.5.4)," for instructions on configuring the switch settings.

Step 2. Configure each of the hosts with an IP address, subnet mask, and default gateway.

Host H1:

IP Address: 192.168.1.2

Subnet mask: 255.255.255.0

Default Gateway: 192.168.1.1

Host H2:

IP Address: 192.168.2.2

Subnet mask: 255.255.255.0

Default Gateway: 192.168.2.1

Host H3:

IP Address: 192.168.3.2

Subnet mask: 255.255.255.0

Default Gateway: 192.168.3.1

Step 3. Verify end-to-end connectivity.

    a. On host H1, open a command prompt window by choosing **Start > Run** and entering **cmd**. Alternatively, you can choose **Start > All Programs > Accessories > Command Prompt**.

    b. Use the **ping** command to test end-to-end connectivity. Ping from host H1 on the R1 LAN to host H3 on the R3 LAN (192.168.3.2):

```
C:\> ping 192.168.3.2
```

    c. If host H3 is not attached to router R3, ping the R3 Serial 0/0/0 interface IP address 172.16.1.2:

```
C:\> ping 172.16.1.2
```

If the pings are unsuccessful, troubleshoot router and host configurations and connections as necessary.

Task 2: Establish a Telnet Session from a Host Computer

Step 1. Telnet from host H1 to remote router R2.

The Cisco router IOS has built-in Telnet client and server software. Nearly all computer operating systems have a Telnet client. Many server operating systems also have a Telnet server, although Microsoft Windows desktop operating systems typically do not.

In many cases you will not have direct access to a router through the console so that you can telnet to other routers. You will most often telnet to a router from a host computer. From the router command prompt you can telnet to other routers that are accessible via the network.

a. On host H1, open a command prompt window by choosing **Start > Run** and entering **cmd**. Alternatively, you can choose **Start > All Programs > Accessories > Command Prompt**.

b. Use the **telnet** command to telnet to the R1 router FastEthernet 0/0 interface:

```
C:\> telnet 192.168.2.1
```

Enter the vty password (**cisco** or other password) to access the router.

What prompt does the router display?

Step 2.   End the Telnet session from host H1 to remote router R2. Exit the Telnet session from host H1 to R1 by entering **exit**.

Task 3: Perform Basic Telnet Operations Between Two Routers

Step 1.   Use help with the **telnet** command.

From the router R1 HyperTerminal session, enter **telnet ?** at either the user EXEC or privileged EXEC router prompt.

What does the router reply with?

What happens if you just enter **telnet** and press **Enter**?

Step 2.   Telnet from R1 to remote router R2.

The Telnet application uses the vty lines on the remote router to connect. If the vty lines on the remote router are not configured for login or no password is set on them, you cannot connect to the remote router using Telnet.

a. Enter **telnet** followed by the IP address of the R2 serial 0/0/0 interface 10.10.10.2:

```
R1> telnet 10.10.10.2
Trying 10.10.10.2 ... Open
User Access Verification
Password:
```

b. Enter the password **cisco** to enter the router. What prompt does the router display?

Step 3.   Display the status of the interfaces on remote router R2.

a.   Enter **show ip interface brief** at the remote router prompt:

```
R2> show ip interface brief
```

b.   List the interfaces that are up on remote router R2.

_____

Another command that provides interface status information is **show protocols**. This command lists all interfaces for the Internet protocol. What information does this command provide that the **show ip interface brief** command does not?

```
R2> show protocols
```

_____

Step 4.   Display the routing table on remote router R2.

Enter **show ip route** at the router prompt. What routes has router R2 learned from RIP?

```
R2> show ip route
```

_____

Step 5.   Display the CDP neighbors for router R2.

a.   Use Cisco Discovery Protocol (CDP) to view information about Cisco devices directly attached to R2. Enter the **show cdp neighbors** command at the router prompt.

```
R2> show cdp neighbors
```

b.   List all device IDs that are connected to the remote router. What is the platform for each device?

_____

_____

Step 6.   Enter privileged EXEC mode.

_____

Note: The previous commands could be issued at the user EXEC mode prompt R2>. To display the running configuration for a router, you must be in privileged EXEC mode.

_____

Enter **enable** at the R2> command prompt, and enter the password **class**.

What prompt does the router display?

_____

What mode is this?

_____

Step 7.   View the running configuration on remote router R2. By Telnetting to another router and issuing the **show running-config** command you can see how a remote router is configured just as though you were connected to it using the console.

Enter **show running-config** at the remote router R2 prompt:

```
R2# show running-config
```

Where is this file located?

Step 8.   Activate console message monitoring on remote router R2.

While telnetted to R2, turn on RIP debugging using the **debug ip rip** command in privileged EXEC mode. This allows you to see the periodic routing updates sent between RIP routers. Do you see any RIP messages?

```
R2# debug ip rip
RIP protocol debugging is on
```

---

a. To see console messages from R2 while connected from R1 via Telnet, issue the **terminal monitor** command from the R2 privileged prompt. Without this command, no R2 console messages or debug output can be viewed remotely from R1. Do you see any RIP messages now?

```
R2# terminal monitor
```

---

b. Turn off RIP debugging on R2 using either the **no debug ip rip** or **undebug all** command. Deactivate terminal monitoring on R2 using the **terminal no monitor** command.

```
R2# no debug ip rip
RIP protocol debugging is off

R2# terminal no monitor
```

Step 9.   Suspend the current Telnet session on remote router R2.

Press the **Ctrl-Shift-6** keys simultaneously, release them, and then press the **x** key. This only suspends the session and returns to the previous router. It does not disconnect from this router.

What prompt does the router display?

Step 10.   Resume the Telnet session to router R2.

Press the **Enter** key at the router prompt. What does the router respond with?

Pressing the **Enter** key resumes the Telnet session that was suspended in Step 9.

What prompt does the router display?

Step 11.   Close the Telnet session to R2.

Enter the command **exit** while in a Telnet session. This terminates the Telnet session.

What does the router respond with?

_____

What prompt does the router display?

_____

Note: To disconnect from a suspended Telnet session, enter **disconnect** and press **Enter**. Do not do this now, however.

Task 4: Perform Telnet Operations Between Multiple Routers

Step 1.   Telnet from R1 to remote router R2.

a. From router R1, enter **telnet** followed by the IP address of the R2 serial 0/0/0 interface 10.10.10.2.

b. Enter the password **cisco** to enter the router.

Step 2.   Suspend the current Telnet session to remote router R2.

Press the **Ctrl-Shift-6** keys simultaneously, release them, and then press the **x** key. This only suspends the session and returns to the previous router. It does not disconnect from this router.

What prompt does the router display?

_____

Step 3.   Establish an additional Telnet session from R1 to R3.

a. Enter **telnet** followed by the IP address of the R3 serial 0/0/0 interface 172.16.1.2.

b. Enter the password **cisco** to access the router.

What prompt does the router display?

_____

Step 4.   Suspend the Telnet session to R3.

Press **Ctrl-Shift-6** followed by the **x** key.

What prompt does the router display?

_____

Step 5.   View the active Telnet sessions.

Enter the **show sessions** command at the R1 command prompt. How many sessions are in use?

```
R1> show sessions
```

_____

Note: The default session is indicated by an asterisk (*). This is the session that you resume if you press **Enter**.

Step 6.   Resume the previously suspended Telnet session.

Enter **resume** and the number of the session that is to be resumed (1), and press **Enter** at the router prompt. What does the router respond with?

_____

Step 7.   View the active Telnet sessions.

Enter **show sessions** at the command prompt.

How many sessions are shown?

_____

There were two the last time. What is the difference?

_____

_____

Step 8.   Suspend the Telnet session to R3.

Press **Ctrl-Shift-6** followed by the **x** key.

What prompt does the router display?

_____

Step 9.   Disconnect the sessions from R1 to R2 and R3.

Enter the command **disconnect 1** at the R1 prompt and press **Enter**. This disconnects session 1 to R2 and leaves one session to R3 still open. Enter the command again to disconnect the Telnet session to R3.

```
R1> disconnect 1
Closing connection to 10.10.10.2 [confirm]
R1> disconnect 1
Closing connection to 172.16.1.2 [confirm]
```

Task 5: Experiment with Multiple Linked Telnet Sessions

When working with Telnet, one of the most common problems is remembering the focus of the session. Focus means the device that is the focus of the commands that are being issued. Many times people telnet to a router, and then telnet from that router to another, and so on. Without hostnames, or if the routers have similar hostnames, confusion can result. The following steps provide an example:

Step 1.   Telnet to the R3 router.

a. From R1, telnet to the R3 router.

b. From the configuration prompt, enter **no hostname**.

Step 2.   Telnet to the R2 router.

a. From R3, telnet to the R2 router.

b. From the configuration prompt, enter **no hostname**.

Step 3.   Telnet back to the R3 router.

From R2, telnet back to the R3 router. By looking at the prompt, is it evident whether the Telnet worked?

_____

Step 4.   Telnet to the R1 router.

From R3, telnet to the R1 router.

Step 5.   Exit from all sessions.

a. Keep entering **exit** until the following prompt appears:

```
Router con0 is now available
Press RETURN to get started.
```

b. Scroll back up the HyperTerminal listing. How many session closed messages are displayed?

_____

Task 6: Reflection

What are some advantages and disadvantages of using Telnet?

_____

_____

_____

_____

_____

_____

Lab 8-7: Configuring a Remote Router Using SSH (8.3.3b)

Objectives

- Configure a router to accept SSH connections.
- Configure SSH client software on a PC.
- Establish a connection to a Cisco ISR using SSH version 2.
- Check the existing running configuration.

Background/Preparation

Traditionally, the most common network protocol used to remotely configure network devices has been Telnet. However, protocols such as Telnet do not authenticate or encrypt the information between a Telnet client and server. As a result, a network sniffer can be used to intercept passwords and configuration information.

Secure Shell (SSH) is a network protocol that can be used to establish a secure terminal emulation connection to a router or other networking device. SSH encrypts all information that passes over the network link and provides authentication of the remote computer. SSH is rapidly replacing Telnet as the remote login tool of choice for network professionals. SSH is most often used to log in to a remote machine and execute commands; however, it can also transfer files using the associated SFTP or SCP protocols.

For SSH to function, the network devices that are communicating must support it. In this lab, you will enable the SSH server on a router to be configured and then connect to that router using a PC with an SSH client installed. For use on a local network, the connection normally is made using Ethernet and IP. Network devices connected via other types of links, such as serial, also can be managed using SSH, as long as they support IP. Like Telnet, SSH is an in-band, TCP/IP-based Internet protocol.

In this lab, you can use either Cisco SDM or Cisco IOS CLI commands to configure SSH on the router. Refer to the topology shown in Figure 8-18.

Figure 8-18   Lab 8-7 Topology Diagram

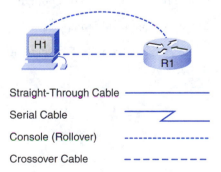

The Cisco 1841 ISR supports the use of SSH versions 1 and 2; version 2 is preferred. The SSH client used in this lab is PuTTY, which can be downloaded free of charge.

The Cisco SDM is supported on a wide range of Cisco routers and Cisco IOS software releases. Many newer Cisco routers come with SDM preinstalled. If you are using an 1841 router, SDM (and SDM Express) is preinstalled. This lab assumes the use of a Cisco 1841 router. You can use another router model as long as it can support SDM. If you are using a supported router that does not have SDM installed, you can download the latest version free of charge from http://www.cisco.com/pcgi-bin/tablebuild.pl/sdm.

From this URL, view or download the document "Downloading and Installing Cisco Router and Security Device Manager." This document provides instructions for installing SDM on your router. It lists specific model numbers and IOS versions that can support SDM, and the amount of memory required.

Note: If you are using SDM to configure SSH, you must complete Lab 5-2, "Configuring an ISR with SDM Express (5.2.3)," on the router to be used, before performing this lab. This lab assumes that the router was previously configured with basic settings.

If you are working with a router that does not have SDM installed, use Cisco IOS CLI commands to configure SSH. Task 2 of this lab tells you how to manually configure SSH using Cisco IOS CLI commands for routers that are not running SDM. To perform the basic router configuration, refer to Lab 5-4, "Configuring Basic Router Settings with the IOS CLI (5.3.5)."

If the startup-config is erased in an SDM router, SDM will no longer come up by default when the router is restarted. You will need to build a basic router configuration using IOS commands. Refer to the procedure in Appendix C, or contact your instructor.

The following resources are required:

- Cisco 1841 ISR router with SDM version 2.4 installed and with basic configuration completed (This is critical. See the note in Task 1.)

- Other Cisco router model with SDM installed (optional)

- Other Cisco router model without SDM installed (IOS version 12.2 or higher—must support SSH) (optional)

- Windows XP computer with Internet Explorer 5.5 or higher and Sun Java Runtime Environment (JRE) version 1.4.2_05 or later (or Java Virtual Machine [JVM] 5.0.0.3810)

- Latest release of putty.exe client installed on the PC and accessible on the desktop

- Straight-through or crossover Category 5 Ethernet cable (for SDM and SSH)

- Console cable if the router is to be configured using the CLI (optional)

- Access to the PC command prompt

- Access to the PC network TCP/IP configuration

Task 1: Configure the ISR to Accept SSH Connections Using SDM

Note: If you are configuring a router for SSH that does not have SDM installed, read through Task 1 to see how SSH is set up as a separate task when using SDM, and then go to Task 2.

Step 1. Open the web browser and connect to http://192.168.1.1. When prompted, enter **admin** for the username and **cisco123** for the password. Click **OK**. Cisco SDM loads. After SDM is loaded, click the **Configure** button on the toolbar. On the Tasks pane, click **Additional Tasks**. On the Additional Tasks pane, expand **Router Access** and click the **SSH** task. You should see a screen similar to that shown in Figure 8-19. Click the **Generate RSA Key** button if required.

Do not select HTTPS if prompted. If SDM Express comes up, select SDM from the Tools section of the Task Panel.

If the SSH Key Setup message says: "RSA key exists and SSH is enabled in your router" and Status is "RSA key is set on this router," it is probably because you completed Lab 5-2, "Configuring an ISR with SDM Express (5.2.3)." Recall that in that lab, when you configured security, one of the recommended security settings enabled by default is "Enhance security on this router." If this box is checked, it automatically configures SSH for router access, sets the banner to warn intruders, enforces minimum password length, and restricts the number of unsuccessful login attempts. If this is the case then read through this task to see how SSH is configured and then proceed to Task 3.

Figure 8-19 SDM SSH Configuration

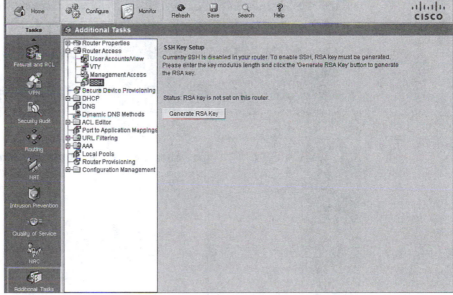

Step 2. In the Key modulus size dialog box, shown in Figure 8-20, enter a key size of **1024** bits and click **OK**.

Figure 8-20   RSA Key Modulus Size

Step 3.   In the Enter SSH Credentials dialog box, shown in Figure 8-21, enter **admin** for the user-name and **cisco123** for the password and click **OK**. After this is done, notice that the Rivest, Shamir, and Adelman (RSA) key is now set on the router.

Figure 8-21   SSH Credentials

Step 4.   In the Additional Tasks pane, shown in Figure 8-22, click the **VTY** option. Select **Input Protocols Allowed**, and then click the **Edit** button.

Figure 8-22   Specifying the Allowed Input Protocols

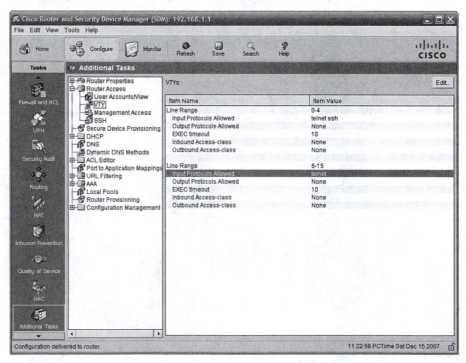

Step 5.   When the Edit VTY Lines dialog box appears, as shown in Figure 8-23, check the box next to **SSH**, and then click **OK**.

Figure 8-23   Allowing SSH

Step 6.   When the Commands Delivery Status window opens, click **OK**.

Step 7.   Close the Cisco SDM by clicking the **X** in the upper-right corner of the window.

Task 2: Configure SSH on a Non-SDM Router (Optional)

Note: If you are configuring a router for SSH that already has SDM installed, you can skip Task 2 and go directly to Task 3.

Step 1.   If you are configuring a router to receive SSH connections that does not have SDM installed, connect the router console port with a PC and the HyperTerminal program, as described in Lab 5-1, "Powering Up an Integrated Services Router (5.1.3)."

Step 2.   Log in to the router. From the privileged EXEC mode prompt, enter the Cisco IOS CLI commands as shown in the following steps. These commands do not include all the passwords that need to be set. Refer to Lab 5-4, "Configuring Basic Router Settings with Cisco IOS CLI (5.3.5)," for additional information on configuration settings.

Note: The router should be running IOS 12.0 or higher. In this example, the router is a Cisco model 2620XM with IOS 12.2(7r).

Step 3.   Configure the basic router and interface information:

```
Router# config terminal
Router(config)# hostname CustomerRouter
CustomerRouter(config)# ip domain-name customer.com
CustomerRouter(config)# username admin privilege 15 password 0 cisco123
CustomerRouter(config)# interface FastEthernet 0/0
```

```
CustomerRouter(config-if)# ip address 192.168.1.1 255.255.255.0
CustomerRouter(config-if)# no shutdown
CustomerRouter(config-if)# exit
```

Step 4.   Configure the remote incoming vty terminal lines to accept Telnet and SSH:

```
CustomerRouter(config)# line vty 0 4
CustomerRouter(config-line)# privilege level 15
CustomerRouter(config-line)# login local
CustomerRouter(config-line)# transport input telnet ssh
CustomerRouter(config-line)# exit
```

Step 5.   Generate the RSA encryption key pair for the router to use for authentication and encryption of SSH data that is transmitted. Enter **768** for the number of modulus bits. The default is 512.

```
CustomerRouter(config)# crypto key generate rsa
How many bits in the modulus [512] 768
CustomerRouter(config)# exit
```

Step 6.   Verify that SSH has been enabled, and check the version being used:

```
CustomerRouter# show ip ssh
```

Fill in the following information based on the output of the **show ip ssh** command:

SSH version enabled:

_____

Authentication timeout:

_____

Authentication retries:

_____

Step 7.   Save the running-config to the startup-config:

```
CustomerRouter# copy running-config startup-config
```

Task 3: Configure the SSH Client, and Connect the PC to the ISR

Step 1.   If PuTTY is not installed on the local PC, obtain a copy of putty.exe and place the application on the desktop. Launch PuTTY by double-clicking the **putty.exe** icon, as shown in Figure 8-24.

Figure 8-24   Starting PuTTY

Step 2.   From the Category pane, as shown in Figure 8-25, select SSH, and verify that the preferred SSH protocol version is set to 2.

Note: The PuTTY client will still connect even if the SSH server is running SSH version 1.

Figure 8-25   PuTTY Configuration

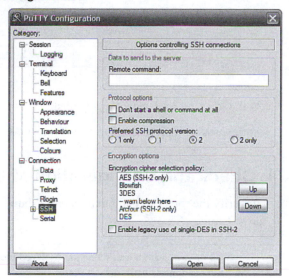

Step 3.   In the Category pane, select **Session** and enter the IP address of the router LAN interface, which is 192.168.1.1, as shown in Figure 8-26. Verify that SSH is selected as the connection type, and click **Open**.

Figure 8-26   PuTTY Session Setup

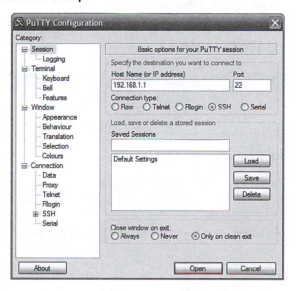

Step 4.   The first time a connection is made to the SSH service on the Cisco 1841 ISR using an SSH client, a connection key is cached in the local machine registry. In the PuTTY Security Alert window, shown in Figure 8-27, click **Yes** to continue.

Figure 8-27   Caching the Host Key

Step 5.   At the login prompt, enter the administrator username, **admin**, and press **Enter**.

Step 6.   At the password prompt, enter the administrator password, **cisco123**, and click **Enter**.

Task 4: Check the Configuration of the Cisco 1841 ISR

Step 1.   To verify the router's configuration, enter **show run** at the privileged mode prompt, and press **Enter**.

Note: There is no need to switch from user mode to privileged mode, because after you configure from SDM Express and SDM, privileged mode is the default mode.

Step 2.   Press the **Spacebar** to scroll through the router's current configuration.

Task 5: Log Out of the Cisco 1841 ISR

To log out of the router when you are finished verifying the configuration, enter **logout** at the privileged mode prompt, and then press **Enter**.

Task 6: Reflection

When comparing Telnet and SSH, what are some advantages and disadvantages?

_____

_____

What is the default port for SSH?

What is the default port for Telnet?

_____

What Cisco IOS software version is displayed in the running-config?

_____

Lab 8-8: Planning a Backup Solution (8.4.2)

Objective

- Based on the business scenario, plan an appropriate backup solution.

Background/Preparation

You have been asked to plan and propose a backup solution for a small business customer of the ISP for which you work. The small business is concerned about losing valuable company data. In the last three years, it has lost data due to hardware failure and user error. The business wants to ensure that it has the quickest data recovery plan available built into the solution. The customer is willing to take on all local administrative tasks to monitor and manage the local backup system.

Current data requirements:

- Server 1: 50 GB
- Server 2: 100 GB
- Server 3: 10 GB

Based on its current growth in the amount of data, the company anticipates 10% growth in total volume of data each year.

The company has decided that it wants a backup solution that allows it to have four weeks of daily backups and an additional 12 months of monthly archives. It also would like a solution that will last five years without outgrowing its capacity.

Note: You can assume that the business cannot purchase a tape autoloader or library system. This means that the capacity of the backup medium needs to accommodate all the data in one unit.

Task 1: Choose the Media and Backup Hardware

Based on the media types described in this course, use the Internet to identify a suitable medium that has the capacity to meet the requirements of the business. You are also required to investigate the cost of purchasing additional hardware, if required, and the price of the medium. Also based on the history requirements, identify the number of backup media. Enter your recommendations in Table 8-2.

Note: The company's normal business hours are Monday through Friday, 8 a.m. to 6 p.m., but employees can come in as early as 7 a.m. and stay as late as 8 p.m. Therefore, the company has decided that backups cannot start until after 10 p.m. and must be completed before 6 a.m. The equipment and backup media selected must be fast enough to back up all data from all servers within this time period.

Table 8-2   Equipment/Media Price Comparison

Equipment/Media	Price	Quantity

Task 2: Design a Backup Plan and Procedure

Now that you have chosen the backup medium, it is time to assemble the backup proposal and procedure for the company to manage its backup system. You need to decide what backup type is most appropriate for the business and how the business should schedule the swapping of the media. The business needs a procedure that is simple and easy to follow. Media need to be labeled properly so that the customer knows what is backed up on each day. Be sure to address the customer's needs in your proposed backup plan. Also identify any other open issues or questions that may still need to be asked to achieve a good solution for the customer. Describe your plan in the following steps:

Step 1.   Describe the equipment recommended, and explain why you selected this equipment.

_____

_____

_____

Step 2.   Describe the location of the equipment in the network and the network link speeds to the equipment.

_____

_____

Step 3.   Describe the backup medium to be used, and explain why you selected it.

_____

_____

Step 4.   Describe the backup schedule.

_____

_____

Step 5.   Describe the backup-and-restore procedure, including what kind of backup (normal, differential, incremental) will be used, how it will be tested, and what kind of maintenance the equipment requires. Explain how tapes will be labeled and where tapes or other media that have been backed up will be stored. When backups need to be restored, what is the specific procedure for a file, a folder, and a drive? (Use extra sheets if necessary.)

_____

_____

_____

_____

_____

Lab 8-9: Managing Cisco IOS Images with TFTP (8.4.3a)

Objectives

- Analyze the IOS image and router flash memory.

- Use TFTP to copy the IOS software image from a router to a TFTP server.

- Reload the backup IOS software image from a TFTP server into flash on a router.

Background/Preparation

In this lab you will use the **show flash** command to view the files in the router flash memory and determine the amount of flash available. You will use Trivial File Transfer Protocol (TFTP) server software to back up the router IOS image to the TFTP server. You will then copy the IOS image from the TFTP server back to the router.

Set up a network similar to the one shown in Figure 8-28 and described in Table 8-3. You can use any router or combination of routers that meets the interface requirements shown in the figure, such as 800, 1600, 1700, 1800, 2500, or 2600 routers. Refer to Table C-1 in Appendix C to correctly identify the interface identifiers to be used based on the equipment in the lab. Depending on the model of router, your output may vary from the output shown in this lab.

Figure 8-28   Lab 8-9 Topology Diagram

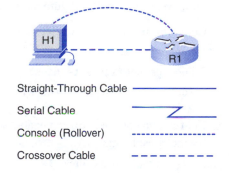

Table 8-3   Router Interface and IP Address Information

Device	Hostname	Interface	IP Address	Subnet Mask
R1	R1	FastEthernet 0/0	172.17.0.1	255.255.0.0

Note: Instead of using a PC and installing TFTP server software, you may use the Discovery Server, because it has Linux-based TFTP server software preinstalled. Check with your instructor on the availability of a Discovery Server CD. The Discovery Server can take the place of host H1 in Figure 8-28. The IP addresses used to configure host H1 and R1 in this lab are compatible with Discovery Server.

The following resources are required:

- One router with an Ethernet interface

- One Windows XP computer (or Discovery Server)

- Crossover Category 5 Ethernet cable (H1 to router R1)

- Console cable (from H1 to R1)

- Access to the computer host command prompt

- Access to the computer host network TCP/IP configuration

Note: Before you begin the lab, start a HyperTerminal session, and use the "Erasing and Reloading the Router" and "Erasing and Reloading the Switch" instructions in Appendix C on all routers and switches before continuing.

Task 1: Build the Network and Verify Connectivity

Step 1.   Configure the TFTP server host.

Connect the router and host H1 according to Figure 8-28. Configure the host H1 IP address as follows:

- IP address: 172.17.0.2

- Subnet mask: 255.255.0.0

- Default gateway: 172.17.0.1

Step 2.   Log in to router R1, and configure the basic settings.

a. Configure the hostname for R1:

```
Router> enable
Router# configure terminal
Router(config)# hostname R1
```

b. Configure a console, vty, and enable secret passwords. Configure logging synchronous for the console line:

```
R1(config)# line console 0
R1(config-line)# password cisco
R1(config-line)# login
R1(config-line)# logging synchronous
R1(config-line)# line vty 0 4
R1(config-line)# password cisco
R1(config-line)# login
R1(config-line)# exit
R1(config)# enable secret class
R1(config)# exit
```

c. Configure a message-of-the-day (MOTD) banner and **no ip domain lookup**:

```
R1(config)# banner motd #Unauthorized Use Prohibited#
R1(config)# no ip domain lookup
```

d. Configure the R1 FastEthernet interface:

```
R1(config)# interface FastEthernet 0/0
R1(config-if)# description R1 LAN Default Gateway
R1(config-if)# ip address 172.17.0.1 255.255.0.0
R1(config-if)# no shutdown
R1(config-if)# end
```

Step 3.   Display the R1 router configuration.

Issue the **show running-config** command in privileged EXEC mode, and verify all the configuration commands you have entered so far. Note that this command can be abbreviated as **sh run**.

```
R1# show running-config
```

Step 4.   Verify basic connectivity.

Host H1 will be the TFTP server, and router R1 will be the TFTP client. To copy files to and from a TFTP server, you must have IP connectivity between the server and the client.

From host H1, ping the router FastEthernet interface at IP address 172.17.0.1.

Are the pings successful?

_____

If the pings are unsuccessful, troubleshoot the host and router configs until they are.

Step 5.   Save the configuration on R1.

Save the running configuration to the startup configuration from the privileged EXEC prompt:

```
R1# copy running-config startup-config
```

Task 2: Collect Information About the Router Memory and IOS Image

Step 1.   Collect information to document the router using the **show version** command.

_____

From the router HyperTerminal session, issue the **show version** command.

```
Router> show version
```

What is the current value of the config-register?

_____

How much flash memory does this router have?

_____

Is there at least 4 MB (4096 KB) of flash?

_____

(This lab requires at least 4 MB of flash.)

What is the version number of boot ROM?

_____

Is the boot ROM version 5.2 or later?

_____

(This lab requires 5.2 or later.)

```
R1# show version
Cisco IOS Software, 1841 Software (C1841-ADVIPSERVICESK9-M), Version
  12.4(10b),
  RELEASE SOFTWARE (fc3)
Technical Support: http://www.cisco.com/techsupport
Copyright  1986-2007 by Cisco Systems, Inc.
Compiled Fri 19-Jan-07 15:15 by prod_rel_team


ROM: System Bootstrap, Version 12.4(13r)T, RELEASE SOFTWARE (fc1)


R1 uptime is 13 minutes
System returned to ROM by reload at 23:45:37 UTC Sat Feb 23 2008
System image file is "flash:c1841-advipservicesk9-mz.124-10b.bin"


<Output Omitted>


Cisco 1841 (revision 6.0) with 174080K/22528K bytes of memory.
Processor board ID FTX1111W0QF
6 FastEthernet interfaces
2 Serial(sync/async) interfaces
1 Virtual Private Network (VPN) Module
DRAM configuration is 64 bits wide with parity disabled.
191K bytes of NVRAM.
62720K bytes of ATA CompactFlash (Read/Write)


Configuration register is 0x2102
```

Step 2.   Collect more information to document the router using the **show flash** command.

Issue the **show flash** command:

```
Router> show flash
```

Is the IOS image already stored in flash?

_____

If so, what is the exact name of that file?

_____

What is the size of the IOS image currently in flash?

_____

How much of flash is available or unused?

_____

Note: There must be enough total flash to hold the new IOS image.

Task 3: Use TFTP to Save the Cisco IOS Image

Step 1.   Obtain and install the TFTP server application.

Many free TFTP servers are available. A search for "free tftp server" will identify several that you can choose from to download. This lab uses the SolarWinds TFTP Server 9.1 application. SolarWinds' free TFTP Server is a multithreaded TFTP server commonly used to upload and download executable images and configurations to routers and switches. The free TFTP Server runs on most Microsoft operating systems, including Windows XP, Vista, 2000, and 2003. The SolarWinds software requires the Microsoft .NET 2.0 framework to install. The .NET software can be downloaded free from www.microsoft.com.

Check with your instructor for a copy of SolarWinds or another TFTP server that you can install.

a.   Go to the SolarWinds website, download the free TFTP server software, and save it to your desktop:

http://www.solarwinds.com/downloads/

b.   Double-click the SolarWinds TFTP application to begin installation. Click **Next**. Agree to the license agreement, and accept the default settings. After SolarWinds has finished installing, click **Finish**.

Step 2.   Start the TFTP application.

Start the TFTP server by choosing **Start > Programs > SolarWinds TFTP Server > TFTP Server**. The main application window is shown in Figure 8-29.

Figure 8-29   SolarWinds TFTP Server Main Window

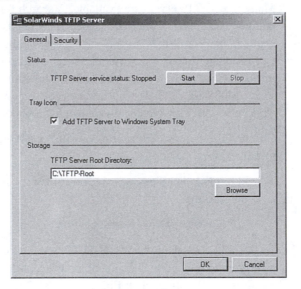

Step 3.   Configure the TFTP server.

    a. To configure the TFTP server, choose **File > Configure**. On the **General** tab, shown in Figure 8-30, ensure that the default TFTP Server Root Directory is set to C:\TFTP-Root.

Figure 8-30   TFTP Server: General Tab

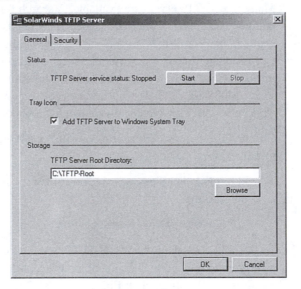

    b. Click the **Security** tab, shown in Figure 8-31, and ensure that **Permitted Transfer Types** is set to **Send and Receive files**. Set **IP Address Restrictions** to allow transfers from only the router R1 FastEthernet 0/0 IP address (From 172.17.0.1 To 172.17.0.1). Click **OK** when finished.

Figure 8-31   TFTP Server: Security Tab

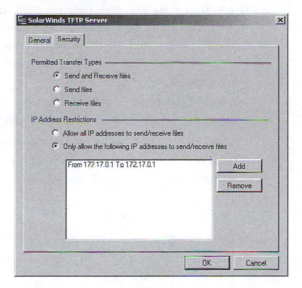

c. On the **General** tab, click the **Start** button to activate the TFTP Server.

d. When you're finished, click **OK**. The screen should look like Figure 8-32.

Figure 8-32   TFTP Server Service Started Message

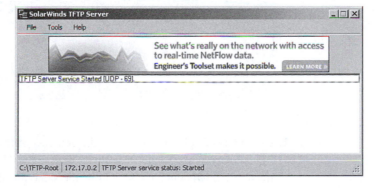

On which well-known UDP port number is the TFTP server operating?

_____

e. Leave the TFTP Server GUI window open so that you can view the activity as the file is copied.

Step 4.   Save the R1 IOS image file to the TFTP server.

a. Verify the IOS image filename that you will be copying. Write it here:

_____

b. From the HyperTerminal session on router R1, begin the IOS image upload to the TFTP server using the command **copy flash tftp**. Respond to the prompts as shown next, but replace the IOS image filename shown with the one in your router. If you're successful, the output from the router terminal window should look similar to the following:

```
R1# copy flash tftp
Source filename []? c1841-advipservicesk9-mz.124-10b.bin
Address or name of remote host []? 172.17.0.2
Destination filename [c1841-advipservicesk9-mz.124-10b.bin]?
!!!!!!!!!!!!!!!!!!!!!!!!!!!!!!!!!!!!!!!!!!!!!!!!!!!!!!!!!!!!!!!!!!!!!!!!!!!
22063220 bytes copied in 58.264 secs (378677 bytes/sec)
```

Step 5.   Verify the TFTP server activity.

a. Observe the TFTP Server GUI window, which should show the connection entries for the transfer of the running-config file to the server. The output should look similar to that shown in Figure 8-33.

Figure 8-33   TFTP Server: Connection and File Transfer Messages

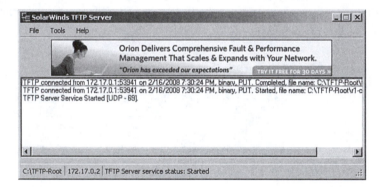

b. Use Windows Explorer to examine the contents of folder C:\TFTP-Root\ on the host H1 TFTP server. Verify the flash image size in the TFTP server directory. The file size in the **show flash** command should be the same file size as the file stored on the TFTP server. If the file sizes are not identical, check with the instructor. The IOS image file should be listed similar to what is shown in Figure 8-34.

Figure 8-34   IOS Image File Stored on the TFTP Server

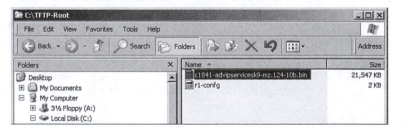

Task 4: Use TFTP to Update a Cisco IOS Image

Step 1.   Copy the IOS image from the TFTP server.

a. Now that the IOS is backed up, the image must be tested and the IOS restored to the router.

b. When prompted for "Destination filename," use the filename from Task 3, Step 4.

c. Start the copy from the privileged EXEC prompt.

```
R1# copy tftp flash
Address or name of remote host []? 172.17.0.2
Source filename []? c1841-advipservicesk9-mz.124-10b.bin
Destination filename [c1841-advipservicesk9-mz.124-10b.bin]?
%Warning:There is a file already existing with this name
Do you want to over write? [confirm]
Accessing tftp://172.17.0.2/c1841-advipservicesk9-mz.124-10b.bin...
Loading c1841-advipservicesk9-mz.124-10b.bin from 172.17.0.2
  (via FastEthernet0/0):
!!!!!!!!!!!!!!!!!!!!!!!!!!!!!!!!!!!!!!!!!!!!!!!!!!!!!!!!!!!!!!!!!!!!!!!!!!
[OK - 22063220 bytes]


22063220 bytes copied in 70.036 secs (315027 bytes/sec)
```

The router may prompt you to erase flash. Will the image fit in the available flash?

_____

What is the size of the file being loaded?

_____

What happened on the router console screen as the file was being downloaded?

_____

Step 2.   Verify that the IOS image file transfer was successful.

_____

a. Restart the router using the **reload** command, and observe the startup process to confirm that no flash errors occurred. If there are none, the router IOS should have started correctly.

b. Verify the new IOS image in flash using the **show flash** command. How can you tell that the previous IOS image was overwritten?

```
R1# show flash
-#- --length-- -----date/time------ path
1     22063220 Feb 23 2008 01:25:20 c1841-advipservicesk9-mz.124-10b.bin
2         1038 May 18 2007 14:25:40 home.shtml
3         1821 May 18 2007 14:25:40 sdmconfig-18xx.cfg
4       113152 May 18 2007 14:25:42 home.tar
```

```
5        1164288 May 18 2007 14:25:44 common.tar
6        6036480 May 18 2007 14:25:54 sdm.tar
7         861696 May 18 2007 14:26:04 es.tar
8         527849 May 18 2007 14:25:42 128MB.sdf
9        1684577 Mar 15 2007 07:23:20 securedesktop-ios-3.1.1.27-k9.pkg
10        398305 Mar 15 2007 07:23:54 sslclient-win-1.1.0.154.pkg


31121408 bytes available (32874496 bytes used)
```

Task 5: Reflection

How do you think TFTP could be used to manage networking device files in an Enterprise network?

_____

_____

_____

Lab 8-10: Managing Cisco IOS Images with ROMmon and TFTP (8.4.3b)

Objectives

- Analyze the IOS image and router flash memory.

- Use TFTP to copy the IOS software image from a router to a TFTP server.

- Reload the backup IOS software image from a TFTP server into flash on a router.

Background/Preparation

In this lab you will use the **show flash** command to view the IOS image in the router flash memory. You will use TFTP server software to back up the router IOS image to the TFTP server. You will then simulate the loss of the IOS and use the ROMmon tftpdnld command to copy the IOS image from the TFTP server back to the router.

Caution: Check with your instructor before performing Task 6 in this lab. The **tftpdnld** command will erase all existing files in flash memory before downloading a new software image to the router. If there are files in the router flash memory that you do not want to lose, they must be backed up to the TFTP server and then copied back to the router flash after the IOS has been restored. The process of copying files to and from a TFTP server is described in Lab 8-9, "Managing Cisco IOS Images with TFTP (8.4.3a)."

If performing this lab presents a problem in your lab environment, you can do all the tasks except Task 6 and read through the steps in Task 6 to become familiar with the procedure.

Set up a network similar to the one shown in Figure 8-35 and described in Table 8-4. You can use any router or combination of routers that meets the interface requirements shown in the figure, such as 800, 1600, 1700, 1800, 2500, or 2600 routers. Refer to Table C-1 in Appendix C to correctly identify the interface identifiers to be used based on the equipment in the lab. Depending on the model of router, your output may vary from the output shown in this lab.

Figure 8-35   Lab 8-10 Topology Diagram

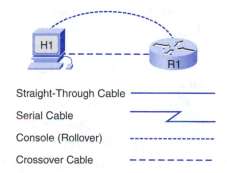

Table 8-4   Router Interface and IP Address Information

Device	Hostname	Interface	IP Address	Subnet Mask
R1	R1	FastEthernet 0/0	172.17.0.1	255.255.0.0

Note: Instead of using a PC and installing TFTP server software, you may use the Discovery Server, because it has Linux-based TFTP server software preinstalled. Check with your instructor on the availability of a Discovery Server CD. The Discovery Server can take the place of host H1 in Figure 8-35. The IP addresses used to configure host H1 and R1 in this lab are compatible with Discovery Server.

The following resources are required:

- One router with an Ethernet interface

- One Windows XP computer (or Discovery Server)

- Crossover Category 5 Ethernet cable (H1 to router R1)

- Console cable (from H1 to R1)

- Access to the computer host command prompt

- Access to the computer host network TCP/IP configuration

Note: Before you begin the lab, start a HyperTerminal session, and use the "Erasing and Reloading the Router" and "Erasing and Reloading the Switch" instructions in Appendix C on all routers and switches before continuing.

Task 1: Build the Network and Verify Connectivity

Step 1.   Configure the TFTP server host.

Connect the router and host H1 according to Figure 8-35. Configure the host H1 IP address as follows:

- IP address: 172.17.0.2

- Subnet mask: 255.255.0.0

- Default gateway: 172.17.0.1

Step 2.   Log in to router R1, and configure the basic settings.

a. Configure the hostname for R1:

```
Router> enable
Router# configure terminal
Router(config)# hostname R1
```

b. Configure console, vty, and enable secret passwords. Configure logging synchronous for the console line:

```
R1(config)# line console 0
R1(config-line)# password cisco
R1(config-line)# login
R1(config-line)# logging synchronous
R1(config-line)# line vty 0 4
R1(config-line)# password cisco
R1(config-line)# login
R1(config-line)# exit
R1(config)# enable secret class
R1(config)# exit
```

c. Configure a message-of-the-day (MOTD) banner and **no ip domain lookup**:

```
R1(config)# banner motd #Unauthorized Use Prohibited#
R1(config)# no ip domain lookup
```

d. Configure the R1 FastEthernet interface:

```
R1(config)# interface FastEthernet 0/0
R1(config-if)# description R1 LAN Default Gateway
R1(config-if)# ip address 172.17.0.1 255.255.0.0
R1(config-if)# no shutdown
R1(config-if)# end
```

Step 3.   Display the R1 router configuration.

Issue the **show running-config** command in privileged EXEC mode, and verify all the configuration commands you have entered so far. Note that this command can be abbreviated as **sh run**.

```
R1# show running-config
```

Step 4.   Verify basic connectivity.

Host H1 will be the TFTP server, and router R1 will be the TFTP client. To copy files to and from a TFTP server, you must have IP connectivity between the server and the client.

From host H1, ping the router FastEthernet interface at IP address 172.17.0.1. Are the pings successful?

_____

If the pings are unsuccessful, troubleshoot the host and router configs until they are.

Step 5.   Save the configuration on R1.

Save the running configuration to the startup configuration from the privileged EXEC prompt:

```
R1# copy running-config startup-config
```

Task 2: Collect Information About the Router Memory and IOS Image

Step 1.   Collect information to document the router using the **show version** command.

_____

From the router HyperTerminal session, issue the **show version** command:

```
Router> show version
```

What is the current value of the config-register?

_____

How much flash memory does this router have?

_____

What is the version number of boot ROM?

_____

Step 2. Collect more information to document the router using the **show flash** command.

Issue the **show flash** command:

```
Router> show flash
```

Is the IOS image already stored in flash?

_____

If so, what is the exact name of that file?

_____

What is the size of the IOS image currently in flash?

_____

How much of flash is available or unused?

_____

To what value is the configuration register set?

_____
_____

Note: There must be enough flash to hold the new IOS image.

How many files are in flash memory?

_____

Task 3: Use TFTP to Save the Current Cisco IOS Image

Step 1. Obtain and install the TFTP server application.

Many free TFTP servers are available. A search for "free tftp server" will identify several that you can choose from to download. This lab uses the SolarWinds TFTP Server application. SolarWinds' free TFTP Server is a multithreaded TFTP server commonly used to upload and download executable images and configurations to routers and switches. The free TFTP Server runs on most Microsoft operating systems, including Windows XP, Vista, 2000, and 2003. The SolarWinds software requires the Microsoft .NET 2.0 framework to install. The .NET software can be downloaded free from www.microsoft.com.

Check with your instructor for a copy of SolarWinds or another TFTP server that you can install.

a. Go to the SolarWinds website, download the free TFTP server software, and save it to your desktop:

http://www.solarwinds.com/downloads/

b. Double-click the SolarWinds TFTP application to begin installation. Click **Next**. Agree to the license agreement, and accept the default settings. After SolarWinds has finished installing, click **Finish**.

Step 2. Start the TFTP application. You should see the main application window, as shown in Figure 8-36.

Start the TFTP server by choosing **Start > Programs > SolarWinds TFTP Server > TFTP Server**.

Figure 8-36   SolarWinds TFTP Server Main Window

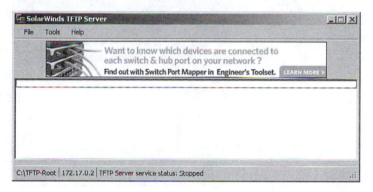

Step 3. Configure the TFTP server.

a. To configure the TFTP server, choose **File > Configure**. On the **General** tab, shown in Figure 8-37, ensure that the default TFTP Server Root Directory is set to C:\TFTP-Root.

Figure 8-37   TFTP Server: General Tab

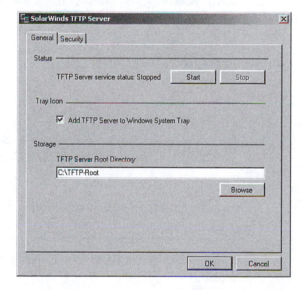

b. Click the **Security** tab, shown in Figure 8-38, and ensure that **Permitted Transfer Types** is set to **Send and Receive files**. Set **IP Address Restrictions** to allow transfers from only the router R1 FastEthernet 0/0 IP address (From 172.17.0.1 To 172.17.0.1).

Figure 8-38   TFTP Server: Security Tab

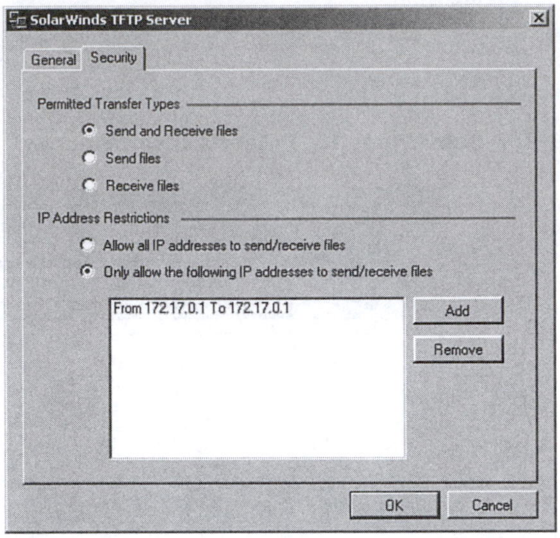

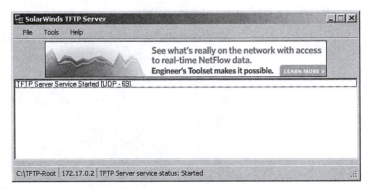

c. On the **General** tab, click the **Start** button to activate the TFTP Server.

d. When you're finished, click **OK**. The screen should look like Figure 8-39.

Figure 8-39   TFTP Server Service Started Message

On which well-known UDP port number is the TFTP server operating?

_____

e. Leave the TFTP Server GUI window open so that you can view the activity as the file is copied.

Step 4. Save the R1 IOS image file to the TFTP server.

a. Verify the IOS image filename that you will be copying. Write it here:

_____

b. From the HyperTerminal session on router R1, begin the IOS image upload to the TFTP server using the command **copy flash tftp**. Respond to the prompts as shown next, but replace the IOS image filename shown with the one in your router. If you're successful, the output from the router terminal window should look similar to the following:

```
R1# copy flash tftp
Source filename []? c1841-advipservicesk9-mz.124-10b.bin
Address or name of remote host []? 172.17.0.2
Destination filename [c1841-advipservicesk9-mz.124-10b.bin]?
!!!!!!!!!!!!!!!!!!!!!!!!!!!!!!!!!!!!!!!!!!!!!!!!!!!!!!!!!!!!!!!!!!!!!!!!!!!!!!!!!!!
22063220 bytes copied in 58.264 secs (378677 bytes/sec)
```

Step 5.   Verify the TFTP server activity.

a. Observe the TFTP Server GUI window, which should show the connection entries for the transfer of the running-config file to the server. The output should look similar to that in Figure 8-40.

Figure 8-40   TFTP Server: Connection and File Transfer Messages

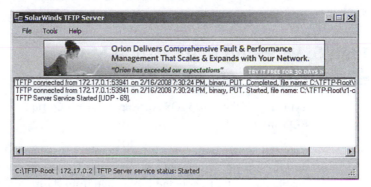

b. Use Windows Explorer to examine the contents of folder C:\TFTP-Root\ on the host H1 TFTP server. Verify the flash image size in the TFTP server directory. The file size in the **show flash** command should be the same file size as the file stored on the TFTP server. If the file sizes are not identical, check with the instructor. The IOS image file should be listed similar to what is shown in Figure 8-41.

Figure 8-41   IOS Image File Stored on the TFTP Server

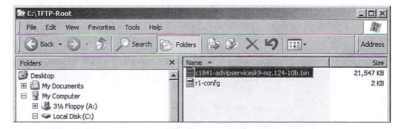

Task 4: Consider IOS Restoration Options

You have several options for restoring a corrupted or missing IOS image:

Option 1. Using ROMmon and tftpdnld (part of this lab): This option can be used if the IOS image is missing or corrupt. The router boots up in ROMmon mode if this is the case. Ethernet and IP connectivity must be available to access the TFTP server.

Option 2. Using ROMmon and XMODEM (not part of this lab): This option is needed only as an emergency when the IOS is missing or corrupt and there is no possibility of being able to download a new version of the IOS from a TFTP server. The router only comes up in ROMmon mode. The **xmodem** command is used at the console to download Cisco IOS software using the ROM monitor (ROMmon) and HyperTerminal. This procedure can also be used where there are no TFTP servers or network connections, and a direct PC connection through the console (or through a modem connection) is the only viable option. Because this procedure relies on the router's console speed and the PC's serial port, it can take a long time to download an image using this method. Depending on the size of the IOS image and the console baud rate, the download can take several hours.

Option 3. Replacing the flash card (not part of this lab): If the router will boot up only in ROMmon mode, you may be able to recover if you have a similar router with a compatible flash card. You can download the correct IOS image on that router and then move the flash card to the router that has a problem.

Task 5: Working in ROMmon Mode

Step 1.   Configure the boot register to enter ROMmon mode.

Typically, if the Cisco IOS software image is corrupt, the router boots up only in ROMmon mode.

You will simulate the loss of the IOS image by changing the router config-register so that it will come up to the rommon > prompt. The config register normally is set to 0x2102 to enable the router to boot the IOS image from flash. Refer to the **show version** command output in Task 2, Step 1 to see the config-register setting.

a. Change the configuration register to 0x2100 to cause the router to start up in ROMmon mode:

```
Router> enable
Router# configure terminal
Enter configuration commands, one per line. End with CNTL/Z.
Router(config)# config-register 0x2100
Router(config)# exit
Router#
```

b. Issue the **show version** command to verify that the new config register setting will take effect at the next reload. What is the last line of the **show version** output?

_____

c. Issue the **reload** command to restart the router:

```
Router# reload
System Bootstrap, Version 12.4(13r)T, RELEASE SOFTWARE (fc1)
Technical Support: http://www.cisco.com/techsupport
```

```
Copyright  2006 by cisco Systems, Inc.
PLD version 0x10
GIO ASIC version 0x127
c1841 platform with 196608 Kbytes of main memory
Main memory is configured to 64 bit mode with parity disabled


Upgrade ROMMON initialized
rommon 1 >
```

Step 2.   View available commands from the rommon prompt.

Enter a question mark (?) at the ROM monitor prompt:

```
rommon 2 > ?
alias            set and display aliases command
boot             boot up an external process
break            set/show/clear the breakpoint
confreg          configuration register utility
cont             continue executing a downloaded image
context          display the context of a loaded image
cookie           display contents of motherboard cookie PROM in hex
dev              list the device table
dir              list files in file system
dis              disassemble instruction stream
dnld             serial download a program module
frame            print out a selected stack frame
gioshow          show the gio version
help             monitor builtin command help
history          monitor command history
iomemset         set IO memory percent
meminfo          main memory information
repeat           repeat a monitor command
reset            system reset
rommon-pref      Select ROMMON
set              display the monitor variables
showmon          display currently selected ROM monitor
stack            produce a stack trace
sync             write monitor environment to NVRAM
sysret           print out info from last system return
tftpdnld         tftp image download
unalias          unset an alias
unset            unset a monitor variable
xmodem           x/ymodem image download
```

Step 3. Find a valid image in flash.

In some cases an IOS image fails to load properly, and the router boots to the ROMmon prompt, but the IOS image may still be a valid image. There may also be more than one image in flash memory. You can use the **boot** command at the rommon x > prompt to attempt to load a single IOS image, or you can select from multiple images in flash if they exist.

a. From the ROM Monitor prompt, issue the **dir flash:** command. Look for a valid Cisco IOS software image:

```
rommon 3 > dir flash:
program load complete, entry point: 0x8000f000, size: 0xcb80
Directory of flash:

2         22063220    -rw-      c1841-advipservicesk9-mz.124-10b.bin
5389      491213      -rw-      128MB.sdf
5509      1052160     -rw-      common.tar
5766      833024      -rw-      es.tar
5970      1038        -rw-      home.shtml
5971      4734464     -rw-      sdm.tar
7127      1821        -rw-      sdmconfig-18xx.cfg
7128      1684577     -rw-      securedesktop-ios-3.1.1.27-k9.pkg
7540      398305      -rw-      sslclient-win-1.1.0.154.pkg
rommon 4 >
```

b. You might be able to recover using one of the listed images (if there are any). Boot from any image that is listed in the preceding step (typically files with a .bin extension). If the image is valid, it will bring back normal operation.

```
rommon 4 > boot flash:c1841-advipservicesk9-mz.124-10b.bin
program load complete, entry point: 0x8000f000, size: 0x150a6d4
Self decompressing the image :

################################################################## ...
```

c. Restart the router using the **reload** command. It will come up in ROMmon mode again, because the config register is still set to 0x2100.

Step 4. Reset the config register so that the router will boot from flash on the next reload.

From the ROMmon prompt, set the boot register back to 0x2102, before the IOS image transfer, using the **confreg** command. Depending on the router model and ROMmon prompt, you may need to use the **o/r** command.

Note: The rommon # prompt increments the number with each command issued.

```
rommon 5 > confreg 0x2102
```

or

```
> o/r 0x2102
```

The router responds with the following:

```
You must reset or power cycle for new config to take effect
rommon 6 >
```

Note: Do not reset the router at this time.

Task 6: Use ROMmon and tftpdnld to Restore an IOS Image (Optional)

Caution: Check with your instructor before performing this task. The **tftpdnld** command will erase all existing files in flash memory before downloading a new software image to the router. If there are files in the router flash memory that you do not want to lose, you must back them up to the TFTP server *before* you start this procedure and then copy them back to the router flash after the IOS has been restored. The process of copying files to and from a TFTP server is described in Lab 8-9, "Managing Cisco IOS Images with TFTP (8.4.3a)."

If performing this task presents a problem in your lab environment, just read through the steps to become familiar with the procedure.

Step 1.   Use the **tftpdnld** command to transfer the IOS image (optional).

a. Note the name of the IOS image displayed in the **show flash** output in Task 2, Step 2, and record it here. This file was saved to the TFTP server in the previous task.

The ROMmon TFTP transfer works only on the first LAN port. To use TFTP in ROMmon mode, you must first set a few environmental variables, including the IP address of the LAN interface, and then use the **tftpdnld** command to restore the image. To set a ROMmon environment variable, enter the variable name, an equals sign (=), and the value for the variable. For example, to set the IP address to 172.17.0.1, enter IP_ADDRESS=172.17.0.1.

Here are some commonly required environment variables:

IP_ADDRESS: IP address on the LAN interface

IP_SUBNET_MASK: Subnet mask for the LAN interface

DEFAULT_GATEWAY: Default gateway for the LAN interface

TFTP_SERVER: IP address of the TFTP server

TFTP_FILE: Cisco IOS filename on the server

b. Enter the environment variables as follows (be sure to replace the IOS image name with the one for your router):

```
rommon 7 > IP_ADDRESS=172.17.0.1
rommon 8 > IP_SUBNET_MASK=255.255.0.0
rommon 9 > DEFAULT_GATEWAY=172.17.0.1
rommon 10 > TFTP_SERVER=172.17.0.2
rommon 11 > TFTP_FILE=c1841-advipservicesk9-mz.124-10b.bin
```

c. Use the **set** command to view and verify the ROMmon environment variables:

```
rommon 12 > set
PS1=rommon ! >
BSI=0
RANDOM_NUM=1770598170
WARM_REBOOT=
RET_2_RTS=18:04:12 UTC Mon Feb 25 2008
RET_2_RCALTS=1203962657
?=0
IP_ADDRESS=172.17.0.1
IP_SUBNET_MASK=255.255.0.0
TFTP_SERVER=172.17.0.2
TFTP_FILE=c1841-advipservicesk9-mz.124-10b.bin
```

d. Use the **tftpdnld** command to start the IOS image transfer from the TFTP server. As each datagram of the Cisco IOS file is received, an exclamation point (!) is displayed. When the entire Cisco IOS file is copied, the flash is erased, and the new image file is written.

```
rommon 13 > tftpdnld
          IP_ADDRESS: 172.17.0.1
      IP_SUBNET_MASK: 255.255.0.0
     DEFAULT_GATEWAY: 172.17.0.1
         TFTP_SERVER: 172.17.0.2
           TFTP_FILE: c1841-advipservicesk9-mz.124-10b.bin
        TFTP_MACADDR: 00:1b:53:25:25:6e
        TFTP_VERBOSE: Progress
    TFTP_RETRY_COUNT: 18
        TFTP_TIMEOUT: 7200
       TFTP_CHECKSUM: Yes
             FE_PORT: 0
        FE_SPEED_MODE: Auto Detect

Invoke this command for disaster recovery only.
WARNING: all existing data in all partitions on flash: will be lost!
Do you wish to continue? y/n:  [n]:  y
.
Receiving c1841-advipservicesk9-mz.124-10b.bin from 172.17.0.2
!!!!!!!!!!!!!!!!!!!!!!!!!!!!!!!!!!!!!!!!!!!!!!!!!!!!!!!!!!!!!!!!!!!!!!!!!!!
!!!!!!!!!!!!!!!!!!!!!!!!!!!!!!!!!!!!!!!!!!!!!!!!!!!!!!!!!!!!!!!!!!!!!!!!!!!
<output omitted>
```

```
!!!!!!!!!!!!!!!!!!!!!!!!!!!!!!!!!!!!!!!!!!!!!!!!!!!!!!!!!!!!!!!!!!!!!!!!!!!!!!
!!!!!!!!!!!!!!!!!!!!!!!!!!!!!!!!!!!!!!!!!!!!!!!!!!!!!!!!!!!!!!!!!!!!!!!!!!!!!!
File reception completed.
Validating checksum.
Copying file c1841-advipservicesk9-mz.124-10b.bin to flash:.
program load complete, entry point: 0x8000f000, size: 0xcb80

Format: Drive communication & 1st Sector Write OK...
Writing Monlib sectors.
.............................................................
.............................................................
.....................
Monlib write complete

Format: All system sectors written. OK...
Format: Operation completed successfully.

Format of flash: complete
program load complete, entry point: 0x8000f000, size: 0xcb80
```

e. When the ROMmon prompt appears (rommon 1>), restart the router using the **reset** command, or enter the letter i. The router should now boot from the new Cisco IOS image in flash.

```
rommon 14 > reset
```

Step 5.   Verify that the IOS image file transfer was successful.

---

a. Restart the router using the **reload** command, and observe the startup process to confirm that there were no flash errors. If there are none, the router IOS should have started correctly.

b. Verify the new IOS image in flash using the **show flash** command:

```
R1# show flash
-#- --length-- -----date/time------ path
1    22063220 Feb 23 2008 01:25:20 c1841-advipservicesk9-mz.124-10b.bin

41947136 bytes available (22065152 bytes used)
```

How many files are in flash memory now?

Task 7: Reflection

What are some advantages and disadvantages of using ROMmon and **tftpdnld** to restore an IOS image?

_____

_____

_____

_____

_____

## CHAPTER 9

Lab: Troubleshooting

The lab exercises included in this chapter cover the Chapter 9 online curriculum labs and ensure that you have mastered the practical, hands-on skills needed to perform basic troubleshooting. As you work through this lab, use Chapter 9 in Part I of this book, or use the corresponding Chapter 9 in the *Working at a Small-to-Medium Business or ISP CCNA Discovery* online curriculum, for assistance.

Lab 9-1: Organizing CCENT Objectives by OSI Layer (9.1.1)

Objectives

- Organize the Cisco Certified Entry Networking Technician (CCENT) exam objectives by which layer or layers they address.

Background/Preparation

In this lab, you associate the objectives of the CCENT exam with the corresponding OSI model layers. Some objectives are associated with more than one layer.

Note: The CCENT exam is the same as the ICND1 exam. The ICND1 and ICND2 exams together equal the CCNA exam.

This lab requires a computer with browser and Internet access.

Task 1: Access the CCENT Exam Web Page

Note: Steps 1 and 2 use the 640-822 ICND1 exam page that is accessed via the CCNA Prep Center website and requires a Cisco.com login account. You can also go directly to the 640-822 ICND1 exam page located at http://www.cisco.com/web/learning/le3/current_exams/640-822.html, which does not require a login.

Step 1. Log in to the Cisco CCNA Prep Center website, as shown in Figure 9-1.

Registered Cisco.com users can access this website for help in preparing for CCNA certification exams:

http://forums.cisco.com/eforum/servlet/PrepCenter?page=main

In the Member Login area, enter your Cisco.com username and password, and click **Go.** If you do not have a Cisco.com user ID, click on the link for Cisco.com Registration in the How to Log In area.

Figure 9-1   CCNA Prep Center Login

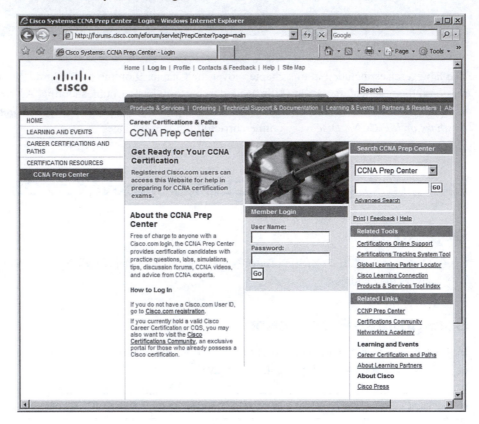

Step 2.   View the ICND1/CCENT exam description and exam topics.

From the CCNA Prep Center main screen, click the **CCNA Paths** button, as shown in Figure 9-2.

In the next screen, click the **640-822 ICND1** exam link. The 640-822 ICND1 screen appears. It contains a description of the exam and a list of exam topics, as shown in Figure 9-3.

Note: The following screen shot shows only a portion of the exam topics.

Figure 9-2   CCNA Paths

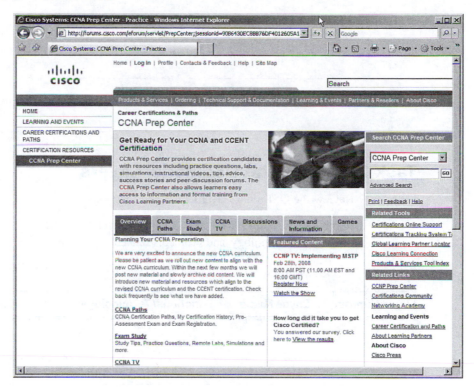

Figure 9-3   ICND1 Exam Topics

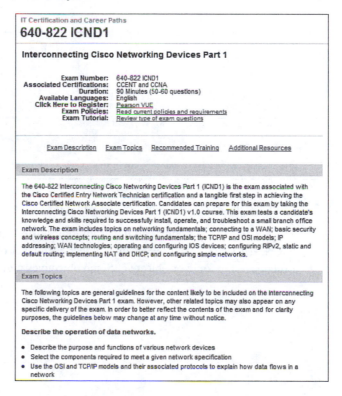

What are some of the main topic areas covered?

_____

_____

_____

_____

_____

Task 2: Review the OSI Model Layers

Step 1.   Review the OSI model layer names and functions.

In Table 9-1, indicate the name of the OSI layer associated with each layer number and the functions, terminology, and protocols related to each layer.

Table 9-1   OSI Model

Layer Number	Layer Name	Functions/Terminology	Technologies/Protocols
7			
6			
5			
4			
3			
2			
1			

Step 2.   Review the exam topics associated with OSI layers.

Tables 9-2 to 9-8 address all the exam topics listed on the Cisco.com website for the ICND1/CCENT exam. Place an X under each layer of the OSI model that most closely relates to the topic or objective. Some objectives may apply to more than one layer.

Table 9-2   Exam Objective: Describe the Operation of Data Networks

640-822 CCENT Topic/Objective	Layer 1	Layer 2	Layer 3	Layer 4	Upper Layers
Describe the purpose and functions of various network devices.					
Select the components required to meet a given network specification.					
Use the OSI and TCP/IP models and their associated protocols to explain how data flows in a network.					
Describe common networking applications, including web applications.					
Describe the purpose and basic operation of the protocols in the OSI and TCP models.					
Describe the impact of applications (Voice Over IP and Video Over IP) on a network.					
Interpret network diagrams.					
Determine the path between two hosts across a network.					
Describe the components required for network and Internet communications.					
Identify and correct common network problems at Layers 1, 2, 3, and 7 using a layered model approach.					
Differentiate between LAN/WAN operation and features.					

Table 9-3   Exam Objective: Implement a Small Switched Network

640-822 CCENT Topic/Objective	Layer 1	Layer 2	Layer 3	Layer 4	Upper Layers
Select the appropriate media, cables, ports, and connectors to connect switches to other network devices and hosts					
Explain the technology and Media Access Control (MAC) method for Ethernet technologies					
Explain network segmentation and basic traffic management concepts					
Explain the operation of Cisco switches and basic switching concepts					
Perform, save, and verify initial switch configuration tasks, including remote access management					

continues

Table 9-3   Exam Objective: Implement a Small Switched Network   *continued*

640-822 CCENT Topic/Objective	Layer 1	Layer 2	Layer 3	Layer 4	Upper Layers
Verify network status and switch operation using basic utilities, including ping, traceroute, Telnet, SSH, ARP, ipconfig, and show and debug commands					
Implement and verify basic security for a switch (port security, deactivate ports)					
Identify, prescribe, and resolve common switched-network media issues, configuration issues, autonegotiation, and switch hardware failures					

Table 9-4   Exam Objective: Implement an IP Addressing Scheme and IP Services to Meet Network Requirements for a Small Branch Office

640-822 CCENT Topic/Objective	Layer 1	Layer 2	Layer 3	Layer 4	Upper Layers
Describe the need and role of addressing in a network; create and apply an addressing scheme to a network					
Assign and verify valid IP addresses to hosts, servers, and networking devices in a LAN environment					
Explain the basic uses and operation of NAT in a small network connecting to one ISP					
Describe and verify DNS operation					
Describe the operation and benefits of using private and public IP addressing					
Enable NAT for a small network with a single ISP and connection using SDM, and verify operation using the CLI and ping					
Configure, verify, and troubleshoot DHCP and DNS operation on a router using the CLI and SDM					
Implement static and dynamic addressing services for hosts in a LAN environment					
Identify and correct IP addressing issues					

Table 9-5   Exam Objective: Implement a Small Routed Network

640-822 CCENT Topic/Objective	Layer 1	Layer 2	Layer 3	Layer 4	Upper Layers
Describe basic routing concepts, including packet forwarding and the router lookup process					
Describe the operation of Cisco routers, including the router bootup process, POST, and router components					
Select the appropriate media, cables, ports, and connectors to connect routers to other network devices and hosts					
Configure, verify, and troubleshoot RIPv2					
Access and utilize the router CLI to set basic parameters					
Connect, configure, and verify the operation status of a device interface					
Verify device configuration and network connectivity using ping, traceroute, Telnet, SSH, and other utilities					
Perform and verify routing configuration tasks for a static or default route given specific routing requirements					
Manage Cisco IOS configuration files, including saving, editing, upgrading, and restoring					
Manage the Cisco IOS Software					
Implement password and physical security					
Verify network status and router operation using basic utilities, including **ping**, **traceroute**, Telnet, SSH, ARP, **ipconfig**, and **show** and **debug** commands					

Table 9-6   Exam Objective: Explain and Select the Appropriate Administrative Tasks Required for a WLAN

640-822 CCENT Topic/Objective	Layer 1	Layer 2	Layer 3	Layer 4	Upper Layers
Describe standards associated with wireless media, including IEEE WiFi Alliance, ITU/FCC					
Identify and describe the purpose of the components in a small wireless network, including SSID, BSS, and ESS					
Identify the basic parameters to configure on a wireless network to ensure that devices connect to the correct access point					

continues

Table 9-6   Exam Objective: Explain and Select the Appropriate Administrative Tasks Required for a WLAN
continued

640-822 CCENT Topic/Objective	Layer 1	Layer 2	Layer 3	Layer 4	Upper Layers
Compare and contrast wireless security features and capabilities of WPA security, including open, WEP, and WPA-1/2					
Identify common issues when implementing wireless networks					

Table 9-7   Exam Objective: Identify Security Threats to a Network and Describe General Methods to Mitigate Those Threats

640-822 CCENT Topic/Objective	Layer 1	Layer 2	Layer 3	Layer 4	Upper Layers
Explain today's increasing network security threats and the need to implement a comprehensive security policy to mitigate the threats					
Explain general methods to mitigate common security threats to network devices, hosts, and applications					
Describe the functions of common security appliances and applications					
Describe security recommended practices, including initial steps to secure network devices					

Table 9-8   Exam Objective: Implement and Verify WAN Links

640-822 CCENT Topic/Objective	Layer 1	Layer 2	Layer 3	Layer 4	Upper Layers
Describe different methods for connecting to a WAN					
Configure and verify a basic WAN serial connection					

Task 3: Reflection

Why is it useful to categorize the exam topics by the OSI layers with which they are associated?

_____

_____

_____

Lab 9-2: Using Wireshark to Observe the TCP Three-Way Handshake (9.1.3)

Objectives

- Use Wireshark to monitor an Ethernet interface for recording packet flows
- Generate a TCP connection using a web browser
- Observe the initial TCP/IP three-way handshake

Background/Preparation

In this lab, you use the Wireshark network packet analyzer (also called a packet sniffer) to view the TCP/IP packets generated by the TCP three-way handshake. When an application that uses TCP first starts on a host, the protocol uses the three-way handshake to establish a reliable TCP connection between two hosts. You will observe the initial packets of the TCP flow: the SYN packet, then the SYN ACK packet, and finally the ACK packet.

Caution: Installing or using a packet sniffer application can be considered a breach of the security policy of an organization, leading to serious legal and financial consequences. It is recommended that you obtain permission before downloading, installing, or running a packet sniffer application.

Note: The term *packet* is used in this lab. Wireshark actually captures Ethernet frames, which contain IP packets. The Wireshark application uses the term *frame* when analyzing captures. The two terms are often used interchangeably, but recall that a frame is a data link Layer 2 encapsulation package and a packet is a network Layer 3 encapsulation.

Task 1: Prepare Wireshark to Capture Packets

Step 1.   Start Wireshark.

Double-click the Wireshark icon, located on the desktop.

Step 2.   Select an interface to use for capturing packets.

From the Capture menu, choose **Interfaces**, as shown in Figure 9-4.

Figure 9-4   Selecting an Interface for Wireshark

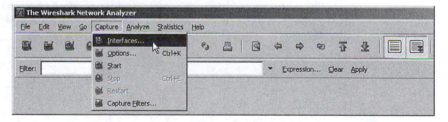

Step 3. Start a network capture.

Choose the local network Ethernet interface adapter for capturing network traffic. Click the **Start** button of the chosen interface, as shown in Figure 9-5.

Figure 9-5 Selecting the Ethernet Interface

Write down the IP address associated with the selected Ethernet adapter. This address is the source IP address to look for when examining captured packets.

The host IP address is

Task 2: Generate and Analyze Captured Packets

Step 1. Open a browser and access a website.

Go to www.google.com. Minimize the Google window and return to Wireshark. You should see captured traffic similar to that shown in Figure 9-6.

Your instructor might provide you with a different website. If so, enter the website name or address here:

The capture windows are now active. Locate the Source, Destination, and Protocol columns on the Wireshark display screen as shown in Figure 9-6. The HTTP data that carries web page text and graphics uses TCP for reliability.

Figure 9-6 Wireshark Capture Window

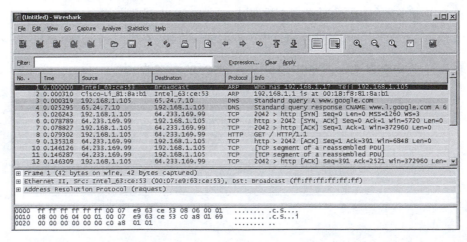

Step 2.   Stop the capture.

From the Wireshark Capture menu, choose **Stop**, as shown in Figure 9-7.

Figure 9-7   Stopping the Packet Capture

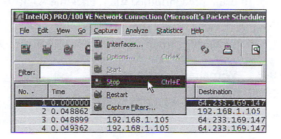

Step 3.   Analyze the captured output.

If the computer was recently started and there has been no activity in accessing the Internet, you can see the entire process in the captured output, including ARP, DNS, and the TCP three-way handshake.

The capture screen in Task 2, Step 1 shows all the packets the computer needs to get to a website, starting with the initial ARP for the gateway router interface MAC address. (Your screen capture may vary.)

In the screen capture, the process starts with frame 1, which is an ARP broadcast from the source computer to determine the MAC address of the router default gateway. The gateway is the local LAN Fast Ethernet interface on the router. The computer must resolve the default gateway IP address to the interface MAC address before it can send the first frame or packet to the router.

What is the IP address of the router default gateway?

_____

The second frame is the reply from the router telling the computer the MAC address of its Fast Ethernet interface. What is the MAC address?

_____

The third frame is a DNS query from the computer to the configured DNS server, attempting to resolve the domain name www.google.com to the IP address of the web server. The computer must have the IP address before it can send the first frame to the web server.

What is the IP address of the DNS server that the computer queried?

_____

The fourth frame is the response from the DNS server with the IP address of www.google.com. You must scroll to the right to see the IP address of the Google server in the DNS response, but you can see it in the next frame.

The fifth frame is the start of the TCP three-way handshake [SYN]. What is the IP address of the Google web server?

_____

Step 4.   Filter the capture to view only TCP packets.

If you have many packets that are unrelated to the TCP connection, it might be necessary to use the Wireshark filter capability.

To use a preconfigured filter, click the **Analyze** menu option, and then click **Display Filters**.

In the Display Filter window shown in Figure 9-8, click **TCP only**, and then click **OK**.

Figure 9-8   Wireshark Display Filters

In the Wireshark window, scroll to the first captured TCP packet as shown in Figure 9-9. This should be the first packet in the flow.

Figure 9-9   Selecting the First Packet in the Flow

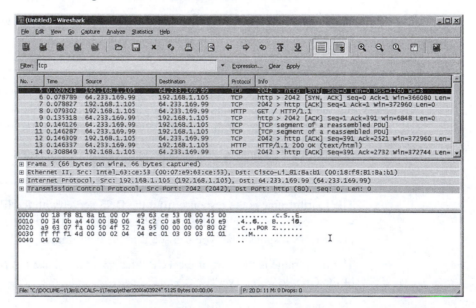

In the Info column, look for three packets similar to the first three shown in Figure 9-9. The first TCP packet is the [SYN] packet from the initiating computer. The second is the [SYN, ACK] response from the web server. The third packet is the [ACK] from the source computer, which completes the handshake.

Step 5.   Inspect the TCP initialization sequence.

In the top Wireshark window, click on the line containing the first packet identified in Step 4. This highlights the line and displays the decoded information from that packet in the two lower windows. This is shown in Figure 9-10.

Figure 9-10   Examining the First Packet in the Flow

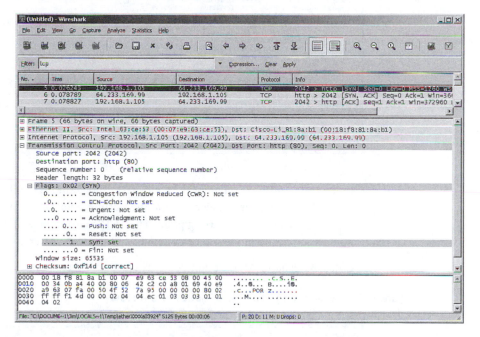

Note: The Wireshark windows shown in Figures 9-10, 9-11, and 9-12 were adjusted to allow the information to be viewed in a compact size. The middle window contains the detailed decoding of the packet.

Click the + icon to expand the view of the TCP information. To contract the view, click the − icon. Expand the contents of the middle window by clicking on the + icons. You may have to scroll to see all the information.

In the first TCP packet, notice that the relative sequence number is set to 0 and the SYN bit is set to 1 in the Flags field.

In the second TCP packet of the handshake, shown in Figure 9-11, notice that the relative sequence number is set to 0 and the SYN bit and the ACK bit are set to 1 in the Flags field.

Figure 9-11   Examining the Second Packet in the Flow

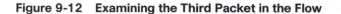

In the third and final frame of the handshake, shown in Figure 9-12, only the ACK bit is set, and the sequence number is set to the starting point of 1. The acknowledgement number is also set to 1 as a starting point. The TCP connection is now established, and communication between the source computer and the web server can begin.

Close Wireshark. At this point you may close the Wireshark application.

Figure 9-12   Examining the Third Packet in the Flow

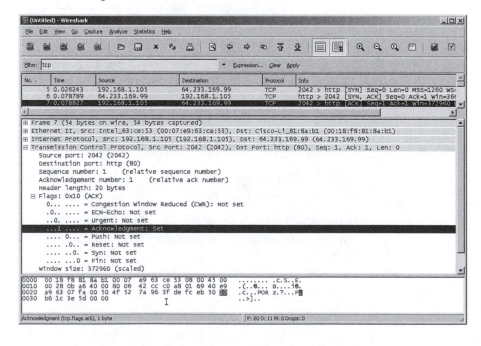

Task 3: Reflection

Hundreds of filters are available in Wireshark. A large network could have numerous filters and many different types of traffic. Which three filters in the list might be the most useful to a network administrator?

_____

Is Wireshark a tool for out-of-band or in-band network monitoring? Explain your answer.

_____

_____

Lab 9-3: Identifying Cabling and Media Errors (9.2.3)

Objectives

- Identify Ethernet device and cabling connectivity.

- Build a simple, routed multi-LAN network and verify connectivity.

- Use the **show interfaces** and **show ip interface** Cisco IOS commands to observe the symptoms when using the wrong cable.

Background/Preparation

In this lab, you build a simple, multi-LAN routed Ethernet network using different types of cables to connect hosts and networking devices, while observing symptoms of connectivity problems.

The following are common cable or media issues that can cause connectivity problems:

- **Loose cable or too much tension on the cable:** If all the pins cannot make a good connection, the circuit is down.

- **Incorrect termination:** Ensure that the correct standard is followed and that all pins are correctly terminated in the connector.

- **Damaged serial interface connector:** Pins on the interface connection are bent or missing.

- **Break or short in the cable:** If there are problems along the circuit, the interface cannot sense the correct signals.

- **Incorrect cable used:** Interchanging straight-through, crossover, and rollover cables can produce unpredictable results and cause lack of connectivity.

Set up a network similar to the one in the topology diagram shown in Figure 9-13 and described in Table 9-9. Any router that meets the interface requirements displayed in that diagram—such as 800, 1600, 1700, 1800, 2500, 2600, or 2800 routers, or a combination of these—can be used. Depending on the model of the router, output may vary from what is shown in this lab.

Figure 9-13 Lab 9-3 Topology

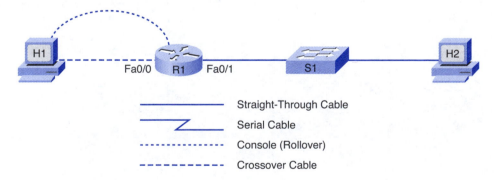

Table 9-9   Device Summary Table

Device	Hostname	Interface	IP Address	Subnet Mask	Default Gateway	Switch Port
R1	R1	Fa0/0	192.168.1.1	255.255.255.0	—	—
		Fa0/1	192.168.2.1	255.255.255.0	—	Fa0/1
S1	S1	VLAN 1	192.168.2.99	255.255.255.0	192.168.2.1	—
H1	H1	NIC	192.168.1.11	255.255.255.0	192.168.1.1	—
H2	H2	NIC	192.168.2.22	255.255.255.0	192.168.2.1	Fa0/2

The following resources are required:

- One 1841 router or other router with two Fast Ethernet interfaces
- One 2960 switch or comparable switch with Fast Ethernet interfaces
- Two Windows XP computers
- Two straight-through Category 5 Ethernet cables
- One crossover Category 5 Ethernet cable
- One RJ-45 rollover console cable
- Access to the command prompts for each host
- Access to the network TCP/IP configuration host

From a host computer, start a HyperTerminal session to the router and switch.

Note: Before starting this lab, make sure the routers and switches have been erased and have no startup configurations.

Task 1: Review Ethernet Device Cabling

Step 1.   Complete the Ethernet device interconnection table (Table 9-10).

Enter the type of cable required to interconnect the devices listed. Use C for crossover and S for straight-through.

Table 9-10   Ethernet Device Interconnections

	Hub	Switch	Router	Workstation
Hub				
Switch				
Router				
Workstation				

Step 2.   Analyze the cabling requirements for this lab.

Which cable type is needed to connect host H1 to router R1, and why?

_____

Which cable type is needed to connect host H2 to S1 and S1 to R1, and why?

_____

_____

Task 2: Build the Network and Configure Devices

Step 1.   Configure basic information on the router and switch.

a.   Build and configure the network according to the topology diagram and device configuration table. Configure basic settings on R1. If necessary, see Lab 5-4, "Configuring Basic Router Settings with the Cisco IOS CLI (5.3.5)," for instructions on setting the hostname, passwords, and interface addresses.

b.   Configure the basic settings on S1 to include the hostname, passwords, and VLAN 1 IP address. If necessary, see Lab 5-11, "Configuring the Cisco 2960 Switch (5.5.4)," for instructions on configuring the switch settings.

c.   Save the running configuration on R1 and S1 using the **copy running-config startup-config** command from privileged EXEC mode.

Step 2.   Configure the hosts.

Configure H1 and H2 with an IP address, subnet mask, and default gateway, according to the device configuration table.

Task 3: Verify Cabling and Interface Link LEDs

Step 1.   Visually inspect the network connections.

After cabling the network devices, verify the connections. Attention to detail now minimizes the time required to troubleshoot network connectivity issues later.

Are all cables and terminations in good condition?

_____

Step 2.   Visually inspect the interface link LEDs.

What is the color of the link light for the switch port to which H2 is attached?

_____

_____

_____

What is the color of the link light on the H1 NIC?

_____

_____

_____

Task 4: Verify Interface Status and Connectivity

Step 1.   Verify the interface status using the **show ip interface brief** command.

a.   From the HyperTerminal session on R1, use the **show ip interface brief** command to view a summary of the device interfaces. This command may be abbreviated **sh ip int br**.

```
R1# show ip interface brief
Interface        IP-Address     OK? Method Status                 Protocol
FastEthernet0/0  192.168.1.1    YES manual up                     up
FastEthernet0/1  192.168.2.1    YES manual up                     up
Serial0/0/0      unassigned     YES NVRAM  administratively down down
Serial0/0/1      unassigned     YES NVRAM  administratively down down
Vlan1            unassigned     YES NVRAM  up                     down
```

What is the interface and protocol status of Fast Ethernet 0/0 and 0/1?

_____

What does Status in column 4 show with regard to cabling and keepalives?

_____

_____

What does Protocol in column 5 refer to?

_____

_____

Why is the status for Serial0/0/0 shown as administratively down?

_____

b.   On router R1, enable the Serial0/0/0 interface using the **no shutdown** command.

```
R1(config)# interface s0/0/0
R1(config-if)# no shutdown
*Mar 1 16:00:02.707: %LINK-3-UPDOWN: Interface Serial0/0/0, changed
  state to down
```

c.   Issue the **show ip interface brief** command again. What is the status for Serial0/0/0 now, and why?

_____

_____

_____

_____

_____

```
R1# show ip interface brief
Interface        IP-Address     OK? Method Status    Protocol
FastEthernet0/0  192.168.1.1    YES manual up        up
FastEthernet0/1  192.168.2.1    YES manual up        up
```

```
Serial0/0/0        unassigned     YES NVRAM  down                    down
Serial0/0/1        unassigned     YES NVRAM  administratively down   down
Vlan1              unassigned     YES NVRAM  up                      down
```

Why is the protocol down for the Serial0/0/0 interface?

_____

_____

Step 2.   Verify the Fast Ethernet interface status using the **show interfaces** command.

a.   On R1, use the **show interfaces** command to view detailed information for interface Fast Ethernet 0/0.

```
R1# show interfaces fastEthernet 0/0
FastEthernet0/0 is up, line protocol is up
  Hardware is Gt96k FE, address is 001b.5325.256e (bia 001b.5325.256e)
  Description: LAN 192.168.1.0/24 Default Gateway
  Internet address is 192.168.1.1/24
  MTU 1500 bytes, BW 100000 Kbit, DLY 100 usec,
     reliability 255/255, txload 1/255, rxload 1/255
  Encapsulation ARPA, loopback not set
  Keepalive set (10 sec)
  Full-duplex, 100Mb/s, 100BaseTX/FX
  ARP type: ARPA, ARP Timeout 04:00:00
  Last input 00:00:50, output 00:00:07, output hang never
  Last clearing of "show interface" counters never
  Input queue: 0/75/0/0 (size/max/drops/flushes); Total output drops: 0
  Queueing strategy: fifo
  Output queue: 0/40 (size/max)
  5 minute input rate 0 bits/sec, 0 packets/sec
  5 minute output rate 0 bits/sec, 0 packets/sec
     142 packets input, 20117 bytes
     Received 135 broadcasts, 0 runts, 0 giants, 0 throttles
     0 input errors, 0 CRC, 0 frame, 0 overrun, 0 ignored
     0 watchdog
     0 input packets with dribble condition detected
     693 packets output, 70950 bytes, 0 underruns
     0 output errors, 0 collisions, 2 interface resets
     0 babbles, 0 late collision, 0 deferred
     0 lost carrier, 0 no carrier
     0 output buffer failures, 0 output buffers swapped out
```

What is the status and line protocol of this interface?

_____

What is the reliability of this interface?

_____

What is the encapsulation of this interface?

_____

What are the duplex and speed settings of this interface?

_____

Are there any runts, giants, input errors, CRC errors, output errors, collisions, or interface resets?

_____

b. On R1, use the **show interfaces** command to view detailed information for interface Fast Ethernet 0/1.

```
R1# show interfaces fastEthernet 0/1
FastEthernet0/1 is up, line protocol is up
  Hardware is Gt96k FE, address is 001b.5325.256f (bia 001b.5325.256f)
  Description: LAN 192.168.2.0/24 Default Gateway
  Internet address is 192.168.2.1/24
  MTU 1500 bytes, BW 100000 Kbit, DLY 100 usec,
     reliability 255/255, txload 1/255, rxload 1/255
  Encapsulation ARPA, loopback not set
  Keepalive set (10 sec)
  Full-duplex, 100Mb/s, 100BaseTX/FX
  ARP type: ARPA, ARP Timeout 04:00:00
  Last input 00:00:00, output 00:00:03, output hang never
  Last clearing of "show interface" counters never
  Input queue: 0/75/0/0 (size/max/drops/flushes); Total output drops: 0
  Queueing strategy: fifo
  Output queue: 0/40 (size/max)
  5 minute input rate 0 bits/sec, 1 packets/sec
  5 minute output rate 0 bits/sec, 0 packets/sec
     5659 packets input, 536086 bytes
     Received 5642 broadcasts, 0 runts, 0 giants, 0 throttles
     0 input errors, 0 CRC, 0 frame, 0 overrun, 0 ignored
     0 watchdog
     0 input packets with dribble condition detected
     775 packets output, 68357 bytes, 0 underruns
     0 output errors, 0 collisions, 1 interface resets
     0 babbles, 0 late collision, 0 deferred
     0 lost carrier, 0 no carrier
     0 output buffer failures, 0 output buffers swapped out
```

Are there any runts, giants, input errors, CRC errors, output errors, collisions, or interface resets?

_____

Step 3.   Verify connectivity.

a.   On host H1, open a command prompt window by selecting **Start > Run** and typing **cmd**. Alternatively, you can select **Start > All programs > Accessories > Command Prompt**.

b.   Ping from H1 to the R1 LAN default gateway.

```
C:\>ping 192.168.1.1
```

c.   Use the **ping** command to test end-to-end connectivity. Ping from host H1 on the R1 192.168.1.0/24 LAN to host H2 on the R1 192.168.2.0/24 LAN.

```
C:\>ping 192.168.2.22
```

Were the pings successful?

_____

_____

Note: If the pings are not successful, troubleshoot the router and host configurations and connections.

Task 5: Observe the Effects of Using Different Cable

Note: The results of this task depend on the type of NIC on the host. If it is a newer NIC, it might be able to autodetect the transmit (TX) and receive (RX) pairs and adjust accordingly. If this is the case, regardless of whether a straight-through or crossover cable is used, the link lights remain lit on the Fa0/0 interface, and the NIC and the **show ip interface brief** command shows up/up after a brief adjustment period.

Step 1.   Change the cable from host H1 to router R1.

Replace the crossover cable from H1 to the R1 Fa0/0 interface with a straight-through cable.

Step 2.   Visually inspect the interface link LEDs.

What is the color of the link light on the R1 interface Fa0/0 to which host H1 is attached?

_____

What is the color of the link light on the host H1 NIC?

_____

Step 3.   Verify interface status.

a.   From the HyperTerminal session on R1, use the **show ip interface brief** command to view a summary of the device interfaces.

```
R1# show ip interface brief
Interface        IP-Address     OK? Method Status                Protocol
FastEthernet0/0  192.168.1.1    YES manual up                    down
FastEthernet0/1  192.168.2.1    YES manual up                    up
Serial0/0/0      unassigned     YES NVRAM  down                  down
Serial0/0/1      unassigned     YES NVRAM  administratively down down
Vlan1            unassigned     YES NVRAM  up                    down
```

What is the interface and protocol status of Fast Ethernet 0/0 and 0/1?

---

b. On R1, use the **show interfaces fastEthernet 0/0** command to view detailed information for each router Fast Ethernet interface.

```
R1#show interfaces fastEthernet 0/0
FastEthernet0/0 is up, line protocol is down
  Hardware is Gt96k FE, address is 001b.5325.256e (bia 001b.5325.256e)
  Description: LAN 192.168.1.0/24 Default Gateway
  Internet address is 192.168.1.1/24
  MTU 1500 bytes, BW 100000 Kbit, DLY 100 usec,
     reliability 255/255, txload 1/255, rxload 1/255
  Encapsulation ARPA, loopback not set
  Keepalive set (10 sec)
  Auto-duplex, 100Mb/s, 100BaseTX/FX
  ARP type: ARPA, ARP Timeout 04:00:00
  Last input 00:12:15, output 00:12:19, output hang never
  Last clearing of "show interface" counters never
  Input queue: 0/75/0/0 (size/max/drops/flushes); Total output drops: 0
  Queueing strategy: fifo
  Output queue: 0/40 (size/max)
  5 minute input rate 0 bits/sec, 0 packets/sec
  5 minute output rate 0 bits/sec, 0 packets/sec
     348 packets input, 42237 bytes
     Received 327 broadcasts, 0 runts, 0 giants, 0 throttles
     0 input errors, 0 CRC, 0 frame, 0 overrun, 0 ignored
     0 watchdog
     0 input packets with dribble condition detected
     1022 packets output, 101376 bytes, 0 underruns
     0 output errors, 0 collisions, 2 interface resets
     0 babbles, 0 late collision, 0 deferred
     0 lost carrier, 0 no carrier
     0 output buffer failures, 0 output buffers swapped out
```

Are there any runts, giants, input errors, CRC errors, output errors, collisions, or interface resets?

Step 4. Change the cable again from host H1 to router R1.

Replace the cable from H1 to the R1 Fa0/0 interface with a rollover cable.

Step 5. Visually inspect the interface link LEDs.

What is the color of the link light on the R1 interface Fa0/0 to which host H1 is attached?

_____

What is the color of the link light on the host H1 NIC?

_____

Step 6.   Verify interface status.

a.   View a summary of the device interfaces.

```
R1# show ip interface brief
Interface        IP-Address     OK? Method Status                   Protocol
FastEthernet0/0  192.168.1.1    YES manual up                       down
FastEthernet0/1  192.168.2.1    YES manual up                       up
Serial0/0/0      unassigned     YES NVRAM  down                     down
Serial0/0/1      unassigned     YES NVRAM  administratively down down
Vlan1            unassigned     YES NVRAM  up                       down
```

What is the interface and protocol status of Fast Ethernet 0/0 and 0/1?

_____

b.   View detailed information for each router Fast Ethernet interface.

```
R1# show interfaces fastEthernet 0/0
FastEthernet0/0 is up, line protocol is down
  Hardware is Gt96k FE, address is 001b.5325.256e (bia 001b.5325.256e)
  Description: LAN 192.168.1.0/24 Default Gateway
  Internet address is 192.168.1.1/24
  MTU 1500 bytes, BW 100000 Kbit, DLY 100 usec,
     reliability 255/255, txload 1/255, rxload 1/255
  Encapsulation ARPA, loopback not set
  Keepalive set (10 sec)
  Auto-duplex, 100Mb/s, 100BaseTX/FX
  ARP type: ARPA, ARP Timeout 04:00:00
  Last input 00:12:15, output 00:12:19, output hang never
  Last clearing of "show interface" counters never
  Input queue: 0/75/0/0 (size/max/drops/flushes); Total output drops: 0
  Queueing strategy: fifo
  Output queue: 0/40 (size/max)
  5 minute input rate 0 bits/sec, 0 packets/sec
  5 minute output rate 0 bits/sec, 0 packets/sec
     348 packets input, 42237 bytes
     Received 327 broadcasts, 0 runts, 0 giants, 0 throttles
     0 input errors, 0 CRC, 0 frame, 0 overrun, 0 ignored
     0 watchdog
     0 input packets with dribble condition detected
     1022 packets output, 101376 bytes, 0 underruns
     0 output errors, 0 collisions, 4 interface resets
```

```
                       0 babbles, 0 late collision, 0 deferred

                       0 lost carrier, 0 no carrier

                       0 output buffer failures, 0 output buffers swapped out
```

Are there any runts, giants, input errors, CRC errors, output errors, collisions, or interface resets?

_____

_____

Step 7.   Change the cable from host H2 to switch S1.

Replace the straight-through cable from host H2 to the switch S1 Fa0/2 interface with a crossover cable.

Step 8.   Visually inspect the interface link LEDs.

What is the color of the link light on the S1 interface Fa0/2 to which host H2 is attached?

_____

What is the color of the link light on the host H2 NIC?

_____

Step 9.   Verify interface status.

a.   From the HyperTerminal session on S1, use the **show ip interface brief** command to view a summary of the device interfaces.

```
S1# show ip interface brief
Interface          IP-Address      OK? Method Status      Protocol
Vlan1              192.168.2.99    YES NVRAM  up          up
FastEthernet0/1    unassigned      YES unset  up          up
FastEthernet0/2    unassigned      YES unset  down        down
```

What is the interface and protocol status of FastEthernet 0/1 and 0/2?

_____

Note: Depending on the switch model and NIC, the LED might be green and the interface may show as up/up. Some switch ports and NICs will automatically adjust to either a straight-through or crossover cable.

b.   On switch S1, use the **show interfaces fastethernet 0/2** command to view detailed information for that interface.

```
S1# show interfaces fastethernet 0/2
FastEthernet0/2 is down, line protocol is down (notconnect)
   Hardware is Fast Ethernet, address is 001d.4635.0c98 (bia
001d.4635.0c98)
   MTU 1500 bytes, BW 10000 Kbit, DLY 1000 usec,
      reliability 255/255, txload 1/255, rxload 1/255
   Encapsulation ARPA, loopback not set
   Keepalive set (10 sec)
   Auto-duplex, Auto-speed, media type is 10/100BaseTX
```

```
      input flow-control is off, output flow-control is unsupported
      ARP type: ARPA, ARP Timeout 04:00:00
      Last input never, output never, output hang never
      Last clearing of "show interface" counters never
      Input queue: 0/75/0/0 (size/max/drops/flushes); Total output drops: 0
      Queueing strategy: fifo
      Output queue: 0/40 (size/max)
      5 minute input rate 0 bits/sec, 0 packets/sec
      5 minute output rate 0 bits/sec, 0 packets/sec
         0 packets input, 0 bytes, 0 no buffer
         Received 0 broadcasts (0 multicast)
         0 runts, 0 giants, 0 throttles
         0 input errors, 0 CRC, 0 frame, 0 overrun, 0 ignored
         0 watchdog, 0 multicast, 0 pause input
         0 input packets with dribble condition detected
         0 packets output, 0 bytes, 0 underruns
         0 output errors, 0 collisions, 1 interface resets
         0 babbles, 0 late collision, 0 deferred
         0 lost carrier, 0 no carrier, 0 PAUSE output
         0 output buffer failures, 0 output buffers swapped out
```

Task 7: Reflection

The note in Task 5 indicated that a modern NIC might be able to sense whether the cable is a straight-through or crossover and adjust accordingly. Why would a NIC not be able to adjust when a rollover cable was used instead of a straight-through or crossover?

_____

_____

_____

Lab 9-4: Troubleshooting LAN Connectivity (9.2.4)

Objectives

- Build a simple, switched network and verify connectivity.

- Troubleshoot LAN connectivity using the LEDs and **show** commands to find link problems and duplex and speed mismatches.

Background/Preparation

LAN troubleshooting usually centers on switches, because the majority of LAN users connect to the network via switch ports. Duplex and speed mismatches are more common on switches than on routers. Many devices are set to autonegotiate speed and duplex settings. If one device on a link is configured to autonegotiate and the other side is manually configured with speed and duplex settings, mismatches may occur, leading to collisions and dropped packets.

In this lab you build a small, switched network with a router and a hub, in addition to workstations. You will alter the speed and duplex settings of device interfaces and observe the effects on link lights and interface status.

Set up a network similar to the one in the topology diagram shown in Figure 9-14 and described in Table 9-11. Any router that meets the interface requirements displayed in that diagram—such as 800, 1600, 1700, 1800, 2500, 2600 or 2800 routers, or a combination of these—can be used. Depending on the model of the router and switch, output may vary from what is shown in this lab.

Figure 9-14   Lab 9-4 Topology

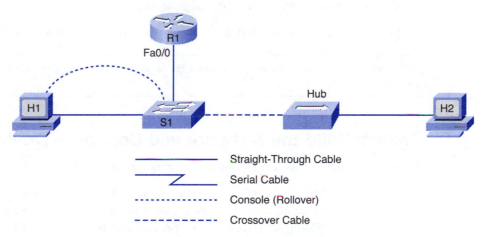

Table 9-11   Device Summary Table

Device	Hostname	Interface	IP Address	Subnet Mask	Default Gateway	Switch Port
R1	R1	Fast Ethernet 0/0	192.168.1.1	255.255.255.0	—	Fast Ethernet 0/2
S1	S1	VLAN 1	192.168.1.99	255.255.255.0	192.168.1.1	—
H1	H1	NIC	192.168.1.11	255.255.255.0	192.168.1.1	Fast Ethernet 0/1
H2	H2	NIC	192.168.1.22	255.255.255.0	192.168.1.1	—
Hub	Hub	1	—	—	—	Fast Ethernet 0/3

The following resources are required:

- One 1841 router or other router with a Fast Ethernet interface

- One 2960 switch or comparable switch with Fast Ethernet interfaces

- One hub with Ethernet interfaces

- Two Windows XP computers

- Three straight-through Category 5 Ethernet cables

- One crossover Category 5 Ethernet cable (optional if the hub has an uplink port)

- One console cable

- Access to the command prompts for each host

- Access to the network TCP/IP configuration for each host

From the host computer, start a HyperTerminal session to the router and switch.

Note: Make sure the routers and switches have been erased and have no startup configurations before beginning this lab.

Task 1: Build the Network and Configure Devices

Step 1.   Configure basic information on the router and switch.

    a.   Build and configure the network according to the topology diagram and device configuration table. Configure basic settings on router R1. If necessary, see Lab 5-4, "Configuring Basic Router Settings with the Cisco IOS CLI (5.3.5)," for instructions on setting the hostname, passwords, and interface addresses.

    b.   Configure the basic settings on switch S1 to include the hostname, passwords, and VLAN 1 IP address. If necessary, see Lab 5-11, "Configuring the Cisco 2960 Switch (5.5.4)," for instructions on configuring the switch settings.

    c.   Save the running configuration on R1 and S1 using the **copy running-config startup-config** command from privileged EXEC mode.

    d.   Connect the hub to switch S1 using a regular port on the hub and a crossover cable, or using the hub uplink port (if present) and a straight-through cable.

Step 2.   Configure the hosts.

Configure H1 and H2 with an IP address, subnet mask, and default gateway, according to the device configuration table.

Task 2: Verify Cabling, Interface LEDs, and Link Speed

Step 1.   Visually inspect the network connections.

After cabling the network devices, verify the connections. Attention to detail now minimizes the time required to troubleshoot network connectivity issues later. Are all cables and terminations in good condition?

_____

Step 2.   Visually inspect the interface link LEDs.

What is the color of the link light for the switch port to which H1 is attached?

_____

_____

_____

What is the color of the link light on the H1 NIC?

_____

Step 3.   View the link speed for host H1 with local area connections as shown in Figure 9-15.

On H1, choose **Start > Settings > Control Panel > Network Connections > Local Area Connection**.

What is the connection speed?

_____

Figure 9-15   Link Speed

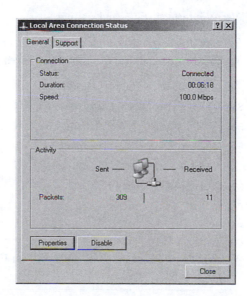

Task 3: Verify Switch Interface Information

Step 1.   Verify interface status.

From the HyperTerminal session on S1, use the **show ip interface brief** command to see the status summary of all interfaces.

Which interfaces have a status of up and a protocol that is up?

```
Interface          IP-Address      OK? Method Status        Protocol

Vlan1              192.168.1.99    YES manual up            up

FastEthernet0/1 unassigned         YES unset  up            up

FastEthernet0/2 unassigned         YES unset  up            up

FastEthernet0/3 unassigned         YES unset  up            up

FastEthernet0/4 unassigned         YES unset  down          down

FastEthernet0/5 unassigned         YES unset  down          down
```

Step 2.   Verify end-to-end connectivity.

a.   On H1, open a command prompt window by choosing **Start > Run** and typing **command** or **cmd**. Alternatively, you can choose **Start > All programs > Accessories > Command Prompt**.

b.   Use the **ping** command to test end-to-end connectivity. Ping from H1 to the default gateway.

```
C:\>ping 192.168.1.1
```

c.   Ping from host H1 to host H2.

```
C:\>ping 192.168.1.22
```

Note: If the pings are not successful, troubleshoot the router and host configurations and connections.

Step 3.   Verify interface status and settings.

To view the speed and duplex settings on a port and whether manual or autonegotiation features were used, use the **show interfaces** *port* **status** command.

Display the status for port numbers Fast Ethernet 0/1 and Fast Ethernet 0/3.

```
S1# show interfaces FastEthernet 0/1 status

Port       Name        Status       Vlan    Duplex  Speed   Type
Fa0/1                  connected    1       a-full  a-100   10/100BaseTX


S1#sh int f0/3 status

Port       Name        Status       Vlan    Duplex  Speed   Type
Fa0/3                  connected    1       a-half  a-10    10/100BaseTX
```

What is the duplex and speed for port Fast Ethernet 0/1?

What does the "a-" at the beginning of "full" and "100" mean?

_____

What is the interface type?

_____

What is the duplex and speed for port Fast Ethernet 0/3?

_____

Why is the duplex and speed for Fast Ethernet 0/3 different than Fast Ethernet 0/1?

_____

_____

Step 4. View interface error statistics.

a. To get a quick view of switch port error statistics, use the **show interfaces** *port* **counters errors** command.

```
S1# show interfaces f0/1 counters errors
Port    Align-Err    FCS-Err    Xmit-Err    Rcv-Err UnderSize
Fa0/1           0          0           0          0         0


Port    Single-Col Multi-Col  Late-Col Excess-Col Carri-Sen Runts Giants
Fa0/1            0         0          0          0         0     0      0
```

Are there any errors or collisions for Fast Ethernet 0/1?

_____

b. Repeat the command for ports Fast Ethernet 0/2 and Fast Ethernet 0/3.

Task 4: Change Duplex Settings

Step 1. Set the duplex setting to full.

a. Change the duplex setting on Fast Ethernet 0/3 to force it to operate at full duplex.

```
S1(config)# interface FastEthernet 0/3
S1(config-if)# duplex full
S1(config-if)# end
S1#
```

What is the result of setting the port Fast Ethernet 0/3 duplex to full?

_____

b. Issue the **show ip interface brief** command. What is the status and protocol for interface 0/3?

_____

Why did this happen?

_____

_____

_____

_____

Step 2.   Set the duplex setting to half duplex.

a.   Change the duplex setting on Fast Ethernet 0/3 to force it to operate at half duplex.

```
S1(config)# interface FastEthernet 0/3
S1(config-if)# duplex half
S1(config-if)# end
S1#
```

What is the result of setting the port Fast Ethernet 0/3 duplex to half?

_____

b.   Issue the **show ip interface brief** command again. What is the status and protocol for interface Fast Ethernet 0/3?

_____

Why did this happen?

_____

Step 3.   Set the duplex setting to autonegotiate.

Change the duplex setting on Fast Ethernet 0/3 back to autonegotiate.

```
S1(config)# interface FastEthernet 0/3
S1(config-if)# duplex auto
S1(config-if)# end
S1#
```

What is the result of setting the port Fast Ethernet 0/3 duplex back to auto?

_____

Task 5: Change Speed Settings

Step 1.   Set the speed to 100 Mbps.

a.   Change the speed setting on Fast Ethernet 0/3 to 100 Mbps.

```
S1(config)# interface FastEthernet 0/3
S1(config-if)# speed 100
S1(config-if)# end
S1#
```

What is the result of setting the speed to 100?

_____

b. Issue the **show ip interface brief** command. What is the status and protocol for interface Fast Ethernet 0/3?

_____

Why did this happen?

_____

_____

_____

_____

Step 2. Set the speed setting to autonegotiate.

a. Change the duplex setting on Fast Ethernet 0/3 back to autonegotiate.

```
S1(config)# interface FastEthernet 0/3
S1(config-if)# speed auto
S1(config-if)# end
S1#
```

b. What is the result of setting the port Fast Ethernet 0/3 speed back to auto?

_____

Task 6: Set Both Duplex and Speed Settings

Step 1. Set the duplex and speed settings for Fast Ethernet 0/1 to full and 100 Mbps.

It is sometimes necessary to set the speed and duplex of a port to ensure that it operates in a particular mode. To force Fast Ethernet port 0/1 to operate at full duplex and 100 Mbps, issue the following commands:

```
S1(config)# interface FastEthernet 0/1
S1(config-if)# duplex full
S1(config-if)# speed 100
S1(config-if)# end
S1#
```

Step 2. Verify the new settings.

When a port is in the default state of auto duplex and auto speed, **duplex** and **speed** commands do not appear in the running configuration for the interface. When the duplex and speed are set to force the port to operate in a particular mode, the commands used are displayed. Use the **show run interface** command to view only the portion of the running configuration that is associated with Fast Ethernet 0/1.

```
S1(config)# show run interface FastEthernet 0/1
Building configuration...

Current configuration : 57 bytes
!
interface FastEthernet0/1
```

```
 speed 100
 duplex full
end
```

Are there any console messages regarding the link status of Fast Ethernet 0/1? Why or why not?

_____

_____

Task 7: Check Settings and Characteristics of Neighboring Devices and Interfaces

Step 1.   Check the characteristics of the neighbor attached to switch port Fast Ethernet 0/2.

a.   Issue the **show cdp neighbors** command for the S1 Fast Ethernet 0/2 port.

```
S1# show cdp neighbors FastEthernet 0/2 detail
-----------------------
Device ID: R1
Entry address(es):
  IP address: 192.168.2.1
Platform: Cisco 1841,  Capabilities: Router Switch IGMP
Interface: FastEthernet0/2,  Port ID (outgoing port): FastEthernet0/1
Holdtime : 145 sec

Version :
Cisco IOS Software, 1841 Software (C1841-ADVIPSERVICESK9-M), Version 12.4(10b),
RELEASE SOFTWARE (fc3)
Technical Support:
Copyright (c) 1986-2007 by Cisco Systems, Inc.
Compiled Fri 19-Jan-07 15:15 by prod_rel_team

advertisement version: 2
VTP Management Domain: ''
Duplex: full
Management address(es):
```

What is the name and platform of the attached device?

_____

What is the Cisco IOS version?

_____

What is the duplex setting for the attached port?

_____

b. Issue the **show cdp neighbors** command for S1 Fast Ethernet 0/3.

```
S1# show cdp neighbors f0/3
Capability Codes: R - Router, T - Trans Bridge, B - Source Route Bridge
                  S - Switch, H - Host, I - IGMP, r - Repeater, P - Phone
Device ID    Local Intrfce  Holdtme    Capability    Platform    Port ID
```

Why is no information shown for the attached device?

_____

_____

Task 8: Change Router Duplex Settings

Step 1.   Set the duplex setting for R1 Fast Ethernet 0/0 to half duplex.

a. To force R1 Fast Ethernet port 0/0 to operate at half duplex, issue the following commands:

```
R1(config)# interface FastEthernet 0/0
R1(config-if)# duplex half
R1(config-if)# end
```

b. Issue the **show ip interface brief** command on R1.

What is the status of Fast Ethernet 0/0?

_____

c. Issue the **show ip interface brief** command on S1.

What is the status of Fast Ethernet 0/2 (the port to which R1 is attached)?

_____

Can you ping the switch VLAN 1 address (192.168.1.99)? Why or why not?

_____

_____

Task 9: Reflection

When LAN connectivity problems exist, always check link lights first, and then check the cabling and terminations. Verify that interfaces are not shut down. Verify that ports are set to autonegotiate, if possible. If a device connected to a port cannot autonegotiate or connectivity problems exist, forcing the port to operate at the specific duplex and speed of the attached device might be required. Check interface errors to determine whether there is a problem with the physical interface itself. Always check both ends of the connection if possible.

Lab 9-5: Troubleshooting WAN Connectivity (9.2.5)

Objectives

- Build a multirouter network and verify connectivity.

- Troubleshoot WAN connectivity using the LEDs and **show** commands to find link problems and encapsulation and timing mismatches.

Background/Preparation

Troubleshooting a serial WAN connection is different from troubleshooting Ethernet LAN connections. Most serial interface and line problems can be identified and corrected using information gathered from the **show interface** serial command. In addition to the transmission errors shown in the error counters, serial connections can experience problems caused by errors or mismatches in encapsulation and timing. In prototype networks, such as those created in a lab environment, a router can be configured to provide DCE clocking functions, eliminating the CSU or modem.

In this lab, you build a multirouter network with a serial WAN link. You will alter the encapsulation and clock speed settings for the serial interfaces and observe the effects on link lights and interface statuses.

Set up a network similar to the one in the topology diagram shown in Figure 9-16 and described in Table 9-12. Any router that meets the interface requirements displayed in that diagram—such as 800, 1600, 1700, 1800, 2500, 2600, or 2800 routers, or a combination of these—can be used. Depending on the model of the router, output may vary from what is shown in this lab.

Figure 9-16   Lab 9-5 Topology

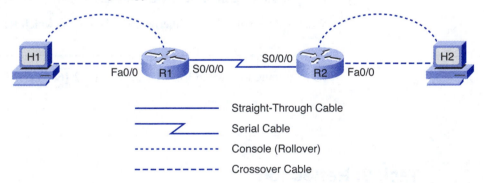

Table 9-12   Device Summary Table

Device	Hostname	Interface	IP Address	Subnet Mask	Default Gateway
R1	R1	Fast Ethernet 0/0	192.168.1.1	255.255.255.0	—
		Serial 0/0/0 (DCE)	192.168.3.1	255.255.255.252	—
R2	R2	Fast Ethernet 0/0	192.168.2.1	255.255.255.0	—
		Serial 0/0/0 (DTE)	192.168.3.2	255.255.255.252	—
H1	H1	NIC	192.168.1.11	255.255.255.0	192.168.1.1
H2	H2	NIC	192.168.2.22	255.255.255.0	192.168.2.1

The following resources are required:

- Two 1841 routers or other routers with one Fast Ethernet and one serial interface

- Two Windows XP computers

- Two crossover Category 5 Ethernet cables

- Null serial cable (R1 to R2)

- At least one console cable

- Access to the command prompt for each host

- Access to the network TCP/IP configuration host

From the host computer, start a HyperTerminal session to the router.

Note: Make sure the routers have been erased and have no startup configurations.

Task 1: Build the Network and Configure Devices

Step 1.   Configure the basic information on the routers.

a.   Build and configure the network according to the topology diagram and device configuration table. Configure basic settings on router R1 and R2. If necessary, see Lab 5-4, "Configuring Basic Router Settings with the Cisco IOS CLI (5.3.5)," for instructions on setting the hostname, passwords, and interface addresses.

Note: Be sure to configure the clock rate for the R1 Serial 0/0/0 interface (DCE).

b.   Save the running configuration on router R1 and R2 using the **copy running-config startup-config** command from privileged EXEC mode.

Step 2.   Configure the hosts.

Configure H1 and H2 with an IP address, subnet mask, and default gateway according to the device configuration table.

Task 2: Verify Cabling and Interface LEDs

Step 1.   Visually inspect the network connections.

After cabling the network devices, verify the connections. Attention to detail now minimizes the time required to troubleshoot network connectivity issues later. Are all cables and terminations in good condition?

Step 2.   Visually inspect interface link LEDs.

What is the color of the link lights for the router R1 Fast Ethernet interface to which host H1 is attached?

What is the color of the link light on the host H1 NIC?

What is the color of the link light for the router R1 Serial 0/0/0 to which router R2 is attached?

Task 3: Verify Router Interface Status and Connectivity

Step 1.   Verify the status of the interfaces on R1.

From the HyperTerminal session on router R1, use the **show ip interface brief** command to see the status summary of all interfaces.

```
R1# show ip interface brief
Interface        IP-Address    OK? Method Status                Protocol
FastEthernet0/0  192.168.1.1   YES NVRAM  up                    up
FastEthernet0/1  unassigned    YES manual administratively down down
Serial0/0/0      192.168.3.1   YES manual up                    up
Serial0/0/1      unassigned    YES NVRAM  administratively down down
Vlan1            unassigned    YES NVRAM  up                    down
```

Which interfaces have a status of up and a protocol that is up?

Step 2.   View the details of the Serial 0/0/0 interface on R1.

Issue the **show interfaces serial 0/0/0** command to view the details of the interface.

```
R1# show interfaces serial 0/0/0
Serial0/0/0 is up, line protocol is up
  Hardware is GT96K Serial
  Description: WAN link to R2
  Internet address is 192.168.3.1/30
  MTU 1500 bytes, BW 1544 Kbit, DLY 20000 usec,
     reliability 255/255, txload 1/255, rxload 1/255
  Encapsulation HDLC, loopback not set
  Keepalive set (10 sec)
  Last input 00:00:05, output 00:00:08, output hang never
  Last clearing of "show interface" counters never
  Input queue: 0/75/0/0 (size/max/drops/flushes); Total output drops: 0
  Queueing strategy: weighted fair
  Output queue: 0/1000/64/0 (size/max total/threshold/drops)
     Conversations  0/1/256 (active/max active/max total)
     Reserved Conversations 0/0 (allocated/max allocated)
     Available Bandwidth 1158 kilobits/sec
  5 minute input rate 0 bits/sec, 0 packets/sec
  5 minute output rate 0 bits/sec, 0 packets/sec
     1154 packets input, 75892 bytes, 0 no buffer
     Received 914 broadcasts, 0 runts, 0 giants, 0 throttles
     0 input errors, 0 CRC, 0 frame, 0 overrun, 0 ignored, 0 abort
```

```
                       908 packets output, 63486 bytes, 0 underruns
                       0 output errors, 0 collisions, 8 interface resets
                       0 output buffer failures, 0 output buffers swapped out
                       25 carrier transitions
                       DCD=up  DSR=up  DTR=up  RTS=up  CTS=up
```

What is the status of Serial 0/0/0?

_____

What is the status of the line protocol?

_____

What is the Internet address?

_____

What is the encapsulation?

_____

Step 3.   Verify the status of the interfaces on R2.

From the HyperTerminal session on router R2, use the **show ip interface brief** command to see the status summary of all interfaces.

```
R2# show ip interface brief
Interface        IP-Address     OK? Method Status                 Protocol
FastEthernet0/0  192.168.2.1    YES NVRAM  up                     up
FastEthernet0/1  unassigned     YES manual administratively down  down
Serial0/0/0      192.168.3.2    YES manual up                     up
Serial0/0/1      unassigned     YES NVRAM  administratively down  down
Vlan1            unassigned     YES NVRAM  up                     down
```

Which interfaces have a status of up and a protocol that is up?

_____

Step 4.   View the details of Serial 0/0/0 interface on R2.

Enter the **show interfaces serial 0/0/0** command to view the details of the interface.

```
R2# show interfaces serial 0/0/0
Serial0/0/0 is up, line protocol is up
  Hardware is GT96K Serial
  Description: WAN link to R1
  Internet address is 192.168.3.2/30
  MTU 1500 bytes, BW 1544 Kbit, DLY 20000 usec,
     reliability 255/255, txload 1/255, rxload 1/255
  Encapsulation HDLC, loopback not set
  Keepalive set (10 sec)
  Last input 00:00:02, output 00:00:00, output hang never
  Last clearing of "show interface" counters never
  Input queue: 0/75/0/0 (size/max/drops/flushes); Total output drops: 0
```

```
        Queueing strategy: weighted fair
        Output queue: 0/1000/64/0 (size/max total/threshold/drops)
            Conversations  0/1/256 (active/max active/max total)
            Reserved Conversations 0/0 (allocated/max allocated)
            Available Bandwidth 1158 kilobits/sec
        5 minute input rate 0 bits/sec, 0 packets/sec
        5 minute output rate 0 bits/sec, 0 packets/sec
            179 packets input, 13104 bytes, 0 no buffer
            Received 169 broadcasts, 0 runts, 0 giants, 0 throttles
            0 input errors, 0 CRC, 0 frame, 0 overrun, 0 ignored, 0 abort
            195 packets output, 13252 bytes, 0 underruns
            0 output errors, 0 collisions, 3 interface resets
            0 output buffer failures, 0 output buffers swapped out
            0 carrier transitions
            DCD=up  DSR=up  DTR=up  RTS=up  CTS=up
```

What is the status of Serial 0/0/0?

_____

What is the status of the line protocol?

_____

What is the Internet address?

_____

What is the encapsulation?

_____

Step 5.   Verify serial link connectivity between the routers.

From the HyperTerminal session on R1, ping the IP address of the R2 Serial 0/0/0 interface.

```
R1# ping 192.168.3.2
```

Note: If the ping is not successful, troubleshoot the router configurations and connections.

Task 4: Change the Clock Rate

Step 1.   On router R1, remove the clock rate from Serial 0/0/0.

The R1 Serial 0/0/0 interface is currently providing the DCE clock signal for the serial WAN link.

Use the **no clock rate** command to remove the clock from Serial 0/0/0.

```
R1(config)# interface serial 0/0/0
R1(config-if)# no clock rate
R1(config-if)# end
```

Which console messages, if any, are displayed when the clock rate is removed?

_____

_____

_____

_____

_____

Step 2.   View the details of the interface.

Issue the **show interfaces serial 0/0/0** command on R1.

Note: The following output is from a Cisco 1841 router. If you are not using an 1841 router and you received an error message in the previous step, the line protocol is down.

```
R1# show interfaces serial 0/0/0
Serial0/0/0 is up, line protocol is up
  Hardware is GT96K Serial
  Description: WAN link to R2
  Internet address is 192.168.3.1/30
  MTU 1500 bytes, BW 1544 Kbit, DLY 20000 usec,
     reliability 255/255, txload 1/255, rxload 1/255
  Encapsulation HDLC, loopback not set
  Keepalive set (10 sec)
  Last input 00:00:00, output 00:00:01, output hang never
  Last clearing of "show interface" counters never
  Input queue: 0/75/0/0 (size/max/drops/flushes); Total output drops: 0
  Queueing strategy: weighted fair
  Output queue: 0/1000/64/0 (size/max total/threshold/drops)
     Conversations  0/1/256 (active/max active/max total)
     Reserved Conversations 0/0 (allocated/max allocated)
     Available Bandwidth 1158 kilobits/sec
  5 minute input rate 0 bits/sec, 0 packets/sec
  5 minute output rate 0 bits/sec, 0 packets/sec
     80 packets input, 6205 bytes, 0 no buffer
     Received 80 broadcasts, 0 runts, 0 giants, 0 throttles
     0 input errors, 0 CRC, 0 frame, 0 overrun, 0 ignored, 0 abort
     81 packets output, 6229 bytes, 0 underruns
     0 output errors, 0 collisions, 5 interface resets
     0 output buffer failures, 0 output buffers swapped out
     1 carrier transitions
     DCD=up  DSR=up  DTR=up  RTS=up  CTS=up
```

What is the status of the R1 Serial 0/0/0 interface and line protocol?

_____

Note: This lab uses Cisco 1841 routers with Cisco IOS Software release 12.4(10). When the clock rate is removed from the DCE Serial 0/0/0 interface, the 1841 router automatically reinserts the clock rate at a default speed of 2,000,000 bps (2 Mbps).

If a router such as a 2600 series is used, the Serial 0/0/0 interface goes to up/down status when the clock rate is removed from the DCE interface Serial 0/0/0.

Step 3.   On router R1, reset the clock rate on Serial 0/0/0.

    a.   Use the Cisco IOS help feature with the **clock rate** command to determine the range of clock rate settings.

```
R1(config)# interface serial 0/0/0
R1(config-if)# clock rate ?
```

What is the highest setting listed?

_____

    b.   On router R1, apply a clock rate of 128,000 bps to Serial 0/0/0.

```
R1(config)# interface serial 0/0/0
R1(config-if)# clock rate 128000
R1(config-if)# end
```

Note: Even though the **clock rate** command lists settings up to 8,000,000, depending on the router model and serial interface type, the router interface might not be able to support speeds above 128,000. The 1841 router with a WIC 2T modular serial interface can support speeds of up to 8,000,000 bps.

The following message is from a 2600 router with Cisco IOS Software release 12.2 and a WIC 2A/S modular serial interface. The WIC 2A/S interface supports speeds up to 128,000 but displays an error message when attempting to set the clock rate to anything higher.

```
R1(config-if)# clock rate 148000
%Error: Unsupported clock rate for this interface
```

Task 5: Remove the Serial Cable and Observe the Effects

Step 1.   Remove the cable from router R1 Serial 0/0/0.

Which console messages, if any, are displayed when the cable is removed?

_____

_____

Step 2.   On router R1, use the **show interfaces serial** command.

Issue the **show interfaces serial 0/0/0** command to view the details of the interface.

```
R1# show interfaces serial 0/0/0
Serial0/0/0 is down, line protocol is down
  Hardware is GT96K Serial
  Description: WAN link to R2
```

```
Internet address is 192.168.3.1/30
MTU 1500 bytes, BW 1544 Kbit, DLY 20000 usec,
    reliability 255/255, txload 1/255, rxload 1/255
Encapsulation HDLC, loopback not set
Keepalive set (10 sec)
Last input 00:04:03, output 00:03:56, output hang never
Last clearing of "show interface" counters 01:36:07
Input queue: 0/75/0/0 (size/max/drops/flushes); Total output drops: 0
Queueing strategy: weighted fair
Output queue: 0/1000/64/0 (size/max total/threshold/drops)
    Conversations  0/1/256 (active/max active/max total)
    Reserved Conversations 0/0 (allocated/max allocated)
    Available Bandwidth 1158 kilobits/sec
5 minute input rate 0 bits/sec, 0 packets/sec
5 minute output rate 0 bits/sec, 0 packets/sec
    954 packets input, 36318 bytes, 0 no buffer
    Received 0 broadcasts, 0 runts, 0 giants, 0 throttles
    0 input errors, 0 CRC, 0 frame, 0 overrun, 0 ignored, 0 abort
    1163 packets output, 37144 bytes, 0 underruns
    0 output errors, 0 collisions, 119 interface resets
    0 output buffer failures, 0 output buffers swapped out
    145 carrier transitions
    DCD=up  DSR=up  DTR=down  RTS=down  CTS=up
```

What is the status of the R1 Serial 0/0/0 interface and line protocol?

_____

Step 3.   Reconnect the serial cable to the R1 Serial 0/0/0 interface.

Did the interface and line protocol come back up?

_____

Are there any runts, giants, input errors, CRC errors, output errors, collisions, or interface resets?

_____

Step 4. On router R1, clear the counters on Serial 0/0/0.

a.   Use the **clear counters serial 0/0/0** command to reset the interface statistics.

```
R1# clear counters serial 0/0/0
Clear "show interface" counters on this interface [confirm]
R1#

*Mar  5 21:30:54.258: %CLEAR-5-COUNTERS: Clear counter on
    interface Serial0/0/0 by console
```

b.   Issue the **show interfaces serial 0/0/0** command to view the details of the interface. Have the interface statistics been reset?

_____

Task 6: Change the Encapsulation Type

Step 1.   Verify the current serial status and data link Layer 2 encapsulation.

Issue the **show interfaces serial 0/0/0** command to view the details of the interface on R1.

```
R1# show interfaces serial 0/0/0
Serial0/0/0 is up, line protocol is down
  Hardware is GT96K Serial
  Description: WAN link to R2
  Internet address is 192.168.3.1/30
  MTU 1500 bytes, BW 1544 Kbit, DLY 20000 usec,
     reliability 255/255, txload 1/255, rxload 1/255
  Encapsulation HDLC, loopback not set
  Keepalive set (10 sec)
  Last input 00:00:08, output 00:00:17, output hang never
  Last clearing of "show interface" counters 00:01:25
  Input queue: 0/75/0/0 (size/max/drops/flushes); Total output drops: 0
  Queueing strategy: weighted fair
  Output queue: 0/1000/64/0 (size/max total/threshold/drops)
     Conversations  0/1/256 (active/max active/max total)
     Reserved Conversations 0/0 (allocated/max allocated)
     Available Bandwidth 1158 kilobits/sec
  5 minute input rate 0 bits/sec, 0 packets/sec
  5 minute output rate 0 bits/sec, 0 packets/sec
     9 packets input, 206 bytes, 0 no buffer
     Received 0 broadcasts, 0 runts, 0 giants, 0 throttles
     0 input errors, 0 CRC, 0 frame, 0 overrun, 0 ignored, 0 abort
     20 packets output, 280 bytes, 0 underruns
     0 output errors, 0 collisions, 4 interface resets
     0 output buffer failures, 0 output buffers swapped out
     6 carrier transitions
     DCD=up  DSR=up  DTR=up  RTS=up  CTS=up
```

What is the status of Serial 0/0/0?

_____

What is the status of the line protocol?

_____

What is the encapsulation?

_____

Step 2.   Change the serial interface encapsulation on R1.

a.   Use the Cisco IOS help feature with the **encapsulation** command to see which encapsulation type settings are available.

```
R1(config)# interface serial 0/0/0
R1(config-if)# encapsulation ?
```

Which encapsulation choices are available?

_____

_____

b. Change the encapsulation type to PPP.

```
R1(config)# interface serial 0/0/0
R1(config-if)# encapsulation ppp
```

What console messages are displayed?

_____

_____

Step 3.   Verify the interface status and encapsulation on R1.

Issue the **show interfaces serial 0/0/0** to view the details of the R1 Serial 0/0/0 interface.

```
R1# show interfaces serial 0/0/0
Serial0/0/0 is up, line protocol is down
  Hardware is GT96K Serial
  Description: WAN link to R2
  Internet address is 192.168.3.1/30
  MTU 1500 bytes, BW 1544 Kbit, DLY 20000 usec,
      reliability 255/255, txload 1/255, rxload 1/255
  Encapsulation PPP, LCP Listen, loopback not set
  Keepalive set (10 sec)
  Last input 00:00:08, output 00:00:17, output hang never
  Last clearing of "show interface" counters 00:01:25
  Input queue: 0/75/0/0 (size/max/drops/flushes); Total output drops: 0
  Queueing strategy: weighted fair
  Output queue: 0/1000/64/0 (size/max total/threshold/drops)
     Conversations  0/1/256 (active/max active/max total)
     Reserved Conversations 0/0 (allocated/max allocated)
     Available Bandwidth 1158 kilobits/sec
  5 minute input rate 0 bits/sec, 0 packets/sec
  5 minute output rate 0 bits/sec, 0 packets/sec
     9 packets input, 206 bytes, 0 no buffer
     Received 0 broadcasts, 0 runts, 0 giants, 0 throttles
     0 input errors, 0 CRC, 0 frame, 0 overrun, 0 ignored, 0 abort
     20 packets output, 280 bytes, 0 underruns
     0 output errors, 0 collisions, 4 interface resets
     0 output buffer failures, 0 output buffers swapped out
     6 carrier transitions
     DCD=up  DSR=up  DTR=up  RTS=up  CTS=up
```

What is the status of Serial 0/0/0?

_____

What is the status of the line protocol?

_____

What is the encapsulation?

_____

Step 4.   Check the serial interface encapsulation on R2.

Issue the **show interfaces serial** command to view the details of the R2 Serial 0/0/0 interface.

```
R2# show interfaces serial 0/0/0
Serial0/0/0 is up, line protocol is down
  Hardware is GT96K Serial
  Description: WAN link to R1
  Internet address is 192.168.3.2/30
  MTU 1500 bytes, BW 1544 Kbit, DLY 20000 usec,
     reliability 255/255, txload 1/255, rxload 1/255
  Encapsulation HDLC, loopback not set
  Keepalive set (10 sec)
  Last input 00:00:03, output 00:00:01, output hang never
  Last clearing of "show interface" counters never
  Input queue: 0/75/0/0 (size/max/drops/flushes); Total output drops: 0
  Queueing strategy: weighted fair
  Output queue: 0/1000/64/0 (size/max total/threshold/drops)
     Conversations  0/1/256 (active/max active/max total)
     Reserved Conversations 0/0 (allocated/max allocated)
     Available Bandwidth 1158 kilobits/sec
  5 minute input rate 0 bits/sec, 0 packets/sec
  5 minute output rate 0 bits/sec, 0 packets/sec
     729 packets input, 30809 bytes, 0 no buffer
     Received 729 broadcasts, 0 runts, 0 giants, 0 throttles
     0 input errors, 0 CRC, 0 frame, 0 overrun, 0 ignored, 0 abort
     548 packets output, 30055 bytes, 0 underruns
     0 output errors, 0 collisions, 63 interface resets
     0 output buffer failures, 0 output buffers swapped out
     204 carrier transitions
     DCD=up  DSR=up  DTR=up  RTS=up  CTS=up
```

What is the status of Serial 0/0/0?

_____

What is the status of the line protocol?

_____

What is the encapsulation?

_____

Why is the line protocol for both R1 and R2 now down?

_____

_____

Step 5.   Change the serial interface encapsulation on R2.

Now change the encapsulation type on the R2 interface to PPP.

```
R2(config)# interface serial 0/0/0
R2(config-if)# encapsulation ppp
```

What console messages are displayed?

_____

_____

Step 6.   Check the interface status on R2.

Issue the **show ip interface brief** command to view the status of all R2 interfaces.

```
R2# show ip interface brief
Interface        IP-Address      OK? Method  Status                 Protocol
FastEthernet0/0  192.168.2.1     YES NVRAM   up                     up
FastEthernet0/1  unassigned      YES NVRAM   administratively down  down
Serial0/0/0      192.168.3.2     YES NVRAM   up                     up
Serial0/0/1      unassigned      YES NVRAM   administratively down  down
Vlan1            unassigned      YES NVRAM   up                     down
```

What is the status of Serial 0/0/0?

_____

What is the status of the line protocol?

_____

Step 7.   Check the interface status on R1.

a.   Issue the **show ip interface brief** command to view the status of all R1 interfaces.

```
R1# show ip interface brief
Interface        IP-Address      OK? Method  Status                 Protocol
FastEthernet0/0  192.168.1.1     YES NVRAM   up                     up
FastEthernet0/1  unassigned      YES NVRAM   administratively down  down
Serial0/0/0      192.168.3.1     YES NVRAM   up                     up
Serial0/0/1      unassigned      YES NVRAM   administratively down  down
Vlan1            unassigned      YES NVRAM   up                     down
```

What is the status of Serial 0/0/0?

_____

What is the status of the line protocol?

_____

b. Issue the **show running-config interface serial 0/0/0** command to view the commands used to configure the R1 Serial 0/0/0 interface.

```
R1(config)# show running-config interface Serial 0/0/0

Building configuration...

Current configuration : 137 bytes
!
interface Serial0/0/0
 description WAN link to R2
 ip address 192.168.3.1 255.255.255.252
 encapsulation ppp
 clockrate 128000
end
```

Step 8. Verify that the serial connection is functioning.

Ping from R1 to R2 to verify that there is connectivity between the two routers.

```
R1# ping 192.168.3.2
R2# ping 192.168.3.1
```

Can the serial interface on R2 be pinged from R1?

_____

Can the serial interface on R1 be pinged from R2?

_____

Note: If the answer is no for either question, troubleshoot the router configurations to find the error. Repeat the pings until they are successful.

Task 7: Reflection

When WAN connectivity problems exist, always check link lights first, and then check the cabling and terminations. Verify that interfaces are not shut down. Verify that interfaces are set to the proper encapsulation and clock rate (if applicable). Check interface errors to determine whether there is a problem with the physical interface itself. Always check both ends of the connection if possible.

Lab 9-6: Designing an IP Subnetting Scheme for Growth (9.3.3)

Objectives

- Analyze the subnetting requirements for a small company with multiple networks.

- Design a subnetting scheme that allows for 20% growth in the number of subnets and the number of hosts per subnet.

- Develop an IP addressing plan to apply addresses to networking devices and host computers.

Background/Preparation

When developing IP addressing schemes for subnetting, it is important to look at the subnet requirements of the network and plan for potential growth in the number of subnets and the number of hosts per subnet.

Figure 9-17 shows the topology for this lab.

Figure 9-17   Lab 9-6 Topology

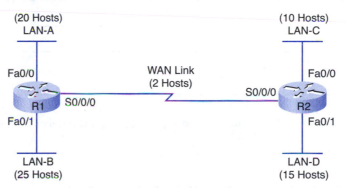

In this lab, you are given a block of addresses to work with. Based on the network requirements of the organization, subnet the block of addresses and allocate a subnet to each segment of the network. In the subnet scheme, you must allow for 20% growth in the number of subnets and in the number of hosts for a given subnet. After you have created the subnets, assign IP addresses to each router interface and allocate blocks of addresses for the hosts on each LAN.

This is a paper-based lab. Use the worksheets to complete the lab.

Task 1: Analyze the Network Topology for Subnetting Requirements

Step 1.   Examine the network topology to determine the number of segments.

How many Ethernet networks currently exist?

_____

How many WAN links currently exist?

_____

How many total networks currently exist?

_____

How many subnets currently exist?

_____

How many subnets have 20% growth?

_____

Step 2.   Document the current number of hosts on each network segment.

Enter the network segment names in Table 9-13. Enter the number of hosts on each subnet, and then calculate the number of hosts the subnet must support if the number grows by 20%.

Table 9-13   Network Host Summary

Segment Name	Current Number of Hosts	Number of Hosts After 20% Growth

Which subnet must support the largest number of hosts?

_____

Task 2: Develop the Subnet Scheme

Step 1.   Determine the number of subnets and hosts.

The customer has been assigned IP address block 172.20.99.0 /24 by their ISP. This provides 8 bits for hosts. How many total addresses do they have to work with before subnetting?

_____

What is the decimal subnet mask for a /24 mask?

_____

What is the minimum number of subnets required for the network design to allow for 20% growth?

_____

How many bits must be borrowed from the host portion of the IP address to allow for that number of subnets, and how many total subnets can be created?

_____

How many hosts (including the 20% growth) must the largest subnet support?

_____

To support that many hosts, the number of host bits required is

_____

Does this subnet scheme allow for the number of subnets and hosts per subnet needed?

_____

Step 2.   Calculate the custom subnet mask.

The address block assigned by the ISP is a /24 or 255.255.255.0. What is the custom subnet mask? _____._____._____._____, or /_____

_____

To which devices and interfaces is this mask assigned?

_____

_____

Step 3.   Identify the subnet and host IP addresses.

Now that the subnet mask is identified, the network addressing scheme can be created. The addressing scheme includes the subnet numbers, the subnet broadcast address, and the range of IP addresses that can be assigned to hosts.

Complete Table 9-14, showing all possible subnets for the 172.20.99.0 network. In the last column, enter the name of the network segment to which you are assigning the subnet.

Table 9-14   Network Host Summary

Subnet	Subnet Address	Host IP Address Range	Broadcast Address	Network Segment
0				
1				
2				
3				
4				
5				
6				
7				

Task 3: Document Network Device and Host Interfaces

Step 1.   Document the network device interface IP addresses.

Fill in Table 9-15 with the IP addresses and subnet masks for the router interfaces.

Table 9-15   Network Device Interface Addresses

Device	Network Segment	Interface	IP Address	Subnet Mask
R1	LAN-A	Fast Ethernet 0/0		
	LAN-B	Fast Ethernet 0/1		
	WAN	Serial 0/0/0		
R2	LAN-C	Fast Ethernet 0/0		
	LAN-D	Fast Ethernet 0/1		
	WAN	Serial 0/0/0		

Step 2.   Document the host IP addresses.

Fill in Table 9-16 with the IP addresses and subnet masks for the first host on each LAN. Assign the next available address to the first host computer on the LAN.

Table 9-16   Host Computer Interface Addresses

Device	Network Segment	Interface	IP Address	Subnet Mask	Default Gateway
Host 1	LAN-A	NIC			
Host 1	LAN-B	NIC			
Host 1	LAN-C	NIC			
Host 1	LAN-D	NIC			

Task 4: Reflection

With the initial block of addresses assigned by the ISP and the requirements for future growth, would any other subnetting scheme have worked?

If the maximum number of hosts per network segment were only 14, could you have used another scheme? Why or why not?

Although it works for this scenario, would it be a good idea to use 4 bits for subnets and 4 bits for hosts? Why or why not?

Lab 9-7: Correcting RIPv2 Routing Problems (9.4.2)

Objectives

- Cable a network according to the topology diagram.

- Load the routers with supplied scripts.

- Gather information about the nonconverged portion of the network, along with any other errors.

- Analyze information using Cisco IOS **show** and **debug** commands to determine network errors.

- Propose solutions to network errors.

- Implement solutions to network errors.

- Document the corrected network.

Background/Preparation

Many different types of problems can prevent dynamic routes from appearing in the routing table. With dynamic routing, routers receive routing updates from neighbors. If an expected route does not appear in the routing table of one of the routers, the cause is most likely a configuration error. This configuration error could occur on any of the routers connected between the source and the destination.

In this lab, you begin by loading configuration scripts on each router. These scripts contain errors that prevent end-to-end communication across the network. After loading the corrupted scripts, troubleshoot each router to determine the configuration errors, and then use the appropriate commands to correct the configurations. When you have corrected all the configuration errors, all the hosts on the network should be able to communicate with each other.

The network should also meet the following requirements:

- RIPv2 routing is configured on all routers.

- RIP updates must be disabled on all router LAN interfaces.

Figure 9-18 shows the topology for this lab, and Table 9-17 provides a device configuration summary.

Figure 9-18   Lab 9-7 Topology

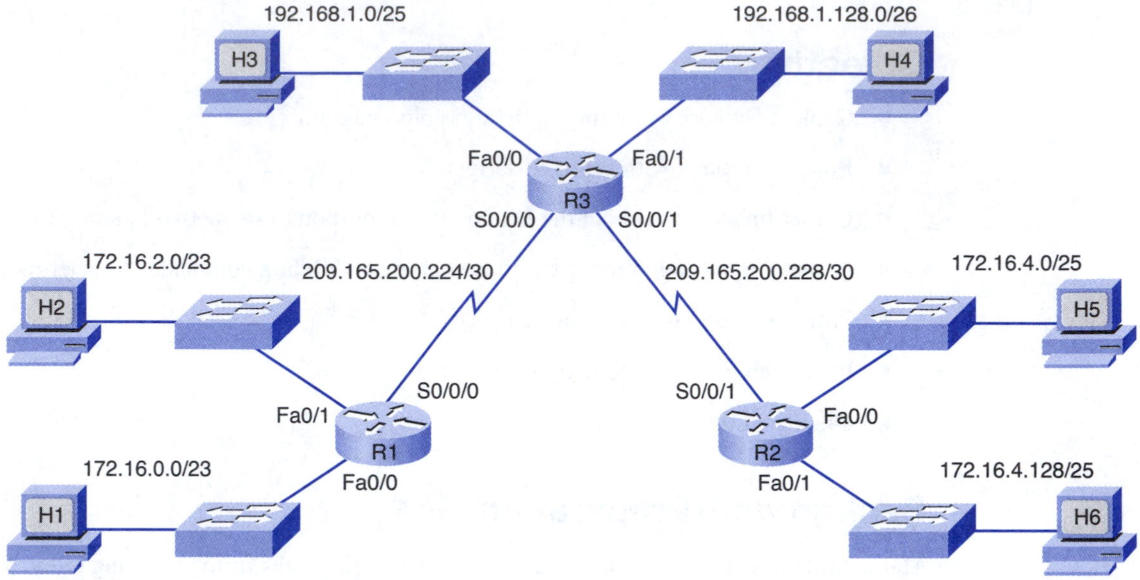

Table 9-17   Device Configuration Summary

Device	Hostname	Interface	IP Address	Subnet Mask	Default Gateway
R1	BRANCH1	Fast Ethernet 0/0	172.16.0.1	255.255.254.0	—
		Fast Ethernet 0/1	172.16.2.1	255.255.254.0	—
		Serial 0/0/0 (DCE)	209.165.200.226	255.255.255.252	—
R2	BRANCH2	Fast Ethernet 0/0	172.16.4.1	255.255.255.128	—
		Fast Ethernet 0/1	172.16.4.129	255.255.255.128	—
		Serial 0/0/1	209.165.200.230	255.255.255.252	—
R3	HQ	Fast Ethernet 0/0	192.168.1.1	255.255.255.128	—
		Fast Ethernet 0/1	192.168.1.129	255.255.255.192	—
		Serial 0/0/0	209.165.200.225	255.255.255.252	—
		Serial 0/0/1 (DCE)	209.165.200.229	255.255.255.252	—
H1	H1	NIC	172.16.0.10	255.255.254.0	172.16.0.1
H2	H2	NIC	172.16.2.10	255.255.254.0	172.16.2.1
H3	H3	NIC	192.168.1.10	255.255.255.128	192.168.1.1
H4	H4	NIC	192.168.1.138	255.255.255.192	192.168.1.129
H5	H5	NIC	172.16.4.10	255.255.255.128	172.16.4.1
H6	H6	NIC	172.16.4.138	255.255.255.128	172.16.4.129

The following resources are required:

- Two routers, each with two Fast Ethernet and one serial interface
- One router, with two Fast Ethernet and two serial interfaces
- Six switches or hubs (or crossover cables from hosts to routers)
- Six Windows XP computers
- Straight-through Category 5 Ethernet cables, as required
- Two null serial cables
- Console cables, as required
- Access to the host command prompt
- Access to the host network TCP/IP configuration

Note: Make sure the routers and the switches have been erased and have no startup configurations.

Task 1: Build the Network and Configure Devices

Step 1. Build a network similar to the one shown in the topology diagram.

Step 2. Configure the hosts.

Configure each host IP address, subnet mask, and default gateway according to the device configuration chart.

Task 2: Load Routers with the Supplied Scripts

Step 1. Load the script onto the BRANCH1 router. Note that this script is for an 1841 router and may require modification to run on other models.

```
hostname BRANCH1
!
line console 0
password cisco
login
logging synchronous
line vty 0 4
password cisco
login
enable secret class
banner motd #Unauthorized Use Prohibited#
no ip domain lookup
!
interface FastEthernet0/0
ip address 172.16.0.1 255.255.254.0
duplex auto
speed auto
no shutdown
```

```
!
interface FastEthernet0/1
ip address 172.16.2.1 255.255.254.0
duplex auto
speed auto
no shutdown
!
interface Serial0/0/0
ip address 209.165.200.226 255.255.255.252
clock rate 64000
no shutdown
!
router rip
passive-interface FastEthernet0/0
passive-interface FastEthernet0/1
network 172.16.0.0
network 209.165.200.0
!
ip classless
!
line con 0
line vty 0 4
login
!
end
```

Step 2.   Load the script onto the BRANCH2 router. Note that this script is for an 1841 router and may require modification to run on other models.

```
hostname BRANCH2
!
line console 0
password cisco
login
logging synchronous
line vty 0 4
password cisco
login
enable secret class
banner motd #Unauthorized Use Prohibited#
no ip domain lookup
!
interface FastEthernet0/0
ip address 172.16.4.129 255.255.255.128
duplex auto
speed auto
```

```
no shutdown
!
interface FastEthernet0/1
ip address 172.16.4.1 255.255.255.128
duplex auto
speed auto
no shutdown
!
interface Serial0/0/1
ip address 209.165.200.230 255.255.255.252
no shutdown
!
router rip
version 2
passive-interface FastEthernet0/0
passive-interface FastEthernet0/1
network 209.165.200.0
!
ip classless
!
line con 0
line vty 0 4
login
!
end
```

Step 3.   Load the script onto the HQ router. Note that this script is for an 1841 router and may require modification to run on other models.

```
hostname HQ
!
line console 0
password cisco
login
logging synchronous
line vty 0 4
password cisco
login
enable secret class
banner motd #Unauthorized Use Prohibited#
no ip domain lookup
!
interface FastEthernet0/0
ip address 192.168.1.1 255.255.255.128
duplex auto
```

```
speed auto
no shutdown
!
interface FastEthernet0/1
ip address 192.168.1.129 255.255.255.192
duplex auto
speed auto
no shutdown
!
interface Serial0/0/0
ip address 209.165.200.225 255.255.255.252
no shutdown
!
interface Serial0/0/1
ip address 209.165.200.229 255.255.255.252
clock rate 64000
no shutdown
!
router rip
version 2
passive-interface FastEthernet0/0
passive-interface FastEthernet0/1
network 192.168.1.0
network 209.165.200.0
!
ip classless
!
line con 0
line vty 0 4
login
!
end
```

Task 3: Troubleshoot the BRANCH1 Router

Step 1.   Begin troubleshooting at the host connected to BRANCH1.

From H1, is it possible to ping H2 (172.16.0.10)?

_____

From H1, is it possible to ping H3 (192.168.1.10)?

_____

From H1, is it possible to ping H5 (172.16.4.10)?

_____

From H1, is it possible to ping the default gateway (172.16.0.1)?

_____

Step 2.   Examine BRANCH1 to find possible interface configuration errors.

View the status information summary for the router interfaces.

Are there any problems with the interface configurations?

_____

If there are problems with the interface configurations, record the commands necessary to correct the configuration errors.

_____

If you have recorded any commands, apply them to the router configuration now.

If any changes were made to the configuration, view the status information summary for the router interfaces again.

Does the information in the summary indicate any configuration errors?

_____

If the answer is yes, troubleshoot the status of the interfaces again.

Step 3.   Troubleshoot the routing configuration on BRANCH1.

What command displays the routing table?

_____

Which networks and routes are shown in the routing table?

_____

_____

_____

_____

_____

_____

_____

_____

_____

Which command displays the commands used to configure the routing protocol on this router?

_____

Are there any problems with the routing table because of the routing configuration?

_____

If there are any problems, record the commands necessary to correct the configuration errors.

_____

Are there any problems with the routing table that could be caused by errors in other parts of the network?

_____

_____

Which version of RIP and which local networks are included in the RIP updates being sent from BRANCH1?

_____

_____

Which commands could you use to determine the version of RIP updates?

_____

Use the **debug ip rip** command to determine which networks are included in the RIP updates being sent from BRANCH1.

_____

_____

_____

_____

_____

_____

_____

_____

_____

_____

_____

Are there any problems with the version of RIP updates that are being sent out from the router?

_____

If there are additional problems with the RIP configuration, record the commands necessary to correct the configuration errors.

_____

_____

Note: Do not turn off auto summary at this time.

Step 4.   Fix the router configuration.

If you have recorded any commands in the previous step, apply them to the router configuration.

If any changes were made to the configuration, view the routing information again.

Does the information in the routing table indicate any configuration errors?

_____

Does the information included in the RIP updates that are sent out indicate any configuration errors?

_____

If the answer to either of these questions is yes, troubleshoot the routing configuration again.

Which networks and routes are shown in the routing table?

_____

_____

_____

_____

_____

_____

_____

_____

_____

_____

_____

Step 5.   Ping between the hosts again.

From H1, is it possible to ping H3 (192.168.1.10)?

_____

From H1, is it possible to ping H4 (192.168.1.138)?

_____

From H1, is it possible to ping H5 (172.16.4.10)?

_____

From H1, is it possible to ping the Serial 0/0/1 interface of the HQ router (209.165.200.229)?

_____

Task 4: Troubleshoot HQ

Step 1.   Begin troubleshooting at host H3.

From H3, is it possible to ping H1 (172.16.0.10)?

_____

From H3, is it possible to ping H5 (172.16.4.10)?

_____

From H3, is it possible to ping the default gateway (192.168.1.1)?

_____

Step 2.   Examine the HQ router to find possible configuration errors.

View the status information summary for the router interfaces. Are there any problems with the interface configurations?

_____

If there are problems with the interface configurations, record the commands necessary to correct the configuration errors.

_____

If you have recorded any commands, apply them to the router configuration now.

Step 3.   Troubleshoot the routing configuration on HQ.

Which networks and routes are shown in the routing table?

_____

_____

_____

_____

_____

_____

_____

_____

_____

_____

If there are any problems with the routing table, list them.

_____

If there are problems, record the commands necessary to correct the configuration errors.

_____

_____

Which networks are included in the RIP updates?

_____

_____

_____

Are there problems with the RIP updates that are being sent out from HQ?

_____

If there are problems, record the commands necessary to correct the configuration errors.

_____

If you have recorded any commands, apply them to the router configuration now.

Step 4.   View the routing information.

If any changes were made to the configuration, view the routing information again.

Does the information in the routing table indicate any configuration errors on HQ?

_____

Does the information included in the RIP updates that are sent out indicate any configuration errors on HQ?

_____

If the answer to either of these questions is yes, troubleshoot the routing configuration again.

Step 5.   Ping between the hosts again.

From H3, is it possible to ping H1 (172.16.0.10)?

_____

From H3, is it possible to ping H5 (172.16.4.10)?

_____

From H3, is it possible to ping the default gateway (192.168.1.1)?

_____

Task 5: Troubleshoot BRANCH2

Step 1.   Begin troubleshooting at host H5.

From H5, is it possible to ping H6 (172.16.4.138)?

_____

From H5, is it possible to ping H1 (172.16.0.10)?

_____

From H5, is it possible to ping the default gateway (172.16.4.1)?

_____

Step 2.   Examine BRANCH2 to find possible configuration errors.

View the status information summary for each interface on the router. Are there any problems with the configuration of the interfaces?

_____

If there are problems, record the commands necessary to correct the configuration errors.

_____

_____

_____

_____

_____

_____

_____

_____

_____

_____

_____

If you have recorded any commands, apply them to the router configuration now.

If any changes were made, view the summary of the status information for the router interfaces again.

Does the information in the interface status summary indicate any configuration errors?

_____

If the answer is yes, troubleshoot the interface status of the interfaces.

Step 3.   Troubleshoot the routing configuration on BRANCH2.

View the routing table.

Which networks and routes are shown in the routing table?

_____

_____

_____

_____

_____

_____

_____

_____

_____

_____

Step 4.   Examine the routes that are being sent out in the routing updates from BRANCH2.

Are there any problems with the routing updates? If so, list them.

_____

If there are problems, record the commands necessary to correct the configuration errors.

_____

_____

_____

Apply any recorded commands to the router configuration.

Step 5.   Ping the hosts again.

From H5, is it possible to ping H6 (172.16.4.138)?

From H5, is it possible to ping H1 (172.16.0.10)?

_____

From H5, is it possible to ping the default gateway (172.16.4.1)?

_____

From the HQ router, is it possible to ping H1 (172.16.0.10)?

_____

From the HQ router, is it possible to ping H5 (172.16.4.10)?

_____

Step 6.   Examine the routing updates that are being received on BRANCH2.

Which networks are being received in the RIP updates on BRANCH2?

_____

_____

Are there any problems with these routing updates? If so, list them.

_____

_____

_____

Display the routing table for the BRANCH2 router.

Is there a route to network 172.16.0.0 or 172.16.2.0 on BRANCH1? Why or why not?

_____

_____

_____

Display the routing table for the HQ router.

How many routes does HQ have to the 172.16.0.0/16 network?

_____

If there are problems with the routing configuration on BRANCH2, record the commands necessary to correct the configuration errors.

_____

_____

Do these commands need to be applied only to BRANCH2, or do they also need to be applied to any other routers in the network?

_____

Task 6: Remove Auto-Summary

Step 1.   Remove auto-summary from all three routers.

Use the **no auto-summary** command in router RIP configuration mode to disable auto-summary and allow the routers to advertise the individual subnets on each router.

Step 2.   View the routing information for BRANCH2.

View the routing table for BRANCH2. Does the information in the routing table indicate any configuration errors?

_____

If the answer is yes, troubleshoot the routing configuration.

Step 3.   View the routing information for BRANCH1.

Are routes to all networks and subnets now present?

_____

Step 4.   View the routing information for HQ.

Are routes to all networks and subnets now present?

_____

Step 5.   Test overall network connectivity by pinging between the hosts.

From H5, is it possible to ping H6 (172.16.4.138)?

_____

From H5, is it possible to ping H1 (172.16.0.10)?

_____

From H5, is it possible to ping H3 (192.168.1.10)?

_____

From H1, is it possible to ping H3 (192.168.1.10)?

_____

From the HQ router, is it possible to ping H1 (172.16.0.10)?

_____

From the HQ router, is it possible to ping H5 (172.16.4.10)?

_____

Task 7: Reflection

There were several configuration errors in the scripts provided for this lab. Use the following space to write a brief description of the errors that you found.

_____

_____

_____

_____

_____

_____

_____

_____

_____

_____

_____

_____

Task 8: Documentation

On each router, use the following commands and capture the output to a text (.txt) file. Save the file for future reference.

- **show running-config**
- **show ip route**
- **show ip interface brief**
- **show ip protocols**

Lab 9-8: Using Telnet and SSH to Access Networking Devices (9.5.3)

Objectives

- Establish and manage Telnet connections to a remote router and switch.

- Verify that the application layer between the source and destination is working properly.

- Retrieve information about remote routers using **show** commands.

- Configure a router to accept SSH connections using the Cisco IOS CLI.

- Connect from one router using the SSH CLI client to a remote router running the SSH server.

Background/Preparation

Telnet is an excellent tool to use when troubleshooting problems with upper-layer functions. Using Telnet to access networking devices enables technicians to enter commands on each device as if they were locally attached. In addition, the ability to reach devices using Telnet indicates that lower-layer connectivity exists between the devices. Telnet is widely available on nearly any networking device.

Telnet is an unsecure protocol, which means that all data communicated can be captured and read. SSH is a more secure method for remote device access. Most newer versions of the Cisco IOS Software contain an SSH server and an SSH client. In some devices, this service is enabled by default. Other devices require the SSH server to be manually enabled. Similarly, a remote computer with an SSH client installed can be used to start a secure CLI session.

This lab focuses on using Telnet and SSH to access routers remotely to gather information about them and verify upper-layer connectivity. In this lab, you telnet from the workstation as a client and from a router into another remote router. In addition, you will configure SSH access on a router and connect using a router-based Cisco IOS CLI client.

Set up a network similar to the one in the topology diagram shown in Figure 9-19 and described in Table 9-18. Any router that meets the interface requirements displayed in that diagram—such as 800, 1600, 1700, 1800, 2500, 2600, or 2800 routers, or a combination of these—can be used. Depending on the model of the router, output may vary from what is shown in this lab. The IOS installed must be able to support SSH.

Figure 9-19   Lab 9-8 Topology

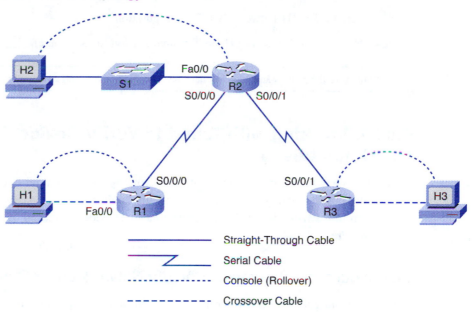

Table 9-18   Device Configuration Summary

Device	Hostname	Interface	IP Address	Subnet Mask	RIPv2 Network Statements
R1	R1	Serial 0/0/0 (DTE)	10.10.10.1	255.255.255.0	10.0.0.0
		Fast Ethernet 0/0	192.168.1.1	255.255.255.0	192.168.1.0
R2	R2	Serial 0/0/0 (DCE)	10.10.10.2	255.255.255.0	10.0.0.0
		Serial 0/0/1 (DCE)	172.16.1.1	255.255.255.0	172.16.0.0
		Fast Ethernet 0/0	192.168.2.1	255.255.255.0	192.168.2.0
R3	R3	Serial 0/0/1 (DTE)	172.16.1.2	255.255.255.0	172.16.0.0
		Fast Ethernet 0/0	192.168.3.1	255.255.255.0	192.168.3.0
S1	S1	VLAN 1 (mgmt)	192.168.2.99	255.255.255.0	—

The following resources are required:

- One router with two serial interfaces and one Fast Ethernet (1841 or other)

- Two routers with one serial interface and one Fast Ethernet (1841 or other)

- One 2960 switch (or comparable) for the R2 LAN

- Three Windows XP computers (hosts H2 and H3 are mainly for configuring routers R2 and R3)

- Straight-through and crossover Category 5 Ethernet cables, as required

- Two null serial cables

- Console cable to configure routers

- Access to host H1 command prompt
- Access to host H1 network TCP/IP configuration

On hosts H1, H2, and H3, start a HyperTerminal session to each router.

Note: Make sure the routers and switches have been erased and have no startup configurations.

Part 1. Working with Telnet to Verify Device Configurations and Connectivity

Telnet allows a remote user to connect into a networking device to monitor or configure it. Telnet is not a secure protocol and any information, including login names and passwords, can be easily "sniffed" from the wire. Because of this, telnet has been widely replaced by SSH on devices that support this secure protocol.

Task 1: Build the Network and Verify Network Layer Connectivity

Step 1.   Configure the basic information on each router and the switch.

a.   Build and configure the network according to the topology diagram and device configuration table. If necessary, see Lab 5-4, "Configuring Basic Router Settings with the Cisco IOS CLI (5.3.5)," for instructions on setting the hostname, passwords, and interface addresses.

b.   Configure RIPv2 on each router, and advertise the networks shown in the device configuration table. If necessary, refer to Lab 6-2, "Configuring and Verifying RIP (6.1.5)," for instructions on configuring the RIP routing protocol.

c.   Configure basic settings on the switch S1 to include hostname, passwords, and VLAN 1 IP addresses. If necessary, see Lab 5-11, "Configuring the Cisco 2960 Switch (5.5.4)."

Step 2.   Configure the hosts.

Configure H1, H2, and H3 with an IP address, subnet mask, and default gateway that is compatible with the IP address of the router default gateway interface address for the LAN to which they are attached.

Step 3.   Verify end-to-end network layer connectivity.

a.   On H1, open a command prompt window by choosing **Start > Run** and typing **cmd**. Alternatively, choose **Start > All programs > Accessories > Command Prompt**.

b.   Use the **ping** command to test end-to-end connectivity. Ping from H1 on the R1 LAN to H3 on the R3 LAN (for example, 192.168.3.2).

```
C:\>ping 192.168.3.2
```

If H3 is not attached to R3, ping the R3 Serial 0/0/1 interface IP address 172.16.1.2.

```
C:\>ping 172.16.1.2
```

If the pings to R3 are successful, what does that indicate about the OSI layer connectivity between H1 and R3?

_____

_____

Note: If the pings are not successful, troubleshoot the router and host configurations and connections.

Task 2: Establish a Telnet Session from a Host Computer

Step 1.   Telnet from H1 to remote router R2.

The Cisco router IOS software has built-in Telnet client and server software. Nearly all computer operating systems have a Telnet client. Many server operating systems also have a Telnet server, although Microsoft Windows desktop operating systems typically do not.

In many cases, you will not have direct access to a router through the console so that you can telnet to other routers. Usually, you telnet to a router from a host computer. From there, you can telnet to other routers that are accessible via the network.

a.   From the command prompt on H1, telnet to the R2 router Fast Ethernet 0/0 interface.

```
C:\>telnet 192.168.2.1
```

b.   Enter the password **cisco** to access the router.

What prompt did the router display?

_____

c.   Issue the **show version** command.

What is the Cisco IOS Software version for the remote router R2?

_____

How many and what type of interfaces does remote router R2 have?

_____

_____

If the Telnet from H1 to R2 is successful, what does that indicate about the OSI layer connectivity between the devices?

_____

_____

_____

Step 2.   End the Telnet session from H1 to remote router R2.

Exit the Telnet session from host H1 to R2 by typing **exit**.

Task 3: Perform Basic Telnet Operations Between the Routers

Step 1.   Telnet from R1 to remote router R2.

Note: Telnet uses the vty lines on the remote router to connect. If the vty lines are not configured for login or no password is set, you cannot connect to the remote router using Telnet.

Telnet to the IP address of the R2 Serial 0/0/0 interface 10.10.10.2.

```
R1> telnet 10.10.10.2
Trying 10.10.10.2 ... Open
User Access Verification
Password:
```

Use the password **cisco** to enter the router.

What prompt did the router display?

Step 2.   Look at the interfaces on remote router R2.

Issue the **show ip interface brief** command at the remote router prompt.

```
R2> show ip interface brief
```

List the interfaces that are up on remote router R2.

Step 3.   Display the routing table on the remote router.

Issue the **show ip route** command at the router prompt. Which routes has R2 learned from RIP?

Step 4.   Display the CDP neighbors for R2.

Use the Cisco Discovery Protocol (CDP) to view information about Cisco devices directly attached to R2. Enter the **show cdp neighbors** command at the router prompt.

List all device IDs that are connected to the remote router. What is the platform for each device?

Step 5.   Suspend the current Telnet session on R2.

Press **Ctrl-Shift-6,** and then press the **x** key. This action only suspends the session and returns to the previous router. It does not disconnect from this router.

What prompt did the router display?

Step 6.   Resume the Telnet session to R2.

Press the **Enter** key at the router prompt. What does the router respond with?

_____

Pressing the **Enter** key resumes the Telnet session that was previously suspended. What prompt did the router display?

_____

Step 7.   Close the Telnet session to R2.

Terminate the Telnet session by typing **exit**.

What does the router respond with?

_____

What prompt did the router display?

_____

Note: When the Telnet session is suspended, you can disconnect from that session using the **disconnect** command and the session number.

Task 4: Perform Telnet Operations Between Multiple Routers

Step 1.   Telnet from R1 to remote router R2.

From R1, telnet to the IP address of the R2 Serial 0/0/0 interface 10.10.10.2.

Use the password **cisco** to enter the router.

Step 2.   Establish an additional Telnet session from R2 to R3.

From R2, telnet to the IP address of the R3 Serial 0/0/1 interface 172.16.1.2.

Use the password **cisco** to access the router.

What prompt did the router display?

_____

Step 3.   Suspend the Telnet session to R3.

Press **Ctrl-Shift-6,** and then press the **x** key.

What prompt did the router display?

_____

Step 4.   View the active Telnet sessions.

Enter the **show sessions** command at the R1 command prompt. How many sessions are in use?

_____

The default session is indicated by an asterisk (*). This is the session that resumes when you press **Enter**.

Step 5.   Resume the Telnet session to R2.

Press **Enter** at the router prompt. What does the router respond with?

_____

What prompt did the router display?

_____

Why does the prompt say R3?

_____

_____

Step 6.   Disconnect the sessions from R1 to R2 and R3.

Enter the **exit** command at the R3 prompt, and then press **Enter** to close the connection to R3.

```
R3>exit
[Connection to 172.16.1.2 closed by foreign host]
R2>
```

Suspend the R2 session from R1 (session 1 on R1) by pressing **Ctrl-Shift-6,** followed by the **x** key. Use the **disconnect** command to end the connection to R2.

```
R1>disconnect 1
Closing connection to 10.10.10.2 [confirm]
```

Task 5: Remove the vty Password from R3

Step 1.   Telnet from R1 to remote router R3.

Telnet to the IP address of the R3 Serial 0/0/1 interface 172.16.1.2.

```
R1>telnet 172.16.1.2
Trying 172.16.1.2 ... Open
User Access Verification
Password:
```

Use the password **cisco** to enter the router.

What prompt did the router display?

_____

Step 2.   Remove the vty password from R3.

Issue the **enable** command at the R3> command prompt, and enter the password **class**.

What prompt did the router display?

_____

Remove the password for the vty lines on R3.

```
R3>enable
R3# config t
R3(config)# line vty 0 4
```

```
R3(config-line)# no password
R3(config-line)# end
R3#
```

Exit from the Telnet session on R3, and return to R1.

```
R3# exit
[Connection to 172.16.1.2 closed by foreign host]
R1#
```

Step 3.   Telnet from R1 to remote router R3 again.

Telnet to the IP address of the R3 Serial 0/0/1 interface 172.16.1.2.

```
R1>telnet 172.16.1.2
```

Are you able to telnet to R3?

_____

What message did you receive and why?

_____

_____

_____

_____

_____

Step 4.   Connect to R3 via the console and reset the vty password.

Issue the **enable** command at the R3> command prompt, and enter the password **class**.

Reestablish the password for the vty lines on R3.

```
R3>enable
R3# config t
R3(config)# line vty 0 4
R3(config-line)# password cisco
R3(config-line)# end
R3#
```

Part 2. Working with SSH to Verify Device Configurations and Connectivity

Secure Shell (SSH) is an RSA-encrypted version of Telnet. All information that passes between an SSH client and SSH server, including user IDs, passwords, and data, is encrypted. Because SSH is an application layer protocol, a successful SSH connection demonstrates that all OSI layers are functioning, including encryption at the presentation layer.

Task 1: Configure SSH on Router R2

Step 1. Telnet from R1 to remote router R2.

Telnet to the IP address of the R2 Serial 0/0/0 interface 10.10.10.2.

```
R1>telnet 10.10.10.2
Trying 10.10.10.2 ... Open
User Access Verification
Password:
```

Use the password **cisco** to enter the router.

What prompt did the router display?

_____

Step 2. Configure the SSH server on R2.

Create a domain name and a Telnet/SSH user ID and password for remote vty connections.

Note: By creating a user ID and password and specifying local login for the vty lines, any attempt to telnet or SSH to this router requires entry of the username and password created.

a. Because the admin user has a privilege level of 15 (the highest), and privilege level 15 is configured for the vty lines, the router prompt goes directly into privileged EXEC (enable) mode when connecting to R2 using either Telnet or SSH.

The use of a special user ID and password to secure Telnet and SSH vty access to the router does not affect the console (line con 0) password or the enable secret password.

```
Router# config terminal
R2(config)# ip domain-name customer.com
R2(config)# username admin privilege 15 password 0 cisco123
R2(config)# exit
```

b. Configure the vty terminal lines to accept incoming remote connections from Telnet and SSH clients, and validate the user ID against the local router username database.

```
R2(config)# line vty 0 4
R2(config-line)# privilege level 15
R2(config-line)# login local
R2(config-line)# transport input telnet ssh
R2(config-line)# exit
```

Note: If Telnet is not specified in the **transport input** command, only SSH remote connections will be allowed to this router.

c. Generate the RSA encryption key pair for the router to use for authentication and encryption of transmitted SSH data. Enter **768** for the number of modulus bits. The default is 512.

```
R2(config)# crypto key generate rsa
The name for the keys will be: R2.customer.com
Choose the size of the key modulus in the range of 360 to 2048 for your
General Purpose Keys. Choosing a key modulus greater than 512 may take
a few minutes.

How many bits in the modulus [512] 768
% Generating 768 bit RSA keys, keys will be non-exportable...[OK]
*Mar 20 13:17:50.123: %SSH-5-ENABLED: SSH 1.99 has been enabled

R2(config)#exit
```

d. Verify that SSH is enabled and which version is used with the **show ip ssh** command.

```
R2# show ip ssh
SSH Enabled - version 1.99
Authentication timeout: 120 secs; Authentication retries: 3
```

Fill in the following information based on the output of the **show ip ssh** command.

SSH version enabled:

_____

Authentication timeout:

_____

Authentication retries:

_____

e. Issue the **show running-config** command. What indication is there that the SSH server has been configured on R2?

_____

_____

f. Save the running-config to the startup-config.

```
R2# copy running-config startup-config
```

g. Exit the Telnet session on R2, and return to R1.

```
R2# exit
[Connection to 10.10.10.2 closed by foreign host]
R1#
```

Task 2: Log In to R2 Using the R1 CLI SSH Client

Note: You can also log in to an SSH-enabled router or switch using a computer with a GUI client, such as PuTTY. This procedure is described in Lab 8-7, "Configuring a Remote Router Using SSH (8.3.3b)."

Step 1.   Use the Cisco IOS CLI help feature with the **ssh** command.

From the R1 terminal session, use the Cisco IOS help feature to display the login options for the R1 SSH client.

```
R1# ssh ?
 -c    Select encryption algorithm
 -l    Log in using this user name
 -m    Select HMAC algorithm
 -o    Specify options
 -p    Connect to this port
 -v    Specify SSH Protocol Version
 WORD  IP address or hostname of a remote system


R1# ssh -l admin ?
 -c    Select encryption algorithm
 -m    Select HMAC algorithm
 -o    Specify options
 -p    Connect to this port
 -v    Specify SSH Protocol Version
 WORD  IP address or hostname of a remote system
```

Step 2.   Log in to R2 using SSH.

In this step, you log in to the R2 SSH server from the R1 CLI SSH client. You establish a secure remote session with R2 from which you can issue show and configuration commands.

a.   Log in to R2 specifying the login username **admin** and password **cisco123,** which were configured earlier, and the IP address of the R2 S0/0/0 interface.

```
R1# ssh -l admin 10.10.10.2

Password:
Unauthorized Use Prohibited
R2#
```

Why did you get the privileged EXEC (enable) mode router prompt?

_____

_____

b.   On R2, issue the **show ssh** command to see the SSH connections to the router.

```
R2# show ssh
Connection Version Mode Encryption   Hmac       State            Username
0          1.99    IN   aes128-cbc   hmac-sha1  Session started  admin
0          1.99    OUT  aes128-cbc   hmac-sha1  Session started  admin
%No SSHv1 server connections running.
```

    c.   Exit from the SSH session on R2, and return to R1.

```
R2# exit
[Connection to 10.10.10.2 closed by foreign host]
R1>
```

Note: **Ctrl-Shift-6** followed by the **x** key, and the commands used previously with Telnet, are the same for SSH.

Task 3: Reflection

Step 1.   Compare the advantages and disadvantages of Telnet and SSH.

_____

_____

_____

_____

_____

Step 2.   If you can ping to a router interface but cannot connect to it using Telnet or SSH, what could the problem be, and which layers of the OSI model are affected?

_____

_____

_____

_____

_____

_____

_____

_____

_____

_____

_____

_____

Lab 9-9: Identifying Necessary Knowledge, Skills, and Abilities (9.6.2)

Objectives

Identify the knowledge, skills, and abilities needed to perform the tasks for a specific hands-on lab.

Background/Preparation

In this lab, you review an existing hands-on lab, which you completed in a previous chapter, and analyze it to identify the types of knowledge, skill, and abilities required to successfully complete the lab.

This lab requires access to Lab 5-6, "Configuring PAT with SDM and Static NAT with IOS (5.3.8)."

Task 1: Review the Definitions for KSAs

The CDC website (http://www.cdc.gov/hrmo/ksahowto.htm) describes the importance of Knowledge, Skills, and Abilities (KSA) in the federal job application process. These concepts are equally applicable to networking job applicants. Understanding the knowledge, skills, and abilities that are required for a position, and showing how you match those KSAs, will be very helpful in making you a strong candidate for that position.

Review the definitions of these terms from the CDC website:

- **Knowledge** statements refer to an organized body of information, usually of a factual or procedural nature which, if applied, make adequate performance on the job possible. A body of information applied directly to the performance of a function.

- **Skill** statements refer to the proficient manual, verbal, or mental manipulation of data or things. Skills can be readily measured by a performance test where quantity and quality of performance are tested, usually within an established time limit. Examples of proficient manipulation of things are skill in typing or skill in operating a vehicle. Examples of proficient manipulation of data are skill in computation using decimals, skill in editing for transposed numbers, and so on.

- **Ability** statements refer to the power to perform an observable activity at the present time. This means that abilities have been evidenced through activities or behaviors that are similar to those required on the job; for example, the ability to plan and organize work. Abilities are different from aptitudes. Aptitudes are only the potential for performing the activity.

List at least one example for each term from your own networking or other area of personal experience.

Knowledge examples:

_____

_____

Skill examples:

_____

_____

_____

Ability examples:

_____

_____

_____

Task 2: Review an Existing Lab

Locate Lab 5-6, "Configuring PAT with SDM and Static NAT with IOS (5.3.8)." Read through the lab to become familiar with the tasks and steps performed. You may also review a different lab with the approval of the instructor.

Task 3: Identify the Knowledge, Skills, and Abilities Required for the Lab

The tasks and steps from the lab are listed in Table 9-19. Fill in the table with the knowledge, skills, and abilities required to perform each step.

Table 9-19   Lab Knowledge/Skills/Ability Summary

Task/Step	Knowledge/Skills/Abilities Required
Task 1: Configure basic router settings and PAT.	—
Step 1: Build the network and configure host computer IP settings.	
Step 2: Configure CustomerRouter basic settings with the Cisco IOS CLI.	
Step 3: Configure the ISP router basic settings with the Cisco IOS CLI.	
Step 4: Connect to CustomerRouter using SDM.	
Step 5: Configure SDM to show Cisco IOS CLI commands.	
Step 6: Launch the Basic NAT wizard.	
Step 7: Select the WAN interface for NAT.	
Step 8: Verify NAT functionality.	
Task 2: Configure and verify static NAT using the Cisco IOS CLI.	—
Step 1: Configure a static mapping for the server.	
Step 2: Test static NAT functionality.	
Step 3: Save the router configurations.	

Lab 9-10: Exploring the CCNA Prep Center (9.6.5)

Objectives

- Use the Cisco CCNA Prep Center website to find study materials and tools to help prepare for the CCENT exam.

- Take an exam interface tutorial and a sample ICND1/CCENT exam.

- Use the tools discovered to help develop an exam preparation plan.

Background/Preparation

In this lab, you explore the CCNA Prep Center and identify some of the tools and resources that are available. You also take an exam interface tutorial and a sample ICND1/CCENT exam. You access the Cisco Career Certifications website for a description of the ICND1/CCENT exam and a list of exam topics. You describe the use of the tools and resources discovered to help develop your exam preparation plan.

Note: The CCENT exam is the same as the ICND1 exam. The ICND1 and ICND2 exams together equal the CCNA exam.

This lab requires a computer with a browser and Internet access.

Task 1: Identify the Tools and Resources Available

Step 1.   Review Cisco and Cisco Press resources.

Investigate all the tools and resources that are available to help you study. The CCENT tests the knowledge and skills obtained during this course, and all the content from Discovery 1.

- **Cisco CCNA Prep Center:** Free to anyone with a Cisco.com login. The CCNA Prep Center provides certification candidates with practice questions, labs, simulations, tips, discussion forums, CCNA videos, and advice from CCNA experts.

- **Cisco Press Exam Certification Books:** Cisco Press publishes several books that cover the CCENT exam objectives. These titles can be purchased through the Cisco Marketplace Bookstore and directly from Cisco Press:

  http://www.cisco.com/pcgi-bin/marketplace/welcome.pl?STORE_ID=CISCO_BOOKSTORE&KEYCODE=Certifications

  http://www.ciscopress.com/markets/detail.asp?st=44711

- **Cisco Press CCNA Discovery Learning Guides:** The Cisco Press Learning Guides for the Discovery courses are the official supplemental textbooks for these courses and provide additional examples, challenge questions, and activities.

Step 2.   Identify other sources of exam prep information.

Open a browser and use a search engine to search for **cisco ccent exam prep**. List some of the websites found here.

_____

_____

_____

_____

List the various resources, including Cisco and Cisco Press, that you plan to use for CCENT exam preparation.

_____

_____

_____

_____

_____

_____

_____

_____

_____

_____

Task 2: Explore the Cisco CCNA Prep Center Website

Step 1.   Log in to the Cisco CCNA Prep Center website.

Registered Cisco.com users can access the website for help in preparing for CCNA certification exams.

http://forums.cisco.com/eforum/servlet/PrepCenter?page=main

In the Member Login area shown in Figure 9-20, enter your Cisco.com username and password, and click **Go.** If you do not have a Cisco.com user ID, click on the link for Cisco.com registration in the **How to Log In** area.

Figure 9-20   CCNA Prep Center Login Page

Step 2.   Identify the various resources available.

Examine the CCNA Prep Center main window as shown in Figure 9-21.

Figure 9-21   CCNA Prep Center Main Screen

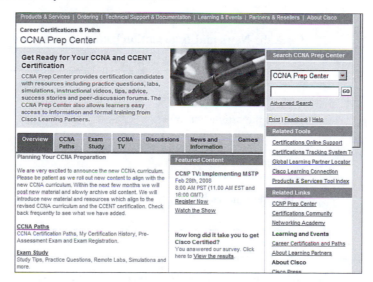

What are the main options available to help with exam preparation?

_____

Step 3.   Explore various resource topics.

Click the **Exam Study** button. What are some of the main areas included here?

_____

_____

_____

What are some of the resources available under the Cisco Resources main heading?

_____

_____

Click the **CCNA TV** button. What are some of the shows that can be selected?

_____

_____

_____

_____

Are all the videos listed appropriate CCENT study topics?

_____

_____

Click the **Discussions** button. What are some of the discussion forums available?

_____

_____

Click the **News and Information** button. What are some of the articles available?

_____

_____

Are all the articles current?

_____

_____

Click the **Games** button. What are some of the games available?

_____

_____

Which of these games could be part of your ICND1/CCENT exam preparation plan?

_____

_____

_____

Task 3: Explore the Exam Study Area and Take Practice Exams

Step 1.   Identify topics and take the Exam Interface Tutorial.

Click the **Exam Study** button. What topics are available?

_____

_____

_____

Under the Practice Taking Exams heading, click **Exam Interface Tutorial**. The Cisco Learning and Assessment Team has developed this tutorial to help prepare for the Cisco certification exams.

Go through the tutorial to see the various types of questions that can appear on the CCENT and CCNA exams.

What are the different types of questions presented?

_____

_____

_____

_____

_____

_____

_____

Step 2.   Take a practice ICND1/CCENT exam.

Under the Practice Taking Exams heading, click **ICND1 and ICND2 Practice Questions**. How many ICND1 test modules are there?

_____

Click **ICND1, Module 1** to start the practice questions for the first module. The correct answers and solutions are located in the Module Self-Check Answer Key. How many questions are there?

_____

How many answers did you get correct?

_____

If time permits, take the other ICND1 module practice questions.

Step 3.   View the ICND1/CCENT exam descriptions and exam topics.

From the CCNA Prep Center main screen, click the **CCNA Paths** button, and then click the **640-822 ICND1** exam link. The 640-822 ICND1 screen appears as shown in Figure 9-22. It contains a description of the exam and a list of exam topics. You can also register to take the exam at an approved testing center by clicking the **Pearson VUE** link.

Note: The following screen shot shows only a portion of the exam topics.

Figure 9-22   ICND1 Exam Information

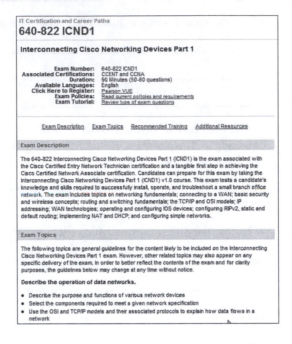

What is the length of the exam?

_____

What are some of the main topic areas covered?

_____

_____

_____

_____

_____

Task 4: Reflection

What is the benefit of taking the exam interface tutorial and sample exam questions?

_____

_____

_____

How will you use the tools identified in your exam preparation plan?

_____

_____

_____

_____

_____

_____

## CHAPTER 10

Capstone Project: Putting It All Together

This lab is a final, summary exercise based on the concepts and tools you have learned throughout this book. Complete this lab to ensure that you have mastered the practical, hands-on skills presented in the *Working at a Small-to-Medium Business or ISP* course of the *CCNA Discovery* curriculum.

Objectives

- Create an IP addressing plan for a small network.
- Implement a network equipment upgrade.
- Verify device configurations and network connectivity.

Background/Preparation

In this activity, you will play the role of an onsite installation and support technician from an ISP. You receive a work order specifying your responsibilities, which include analyzing the customer's existing network configuration and implementing a new configuration to improve network performance. You will use additional equipment as necessary and develop an IP subnetting scheme to address the customer's needs. On an earlier site visit, one of the ISP technicians created a diagram of the customer's existing network; it is shown in Figure 10-1. The following resources are required:

- ISP router with two serial interfaces and one FastEthernet interface (preconfigured by the instructor)
- Ethernet 2960 switch to connect to the ISP router (preconfigured by the instructor)
- Customer 1841 router (or another router with two FastEthernet interfaces and at least one serial interface to connect to the ISP)
- Linksys WRT300N (or another Linksys that supports wireless)
- Ethernet 2960 switch to connect wired PCs
- Windows XP-based PC to act as a wireless client (wireless NIC)
- Windows XP-based PC to act as a wired client (Ethernet NIC)
- Category 5 cabling as necessary
- Serial cabling as necessary
- ISP work order (in this lab)
- Device Configuration Checklist (in this lab)
- Network Equipment Installation Checklist (in this lab)
- Configuration Verification and Connectivity Checklist (in this lab)

Figure 10-1   Customer's Existing Network

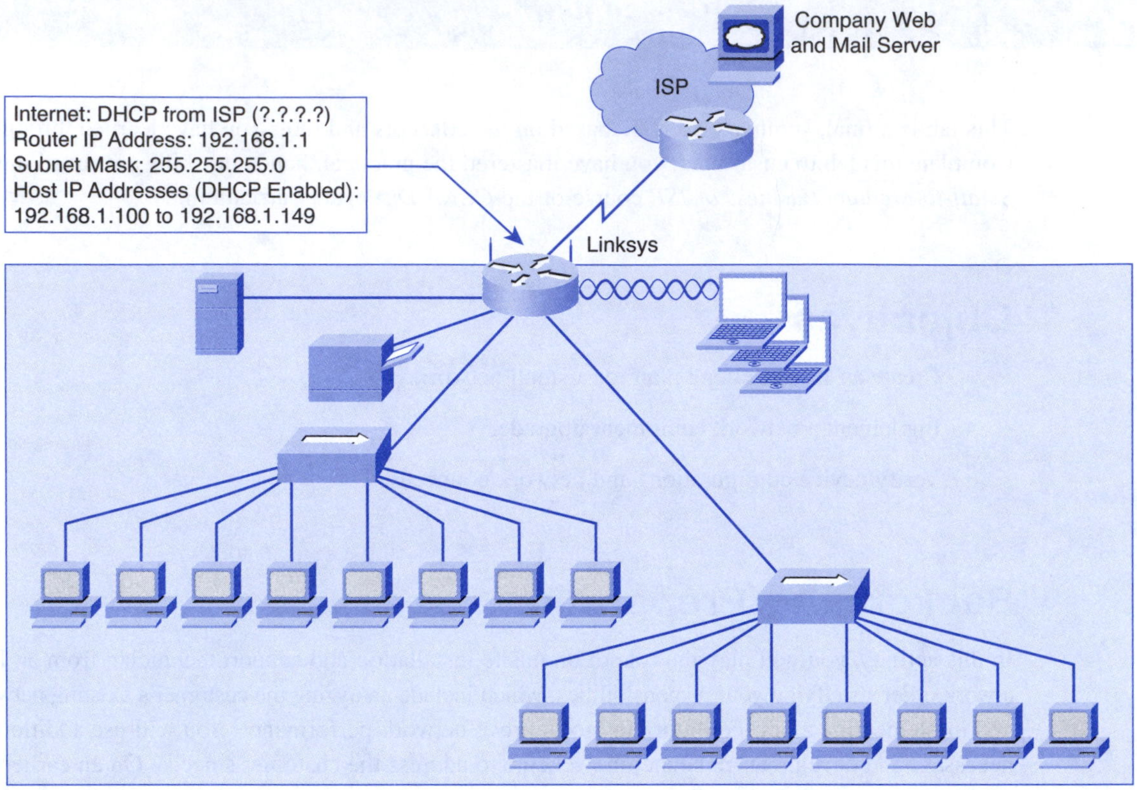

Company Web
and Mail Server

ISP

Internet: DHCP from ISP (?.?.?.?)
Router IP Address: 192.168.1.1
Subnet Mask: 255.255.255.0
Host IP Addresses (DHCP Enabled):
192.168.1.100 to 192.168.1.149

Linksys

Part A: Review the Existing Network and Customer Work Order

Review the work order to get a general understanding of what is to be done for the customer.

ABC-XYZ-ISP Inc.
Official Work Order

Customer: AnyCompany1 or AnyCompany2   **Date:** _____

(Circle the customer name assigned by your instructor)

Address: 1234 Fifth Street, Anytown

Customer contact: Fred Pennypincher, Chief Financial Officer

Phone number: 123-456-7890

Description of Work to Be Performed

Review the existing network shown in Figure 10-1, and upgrade it by adding a Cisco 1841 router and a standalone Cisco 2960 switch to supplement and offload the existing Linksys WRT300N. The new switch will support connections from wired clients on one subnet. The existing Linksys will support wireless clients on another subnet. Configure the Cisco 1841 router as a DHCP server for the wired network and the Linksys, which supports wireless users.

The wired and wireless client traffic from each subnet will be routed through the new Cisco 1841 customer router. The RIPv2 routing protocol is to be used between the 1841 router and the ISP, and PPP is the encapsulation on the WAN link between. The customer router must use a static address. The ISP router serial interface IP address the customer must communicate with is one of the following:

- If your local network is connected to the ISP as AnyCompany1, the IP address of the ISP serial 0 interface is 10.100.1.5 /22.

- If your local network is connected to the ISP as AnyCompany2, the IP address of the ISP serial 1 interface is 172.27.100.25 /22.

Assigned to: Approved by:

Guy Netwiz   Bill Broadband, ISP Manager

Part B: Develop the Subnet Scheme

The customer has been assigned an IP address and subnet mask as follows:

- If the local network customer is AnyCompany1, use 192.168.111.0 /24.

- If the local network customer is AnyCompany2, use 192.168.222.0 /24.

Develop a subnet scheme using this address that will allow the customer network to support two subnets of up to 30 clients each, and allow for growth to as many as six subnets in the future.

The first available subnet will be used for the wired clients. The second available subnet will be used to assign an IP address to the Linksys external Internet interface. The internal wireless network clients will use the default IP addressing (network 192.168.1.0 /24) assigned by the Linksys. The Linksys will use NAT/PAT to convert internal wireless client addresses to the external address. The internal wireless clients will not require a subnet from the base address.

Task 1: Determine the Number of Hosts and Subnets

The largest subnet must be able to support 30 hosts. To support that many hosts, how many host bits are required?

_____

What is the minimum number of subnets required for the new network design that also allows for future growth?

_____

How many host ID bits are reserved for the subnet ID to allow for this number of subnets, with each subnet having 30 hosts?

_____

What is the maximum possible number of subnets with this scheme?

_____

Task 2: Calculate the Custom Subnet Mask

Now that you know the number of subnet ID bits, you can calculate the subnet mask. A Class C network has a default subnet mask of 24 bits, or 255.255.255.0. Determine what the custom subnet mask will be.

The custom subnet mask for this network will be _____._____._____._____, or /_____.

Task 3: Identify Subnet and Host IP Addresses

Now that you have identified the subnet mask, you can create the network addressing scheme. The addressing scheme includes the network number of the subnets, the subnet broadcast address, and the range of IP addresses that can be assigned to hosts.

Complete Table 10-1, showing all the possible subnets for the 192.168.111.0 network (if you are working with AnyCompany1) or the 192.168.222.0 network (if you are working with AnyCompany2).

Table 10-1   Subnet Identification

Subnet	Subnet Address	Host IP Address Range	Broadcast Address

Part C: Document Network Device Interfaces and Physical Topology

In this part of the lab, you will use the IP addressing scheme developed in Part B to assign addresses to device interfaces and hosts. You will also create a topology diagram of the updated network.

Task 1: Document the Cisco 1841 Router Interfaces and Host IP Addresses

Fill in Table 10-2 with the IP addresses, subnet masks, and connection information for the customer router interfaces. If an interface is not used, enter N/A. This information will be used to configure the customer router. If you are using a router other than a Cisco 1841, use the interface chart in Appendix C, "Lab Equipment Interfaces and Initial Configuration Restoration," to determine the proper interface designations.

Table 10-2   1841 Interfaces and IP Addresses

Interface (1841)	IP Address/ Subnet Mask	Connects to Device/Interface	Connects to Device IP Address (If Applicable)
Serial 0/0/0			
Serial 0/0/1			
Fa 0/0			
Fa 0/1			

Task 2: Document the Linksys Interfaces and Host IP Addresses

Fill in Table 10-3 with the IP addresses, subnet masks, and connection information for the Linksys interfaces.

Note: The Linksys should be reset to its factory default setting and should not be configured, except for changing the SSID.

Table 10-3   Linksys Interfaces and IP Addresses

Interface (Linksys)	IP Address/ Subnet Mask	Connects to Device/Interface	Connects to Device IP Address (if Applicable)
Internet interface (external address)			
LAN gateway (internal address)			
DHCP wireless hosts address range			

Task 3: Diagram the Upgraded Network

In the space provided here, draw a physical network diagram, showing all network devices, PCs, and cabling. Identify all devices and interfaces according to the interface chart, and indicate the IP address and subnet mask (using the /xx format) for each interface, based on the entries from the previous steps.

Figure 10-2   Complete Lab Diagram (Both Companies)

Part D: Configure Devices, and Verify Default Settings

In Part D you will configure networking devices and hosts. Before configuring devices, you will verify that they are in their default state.

Task 1: Verify the Default Settings for the Cisco 1841 Customer Router

Step 1.   Connect to the customer router, and verify that it is in the factory default state.

Step 2.   If you're using Cisco Security and Device Manager (SDM) to configure basic settings, use the Reset to Factory Defaults option on the SDM GUI main menu. Also verify that your router has SDM version 2.4 or later installed. If it doesn't, contact your instructor.

Step 3.   If you're using IOS CLI to configure the router, erase the startup-config and issue the **reload** command from privileged mode.

Note: If the startup-config is erased in an SDM router, SDM no longer comes up by default when the router is restarted. It will be necessary to build a basic config. Contact your instructor if this is the case.

Task 2: Configure the Cisco 1841 Customer Router

Step 1.   Use the checklist shown in Table 10-4 to help configure the 1841 customer router. Check off the configuration tasks as you complete them. Note that some of the basic router settings can be configured using SDM if it's available.

Step 2.   Display the running-config of the router, and save it as a file for reference.

Device Configuration Checklist

Device manufacturer and model number: _____

Cisco IOS version: _____

Table 10-4   1841 Router Configuration Checklist

✔	Configuration Task	Configuration Value	Notes/IOS Commands or SDM Used
❑	Configure the router hostname.	AnyCompany1 or AnyCompany2	
❑	Configure the passwords.	Console: cisco Enable: cisco Enable secret: class VTY terminals: cisco	
❑	Configure FastEthernet . interface 0/0	IP address: _____ Subnet mask: _____	
❑	Configure FastEthernet interface 0/1.	IP address: _____ Subnet mask: _____	
❑	Configure the WAN interface serial 0/0/0. (The ISP provides clock rate, encapsulation PPP.)	IP address: _____ Subnet mask: _____	
❑	Configure the DHCP server for internal networks (wired and Linksys Internet interface pools).	Wired subnet 1: _____ Linksys subnet 2: _____	
❑	Configure a static route to the wireless network.		
❑	Configure a default route to the ISP router.		
❑	Configure RIP version 2 to advertise the customer networks.	Net: _____ Net: _____ Net: _____	

❏   Display the running-config,
and verify all settings.

❏   Save the running-config to
the startup-config.

Task 3: Verify Default Settings for the Linksys, and Set the SSID

Step 1.   Log in to the Linksys, and verify that it is in the factory default state. Use the factory default of no user ID and a password of admin. The router internal IP address should be set to 192.168.1.1 and should have a subnet mask of 255.255.255.0. The DHCP address range should be 192.168.1.100 to 192.168.1.149. All security settings should be the defaults, with no MAC filtering and so on.

Step 2.   If necessary, reset the ISR using the Administration tab and the Factory Defaults option.

Step 3.   Change the default Service Set Identifier (SSID) of Linksys to AnyCompany1 or AnyCompany2, depending on which company your instructor has chosen, and ensure that it is broadcast.

Task 4: Verify Default Settings for the Cisco 2960 Switch

Log in to the switch, and verify that it is in the factory default state. Use the IOS CLI to reset the switch by deleting vlan.dat, erasing the startup-config, and issuing the **reload** command from privileged mode. You might need to power-cycle the switch for the changes to take effect.

Task 5: Verify That Host PCs Are DHCP Clients

Choose **Control Panel > Network Connections** to verify that both the wired and wireless host PCs are set to obtain their IP addresses automatically via DHCP.

Part E: Connect Network Devices, and Verify Connectivity

In Part E you will cable the network and verify connectivity between hosts and network devices.

Task 1: Connect the Network Devices

Use the checklist shown in Table 10-5 to help connect network devices using the proper cables. Check off the installation tasks as you complete them.

Table 10-5   Network Equipment Installation Checklist

✔	Devices Connected	From Device/ Interface	To Device/ Interface	Cable Type
❑	Connect the Linksys to the 1841.			
❑	Connect the 1841 to the ISP router.			
❑	Connect the 1841 to the switch.			
❑	Connect the wired PC to the switch.			
❑	Connect the wireless PC to the Linksys SSID entered in Part D, Task 3.			

Task 2: Verify Device Configurations and Network Connectivity

Use the checklist shown in Table 10-6 to verify the IP configuration of each host and test network connectivity. You will also display the various running-configs and routing tables. Check off the tasks as you complete them.

Table 10-6   Configuration Verification and Connectivity Checklist

✔	Verification Task	Record Results Here
❑	From the command prompt of the wired PC, display the IP address, subnet mask, and default gateway.	
❑	From the command prompt of the wireless PC, display the IP address, subnet mask, and default gateway.	
❑	Log in to the Linksys GUI from the wireless host. Record the LAN IP address and subnet mask, Internet IP address, and subnet mask and default gateway.	
❑	Ping from the wired host to the 1841 default gateway.	
❑	Ping from the wired host to the ISP S0/0 interface.	
❑	Ping from the wired host to the ISP Lo0 interface.	
❑	Ping from the wireless host to the 1841 default gateway.	
❑	Ping from the wireless host to the ISP S0/0 . interface	
❑	Ping from the wireless host to the ISP Lo0 interface.	

continues

Table 10-6   Configuration Verification and Connectivity Checklist   *continued*

✔	Verification Task	Record Results Here
☐	Display the IP routing table for the customer router. What routes are known, and how were they learned?	
☐	Capture the running-config from the customer 1841 router in a text file on the desktop to show to the instructor. Name the file using your initials.	

Part F: Configure Port Security for the Switch

In this part you configure port security and test it by connecting a different host than the original.

Task 1: Display the MAC Address Table Entry for the Port to Which the Wired Host Is Connected

Use the **show mac-address-table int fa0/***X* command, where *X* is the port number to which the wired host is connected. You might need to ping from the host to the router default gateway IP address to refresh the MAC address table entry. In this example, the port number is Fa0/2.

```
S1#show mac-address-table int fa0/2
        Mac Address Table

Vlan    Mac Address      Type       Ports
----    -----------      --------   -----
  1     000b.db04.a5cd   DYNAMIC    Fa0/2
Total Mac Addresses for this criterion: 1
```

Task 2: Clear the Dynamically Learned MAC Address Entry

Issue the **clear mac-address-table dynamic interface fa0/***X* command and replace the *X* with the port number to which the wired host is attached.

```
Switch#clear mac-address-table dynamic interface fa0/2
```

Task 3: Shut Down the Port, Configure It as an Access Port, and Then Issue the Port Security Commands

The **switchport port-security** command enables port security on the port using the defaults. The defaults are one MAC address allowed and **shutdown** as the violation action to be taken.

The **switchport port-security mac-address sticky** command allows the switch to learn the MAC address currently associated with the port. This address will become part of the running configuration. If the running–config is saved to the startup-config, the MAC address will be retained when the switch is reloaded.

First shut down the port to which the wired host is attached. Use the **switchport mode access** command to force the port to be an access port to configure port security. Use the command **switchport port-security** to enable port security, and then use the **switchport port-security mac-address sticky** command to enable the port to learn the MAC address of the connected host. Finally, enter the **no shutdown** command to reenable the port so that it can learn the MAC address of the host.

```
Switch(config)#interface fa0/2
Switch(config-if)#shutdown
Switch(config-if)#switchport mode access
Switch(config-if)#switchport port-security
Switch(config-if)#switchport port-security mac-address sticky
Switch(config-if)#no shutdown
Switch(config-if)#end
```

Task 4: Ping from the Wired Host to the AnyCompanyX Router Default Gateway

Allow some time to pass, and then issue the **show running-config interface Fa0/***X* command to see the MAC address that the switch learned. Replace the *X* with the port number to which the wired host is attached.

```
S1#show run interface Fa0/2
<output omitted>
!
interface FastEthernet0/2
 switchport access vlan 1
 switchport mode access
 switchport port-security
 switchport port-security mac-address sticky
 switchport port-security mac-address sticky 000b.db04.a5cd
```

Task 5: Display the Port Security Using the show port-security interface Command

Issue the **show port-security interface Fa0/**X command and replace the X with the port number to which the wired host is attached.

What is the Port Status?

_____

What is the Security Violation Count?

_____

What is the Source Address:Vlan?

_____

Task 6: Remove the Wired Host Cable from the Switch Port and Connect the Cable from Another PC

Step 1.   Ping from the new wired host to any IP address to cause a security violation on port Fa0/X. You should see security violation messages.

Step 2.   Issue the **show port-security interface** command again for Fa0/X.

What is the Port Status?

_____

What is the Security Violation Count?

_____

What is the Source Address?

_____

Task 7: Reconnect the Original Host to Its Port and Restore the Port

Step 1.   Clear the sticky address entry for port Fa0/X using the command **clear port-security sticky interface fa0/**X **access**. Replace the X with the port number to which the wired host is attached.

Step 2.   To return the interface from **error disable** to **administratively up**, enter the **shutdown** command followed by the **no shutdown** command.

```
S1#clear port-security sticky interface fa0/2 access

S1(config)#interface fa0/9
S1(config-if)#shutdown
S1(config-if)#no shutdown
```

Check Your Understanding and Challenge Questions Answer Key

Chapter 1

Check Your Understanding

1. A, B, C, D. E-commerce, communication, collaboration, and training are all common business uses for the Internet.

2. A, B, C, D, E, F. All the answers are services that most ISPs provide.

3. E. In remote regions, the only option available to connect to the Internet may be through a satellite. The other options depend on physical cables that may not be available in remote regions.

4. E. Metro Ethernet is a high-bandwidth connection used to connect sites in the same urban area.

5. A. Tier 1 ISPs form the Internet backbone and normally control the links between the continents. Tier 2 and Tier 3 ISPs often purchase this service from the Tier 1 ISP.

6. C. An IXP or NAP is where multiple ISPs are joined to gain access to each others' networks and exchange information. Currently more than 100 major exchange points exist worldwide.

7. B. The planning and provisioning team within an ISP is responsible for determining which equipment is in use and which must be installed to provide a required service. It accepts the request from the customer service team. After services are provisioned, the planning and provisioning team passes the information on to the onsite installation team for installation.

8. E. The help desk is responsible for working with the customer after the service has been provisioned, installed, and tested.

9. D. After the onsite installation team connects the services, the network operations center tests the service to make certain that it is functioning as expected. As soon as this team is certain that the service is properly provisioned and installed, it passes the information to the help desk, which then works with the customer to get the service properly configured from the customer's perspective.

10. A medium-sized business might require dedicated bandwidth that a T1 connection can provide rather than the shared bandwidth available via cable. Depending on the technology used on the T1, this type of connection can also provide an enhanced level of security over a cable Internet connection.

11. As more customers connect to the network, increased traffic may overload the network, causing router errors, lost packets, and excessive delays. In an overloaded network, subscribers can wait for minutes for a web page to load, or they may even lose network connectivity. These customers may choose to switch to a competing ISP to get better performance. Loss of customers directly translates into loss of income for an ISP. For this reason, it is important that the ISP provide a reliable and scalable network.

Challenge Questions and Activities

1. The answer to this question depends very much on the individual. Some of the areas that may be included are online research, e-mail, instant messaging (IM) communications, downloading files such as device drivers and audio and video files, and online gaming. VoIP service may also be included; it is becoming increasingly common as a method of saving long-distance toll charges.

2. Customer service receives the order for the new T1 from the customer and enters the requirements into an order-tracking database.

   Planning and provisioning determines whether the new customer has existing network hardware and circuits that will meet the customer's requirements or if additional circuits and/or services must be installed. Circuits and services are assigned to the customer.

   The onsite installation team is advised of which circuits and equipment to use and then installs them at the customer site.

   The installation team informs the network operations center (NOC) as soon as the circuits and equipment have been installed. The NOC monitors and tests the new connection and ensures that it is performing properly.

   The NOC notifies the help desk when the circuit is ready for operation. Then the help desk contacts the customer to guide the customer through the process of setting up passwords and other necessary account information.

Chapter 2

Check Your Understanding

1. A. The transport layer divides data into segments. (T)

   B. The network layer uses IP addresses to route packets. (N)

   C. The network layer encapsulates TCP or UDP segments into packets for transmission. (N)

   D. The transport layer uses UDP for real-time data streaming. (T)

   E. The transport layer uses source and destination port numbers in the segment header. (T)

   F. The network layer uses source and destination IP addresses in the packet header. (N)

2. A, D. Layer 3 deals with IP addressing, so questions should be related to this area. DHCP is used to obtain a Layer 3 IP address automatically. Ping is used to test Layer 3 IP connectivity to a host. Browsing is associated with the upper layers (applications). The network cable is a Layer 1 issue, and link lights are a Layer 1 or 2 issue.

3. A. Is your network cable securely connected? (L1)

   B. What mail server is listed in the outgoing server setting? (L5-7)

   C. Is your Windows firewall blocking port 25? (L4)

   D. Do you see a link light on your network card? (L2)

   E. What is the subnet mask on local area connection 2? (L3)

   Bottom-up means starting with the lowest OSI layers and working your way up. Cabling is Layer 1 (physical), link lights are Layer 2 (data link), the subnet mask is IP-related at Layer 3 (network), firewall port blocking is Layer 4 (transport), and e-mail server setup in the mail client is application Layers 5 through 7 (session, presentation, application).

4. B, D, E. An onsite technician would replace cables, correct PC settings, and swap out hardware. Opening a trouble ticket and checking the account payment status are Level 1, and checking the ISP's mail server could be Level 1 or 2.

5. B, E. Always document the solution in the trouble ticket and knowledge base for future reference. As soon as a solution is found, the other possible answers are not appropriate.

6. B, E. Only the Ethernet cable-related issues are physical network problems.

7. A. Twisted-pair cable: Cable is physical Layer 1 (P).

   B. IP address: IP addressing is network Layer 3 (N).

   C. Routing: Routing is network Layer 3 (N).

   D. Switching: Switching is data link Layer 2 (D).

   E. MAC address: MAC addresses are data link Layer 2 (D).

   F. Hub: Hubs operate at physical Layer 1 (P).

8. A, D. The technician should first provide identification and then review the trouble ticket with the customer before starting.

9. Answer:

Skill	Desk Activity
Make notes about the resolution of a help desk case	Logging the call
Answer calls in a friendly, professional manner	Providing a courteous greeting
Speak in a calm, reassuring manner	Adapting to the customer's temperament
Get all relevant information from the customer	Listening to the customer
Use analytical tools to provide a problem resolution	Diagnosing a problem correctly

10. A, D. Successful pings to the web server IP address indicate that it can be reached from the source host. When the host is pinged using its hostname, DNS is unable to resolve the name. This could result from an improper TCP/IP configuration on the source host or a problem with the DNS server (down or unreachable). If the default gateway, an intermediate router, or the web server were down, pings to the web server IP address would not work.

11. B. This is an example of the divide-and-conquer approach. She starts at the middle with OSI Layer 3 by pinging the server. This demonstrates that Layers 1, 2, and 3 are functional. She then moves up to check Layer 4 (firewall blocking port 23) and then to Layer 7 on the target server to see if the Telnet service application is actually running on the destination server.

12. C. The **nslookup** command is used to query the DNS server to determine whether it is up and how it is resolving names and addresses.

13. Automatic Private IP Addressing (APIPA) in the range 169.254.0.1 to 169.254.255.254. Link local is also an appropriate answer.

14. Loopback address in the 127.0.0.1 to 127.255.255.254 range. Address 127.0.0.1 is the most common one used for testing.

Challenge Questions and Activities

1. Answers:

   A. The top-down approach is probably best in this case.

   B. Possible answers include the following:
      When did she first notice the problem?

      Has this occurred before?

      Can she get to the Internet?

      Can she get to other servers she uses?

      Can she access her e-mail?

      Has a technician or someone else recently worked in her work area?

   C. Possible answers:
      Consult the problem log to check for a history with this user or server.

      Check with other members of the IT staff to determine if there are known outages or problems in the user's area.

2. Answers:

   A. The bottom-up or top-down approach could be used, but bottom-up is probably best in this case.

   B. Possible answers:
      Is the access light on the DSL/cable modem on?

      Is he using a router to share the Internet connection?

      Can other local users access the Internet?

      Has he or a technician moved equipment in the area?

   C. Possible answers:
      Check the customer's account to verify that he is a current customer and that his account has not been deactivated due to nonpayment or some other reason.

      Check with other members of the ISP network operations center staff or use a network management application to determine if there are known outages or problems in the user's service area.

      Ask the customer to turn off the power to the DSL/cable modem, the router (if present), and the PC. Then have the person turn the power back on in the order of DSL/cable modem, router, and PC.

      Ask the customer to disconnect the router and connect his PC directly to the DSL/cable modem to determine if the problem is with the modem or the router.

3. Answers will vary.

Chapter 3

Check Your Understanding

1. A, B. The purpose of a site survey is to accurately determine current resources and current and future network requirements.

2. D. When networks grow unexpectedly, standards are not always followed. It is important to alert the company's management so that they are aware of the situation, but blame should never be assigned.

3. B. The contents of the site survey should be reviewed with the customer to make sure that all information is accurate and complete.

4. C, D. The logical topology is concerned with the flow of information within the network, not the physical location of cables, wiring closets, and other networking devices.

5. A, B, C, D, E, F. All answers are correct. You should record all this information when doing an inventory of network devices during a site survey.

6. C. The correct sequence starts with a gathering of requirements and ends with a review and evaluation of the upgraded network.

7. D. The main distribution facility (MDF) is the point at which all network cable is concentrated in a single point. Intermediate distribution facilities (IDF) are usually smaller wiring closets that connect back to the main MDF through backbone cabling. Internet service providers (ISP) connect at Internet Exchange Points (IXP). An MFD is a multifunction device.

8. B. Unshielded twisted-pair (UTP) cabling is the most common type of LAN cabling and normally is used to connect a workstation NIC to the wall outlet.

9. A, C, E. PCs and routers have similar network interfaces. Hubs and switches normally have interfaces that cross the transmit and receive wires. If devices with similar interfaces are connected, a crossover cable must be used.

10. Type of connectivity: Routers have both LAN and WAN interfaces. UTP is the most common type of LAN medium, but you can buy interfaces to support other technologies that use different media, such as coaxial or fiber-optic cables.

   Available features: Routers are used mainly to interconnect separate networks, but they also may perform many additional functions. Among these are security, QoS, NAT/PAT, and DHCP.

   Cost: Modular devices generally are more cost-efficient than those with fixed configurations. As requirements change, modules can be added to provide the required connectivity.

Challenge Questions and Activities

1. For this company, a managed solution is probably the most appropriate choice. In-house solutions require that the company have both the financial and technical resources to purchase and manage the network. This company appears to have neither. A managed solution would allow it to clearly budget a fixed amount each month for providing network services without having to incur any unexpected expenses should network devices and/or services fail. A managed solution would also eliminate the requirement for hiring and training additional technical staff.

2. Even though both switches allow for growth within the department by having extra ports, only the second switch allows for an increase in speed to 1000 Mbps without replacing the device. In addition, the second switch has high-speed uplink ports to connect to server farms or the Internet, thus reducing the potential for a bottleneck. Because networks continue to evolve, it is not unlikely that the company will eventually move to 1 Gbps. Therefore, in this case the more expensive switch is probably the better choice if the budget will support its purchase.

Chapter 4

Check Your Understanding

1. A, D, E. NAT in conjunction with private addressing can hide internal addresses from the Internet and reduces the need for public IP addresses. It increases CPU usage on routers running NAT and does not create multiple addresses.

2. B. IP address 172.31.18.222 is a Class B address, and the default for a Class B is 255.255.0.0. 255.0.0.0 is the default subnet mask for a Class A address. 255.255.255.0 is the default subnet mask for a Class C address. 255.255.255.254 is an unused mask (no valid hosts), and 255.255.255.255 is the all-networks broadcast address.

3. A, C, E. Borrowing 4 bits from the 172.25.15.0/24 network results in 16 subnets (2^4 = 16) and 16 possible addresses. There are only 14 valid hosts per subnet, however (2^4–2 = 16–2 = 14). With 16 possible addresses per subnet, the subnet numbers will increment in multiples of 16. The subnet numbers shown (fourth octet) must be divisible by 16 with no remainder to be a valid subnet number. Starting with the base address of 172.25.15.0, the first seven subnets are as follows (with the 172.25.15.248 network, 248 is not evenly divisible by 16):

   Subnet 0: 172.25.15.0/28

   Subnet 1: 172.25.15.16/28

   Subnet 2: 172.25.15.32/28

   Subnet 3: 172.25.15.48/28

   Subnet 4: 172.25.15.64/28

   Subnet 5: 172.25.15.96/28

   Subnet 6: 172.25.15.128/28

4. D. The first bit value is 128, and the second is 64, for a total of 192, which is the first Class C network address.

5. D. A router is required because the two hosts are on different subnets. Host 192.168.75.34/28 is on subnet 192.168.75.32, and host 192.168.75.50/28 is on subnet 192.168.75.48.

6. A, B. This is a Class C address if the first 3 (high-order) bits are binary 110, which equals 192. The default mask for a Class C is /24, or 255.255.255.0. The host portion is the fourth octet, not the third and fourth octets. The second HOB is not a 0, so this is not a Class B. The parent network is 192.168.42.0, not 192.168.0.0. A Class C address has 254 possible host addresses, not 65,534 addresses as with a Class B.

7. B. The subnet mask /18 on a Class B network borrows 2 bits from the third octet. The value of these bits is 128 + 64 = 192.

8. Answer:

127.0.0.0	Loopback testing address
223.14.6.95	Class C host address
191.82.0.0	Class B network address
255.255.0.0	Class B default subnet mask
124.255.255.255	Class A broadcast address
224.100.35.76	Multicast address
61.0.0.255	Class A host address

9. B. Static NAT is required to provide a one-to-one direct mapping from outside the network to a local internal host.

10. A. Borrowing 5 bits from the fourth octet leaves 3 bits for hosts. This creates 32 subnets ($2^5 = 32$) of six hosts each ($2^3 - 2 = 8 - 2 = 6$). A quick way to determine the number of hosts per subnet is to subtract the non-255 part of the subnet mask (in this case, 248) from 256 and then subtract 2; $256 - 248 = 8$ hosts; $8 - 2 = 6$.

11. C. Borrowing 3 bits from the fourth octet results in a subnet mask of 255.255.255.224. This leaves 5 bits for hosts. This creates eight subnets ($2^3 = 8$) of 30 hosts each ($2^5 - 2 = 32 - 2 = 30$).

12. Answer:

Characteristics	IPv4	IPv6
Uses a 32-bit address	✔	
Is usually expressed in dotted-decimal notation	✔	
Contains a 24-bit global prefix		✔
Is usually expressed in hexadecimal notation		✔
Is in widespread use on the Internet	✔	
Uses a 128-bit address		✔

13. B. The broadcast address for a network is the main network address with a host portion of all 1s. A basic Class B uses the first two octets for the network number and the last two octets for hosts, so the broadcast would be 172.17.255.255.

14. C. A Class C network uses the fourth octet for host addresses. With 8 bits, 254 hosts are possible ($2^8 - 2 = 256 - 2 = 254$ hosts).

15. PAT or NAT overload

16. C. A mask of 255.255.255.192 is a /26 and borrows 2 bits from the host portion when starting with a /24. This leaves 6 bits for hosts. This results in four subnets ($2^2 = 4$) with 62 hosts per subnet ($2^6 - 2 = 64 - 2 = 62$).

17. Class B. A Class B provides 65,534 host addresses. Class A provides 16,777,214, and Class C provides 254.

Challenge Questions and Activities

1. Answer:

Host IP Address	CIDR Prefix	Dotted-Decimal Mask	Network/ Subnet Number	Total Number of CIDR Host Addresses on This Network/ Subnet
172.27.130.53	/22	255.255.252.0	172.27.128.0	$2^{10}-2 = 1022$
192.168.117.40	/27	255.255.255.224	192.168.117.32	$2^5-2 = 30$
10.5.93.226	/24	255.255.255.0	10.5.93.0	$2^8-2 = 254$
172.18.21.138	/20	255.255.240.0	172.18.16.0	$2^{12}-2 = 4094$
192.168.117.5	/30	255.255.255.252	192.168.117.4	$2^2-2 = 2$

2. Answers:

   A. 209.165.202.65

   B. Inside global address

   C. 192.168.1.27

   D. Inside local address

   E. 209.165.200.229 (server)

   F. Outside local or outside global address

   G. 209.165.200.229 (server IP)

   H. 209.165.202.65 (router S0/0/0 interface address)

   I. 192.168.1.27 (internal Host-A IP address)

3. Answers:

   A. Varies

   B. Varies

   C. Varies

   D. Use the ANDing process to compare the 32 bits of the host IP address to the 32 bits of the sub-net mask.

   E. 2 to the power of the number of bits left for hosts by the mask minus 2.

   F. Varies

   G. Either by static entry or through DHCP. If DHCP, a DHCP server IP address is displayed in the **ipconfig /all** output.

   H. If it starts with 10, 172.16 through 172.31, or 192.168, it is private.

   I. If the PC has a private IP address and can access the Internet, NAT or PAT probably is being used.

   J. Varies

   K. If they are private, the organization is using internal DNS servers. If public, they are probably the ISP's DNS servers.

   Answers will vary, depending on which PC is investigated and how it is connected to the Internet.

Chapter 5

Check Your Understanding

1. B. The modular format of the Cisco IOS allows businesses to select the image that is optimal for them. Current ISRs can handle most IOSs. It is not possible to mix and match modules for functionality.

2. A. Most new ISRs come with SDM installed. This is the preferred tool for configuring new devices. SDM works through the Ethernet port and is an in-band configuration tool.

3. The startup-config file is stored in NVRAM so that it is retained even when the power is removed.

4. A, C, D. The domain name, SDM username and password, and enable password are required on the Basic Configuration page. DHCP information is requested on the DHCP page, and the WAN interface information is on the WAN (Internet) Configuration page.

5. C. HDLC is the default serial line encapsulation used on Cisco routers. Although HDLC is standards-based, Cisco HDLC is not the same as other HDLC implementations. Cisco HDLC should be used only when connecting to another Cisco router.

6. IP Unnumbered sets the serial interface address to match the IP address on one of the router's other functional interfaces. This feature is often used to save address space by allowing a serial interface to "borrow" one of the router's other addresses when required.

7. B. Dynamic NAT is configured by default when the Cisco SDM Basic NAT Wizard is used. Dynamic NAT enables the hosts on the internal local network to share the registered IP address assigned to the WAN interface. In this manner, hosts with internal private addresses can have access to the Internet.

8. C. Addresses are excluded in global configuration mode.

9. This command creates a static NAT translation. The machine with an internal IP address of 172.31.232.14 would have its source address rewritten as 10.114.11.14 as the packets moved through the serial interface.

10. E.

    show running-configuration displays the current operating configuration.

    show interfaces displays interface status and configuration.

    show arp displays the ARP table.

    show ip route displays the IP routing table.

    show version displays system hardware and software status.

11. The **enable secret** command encrypts the password in the configuration file, but the **enable password** does not. If the router is compromised, the password can be read unless it is encrypted. Always use **enable secret** when configuring a device.

12. A. The DHCP server will hand out the first address in the pool that is not excluded or already in use.

13. C. A port that is receiving data flashes green. A steady green color indicates a connection to an end device, but no data is flowing through the interface. Amber or red colors indicate a problem with the port or that STP is functioning. No light indicates that the port is not terminated (nothing is connected).

14. D. To recall the most recent command in the history buffer, press **Ctrl-P** or the **up arrow** key. Repeat this process to recall successively older commands. To return to a more recent command in the history buffer, press **Ctrl-N** or the **down arrow** key. Repeat this process to recall successively more recent commands.

15. A router forwards packets from one network to another based on the destination IP address specified in the packet. It examines the routing table to determine where to forward the packet to reach the destination network. If the router does not have a route to a specific network in its routing table, a default route can be configured to tell the router how to forward the packet. The default route is used on a router only if the router does not know where to send a packet.

Challenge Questions and Activities

1. For most new device configurations, SDM is recommended. SDM eliminates the need for extensive knowledge of the CLI commands and provides guided step-by-step configuration instructions. The IOS CLI normally is used on older devices that do not support SDM, for advanced configurations, or by people with extensive knowledge of the IOS CLI commands. Because this technician is new, she might not be comfortable with the IOS CLI commands. Because the device is an ISR, it supports SDM.

2. Cisco Discovery Protocol (CDP) is an information-gathering tool used on a switch, ISR, or router to share information with other directly connected Cisco devices. By default, CDP begins running when the device boots up. It then sends periodic messages, known as CDP advertisements, to its directly connected networks. This tool gathers information about any directly connected devices, including their IP address, platform, and IOS version. The user does not have to log in to the connected device to gather this information. Because CDP works at Layer 2, IP addressing does not need to be configured. This presents a serious security risk on the network.

To disable CDP on a device, issue the **no cdp run** command from the global configuration prompt. To disable CDP on an interface, use the interface-specific command **no cdp enable**.

Chapter 6

Check Your Understanding

1. B, D. Interior routers use Interior Gateway Protocols (IGP) to exchange information on local routes. Exterior routers, also known as border gateways, use BGP to route between autonomous systems.

2. A, B. Routes can be entered by an administrator or learned through a routing protocol. None of the other answers are related to routers or routing protocols.

3. B. The routing table, which is built in RAM, contains network numbers and path information that are either entered manually or learned through a routing protocol. The IOS and router configuration files are important to router operation but do not contain best path route information. The router uses the destination address in IP packets to route packets, but this does not affect the routing table or best path selection.

4. B, E. ISPs can choose to allow transit traffic or not. Excessive transit traffic can overload an Internet router. By its nature, transit traffic is destined for a network in another AS and passes through an intermediate AS to get there.

5. The directly connected router AS number. The neighbor IP address is the border router for that AS.

6. Answer:

AS	A group of networks administered by a single entity
ASN	A registered number that identifies a particular set of networks
ISP	A provider of Internet access
IGP	Examples include RIP, EIGRP, and OSPF
EGP	An example is BGP

7. A, B, D. The first step is to select the routing protocol to be configured. To route packets, the interface that is to participate in the routing process must be assigned an IP address and subnet mask. Finally, the routing protocol is configured with the new network IP address. The other answers are not related to configuring a new network on a router.

8. D. The **network** command specifies which interfaces will exchange RIP routing updates. If the interface IP address is in the network number specified, the interface will send and receive updates. The **router rip** and **version 2** commands specify RIP v2 as the routing protocol. The **network** command has nothing to do with VLSM and does not accomplish the other goals indicated.

9. Answer:

debug ip rip	Displays the networks advertised in the updates as the updates are sent and received.
show ip protocols	Verifies the routing protocol process running and that the correct networks are advertised.
show running-config	Displays current configuration information for configured routing protocols and interfaces.
show ip route	Verifies that routes received are installed in the routing table.
show interfaces	Checks to see that the interfaces are up and operational.

10. **show ip route**

11. A, C, D. The command must specify the network to be reached, the subnet mask, and either the next-hop router interface IP address or the exit interface for the router being configured.

12. C. If an interface has an IP address, and the status of the interface and its data link protocol is

up/up, the directly connected classful network associated with the interface appears in the routing table. No other entries appear in the routing table unless a routing protocol is activated or the static route is configured.

13. A, D, E. Routing protocols learn available routes to destinations. They place the best routes in the routing table and remove routes from the routing table when they are no longer valid.

14. Border gateway router

15. BGP

16. Convergence

17. A, C. EIGRP uses bandwidth and delay by default. Hop count and cost are optional metrics but must be configured. Interface type is not an EIGRP metric.

18. **debug ip rip**

19. No. The interface protocol is down.

Chapter 7

Check Your Understanding

1. B. Managed services allow a company to budget a fixed amount each month to manage its network. The ISP is responsible for any unexpected expenses and for keeping the network performing at the level specified in the service-level agreement. In-house management implies that the company is responsible for all expenses occurred in relation to the network. A high mean time between failures may reduce the total costs, but the company would still be responsible for all expenses incurred.

2. This means that the network is available and performing as designed 99.999% of the time. Most business-critical networks are designed to meet this level of system availability. To achieve this, high-quality enterprise-class equipment is used throughout the network. Redundancy in all critical components and links is also necessary to achieve this level of reliability.

3. D, E. TCP and UDP are the two transport layer protocols. IP is an internetwork layer protocol, and DNS and HTTPS are application layer protocols.

4. A, B, C. The top three layers of the OSI model equate to the application layer in the TCP/IP model.

5. E. The three-way handshake starts with the source host sending a SYN to the destination host. The destination host then replies by sending a SYN-ACK back to the source. The source acknowledges this by sending an ACK back to the destination. At this point the three-way handshake is complete, and communication can occur.

6. D. UDP relies on upper-layer protocols to compensate for any lost data. UDP does not retransmit any lost data.

7. A, D, E, F. All these types of traffic use UDP. FTP and e-mail use TCP to ensure reliable delivery of all information.

8. E. The socket is a combination of IP address and port. It uniquely identifies a particular application process running on a host device.

9. A. A DNS forward lookup searches the DNS database for an IP address.

10. D. SMTP is used to send e-mail, and HTTPS is used to securely transfer hypertext documents. POP3 and IMAP4 are used to retrieve e-mail from a server. POP3 does not leave a copy on the server, but IMAP4 does. If the company does centralized backup and storage, it is important that the messages remain on the server.

11. In an active data connection, a client initiates a request to the server and opens a port for the expected data. The server then connects to the client on that port, and the data transfer begins. With a passive data connection, the FTP server opens a random source port (greater than 1023). The server forwards its IP address and this random port to the FTP client over the control stream. The server then waits for a connection from the FTP client to begin the data file transfer. The client initiates the data transfer connection.

Challenge Questions and Activities

1. The fact that the web server's IP address was recently changed and that the URL was working fine before this change could indicate a problem with the name resolution. To verify this, try connecting to the web server using the new IP address instead of the URL. If this works, the problem is with the DNS resolution. The DNS server probably is handing out stale information. DNS entries normally expire in caching name servers, so the problem may correct itself with time. If the entry in the DNS database was statically assigned, make sure that the administrator has updated the information. You could use **nslookup** to query the name server to determine what information is being supplied. If you have access to the company DNS server, you could flush the cache and force it to update with new information.

2. HTTPS is a secure protocol that uses SSL to encrypt information to protect it during transmission. This encryption and decryption of information puts a substantial load on the server. HTTP does not encrypt data and would decrease the burden on the overtaxed server.

   The two possible solutions are to invest in a more powerful server or to change the protocol from HTTPS to HTTP. Purchasing and installing new servers takes time and costs money. Changing the protocol from HTTPS to HTTP costs nothing but puts customer information at risk. If customer information is compromised, legal action can be taken, and this could force the company out of business. This is an excellent example of why networks must be continually monitored and upgraded to keep pace with demand. It is highly recommended that HTTP not be used and new equipment be purchased and installed as soon as possible.

Chapter 8

Check Your Understanding

1. C. Accounting keeps track of who uses what resource and when. Authentication validates user credentials, and authorization controls access to resources. Assigning permissions by itself does not track usage.

2. C, D. Out-of-band network management requires a physical connection. It is not preferred over in-band management for managing services. It is commonly used for initial device configuration, because the device may not have network connectivity yet, and it uses either a direct console or dial-in connection. It is a non-GUI method and does not provide greater functionality than in-band management.

3. C, E. The SNMP agent reports to the management station by responding to polls. It can send an alert message to the management station if a threshold is exceeded, known as a trap. The agent does not poll devices, assign community IDs, or run the SNMP applications that the admin uses.

4. B. Assign users the minimum privileges required, and increase those privileges if necessary.

5.

Accounting	Who used what network resource
Authorization	Permissions to a specific network resource
Authentication	Username and password

6. C. Magnetic tape has the lowest cost per megabyte of any storage medium and can hold huge quantities of data in a very small package. If data is to be recorded and read sequentially, tape is also the fastest.

7. Full. Full backup takes longer than either differential or incremental but allows access to all data backed up on a given day.

8. C. It would be necessary to start with the last full backup from Monday and then add the most recent differential tape from Thursday, because the server crashed on Friday.

9. D. If a disaster such as a fire destroys a facility, the backup media probably would also be destroyed, unless it is kept offsite.

10. B. Stateful filtering or stateful packet inspection (SPI) keeps track of communications between internal and external hosts and allows incoming packets back into the internal network if they are a response to an internal request.

11. D. Risk assessment identifies potential problems that can occur and their effect on the business.

12. A, C. An IPS can detect and prevent malicious activity before it reaches a network target. An IDS cannot stop some malicious traffic from getting through. The downside of an IPS is that all traffic must be inspected before it is allowed into the network, even though the vast majority of traffic is normal. This requires a faster, more sophisticated device.

13. Answers could include SNMP, HTTP, or Telnet. All require a network connection such as Ethernet or a serial WAN link and use the IP network protocol.

14. A, E, F. POP3, SMTP, and IMAP can use SSL. HTTPS can be used to secure websites. IPsec can be used with various network applications.

15. Syslog is a networking standard protocol that allows servers and other networking devices to specify a centralized syslog server that can maintain a list of any or all messages generated. GUI and CLI versions of syslog management applications allow the messages to be analyzed.

16. D. Allowing web access to the server on port 80 and preventing access on other ports is called port filtering.

17. B. An intrusion detection system is a security system to help protect against attacks and is unrelated to SNMP. The MIB stores SNMP data for a device. A trap is an SNMP alert threshold. An agent is software that collects MIB data and communicates with the management station. The community ID or string permits access to the devices running SNMP agents.

18. E. WPA2 uses the more secure Advanced Encryption Standard (AES) encryption technology. WiFi Protected Access 2 (WPA2) is an improved version of WPA. Wired Equivalent Privacy (WEP) is used with older equipment that does not support newer wireless security protocols. WiFi Protected Access (WPA) preceded WPA2. WLAN is not an encryption protocol. WEP2 was a stopgap enhancement to WEP.

19. TFTP server

20. ROMmon and **tftpdnld**

21. A, C, E. Open authentication, preshared key (PSK), and Extensible Authentication Protocol (EAP) are all wireless authentication methods. Wired Equivalent Privacy (WEP) and WiFi Protected Access (WPA) are encryption techniques.

Chapter 9

Check Your Understanding

1. Answer:

Networking Tool	Description
Cable tester	Detects broken wires, crossed-over wiring, shorted connections, and improperly paired connections.
Digital multimeter	Checks power-supply voltage levels and verifies that network devices are receiving power.
Network analyzer	Graphically displays a physical view of network devices and can locate the source of a failed device.
Network management system	Identifies devices producing the most network traffic, analyzes network traffic by protocol, and views interface details.
Protocol analyzer	Filters traffic that meets certain criteria so that all traffic between two devices can be captured.

2. B. IP addressing issues are associated with network Layer 3. Layer 1 is physical, Layer 4 deals with transport protocol such as TCP and UDP, and Layer 7 is application.

3. Answer:

Device Pair	Cable Type (S or C)
Host to switch	S
Hub to switch	C
Router to switch	S
Routers Fa0/0 to host	C
Hub to router	S
Switch to switch	C

4. Answer:

Network Situation	Layer (1 or 2)
Excessive broadcasts	2
Encapsulated error	2
Loose cable connection	1
Fluctuating power supply	1
Serial 0/0/0 is up, protocol is down	2
Misconfigured NIC	2
Incorrect cable type	1
Damaged serial interface connector	1

5. A. The **show interface serial 0/0/0** output shows encapsulation type. It does not show CSU/DSU or routing information.

6. D. The router may disable an interface with a high error rate. Choice A indicates that there is a physical problem with the interface or cable on this interface or the opposite end. Choice B indicates a framing or encapsulation problem. Choice C indicates the interface has been placed in loopback mode, and Choice E indicates that the interface is shut down.

7. D. The LAN subnet is 192.168.1.0/28, which has a range of 192.168.1.1–192.168.1.15. The DNS server IP address is 192.168.1.30, which is on the 192.168.1.16 subnet, a different network.

8. D, E. R1 sent an update to broadcast address 255.255.255.255 and received a v1 update from 10.0.15.2. Answer A is incorrect because the update entry shows the 10.0.0.0 network at a metric of 1. Answer B is incorrect because the 192.168.168.0 network is inaccessible. Answer C is incorrect because R1 sent information about two networks, not five.

9. D. The helper address allows the router to forward DHCP requests broadcast from hosts on the 192.168.1.0/24 network, which would normally be blocked, to the DHCP server on the 192.168.2.0/24 network.

10. B. If pings from 192.168.1.20 to 192.168.1.1 and 192.168.3.16 are successful, that demonstrates basic IP connectivity. If Telnet is not successful, it must be getting blocked by a firewall.

Router Boot and Password Recovery Labs

The labs in this appendix are excerpted from Chapter 5, "Managing Cisco IOS Software," of *Routers and Routing Basics, CCNA 2 Labs and Study Guide*, by Allan Johnson (Cisco Press, ISBN 1-58713-167-6). This appendix supplements the labs that appear in this book in Chapter 5, "Labs: Configuring Network Devices."

Lab B-1: Using the boot system Command

Figure B-1   Topology for Lab B-1

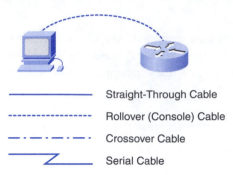

——————— Straight-Through Cable

------------------ Rollover (Console) Cable

— · — · — · Crossover Cable

————— Serial Cable

Table B-1   Lab Equipment Configuration

Router Designation	Router Name	Enable Secret Password	Enable/vty/ Console Password
Router 1	GAD	class	cisco

Objectives

- Display information about the Cisco IOS Software image that is currently running.

- Determine where the IOS image is booting from.

- Check the amount of RAM, Flash memory, and nonvolatile RAM (NVRAM) memory the router has.

- Check the IOS image and Flash memory for space used and availability.

- Document the parts of the IOS image filename.

- Check and document the configuration register settings related to the boot method.

- Document a fallback boot sequence.

Background/Preparation

Cable a network similar to the one in Figure B-1. Refer to the Information in Appendix C, "Lab Equipment Interfaces and Initial Configuration Restoration." You can use any router that meets the interface requirements in Figure B-1 (that is, 800, 1600, 1700, 1800, 2500, 2600, and 2800 series routers or a combination). The 2600 Series routers produced the configuration output in this lab. Any other router might produce slightly different output.

Start a HyperTerminal session. Implement the procedure documented in Appendix C before continuing with this lab.

Task 1: Log in to the Router

Connect to the router and log in.

Task 2: Enter Privileged EXEC Mode

Type **enable** at the command prompt.

Task 3: Save the Existing running-config to the startup-config

At the privileged EXEC command prompt, enter the following:

```
Router#copy running-config  startup-config

Destination filename [startup-config]?
  Enter
```

This task saves the current blank configuration.

Task 4: Configure the Router and View the Running Configuration File

Step 1.   Configure the router with the information in Table B-1.

Step 2.   Enter **show running-config** at the router prompt. The router displays information on the running configuration file stored in RAM.

Do you see the configuration that you just entered?

_____

Task 5: Show Information About the Backup Configuration File

Enter **show startup-config** at the router prompt. The router displays information on the backup configuration file stored in NVRAM.

Do you see the configuration that you just entered?

_____

If not, why?

_____

What command would make the running-config file and startup-config file identical?

_____

Why is the startup-config file so important?

_____

Is there any indication of the configuration register setting?

_____

Task 6: Display the IOS Version and Other Important Information

Enter **show version** at the router prompt. The router returns information about the IOS image that is running in RAM.

What is the IOS version and revision level?

_____

What is the name of the system image (IOS) file?

_____

Where was the router IOS image booted from?

_____

What type of processor and how much RAM does this router have?

_____

What kind of router (platform type) is this?

_____

The router backup configuration file is stored in NVRAM. How much NVRAM does this router have?

_____

The router operating system (IOS) is stored in flash memory. How much flash memory does this router have?

_____

What is the configuration register set to? What boot type does this setting specify?

_____

Task 7: Create the Statements to Perform the Following Functions

Assuming that in Task 6, the configuration register was set to 0x2102, write the configuration mode commands to specify that the IOS image should be loaded from the following:

- ROM monitor:

    _____

- Flash (without checking for **boot system** commands):

    _____

- Flash (checks for **boot system** commands first):

    _____

- ROM IOS:

    _____

Note: ROM IOS is the default on older platforms.

Task 8: Show Information About the Flash Memory Device

Step 1.   Enter **show flash** at the router prompt.

The router responds with information about the flash memory and what IOS image files are stored there.

Step 2.   Document the following information:

How much flash memory is available and used?

_____

_____

What is the file that is stored in flash memory?

_____

What is the size in bytes of the flash memory?

_____

Task 9: Specify a Fallback Boot Sequence

Step 1.   Write the **boot system** command to specify that the IOS image should be loaded from the following:

■ Flash memory:

_____

■ A Trivial File Transfer Protocol (TFTP) server:

_____

■ ROM:

_____

Will this be a full IOS image? ____

To ensure that these commands are available for the router to use the next time you restart it, which task would need to be completed before reloading or power-cycling the router?

_____

Step 2.   When you finish the preceding tasks, log off (by typing **exit**) and turn off the router.

Lab B-2: Troubleshooting Configuration Register Boot Problems

Note: Before beginning this lab, make sure your instructor has prepared the router that you will be using.

Figure B-2   Topology for Lab B-2

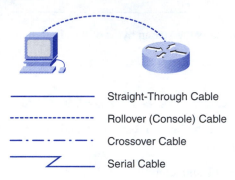

—————————— Straight-Through Cable

------------------ Rollover (Console) Cable

— · — · — · Crossover Cable

———— Serial Cable

Table B-2   Lab Equipment Configuration

Router Designation	Router Name	Enable Secret Password	Enable/vty/Console Password
Router 1	GAD	class	cisco

Objectives:

- Check and document the configuration register settings related to the boot method.

- Configure the router to boot using the configuration file in NVRAM, and reload the router.

Background/Preparation

Cable a network similar to the one in Figure B-2. You can use any router that meets the interface requirements in Figure B-2 (that is, 800, 1600, 1700, 1800, 2500, 2600, and 2800 routers or a combination). Refer to the information in Appendix C to correctly specify the interface identifiers based on the equipment in your lab. The 1721 series routers produced the configuration output in this lab. Any other router might produce slightly different output.

Start a HyperTerminal session.

Implement the procedure documented in Appendix C before continuing with this lab.

Task 1: Log in to the Router

Connect to the router and log in.

Task 2: Configure the Router Name and Configuration Register Setting

Enter the following commands:

```
Router>enable
Router#configure terminal
Router(config)#hostname GAD
GAD(config)#config-register 0x2142
GAD(config)#exit
```

Task 3: Save the Existing running-config to the startup-config

At the privileged EXEC command prompt, enter the following:

```
GAD#copy running-config startup-config
Destination filename [startup-config]? Enter
```

Task 4: Restart the Router

At the privileged EXEC command prompt, enter the following:

```
GAD#reload
Proceed with reload? [confirm]  Enter
After the reload, the router responds with the following:
-- System Configuration Dialog --
Would you like to enter the initial configuration dialog? [yes/no]:  n
Type n and press  Enter.
```

Task 5: View the Running Configuration File

Enter **show running-config** at the privileged EXEC mode prompt. The router displays information on the running configuration file stored in RAM.

Do you see the configuration that you just entered?

Task 6: Reload the Saved Configuration

At the privileged EXEC command prompt, enter the following:

```
Router#copy startup-config running-config
Destination filename [running-config]? Enter
```

Notice that the router name that was configured in Task 2 (GAD) is now displayed. Why did the Startup config file not load when you reloaded the router?

Task 7: Display the IOS Version and Other Important Information

Enter **show version** at the router prompt.

The router displays information about the IOS image that is running in RAM.

Notice that the end of the output shows a configuration register setting of 0x2142. This setting is the problem. The setting configures the router to ignore the Startup configuration file on bootup. The setting will be useful to boot up in the password recovery mode.

Task 8: Change the Configuration Register to Load the Startup Configuration File from NVRAM, Save, and Reload the Router

Enter global configuration mode and enter the following commands:

```
Router>enable
GAD#configure terminal
GAD(config)#config-register 0x2102
GAD(config)#exit
GAD#copy running-config  startup-config Destination filename [startup-config]?
  Enter
GAD#reload
Proceed with reload? [confirm]Enter
```

Task 9: Verify the Configuration Register Setting and Log Out of the Router

After the router reboots, it should look to NVRAM for the Startup Configuration. Verify it by issuing the command **show version**:

```
GAD#show version
```

The results will be shown. You should be able to see the config-register 0x2102. When you finish these tasks, log off (by typing **exit**) and turn off the router.

Lab B-3: Password Recovery Procedures

Figure B-3 Topology for Lab B-3

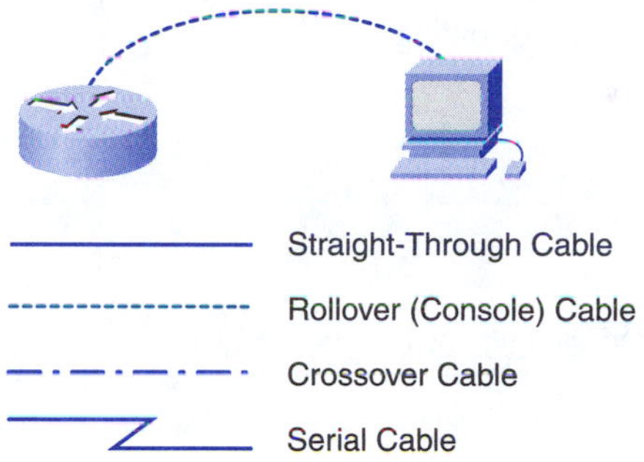
Straight-Through Cable
Rollover (Console) Cable
Crossover Cable
Serial Cable

Table B-3 Lab Equipment Configuration

Router Designation	Router Name	Enable Secret Password	Enable/vty/Console Passwords
Router 1	GAD	class	cisco

Objective

- Gain access to a router with an unknown privileged EXEC mode (enable) password.

Background/Preparation

This lab demonstrates how you gain access to a router with an unknown privileged EXEC mode (enable) password. Anyone with this procedure and access to a console port on a router can change the password and take control of the router. That is why routers must also have physical security to prevent unauthorized access.

Cable a network similar to the one in Figure B-3. You can use any router that meets the interface requirements in the diagram (that is, 800, 1600, 1700, 1800, 2500, 2600, or 2800 series routers or a combination). Refer to the information in Appendix C to correctly specify the interface identifiers to be used based on the equipment in your lab. The 1721 series routers produced the configuration output in this lab. Any other router might produce slightly different output.

Start a HyperTerminal session.

Note: Configure the hostname and passwords on the router. Let an instructor, lab assistant, or other student configure a basic configuration, change the enable secret password, perform **copy running-config startup-config**, and reload the router.

Note: The version of HyperTerminal with Windows 95, 98, NT, and 2000 was developed for Microsoft by Hilgraeve. Some versions might not issue a "break" sequence as required for the Cisco router password-recovery technique. If you have this version, upgrade to HyperTerminal Private Edition (PE), which is free for personal and educational use. You can download the program at http://www.hilgraeve.com.

Task 1: Attempt to Log in to the Router

Make the necessary console connections and establish a HyperTerminal session with the router. Attempt to log in to the router using the privileged mode password **class**. Your output should look something like the following:

```
Router>enable
Password:
Password:
Password:
% Bad secrets
Router>
```

Task 2: Document the Current Configuration Register Setting

Step 1. At the user EXEC prompt, type **show ver**.

Step 2. Record the value displayed for the configuration register (for example, 0x2102):

_____

Task 3: Enter ROM Monitor Mode

Turn the router off, wait a few seconds, and turn it back on. When the router starts displaying "System Bootstrap, Version …" on the HyperTerminal screen, press the **Ctrl** key and the **Break** key together. The router will boot in ROM monitor mode. Depending on the router hardware, you get one of several prompts, such as **rommon 1 >** or simply **>**.

Task 4: Examine the ROM Monitor Mode Help

Type **?** at the prompt. The output should be similar to the following:

```
rommon 1 >?
alias              set and display aliases command
boot               boot up an external process
break              set/show/clear the breakpoint
confreg            configuration register utility
context            display the context of a loaded image
dev                list the device table
dir                list files in file system
dis                display instruction stream
help               monitor builtin command help
history            monitor command history
meminfo            main memory information
repeat             repeat a monitor command
reset              system reset
set                display the monitor variables
sysret             print out info from last system return
tftpdnld           tftp image download
xmodem             x/ymodem image download
```

Task 5: Change the Configuration Register Setting to Boot Without Loading the Configuration File

From ROM monitor mode, type **confreg 0x2142** to change the configuration register.

```
rommon 2>confreg 0x2142
```

Task 6: Restart the Router

Step 1. From ROM monitor mode, type **reset** or power-cycle the router:

```
rommon 2>reset
```

Step 2. Because of the new configuration register setting, the router will not load the configuration file. When the system prompts, "Would you like to enter the initial configuration dialog? [yes]," enter **no** and press **Enter**.

Task 7: Enter Privileged EXEC Mode and Change the Password

Step 1. At the user EXEC mode prompt, type **enable** and press **Enter** to go to privileged EXEC mode without a password.

Step 2. Use the command **copy startup-config running-config** to restore the existing configuration. Because you are already in privileged EXEC mode, you do not need a password.

Step 3. Type **configure terminal** to enter global configuration mode.

Step 4. In global configuration mode, type **enable secret class** to change the secret password.

Step 5. While still in global configuration mode, type **config-register** *xxxxxx*, where *xxxxxx* is the original configuration register value recorded in Task 2, and press **Enter**.

Step 6. Press **Ctrl-Z** to return to privileged EXEC mode.

Step 7. Use the **copy running-config startup-config** command to save the new configuration.

Step 8. Before restarting the router, verify the new configuration setting. From the privileged EXEC prompt, enter the **show version** command and press **Enter**.

Step 9. Verify that the last line of output is the following:

```
Configuration register is 0x2142 (will be 0x2102 at next reload)
```

Step 10. Use the **reload** command to restart the router.

Task 8: Verify the New Password and Configuration

When the router reloads, the enable password will be **class**.

When you complete all eight tasks, log off (by typing **exit**) and turn the router off.

Lab Equipment Interfaces and Initial Configuration Restoration

This appendix provides a reference for router interface designations and instructions for restoring routers and switches to their default configurations. This appendix includes the following instruction sections:

- Router Interface Summary
- Erasing and Reloading the Router
- Erasing and Reloading the Switch
- SDM Router Basic IOS Configuration

Router Interface Summary

To find out exactly how the router is configured, look at the interfaces. This will identify the type of router as well as how many interfaces the router has. There is no way to effectively list all the combinations of configurations for each router class. The interface chart shown in Table C-1 provides the identifiers for the possible combinations of Ethernet and Serial interfaces applicable to CCNA Discovery. This interface chart does not include any other type of interface a specific router may contain; for example, ISDN BRI interfaces are not shown. The string in parentheses is the legal abbreviation that can be used in a Cisco IOS command to represent the interface.

Table C-1   Router Interface Summary

Router Model	Ethernet Interface #1	Ethernet Interface #2	Serial Interface #1	Serial Interface #2
800 (806)	Ethernet 0 (E0)	Ethernet 1 (E1)	–	–
1600	Ethernet 0 (E0)	Ethernet 1 (E1)	Serial 0 (S0)	Serial 1 (S1)
1700	Fast Ethernet 0 (FA0)	Fast Ethernet 1 (FA1)	Serial 0 (S0)	Serial 1 (S1)
1800	Fast Ethernet 0/0 (FA0/0)	Fast Ethernet 0/1 (FA0/1)	Serial 0/0/0 (S0/0/0)	Serial 0/0/1 (S0/0/1)
2500	Ethernet 0 (E0)	Ethernet 1 (E1)	Serial 0 (S0)	Serial 1 (S1)
2600	Fast Ethernet 0/0 (FA0/0)	Fast Ethernet 0/1 (FA0/1)	Serial 0/0 (S0/0)	Serial 0/1 (S0/1)

Erasing and Reloading the Router

For the majority of the labs in *CCNA Discovery*, it is necessary to start with an unconfigured router. Using a router with an existing configuration may produce unpredictable results. The following instructions prepare the router before you perform the lab so that previous configuration options do not interfere. These instructions apply to most Cisco routers.

Step 1.   Enter privileged EXEC mode by entering **enable**:

```
Router> enable
```

Step 2.   In privileged EXEC mode, enter the **erase startup-config** command:

```
Router# erase startup-config
```

Step 3.   Press **Enter** to confirm.

The response is

```
Erase of nvram: complete
```

Step 4.   In privileged EXEC mode, enter the **reload** command:

```
Router# reload
```

The responding line prompt is

```
System configuration has been modified. Save? [yes/no]:
```

Step 5.   Enter **n** and press **Enter**.

The responding line prompt is

```
Proceed with reload? [confirm]
```

Step 6.   Press **Enter** to confirm.

The first line of the response is

```
Reload requested by console.
```

After the router has reloaded, the line prompt is

```
Would you like to enter the initial configuration dialog? [yes/no]:
```

Step 7.   Enter **n** and press **Enter**.

The responding line prompt is

```
Press RETURN to get started!
```

Step 8.   Press **Enter**.

The router is ready for the assigned lab to be performed.

Erasing and Reloading the Switch

For the majority of the labs in *CCNA Discovery*, it is necessary to start with an unconfigured switch. Using a switch with an existing configuration may produce unpredictable results. The following instructions prepare the switch before you perform the lab so that previous configuration options do not interfere. Instructions are provided for the 29xx series of switches.

Step 1.   Enter privileged EXEC mode by entering **enable**. If you're prompted for a password, enter **class**. (If that doesn't work, ask the instructor.)

```
Switch> enable
```

Step 2.   Remove the VLAN database information file:

```
Switch# delete flash:vlan.dat
```

```
Delete filename [vlan.dat]?[Enter]
Delete flash:vlan.dat? [confirm] [Enter]
```

If there was no VLAN file, you see this message:

```
%Error deleting flash:vlan.dat (No such file or directory)
```

Step 3.   Remove the switch startup configuration file from NVRAM:

```
Switch# erase startup-config
```

The responding line prompt is

```
Erasing the nvram filesystem will remove all files! Continue? [confirm]
```

Press **Enter** to confirm.

The response should be

```
Erase of nvram: complete
```

Step 4.   Check that the VLAN information was deleted.

Verify that the VLAN configuration was deleted in Step 2 using the **show vlan** command. If previous VLAN configuration information (other than the default management VLAN 1) is still present, you must power-cycle the switch (hardware restart) instead of issuing the **reload** command. To power-cycle the switch, remove the power cord from the back of the switch or unplug it, and then plug it back in. If the VLAN information was successfully deleted in Step 2, go to Step 5 and restart the switch using the **reload** command.

Step 5.   Restart the software using the **reload** command.

Note

This step is not necessary if the switch was restarted using the power-cycle method.

a.   In privileged EXEC mode, enter the reload command:

```
Switch# reload
```

The responding line prompt is

```
System configuration has been modified. Save? [yes/no]:
```

b.   Enter n and press Enter.

The responding line prompt is

```
Proceed with reload? [confirm] [Enter]
```

The first line of the response is

```
Reload requested by console.
```

c.   After the switch has reloaded, the line prompt is

```
Would you like to enter the initial configuration dialog? [yes/no]:
```

Enter n and press Enter.

The responding line prompt is

```
Press RETURN to get started! [Enter]
```

SDM Router Basic IOS Configuration

If the startup-config is erased in an SDM router, SDM will no longer come up by default when the router is restarted. You must build a basic config as follows. Further details about the setup and use of SDM can be found in the SDM Quick Start Guide:

http://www.cisco.com/en/US/products/sw/secursw/ps5318/products_quick_start09186a0080511c89.html#wp44788

Step 1. Configure the router and PC IP addresses.

A PC-based web browser uses the router interface to bring up SDM. The PC IP address should be set to 10.10.10.2 255.255.255.248.

Note:

An SDM router other than the 1841 may require connection to a different port to access SDM.

```
Router(config)#interface fastethernet 0/0
Router(config-if)#ip address 10.10.10.1 255.255.255.248
Router(config-if)#no shutdown
```

Step 2. Enable the HTTP/HTTPS server on the router.

```
Router(config)#ip http server
Router(config)#ip http secure-server
Router(config)#ip http authentication local
```

Step 3. Create a user account with privilege level 15 (enable privileges):

```
Router(config)#username username privilege 15 password 0 password
```

Replace *username* and *password* with the username and password you want to configure.

Step 4. Configure SSH and Telnet for local login and privilege level 15:

```
Router(config)#line vty 0 4
Router(config-line)#privilege level 15
Router(config-line)#login local
Router(config-line)#transport input telnet
Router(config-line)#transport input telnet ssh
Router(config-line)#exit
```

Glossary

A

access control list (ACL)   A list kept by a network device (such as a router or switch) to control access to or from the device for a number of services. For example, it prevents packets with a certain IP address from leaving a particular interface on the device.

acknowledgment (ACK)   A transmission control character (or transmission frame) that confirms that a transmitted message was received uncorrupted or without errors or that the receiving station is ready to accept transmissions.

administrative distance   Used by Cisco routers to determine the trustworthiness of the routing source. When two router sources—routing protocols, static routes, connected routes—offer the same route to the Cisco router, the source with the lowest administrative distance is placed in the routing table.

Advanced Encryption Standard (AES)   A symmetric cipher defined in Federal Information Processing Standard (FIPS) Number 197 in 2001 as the federal government-approved encryption algorithm. The U.S. government adopted AES to replace Data Encryption Standard (DES).

algorithm   A step-by-step procedure for solving a mathematical problem. Algorithms and route metrics are used by routing protocols to determine the best path to a destination.

application layer   Layer 7 of the OSI model. It interfaces directly to and performs common application services for the application processes. It also issues requests to the presentation layer (Layer 6).

ATM   Asynchronous Transfer Mode. The international standard for cell relay in which multiple service types (such as voice, video, or data) are conveyed in fixed-length (53-byte) cells. Fixed-length cells allow cell processing to occur in hardware, thereby reducing transit delays. ATM is designed to take advantage of high-speed transmission media, such as E3, SONET, and T3.

authentication   A process implemented on a network to verify a user's identity.

authentication, authorization, and accounting (AAA)   A protocol, specified in RFC 2903 and several other RFCs, for controlling who can access a system or network and how they can access it, and determining what they did while connected.

Automatic Private IP Addressing (APIPA) A link-local address automatically assigned to a DHCP client by the operating system if a DHCP server is unavailable or unreachable. IPv4 addresses in the address block 169.254.0.1 to 169.254.255.254 (169.254.0.0 /16).

autonegotiation   A feature of Ethernet switches that allows ports to adjust their speed and duplex settings automatically based on the capabilities of connected devices. Autonegotiation occurs when a switch port can autodetect the speed and duplex of the device that is connected to the port.

autonomous system (AS)   A collection of networks under a common administration sharing a common routing strategy.

autonomous system number (ASN)   A unique number assigned to an autonomous system (AS) for use when routing packets through the Internet.

availability   With networking resources, the condition of being accessible to users.

B

bandwidth   1) Digital: A measurement of the amount of data that can be transmitted on a given networking medium within a given amount of time. 2) Analog: The range of frequencies transmitted on a medium.

border gateway   A device, such as a router, that provides access to the Internet or another external network for internal users.

Border Gateway Protocol (BGP)   An inter-AS (autonomous system) routing protocol, also called an exterior gateway protocol. It is used to connect Internet service providers (ISPs) to the Internet.

bottom-up approach   A troubleshooting technique used in a layered concept of networking that starts with the physical or lowest layer and works up.

C

cable   1) An abbreviated term for cable modem, an Internet and WAN connectivity option offered by cable providers. 2) A wired medium used to interconnect hosts and networking devices.

cable modem termination system (CMTS)   A component located at the local cable television company that exchanges digital signals with cable modems on a cable network.

Channel Service Unit/Data Service Unit (CSU/DSU)   A network device that connects an organization to a digital circuit such as a T1.

Cisco IOS   Operating system software installed in Cisco networking devices, such as routers and switches, that controls the operation and interaction between the CPU, memory, and interfaces.

Cisco Network Assistant (CNA)   A PC-based GUI network management application that simplifies configuration, deployment, and ongoing management and maintenance of Cisco devices. The application provides a centralized network view that allows network administrators to apply common services, generate inventory reports, synchronize passwords, and employ features across Cisco switches, routers, and access points. Cisco Network Assistant is available at no cost and can be downloaded from the Cisco Systems website.

Cisco Router and Security Device Manager (SDM)   A web-based device-management tool for a Cisco IOS software-based router. Simplifies router and security configuration through smart wizards used to deploy, configure, and monitor a Cisco router without requiring knowledge of the CLI.

CiscoWorks   A series of SNMP-based internetwork management software applications developed by Cisco. CiscoWorks includes applications for monitoring router and access server status, managing configuration files, and troubleshooting network problems. CiscoWorks applications are integrated on several SNMP-based network management platforms, including SunNet Manager, HP OpenView, and IBM NetView.

classful   The division of IP addresses into five classes: A, B, C, D, and E. A fixed number of networks and hosts is associated with each class.

classless   A system of IP addressing that does not rely on class boundaries but instead treats all address space as equal. Any number of bits can be assigned to represent the network portion of an address, leaving the rest to represent hosts.

classless interdomain routing (CIDR)   A technique supported by border gateway protocols and based on route aggregation. CIDR allows routers to group routes to reduce the quantity of routing information carried by the core Internet routers. With CIDR, several IP networks appear to networks outside the group as a single, larger entity. With CIDR, IP addresses and their subnet masks are written as four octets, separated by periods, followed by a slash and a two-digit number that represents the subnet mask.

command-line interface (CLI)   A user interface to a computer operating system or application that depends on textual commands being entered by the user.

connection-oriented   A term applied to protocols that establish an end-to-end connection before data is sent so that data arrives in the proper sequence. TCP is a connection-oriented protocol.

context-sensitive   A type of software help feature available with Cisco IOS CLI that provides assistance when entering commands, depending on the location in the command structure.

converged IP network   Enables a combination of voice, video, and data services to be delivered over a common network using Internet Protocol (IP).

convergence   The process of exchanging routing updates between routers running a dynamic routing protocol so that each router in the system has the most current information on network reachability.

customer premises equipment (CPE)   Terminating equipment, such as terminals, telephones, and modems, supplied by the telephone company, installed at customer sites, and connected to the telephone company network.

D

data communications equipment (DCE)   A physical connection to a communications network in an EIA expansion environment. The DCE forwards traffic and provides a clocking signal used to synchronize data transmission between DCE and DTE devices. Examples of DCE devices include a modem and an interface card. DCE is also known as data circuit-terminating equipment when used in an ITU-T expansion environment.

datagram   Another term for an IP packet containing user data.

data link layer   Layer 2 of the OSI model. It responds to service requests from the network layer (Layer 3) and issues service requests to the physical layer (Layer 1). An Ethernet MAC address is a data-link address.

data terminal equipment (DTE)   A physical connection to the user end in an EIA expansion environment. The DTE serves as a data source, destination, or both. It connects to a data network through a DCE device, such as a modem, and typically uses clocking signals generated by the DCE. Examples of DTE devices include computers, protocol translators, multiplexers, and routers.

data transfer process (DTP)   Establishes and manages the data connection. The DTP can be passive or active.

de facto standard   An unofficial standard that evolves over time to become more common than the others. Ethernet is an example of a de facto standard.

default gateway   The address of the router interface connected to the same local network as a source host. All hosts on the local network use the default gateway address to send data outside the LAN.

default route   The interface through which the router forwards a packet containing an unknown destination IP network address. The default route usually connects to another router that can forward the packet toward its final destination network.

demilitarized zone (DMZ)   A term borrowed from the military. A DMZ is a designated area between two powers where military activity is not permitted. In computer networking, a DMZ refers to an area of the network that is accessible to both internal and external users. It is more secure than the external network but not as secure as the internal network. It is created by one or more firewalls to separate the internal, DMZ, and external networks. Web servers for public access are frequently placed in a DMZ.

denial-of-service (DoS) attack   A single system on a network that floods the bandwidth or resources of the targeted system, such as a web server, with the intent to shut it down.

dialup   An Internet access technology that uses a dialup analog modem and a conventional phone line to contact the ISP using the public switched telephone network (PSTN).

differential backup   A backup type that contains all files that have changed since the last full backup. The advantage of differential backup is that it has a shorter backup and restore time than a full backup.

Diffusing Update Algorithm (DUAL)   Mathematical process used in the EIGRP routing protocol that provides loop-free operation at every instant throughout a route computation. DUAL allows routers involved in a topology change to synchronize at the same time, while not involving routers that are unaffected by the change.

digital subscriber line (DSL)   A public network technology that delivers high bandwidth over conventional copper wiring at limited distances. It is an always-on technology that allows users to connect to the Internet.

Direct Attached Storage (DAS)   A digital storage system directly attached to a host (server or workstation). The connection between the DAS and the host could be SCSI or fiber-optic cable. It is used to differentiate non-networked storage from SAN and NAS.

distributed denial-of-service (DDoS) attack   Designed to saturate and overwhelm network links with useless data. DDoS operates on a much larger scale than DoS attacks. Typically hundreds or thousands of attack points attempt to overwhelm a target simultaneously. The attack points might be unsuspecting computers that have been previously infected by the DDoS code.

distributed reflected denial-of-service (DRDoS) attack   Occurs when an attacker sends a spoofed, or mock, request to many computer systems on the Internet, with the source address modified to be the targeted computer system. When the computer systems respond to the request, all the requests are directed at the target computer system. Because of the attack's reflection, it is very difficult to determine the attack's originator.

divide-and-conquer approach   A troubleshooting technique in a layered concept of networking that can start at any layer and work up or down, depending on the outcome.

DNS name   A name assigned to a device within a DNS domain that identifies the device. DNS names usually are of the format *servername.domainname.domaintype*. For example, www.cisco.com identifies a web server in the cisco.com domain.

DNS server   A local or remote physical server that resolves a DNS name to an IP address for hosts on a network.

domain name service   A service daemon running on a DNS server that resolves a DNS name to an IP address for hosts on a network.

domain namespace   The hierarchical naming structure for organizing resource records. The domain namespace is made up of various domains, or groups, and the resource records within each group.

Domain Name System (DNS)   A system that provides a way to map hostnames, or URLs, to IP addresses.

dotted-decimal notation   A method of common notation for IP addresses and subnet masks in the form *a.b.c.d*. For IP addresses, each number represents, in decimal (from 0 to 255), 1 byte (8 bits) of the 4-byte IP address. Also called a dot address.

digital subscriber line (DSL)   A public network technology that delivers high bandwidth over conventional copper twisted-pair wiring at limited distances. An always-on technology that allows users to connect to the Internet.

DSL access multiplexer (DSLAM)   A device that allows two or more data sources to share a common transmission medium. DSLAM separates DSL phone and data signals and directs them onto networks. A DSLAM contains a bank of DSL modems to accept the connections from DSL customers.

Dynamic Host Configuration Protocol (DHCP)   Requests and assigns an IP address, default gateway, and DNS server address to a network host automatically.

dynamic NAT   A form of network address translation in which an internal address is converted automatically to a single public address or one of a pool of public addresses.

E

electronic commerce (e-commerce)   The buying and selling of goods and services on the Internet, especially the World Wide Web.

encapsulation   The wrapping of data in a particular protocol header.

encryption   A process to transform data during its transmission to prevent the data's content from being read by anyone but the intended recipient.

Enhanced Interior Gateway Routing Protocol (EIGRP)   A Cisco-proprietary routing protocol that is a mix of a distance vector routing protocol and a link-state routing protocol.

escalation   The process of raising a problem or issue to the next level of support if the previous level is unable to resolve it.

Extensible Authentication Protocol (EAP)   A wireless security protocol that provides mutual, or two-way, authentication and user authentication. An EAP client communicates with a backend authentication server, such as RADIUS.

exterior gateway protocol (EGP)   A type of routing protocol that performs routing between multiple autonomous systems and exchanges routing and reachability information with other routers. The most common example of EGP is Border Gateway Protocol (BGP).

external interface   Relative to network address translation, the device (usually a router) interface that connects to or faces the public Internet.

F

failure domain   An area of a network that is affected when a piece of networking equipment malfunctions or fails.

fault tolerance   The ability of a computer, server, or network to continue operating properly in the event of a failure of one or more of its components.

File Transfer Protocol (FTP)   An application protocol that is part of the TCP/IP protocol stack, used to transfer files between network devices.

flow control   1) The ability to maintain the rate of activity on a network. 2) A method of controlling the amount of data sent to a receiving device so that its buffers do not become overloaded.

forward lookup zone   A standard DNS zone that resolves fully qualified domain names to IP addresses. This zone type is most commonly found when surfing the Internet.

frame A logical grouping of information sent over a transmission medium as a data link layer unit. Often refers to the header and trailer, used for synchronization and error control, that surround the user data contained in the unit. Known as the data link layer protocol data unit (PDU).

frequently asked question (FAQ) A question that customers often ask. FAQs are usually posted by a company on the Internet to assist with common questions and problem resolution.

full backup A data backup method that copies all data to be backed up each time the backup is run, regardless of whether the data was backed up previously.

full duplex Data transmission that can go two ways at the same time, both transmit and receive. An Internet connection using DSL service is an example of full duplex.

fully qualified domain name (FQDN) The complete expression of a host or server's location on the Internet. An FQDN includes both the hostname and domain name.

G–H

graphical user interface (GUI) A user-friendly interface that uses graphical images and widgets, along with text, to indicate the information and actions available to a user when interacting with a computer.

half duplex Data transmission that can go two ways, but not at the same time. Two-way radios and early shared Ethernet networks are examples of half duplex.

help desk A person or department in an organization that supports end users and resolves network issues.

hierarchy In IP addressing, the address has two parts—a network portion and a host portion—and is an example of a hierarchical addressing system. All hosts on the same network have the same network portion of the address and different host portions.

high-order bits (HOB) The first few bits of an IP address. The high-order bit of a binary number is the one that carries the most weight—the one written farthest to the left. High-order bits are the 1s in the network mask, sometimes called the network portion of the mask. In classful addressing, the high-order bits identify the class of the address.

hop A router or Layer 3 device that a packet passes through on its way to a destination.

hop count The metric used by RIP and some other distance-vector routing protocols.

Hypertext Transfer Protocol (HTTP) The application layer protocol used by web browsers and web servers to transfer/convey files, such as text and graphics files.

I–K

in-band management A management technique for connecting a computer to a network device. In-band management is used to monitor and make configuration changes to a network device over a network connection. Using Telnet over a LAN or WAN link to access and configure a network device is an example of in-band network management.

incident management A basic procedure that should be followed every time a help desk technician initiates a problem-solving process.

incremental backup A backup method in which multiple backups are kept. A full backup is performed initially, and then successive incremental backups contain only the information that has changed since the previous backup. The advantage of incremental backup is that it takes the least time to complete.

inside global address With NAT, the router's public address, normally assigned to the external interface connected to the ISP.

inside local address With NAT, the internal (usually private) address of an internal host that will be translated into the inside global (public) address.

integrated services router (ISR) A device that forwards packets from one network to another based on network layer information. An ISR provides secure Internet and intranet access and can combine routing, switching and wireless capabilities in a single device. Normally used in home and small office environments.

interior gateway protocol (IGP) Used to exchange routing information within a company or within a set of routers under the same administration.

internal interface Relative to Network Address Translation, the device (usually a router) interface that faces the internal (normally private) network.

Internet   A publicly accessible network of interconnected computer networks that transmit data by using Internet Protocol (IP).

Internet Control Message Protocol (ICMP)   A network layer Internet protocol that reports errors and provides other information relevant to IP packet processing. Documented in RFC 792.

Internet Engineering Task Force (IETF)   The body that defines standard Internet operating protocols such as TCP/IP.

Internet Exchange Point (IXP)   Physical locations and equipment where multiple ISPs can exchange traffic between their networks.

Internet Message Access Protocol (IMAP4)   An application layer Internet protocol that allows a local client to access e-mail on a remote server. The latest version is IMAP4.

Internet Protocol version 4 (IPv4)   The current Internet Protocol version. Uses a 32-bit addressing structure.

Internet Protocol version 6 (IPv6)   The next generation of Internet Protocol. Uses a 128-bit addressing structure.

Internet service provider (ISP)   A company that provides Internet access to individuals and organizations. ISPs can provide services and equipment.

intrusion detection system (IDS)   A combination of a sensor, console, and central engine in a single device installed on a network to protect against the attacks that a conventional firewall can miss.

Intrusion Prevention System (IPS)   An extension of IDS. Based on application content, IPS enhances access control to protect computers from exploitation.

IP security (IPsec)   A framework of open standards that provides data confidentiality, data integrity, and data authentication between participating peers. IPsec provides security services at the IP layer. IPsec can protect one or more data flows between a pair of hosts, between a pair of security gateways, or between a security gateway and a host.

L

LAND attack   A DoS security attack that can cause a computer to lock up.

link-local address   A private address automatically assigned to a DHCP client by the operating system if a DHCP server is unavailable or unreachable. An IPv4 address in the address block 169.254.0.1 to 169.254.255.254 (169.254.0.0 /16).

link state   A class of routing algorithm in which each router broadcasts or multicasts information about the cost of reaching each of its neighbors to all nodes in the internetwork.

link-state advertisement (LSA)   A broadcast packet used by link-state routing protocols such as OSPF that contains information about neighbors and path costs.

local traffic   Packets generated and managed by a company's routers and routing protocol(s). Local packets stay within one autonomous system (AS).

lower layers   OSI model Layers 1 (physical), 2 (data link), 3 (network), and 4 (transport). The lower layers of the OSI model handle data transport functions.

M

main distribution facility (MDF)   The primary communications room for a building. Also, the central point of a star networking topology in which patch panels, hubs, and routers are located.

malware   Malicious software designed to infiltrate or damage a computer system without the owner's knowledge. It is a general term used to mean a variety of hostile, intrusive, or annoying software.

managed services   Service providers that offer onsite support of a customer network.

Management Information Base (MIB)   A database of network management information that is used and maintained by a network management protocol such as SNMP or CMIP.

mean time between failures (MTBF)   Calculates the average length of time a device will perform before it fails. This term is used to estimate the average "life span" of hard disks and other computer elements.

mean time between repairs (MTBR)   Calculates how much time passes between device repairs. A longer MTBR means that the device requires repair less often. In a maintenance contract, the user would pay more for a system whose MTBR is longer than that of another system.

mean time to repair (MTTR)   Calculates how long it takes to repair a device. MTTR is also an abbreviation for mean time to recovery, which calculates how long a device will take to recover from a nonterminal failure. In a maintenance contract, the user would pay more for a system whose MTTR is shorter than that of another system.

medium   A physical environment through which transmission signals pass.

metric   A method or measure by which a routing algorithm determines that one route is better than another.

Metro Ethernet   A computer network based on the Ethernet standard and that covers a metropolitan area. It is commonly used as a metropolitan-area network (MAN) to connect subscribers and businesses to a wide-area network (WAN), such as the Internet.

Microsoft Baseline Security Analyzer (MBSA)   A Microsoft tool that helps analyze security problems in Microsoft Windows by scanning for security problems such as those found in the operating system and Windows components such as IIS web server, Microsoft SQL Server, and Microsoft Office.

multicast   Sending a message to selected hosts that are part of a group.

N

Nessus Vulnerability Scanner   Network scanning s oftware, developed by Tenable Network Security, that network administrators can use to help identify network and server vulnerabilities.

Network Access Point (NAP)   The point at which access providers are interconnected. This term was replaced by Internet Exchange Point (IXP).

Network Address Translation (NAT)   The process of rewriting the source or destination address of IP packets as they pass through a router or firewall so that multiple hosts on a private network can access the Internet using one or more public IP addresses.

Network Attached Storage (NAS)   A dedicated, high-speed, high-capacity data storage technology that any server can use. NAS groups large numbers of disk drives that are connected directly to a computer network to provide centralized data access and storage to heterogeneous network hosts (various hardware and operating system platforms). A NAS device typically is attached to an Ethernet network and is assigned its own IP address.

network ID   The portion of an IPv4 address that identifies the network to which the host belongs.

network layer   Layer 3 of the OSI model. It responds to service requests from the transport layer (Layer 4) and issues service requests to the data link layer (Layer 2).

nonvolatile random-access memory (NVRAM)   Memory that retains content, such as configuration information, when a device is powered off.

normal backup   A term used by Windows 2003 Server that refers to the more widely used term "full backup," which is a backup of all or selected files on the system, regardless of their archive attribute status.

O

octet   A decimal number in the range of 0 to 255 that represents 8 bits.

octet boundary   A 32-bit IPv4 address has four 8-bit octets, and network classes change on the boundaries between the octets.

Open Shortest Path First (OSPF)   A link-state interior routing protocol that uses Dijkstra's algorithm to calculate the shortest-path tree.

Open Systems Interconnection (OSI) model   An international standardization program created by ISO and ITU-T to develop standards for data networking that facilitate multivendor equipment interoperability.

optical medium   A data storage medium that holds content in a digital format. The content is written and read using laser technology. Examples of optical media are CD and DVD.

out-of-band management   A transmission method using frequencies or channels outside the frequencies or channels normally used for information transfer. Out-of-band signaling is often used for error reporting in situations in which in-band signaling can be affected by whatever problems the network might be experiencing.

An example is connecting to a device (router or switch) through the console or AUX port to configure or diagnose problems.

outside global address   The actual public IP address of an external host. The address is allocated from a globally routable address or network space.

outside global network   Any network attached to the router that is external to the LAN and that does not recognize the private addresses assigned to hosts on the LAN.

outside local address   The IP address of an outside host as it appears to hosts on the inside network.

outsourcing   With regard to networks, delegating responsibility for network support to an external organization.

P–Q

packet   A logical grouping of information that includes a header that contains control information and usually user data. Packets are most often used to refer to network layer units of data.

phishing   Fraudulent acquisition of sensitive information through the impersonation of a trustworthy source.

physical layer   Layer 1 of the OSI model. Responds to service requests from the data link layer and encodes data onto the physical medium.

physical topology   A diagram created to record where each host is located and how it is connected to the network. The physical topology map also shows where the wiring is installed, the location of wiring closets, and the locations of the networking devices that connect the hosts. The physical topology map usually is based on a building floor plan.

point of presence (POP)   A point of interconnection between the communication facilities provided by the telephone company and the building's main distribution facility.

port   When using transport layer protocols (TCP and UDP), ports are logical communication channels identifying source and destination. Each side of a TCP or UDP connection has a port number assigned to it. Servers use ports to handle multiple requests for services.

Port Address Translation (PAT)   The translation of multiple internal private IP addresses to a single external public IP address using port number to distinguish individual conversations. Also called NAT overload.

port filter   The practice of access control by selectively enabling or disabling TCP ports and/or UDP ports.

port number   A number for a software function that uniquely identifies a process on a computer using TCP or UDP. For example, Telnet is port 23, and SMTP is port 25.

Post Office Protocol version 3 (POP3)   A protocol used when retrieving e-mail messages from a server.

power-on self-test (POST)   A process used to test the device hardware after the power is turned on.

presentation layer   Layer 6 of the OSI model. The presentation layer responds to service requests from the application layer (Layer 7) and issues service requests to the session layer (Layer 5).

preshared key (PSK)   A secret code shared between a wireless client and an access point. The preshared key is used to control access to the network.

primary DNS zone   A zone that can be modified as needed when a new resource record needs to be added or an existing record needs to be updated or deleted. There are primary forward and reverse lookup zones. When you have a primary zone on a DNS server, that server is said to be authoritative for that DNS zone, because it has the answer for DNS queries for records within that zone. There can be only one primary DNS zone for any given DNS domain.

private IP address   An IP address that is reserved for internal network use and that cannot be routed on the Internet. The ranges for IP addresses are 10.0.0.0 to 10.255.255.255, 172.16.0.0 to 172.31.255.255, and 192.168.0.0 to 192.168.255.255.

production environment   A network that is in service and being accessed by users. The software, equipment, documentation, and procedures used in support of live business operations.

protocol interpreter (PI)   In relation to FTP, the PI functions as the main control connection between the FTP client and the FTP server. It establishes the TCP connection and passes control information to the server.

protocol stack   A software implementation of a computer networking protocol suite.

prototype   The process of putting together a working model to test design aspects, demonstrate features, and gather feedback, which can help reduce project risk and cost.

proxy server   Using a server that, in the interest of efficiency, essentially stands in for another server. A client connects to the proxy server, requesting resources that are available from a different server.

public IP address   All IP addresses except those reserved for private IP addresses.

public peer   A process by which multiple ISPs interconnect with each other across a single physical port, known as an exchange point.

quality of service (QoS)   The ability to provide different priority to different applications, users, or data flows, or to guarantee a certain level of performance to a data flow.

queue   Generally, an ordered list of elements waiting to be processed. In routing, a backlog of packets waiting to be forwarded over a router interface.

R

reachability   A measurement used by routing protocols to determine whether a remote network is accessible.

redundancy   The use of multiple components, such as network devices, links, and servers, in network design to help ensure accessibility. In redundant configurations, if one device fails, the other one can take over the functions automatically with little or no disruption in service.

reliability   When a program sends a message whose delivery is guaranteed. This term also refers to the ability of a system or component to perform its required functions under stated conditions for a specified period of time.

remote desktop sharing   Software that runs on both a local and remote computer. It allows the remote computer to access the local one and take it over as though the remote user were sitting at the local computer.

Request for Comments (RFC)   A document series used as the primary means to communicate information about the Internet. Most RFCs document protocol specifications such as Telnet or File Transfer Protocol (FTP), but some are humorous or historical. RFCs are available online from numerous sources.

Resolver   An application that runs on a DNS client or server. When a domain name is used, the Resolver queries the DNS server to translate that name to an IP address. A Resolver creates the DNS name query that is sent to a DNS server.

resource record   DNS servers store and maintain resource records that contain domain names that the server can resolve, and alternative servers that can also process requests.

reverse lookup   A process to determine the hostname or host associated with a given IP address or host address.

reverse lookup zone   A special zone type that allows you to resolve an IP address to a fully qualified domain name. Some applications use reverse lookups to identify computer systems that are actively communicating with them. An entire reverse lookup DNS hierarchy on the Internet enables any publicly registered IP address to be resolved. Reverse lookups on IP addresses can be found using the **ping -a** *ip-address* command.

RFC 791   An IETF standard that defines the Internet Protocol.

RFC 917   An IETF standard that defines Internet subnets.

RFC 1519   An IETF standard that defines classless interdomain routing (CIDR).

RFC 1878   An IETF standard that defines a variable-length subnet table for IPv4.

RFC 1918   An IETF standard that defines private address ranges for use in IP networks. These addresses cannot be routed on the Internet. They include 10.0.0.0/8 (a single 10.0.0.0 network), 172.16.0.0/12 (networks 172.16.0.0 to 172.31.0.0), and 192.168.0.0/24 (networks 192.168.0.0 to 192.168.255.0).

RFC 2460   An IETF standard that defines Internet Protocol version 6 (IPv6).

ROMmon mode   A basic mode of operation used by a Cisco network device if it is unable to load the IOS image.

route cost   A value typically based on hop count, media bandwidth, or other measures that is assigned by a network administrator and used to compare various paths through an internetwork environment.

routing algorithm   A mathematical formula and procedures used to determine the best route for traffic from a particular source to a particular destination.

Routing Information Protocol (RIP)   A common interior routing protocol that uses only hop count as a metric. RIP is a distance vector routing protocol.

running configuration   With Cisco IOS and networking devices (such as routers and switches), the running configuration is the one currently operating in the device memory (RAM). Changes to the running configuration take immediate effect on the network device.

S

scalable network   A network's capability to adapt to increased demands without suffering negative effects on performance.

SDM   Cisco Security Device Manager. A web-based device-management tool for a Cisco IOS software-based router. Simplifies router and security configuration through smart wizards used to deploy, configure, and monitor a Cisco router without requiring knowledge of the CLI.

secondary DNS zone   A read-only backup zone maintained on a DNS server separate from the primary zone. The secondary zone is a copy of the primary zone and receives updates to the zone information from the primary server through zone transfers.

second-level domain   In the DNS hierarchy, a second-level domain (SLD) is directly below a top-level domain (TLD). For example, in cisco.com, cisco is the second-level domain of the .com TLD. Second-level domains commonly refer to the organization that registered the domain name with a domain name registrar.

Secure HTTP (HTTPS)   A protocol used to access or post web server information. HTTPS can use authentication and encryption to secure data as it travels between the client and server.

Secure Shell (SSH)   A protocol that functions similarly to Telnet. SSH protects all authentication and transmitted data using encryption. SSH allows safe access to a remote device over an insecure network, such as the Internet.

Secure Socket Layer (SSL)   A cryptographic protocol that provides secure communications on the Internet for such things as web browsing, e-mail, Internet faxing, instant messaging, and other data transfers.

sequencing   With transport protocols, the numbering of packets so that they can be transmitted and received in the correct order.

serial cable   A cable used to sequentially transmit the bits of a data character over a single channel.

service-level agreement (SLA)   A contract that defines expectations between an organization and the service vendor to provide an agreed-upon level of support.

session layer   Layer 5 of the OSI model. It responds to service requests from the presentation layer and issues service requests to the transport layer.

Shortest Path First (SPF) algorithm   A routing algorithm that uses path cost to determine a shortest-path spanning tree. Commonly used in link-state routing algorithms. Sometimes called Dijkstra's algorithm.

signature   In antivirus and intrusion detection systems, a pattern that the security system looks for when scanning files or network traffic.

Simple Mail Transfer Protocol (SMTP)   A protocol that allows e-mail to be transmitted over the Internet using the *username@domainname* format.

Simple Network Management Protocol (SNMP)   A series of network management protocols used in TCP/IP networks. SNMP provides a means to monitor and control network devices and to manage configurations, statistics collection, performance, and security.

socket   A communication endpoint unique to a machine communicating on an Internet Protocol-based network, such as the Internet. An Internet socket is composed of a protocol (TCP, UDP, raw IP), local IP address, local port, remote IP address, and remote port.

solid-state medium   A type of nonvolatile memory that includes devices such as flash drives. Solid-state storage devices use integrated circuits (IC) instead of magnetic or optical media (such as those used by hard drives and CD/DVD drives) to store data.

SPF tree   The result of running the SPF algorithm to find the best route from any router to a particular destination.

startup configuration   With Cisco IOS and networking devices, the startup configuration is stored in nonvolatile RAM (NVRAM). Changes to the running configuration must be saved to the startup configuration to take effect when the device is restarted.

stateful packet inspection (SPI)   A function of a stateful firewall that distinguishes legitimate packets and allows only packets that match assigned attributes.

static NAT   A mechanism of Network Address Translation (NAT) in which an internal host with a fixed private IP address is permanently mapped with a fixed public IP address.

storage-area network (SAN)   An architecture used to attach remote data storage devices such as disk arrays, tape libraries, and CD arrays to servers in such a way that the SAN storage devices appear as locally attached to the operating system.

subnet   A portion of a network that has been partitioned, or subdivided; a mini-network.

subnet mask   A 32-bit address mask used in IP to indicate the bits of an IP address that are being used to identify the network or subnet address.

SWOT   Strengths, weaknesses, opportunities, and threats analysis. An extensive planning tool used to evaluate these aspects of designing a network or planning for a network upgrade.

SYN (synchronous) flood   A form of network attack in which a flood of packets is sent to a server requesting a client connection. The packets contain invalid source IP addresses. The server becomes occupied with trying to respond to these fake requests from the SYN flood and therefore cannot respond to legitimate ones.

Synchronous Optical Network (SONET)   A standard format for transporting a wide range of digital telecommunications services over optical fiber. SONET is characterized by standard line rates, optical interfaces, and signal formats.

syslog   A standard for forwarding host log messages to a centralized storage location such as a server found on an IP network.

syslog daemon   A syslog server that receives syslog messages from syslog senders.

T

T3 connection   Used mainly by Internet service providers (ISPs) connecting to the Internet backbone and for the backbone itself. T3 circuit channels carry multiple T1 channels multiplexed, resulting in transmission rates of up to 44.736 Mbps.

TCP/IP   An Internet protocol suite that is the set of communications protocols that implement the protocol stack on which the Internet and many commercial networks run. The TCP/IP protocol suite is named after two of the most important protocols that comprise the Internet protocol suite: Transmission Control Protocol (TCP) and Internet Protocol (IP), which were also the first two networking protocols defined.

telecommunication room   Also called a riser, distribution, or wiring closet. It contains network and telecommunications equipment, vertical and horizontal cable terminations, and cross-connect cables. May also be called a Main Distribution Facility (MDF).

telecommunications service provider (TSP)   A company that offers communications services to connect networks, usually over a distance, as with a WAN.

TFTP server   A server running Trivial File Transfer Protocol. Uses UDP for fast transfer of files to and from networking devices with little overhead.

three-way handshake   A process that establishes a TCP session between two endpoints. The process is as follows: 1. A client wants to communicate with a server. The client sends a segment with the SYN flag marked. 2. The server responds with a SYN-ACK. 3. The client sends back an ACK to the other end, and the session is established.

throughput   The rate at which a computer or network sends or receives data, measured in bits per second (bps).

Tier 1 ISP   The group of very large Internet service providers that connect directly to the Internet backbone and that can be considered part of the backbone itself.

Tier 2 ISP   The group of Internet service providers that cover more limited geographic areas and that purchase their Internet access from Tier 1 ISPs.

Tier 3 ISP   The group of Internet service providers that typically cover smaller geographic areas than Tier 2 ISPs and that purchase their Internet access from either Tier 1 or Tier 2 ISPs.

tiered backup   A disaster recovery strategy that identifies various methods for preserving mission-critical data required by business continuity planning.

top-down approach   A troubleshooting technique in a layered concept of networking that starts with the application or highest layer and works down.

top-level domain   The last part of an Internet domain name—that is, the letters that follow the final dot of any domain name. For example, in a domain name the top-level domain is com (or COM, because domain names are not case-sensitive).

topological database   A database created using received information from other routers. Used to build a routing table and select the best path to a destination network.

traffic   The number of packets traversing through a router or network at one time.

transit traffic   Packets that are generated by outside hosts or routers that travel through an autonomous system (AS) destined for another AS. A border gateway can be configured to allow or deny transit traffic.

Transmission Control Protocol (TCP)   The primary Internet protocol for the delivery of data. TCP includes facilities for end-to-end connection establishment, error detection and recovery, and controlling the rate of data flow into the network. Many standard applications—such as e-mail, web browsers, file transfer, and Telnet—depend on the services of TCP.

transport layer   Layer 4 of the OSI model. Responds to service requests from the session layer (Layer 5) and issues service requests to the network layer (Layer 3).

transport network   The network of interconnecting networks that allow ISPs to communicate with each other.

trap   In SNMP, a message sent by an SNMP agent to a network management system (NMS), console, or terminal to indicate the occurrence of a significant event, such as a specifically defined condition or a threshold that has been reached.

trigger update   When a router sends updated information as soon as a change in the network occurs.

Trivial File Transfer Protocol (TFTP)   A simplified version of FTP that allows files to be transferred from one computer to another over a network, usually without the use of client authentication (for example, username and password).

Trojan   A program that contains or installs malicious program code while under the guise of being something interesting or useful to an unsuspecting user. When the user executes the program, the malicious code is released.

trouble ticket   A document that help desk personnel use to record a reported network issue or problem. Also used to track the problem's status and document its resolution.

U

uniform resource locator (URL)   An alphanumeric string in a specific format that represents a device, file, or web page located on the Internet.

upper layers   A term sometimes used to refer to any layer above the transport layer of the OSI model. The upper layers of the OSI model deal with application functionality and generally are implemented only in software. The highest layer, the application layer, is closest to the end user.

User Datagram Protocol (UDP)   A simple transport layer protocol that exchanges data without acknowledgments or guaranteed delivery. UDP relies on applications to handle error processing and retransmission.

user EXEC mode   The default mode when a user first logs in to a Cisco device with an IOS.

V

variable-length subnet mask (VLSM)   A means of allocating IP addressing resources to subnets according to their individual need rather than along octet boundaries.

virtual circuit   A logical circuit created to ensure reliable communication between two network devices. A virtual circuit can be either permanent (PVC) or switched (SVC). Virtual circuits are used in Frame Relay and X.25. In ATM, a virtual circuit is called a virtual channel.

virtual local-area network (VLAN)   A network of hosts that communicate as if they are connected to the same physical network even though they may actually be physically located on different segments of a LAN. A VLAN is configured via software on switches and routers. It is made up of a group of ports defined on one or more switches that create an independent broadcast domain and that can span multiple LANs or WANs.

virtual machine   A technique deployed on servers to enable multiple copies of an operating system to run on a single set of hardware, thus creating many virtual machines, each one treated as a separate computer. This enables a single physical resource to appear to function as multiple logical resources.

Virtual Private Network (VPN)   Makes use of the public telecommunication infrastructure while maintaining privacy through the use of a tunneling protocol and security procedures.

virtual terminal   Allows users to remotely log in to a host and interact with the operating system as if they are physically in front of the host.

virus   A malicious program that infects a computer without the user's permission or knowledge. The virus program copies itself and attaches the copies to executable programs or files in the computer.

VLAN 1   A switch's IP address is assigned to a virtual interface represented as a virtual LAN (VLAN) interface. By default, this is interface VLAN 1.

voice over IP (VoIP)   A standard for transmitting voice data encapsulated in an IP packet on an existing IP network without needing its own network infrastructure. In VoIP, the digital signal processor divides the voice signal into frames, which are paired and stored in voice packets. The voice packets are transported using IP in compliance with ITU-T specification H.323.

Wireshark   A packet-sniffing application used for network troubleshooting and analysis. This program captures packets coming into or going out of the network interface card (NIC) and decodes the packet contents for readability.

zone   A portion of the global DNS namespace. DNS zones are laid out in a tree structure from right to left, such that divisions of the namespace are performed by prepending a series of characters followed by a period (.) to the upper namespace.

zone database   The DNS naming structure is broken into small, manageable zones. Each DNS server maintains a specific zone database file and is responsible for managing name-to-IP mappings for only that small portion of the entire DNS structure.

W–Z

WAN   Wide-area network. A data communications network that serves users across a broad geographic area and that often uses transmission devices provided by telecommunications providers. Frame Relay, T1, and ATM are examples of WAN technologies.

well-known port   A TCP or UDP port in the range of 0 to 1023.

Wired Equivalent Privacy (WEP)   Part of the IEEE 802.11 wireless networking standard that provides a low level of security.

wireless local-area network (WLAN)   Two or more computers or devices equipped to use spread-spectrum technology based on radio waves to communicate within a limited area.

Symbols

^ (caret symbol), 131

A

AAA, 246

access lists, 251

active data connections, 230

address translation (NAT), troubleshooting, 321-323

administratively down interfaces, 315

ADSL (Asymmetric Digital Subscriber Line), 6

Anti-X software, 259

application layer, 25

    OSI model, 286
    protocols, 210

application security, 244

ASN (AS number), 193

assigning permissions, 245

attacks, 249-250

autonomous systems, 193-194

    reachability, 196
    routing between, 195

availability, 67, 208

B

back doors, 260

backing up Cisco router configuration files, 146-148

backup solutions

    differential backups, 272
    full backups, 271
    hard disk media, 270
    incremental backups, 273
    maintenance, 273-275
    optical media, 270
    solid state media, 271
    tape media, 270

bandwidth, 4

banners, configuring on Cisco routers, 137

baseline tools, 291

Basic Configuration window (SDM Express), 121

BGP (Border Gateway Protocol), 195, 199-200

boot errors, troubleshooting, 298-301

bootup process, Cisco ISR, 114

    running configuration, 115-116
    startup configuration, 114
    troubleshooting, 116

bottom-up troubleshooting methodology, 30-34, 289

building distributors, 58

C

cable modems, 6

cable testers, 294

cables, 58, 60, 301

    excessive collisions, troubleshooting, 303
    excessive noise, troubleshooting, 302
    excessive runt frames, troubleshooting, 303
    late collisions, troubleshooting, 303
    structured, 60-61

Catalyst 2960 switches. *See* Cisco Catalyst 2960 series switches

Catalyst switches. *See* Cisco Catalyst switches

CCENT exam, preparing for, 336-340

    commitment, 341
    creating a plan, 341-342
    practicing test taking, 342-344

CDP (Cisco Discovery Protocol), configuring on Cisco Catalyst switches, 164-166

certification exams, format of, 343

CIDR (Classless Interdomain Routing), 79-82

circuit-switched WAN connections, 152

Cisco Catalyst 2960 series switches, 66

    CDP, configuring, 164-166
    configuring, 156-160
    connecting to router, 161-162
    powering up, 159
    switch port security, 162-164

Cisco Catalyst switches

    LAN connectivity, troubleshooting, 304-305
    LED lights, 157
    switch port modes, 158-159

Cisco IOS Firewall software, 252

Cisco IOS Software

    CLI

        Cisco ISR, configuring, 118
        commands, recalling, 131-132
        global configuration mode, 129
        help system, 129-130
        router configuration submode, 129
        routers, configuring, 128, 137-146
        banners, 137
        show commands, 132-136
    image files
        corrupt images, troubleshooting, 301
        IP Base image, 111
        recovering, 276-277
        updating, 275

Cisco ISR (Integrated Services Router)

    bootup process, 114
        running configuration, 115-116
        startup configuration, 114
        troubleshooting, 116

configuring, 110
  with CLI, 118
  with SDM, 118-120
  with SDM Express, 121-124
  in-band management, 117
  initial setup, 112-113
  out-of-band management, 117
Cisco routers
  configuration files, backing up, 146-148
  connecting to Cisco Catalyst switches, 161-162
  WAN connections, configuring PPP, 154-155
Cisco SDM (Security Device Manager), configuring dynamic NAT, 127
Class A addresses, 76
Class B addresses, 77
Class C addresses, 77
classful addressing, 75-77
classful subnetting, 85-86
CLI (command-line interface), 128
  help system, 129-130
    commands, recalling, 131-132
  routers, configuring, 128
  show commands, 132-136
  versus SDM, 119-120
CMTS (cable modem termination system), 13
collisions
  effect on network performance, 296
  troubleshooting, 303
commands
  copy running-config startup config, 115
  copy tftp flash, 275
  debug ip rip, 193, 330
  enable password, 137
  enable secret, 137
  ipconfig, 93
  ping, 9
  recalling, 131-132
  router bgp, 199
  service password encryption, 138
  show, 132-133
  show arp, 135
  show flash, 300
  show history, 131-132
  show interfaces, 134-135, 329
  show interfaces serial, 306-307
  show ip dhcp binding, 317
  show ip interface, 329
  show ip interfaces brief, 300-303
  show ip nat translation, 322
  show ip protocols, 192, 327
  show ip route, 135, 175-177, 323, 330
  show protocols, 136
  show running-config, 328-329
  show running-config interface, 304
  show running-configuration, 138, 300
  show startup-configuration, 300
  show version, 115-116, 136, 299
  tracert, 11-12
  Windows, ipconfig /all, 318-320
committing to exam preparation, 341
communicating between subnets, 90-91

community strings, 266
comparing
  CLI and SDM, 119-120
  TCP/IP and OSI models, 211
  UDP and TCP, 214
configuration files
  backing up, 146-148
  corrupt configuration files, troubleshooting, 301
configuring
  BGP, 199-200
  Cisco Catalyst 2960 switches, 156-160
    CDP, 164-166
    router connection, 161-162
    switch port security, 162-164
  Cisco ISR, 110
    bootup process, 114-116
    in-band management, 117
    initial setup, 112-113
    out-of-band management, 117
    with CLI, 118
    with SDM, 118-120
    with SDM Express, 121-124
  Cisco routers with CLI, 128, 137
    banners, 137
    console port, 138-139
    default routes, 141
    DHCP services, 141-144
    interfaces, 139-140
    static NAT, 144-146
  dynamic NAT with Cisco SDM, 127
  NAT, 321
  RIP, 190-193
  serial WAN connections
    IP address, 125-126
    serial line encapsulations, 124-125
  static routes, 178-179
connecting CPE over WAN
  connection type, selecting, 153-154
  via circuit-switched connection, 152
  via packet-switched connection, 152
  via point-to-point connection, 151
connecting to Internet, 5-7
connection-oriented protocols, 212
connectivity
  duplex mismatches, troubleshooting, 305
  troubleshooting, 36, 304
  verifying with ping command, 9
  verifying with tracert command, 11-12
console port, configuring on Cisco routers, 138-139
context-sensitive help (CLI), 130
convergence, 180
copy running-config startup-config command, 115
copy tftp flash command, 275
corrupt Cisco IOS images, troubleshooting, 301
CPE (customer premises equipment)
  connecting over WAN, 151
    connection type, selecting, 153-154
    via circuit-switched connection, 152
    via packet-switched connection, 152

via point-to-point connection, 151
installing, 148-151

CSMA/CD (carrier sense multiple access/collision detect), 296

custom subnet masks, 86, 90

customer site troubleshooting procedures, 40-41

D

data encryption, 247-249

data link layer, 25
cables, troubleshooting, 301-303
OSI model, 287
troubleshooting, 295-298

DCE (data circuit-terminating equipment), 139

DDoS attacks, 249

debug ip rip command, 193, 330

decapsulation, 29

default routes, 178
configuring on Cisco routers, 141
troubleshooting, 324

devices
availability, 67
inventory sheets, 55
reliability, 67
routers, selecting, 64-65
switches, selecting, 63-64
upgrading, 66

DHCP (Dynamic Host Configuration Protocol)
configuring on Cisco routers, 141-144
troubleshooting, 318-320

DHCP window (SDM Express), 123-124

dialup access, 5

differential backups, 272

directly connected routes, 178
troubleshooting, 324

disabling privileged EXEC mode, 128

disaster recovery
backup solutions
differential backups, 272
full backups, 271
hard disk media, 270
incremental backups, 273
optical media, 270
solid-state media, 271
tape media, 270
best practices, 277-279
causes of data loss, 268-269

distance vector routing protocols, 180-182
RIP, configuring, 190-193

divide-and-conquer troubleshooting methodology, 289

DMM (digital multimeters), 294

DMZ (demilitarized zone), 252

DNS (Domain Name System), 218-219
domain name servers, 220
implementing
via ISPs, 225
via local DNS servers, 226

name resolution, 33, 221-224
forward lookup zones, 224
primary DNS zones, 225
reverse lookup zones, 224
secondary DNS zones, 225
resolvers, 220-221
resource records, 220
top-level domains, 221
verifying operation, 334

documenting
help desk calls, 37-39
network requirements, 55

domain name servers, 220

domain namespace, 220

DoS (denial-of-service) attacks, 249-250

DRDoS (distributed reflected denial-of-service) attacks, 250

DSL (Digital Subscriber Line), 5

DSLAM (DSL access multiplexer), 13

DTE (data terminal equipment), 139

DTP (Data Transfer Process) function of FTP, 229

DUAL (diffusing update algorithm), 185

duplex settings, displaying, 305

dynamic NAT, 97
configuring with Cisco SDM, 127

dynamic routes, 178
troubleshooting, 324-330

E

e-commerce, 2

EAP (Extensible Authentication Protocol), 257

EGPs (Exterior Gateway Protocols), 195

EIGRP (Enhanced IGRP), 184-185

e-mail, troubleshooting, 35

enable password command, 137

enable secret command, 137

encapsulation, 27, 213

encoding, 27

encryption, 247-249

end systems, 288

equipment, purchasing, 61-62

escalation, 21

evaluating network design and implementation, 57

exam
format of, 343
preparing for, 336-340
commitment, 341
creating a plan, 341-342
practicing test taking, 342-344

exterior routing protocols, autonomous systems, 193-196

external interfaces, 144

F-G

factual knowledge, importance of during exam preparation, 338

failure domains, 64

fault tolerance, 68

firewalls, 251, 253

five 9s, 208

Flash memory, displaying contents of, 300

floor distributors, 58

forward lookup zones, 224

frame headers, 28

FTP (File Transfer Protocol), 229

DTP function, 229

PI function, 229

full backups, 271

global configuration mode (CLI), 129

H

hard disk media, 270

hardware troubleshooting tools, 293-295

help desk technicians, 20

calls, documenting, 37, 39

connectivity issues, troubleshooting, 36

customer interaction, 22-24

customer site troubleshooting procedures, 40-41

e-mail issues, troubleshooting, 35

levels of customer support, 21

roles of, 21-22

help system, Cisco IOS CLI, 129-132

hierarchical addressing, 75, 314

HOB (high-order bits), 75

HOSTS file, 218-219

HTTP (HyperText Transfer Protocol)

proxy servers, 229

URLs, 227

HTTPS (Secure HTTP), 227-229

hubs, 288

I

IDF (intermediate distribution facility), 58

IDS (intrusion detection systems), 254-255

IGPs (Interior Gateway Protocols), 195

image files

corrupt images, troubleshooting, 301

IP Base image, 111

recovering, 276-277

updating, 275

IMAP4 (Internet Message Access Protocol), 234-235

implementing DNS

via ISPs, 225

via local DNS servers, 226

in-band management, 262

Cisco ISR, 117

SNMP, 265

Syslog, 267

Telnet, 264

incident management, 23

incremental backups, 273

inside global addresses, 95

inside local addresses, 95

installing CPE, 148-151

interfaces

administratively down, 315

configuring on Cisco routers, 139-140

troubleshooting, 301

interior routing protocols

EIGRP, 184-185

RIP, 183-184

configuring, 190-193

internal help desk technicians, 20

internal interfaces, 144

Internet, 2-3

internetworking devices, 111

inventory checklists, 150

inventory sheets, 55

IP addresses, 310-311

addressing scheme, developing, 68

assigning to serial WAN connection, 125-126

classful addressing, 75-77

DHCP, troubleshooting, 318-320

DNS resolution, 33

hierarchical addressing, 75, 314

IPv6, 92-93

NAT, 93-96

dynamic NAT, 97

static NAT, 98

troubleshooting, 321-323

PAT, 99-102

subnet masks, troubleshooting, 315-317

subnets, 312

overlapping, 314-315

subnetting, 77-78

CIDR, 79-82

classful, 85-86

communicating between subnets, 90-91

custom subnet masks, 86, 90

network expansion requirements, 82-85

VLSM, 81

unavailable addresses, troubleshooting, 317-318

IP Base image, 111

ipconfig /all command (Windows), 318-320

ipconfig command, 93

IPS (intrusion prevention systems), 255-256

IPv6, 92-93

ISPs, 4, 197-198

backup solutions, maintenance, 273-275

connection methods

cable modem, 6

dialup access, 5

DSL, 5
Metro Ethernet, 7
satellite connection, 6
T1/E1, 7
T3/E3, 7
connectivity, requirements, 13
disaster recovery
   backup media, 270
   best practices, 277-279
   data loss, causes of, 268-269
   file backups, 271-275
   solid-state media, 271
help desk technicians, 20
   calls, documenting, 37-39
   connectivity, troubleshooting, 36
   customer interaction, 22-24
   customer site troubleshooting procedures, 40-41
   e-mail, troubleshooting, 35
   levels of customer support, 21
   roles of, 21-22
host security, 258-260
in-band management
   SNMP, 265
   Syslog, 267
   Telnet, 264
IXPs, 7
link performance, monitoring, 262
POP, 7
roles and responsibilities, 14
security, 242-243
   applications, 244
   extraneous services, 243
   passwords, 243
   user rights, 244
   wireless, 256-257
services, 206
   application layer protocols, 210
   availability, 208
   reliability, 207
   TCP/IP protocols, 208
   transport layer protocols, 211-217
SLAs, 261
Tier 1, 9
Tier 2, 9
Tier 3, 9
ISR. *See* **Cisco ISR**
IXP (Internet Exchange Point), 7

J-K-L

knowledge bases, 292

LAN connectivity, 304-305
LAN IP Address window (SDM Express), 122
Layer 1, 301. *See also* **physical layer**
   troubleshooting, 295-298
Layer 2, 301. *See also* **data link layer**
   devices, selecting, 63-64
   troubleshooting, 295-298

Layer 3, 310. *See also* **network layer**
   devices, selecting, 64-65
   DHCP, troubleshooting, 318-320
   IP addressing
      overlapping subnets, troubleshooting, 314-315
      subnet masks, troubleshooting, 315-317
      unavailable addresses, troubleshooting, 317-318
   NAT, troubleshooting, 321-323
   routing, troubleshooting, 323-330
Layer 4, troubleshooting, 331-332
layers of OSI model, 25-26
   decapsulation, 29
   encapsulation, 27
LED indicators (Cisco routers), 157, 300
link performance, monitoring, 262
link state routing protocols, OSPF, 185, 187
local traffic, 198
logical networks, 291, 310
logical topologies, 52
lower layers, 25, 288
LSAs (link-state advertisements), 186

M

MAC address filtering, 257
malware, 242
managed services, 22
MBSA (Microsoft Baseline Security Analyzer), 244
MDF (main distribution facility), 57
media errors, troubleshooting, 302-303
Metro Ethernet, 7
monitoring ISP link performance, 262
   in-band tools, 264-267
MTBF (mean time between failure), 207
MTTR (mean time to repair), 207
multiple service support at transport layer, 215-217

N

name resolution, DNS, 221-224
   forward lookup zones, 224
   primary zones, 225
   reverse lookup zones, 224
   secondary zones, 225
NAPs (Network Access Points), 7
NAT (Network Address Translation), 93-96
   configuring, 321
   dynamic NAT, 97
   static NAT, 98
      configuring on Cisco routers, 144-146
   troubleshooting, 321-323
Nessus Vulnerability Scanner, 244
network documentation, 291
network layer, 25
   OSI model, 287-288, 310-311
   troubleshooting, 312

network management system tools, 292

network naming systems

DNS, 218-219

domain name servers, 220

implementing via ISPs, 225

implementing via local DNS servers, 226

name resolution, 221-225

resolvers, 220-221

resource records, 220

TCP/IP HOSTS file, 218-219

network prefix, 79

network support services, 14

network topologies

logical, 291

physical, 290

network upgrades, planning, 56-57

NOC (network operations center), 14

NVRAM (non-volatile random access memory), 114

O

open authentication, 257

operating systems

patching, 244

version, displaying, 299

optical media, 270

OSI model, 24, 286

as troubleshooting tool, 25, 29-30

bottom-up approach, 30-34

top-down approach, 30

corresponding TCP/IP model layers, 286

data link layer, troubleshooting, 295-298

decapsulation, 29

encapsulation, 27

encoding, 27

layers of, 25-26

lower layers, 288

network layer, 310-311

routing, troubleshooting, 323-330

troubleshooting, 312

physical layer, troubleshooting, 295-298

transport layer, troubleshooting, 331-332

upper layers, 288

troubleshooting, 332-336

OSPF (Open Shortest Path First), 185-187

out-of-band management, 262

Cisco ISR, 117

outside global address, 95

outside local address, 95

outsourcing, 21

overlapping subnets, troubleshooting, 314-315

P

packet-switched WAN connections, 152

packet trailers, 28

passive data connections, 230

passwords, 243

PAT (Port Address Translation), 99-102

patches, 244

permissions, assigning, 245

physical environment, documenting, 57

physical layer, 25

cables, troubleshooting, 301-303

OSI model, 287-288

troubleshooting, 295-298

physical topologies, 52, 290

PI (Protocol Interpreter) function of FTP, 229

ping command, 9

planning

for exam preparation, 341-342

network upgrades, 56-57

IP addressing, 68

point-to-point WAN connections, 151

POP (point of presence), 7

POP3 (Post Office Protocol version 3), 233

port filtering, 250

portable network analyzers, 295

ports, 215

duplex settings, displaying, 305

POST (power-on self test), 114

failures, troubleshooting, 301

powering up Cisco Catalyst 2960 switches, 159

PPP encapsulation, configuring, 154-155

practicing test taking, 342-344

preparing for CCENT exam, 336-340

commitment, 341

creating a plan, 341-342

factual knowledge, importance of, 338

practicing test taking, 342-344

presentation layer, 25, 286

primary DNS zones, 225

privileged EXEC mode, 128

problem-solving procedures, 29-30

protocol analyzers, 293

protocol stack, 26

proxy servers, 229

PSKs (preshared keys), 257

purchasing equipment, 61-62

Q-R

reachability, 196

recalling commands, 131-132

recovering Cisco IOS images, 276-277

redundancy, 208

reliability, 67

of ISP services, 207

required devices for ISP connectivity, 13

resolvers, 220-221

resource records, 220

reverse lookup zones, 224

RFCs (Requests For Comments), 3

RIP (Routing Information Protocol), 183-184

   configuring, 190-193

roles within ISPs, 14, 21-22

ROMmon, recovering Cisco IOS image, 276-277

router bgp command, 199

router configuration submode (CLI), 129

routers, 128, 137

   banners, configuring, 137
   bootup, troubleshooting, 298-301
   console port, 138-139
   default routes, configuring, 141
   DHCP services, configuring, 141-144
   interfaces, configuring, 139-140
   selecting, 63-65
   static NAT, configuring, 144-146

routes, 174

   default, 178
   directly connected, 178
     troubleshooting, 324
   dynamic, 178
     troubleshooting, 324-330
   static, configuring, 178-179
   troubleshooting, 323

routing protocols, 179

   configuring, 190-193
   distance vector, 180-182
   EIGRP, 184-185
   exterior routing protocols, autonomous systems, 193-195
   link state, OSPF, 185-187
   RIP, 183-184

routing table, 186

running configuration, 115-116

runt frames, troubleshooting, 303

S

satellite Internet connection, 6

scalability, 14

scanning, 244

SDM (Cisco Router and Security Device Manager)

   Cisco ISR, configuring, 118-120
   dynamic NAT, configuring, 127
   versus CLI, 119-120

SDM Express, configuring Cisco ISR

   Basic Configuration window, 121
   DHCP window, 123-124
   LAN IP Address window, 122

SDSL (Symmetric Digital Subscriber Line), 6

secondary DNS zones, 225

security

   access lists, 251
   attacks, 249-250

best practices, 245
   AAA, 246
   permissions, 245
data encryption, 247-249
firewalls, 251-253
host security, 258-260
IDS, 254-255
IPS, 255-256
port filtering, 250
scanning, 244
user rights, 244
wireless, 256-257

selecting

   routers, 64-65
   switches, 63-64
   WAN connection type, 153-154

serial cables, 60

serial line encapsulations, 124-125

serial link problems

   loops, troubleshooting, 308
   troubleshooting, 307-309

serial WAN connections

   configuring, 124
   IP address, assigning, 125-126
   serial line encapsulations, 124-125

service password encryption command, 138

session layer, 25

   OSI model, 286

setting up Cisco ISR, 112-113

show arp command, 135

show commands, 132-133

show flash command, 300

show history command, 131-132

show interfaces command, 134-135, 329

show interfaces serial command, 306-307

show ip dhcp binding command, 317

show ip interface brief command, 300

show ip interface command, 329

show ip interfaces brief command, 301-303

show ip nat translation command, 322

show ip protocols command, 192, 327

show ip route command, 135, 175-177, 323, 330

show protocols command, 136

show running-config command, 328-329

show running-config interface command, 304

show running-configuration command, 300

show running-configuration command, 138

show startup-configuration command, 300

show version command, 115-116, 136, 299

sign-off phase, 150

site surveys, documenting physical environment, 57

SLAs (service-level agreements), 22, 261

SMTP (Simple Mail Transfer Protocol), 231-233

SNMP (Simple Network Management Protocol), 265

sockets, 217

software troubleshooting tools, 291-293

solid-state media, 271

SPF (shortest path first) algorithm, 186

SPI (stateful packet inspection), 252

standards, Internet, 3

startup configuration, 114

static NAT, 98

    configuring on Cisco routers, 144-146

static port security, 162

static routes

    configuring, 178-179

    troubleshooting, 324

structured cable, 60-61

subnet masks, 175

    troubleshooting, 315-317

subnetting, 77-78, 312

    CIDR, 79-82

    classful, 85-86

    communicating between subnets, 90-91

    custom subnet masks, 86, 90

    network expansion requirements, 82-85

    overlapping subnets, troubleshooting, 314-315

    VLSM, 81

swap media, 273

switch port modes, 158-159

switch ports, 158-161

switches, selecting, 63-64

Syslog, 267

T

T1/E1 Internet connections, 7

T3/E3 Internet connections, 7

tape media, 270

TCP (Transport Control Protocol), 212

    and UDP, 214

TCP/IP model, corresponding OSI model layers, 286. *See also* **TCP/IP protocols**

TCP/IP protocols, 208

    application layer, 210

    FTP, 229

        DTP function, 229

        PI function, 229

    HOSTS file, 218-219

    HTTP, 227

        proxy servers, 229

        URLs, 227

    IMAP4, 234-235

    POP3, 233

    SMTP, 231-233

    transport layer, 211

        multiple service support, 215-217

        TCP, 212

        UDP, 212-214

Telnet, 264

    troubleshooting upper-layer problems, 335-336

TFTP servers, backing up Cisco router configuration files, 146-148

three-way handshakes, 213

Tier 1 ISPs, 9

Tier 2 ISPs, 9

Tier 3 ISPs, 9

top-down troubleshooting methodology, 30, 289

top-level domains, 221

topological database, 186

topology maps, creating, 52-54

tracert command, 11-12

traffic, 198

trailers, 28

transit traffic, 198

transport layer, 25

    OSI model, 287-288

    protocols, 211

        multiple service support, 215-217

        TCP, 212

        UDP, 212-214

    troubleshooting, 331-332

traps, 266

Trojans, 260

trouble tickets, 23

troubleshooting. *See also* **troubleshooting tools**

    boot errors, 298-301

    cables, 301-303

    calls, documenting, 37-39

    Cisco ISR bootup process, 116

    connectivity issues, 36

    customer site procedures, 40-41

    data link layer, 295-298

    divide-and-conquer methodology, 289

    e-mail issues, 35

    IP addressing, unavailable addresses, 317-318

    LAN connectivity, 304

        duplex mismatches, 305

    Layer 3

        DHCP, 318-320

        NAT, 321-323

    network layer, 312

    OSI model as framework, 29-30

        bottom-up approach, 30-34

        top-down approach, 30

    overlapping subnets, 314-315

    physical layer, 295-298

    routing, 323

        directly connected routes, 324

        dynamic routes, 324-330

    subnet masks, 315, 317

    transport layer problems, 331-332

    upper-layer problems, 332-335

        with Telnet, 335-336

    WAN connectivity, 305

        serial link problems, 307-309

troubleshooting tools

    baseline tools, 291

    cable testers, 294

digital multimeters, 294
knowledge bases, 292
logical network topologies, 291
network documentation, 291
network management system tools, 292
physical network topologies, 290
portable network analyzers, 295
protocol analyzers, 293

TSPs (telecommunications service providers), 124

U-V

UDP (User Datagram Protocol), 212-214

unavailable IP addresses, troubleshooting, 317-318

unrecognized interface modules, troubleshooting, 301

updating Cisco IOS image, 275

upgrading network devices, 66

cabling, 58-61

upper layers, 25

encoding, 27
OSI model, 288
troubleshooting, 332-335
with Telnet, 335-336

URLs, 227

user EXEC mode, 128

user rights, 244

viruses, 260

VLSM (variable length subnet masking), 79-81

W-X-Y-Z

WANs

connectivity, troubleshooting, 305
CPE, connecting to, 151
connection type, selecting, 153-154
via circuit-switched connection, 152
via packet-switched connection, 152
via point-to-point connection, 151
PPP encapsulation, configuring, 154-155
serial link problems, troubleshooting, 307-309

WEP (Wired Equivalent Privacy), 257

WireShark protocol analyzer, 262, 293

WLANs (wireless LANs), security, 256-257

worldwide enterprise routing, 188-190

worms, 260

WPA (WiFi Protected Access), 258